AMERICA

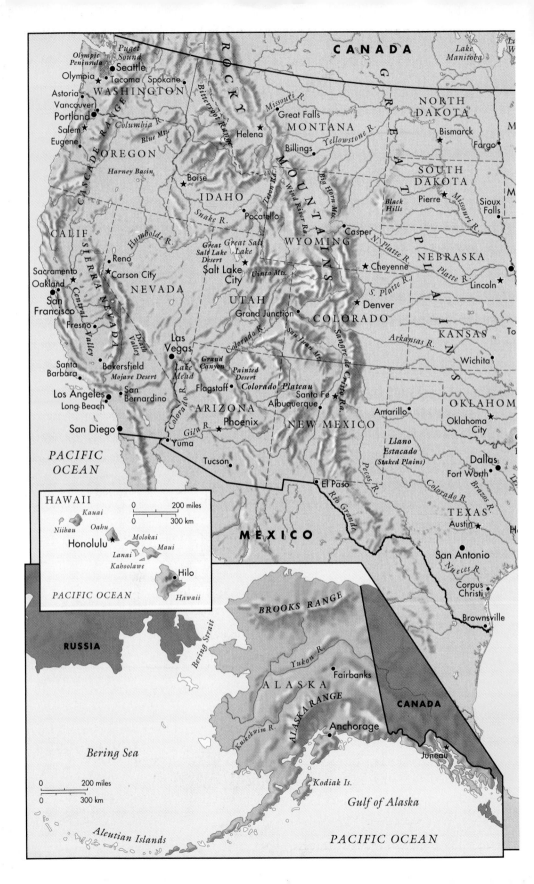

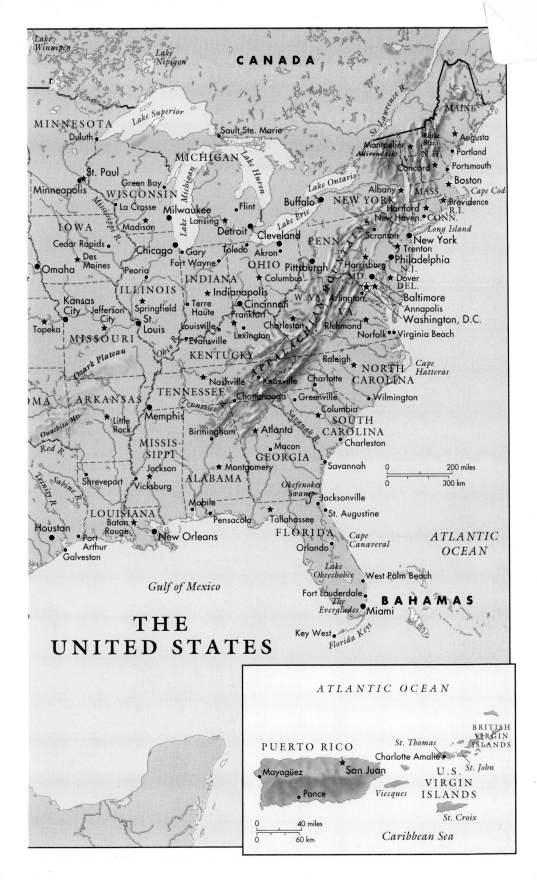

THE UNITED STATES

CANADA

Lake Winnipeg

Lake Nipigon

Lake Superior

MINNESOTA
• Duluth
Sault Ste. Marie
MICHIGAN
Lake Huron

St. Lawrence R.
MAINE
★ Augusta
• Portland
Montpelier ★
Adirondacks
VT. N.H.
Concord •
Portsmouth •

• St. Paul
Minneapolis •
Green Bay •
WISCONSIN
Lake Michigan
• Flint
Lansing
Lake Ontario
Albany ★
Hartford ★
MASS. Boston •
Cape Cod
Providence
R.I.

Mississippi R.
La Crosse •
Madison •
Milwaukee •
Detroit •
Cleveland
Buffalo •
NEW YORK
New Haven •
CONN.
New York
Long Island

IOWA
• Cedar Rapids
Chicago •
• Gary
Toledo •
Akron •
PENN.
Scranton •
Trenton ★
Philadelphia
N.J.

• Omaha
Des Moines
Peoria •
Fort Wayne •
OHIO
Pittsburgh •
Columbus •
Harrisburg •
MD.
Dover •
DEL.

ILLINOIS
INDIANA
• Indianapolis
Cincinnati
W. VA.
Arlington
Baltimore
Annapolis
Washington, D.C.

Kansas City •
Jefferson City •
Springfield •
St. Louis
Terre Haute •
Frankfort •
Charleston •
Richmond •
VA.
Norfolk • Virginia Beach

★ Topeka
MISSOURI
Louisville •
Lexington •
Evansville •
KENTUCKY
Ohio R.

Ozark Plateau
Raleigh •
NORTH CAROLINA
Cape Hatteras

OMA
ARKANSAS
Nashville •
Knoxville •
Charlotte •
TENNESSEE
Chattanooga •
Greenville •
Wilmington •

Ouachita Mts.
Little Rock ★
Memphis •
Tennessee R.
Columbia •
SOUTH CAROLINA
Savannah R.

Red R.
Birmingham •
Atlanta ★
Charleston •

MISSIS-SIPPI
Jackson ★
Macon •
GEORGIA
Savannah •

Shreveport •
Vicksburg •
Montgomery ★
ALABAMA
Okefenokee Swamp
Jacksonville •

Trinity R.
Sabine R.
LOUISIANA
Baton Rouge ★
Mobile •
Pensacola •
Tallahassee ★
FLORIDA
St. Augustine •

Houston •
Port Arthur •
Galveston •
New Orleans •
Orlando •
Cape Canaveral

Gulf of Mexico
Lake Okeechobee
West Palm Beach •
ATLANTIC OCEAN

Fort Lauderdale •
The Everglades
Miami •
BAHAMAS

Key West •
Florida Keys

0 — 200 miles
0 — 300 km

Inset map

ATLANTIC OCEAN

PUERTO RICO
St. Thomas •
Charlotte Amalie •
BRITISH VIRGIN ISLANDS

Mayagüez •
San Juan ★
St. John
U.S. VIRGIN ISLANDS

Ponce •
Vieques
St. Croix

Caribbean Sea

0 — 40 miles
0 — 60 km

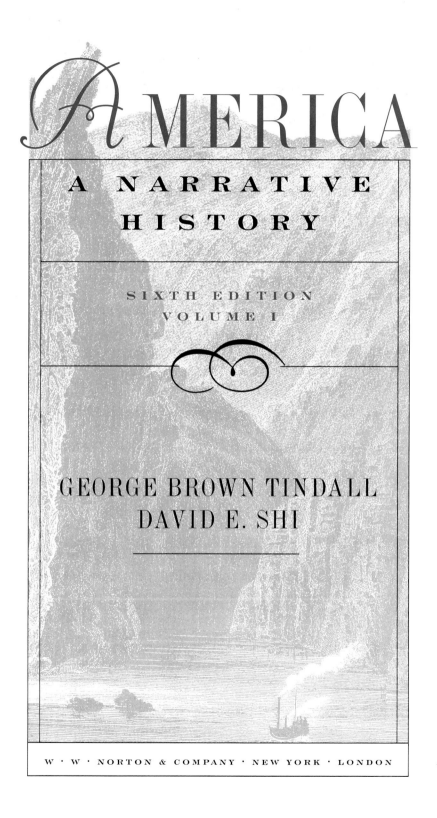

AMERICA

A NARRATIVE HISTORY

SIXTH EDITION
VOLUME I

GEORGE BROWN TINDALL
DAVID E. SHI

W · W · NORTON & COMPANY · NEW YORK · LONDON

Composition by TechBooks
Manufacturing by Courier Westford, Inc.
Book design by Antonina Krass
Editor: Steve Forman
Manuscript editor: Jan Hoeper
Project editor: Lory A. Frenkel
Production manager: JoAnn Simony
Editorial assistant: Sarah England
Cartographer: CARTO-GRAPHICS/Alice Thiede and William Thiede,
with relief maps from Mountain High Maps®, Digital Wisdom, Inc.

Acknowledgements and copyrights continue on page A101,
which serves as a continuation of the copyright page.

The Library of Congress has cataloged the one-volume edition as follows:

Tindall, George Brown.
America : a narrative history / George Brown Tindall,
David Emory Shi.—6th ed.
p.   cm.
Includes bibliographical references and index.
ISBN 0-393-97812-5
1. United States—History.   I. Shi, David E. II.   Title.
E178.1 .T55 2003   2003051038
973—dc21

ISBN 0-393-92426-2 (pbk.)

W. W. Norton & Company, Inc., 500 Fifth Avenue, New York, N.Y. 10110
www.wwnorton.com

W. W. Norton & Company Ltd., Castle House, 75/76 Wells Street, London W1T 3QT

2 3 4 5 6 7 8 9 0

*W. W. Norton & Company has been independent since its founding in
1923, when William Warder Norton and Mary D. Herter Norton first published lectures delivered at the People's Institute, the adult education division of New York City's Cooper Union. The Nortons soon expanded their
program beyond the Institute, publishing books by celebrated academics
from America and abroad. By mid-century, the two major pillars of Norton's
publishing program—trade books and college texts—were firmly established. In the 1950s, the Norton family transferred control of the company
to its employees, and today—with a staff of four hundred and a comparable
number of trade, college, and professional titles published each year—
W. W. Norton & Company stands as the largest and oldest publishing
house owned wholly by its employees.*

For Bruce and Susan
and for Blair

For
Jason and Jessica

CONTENTS

$\mathcal{P}$ART TWO / **BUILDING A NATION**

$\mathscr{P}$ART THREE / **AN EXPANSIVE NATION**

17 | THE WAR OF THE UNION   655

18 | RECONSTRUCTION: NORTH AND SOUTH   713

GLOSSARY   A1

APPENDIX   A41

CREDITS   A101

INDEX   A107

MAPS

PREFACE

Just as history is never complete, neither is a historical textbook. We have learned much from the responses of readers and instructors to the first five editions of *America: A Narrative History.* Perhaps the most important and reassuring lesson is that our original intention has proved valid: to provide a compelling narrative history of the American experience, a narrative animated by human characters, informed by analysis and social texture, and guided by the unfolding of events. Readers have also endorsed the book's distinctive size and format. *America* is designed to be read and to carry a moderate price.

As in previous revisions of *America,* we have adopted an overarching theme that informs many of the new sections we introduce throughout the Sixth Edition. In previous editions we have traced such broad-ranging themes as immigration, the frontier and the West, and popular culture. In each case we blend our discussions of the selected theme into the narrative, where they reside through succeeding editions.

The Sixth Edition of *America* highlights the social, political, cultural, and economic history of work in American life. Frederick Douglass, the former slave who became a leading abolitionist, declared in 1853 that Americans are not valued "for what they are; they are valued for what they can do." Work, of course, is a central aspect of human endeavor; it forms an indelible part of our lives. Labor structures our days and transforms the world we live in. It helps shape our identities and define our possibilities. Through almost four centuries of American history, workers have built, sustained, and transformed the economy. Their everyday lives have helped shape American society and culture. Their needs and aspirations have fueled American politics at every level and have been mediated by the courts. The history of work takes in all dimensions of American history.

The Sixth Edition of *America* includes new material reflecting this expansive sense of the history of work in the United States. Here are some of the highlights:

- Chapter 3 includes a new discussion of shipbuilding in colonial New England that explores maritime work and its significance in the colonial economy
- Chapter 9 explores how the emerging factory system changed the nature of work for many laborers
- Chapter 12 includes an expanded discussion of early labor organization and the rise of professions
- Chapter 14 includes a section on the Spanish missions in California and their use of Indian labor
- Chapter 15 offers a new discussion of slave women and their work
- Chapter 20 has been revised and includes an expanded discussion of the rise of big business after the Civil War, a new section on child labor and its regulation, and a profile of the colorful labor organizer Mother Jones
- Chapter 26 features new sections on women workers and Margaret Sanger's efforts to educate them on the issue of birth control
- Chapter 27 includes a section on the dramatic strike at the Loray textile mills in Gastonia, North Carolina, in 1929
- Later chapters include new discussions of the rise of high-tech industry and how the expanding service sector has compensated for dwindling manufacturing jobs, with widespread effects on work and society.

Beyond these explorations of work in American history, we have introduced other new discussions throughout the Sixth Edition. We have revised the book to reflect the best of recent scholarship and we feel confident that the text provides students an excellent introduction to the current state of scholarship in American history.

We are pleased that even with the addition of rich new material throughout, we have managed to reduce the length of *America* by almost 10 percent in the Sixth Edition. This was not achieved by crash diet, but by the authorial equivalent to regular exercise: the careful pruning of detail throughout the book. We trust that the result retains all the character and color that students and instructors have prized in the book, but in a trimmer form.

To enhance the pedagogical features of the text, we have included a **Glossary** in this new edition. It provides a handy reference for checking basic events, concepts, legal decisions, and so on. The Glossary was researched and drafted by Brenda Eagles with the assistance of Charles Eagles.

A new item to supplement this edition is *The Norton Map Workbook in American History.* It includes a range of work-maps covering the core of American history from the colonial period to the present. Questions for each map reinforce students' skills in geography and probe their knowledge of historical events.

We have also revised the outstanding ancillary package that supplements the text. *For the Record: A Documentary History of America,* Second Edition, by David E. Shi and Holly A. Mayer (Duquesne University), is a rich resource with over 300 primary source readings from diaries, journals, newspaper articles, speeches, government documents, and novels. It also has four special chapters on interpreting illustrations and photographs as historical documents. The *Study Guide,* by Charles Eagles (University of Mississippi), is another valuable resource. This edition contains chapter outlines, learning objectives, timelines, expanded vocabulary exercises, and many new short-answer and essay questions. *America: A Narrative History* Online Tutor prepared by Tom Pearcy (Slippery Rock University), is an online collection of tools for review and research. It includes chapter summaries, review questions and quizzes, interactive map exercises, timelines, and research modules, many new to this edition. *Norton Presentation Maker* is a CD-ROM slide and text resource that includes images from the text, four-color maps, additional images from the Library of Congress archives, and audio files of significant historical speeches. Finally, the *Instructor's Manual and Test Bank,* by Mark Goldman (Tallahassee Community College) includes a test bank of short-answer and essay questions, as well as detailed chapter outlines, lecture suggestions, and bibliographies.

In preparing the Sixth Edition, we have benefited from the insights and suggestions of many people. Some of these insights have come from student readers of the text and we encourage such feedback. Among the scholars and survey instructors who offered us their comments and suggestions are: James C. Cobb (University of Georgia),

Kara Miles Turner (Virginia State University), Vernon Burton (University of Illinois), Blanche Brick, Cathy Lively, Harley Haussman and others at the Bryan campus of Blinn College, Charles Eagles (University of Mississippi), Timothy Gilfoyle (Loyola University), James M. Russell (University of Tennessee, Chattanooga), Matthew Plowman (Waldorf College), and Rand Burnette (MacMurray College). Our special thanks go to Tom Pearcy (Slippery Rock University) for all of his work on the timelines. Once again, we thank our friends at W. W. Norton, especially Steve Forman, Steve Hoge, Sarah England, Neil Hoos, Kate Barry, Lory Frenkel, JoAnn Simony, Karl Bakeman, and Matt Arnold, for their care and attention along the way.

—George B. Tindall
—David E. Shi

PART ONE

A NEW WORLD

Long before Christopher Columbus accidentally discovered the New World in his effort to find a passage to Asia, the tribal peoples he mislabeled "Indians" had occupied and shaped the lands of the Western Hemisphere. The first people to settle the New World were nomadic hunters and gatherers who migrated from northeastern Asia during the last glacial advance of the Ice Age, nearly 20,000 years ago. By the end of the fifteenth century, when Columbus began his voyage west, there were millions of Native Americans living in the Western Hemisphere. Over the centuries, they had developed stable, diverse, and often highly sophisticated societies, some rooted in agriculture, others in trade or imperial conquest.

The Native American cultures were, of course, profoundly affected by the arrival of peoples from Europe and Africa. They were exploited, enslaved, displaced, and exterminated. Yet this conventional tale of conquest oversimplifies the complex process by which Indians, Europeans, and Africans interacted. The Indians were more than passive victims; they were also trading partners and rivals of the transatlantic newcomers. They became enemies and allies, neighbors and advisers, converts and spouses. As such they fully participated in the creation of the new society known as America.

The Europeans who risked their lives to settle in the New World were themselves quite diverse. Young and old, men and women, they came from Spain, Portugal, France, Great Britain, the Netherlands, Italy, and the various German states. A variety of motives inspired them to undertake the transatlantic voyage. Some were adventurers and fortune seekers, eager to find gold and spices. Others were fervent Christians determined to create kingdoms of God in the New World. Still others were convicts, debtors, indentured servants, or political or religious exiles. Many were simply seeking higher wages and greater economic opportunity. A settler in Pennsylvania noted that "poor people (both men and women) of all kinds can here get three times the wages for their labour than they can in England or Wales."

Yet such enticements were not sufficient to attract enough workers to keep up with the rapidly expanding colonial economies. So the Europeans began to force Indians to work for them. But there were never enough of them to meet the unceasing demand. Moreover, they often escaped or were so obstreperous that several colonies banned their use. The Massachusetts legislature did so because Indians were of such "a malicious, surly and revengeful spirit; rude and insolent in their behavior, and very ungovernable."

Beginning early in the seventeenth century, more and more colonists turned to the African slave trade for their labor needs. In 1619 white traders began transporting captured Africans to the English colonies. This development would transform American society in ways that no one at the time envisioned. Few Europeans during the colonial era saw the contradiction between the New World's promise of individual freedom and the expanding institution of race slavery. Nor did they reckon with the problems associated with introducing into the new society peoples they considered alien and unassimilable.

The intermingling of peoples, cultures, and ecosystems from the three continents of Africa, Europe, and North America gave colonial American society its distinctive vitality and variety. In turn, the diversity of the environment and climate led to the creation of quite different economies and patterns of living in the various regions of North America. As the original settlements grew into prosperous and populous colonies, the transplanted Europeans had to fashion social institutions and political systems to manage growth and control tensions.

At the same time, imperial rivalries among the Spanish, French, English, and Dutch produced numerous intrigues and costly wars. The monarchs of Europe had a difficult time trying to manage and exploit this fluid and often volatile colonial society. Many of the colonists, they discovered, brought with them to the New World a feisty independence that led them to resent government interference in their affairs. A British official in North Carolina reported that the residents of the Piedmont region were "without any Law or Order. Impudence is so very high [among them], as to be past bearing." As long as the reins of imperial control were loosely applied, the two parties maintained an uneasy partnership. But as the British authorities tightened their control during the mid–eighteenth century, they met resistance, which became revolt, and culminated in revolution.

1 ⌒ THE COLLISION

OF CULTURES

CHAPTER ORGANIZER

This chapter focuses on:

- the origins and variety of civilizations that existed in pre-Columbian America.

- the European voyages of discovery and explorers who probed the shorelines of America looking for a passage to Asia.

- the exchanges and clashes that came with European contacts with the plants, animals, and people of the New World.

he "New World" discovered by Christopher Columbus was in fact home to civilizations thousands of years old. The Americas were the last regions of the world to be occupied by people. Until recently, archaeologists had long assumed that the first arrivals were Siberians who some 15,000 years ago crossed the Bering Sea on a land bridge to Alaska made accessible by the receding waters during the last ice age. These nomadic hunters and their descendants then drifted south in pursuit of grazing herds of large mammals: mammoths, musk oxen, and woolly rhinoceroses. Over the next 500 years,

5

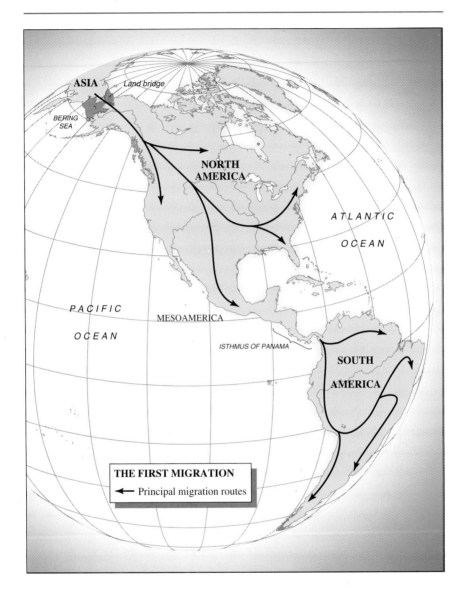

these peoples fanned out in small bands across the entire hemisphere, foraging for food and game. Recent archaeological discoveries in Pennsylvania, Virginia, and Chile, however, suggest that humans may have arrived much earlier in several different waves from various parts of Asia—and some of them may even have come across the Atlantic Ocean from southwestern Europe.

The story of the first peoples to arrive in the Western Hemisphere remains in the realm of prehistory, the domain of archaeologists and anthropologists who must salvage an incomplete record from the rubble of the past: stone tools and weapons, bones, pottery, figurines, ancient dwellings, burial places, scraps of textiles and basketry, and finally bits of oral tradition and the reports of early explorers, all pieced together with the adhesive of informed guesswork.

PRE-COLUMBIAN INDIAN CIVILIZATIONS

The first humans in North America discovered an immense continent with extraordinary climatic and environmental diversity. Coastal plains, broad grasslands, harsh deserts, and soaring mountain ranges all required different modes of living that in turn generated distinct social structures and cultural patterns. By the time Columbus discovered the "New World," the native peoples of North America had developed a diverse array of communities that used almost 400 different languages. Yet despite the distances and dialects separating these different Indian societies, the so-called Paleo-Indians created extensive trading networks that helped diffuse ideas and innovations. Contrary to the romantic myth of early Indian civilizations living in perfect harmony with nature and each other, the native societies exerted great pressure on their environments and engaged in frequent warfare with one another.

EARLY CULTURAL STAGES   After years of nomadic life, the Indians settled in more permanent villages. They invented fiber snares, basketry, and mills for grinding nuts, and they domesticated the dog and the turkey. A new cultural stage arrived with the introduction of farming and pottery. Already by about 5000 B.C., Indians of the Mexican highlands were consuming plant foods that became the staples of the New World: chiefly maize (Indian corn), beans, and squash, but also chili peppers, avocados, and pumpkins.

THE MAYAS, AZTECS, AND INCAS   By about 2000–1500 B.C., permanent towns dependent on farming had appeared in Mexico. The more settled life in turn provided leisure for the cultivation of religion, crafts, art, science, administration—and warfare. From about A.D. 300 to A.D. 900, Middle America (Mesoamerica) developed great city centers complete with gigantic pyramids, temple complexes, and courts for ceremonial games, all supported by the surrounding peasant villages. Moreover, the Mayas developed enough mathematics (including a symbol for zero) and astronomy to devise a calendar more accurate than the one the Europeans were using at the time of Columbus.

About A.D. 900, the complex Mayan culture collapsed. The cause of its collapse remains uncertain. Pollen recovered from underground debris suggests that the Mayas overexploited the rain forest upon whose fragile ecosystem they depended. Overpopulation also placed added strain on Mayan society. The primary factor, however, was unrelenting civil war among the Mayas themselves. Mayan war parties destroyed each other's cities and took prisoners who were then sacrificed to the gods in theatrical rituals. Whatever the reasons for the weakening of

A fresco depicting the social divisions of Mayan society. The king, on the top step, is surrounded by nobles; below, prisoners are guarded by warriors.

Mayan society, it succumbed to the Toltecs, a warlike people who conquered most of the region in the tenth century. But around A.D. 1200, the Toltecs too mysteriously withdrew.

During the time of troubles that followed, the Aztecs arrived from the northwest, founded the city of Tenochtitlán (now Mexico City) in 1325, and gradually expanded their control over central Mexico. When the Spaniards invaded in 1519, the Aztec Empire under Montezuma II ruled over perhaps 5 million people—though estimates range as high as 20 million.

Farther south, in what is now Colombia, the Chibchas built a similar empire on a smaller scale. Still farther south the Quechua peoples (better known by the name of their ruler, the Inca) by the fifteenth century controlled an empire that stretched a thousand miles along the Andes Mountains from Ecuador to Chile. It was connected by an elaborate system of roads and organized under an autocratic government that dominated life.

INDIAN CULTURES OF NORTH AMERICA   The Indians of the present-day United States developed three identifiable cultural peaks: the Adena-Hopewell culture of the Northeast (800 B.C.–A.D. 600); the

Mississippian culture of the Southeast (A.D. 600–1500); and the Pueblo-Hohokam culture of the Southwest (400 B.C.–present). None of these developed as fully as the Mayas, Aztecs, and Incas.

The Adena-Hopewell culture, centered in the Ohio Valley, left behind enormous earthworks and burial mounds—sometimes elaborately shaped like great snakes, birds, or other animals. Evidence from the mounds suggests a complex social structure and a specialized division of labor. Moreover, the Hopewell Indians developed an elaborate trade network that spanned the continent.

The Mississippian culture, centered in the central Mississippi River Valley, resembled the Mayan and Aztec societies in its intensive agriculture, substantial towns built around central plazas, temple mounds (vaguely resembling pyramids), and death cults, which involved human torture and sacrifice. The Mississippian culture peaked in the fourteenth and fifteenth centuries, and finally collapsed because of diseases transmitted from Europe.

The arid Southwest hosted irrigation-based cultures, elements of which persist today and heirs of which (the Hopis, Zunis, and others)

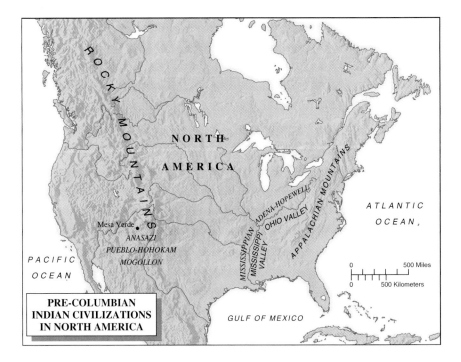

PRE-COLUMBIAN
INDIAN CIVILIZATIONS
IN NORTH AMERICA

still live in the adobe pueblos of their ancestors. The most widespread and best known
of the cultures, the Anasazi ("the ancient
ones," in the Navajo language), developed
in the "four corners" where the states of
Arizona, New Mexico, Colorado, and
Utah meet.

The Anasazis lived in baked-mud
adobe structures built four and
five stories high. In contrast to the
Mesoamerican and Mississippian
cultures, Anasazi society lacked a
rigid class structure. The religious leaders and warriors labored
much as the rest of the people. In
fact, they engaged in warfare only
as a means of self-defense (Hopi
means "the peaceful people"),
and there is little evidence of human sacrifice or human trophies.
Toward the end of the thirteenth
century a lengthy drought and the
pressure of new arrivals from the

*A ceramic vase or urn in the form of
a woman and child, one of only a
few Mississippian artifacts found
in present-day Missouri.*

north began to restrict the territory of the Anasazis. Into their peaceful
world came the aggressive Navajos and Apaches, followed two centuries later by Spaniards marching up from the south.

Even the most developed Indian societies of the sixteenth century
were ill equipped to resist the European cultures invading their world.
There were large and fatal gaps in Indian knowledge and technology.
The Indians of Mexico had copper and bronze but no iron except a few
specimens of meteorites. Messages were conveyed by patterns in beads
in the Northeast and by knotted cords among the Incas, but there was
no true writing except for the hieroglyphs of Mesoamerica. The Indians
had domesticated dogs, turkeys, and llamas, but horses were unknown
until the Spaniards came astride their enormous "dogs."

Disunity everywhere—civil disorders and rebellions plagued the
Aztecs, Mayas, and Incas—left the native peoples of the New World
open to division and conquest. As it turned out, the centralized societies

Ruins of Anasazi cliff dwellings at Mesa Verde, Colorado. The circular chamber to the left is a ceremonial kiva.

in the south were as vulnerable as the scattered tribes farther north. The capture or death of their rulers left them in disarray and subjection. The loosely organized tribes of North America (over 1,000 in all) made the Europeans pay more dearly for their conquest, but when open conflict erupted, arrows and tomahawks were seldom a match for guns.

Despite such disadvantages, the Indians resisted European invaders for centuries. They displayed an amazing capacity for adapting to changing circumstances, incorporating European technology and weaponry, forging new alliances, changing their own community structures, and, in numerous instances, converting the Europeans to their way of life. For centuries, scholars glossed over the awkward fact that many Spanish, English, and French settlers had voluntarily joined Indian society or had chosen to stay after being captured.

EUROPEAN VISIONS OF AMERICA

Long before Columbus set sail, America lived in the fantasies of Europeans. The vast unknown beyond the horizon held a prominent place in the mythology of ancient Greece. In the west, toward the sunset which marked the end of day and symbolically the end of life, was supposedly an earthly paradise. The vision of America as a place of rebirth, a New Eden freed from the historic sins of the Old World, still colors the self-image of the American people.

Norse expeditions to the New World during the tenth and eleventh centuries are the earliest that can be verified, and even they have dissolved into legend. Like Asians crossing the Bering Strait to the east, the Norsemen went island-hopping across the North Atlantic to the west. Before about A.D. 870 they conquered Iceland from Irish settlers while other Vikings terrorized the coasts of Europe. Around A.D. 985 an Icelander named Erik the Red colonized the west coast of a rocky, fogbound island he deceptively called Greenland—Erik was the New World's first real-estate booster—and about a year later a trader missed Greenland and sighted land beyond. Knowing of this, Thorvald Eriksson, son of Erik the Red, sailed out from Greenland about A.D. 1001 and sighted the coasts of Helluland (Baffin Island), Markland (Labrador), and Vinland (Newfoundland), where he settled for the winter. Speculation had long placed Vinland as far south as Rhode Island or Chesapeake Bay, but in 1963 a Norwegian investigator uncovered the ruins of a number of Norse houses at L'Anse-aux-Meadows,

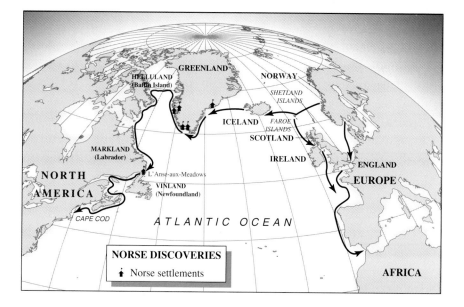

on the northern coast of Newfoundland. This almost surely was the Vinland of the Norse sagas.

The Norse discoveries of the New World are fascinating, but they have no connection to later American history unless Columbus heard of them, which is doubtful. The Norse settlers withdrew from North America in the face of hostile natives, and the Greenland colonies vanished mysteriously in the fifteenth century. Nowhere in Europe had the forces yet developed that would inspire adventurers to subdue the New World.

THE EXPANSION OF EUROPE

During the late fifteenth century, Europeans developed the maritime technology and imperial ambitions to venture around the world. The age of discovery coincided with the opening of the modern period in European history. The peculiar activities and institutions that distinguished modern times from the medieval period included the rise of an inquiring spirit; the growth of trade, towns, and modern corporations; the decline of feudalism and the formation of national states; the Protestant Reformation and the Catholic Counter-Reformation; and, some old sins—greed, conquest, exploitation, oppression, racism, and slavery—that quickly defiled the fancied innocence of the New Eden.

RENAISSANCE GEOGRAPHY   For more than two centuries before Columbus, the mind of Europe quickened with the so-called Renaissance: the rediscovery of ancient texts, the rebirth of secular learning, the spirit of inquiry, all of which spread the more rapidly after Johannes Gutenberg's invention of movable type around 1440. Learned Europeans of the fifteenth century held in almost reverential awe the authority of ancient learning. The age of discovery was especially influenced by ancient concepts of geography. As early as the sixth century B.C., the Pythagoreans had taught the sphericity of the earth, and in the third century B.C., the earth's size was computed very nearly correctly. All this was accepted in Renaissance universities on the word of Aristotle, and the myth that Columbus was trying to prove this theory is one of those durable falsehoods that will not disappear, even in the face of the evidence. No informed person at that time thought the earth was flat.

Progress in the art of navigation accompanied the revival of learning. The precise origin of the magnetic compass is unknown, but the principle was known by the twelfth century, and in the fifteenth century mariners employed the astrolabe and cross-staff long used by landlocked astronomers to sight stars and find the latitude. Steering across the open sea, however, remained a matter of dead reckoning. A ship's master set his course along a given latitude and calculated it from the angle of the North Star, or with less certainty the sun, estimating speed by the eye. Longitude remained a matter of guesswork, since accurate timepieces were needed to obtain it. Ship's clocks were too inaccurate until more precise chronometers were developed in the eighteenth century.

THE GROWTH OF TRADE, TOWNS, AND NATION-STATES The forces that would invade and reshape the New World found their focus in Europe's rising towns, the centers of a growing trade that slowly broadened the narrow horizons of feudal culture. In its farthest reaches, this commerce moved either overland or through the eastern Mediterranean all the way to East Asia, whence Europeans imported medicine, silks, precious stones, dyewoods, perfumes, and rugs. There they also purchased the spices—pepper, nutmeg, clove—so essential to the preserving of food, especially in the countries of southern Europe, where the warm, humid climate accelerated spoilage. The trade gave rise to a merchant class and to the idea of corporations through which stockholders would share risks and profits.

The trade was both chancy and costly. Goods commonly passed from hand to hand, from ships to pack trains and back to ships along the way, subject to levies by all sorts of princes and potentates. The Muslim world, from Spain across North Africa into Central Asia, lay athwart all the important trade routes, and this added to the hazards. Little wonder, then, that Europeans should dream of an all-water route to the coveted spices of East Asia and the Indies. Travelers' stories also stirred interest in the Orient. The Venetian Marco Polo provided the most famous account in 1298–1299. Christopher Columbus owned a Latin version of Polo's travels, with margins heavily annotated in his own hand.

Another spur to exploration was the rise of national states, with kings and queens who had the power and the money to sponsor the search. The growth of the merchant class went hand in hand with the growth of centralized power. Merchants wanted uniform currencies, trade laws, and the elimination of trade barriers. They thus became natural allies of the sovereigns who could meet their needs. In turn, merchants and university-trained professionals supplied the monarchs with money, lawyers, and officials. The Crusades to capture the Holy Land (1095–1270) had also advanced the process of international trade and exploration. They had brought the West into contact with Eastern autocracy and had decimated the ranks of the feudal lords. And new means of warfare—the use of gunpowder and standing armies—further weakened the independence of the nobility.

By 1492 the map of western Europe showed several united kingdoms: France, where in 1453 Louis XI had emerged from the Hundred Years' War as head of a unified state; England, where in 1485 Henry VII emerged victorious after thirty years of civil strife known as the Wars of the Roses; Spain, where in 1469 Ferdinand of Aragon and Isabella of Castile united two great kingdoms in marriage; and Portugal, where even earlier, in 1385, John I had fought off the Castilians and assured national independence.

These factors—urbanization, world trade, the rise of national states, and advances in knowledge and technology—combined with natural human curiosity and greed to create the outburst of energy that led to the discovery and conquest of the New World. Beginning in the late fifteenth century, Europeans set in motion the events that, as one historian has observed, bound together "four continents, three races, and a great diversity of regional parts."

THE VOYAGES OF COLUMBUS

It was in Portugal, with the guidance of King John's son, Prince Henry the Navigator, that exploration and discovery began in earnest. In 1422 Prince Henry dispatched his first expedition to map the African coast. Driven partly by the hope of outflanking the Islamic world, partly by the hope of trade, the Portuguese by 1446 reached Cape Verde, then the equator, and by 1482 the Congo River. In 1488 Bartholomeu Dias rounded the Cape of Good Hope at Africa's southern tip.

Christopher Columbus meanwhile was learning his trade in the school of Portuguese seamanship. Born in 1451, the son of an Italian weaver, Columbus took to the sea at an early age, making up for his lack of formal education by teaching himself geography, navigation, and Latin. By the 1480s, Columbus—a tall, red-haired, long-faced man—was an experienced mariner. Dazzled by the prospect of Asian riches, he hatched a scheme to reach the Indies (India, China, the East Indies, or Japan) by sailing west across the Atlantic. Columbus won the support of Ferdinand and Isabella, the Spanish monarchs, and himself raised much of the money needed to finance the voyage. The legend that

Christopher Columbus.

the queen had to hock the crown jewels is as spurious as the fable that Columbus set out to prove the earth was round.

Columbus chartered one seventy-five-foot ship, the *Santa María*, and the Spanish city of Palos supplied two smaller caravels, the *Pinta* and *Niña*. From Palos this little squadron, with eighty-seven officers and men, set sail westward for what Columbus thought was Asia. The first leg of the journey went well, but then the breeze lagged, the days passed, and the crew began to grumble about their captain's farfetched plan. Columbus finally promised that the expedition would turn back if land were not sighted in three days.

Early on October 12, 1492, after thirty-three days at sea, a lookout on the *Santa María* yelled *"Tierra! Tierra!* [Land! Land!]" It was an island in the Bahamas east of Florida that Columbus named San Salvador (Blessed Savior). Columbus decided they were near the Indies, so he called the island people *los Indios.* He described the "Indians" as naked people, "very well made, of very handsome bodies and very good faces." He added that "with fifty men they could all be subjugated and compelled to do anything one wishes." The natives, Columbus wrote, were "to be ruled and set to work, to cultivate the land and to do all else that may be necessary . . . and to adopt our customs."

At that moment, however, Columbus was not interested in enslaving noble savages; he was seeking the Indies. He therefore continued to search through the Bahamian Cays down to Cuba, a place name that suggested Cipangu (Japan), and then eastward to the island he named Española (or Hispaniola, now the site of Haiti and the Dominican Republic), where he first found significant amounts of gold jewelry. Columbus learned of, but did not encounter until his second voyage, the fierce Caribs of the Lesser Antilles. The Caribbean Sea was named after them, and, because of their alleged bad habits, the word "cannibal" was derived from a Spanish version of their name (Caníbal).

On the night before Christmas, 1492, the *Santa María* ran aground off Hispaniola, and Columbus, still believing he had reached Asia, decided to return home. He left about forty men behind and seized a dozen natives to present as gifts to Spain's royal couple. When Columbus reached Palos, he received a hero's welcome. The news of his discovery spread rapidly throughout Europe, and Ferdinand and Isabella instructed him to prepare for a second voyage. They were eager to acquire gold from the Indians and to convert them to Christianity. The Spanish monarchs also set about shoring up their legal claim against Portugal's pretensions to the newly discovered lands. When the pope, who was Spanish, interceded on Spain's behalf, Spain and Portugal reached a compromise agreement called the Treaty of Tordesillas (1494), which drew an imaginary line west of the Cape Verde Islands and stipulated that the area west of the line would be a Spanish sphere of exploration and settlement.

Columbus returned across the Atlantic in 1493 with seventeen ships, livestock, and some 1,200 men, as well as royal instructions to "treat the Indians very well." Once back in the New World, Admiral Columbus discovered that the camp he had left behind was in chaos. The unsupervised soldiers had run amok, raping native women, robbing Indian villages, and, as Columbus's son later added, "committing a thousand excesses for which they were mortally hated by the Indians." The natives finally struck back and killed ten Spaniards. A furious Columbus immediately attacked the Indian villages. The Spaniards, armed with crossbows, guns, and ferocious dogs, decimated the native defenders and loaded 550 of them onto ships bound for the slave market in Spain.

Columbus then ventured out across the Caribbean Sea. He found the Lesser Antilles, explored the coast of Cuba, discovered Jamaica, and finally returned to Spain in 1496. On a third voyage in 1498 Columbus found Trinidad and explored the northern coast of South

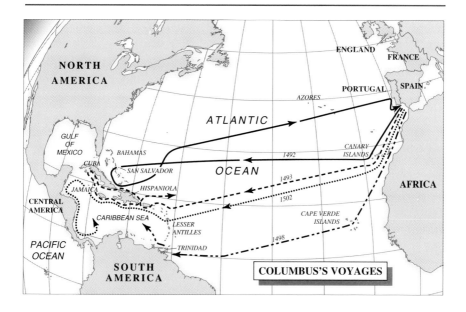

ATLANTIC OCEAN

NORTH AMERICA

ENGLAND
FRANCE
PORTUGAL SPAIN
AZORES

GULF OF MEXICO
BAHAMAS
CANARY ISLANDS
CUBA
SAN SALVADOR
1492
JAMAICA
HISPANIOLA
1493
CENTRAL AMERICA
1502
AFRICA
CARIBBEAN SEA
LESSER ANTILLES
CAPE VERDE ISLANDS
PACIFIC OCEAN
TRINIDAD
1498
SOUTH AMERICA

COLUMBUS'S VOYAGES

America. He led a fourth voyage in 1502, during which he sailed along the coast of Central America, still looking in vain for Asia. Marooned on Jamaica more than a year, he finally returned to Spain in 1504. He died two years later.

To the end, Columbus refused to believe that he had discovered anything other than outlying parts of Asia. Full awareness that a great land mass lay between Europe and Asia dawned on Europeans very slowly. By one of history's greatest ironies, this led the New World to be named not for its discoverer but for another Italian explorer, Amerigo Vespucci, who sailed to the New World in 1499. Vespucci roamed the coast of South America and reported that it was so large it must be a new continent. European mapmakers thereafter began to label the New World using a variant of Vespucci's first name: America.

THE GREAT BIOLOGICAL EXCHANGE

The first European contacts with the New World began a prolonged diffusion of cultures, a complicated worldwide exchange of such magnitude as humanity had never known before. It was in fact more than a diffusion of cultures: it was a diffusion of distinctive biological

A tortoise, drawn by John White, one of the earliest English settlers in America.

systems that ultimately worked in favor of the Europeans at the expense of the native peoples. Indians, Europeans, and eventually Africans intersected to create new religious beliefs and languages, adopt new tastes in food, and develop new modes of dress.

If anything, the plants and animals of the two worlds were more different than the people and their ways of life. Europeans, for instance, had never seen such creatures as the fearsome (if harmless) iguana, flying squirrels, fish with whiskers like cats, rattlesnakes, or anything quite like several other species: bison, cougars, armadillos, opossums, sloths, tapirs, anacondas, American eels, toucans, condors, and hummingbirds. Among the few domesticated animals, they could recognize the dog and the duck, but turkeys, guinea pigs, llamas, and alpacas were all new. Nor did the Native Americans know of horses, cattle, pigs, sheep, goats, and (maybe) chickens, which soon arrived from Europe in abundance. Yet, within a half century, whole islands of the Caribbean would be overrun by pigs, whose ancestors were bred in Spain.

The exchange of plant life between old and new worlds worked an even greater change, a revolution in the diets of both hemispheres. Before the Great Discovery three main staples of the modern diet were unknown in the Old World: maize, potatoes (sweet and white), and many kinds of beans (snap, kidney, lima, and others). The white potato, although commonly called "Irish," actually migrated from South America to Europe and only reached North America with the Scotch-Irish immigrants of the 1700s. Other New World food plants included peanuts, squash, peppers, tomatoes, pumpkins, pineapples, sassafras, papayas, guavas, avocados, cacao (the source of chocolate), and chicle (for chewing gum). Europeans in turn soon introduced rice, wheat, barley, oats, wine grapes, melons, coffee, olives, bananas, "Kentucky" bluegrass, daisies, and dandelions to the New World.

The beauty of the exchange was that the food plants were more complementary than competitive. Indian corn, it turned out, could flourish almost anywhere—high or low, hot or cold, wet or dry. It spread quickly throughout the world. Before the end of the 1500s, American maize and sweet potatoes were staple crops in China. The green revolution exported from the Americas thus helped nourish a worldwide population explosion probably greater than any since the invention of agriculture. The dramatic increase in the British and European populations fueled by such new foods in turn helped provide the surplus of peoples who colonized the New World.

Europeans, moreover, adopted many Native American devices: canoes, snowshoes, moccasins, hammocks, kayaks, ponchos, dogsleds,

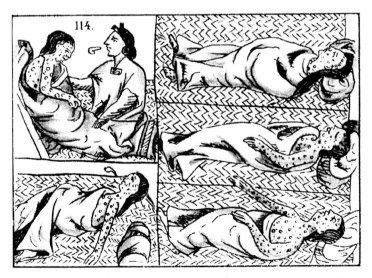

A devastating smallpox epidemic depicted in an Aztec manuscript.

and toboggans. The rubber ball and the game of lacrosse had Indian origins. New words entered the languages of Europeans: wigwam, teepee, papoose, succotash, hominy, tobacco, moose, skunk, opossum, woodchuck, chipmunk, tomahawk, hickory, pecan, raccoon, and hundreds of others—and new terms in translation: warpath, warpaint, paleface, medicine man, firewater. And the natives left the map dotted with place names of Indian origin long after they were gone, from Miami to Yakima, from Penobscot to Yuma.

There were still other New World contributions: tobacco and a number of other drugs, including coca (for cocaine and novocaine), curare (a muscle relaxant), and cinchona bark (for quinine). But Europeans also exposed the New World inhabitants to exotic new illnesses. Even minor European diseases such as measles turned killer in the bodies of Indians who had never encountered them and thus had built up no immunity. Major diseases such as smallpox and typhus killed all the more speedily. In central Mexico alone, some 8 million people, perhaps a third of the entire population, died of disease within a decade after the Spaniards arrived. In what is now Texas, one Spanish explorer noted, "half the natives died from a disease of the bowels and blamed us."

PROFESSIONAL EXPLORERS

Undeterred by new diseases and encouraged by Columbus's discoveries, professional explorers, mostly Italians, hired themselves out to the highest bidder to look for the elusive western passage to Asia. They probed the shorelines of America during the early sixteenth century in the vain search for an opening, and thus increased by leaps and bounds European knowledge of the New World.

The first to sight the North American continent was John Cabot, a Venetian sponsored by Henry VII of England. Cabot sailed across the North Atlantic in 1497. His landfall at what the king called "the new founde lande" gave England the basis for a later claim to all of North America. During the early sixteenth century, however, the English grew so preoccupied with internal divisions and conflicts with France that they failed to capitalize on Cabot's discoveries. Only fishermen exploited

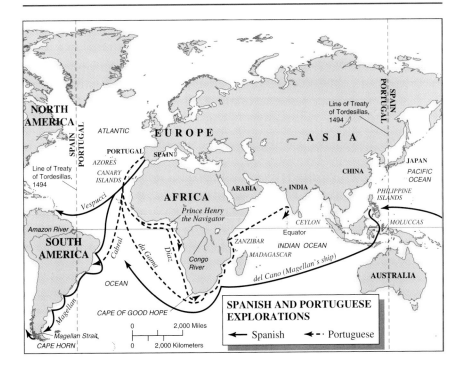

SPANISH AND PORTUGUESE
EXPLORATIONS
← Spanish   ◄-· Portuguese

the teeming waters of the Grand Banks. In 1513 the Spaniard Vasco Núñez de Balboa became the first European to sight the Pacific Ocean, but only after he had crossed the Isthmus of Panama on foot.

The Portuguese, meanwhile, went the other way. In 1498, while Columbus prowled the Caribbean, Vasco da Gama sailed east around Africa and soon set up the trading posts of a commercial empire stretching from India to the Moluccas (or Spice Islands) of Indonesia. The Spaniards, however, reasoned that the line of demarcation established by the Treaty of Tordesillas ran around the other side of the earth as well. Hoping to show that the Moluccas lay near South America within the Spanish sphere, Ferdinand Magellan, a haughty Portuguese seaman in the employ of Spain, set out to find a passage through or around South America. Departing Spain in 1519, he found his way through the dangerous strait that now bears his name, then moved far to the north. On a journey far longer than he had anticipated, he touched upon Guam and eventually made a landfall in the Philippines, where he lost his life in a fight with the natives.

Magellan's remaining crew members made their way to the Moluccas, picked up a cargo of spices, and returned to Spain in 1522. This first voyage around the globe quickened Spanish ambitions for empire in the East, but after some abortive attempts at establishing themselves there, the Spaniards, beset by war with France, sold Portugal their claims to the Moluccas. From 1565, however, Spaniards would begin to penetrate the Philippines, discovered by Magellan and named for the Spanish prince who became King Philip II. In the seventeenth century, the English and the Dutch would oust Portugal from most of its empire, but for a century the East Indies were Portuguese.

THE SPANISH EMPIRE

During the sixteenth century, Spain created the most powerful empire in the world by exploiting its presence in the Americas. The Caribbean Sea served as the funnel through which Spanish power entered the New World. After establishing colonies on Hispaniola and at Santo Domingo, which became the capital of the West Indies, the Spanish proceeded eastward to Puerto Rico (1508) and westward to Cuba (1511–1514). Their motives were explicit. Said one soldier: "We came here to serve God and the king, and also to get rich."

The process of colonizing the New World was difficult and deadly. Most of those in the first wave of settlement died of malnutrition or disease. But the natives suffered even more casualties. A Spaniard on Hispaniola reported in 1494 that over 50,000 Indians had died from infectious diseases carried by Europeans, and more were "falling each day, with every step, like cattle in an infected herd."

A CLASH OF CULTURES The violent encounter between Spaniards and Indians in North America involved more than a clash between different peoples. It also involved contrasting forms of technological development. Where Indians used dugout canoes for transport, Europeans sailed on heavily armed, oceangoing vessels. The Spanish ships not only carried human cargo; they also brought with them steel swords, firearms, explosives, and armor. These advanced military tools struck fear into many Indians. A Spanish priest in Florida observed that gunpowder "frightens the most valiant and courageous Indian and renders him slave to the white man's command." Such weaponry helps explain why the Europeans were able to defeat far superior numbers of Indians.

The Europeans enjoyed other cultural advantages. The only domestic four-legged animal in North America, for example, was the dog. The Spaniards, on the other hand, brought with them horses, pigs, and cattle, all of which offered sources of food and leather. Horses provided greater speed in battle and also introduced a decided psychological advantage. "The most essential thing in new lands is horses," reported one Spanish soldier. "They instill the greatest fear in the enemy and make the Indians respect the leaders of the army." Even more feared among the Indians were the greyhound dogs that the Spaniards used to guard their camps. These incredibly fast canines scared many into surrender; those who did not surrender were often attacked by the ferocious degs.

CORTÉS'S CONQUEST   The first European conquest of a major Indian civilization on the North American mainland began in 1519,

Page from the Tlaxcala Lienzo, a historical narrative from the sixteenth century. The scene, in which Cortés is shown seated on a throne at the center, depicts the arrival of the Spaniards in Tlaxcala.

when Hernando Cortés landed on the coast of Mexico with an unauthorized expedition of 600 Spanish soldiers from Cuba. The soldiers, called conquistadores, received no pay; they were military entrepreneurs willing to risk their lives for a share in the expected plunder and slaves. The brilliant, ruthless Cortés had participated in the military occupation of Cuba and had acquired his own plantations and gold mines. But he yearned for even more wealth and glory. Against the wishes of the Spanish governor in Cuba, who wanted the Aztec Empire for himself, Cortés launched a daring invasion of Mexico. The 200-mile march from Vera Cruz on the coast through difficult mountain passes to the magnificent Aztec capital of Tenochtitlán (Mexico City), and the subjugation of the Aztecs, who thought themselves the "masters of the world," was one of the most remarkable feats in human history.

Tenochititlán, with some 200,000 inhabitants, was much larger than Seville, the most populous city in Spain. Graced by wide canals and boasting beautiful stone pyramids and buildings, the fabled capital seemed impregnable. But Cortés made the most of his assets. He landed in a coastal region where the local Indians were still fighting off the spread of Aztec power and were ready to embrace new allies, especially those possessing strange animals (horses) and powerful weapons. By a combination of threats and deceptions, Cortés entered Tenochtitlán peacefully and made the surprisingly pliant emperor, Montezuma, his puppet. Cortés explained to Montezuma why the invasion was necessary: "We Spaniards have a disease of the heart that only gold can cure."

After taking all the Aztec gold, the Spanish forced Montezuma to provide Indian laborers to produce more gold from the mines. This state of affairs lasted until the spring of 1520, when disgruntled Aztecs, regarding Montezuma as a traitor, rebelled, stoned him to death, and attacked Cortés's forces. The Spaniards lost about a third of their men as they retreated. Their Indian allies remained loyal, however, and Cortés gradually regrouped his men. In 1521, having been reinforced with troops from Cuba and thousands of Indians eager to defeat the Aztecs, he recaptured the city. After that, the resistance collapsed, and Cortés and his officers replaced the former Aztec overlords as rulers over the Indian empire.

In doing so, they set the style for other conquistadores to follow, who within twenty years had established a sprawling Spanish empire in the New World. Between 1522 and 1528, various lieutenants of Cortés conquered the remnants of Indian culture in the Yucatán Peninsula and Guatemala. In 1531 Francisco Pizarro led a band of soldiers down the Pacific coast from Panama toward Peru, where they subdued the Inca Empire. From Peru, conquistadores extended Spanish authority through Chile by about 1553 and to the north, in present-day Colombia, in 1536–1538.

SPANISH AMERICA The Spaniards sought to displace the "pagan" civilizations throughout the Americas with their Catholic-based culture. Believing that God was on their side in this cultural exchange, the Spaniards carried with them a fervent sense of mission that bred both intolerance and zeal. The conquistadores transferred to America a system known as the *encomienda,* whereby favored officers became privileged landowners who controlled Indian villages or groups of villages. As *encomenderos,* they were called upon to protect and care for the villages and support missionary priests. In turn, they could require Indians to provide them with goods and labor. Spanish America therefore developed from the start a society of extremes: conquistadores and *encomenderos* who sometimes found wealth beyond the dreams of avarice, if more often just a crude affluence, and subject native peoples who were held in poverty.

What were left of them, that is. By the mid-1500s, native Indians were nearly extinct in the West Indies, reduced more by European diseases than by Spanish brutalities. To take their place, as early as 1503 the colonizers began to transport slaves from Africa, the first in a wretched traffic that eventually would carry over 9 million people across the Atlantic. In all of Spain's New World empire, by one informed estimate, the Indian population dropped from about 50 million at the outset to 4 million in the seventeenth century, and slowly rose again to 7.5 million by the end of the eighteenth century. Whites, who totaled no more than 100,000 in the mid–sixteenth century, numbered over 3 million by the end of the colonial period.

The Indians, however, did not always lack advocates. In many cases Catholic missionaries offered a sharp contrast to the conquistadores.

Setting examples of self-denial, they ventured into remote areas, usually without weapons or protection, to spread the gospel—and often suffered martyrdom for their efforts. Among them rose defenders of the Indians, the most noted of whom was Bartolomé de las Casas, a priest in Hispaniola and later a bishop in Mexico, author of *A Brief Relation of the Destruction of the Indies* (1552). Las Casas won some limited reforms from the Spanish government, but ironically had a more lasting influence in giving rise to the so-called Black Legend of Spanish cruelty, which the enemies of Spain gleefully spread abroad, often as a cover for their own abuses.

From such violently contrasting forces, Spanish America gradually developed into a settled society. The independent conquistadores were replaced by a second generation of bureaucrats and the *encomienda* was succeeded by the *hacienda* (a great farm or ranch) as the claim to land became a more important source of wealth than the claim to labor. From the outset, in sharp contrast to the later English experience, the Spanish government regulated every detail of colonial administration. After 1524 the Council of the Indies, directly under the crown, issued laws for America, served as the appellate court for civil cases arising in the colonies, and administered the bureaucracy.

The culture of Spanish America would be fundamentally unlike the English-speaking culture that would arise to the north. In fact, a difference already existed among the Indians in pre-Columbian America, with largely nomadic tribes to the north and the more complex civilizations in Mesoamerica. On the latter world, the Spaniards imposed an overlay of their own peculiar ways, but without uprooting the deeply planted cultures they found. Catholicism, which for long centuries had absorbed pagan gods and transformed pagan feasts into such holy days as Christmas and Easter, in turn adapted Indian beliefs and rituals to its own purposes. The Mexican Virgin of Guadalupe Hidalgo, for instance, evoked memories of feminine divinities in native cults. Thus Spanish America, in the words of modern-day Mexican writer Octavio Paz, became a land of superimposed pasts: "Mexico City was built on the ruins of Tenochtitlán, the Aztec city that was built in the likeness of Tula, the Toltec city that was built in the likeness of Teotihuacán, the first great city on the American continent. Every Mexican bears within him this continuity, which goes back two thousand years."

SPANISH EXPLORATIONS   For more than a century after Columbus, no European power other than Spain had more than a brief foothold in the New World. Spain had the advantage not only of having sponsored the discovery, but of having stumbled onto those parts of America that would bring the quickest profits. While France and England struggled with domestic quarrels and religious conflict, Spain had forged an intense national unity. Under Charles V, heir to the throne of Austria and the Netherlands, and Holy Roman Emperor to boot, Spain dominated Europe as well as the New World. The treasures of the Aztecs and the Incas added to Spain's power, but they would prove to be a mixed blessing. The easy reliance on American gold and silver undermined the basic economy of Spain and tempted the government to live beyond its means, while the influx of gold from the New World caused price inflation throughout Europe.

For most of the colonial period, much of what is now the United States belonged to Spain, and Spanish culture has left a lasting imprint upon American ways of life. Spain's colonial presence lasted more than three centuries, much longer than either England's or France's. New Spain was centered in Mexico, but its frontiers extended from the Florida Keys to Alaska and included areas not currently thought of as formerly Spanish, such as the Deep South (Memphis was founded as San Fernando, Vicksburg as Nogales) and the lower Midwest. Hispanic place names—San Francisco, Santa Barbara, Los Angeles, San Diego, Tucson, Santa Fe, San Antonio, Pensacola, and St. Augustine—survive to this day, as do Hispanic influences in art, architecture, literature, music, law, and cuisine.

The Spanish encounter with Native American populations and their diverse cultures produced a two-way exchange by which the two societies blended, coexisted, and interacted. Even when locked in mortal conflict and riven with hostility and mutual suspicion, the two cultures necessarily affected each other. The imperative of survival forced both natives and conquerors to devise creative adaptations. In other words, the frontier world, while permeated with violence, coercion, and intolerance, also produced mutual accommodation that enabled two living traditions to persist side by side. For example, the Pueblo Indians of the Southwest practiced two religious traditions simultaneously, adopting Spanish Catholicism while at the same time retaining the essence of their own inherited animistic faith.

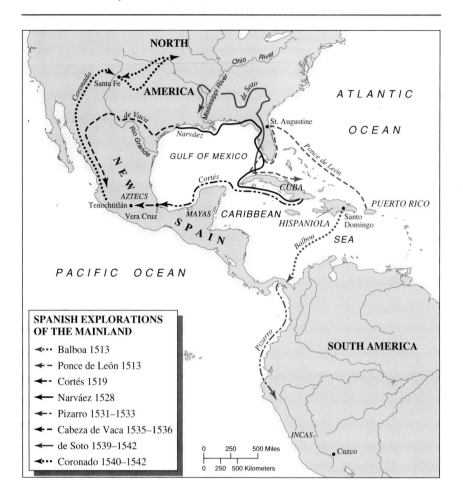

SPANISH EXPLORATIONS OF THE MAINLAND

◀··· Balboa 1513
◀ − Ponce de León 1513
◀· Cortés 1519
◀ Narváez 1528
◀· Pizarro 1531–1533
◀ − Cabeza de Vaca 1535–1536
◀ de Soto 1539–1542
◀··· Coronado 1540–1542

0   250   500 Miles
0   250 500 Kilometers

The "Spanish borderlands" of the southern United States preserve many reminders of the Spanish presence. The earliest known exploration of Florida was made in 1513 by Juan Ponce de León, then governor of Puerto Rico. Meanwhile, Spanish explorers skirted the Gulf coast from Florida to Vera Cruz, scouted the Atlantic coast from Cuba to Newfoundland, and established a short-lived colony on the Carolina coast.

Sixteenth-century knowledge of the North American interior came mostly from would-be conquistadores who sought to plunder the hinterlands. The first, Pánfilo de Narváez, landed in 1528 at Tampa Bay, marched northward to Appalachee, an Indian village in present-day Alabama, then back to the coast near St. Marks, where his party contrived crude vessels in hope of reaching Mexico. Wrecked on the coast of Texas, a few survivors under Núñez Cabeza de Vaca worked their way painfully overland and after eight years stumbled into a Spanish outpost in western Mexico.

Hernando de Soto followed their example. With 600 men he landed on the Florida west coast in 1539, hiked up as far as western North Carolina, then westward beyond the Mississippi, and up the Arkansas River. In the spring of 1542 de Soto died near the site of Memphis; the next year the survivors among de Soto's party floated down the Mississippi, and 311 of the original adventurers found their way to Mexico. In 1540 Francisco Vásquez de Coronado, inspired by rumors of gold, traveled northward into New Mexico and eastward across Texas and Oklahoma as far as Kansas. He returned in 1542 without gold but with a more realistic view of what lay in those arid lands.

The Spanish established provinces in North America not so much as commercial enterprises but as defensive buffers protecting their more lucrative trading empire in Mexico and South America. They were concerned about French traders infiltrating from Louisiana, English settlers crossing into Florida, and Russian seal hunters wandering down the California coast.

Yet the Spanish settlements in what is today the United States never flourished. Preoccupied with exploitative and extractive economic objectives, the Spanish never understood the significance of developing a viable market economy. England and France surpassed Spain in America because Spain mistakenly assumed that developing a thriving trade in goods with the Native Americans was less important than the conversion of "heathens" and the vain search for gold and silver.

The first Spanish outpost in the present United States emerged in response to French encroachments on Spanish claims. In the 1560s French Huguenots (Protestants) established short-lived colonies in South Carolina and Florida. In 1565 a Spanish outpost, St. Augustine, became the first European town in the present-day United States, and is now its oldest urban center except for the pueblos of New Mexico. Spain's colony at St. Augustine included a fort, church, hospital, fish market, and over 100 shops and houses—all built decades before the first English settlements at Jamestown and Plymouth. While other outposts failed, St. Augustine survived as a defensive base perched on the edge of a continent—and the first colonial town in what became the United States.

THE SPANISH SOUTHWEST   The Spanish eventually established other permanent settlements in what is now New Mexico, Texas, and California. Eager to pacify rather than fight the far more numerous Indians of the region, the Spanish used religion as an effective instrument of colonial control. Missionaries, particularly Franciscans and Jesuits, established isolated Catholic missions where they taught Christianity to the Indians. After about ten years, a mission was secularized; its lands were divided among the converted Indians, the mission chapel became a parish church, and the inhabitants were given full Spanish citizenship—including the privilege of paying taxes. The soldiers who were sent to protect the missions were housed in *presidios,* or forts, while their families and the merchants accompanying the soldiers lived in adjacent villages.

The land that would later be called New Mexico was the first center of mission activity in the American Southwest. In 1598 Juan de Oñate, the wealthy son of a Spanish mining family in Mexico, received a patent for the territory north of Mexico above the Rio Grande. With an expeditionary military force made up mostly of Mexican Indians and mestizos (sons of Spanish fathers and native mothers), he took possession of New Mexico, established a capital at San Gabriel, and sent out search parties looking for evidence of gold and silver deposits. He promised the Pueblo Indian leaders that Spanish dominion would bring them peace, justice, prosperity, and protection. Conversion to Catholicism offered even greater benefits: "an eternal life of great bliss" instead of "cruel and everlasting torment." One of Oñate's aides recorded that the Indians thereupon "spontaneously" agreed to become Spanish vassals and Christians.

Some Indians welcomed the missionaries as "powerful witches" capable of easing their burdens. Others tried to use the invaders as allies against rival Indian tribes. Still others saw no alternative but to submit. The Indians living in Spanish New Mexico were required to pay tribute to their *encomenderos.* The annual tribute usually entailed a bushel of maize and a blanket or deer hide. But often Indians were required to perform personal tasks for the *encomenderos,* including sexual favors. Disobedient Indians were flogged, by both soldiers and priests.

Before the end of the province's first year, the Indians revolted, killing several soldiers and incurring Oñate's wrath. During three days of relentless fighting, the army killed 500 Pueblo men and 300 women and children. Survivors were enslaved. Pueblo males over the age of twenty-five had one foot severed in a public ritual intended to strike fear in the hearts of the Indians and to keep them from escaping or resist-

A friar forcing a native woman to weave.

ing. Children were taken from their parents and placed under the care of a Franciscan mission where, Oñate remarked, "they may attain the knowledge of God and the salvation of their souls."

During the first three-quarters of the seventeenth century, Spanish New Mexico expanded very slowly. The hoped-for deposits of gold and silver were never found, and a sparse food supply also helped dull interest among potential colonists. The Spanish king prepared to abandon the colony, only to realize that Franciscan missionaries had baptized so many Pueblo Indians that they could not be deserted. In 1608 the Spanish government decided to turn New Mexico into a royal province. The following year it dispatched a royal governor, and in 1610, at the same time that the English settlers were struggling to survive at Jamestown, the Spanish moved the capital of New Mexico to Santa Fe, the first seat of government in the present-day United States. By 1630 there were fifty Catholic churches and friaries in New Mexico and some 3,000 Spaniards.

The leader of the Franciscan missionaries claimed that 86,000 Pueblo Indians had been converted to Christianity. In fact, however, resentment among the Indians increased with time. In 1680 a charismatic Indian leader named Popé organized a massive rebellion that involved some 17,000 Indians living in separate villages spread across hundreds of miles. Within a few weeks, the Spaniards had been driven from New Mexico. The outraged Indians burned churches, tortured, mutilated, and executed priests, and destroyed all relics of Christianity. It took fourteen years and four military assaults for the Spaniards to reestablish their control over New Mexico. Thereafter, except for sporadic raids by Apaches and Navajos, the Spanish pacified the region. Spanish outposts on the Florida and Texas Gulf coasts and in California did not appear until the eighteenth century.

THE PROTESTANT REFORMATION

While Spain built her empire, a new movement was growing elsewhere in Europe, the Protestant Reformation. It would intensify national rivalries, and, by encouraging serious challenges to Catholic Spain's power, profoundly affect the course of early American history. When Columbus sailed in 1492, all of western Europe acknowledged the Catholic church and its pope in Rome. The unity of Christendom began to crack in 1517, however, when Martin Luther, a German monk, posted his "Ninety-five Theses" in protest against abuses in the church. He especially criticized the sale of indulgences, whereby priests would forgive sins in exchange for money or goods. Sinners, Luther argued, could win salvation neither by good works nor through the mediation of the church, but only by faith in the redemptive power of Christ and through a direct relationship to God—the "priesthood of all believers."

Lutheranism spread rapidly among the people and their rulers—some of them with an eye to seizing church properties. When the pope expelled Luther from the church in 1520, reconciliation became impossible. The German states erupted into conflict over religious differences until 1555, when they finally agreed to let each prince determine the religion of his subjects. Most of northern Germany, along with Scandinavia, became Lutheran. The principle of close association between church and state thus carried over into Protestant lands, but Luther had unleashed volatile ideas that ran beyond his personal control.

Other Protestants pursued Luther's doctrine to its logical end and preached religious liberty for all. Further divisions on doctrinal matters led to the appearance of various sects such as the Anabaptists, who rejected infant baptism and favored the separation of church and state. Other offshoots, including the Mennonites, Amish, Dunkers, Familists, and Schwenkfelders, appeared later in America, but the more numerous like-minded groups would be Baptists and Quakers, who derived from English origins.

CALVINISM   Soon after Luther began his revolt, Swiss Protestants also challenged the authority of Rome. In Geneva the reform movement looked to John Calvin, a French scholar who had fled to Switzerland and who brought his adopted city under the sway of his beliefs. In his great theological work, *The Institutes of the Christian Religion* (1536), Calvin set forth a stern doctrine. All people, he taught, were damned by Adam's original sin, but the sacrifice of Christ made possible their redemption. The experience of faith, however, was open only to those whom God had elected and thus predestined to salvation from the beginning of time. Predestination was a hard doctrine, but the infinite wisdom of God was beyond human understanding.

Calvin insisted upon strict morality and hard work, values that especially suited the rising middle class. Moreover, he taught that people serve God through any legitimate labor, and permitted lay members a share in the governance of the church through a body of elders and ministers called the presbytery. Calvin's doctrines became the basis for the beliefs of the German Reformed and Dutch Reformed churches, the Presbyterians in Scotland, some of the Puritans in England, and the Huguenots in France. Through these and other groups, Calvin exerted more effect upon religious belief and practice in the English colonies than did any other single leader of the Reformation.

THE REFORMATION IN ENGLAND   In England the Reformation followed a unique course. The Church of England, or Anglican church, took form through a gradual process of integrating Calvinism with English Catholicism. In early modern England, church and state were united and mutually supportive. The government required citizens to attend religious services and to pay taxes to support the Church of England. The English monarchs also supervised the hierarchy of church officials: two archbishops, twenty-six bishops, and 8,600 parish clergy. The royal rulers often instructed the religious leaders to preach sermons in support of particular government policies. As one English king explained, "People are governed by the pulpit more than the sword in time of peace."

Purely political reasons initially led to the rejection of papal authority in England. Henry VIII (1509–1547), the second of the Tudor dynasty, had in fact won from the pope the title of Defender of the Faith, for refuting Martin Luther's ideas. But Henry's marriage to Catherine of Aragon had produced no male heir, and to marry again he required an annulment. In the past, popes had found ways to accommodate such requests, but Catherine was the aunt of Charles V, king of Spain and emperor of the Holy Roman Empire, whose support was vital to the church's cause on the continent. So the pope refused to grant an annulment. Unwilling to accept the rebuff, Henry severed England's connection with Rome, named a new archbishop of Canterbury, who granted the annulment, and married the lively Anne Boleyn. In one of history's great ironies, she presented him not with the male heir he sought but with a daughter, who as Elizabeth I would reign from 1558 to 1603 over one of England's greatest eras.

Elizabeth could not be a Catholic, for in the Catholic view she was illegitimate. During her reign, therefore, the Church of England became Protestant, but in its own way. The organizational structure, centered on bishops and archbishops, remained much the same, but the doctrine and practice changed: the Latin liturgy became, with some changes, the English *Book of Common Prayer*, the cult of saints was dropped, and the clergy were permitted to marry. For the sake of unity the "Elizabethan Settlement" allowed some latitude in theology and other matters, but this did not satisfy all. Some tried to enforce the letter of the law, stressing traditional Catholic practices. Many others, however, especially those under Calvinist influence, wished to "purify" the church of all its

Queen Elizabeth I.

Catholic remnants. Some of these Puritans would leave England to build their own churches in America. Those who broke altogether with the Church of England were called Separatists. The religious controversies associated with the English Reformation so dominated the nation's political life that interest in colonizing the New World was forced to the periphery of concern.

CHALLENGES TO THE SPANISH EMPIRE

The Spanish monopoly of New World colonies remained intact throughout the sixteenth century, but not without challenge from national rivals spurred now by the emotion unleashed by the Protestant Reformation. The French were the first to pose a serious threat as Huguenot seamen promised to build France into a major sea power. Spanish treasure ships from the New World were tempting targets for French privateers. In 1524 the French king sent Italian Giovanni da Verrazano in search of a passage to Asia. Sighting land (probably at Cape Fear, North Carolina), Verrazano ranged along the coast as far north as Maine. On a second voyage in 1538, his life met an abrupt end in the West Indies at the hands of the Caribs.

Unlike the Verrazano voyages, those of Jacques Cartier a decade later led to the first French effort at colonization. On three voyages Cartier explored the Gulf of St. Lawrence and ventured up the St. Lawrence River. Twice he got as far as present-day Montreal, and twice wintered at or near the site of Quebec, near which a short-lived French colony appeared in 1542–1543. From that time forward, however, French kings lost interest in Canada. France after mid-century plunged into religious civil wars, and the colonization of Canada had to await the coming of Samuel de Champlain, the "Father of New France," after 1600.

From the mid-1500s, greater threats to Spanish power arose from the growing strength of the Dutch and English. The provinces of the Netherlands, which had passed by inheritance to the Spanish king, and which had become largely Protestant, rebelled against Spanish rule in 1567. A protracted and bloody struggle for independence ensued. Spain did not accept the independence of the Dutch Republic until 1648.

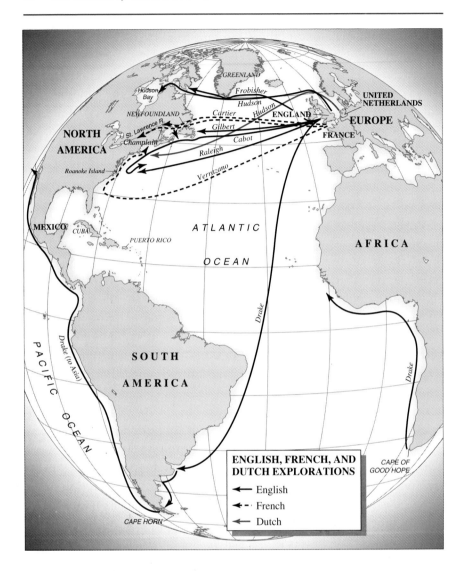

ENGLISH, FRENCH, AND DUTCH EXPLORATIONS

← English
←-· French
← Dutch

Almost from the beginning of the Dutch revolt against Spain, the Dutch "Sea Beggars," privateers working out of both English and Dutch ports, plundered Spanish ships in the Atlantic and carried on illegal trade with Spain's colonies. The Dutch "Sea Beggars" soon had their counterpart in the English "Sea Dogges": John Hawkins, Francis Drake, and others. While Elizabeth steered a tortuous course to avoid open war with Catholic Spain, she encouraged both Dutch and English captains to engage in smuggling and piracy. In 1577 Drake embarked on his famous adventure around South America to raid Spanish towns along the Pacific and surprise a treasure ship from Peru. Continuing in a vain search for a passage back to the Atlantic, he spent seven weeks at Drake's Bay in "New Albion," as he called California. Eventually he found his way westward around the world and back home in 1580. Elizabeth knighted Drake as "Sir Francis" upon his return.

THE ARMADA'S DEFEAT   The plundering of Spanish shipping by English privateers continued for some twenty years before open war erupted. In 1568 Elizabeth's cousin Mary, "Queen of Scots," ousted by Scottish Presbyterians in favor of her infant son, fled to refuge in England. Mary, who was Catholic, had a claim to the English throne by descent from Henry VII, and soon became the focus for Spanish-Catholic intrigues to overthrow Elizabeth. Finally, after the discovery of a plot to kill Elizabeth and elevate Mary to the throne, Elizabeth yielded to the demands of her ministers and had Mary beheaded in 1587.

Seeking revenge for Mary's execution, Spain's king, Philip II, decided to crush the Protestant power of the north and began to gather his ill-fated Armada, whereupon Francis Drake destroyed part of the Spanish

The defeat of the Spanish Armada, depicted in a contemporary English oil painting.

fleet before it was ready to sail. Drake's foray postponed for a year the departure of the "Invincible Armada," which set out to invade England in 1588. The heavy Spanish galleons, however, could not compete with the smaller, faster English vessels. Drake and the English harried the Spanish ships through the English Channel on their way to the Netherlands, where the Armada was to pick up an invasion force. But caught up in a powerful "Protestant Wind" from the south, the storm-tossed fleet was swept into the North Sea instead. What was left of it finally found its way home around the British Isles, leaving wreckage scattered on the shores of Scotland and Ireland.

Defeat of the Spanish Armada marked the beginning of English naval supremacy and cleared the way for English colonization of America. The naval victory was the climactic event of Elizabeth's reign. England at the end of the sixteenth century was in the springtime of its power, filled with a youthful zest for new worlds and new wonders that were opening up before the nation.

ENGLISH EXPLORATIONS   The history of English colonization begins with Sir Humphrey Gilbert and his half-brother, Sir Walter Raleigh. In 1578 Gilbert, who had long been a favorite of the queen, secured a royal patent to possess "heathen and barbarous landes countries and territories not actually possessed of any Christian prince or people." Significantly, the patent guaranteed to settlers and their descendants in such a colony the rights and privileges of Englishmen "in suche like ample manner and fourme as if they were borne and personally residaunte within our sed Realme of England." And laws had to be "agreable to the forme of the lawes and pollicies of England."

Gilbert, after two false starts, finally set out with a colonial expedition in 1583, intending to settle near Narragansett Bay (in present-day Rhode Island). He landed in Newfoundland, and took possession of the land for Elizabeth. With winter approaching and his largest vessels lost, Gilbert resolved to return home. While in transit, however, his ship vanished, and he was never seen again.

RALEIGH'S LOST COLONY   The next year, 1584, Sir Walter Raleigh persuaded the queen to renew Gilbert's colonizing mission in his own name, and he sent out a ship to reconnoiter a site. Sailing by way of the West Indies, the flotilla came to the Outer Banks of North Carolina and

The English arrival at the Outer Banks, with Roanoke Island at left.

discovered Roanoke Island, where the soil seemed fruitful and the natives friendly. After several false starts, Raleigh in 1587 sponsored an expedition of about 100 colonists, including women and children, under Governor John White. After a month in Roanoke, Governor White returned to England to get supplies, leaving behind his daughter Elinor and his grand-daughter Virginia Dare, the first English child born in the New World. White's return, however, was delayed because of the war with Spain. He finally returned in 1590 to find Roanoke abandoned and pillaged.

No trace of the "Lost Colonists" was ever found. Hostile Indians may have destroyed the colony, or hostile Spaniards—who certainly planned to attack—may have done the job. The most recent evidence indicates that the "Lost Colony" fell prey to the region's worst drought in eight centuries. Tree-ring samples reveal that the colonists arrived during the driest seven-year period in 770 years. While some may have gone south, the main body of colonists appears to have gone north to the southern shores of Chesapeake Bay, as they had talked of doing, and lived there for some years until killed by local Indians. Unless some remnant of the Roanoke settlement did survive in the woods, there was still not a single English colonist in North America when Queen Elizabeth died in 1603.

MAKING CONNECTIONS

- The funding of the voyages of discovery by various European nations had implications for the settlement and control of the New World, as will be discussed in later chapters.

- This chapter noted the settlement pattern and plundered wealth obtained by the Spanish in the New World; this will be contrasted in the next chapter with the patterns of English settlement and sources of wealth found in the New World.

- The next chapter describes how the Reformation and religious controversies in Europe led various religious groups to found their own settlements in the New World, where they did not face discrimination and persecution.

FURTHER READING

A fascinating study of pre-Columbian migration is Brian M. Fagan's *The Great Journey: The Peopling of Ancient America* (1987). Alice B. Kehoe's *North American Indians: A Comprehensive Account* (1992) provides an encyclopedic treatment of Native Americans. The best introduction to the prehistory of the American Southwest, its people, and archaeology is Stephen Plog's *Ancient Peoples of the American Southwest* (1997).

The conflict between Native Americans and Europeans is treated well in James Axtell's *The Invasion Within:The Contest of Cultures in Colonial North America* (1986) and *Beyond 1492: Encounters in Colonial North America* (1992). Colin G. Calloway's *New Worlds for All: Indians, Europeans, and the Remaking of Early America* (1997) explores the ecological effects of European settlement.

The most comprehensive overviews of European exploration are two volumes by Samuel E. Morison, *The European Discovery of America: The*

Northern Voyages, A.D. *500–1600* (1971), and *The Southern Voyages, 1492–1616* (1974). David B. Quinn's *North America from Earliest Discovery to First Settlements* (1977) is also useful. A good outline of the forces of exploration is John H. Parry's *The Age of Renaissance* (1963).

The voyages of Columbus are surveyed in William D. Phillips, Jr., and Carla Rahn Phillips's *The Worlds of Christopher Columbus* (1992). David J. Weber examines Spanish colonization in *The Spanish Frontier in North America* (1993). For the French experience, see William J. Eccles's *France in America* (1972).

2 ⌘ ENGLAND AND
ITS COLONIES

CHAPTER ORGANIZER

This chapter focuses on:

- the reasons for the founding of the different colonies in North America.

- the ways in which the British colonists and Native Americans adapted to each other's presence.

- the factors making for England's success in North America.

he England that Queen Elizabeth bequeathed to King James I, like the colonies it would plant, was a unique blend of elements. The language and the people themselves mixed Germanic and Latin ingredients. The Anglican church mixed Protestant theology and Catholic forms. And the growth of royal power paradoxically had been linked with the rise of English liberties, in which even Tudor monarchs took pride. In the course of their history, the English people have displayed a genius for "muddling through," a gift for the pragmatic compromise that defied logic but in the light of experience somehow worked.

THE ENGLISH BACKGROUND

Dominated by England, Great Britain included the distinct kingdoms of Wales, Ireland, and Scotland. England, set off from continental Europe by the English Channel, had safe frontiers after the union of the English and Scottish crowns in 1603. Such comparative isolation enabled the nation to develop institutions unlike those on the continent. Unlike the absolute monarchs of France and Spain, the British rulers had to share power with the aristocracy and a lesser aristocracy known as the gentry, whose representatives formed the bicameral legislature known as Parliament.

By 1600 the decline of feudal practices was far advanced. The great nobles, decimated by the Wars of the Roses, had been brought to heel by Tudor monarchs and their ranks filled with men loyal to the crown. In fact the only nobles left, strictly speaking, were those who sat in the House of Lords. All others were commoners, and among their ranks the aristocratic pecking order ran through a great class of landholding squires, distinguished mainly by their wealth, and bearing the simple titles of "esquire" and "gentleman," as did many well-to-do townsmen. They in turn mingled freely and often intermarried with the classes of yeomen (small freehold farmers) and merchants.

ENGLISH LIBERTIES   It was to these middle classes that the Tudors looked for support and, for want of bureaucrats or a standing army, for local government. Chief reliance in the English counties was on the country gentlemen, who usually served as officials without pay. Government, therefore, allowed a large measure of local initiative. Self-rule in the counties and towns became a habit—one that, along with the offices of justice of the peace and sheriff, English colonists took along to the New World as part of their cultural baggage.

In the making of laws, the monarch's subjects consented through representatives in the House of Commons. Subjects could be taxed only with the consent of Parliament. By its control of the purse strings, Parliament drew other strands of power into its hands. This structure of powers served as an unwritten constitution. The Magna Carta (Great Charter) of 1215 had been a statement of privileges wrested by certain nobles from the king, but it became part of a broader assumption that the people as a whole had rights that even the monarch could not violate.

A further buttress to English liberty was the great body of common law, which had developed since the twelfth century in royal courts established to check the arbitrary power of local nobles. Without laws to cover every detail, judges had to exercise their own ideas of fairness in settling disputes. Decisions once made became precedents for later decisions, and over the years a body of judge-made law developed, the outgrowth more of practical experience than of abstract logic. The courts evolved the principle that people could be arrested or their goods seized only upon a warrant issued by a court, and that individuals were entitled to a trial by a jury of their peers (their equals) in accordance with established rules of evidence.

ENGLISH ENTERPRISE   English liberties inspired a sense of personal initiative and enterprise that spawned prosperity and empire. The ranks of entrepreneurs and adventurers were constantly replenished by the younger sons of the squirearchy, cut off from the estate that the oldest son inherited by the law of primogeniture (or first born). The formation of joint-stock companies spurred commercial expansion. These companies were the ancestors of the modern corporation, in which stockholders shared the risks and profits, sometimes for a single venture but more and more on a permanent basis. In the late sixteenth century, some of the larger companies managed to get royal charters that entitled them to monopolies in certain areas and even governmental powers in their outposts. Such companies would become the first instruments of colonization.

For all the vaunted glories of English liberty and enterprise, it was not the best of times for the common people. During the late sixteenth century, the "lower sort" in Britain experienced a population explosion that outstripped the ability of the economy to accommodate so many workers. An additional strain on the population was the "enclosure" of farmlands where peasants had lived and worked. For more than two centuries, serfdom had been on the way to extinction, as the feudal duties of serfs were transformed into rents and the serfs themselves into tenants. But while tenancy gave a degree of independence, it also allowed landlords to increase demands, and, as the trade in woolen products grew, to "enclose" farmlands and evict the human tenants in favor of sheep. The enclosure movement of the sixteenth century coupled with rising population gave rise to the great numbers of beggars and

(Left) *James I, the successor to Queen Elizabeth and the first of England's Stuart kings.* (Right) *Charles I, in a portrait by Van Dyck.*

rogues who peopled the literature of Elizabethan times and gained immortality in Mother Goose: "Hark, hark, the dogs do bark. The beggars have come to town." The needs of this displaced peasant population, on the move throughout Great Britain, became another powerful argument for colonial expansion. The displaced poor migrated from farms to crowded towns and cities. London became a powerful magnet for vagabonds. By the seventeenth century, the English capital was notorious for its filth, poverty, crime, and class tensions—all of which helped convince the ruling elite to send idle and larcenous commoners abroad to settle new colonies.

PARLIAMENT AND THE STUARTS   With the death of Elizabeth, who never married and did not give birth to an heir, the Tudor line ran out and the throne fell to the first of the Stuarts, whose dynasty spanned most of the seventeenth century, a turbulent time during which the English planted an overseas empire. In 1603 James VI of Scotland, son of the ill-fated Mary, Queen of Scots, and great-grandson of Henry VII, became James I of England—as Elizabeth had planned. A man of ponderous learning, James fully earned his reputation as the "wisest fool in all Christendom." He lectured the people on every topic but remained blind to English traditions and sensibilities. Where the Tudors had wielded absolute power through constitutional forms, James promoted the theory of divine right, by which monarchs answered only to God for their actions. Where the Puritans hoped to find a Presbyterian ally in their opposition to Anglican trappings, they found instead a testy autocrat who promised to banish them. He even offended Anglicans by deciding to end Elizabeth's war with Catholic Spain.

Charles I, who succeeded his father in 1625, proved even more stubborn about royal power. He ruled without Parliament from 1629 to 1640 and levied taxes by decree. In the religious arena, the archbishop of Canterbury, William Laud, directed a systematic persecution of Puritans but finally overreached himself when he tried to impose Anglican worship on Presbyterian Scots. In 1638 Scotland rose in revolt, and in 1640 Charles called Parliament to rally support and raise money for the defense of his kingdom. The "Long Parliament" impeached Laud instead, condemned to death the king's chief minister, and abolished the king's "prerogative courts." In 1642, when the king tried to arrest five members of Parliament, civil war erupted between the "Roundheads," who backed Parliament, and the "Cavaliers," who supported the king.

In 1646 royalist resistance collapsed, and parliamentary forces captured the king. Parliament, however, could not agree on a permanent settlement. A dispute arose between Presbyterians and Independents (who preferred a congregational church government), and in 1648 the Independents purged the Presbyterians, leaving a "Rump Parliament" that then instigated the trial and execution of Charles I on charges of treason.

Oliver Cromwell, commander of the army, operated like a military dictator, ruling first through a council chosen by Parliament (the Commonwealth), and, after forcible dissolution of Parliament, as Lord Protector (the Protectorate). Cromwell extended religious toleration to all except Catholics and Anglicans, but his arbitrary governance and his moralistic codes provoked growing public resentment. When, after his death in 1658, his son proved too weak to carry on, the army once again took control, permitted new elections for Parliament, and in 1660 supported the restoration of the monarchy under Charles II, son of the martyred king.

Charles accepted as terms of the Restoration settlement the principle that he must rule jointly with Parliament. By tact or shrewd maneuvering, he managed to hold his throne. His younger brother, the duke of York (who became James II upon succeeding to the throne in 1685) was less flexible. He openly avowed Catholicism and assumed the same un-yielding stance as the first two Stuarts. The people could bear it so long as they expected one of his Protestant daughters, Mary or Anne, to suc-ceed him. In 1688, however, the birth of a son who would be reared a Catholic finally brought matters to a crisis. Leaders of Parliament in-vited Mary and her husband, William of Orange, a Dutch prince, to as-sume the throne jointly, and James fled the country.

By this "Glorious Revolution," Parliament finally established its free-dom from royal control. Under the Bill of Rights, in 1689, William and Mary gave up the royal prerogatives of suspending laws, erecting special courts, keeping a standing army, or levying taxes except by Parliament's consent. They further agreed to hold frequent legislative sessions and allow freedom of speech in Parliament, freedom of petition to the crown, and restrictions against excessive bail and cruel and unusual punishments. The Toleration Act of 1689 extended a degree of freedom of worship to all Christians except Catholics and Unitarians, although dissenters from the established church still had few political rights. In 1701 the Act of Settlement ensured a Protestant succession through Queen Anne (1702–1714). And by the Act of Union in 1707, England and Scotland became the United Kingdom of Great Britain.

SETTLING THE CHESAPEAKE

During these eventful years all but one of the thirteen North American colonies had their start. In 1606 King James I chartered what was called the Virginia Company, with two divisions, the First Colony of London and the Second Colony of Plymouth. The London group could plant a settlement between the 34th and 38th parallels, the Ply-mouth group between the 41st and 45th parallels, and either between the 38th and 41st parallels, provided they kept a hundred miles apart. The stockholders expected a potential return from gold and other min-erals; products, such as wine, citrus fruits, and olive oil, to free England from dependence on Spain; trade with the Indians; pitch, tar, potash, and other forest products needed for naval use; and perhaps a passage to East Asia. Some investors dreamed of finding another Aztec or Inca Empire. Few if any investors foresaw what the first English colony would actually become: a place to grow tobacco.

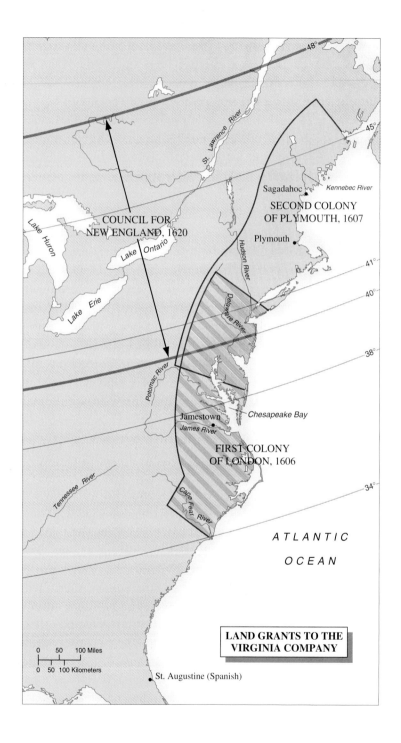

48°

St. Lawrence River

45°

Sagadahoc   *Kennebec River*

**SECOND COLONY
OF PLYMOUTH, 1607**

COUNCIL FOR
NEW ENGLAND, 1620

Plymouth

Lake Huron

Lake Ontario

Hudson River

41°

Lake Erie

40°

Delaware River

38°

Potomac River

Jamestown   *Chesapeake Bay*

James River

**FIRST COLONY
OF LONDON, 1606**

Tennessee River

34°

Cape Fear River

ATLANTIC

OCEAN

**LAND GRANTS TO THE
VIRGINIA COMPANY**

| 0 | 50 | 100 Miles |

| 0 | 50 | 100 Kilometers |

St. Augustine (Spanish)

From the outset, the pattern of English colonization diverged significantly from the Spanish pattern. The Spaniards conquered highly sophisticated peoples and proceeded to regulate all aspects of colonial life. The English had a different model in their experience. While the interest in America was growing, the English were already involved in planting settlements, or "plantations," in Ireland, which the English had conquered by military force under Elizabeth. Within their own pale (or limit) of settlement in Ireland, the English set about transplanting their familiar way of life insofar as possible.

The English would apply the same pattern as they settled North America, subjugating the Indians there as they had the Irish in Ireland. Yet, in America the English settled along the Atlantic seaboard, where the native populations were relatively sparse. There was no Aztec or Inca Empire to conquer and rule. The colonists thus had to establish their own communities within a largely wilderness setting. Describing the "settlement" of the Atlantic seaboard is somewhat misleading, however, for the British colonists who arrived in the seventeenth century rarely *settled* in one place for long. They were migrants more than settlers, people who were already on the move in Britain and who continued to pursue new opportunities in different places once they arrived in America.

VIRGINIA   The London group of the Virginia Company planted the first permanent colony in Virginia, named after Elizabeth I, the "Virgin Queen." On May 6, 1607, three ships carrying about 100 men reached Chesapeake Bay after four storm-tossed months at sea. They chose a river with a northwest bend—in hope of finding a passage to Asia—and settled about 40 miles from the sea to hide from marauding Spaniards.

The river they called the James, and the colony, Jamestown. The sea-weary colonists began building a fort, thatched huts, a storehouse, and a church. They then set to planting, but most were either townsmen unfamiliar with farming or "gentleman" adventurers who scorned manual labor. They had come to find gold, not to establish a farm settlement. Ignorant of woodlore, they did not know how to exploit the area's abundant game and fish. Supplies from England were undependable, and only some effective leadership and their trade with the Indians, who taught the colonists to grow maize, enabled them to survive.

The Indians of the region were loosely organized. Wahunsonacock, called Powhatan by the English after the name of his tribe, was the

Captain Smith taketh the King of Pamaunkee prisoner, *1608, from John Smith's map of "Ould Virginia," 1624.*

powerful, charismatic chief of numerous Algonquian-speaking towns in eastern Virginia representing over 10,000 Indians. The Indians making up the so-called Powhatan Confederacy were largely an agricultural people who focused on the raising of several varieties of corn. They lived along rivers in fortified towns and resided in framed houses sheathed with bark. Despite occasional clashes with the colonists, the Indians of Virginia initially adopted a stance of nervous assistance and watchful waiting. Powhatan developed a lucrative trade with the colonists, exchanging corn and hides for hatchets, swords, and muskets; he realized too late that the newcomers intended to expropriate his lands and subjugate his people.

The colonists, as it happened, had more than a match for Powhatan in Captain John Smith, a swashbuckling soldier of fortune with rare powers of leadership and self-promotion. The Virginia Company, impressed by Smith's exploits in foreign wars, appointed him a member of the resident council to manage the new colony in America. It was a wise decision. Of the original 104 settlers, only 38 survived the first nine months. With the colonists on the verge of starvation, Smith imposed strict discipline and forced all to labor, declaring that "he that will not work shall not eat." Smith also bargained with the Indians and explored and mapped the Chesapeake region.

Through his efforts, Jamestown survived, but Smith's dictatorial acts did not endear him to many of the colonists. One called him "ambitious, unworthy, and vainglorious."

In 1609 the Virginia Company moved to reinforce the Jamestown colony. More colonists were dispatched. A new charter redefined the colony's boundaries and replaced the largely ineffective council with an all-powerful governor whose council was only advisory. The company then lured new investors and attracted new settlers with the promise of free land after seven years of labor. The company in effect had given up hope of prospering except through the sale of lands which would rise in value as the colony grew. The governor, the noble Lord De La Warr (Delaware), sent as interim governor Sir Thomas Gates. In 1609 Gates set out with a fleet of nine vessels and about 500 passengers and crew. On the way Gates was shipwrecked on Bermuda, where he and the other survivors wintered in comparative ease, subsisting on fish, fowl, and wild pigs. (Their story was transformed by William Shakespeare into his play *The Tempest*.)

Most of the fleet, however, did reach Jamestown. Some 400 settlers overwhelmed the remnant of about 80. All chance that John Smith might control things was lost when he suffered a gunpowder burn and sailed back to England. The consequence was anarchy and the "starving time" of the winter of 1609–1610, during which most of the colonists, weakened by hunger, fell prey to pestilence. By May 1610, when Gates and his companions made their way to Jamestown on two small ships built in Bermuda, only about 60 remained alive. All poultry and livestock (including horses) had been eaten. Jamestown was abandoned.

In June 1610, as the colonists made their way down the river, the new governor, Lord Delaware, providentially arrived with three ships and 150 men, whereupon instead

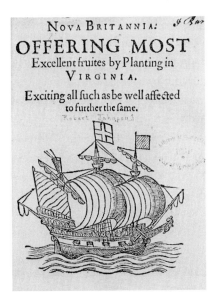

A 1609 handbill of the Virginia Company attempts to lure settlers to Jamestown.

of leaving Virginia, the colonists returned to Jamestown and created the first new settlements upstream at Henrico (Richmond) and two more downstream near the mouth of the river. It was a critical turning point for the colony, whose survival required a combination of stern measures and not a little luck. When Lord Delaware returned to England in 1611, Gates took charge of the colony and established a strict system of *Lawes Divine, Moral, and Martiall,* inaccurately called "Dale's Code," after Thomas Dale who enforced them as marshal. Severe even by the standards of a ruthless age, the code enforced a militaristic discipline needed for survival. When one laborer was caught stealing oatmeal, the authorities had a long needle thrust through his tongue, chained him to a tree, and let him starve to death as a grisly example to the community. Desperate colonists who fled to join the Indians were caught and hanged or burned at the stake. The new colonial regime also assaulted the local Indians. English soldiers attacked Indian villages and destroyed their crops. One commander reported that they marched a captured Indian queen and her children to the river where they "put the Children to death . . . by throwing them overboard and shooting out their brains in the water."

Over the next seven years, the colony limped along until it gradually found a reason for being: tobacco. The plant had been grown in the West Indies for years, and smoking had become a popular habit in Europe and Britain. In 1612 John Rolfe had begun to experiment with the harsh Virginia tobacco. Eventually he got hold of some seed for the more savory Spanish varieties, and by 1616 the weed had become a profitable export staple. Even though King James dismissed smoking as "loathsome to the eye, hateful to the nose, harmful to the brain, and dangerous to the lungs," he swallowed his objections to the "noxious weed" when he realized how much revenue it provided the monarchy. Virginia's tobacco production soared during the seventeenth century. It was such a profitable crop for Virginia planters that they could afford to purchase more indentured servants, thus increasing the flow of emigrants to the colony.

Meanwhile John Rolfe had made another contribution to stability by marrying Pocahontas, the daughter of Powhatan. Pocahontas (a nickname usually translated as "frisky"—her given name was Matowaka) had been a familiar figure in Jamestown almost from the beginning. In

1607, then only eleven, she figured in perhaps the best-known story of the settlement, her plea for the life of John Smith. In 1613, however, on a foray to extort corn from the Indians, settlers captured Pocahontas and held her for ransom. To fend off the crisis, Rolfe proposed marriage to Pocahontas, Powhatan agreed, and a wary peace ensued. By now Pocahontas had been baptized in the Anglican church, and she was given a new name, "Lady Rebecca."

Pocahontas in European garb.

In 1616 Rolfe took Rebecca and their infant son Thomas to London, where the young princess drew excited attention from the royal family and curious Londoners. But only a few months after arriving, Rebecca contracted a lung disease and died at age twenty.

In 1618 Sir Edwin Sandys, a prominent member of Parliament, became head of the Virginia Company and instituted a series of reforms. First of all he inaugurated a new "headright" policy: anyone who bought a share in the company and could get to Virginia could have fifty acres, and fifty more for any additional servants. The following year, 1619, the company relaxed the tight regimen of the *Lawes* and promised that the settlers should have the "rights of Englishmen," including a representative assembly.

A new governor arrived with instructions to put the new order into effect, and on July 30, 1619, the first General Assembly of Virginia, including the governor, six councilors, and twenty-two burgesses, met in the church at Jamestown and deliberated for five days, "sweating & stewing, and battling flies and mosquitoes." It was an eventful year in two other respects. The promoters also saw a need to send out wives for the men. During 1619 a ship arrived with ninety young women who were to be sold to likely husbands of their own choice for the cost of transportation (about 125 pounds of tobacco). And a Dutch ship, according to an ominous note in John Rolfe's diary, stopped by and dropped off "20 Negars," the first blacks known to have reached English America.

The profitable tobacco trade intensified the settlers' lust for land. They especially coveted Indian fields because they had already been cleared and were ready to be planted. In 1622 the Indians, led by Opechancanough, Powhatan's brother and successor, tried to repel the land-grabbing English. They killed a fourth of the settlers, some 350 colonists, including John Rolfe, only to provoke a vengeful counterattack. John Smith denounced the Indian assault as a "massacre" and dismissed the "savages" as "cruel beasts" whose "brutishness" exceeded that of wild animals.

Whatever moral doubts had earlier plagued English settlers were now swept away. The English thereafter sought to wipe out the Indian presence along their frontier. In 1623 Captain William Tucker and a band of soldiers met with a large party of Indian leaders to negotiate a settlement. After signing a treaty, Tucker invited the Indians to drink a toast to celebrate their truce. The Indians drank the proffered wine, only to realize too late that it had been poisoned. Two hundred Indians died from the doctored brew. The soldiers then burned Indian villages and plundered the corn, killed another fifty, and "brought home part of their heads." This process of "continual incursions" into Indian territory persisted throughout the decade.

Yet the English foothold in Virginia remained tenuous. Some 14,000 men, women, and children had migrated to the colony since 1607, but the population in 1624 stood at a precarious 1,132. Despite the broad initial achievements of the company, after about 1617 a handful of insiders had appropriated large estates and began to monopolize the indentured workers. Some made fortunes from the tobacco boom, but most of the thousands sent out died before they could prove themselves. At the behest of Sandys's opponents, the king appointed a commission to investigate the running of the colony by the London Company, and on the recommendation of the commission a court dissolved the company. In 1624 Virginia became a royal colony.

The king did not renew instructions for an assembly, but his governors found it impossible to rule the troublesome Virginians without one. Annual assemblies met after 1629, although they were not recognized by the crown for another ten years. After 1622, relations with the Indians continued in a state of what the governor's council called "perpetual enmity" until the aging Opechancanough staged another concerted attack in 1644. The English suffered as many casualties as they had twenty-two years before, but put down the uprising with such ferocity that nothing quite like it happened again. The combination of warfare and disease decimated the Indians in Virginia. The 24,000 Algonquians who inhabited the colony in 1607 were reduced to 2,000 by 1669.

Sir William Berkeley, who arrived as Virginia's governor in 1642, presided over the colony's growth for most of the next thirty-four years. The instability and turmoil of Virginia's early days gave way to a more settled and stable period. Tobacco prices peaked, and the large planters began to consolidate their economic gains through political action. They assumed key civic roles as justices of the peace and sheriffs, helped initiate internal improvements such as roads and bridges, supervised elections, and collected taxes. They also formed the able-bodied males into local militias. Despite the presence of a royal governor, the elected assembly continued to assert its sovereignty, making laws for the colony and resisting the governor's encroachments.

Virginia at mid-century continued to serve as a magnet for new settlers. As the sharp rise in tobacco profits leveled off, planters began to grow corn and raise cattle. The increase in the food supply helped lower mortality rates and fuel a rapid rise in population. By 1650 there were 15,000 European residents of Virginia. Many former servants became planters in their own right. Women typically improved their status through marriage. If they outlived their husbands—and many did— they inherited the property and often increased their wealth through second and even third marriages.

The relentless stream of new white settlers exerted constant pressure on Indian lands and produced unwanted economic effects. The increase in the number of planters resulted in a dramatic rise in agricultural production. This in turn caused the cost of land to soar and the price of tobacco to plummet. To sustain their competitive advantage, the largest planters bought up the most fertile lands along the coast, thereby forcing freed servants to become tenants or to claim less fertile lands along the frontier. In either case, the tenants found themselves at a disadvantage. They grew dependent on planters for land and credit, while small farmers along the frontier became more vulnerable to Indian attacks.

The plight of common folk worsened after 1660, when a restored monarchy under Charles II instituted new trade regulations for the colonies. By 1676 a fourth of the free white men in Virginia were landless. Vagabonds roamed the roads, squatting on private property, working at odd jobs, or poaching game or engaging in other petty crimes in order to survive. Alarmed by the growing social unrest, the large planters who controlled the assembly—generally ruthless and callous men—lengthened terms of indenture, passed more stringent vagrancy laws, stiffened punishments, and stripped the landless of their political rights. But such efforts only increased social friction.

BACON'S REBELLION A variety of simmering tensions—caused by depressed tobacco prices, rising taxes, and crowds of freed servants greedily eyeing Indian lands—contributed to the tangled events that have come to be labeled Bacon's Rebellion. The roots of the revolt grew out of a festering hatred for the domineering colonial governor William Berkeley. Appointed by the king in 1641, he served as Virginia's governor for most of the next thirty-five years. Berkeley was an unapologetic elitist who limited his circle of friends to the wealthiest and most ambitious planters. He granted them most of the frontier lands and public offices, and he rarely allowed new elections to the assembly for fear that his cronies might be defeated. He despised commoners. He did not want the laboring poor to be educated because literacy only brought "disobedience." The large planters who dominated the assembly levied high taxes to finance Berkeley's regime, which in turn supported their interests at the expense of the small farmers and servants. With little nearby land available, newly freed indentured servants were forced to migrate westward in their quest for farms. Their lust for land led them to displace the Indians. When Governor Berkeley failed to support the aspiring farmers, they rebelled. The tyrannical governor expected as much. Just before the outbreak of rebellion, Berkeley had remarked in a letter: "How miserable that man is that Governes a People where six parts of seaven at least are Poore, Endebted, Discontented and Armed."

The discontent turned to violence in 1675 when a petty squabble between a frontier planter and the Doeg Indians on the Potomac River led to the murder of the planter's herdsman, and in turn to retaliation by frontier militiamen who killed ten or more Doegs and, by mistake, fourteen Susquehannocks. Soon a force of Virginia and Maryland militiamen laid siege to the Susquehannocks, murdered five chieftains who came out to negotiate, and then let the enraged survivors escape to take their revenge on frontier settlements. Scattered attacks continued on down to the James River, where Nathaniel Bacon's overseer was killed.

By then, their revenge accomplished, the Susquehannocks pulled back. What followed had less to do with a state of war than with a state of hysteria. Berkeley proposed that the assembly erect a series of forts along the frontier. But that would not slake the thirst for revenge—nor would it open new lands to settlement. Besides, it would be expensive. Some thought Berkeley was out to preserve a profitable fur trade for himself.

In 1676 Nathaniel Bacon defied Governor Berkeley's authority by assuming command of a group of frontier vigilantes. The tall, slender, twenty-nine-year-old Bacon, a graduate of Cambridge University, had been in Virginia only two years, but he had been well set up by an English father relieved to get his vain, ambitious, hot-tempered son out of the country. Later historians would praise Bacon as the "Torch-bearer of the Revolution" and leader of the first struggle of common folk versus aristocrats. In part this was true. The rebellion he led was largely a battle of servants, small farmers, and even slaves against Virginia's wealthiest planters and political leaders. But Bacon was also the spoiled son of a rich squire who had a talent for trouble. It was his ruthless assaults against peaceful Indians and his desire for power and land rather than any commitment to democratic principles that brought him into conflict with the governing authorities.

Bacon despised the Indians. They were, he said, "all alike," in that they were "wolves, tigers, and bears" who preyed upon "our harmless and innocent lambs," and therefore should be killed. After threatening to kill the governor and members of the assembly if they tried to intervene, Bacon began preparing for a total war against all the local Indians. Berkeley opposed Bacon's genocidal plan, not because he liked Indians but because he wanted to protect his lucrative monopoly over the deerskin trade with the Indians. To prevent any governmental interference, Bacon ordered the governor arrested. Berkeley's forces resisted—but only feebly—and Bacon's men burned Jamestown. Bacon, however, could not savor the victory long; he fell ill and died of dysentery a month later.

Governor Berkeley quickly regained control and subdued the leaderless rebels. In the process, he hanged twenty-three rebel leaders and confiscated several estates. When his men captured one of Bacon's closest lieutenants, Berkeley gleefully exclaimed: "I am more glad to see you than any man in Virginia. Mr. Drummond, you shall be hanged in half an hour." For such severity, the king denounced Berkeley as a "fool" and recalled him to England, where he died within a year. A royal commission made peace treaties with the remaining Indians, about 1,500 of whose descendants still live in Virginia on tiny reservations guaranteed them in 1677. The end result of Bacon's Rebellion was that new lands were opened to the colonists, and the wealthy planters became more cooperative with the small farmers.

MARYLAND   In 1634, ten years after Virginia became a royal colony, a neighboring settlement appeared on the northern shores of Chesapeake Bay. Named Maryland in honor of Queen Henrietta Maria, it was granted to Lord Baltimore by King Charles I and became the first proprietary colony—that is, it was owned by an individual, not a joint-stock company. Sir George Calvert, the first Lord Baltimore, had

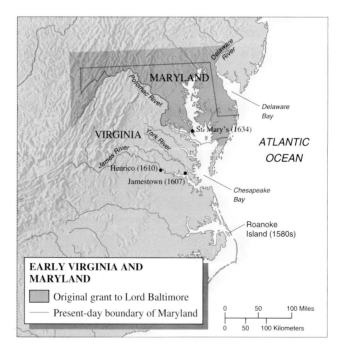

EARLY VIRGINIA AND MARYLAND

Original grant to Lord Baltimore

Present-day boundary of Maryland

announced in 1625 his conversion to Catholicism and sought the colony as a refuge for English Catholics who were subjected to discrimination at home. His son, Cecilius Calvert, the second Lord Baltimore, actually founded the colony. The charter gave the proprietor powers similar to those of an independent monarch, though the charter specified that the laws must be in accordance with those of England. References to religion were vague except for a mention that chapels should be established according to the ecclesiastical law of England.

In 1634 Calvert planted the first settlement in Maryland at St. Mary's on a small stream near the mouth of the Potomac River. Calvert brought Catholic gentlemen as landholders, but a majority of the servants were Protestants. The charter gave Calvert power to make laws with the consent of the freemen (all property holders). The first legislative assembly met in 1635, and divided into two houses in 1650, with governor and council sitting separately. This was instigated by the predominantly Protestant freemen—largely servants who had become landholders, or immigrants from Virginia. The charter also empowered the proprietor to grant huge manorial estates, and Maryland had some sixty before 1676, but the Lords Baltimore soon found that to draw settlers they had to offer small farms. The colony was meant to rely on mixed farming, but its fortunes, like those of Virginia, soon came to depend on tobacco.

SETTLING NEW ENGLAND

Far to the north of the Chesapeake Bay colonies, quite different settlements were emerging. The New England colonists were generally made up of middle-class families who could pay their own way across the Atlantic. In the Northeast there were relatively few indentured servants like those who peopled the Chesapeake region, and there was no planter elite. Most male settlers were small farmers, merchants, seamen, or fishermen. New England also became home to more women than the southern colonies. Although its soil was not as fertile as that of the Chesapeake and its farmers not as wealthy as the southern planters, New England was a much healthier place to settle. Because of its colder climate, the region did not foster the infectious diseases that ravaged the southern colonies. Life expectancy was much longer. During the seventeenth century, only 21,000 colonists arrived in New England, compared to the 120,000 who went to the Chesapeake. But by 1700, New England's white population exceeded that of Maryland and Virginia.

Most early New Englanders were devout Puritans who embraced a much more rigorous faith than the Anglicans of Virginia and Maryland. In 1650, for example, Massachusetts boasted one minister for every 415 persons, compared to one minister per 3,239 persons in Virginia. The Puritans who arrived in America believed themselves to be on a divine mission to create a model society committed to the proper worship of God. In their efforts to separate themselves from a sinful England and its authoritarian Anglican bishops, New England Puritans sought to create "holy commonwealths" that would help inspire a spiritual transformation in their homeland. In the New World, these self-described "saints" could purify their churches of all Catholic and Anglican rituals, supervise one another in practicing a communal faith, and enact a code of laws and a government structure based on biblical principles. Such a holy settlement, they hoped, would provide a beacon of righteousness for a wicked England to emulate.

PLYMOUTH   In 1620 a band of English settlers headed for Virginia strayed off course and made landfall at Cape Cod. There they decided to establish a colony, naming it Plymouth after the English port from which they embarked. The Pilgrims who established Plymouth colony belonged to the most uncompromising sect of Puritans, the Separatists, who had severed all ties with the Church of England. Many of the Separatists fled to Holland in 1607 to escape persecution. The Calvinistic Dutch granted them asylum and toleration, but restricted them mainly to unskilled labor. After ten years in the Dutch city of Leyden, they had wearied of the struggle. Watching their children take up Dutch habits and customs, drifting away to become sailors, soldiers, or worse, so that "their posterity would be in danger to degenerate and be corrupted," they longed for English ways and the English flag. If they could not have them at home, perhaps they might transplant them to the New World.

The Leyden Separatists secured a land patent from the Virginia Company and set up a joint-stock company. In 1620, 102 men, women, and children, led by William Bradford, crammed aboard the three-masted

A sixteenth-century oceangoing vessel.

Mayflower. Their ranks included both "saints" (people recognized as having been elected by God for salvation) and "strangers" (those yet to receive the gift of grace). The latter group included John Alden, a cooper (barrel maker), and Miles Standish, a soldier hired to organize their defenses. A stormy voyage led them to Cape Cod, far north of Virginia. Heading south, they encountered rough waters and turned back to seek safety at Provincetown. "Being thus arrived at safe harbor, and brought safe to land," William Bradford wrote, "they fell upon their knees and blessed the God of Heaven who had brought them over the vast and furious ocean." Since they were outside the jurisdiction of any organized government, forty-one of the Pilgrim leaders entered into a formal agreement to abide by laws made by leaders of their own choosing—the Mayflower Compact.

On December 26 the *Mayflower* reached Plymouth harbor and stayed there until April to give shelter and support while the Pilgrims built dwellings on the site of an abandoned Indian village. Nearly half the colonists died of exposure and disease, but friendly relations with the neighboring Wampanoag Indians proved their salvation. In the spring of 1621 the colonists met Squanto, an Indian who spoke English and showed them how to grow maize. By autumn the Pilgrims had a bumper crop of corn, a flourishing fur trade, and a supply of lumber for shipment.

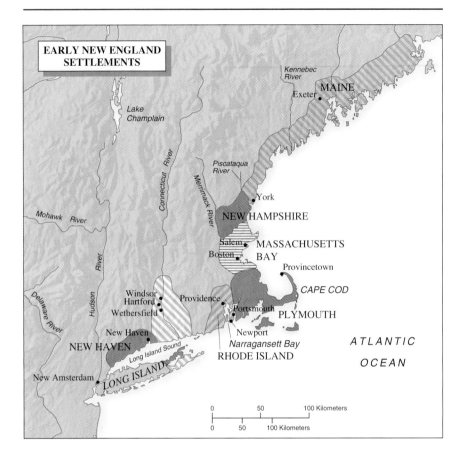

To celebrate, they held a harvest feast in company with Chief Massasoit and the Wampanoags. This event provided the inspiration for what has since become Thanksgiving.

In 1621 Plymouth received a land grant from the Council for New England. Two years later it gave up its original communal economy, and stipulated that now each settler was to provide for his family from his own land. Throughout its separate existence, until absorbed into Massachusetts in 1691, the Plymouth colony remained in the anomalous position of holding a land grant but no charter of government from any English authority. The government grew instead out of the Mayflower Compact, which was neither exactly a constitution nor a precedent for later constitutions. Rather it was the obvious recourse of a group that had made a covenant (or agreement) to form a church and that believed God had made a covenant with them to provide a way to salvation. Thus the civil government grew naturally out of the church government, and the members of each were identical at the start. The signers of the compact at first met as the General Court, which chose the governor and his assistants (or council). Later others were admitted as members, or "freemen," but only church members were eligible. Eventually, as the colony grew, the General Court became a body of representatives from the various towns.

MASSACHUSETTS BAY The Plymouth colony's population never rose above 7,000, and after ten years it was overshadowed by its larger neighbor, the Massachusetts Bay colony. It, too, was originally intended to be a holy commonwealth made up of religious folk bound together in the harmonious worship of God and the pursuit of their "callings." Like the Pilgrims, the Puritans who colonized Massachusetts Bay were primarily Congregationalists who sought to form self-governing churches with membership limited to "visible saints"—those who could demonstrate receipt of the gift of God's grace. But unlike the Plymouth Separatists, the Puritans who settled Massachusetts Bay still hoped to reform the Church of England and therefore they were called Non-Separating Congregationalists.

Governor John Winthrop, in whose vision the Massachusetts Bay colony would be as "a city upon a hill."

In 1628 a group of Puritans and merchants formed the New England Company and got a land patent from the Council for New England. To confirm its legality, the company turned to Charles I, who issued a charter in 1629 under the new name of the Massachusetts Bay Company. Leaders of the company at first looked upon it mainly as a business venture, but a majority faction led by John Winthrop, a well-to-do lawyer from East Anglia recently discharged from a government job, resolved to use the colony as a refuge for persecuted Puritans and as an instrument for building a "wilderness Zion" in America.

Winthrop shrewdly took advantage of a fateful omission in the royal charter for the Massachusetts Bay Company: the usual proviso that the company maintain its home office in England. Winthrop's group took its charter with them, thereby transferring the entire government of the colony to Massachusetts Bay, where they hoped to ensure Puritan control.

In 1630 the *Arbella,* with Governor John Winthrop and the charter aboard, embarked with six other ships for Massachusetts. In a lay sermon, "A Model of Christian Charity," delivered on board, Winthrop told his fellow Puritans "we must consider that we shall be a city upon a hill"—a shining example of what a godly community could be. They landed at Charlestown, Massachusetts. By the end of the year seventeen more ships bearing 1,000 more colonists arrived. As settlers—both Puritan and non-Puritan—poured into the region, Boston became the new colony's chief city and capital.

The *Arbella* migrants proved to be the vanguard of a massive movement, the Great Migration, that carried some 80,000 Britons to new settlements around the world over the next decade. Fleeing persecution and economic depression at home, they gravitated to Ireland, the Netherlands, and the Rhineland. But the majority traveled to the New World. They went not only to New England and the Chesapeake, but also to new English settlements in the Caribbean.

The transfer of the Massachusetts charter, whereby an English trading company evolved into a provincial government, was a unique venture in colonization. Under the royal charter, power in the company rested with the General Court, which elected the governor and assistants. The General Court consisted of shareholders, called freemen (those who had the "freedom of the company"), but only a few besides Winthrop and his assistants had such status. This suited Winthrop and his friends, but then over 100 settlers asked to be admitted as freemen. Rather than risk trouble, the inner group finally admitted 118 in 1631, stipulating that only church members could become freemen.

At first the freemen had no power except to choose "assistants," who in turn chose the governor and deputy governor. The procedure violated provisions of the charter, but Winthrop kept the document hidden and few knew of the exact provisions. Controversy simmered until 1634,

when each town sent two delegates to Boston to confer on matters coming before the General Court. There they demanded to see the charter, which Winthrop reluctantly produced, and they read that the power to pass laws and levy taxes rested in the General Court. Winthrop argued that the body of freemen had grown too large, but when it met, the General Court responded by turning itself into a representative body with two or three deputies to represent each town. They also chose a new governor, and Winthrop did not resume the office until three years later.

A final stage in the evolution of the government, a two-house legislature, came in 1644 when, according to Winthrop, "there fell out a great business upon a very small occasion." The "small occasion" pitted a poor widow against a well-to-do merchant over ownership of a stray sow. The General Court, being the supreme judicial as well as legislative body, was the final authority in the case. Popular sympathy and the deputies favored the widow, but the assistants disagreed. The case was finally settled out of court, but the assistants feared being outvoted on some greater occasion. They therefore secured a separation into two houses, and Massachusetts thenceforth had a bicameral assembly, the deputies and assistants sitting apart, with all decisions requiring a majority in each house.

Thus over a period of fourteen years the Massachusetts Bay Company, a trading corporation, evolved into the governing body of a commonwealth. Membership in a Puritan church replaced the purchase of stock as the means of becoming a freeman, which was to say, a voter. The General Court, like Parliament, became a representative body of two houses: the House of Assistants corresponding roughly to the House of Lords, and the House of Deputies to the House of Commons. The charter remained unchanged, but practice under the charter was quite different from the original expectation.

RHODE ISLAND   More by accident than design Massachusetts became the staging area for the rest of New England as new colonies grew out of religious quarrels within the fold. Young Roger Williams, who arrived in 1631, was among the first to cause problems, precisely because he was the purest of Puritans, troubled by the failure of Massachusetts Nonconformists to repudiate the Church of England entirely. He held a brief pastorate in Salem, then moved to Separatist Plymouth. Governor Bradford found Williams to be gentle and kind in his personal relations as well as a charismatic speaker. But he charged that Williams "began to fall into strange opinions," specifically questioning the king's right to confiscate Indian lands. Williams then returned to Salem. Williams's belief that a true church must include only those who had received God's gift of grace led him eventually to the conclusion that no true church was possible, unless perhaps consisting of his wife and himself.

But eccentric as some of Williams's beliefs may have been, they led him to principles that later generations would honor for other reasons. In his view, the purity of the church required complete separation of church and state and freedom from coercion in matters of faith. "Forced worship," he declared, "stinks in God's nostrils." Williams therefore questioned the authority of government to impose an oath of allegiance and rejected laws imposing religious conformity. Such views were too advanced even for the radical church of Salem, which finally removed him, whereupon Williams retorted so hotly against "ulcered and gangrened" churches that the General Court in 1635 banished him to England. Governor Winthrop, however, out of personal sympathy, permitted Williams to slip away with a few followers among the Narraganset Indians, whom he had befriended. In 1636 Williams established the town of Provi-

Religious quarrels within the Puritan fold led to the founding of new colonies. Here a seventeenth-century cartoon shows wrangling sects tossing a Bible in a blanket.

dence at the head of Narragansett Bay, the first permanent settlement in Rhode Island, and the first in America to legislate freedom of religion.

Anne Hutchinson quarreled with the Puritan leaders for different reasons. The articulate, strong-willed, and intelligent wife of a prominent merchant, she raised thirteen children, served as a healer and midwife, and hosted meetings in her Boston home to discuss sermons. Soon, however, the discussions turned into large forums for Hutchinson to provide her own commentaries on religious matters. She claimed to have experienced direct revelations from the Holy Spirit that convinced her that only two or three Puritan ministers actually preached the appropriate "covenant of grace." The others, she claimed, were godless hypocrites, deluded and incompetent; the "covenant of works" they promoted led people to believe that good conduct would ensure salvation.

Hutchinson's beliefs were provocative for several reasons. Puritan theology was grounded in the Calvinist doctrine that people could be saved only by God's grace rather than through their own willful actions. But Puritanism in practice also insisted that ministers were necessary to interpret God's will for the people so as to "prepare" them for the possibility of their being selected for salvation. In challenging the very legitimacy of the ministerial community as well as the hard-earned assurances of salvation enjoyed by current church members, Hutchinson was undermining the stability of an already fragile social system. More-over, her critics likened her claim of direct revelations from the Holy Spirit to the antinomian heresy, a belief that one is freed from obeying the moral law by one's own faith and by God's grace. And what made the situation worse in the male-dominated society of seventeenth-century New England was that a *woman* was making such charges and asser-tions. Mrs. Hutchinson had both offended authority and sanctioned a disruptive individualism.

A pregnant Hutchinson was hauled before the General Court in 1637, and for two days she sparred on equal terms with the presiding magistrates and testifying ministers. Her skillful deflections of the charges and her ability to cite chapter-and-verse defenses of her actions led an exasperated Governor Winthrop at one point to explode: "We do not mean to discourse with those of your sex." He found Hutchinson to be "a woman of haughty and fierce carriage, of a nimble wit and active spirit, and a very voluble tongue." As the trial continued, an over-wrought Hutchinson was eventually lured into convicting herself by claiming direct divine inspiration—blasphemy in the eyes of orthodox Puritans.

Banished in 1638 as a leper not fit for "our society," Hutchinson set-tled with her family and a few followers on an island south of Provi-dence, near what is now Portsmouth, Rhode Island. But the arduous journey had taken its toll. Hutchinson grew sick and her baby was still-born, leading her critics back in Massachusetts to assert that the "mon-strous birth" was God's way of punishing her for her sins. Hutchinson's spirits never recovered. After her husband's death in 1643, she moved to Long Island, then under Dutch jurisdiction, and the following year she and five of her children were massacred during an Indian attack. Her fate, wrote a vindictive Winthrop, was "a special manifestation of divine justice."

Thus the colony of Rhode Island and Providence Plantations, the smallest in America, grew up in Narragansett Bay, as a refuge for dis-senters who agreed that the state had no right to coerce religious belief. In 1640 they formed a confederation and in 1643 secured their first charter. Roger Williams lived until 1683, an active and beloved citizen of the commonwealth he founded in a society which, during his life-time at least, lived up to his principles of religious freedom and a gov-ernment based on the consent of the people.

CONNECTICUT   Connecticut had a more orthodox beginning than did Rhode Island. In 1633, a group from Plymouth settled in the Connecticut River valley. Three years later Thomas Hooker led three entire church congregations from Massachusetts Bay to the Connecticut River towns of Wethersfield, Windsor, and Hartford, which earlier arrivals had laid out the previous year.

For a year the settlers in the river towns were governed under a commission from the Massachusetts General Court, but the inhabitants organized the self-governing colony of Connecticut in 1637. Two years later, the Connecticut General Court adopted the "Fundamental Orders of Connecticut," a series of laws that provided for a government like that of Massachusetts, except that voting was not limited to church members. New Haven had by then emerged as a major settlement within Connecticut. A group of English Puritans, led by their minister and a wealthy merchant, had migrated first to Massachusetts and then, seeking a place to establish themselves in commerce, to New Haven on Long Island Sound in 1638. Mostly city dwellers, they found themselves reduced to hardscrabble farming, despite their intentions. The New Haven colony became the most rigorously Puritan of all. Like all the other offshoots of Massachusetts, it too lacked a charter and maintained a self-governing independence until 1662, when it was absorbed into Connecticut under the terms of that colony's first royal charter.

NEW HAMPSHIRE AND MAINE   To the north of Massachusetts, most of what are now New Hampshire and Maine was granted in 1622 by the Council for New England to Sir Ferdinando Gorges and Captain John Mason and their associates. In 1629 Mason and Gorges divided their territory at the Piscataqua River, Mason taking the southern part which he named New Hampshire, and Gorges taking the northern part, which became the province of Maine. In the 1630s Puritan immigrants began filtering in, and in 1638 the Reverend John Wheelwright, one of Anne Hutchinson's group, founded Exeter. Maine consisted of a few scattered settlements, mostly fishing stations.

An ambiguity in the Massachusetts charter brought the proprietorships into doubt, however. The charter set the boundary three miles north of the Merrimack River, and the Bay colony took that to mean north of the river's northernmost reach, which gave it a claim on nearly the entire Gorges-Mason grant. During the English time of troubles in the early 1640s, Massachusetts took over New Hampshire, and in the 1650s extended its authority to the scattered settlements in Maine. This led to lawsuits with the heirs of the proprietors, and in 1678 English judges and the Privy Council decided against Massachusetts in both cases. In 1679 New Hampshire became a royal colony, but Massachusetts bought out the Gorges heirs and continued to control Maine as its proprietor. A new Massachusetts charter in 1691 finally incorporated Maine into Massachusetts.

INDIANS IN NEW ENGLAND

The English settlers who poured into New England found not a "virgin land" of uninhabited wilderness but a developed region populated by over 100,000 Indians. To the white colonists, the Native Americans represented both an alien race and an impediment to their economic and spiritual goals. They considered the natives to be wild pagans incapable of fully exploiting nature's bounty. In their view, God meant for the Puritans to take over Indian lands as a reward for their piety and hard work. The town meeting of Milford, Connecticut, for example, voted in 1640 that the land was God's "and that the earth is given to the Saints; voted, we are the Saints."

To the Indians, the newcomers seemed like magical monsters. As one Indian leader explained, the white adventurers "strike awe and terror to our hearts." But the interactions of the two cultures were more complex than the conventional story of conquest and subjugation. Indians coped with the newcomers and changing circumstances in a variety of different ways. Many resisted, others sought accommodation, and still others grew dependent on European culture. In some areas, Indians survived and even flourished in concert with European settlers over long periods of time and with varying degrees of advantage. In other areas, land-hungry newcomers quickly displaced or decimated the native populations. The interactions of the two cultures thus involved misunderstandings, the mutual need for trade and adaptation, and sporadic outbreaks of epidemics and warfare.

In general, the English colonists adopted a quite different strategy for dealing with the Native Americans than that of the French and the Dutch. Merchants from France and the Netherlands were preoccupied with exploiting the fur trade. To do so, they established permanent trading outposts among the Indians. This led them to establish amicable relations with the far more numerous Indians in the region. In contrast, the English colonists were more interested in pursuing their "God-given" right to fish and farms. They were quite willing to manipulate and exploit Indians rather than deal with them on an equal footing. Their goal was subordination rather than reciprocity.

THE NEW ENGLAND INDIANS   In Maine the Abenakis were mainly hunters and gatherers dependent upon the natural offerings of the land and waters. The men did the hunting and fishing while the women retrieved the dead game and prepared it for eating. Women were also responsible for setting up and breaking camp, gathering fruits and berries, and raising the children. The Algonquian tribes of southern New England—the Massachusetts, Nausets, Narragansets, Pequots, and Wampanoags—were more horticultural. Their highly developed agricultural system centered on three primary crops: corn, beans, and pumpkins. While the men still hunted, fished, or traded surplus grain, women planted crops on regularly spaced mounds so as to allow the

Native Americans fishing, in an engraving by Theodor de Bry based on a watercolor by John White.

roots of the plants to intertwine and thereby protect the young tendrils from wind and birds.

For centuries the Indians had used the "slash-and-burn" technique to transform densely wooded forests into fields or parklike hunting preserves. They set fires to burn the underbrush and to nourish the soil. This not only facilitated planting but also allowed for the emergence of succulent new plants that enticed deer. Burning the thick underbrush under the forest canopy also made it easier for Indians to track game and to gather nuts and berries.

The Indians' dependence on nature for their survival shaped their religious beliefs. They believed in a Creator who provided them with the land and its bountiful resources. Many rituals, ceremonies, and taboos acknowledged their dependence on the gods. Rain dances, harvest festivals, and sacrificial offerings bespoke a culture whose fate was dependent on supernatural powers.

Initially, the coastal Indians helped the white settlers develop a subsistence economy. They taught the Europeans how to plant corn and to use fish for fertilizer. They also developed a flourishing trade with the newcomers, exchanging furs for manufactured goods and "trinkets." The various Indian tribes of New England often fought among themselves, usually over disputed land. Had they been able to forge a solid alliance, they would have been better able to resist the encroachments of white settlers. As it was, they not only were fragmented but also vulnerable to the infectious diseases carried on board the ships transporting European settlers to the New World. Epidemics of smallpox soon devastated the Indian population, leaving the coastal areas "a widowed land." Between 1610 and 1675, the Abenakis declined from 12,000 to 3,000, and the southern New England tribes from 65,000 to 10,000. Governor William Bradford of Plymouth reported that the Indians "fell sick of the smallpox, and died most miserably." By the hundreds, they died "like rotten sheep." Many of the Puritan leaders interpreted these epidemics as divine harvests intended to clear the region of Indians and thereby facilitate white settlement. After all, they reasoned, the Indians were heathens doing the devil's work. They must be rooted out.

THE PEQUOT WAR   Those Indians who survived the epidemics and refused to yield their lands were often dislodged by force. In 1636 white settlers in Massachusetts accused a Pequot of murdering a colonist. Joined by Connecticut colonists, they exacted their revenge by setting fire to a Pequot village on the Mystic River. As the Indians fled their burning huts, the Puritans shot and killed them—men, women, and children. In less than an hour, all but seven escapees were dead.

Sassacus, the Pequot chief, then organized the survivors among his followers and attacked the whites. During the Pequot War of 1637, the colonists and their Narraganset allies indiscriminately killed hundreds of Pequots in their village near West Mystic, in the Connecticut River valley. A white participant described the horrible scene: "Many were burnt in the fort, men, women, and children. . . . There were about four hundred souls in this fort, and not above five of them escaped out of our hands. Great and doleful was the bloody sight." The magisterial Puritan minister Cotton Mather described the slaughter as a "sweet sacrifice" and "gave the praise thereof to God." Another Puritan leader justified the massacre of Indians by saying that "Sometimes the Scripture declareth [that] women and children must perish with their parents."

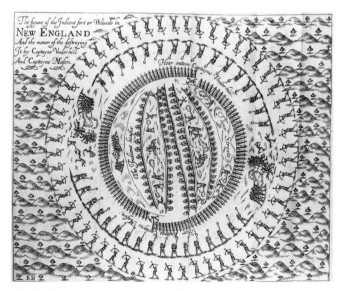

The Puritans and their Indian allies, the Narragansets, mount a ferocious attack on the Pequots at Mystic, Connecticut (1637).

Only a few colonists regretted the massacre. Roger Williams warned that the lust for land would become "as great a God with us English as God Gold was with the Spanish." With poignant clarity, Pequot survivors recognized the motives of the English settlers: "We see plainly that their chiefest desire is to deprive us of the privilege of our land, and drive us to our utter ruin." Indeed, the white colonists captured most of the surviving Pequots and sold them into slavery in Bermuda. Under the terms of the Treaty of Hartford (1638), the Pequot nation was declared dissolved.

KING PHILIP'S WAR   After the Pequot War, the prosperous fur trade contributed to peaceful relations between whites and the remaining Indians, but the relentless growth of the colony and the decline of the animal population began to reduce the eastern tribes to relative poverty. The colonial government repeatedly encroached upon the Indian settlements, forcing them to acknowledge English laws and customs. At the same time that colonial leaders expropriated Indian lands, Puritan missionaries sought to convert the tribes to Christianity. Hundreds of converts settled in special "praying Indian" towns. By 1675 the natives and settlers had come to know each other well—and fear each other deeply.

The era of fairly peaceful coexistence that began with the Treaty of Hartford came to an end during the last quarter of the seventeenth century. In 1675 Philip (Metacom), chief of the Wampanoags and the son of Massasoit, who had helped the original Pilgrims, forged an alliance among the remaining tribes of southern New England—the Narragansets, Mohegans, and Wampanoags. The spark that set New England ablaze resulted from the murder of John Sassamon, a "praying Indian" who had attended Harvard and served as a British spy. He had warned the colonists that Metacom was planning to attack them. The officials of Plymouth colony tried and executed three Wampanoags for the murder of Sassamon. In retaliation the Indians attacked and burned colonial settlements throughout Massachusetts and Plymouth colony.

Both sides suffered incredible losses. It is estimated that some 7,000 people were killed in what came to be called either King Philip's War or Metacomet's War. The fighting killed more people and caused more destruction in New England, in proportion to the population, than any American conflict since. Bands of Indian warriors assaulted thirty separate towns. Within a year, the Indians were threatening Boston itself.

Finally, however, depleted supplies and the casualty toll wore down Indian resistance. Philip's wife and son were captured and sold into West Indian slavery. Some of the tribes surrendered, a few succumbed to disease, while others fled to the west. Those who remained behind were forced to resettle in villages supervised by white settlers. Philip initially escaped, only to be hunted down and killed in 1676 at a battle known as the Great Swamp Fight. The colonists marched his severed head on a pike through their towns. Indian resistance in New England died with King Philip.

THE ENGLISH CIVIL WAR IN AMERICA

Before 1640 English settlers in New England and around Chesapeake Bay had established two great beachheads on the Atlantic coast, separated by the Dutch colony of New Netherland in between. After 1640, however, the struggle between king and Parliament distracted attention from colonization, and migration dwindled to a trickle of emigrants for more than twenty years. During the time of civil war and Oliver Cromwell's Puritan dictatorship, the struggling colonies were left pretty much to their own devices, especially in New England where English Puritans saw little need to intervene.

In 1643 four of the New England colonies—Massachusetts Bay, Plymouth, Connecticut, and New Haven—formed the New England Confederation to provide joint defense against the Dutch, French, and Indians. They also agreed to support the Christian faith, to render up fugitives, and to settle disputes through the machinery of the Confederation. Two commissioners from each colony met annually to transact business. In some ways the Confederation behaved like a sovereign power. It made treaties, and in 1653 it declared war against the Dutch who were supposedly stirring the Indians against Connecticut. Massachusetts, far from the scene of trouble, failed to cooperate, which greatly weakened the Confederation. But the commissioners continued to meet annually until 1684, when Massachusetts lost its charter.

Virginia and Maryland remained almost as independent as New England. At the behest of Governor William Berkeley, the Virginia burgesses in 1649 denounced the execution of Charles and recognized his son, Charles II, as the lawful king. In 1652, however, the assembly yielded to parliamentary commissioners and overruled the governor. In return for the surrender, the commissioners let the assembly choose its own council and governor, and the colony grew rapidly in population during its years of independent government—some of the growth came from the arrival of royalists who found a friendly haven in the Old Dominion, despite its capitulation to the English Puritans.

The parliamentary commissioners who won the submission of Virginia proceeded to Maryland, where the proprietary governor faced particular difficulties with his Protestant majority, largely Puritan but including some earlier refugees from Anglican Virginia. At the governor's suggestion, the assembly had passed, and the proprietor had accepted, the Maryland Toleration Act of 1649, an assurance that Puritans would not be molested in their religion. In 1652 the commissioners revoked the Toleration Act and deprived Lord Baltimore of his governmental rights, though not of his lands and revenues. Still, the more extreme Puritan elements were dissatisfied, and a brief clash in 1654 brought civil war to Maryland, deposing the governor. But Oliver Cromwell took the side of Lord Baltimore and restored him to full rights in 1657, whereupon the Toleration Act was reinstated. The act deservedly stands as a landmark to human liberty, albeit enacted more out of expediency than conviction.

Cromwell let the colonies go their own way, but he was not indifferent to the nascent empire. He fought trade wars with the Dutch and harassed England's traditional enemy, Catholic Spain, in the Caribbean. In 1655 he sent out an expedition that wrested Jamaica from the Spaniards, thereby improving the odds for English privateers and pirates who pillaged Spanish ships.

The Restoration of King Charles II in England in 1660 led to an equally painless restoration of previous governments in the colonies. The process involved scarcely any change, since little had occurred under Cromwell. Emigration rapidly expanded the populations in Virginia and Maryland. Fears of reprisals against Puritan New England proved unfounded, at least for the time being. Agents hastily dispatched by the colonies won reconfirmation of the Massachusetts charter in 1662 and the very first royal charters for Connecticut and Rhode Island in 1662 and 1663. All three retained their status as self-governing corporations. Plymouth still had no charter, but it went unmolested. New Haven, however, disappeared as a separate entity, absorbed into the colony of Connecticut.

Settling the Carolinas

The Restoration of Charles II opened a new season of enthusiasm for colonial expansion, directed mainly by royal favorites. Within twelve years the English had conquered New Netherland, had settled Carolina, and very nearly filled out the shape of the colonies. In the middle region formerly claimed by the Dutch, four new colonies sprang into being: New York, New Jersey, Pennsylvania, and Delaware. Without exception the new colonies were proprietary, awarded by the king to men who had remained loyal, or had brought about his restoration, or in one case to whom he was indebted. In 1663 he granted Carolina to eight prominent allies who became Lords Proprietors of the region.

NORTH CAROLINA Carolina was from the start made up of two widely separated areas of settlement, which finally became separate colonies. The northernmost part, long called Albemarle, had been entered as early as the 1650s by stragglers who drifted southward from Virginia. For half a century Albemarle remained a remote scattering of settlers along the shores of Albemarle Sound, isolated from Virginia by

the Dismal Swamp and lacking easy access for oceangoing vessels. Albemarle had no governor until 1664, no assembly until 1665, and not even a town until a group of French Huguenots founded the village of Bath in 1704.

SOUTH CAROLINA   The eight Lords Proprietors to whom the king gave Carolina neglected Albemarle from the outset, and focused on more promising sites to the south. They recruited settlers who had already been seasoned in the colonies, and from the outset West Indian planters showed a lively interest, for the rise of large-scale sugar production in Barbados had persuaded small planters to try their luck elsewhere. In 1669 three ships left London with about 100 settlers recruited in England. The expedition sailed first to Barbados, to pick up more settlers, then north to Bermuda. They landed in South Carolina at a place several miles up the Ashley River, where Charles Town (later known as Charleston) remained from 1670 to 1680, when it was moved across and downstream to Oyster Point, overlooking Charleston Harbor. There, as proud Charlestonians later claimed, the Ashley and Cooper Rivers "join to form the Atlantic Ocean."

The government of South Carolina rested on one of the most curious documents of colonial history, the "Fundamental Constitutions of Carolina," drawn up by one of the proprietors, Lord Ashley-Cooper, with the help of his secretary, the philosopher John Locke. Its cumbersome frame of government and its provisions for an elaborate nobility had little effect in the colony except to encourage a practice of large land grants. From the beginning, however, smaller "headrights" were given to every immigrant who paid for the cost of transit. The most enticing provision was a grant of religious toleration, designed to encourage immigration, which gave South Carolina a greater degree of indulgence (extending even to Jews and heathens) than either England or any other colony except Rhode Island and, once it was established, Pennsylvania.

The first profitable enterprise in South Carolina was a flourishing trade in deerskins and Indian slaves. Ambitious English planters from crowded Barbados dominated the colony and organized a major trade in Indian slaves, whom the Westo tribe obligingly captured and drove to the coast for shipment to the Caribbean. The first major export other than furs and slaves was cattle, and a staple cash crop was not developed until the introduction of rice in the 1690s. South Carolina became a separate royal colony in 1719. North Carolina remained under the proprietors' rule for ten more years, when they surrendered their governing rights to the crown.

THE SOUTHERN INDIAN TRADE   The major Indian tribes in Florida, the Carolinas, Georgia, and what is today Alabama and Mississippi—the Apalachee, Timucua, Catawba, Cherokee, Chickasaw, Choctaw, Creek, and Tuscarora—combined farming with hunting and fishing to produce a thriving culture. They clustered in matrilineal clans (in which authority and property descended through the maternal line). The women raised beans, potatoes, and especially corn. The men hunted, traded, and made war. Beginning in the late seventeenth century, the Creeks developed a flourishing trade with the British settlers, exchanging deerskins and slaves (mostly women and children from rival tribes) for manufactured goods—hoes, copper kettles, knives, beads, blankets, clothing, and, most precious of all, guns.

In the late seventeenth century English merchants—mostly illiterate adventurers—began traveling southward from Virginia down the Occaneechi trading path into the Piedmont region of Carolina, where they developed a prosperous exchange with the Catawbas. By 1690 traders from Charleston, South Carolina, made their way up the Savannah River to arrange deals with the Cherokees, Creeks, and Chickasaws. Between 1699 and 1715 Carolina exported an average of 54,000 deerskins per year. Europeans transformed the valuable hides

A contemporary print depicting seven "Chiefs of the Cherokee Indians" who had been taken from Carolina to England in 1730.

into bookbindings, gloves, belts, hats, and work aprons. The voracious demand for the soft skins almost exterminated the deer population.

The growing trade with the English exposed the Indians to contagious diseases that decimated their population. Commercial activity also entwined the Indians in a dependent relationship that would prove disastrous to their traditional way of life. Eager to receive more finished goods, weapons, and ammunition, the Indians became pliable trading partners, easily manipulated by wily English entrepreneurs and government officials. The English traders began providing the Indians with firearms and rum as incentives to convince them to capture rivals to be sold as slaves.

During the early eighteenth century, Indians equipped with British weapons and led by English soldiers crossed into Spanish territory in south Georgia and north Florida. They destroyed thirteen Spanish missions, killed several hundred Indians and Spaniards, and enslaved over 300 Indian men, women, and children. By 1710 the Florida tribes were on the verge of extinction. In 1708, when the total population of South Carolina was 9,580, including 2,900 blacks, there were 1,400 Indian slaves. Because the captive Indians frequently escaped or revolted, many were relocated to New England or the West Indies.

The continuing Indian trade led to repeated troubles. In 1711 the Tuscaroras in North Carolina were goaded by the Iroquois to abandon their accommodating ways and oust the Europeans. The catalyst for their uprising was the severe punishment of a Tuscarora accused of a petty offense. In a vengeful outburst, the Tuscaroras captured and killed a white colonist, then assaulted several plantations. In 1713, however, the colonists launched a well-coordinated assault that resulted in hundreds of Tuscaroras being killed or enslaved. Most of the survivors of this Tuscarora War retreated north, where they joined the Iroquois League.

Two years later, in 1715, Creeks, Choctaws, and members of smaller tribes organized a more massive revolt against English control. The so-called Yamasee War began when Indians killed several English traders, including the royal Indian agent for South Carolina. The English attributed the attacks to French and Spanish intrigues, but it now seems likely that the Indians acted on their own. The English colonists won out by playing the Indians against one another, convincing the Cherokees to join their side. When the Creek leaders visited the

Cherokees in an effort to gain their support, the Cherokees killed them, an incident that engendered hatred between the two tribes for years thereafter.

The Yamasee War ended in 1717, but infighting among the Indians continued. For the next ten years or so, the Creeks and Cherokees engaged in a costly blood feud, much to the delight of the English. One Carolinian explained that their challenge was to figure "how to hold both [tribes] as our friends, for some time, and assist them in cutting one another's throats without offending either. This is the game we intend to play if possible." The French played the same brutal game, doing their best to excite hatred between the Choctaws and the Chickasaws. By 1730, the Indian population in the Carolinas had dwindled from 15,000 thirty years before to just 4,000.

SETTLING THE MIDDLE COLONIES AND GEORGIA

NEW NETHERLAND BECOMES NEW YORK Charles II resolved early to pluck out that old thorn in the side of the English colonies— New Netherland. The Dutch colony was older than New England, and had been planted when the two Protestant powers allied in opposition to Catholic Spain. The Dutch East India Company (organized in 1602) had hired an English captain, Henry Hudson, to seek the elusive passage to China. Sailing along the upper coast of North America in 1609, Hudson had discovered Delaware Bay and explored the river named for him, venturing 160 miles upriver to a point probably beyond Albany, where he and a group of Mohawks began a lasting trade relation between the Dutch and the Iroquois nations. In 1614 the Dutch established fur-trading posts on Manhattan Island and upriver at Fort Orange (later Albany). In 1626 Governor Peter Minuit purchased Manhattan from the resident Indians, and a Dutch fort appeared at the lower end of the island. The village of New Amsterdam, which grew up around the fort, became the capital of New Netherland.

Dutch settlements gradually dispersed in every direction where furs might be found. In 1638 a Swedish trading company established Fort Christina at the site of the present Wilmington and scattered a few hundred settlers up and down the Delaware River. The Dutch, at the time allied to the Swedes in the Thirty Years' War, made no move to challenge the claim until 1655, when a force outnumbering the entire Swedish colony subjected them without bloodshed to the rule of New Netherland. The chief contribution of the short-lived New Sweden to American culture was the idea of the log cabin, which the Swedes and a few Finnish settlers had brought from the woods of Scandinavia.

Like the French, the Dutch were interested mainly in the fur trade rather than agricultural settlements. In 1629, however, the Dutch West India Company (organized in 1621) decided that it needed a mass of settlers to help protect the colony's "front door" at the mouth of the Hudson River. It provided that any stockholder might obtain a large estate (a patroonship) if he peopled it with fifty adults within four years. The patroon was obligated to supply cattle, tools, and buildings. His tenants, in turn, paid him rent, used his gristmill, gave him first option on surplus crops, and submitted to a court he established. It amounted to transplanting the feudal manor into the New World, and it met with as little luck as similar efforts in Maryland and South Carolina. Volunteers for serfdom were hard to find when there was land to be had elsewhere; most settlers took advantage of the company's provision that one could have as farms (*bouweries*) all the lands one could improve.

The colony's government was under the almost absolute control of a governor sent out by the Dutch West India Company. The governors were mostly stubborn autocrats, either corrupt or inept, especially at Indian relations. They depended on a small professional garrison for defense, and the inhabitants (including a number of English on Long Island) showed almost total indifference in 1664 when Governor Peter Stuyvesant called them to arms against a threatening British fleet. Almost defenseless, old soldier Stuyvesant blustered and stomped about on his wooden leg, but finally surrendered without a shot and stayed on quietly at his farm in what had become the colony of New York.

The plan of conquest had been hatched by the king's brother, the duke of York and Albany, later King James II. As lord high admiral and an investor in the African trade, he had already harassed Dutch shipping and forts in Africa. When he and his advisers counseled that New Netherland could easily be conquered, Charles II simply granted the region to his brother as proprietor, permitted the hasty gathering of an

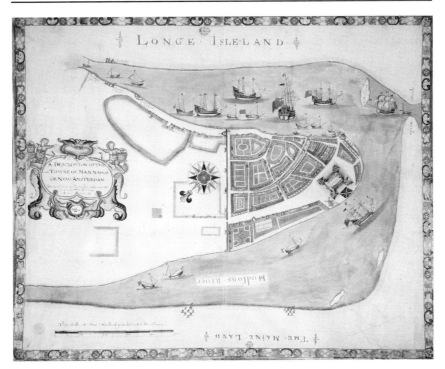

A map of New Amsterdam in 1664, shortly after the English took it away from the Dutch and christened it New York.

invasion force, and the English transformed New Amsterdam into New York and Fort Orange into Albany. The Dutch, however, left a permanent imprint on the land and the language: the Dutch vernacular faded away but place names such as Block Island, Wall Street (the original wall was for protection against Indians), and Broadway (*Breede Wegh*) remained, along with family names like Rensselaer, Roosevelt, and Van Buren. The Dutch presence lingered in the Dutch Reformed church; in words like *boss, cookie, crib, snoop, stoop, spook,* and *kill* (for creek); and in the legendary Santa Claus and Rip Van Winkle.

THE IROQUOIS LEAGUE   One of the most significant effects of European settlement in North America during the seventeenth century was the intensification of warfare between Indian peoples. The same combination of forces that decimated the Indian population of New England and the Carolinas affected the tribes around New York City and the lower Hudson Valley. Dissension among the Indians and susceptibility to infectious disease left them vulnerable to exploitation by whites and by other Indians.

In the interior of New York, however, a different situation arose. There the Iroquois (an Algonquian term signifying "snake" or "terrifying man") nation forged a league so strong and numerous that the outnumbered Dutch and, later, English traders were forced to work with the Indians in exploiting the lucrative fur trade. Initially, the Mahicans (an offshoot of the Pequots) supplied the Dutch with pelts. By 1625, however, the game animals in the Mahican territory had been hunted almost to extinction, so the Dutch turned to the Iroquois, a federation of five tribes that spoke related languages—the Mohawk, Oneida, Onondaga, Cayuga, and Seneca (a sixth tribe, the Tuscaroras, joined them from Carolina in 1712)—for supplies of fur and for allies.

By the early 1600s, some fifty sachems (chiefs) governed the 12,000 members of the Iroquois League. The sachems made decisions for all the villages and mediated tribal rivalries and dissension within the confederacy. The well-organized, firmly knit Iroquois tribes lived in rectangular "longhouses" sheathed in bark. Iroquois men hunted deer, bear, and beaver; women grew corn, beans, and squash. Although a patriarchal society, the Iroquois granted considerable powers to women, who controlled the nominations for the tribal councils and could remove ineffective or corrupt leaders.

When the Iroquois began to deplete the local game during the 1640s, they used firearms supplied by their Dutch trading partners to seize the Canadian hunting grounds of the neighboring Hurons and Eries. During the so-called Beaver Wars, the Iroquois defeated the western tribes and thereafter hunted the region to extinction. Other Indian nations such as the Fox, Sauk, and Kickapoo fled in terror at the approach of the Iroquois.

Iroquois men were proud, ruthless warriors. Participation in a war party served as the crucial rite of passage for young men. They fought opponents to gain status and revenge and to ease the grief caused by the death of friends and relatives. Their skill and courage in battle determined their social status. A warrior's success was not only measured by his fighting prowess but also by his ability to take prisoners and bring them back alive for adoption or ritual execution. This helps explain the Indian preference for surprise attacks and ambushes rather than conventional frontal assaults.

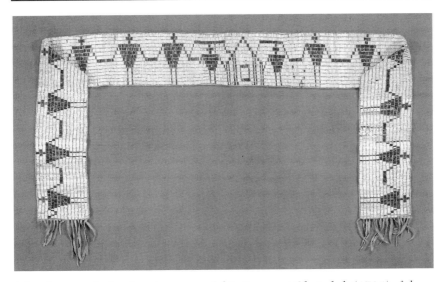

A longhouse is depicted at the center of this Covenant Chain belt (1794) of the Haudenosaunee, otherwise known as the Iroquois. Wampum belts such as this one were often used to certify treaties or record transactions with other Indians and whites.

While providing profitable new hunting grounds, wars against other Indian tribes depleted the Iroquois population. This led them to replace lost relatives by allowing elder women to "adopt" able-bodied captives after they had been tortured so as to break their allegiance to their native group or culture. By the 1660s more than two-thirds of the residents of some Iroquois villages were adoptees.

During the second half of the seventeenth century, the relentless search for furs and captives led Iroquois war parties to range far and wide across what is today eastern North America. They gained control over a huge area from the St. Lawrence River to Tennessee and from Maine to Michigan. These wars helped reorient the political relationships in the whole eastern half of the continent, especially in the area from the Ohio River Valley northward across the Great Lakes basin. Besieged by the Iroquois League, the western tribes forged defensive alliances with the French.

For over twenty years warfare raged across the Great Lakes region. In the 1690s the French and their Indian allies gained the advantage over the Iroquois. They destroyed their crops and villages, infected them with smallpox, and reduced the male population by more than a third.

Facing extermination, the Iroquois made peace with the French in 1701. During the first half of the eighteenth century, they maintained a shrewd neutrality between the two rival European powers that enabled them to play the British off against the French, all the while creating a thriving fur trade for themselves.

NEW JERSEY   Shortly after the conquest of New Netherland, the duke of York granted his lands between the Hudson and the Delaware Rivers to Sir George Carteret and Lord John Berkeley (brother of Virginia's governor), and named the territory for Carteret's native island of Jersey. In 1676, by mutual agreement, the colony was divided by a diagonal line into East and West New Jersey, with Carteret taking the east. Finally in 1682 Carteret sold out to a group of twelve, including William Penn, who in turn brought into partnership twelve more proprietors, for a total of twenty-four! In East New Jersey, peopled at first by perhaps 200 Dutch who had crossed the Hudson, new settlements gradually arose: some disaffected Puritans from New Haven founded Newark, Carteret's brother brought a group to found Elizabethtown (Elizabeth), and a group of Scots founded Perth Amboy. In the west, which faces the Delaware River, a scattering of Swedes, Finns, and Dutch remained, soon to be overwhelmed by swarms of English Quakers. In 1702 East and West New Jersey were united as a single royal colony.

PENNSYLVANIA AND DELAWARE   The Quaker sect, as the Society of Friends was called in ridicule (because they told their followers to "tremble at the word of the Lord"), became the most influential of many radical groups that sprang from the turbulence of the English Civil War. Founded by George Fox in about 1647, the Quakers carried further than any other group the doctrine of individual inspiration and interpretation—the "inner light," they called it. They discarded all formal sacraments and formal ministry, refused deference to persons of rank, used the familiar "thee" and "thou" in addressing everyone, refused to take oaths because that was contrary to Scripture, and embraced pacifism. Quakers were subjected to intense persecution—often in their zeal they seemed to invite it—but never inflicted it on others. Their toleration extended to complete religious freedom for all, of whatever belief or disbelief, and to the equality of the sexes and the full participation of women in religious affairs.

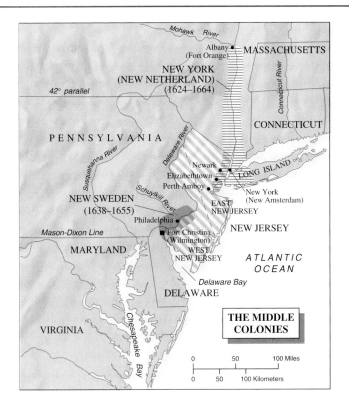

In 1673 George Fox returned from a visit to America with the vision of a Quaker commonwealth in the New World and enticed others with his idea. The entrance of Quakers into New Jersey encouraged other Friends to migrate, especially to the Delaware River side. And soon, across the river, arose William Penn's Quaker commonwealth, the colony of Pennsylvania.

Penn was the son of Admiral Sir William Penn, who had supported Parliament in the Civil War and had led Cromwell's conquest of Jamaica but later helped in the Restoration. Young William was reared as a proper gentleman, but as a student at Oxford he had turned to Quakerism. Upon his father's death, Penn inherited a substantial estate, including proprietary rights to a huge tract in America. The land was named, at the king's insistence, for Penn's father: Pennsylvania (literally Penn's Woods).

When Penn assumed control of the area, there was already a scattering of Dutch, Swedish, and English settlers on the west bank of the

*A Quaker meeting. The presence of women is evidence of
Quaker views on the equality of the sexes.*

Delaware. But Penn also soon made vigorous efforts to bring in more
settlers. He published glowing descriptions of the colony, which were
translated into German, Dutch, and French. By the end of 1681, about
1,000 settlers lived in his province. By that time, a town was growing up
at the junction of the Schuylkill and Delaware Rivers. Penn called it
Philadelphia (the City of Brotherly Love). Because of the generous
terms on which Penn offered land, because indeed he offered aid to
emigrants, the colony grew rapidly.

The relations between the Indians and the Quakers were cordial
from the beginning, because of the Quakers' friendliness and because
of Penn's careful policy of purchasing land titles from the Indians. Penn
even took the trouble to learn the language of the Delawares, something
few colonists even tried. For some fifty years, the settlers and the natives lived side by side in peace, in relationships of such trust that
Quaker farmers sometimes left their children in the care of Indians
when they were away from home.

The government, which rested on three Frames of Government
promulgated by Penn, resembled that of other proprietary colonies,
except that the freemen (taxpayers and property owners) elected the
councilors as well as the assembly. The governor had no veto—

although Penn, as proprietor, did. Penn hoped to show that a government could operate in accordance with Quaker principles, that it could maintain peace and order without oaths or wars, and that religion could flourish without an established church and with absolute freedom of conscience. Because of its tolerance, Pennsylvania became a refuge not only for Quakers but for a variety of dissenters—as well as Anglicans—and early reflected the ethnic mixture of Scotch-Irish and Germans that became common to the middle colonies and the southern backcountry. Penn himself stayed only four years in the colony.

In 1682 the duke of York also granted Penn the area of Delaware, another part of the Dutch territory. At first Delaware became part of Pennsylvania, but after 1701 it was granted the right to choose its own assembly. From then until the American Revolution it had a separate assembly but the same governor as Pennsylvania.

GEORGIA   Georgia was the last of the British continental colonies to be established, half a century after Pennsylvania. During the seventeenth century, English settlers pushed southward into the borderlands between the Carolinas and Florida. They brought with them their African slaves and a desire to win over the Indian trade from the Spanish. Each side used guns, goods, and rum to influence the Indians, and the Indians, in turn, effectively played off the English against the Spanish in order to gain the most favorable terms.

In 1732 George II gave the land between the Savannah and Altamaha Rivers to the twenty-one trustees of Georgia. In two respects Georgia was unique among the colonies: it was set up as both a philanthropic experiment and a military buffer against Spanish Florida. General James E. Oglethorpe, who accompanied the first colonists as resident trustee, represented both concerns: as a soldier who organized the defenses, and as a philanthropist who championed prison reform and sought a colonial refuge for the poor and religiously persecuted.

In 1733 a band of 120 colonists founded Savannah near the mouth of the Savannah River. Carefully laid out by Oglethorpe, the old town with its geometrical pattern and its numerous little parks remains a monument to the city planning of a bygone day. A group of Protestant refugees from Austria began to arrive in 1734, followed by Germans and

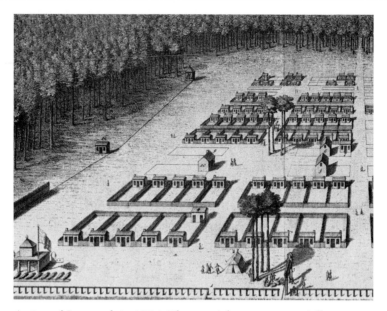

A view of Savannah in 1734. The town's layout was carefully planned.

German-speaking Moravians and Swiss, who made the colony for a time more German than English. The addition of Highland Scots, Portuguese Jews, Welsh, and others gave the early colony a cosmopolitan character much like that of Charleston.

As a buffer against Florida the colony succeeded, but as a philanthropic experiment it failed. Efforts to develop silk and wine production floundered. Land holdings were limited to 500 acres, rum was prohibited, and the importation of slaves was forbidden, partly to leave room for servants brought on charity, partly to ensure security. But the utopian rules soon collapsed. The regulations against rum and slavery were widely disregarded, and finally abandoned. By 1759 all restrictions on landholding were removed.

In 1753 the trustees' charter expired, and the province reverted to the crown. As a royal colony, Georgia acquired for the first time an effective government. The province developed slowly over the next decade, but grew rapidly in population and wealth after 1763. Instead of wine and silk, as was Oglethorpe's plan, Georgians exported rice, indigo, lumber, beef, and pork, and carried on a lively trade with the West Indies. The colony had become a commercial success.

THRIVING COLONIES

By the early eighteenth century, the English had outstripped both the French and the Spanish in the New World. British America became the most populous, prosperous, and powerful region on the continent. The prospect of cheap or free land, greater prosperity, higher social status, and greater religious opportunities attracted thousands of emigrants. By the mid–seventeenth century, American colonists on average were better fed, clothed, and housed than their counterparts in Britain and Europe, where a majority of the people lived in destitution. But the English colonization of North America included many failures as well as successes. Lots of settlers found only hard labor and early deaths in the New World. Others flourished only because they exploited Indians, indentured servants, or slaves.

The British succeeded in creating a lasting American empire because of crucial advantages they had over their European rivals. The centralized control imposed by the monarchs of Spain and France got them off the mark more quickly but eventually hobbled innovation and responsiveness to new circumstances. The British acted by private investment and with a minimum of royal control. Not a single colony was begun at the direct initiative of the crown. In the English colonies, poor immigrants had a much greater chance of getting at least a small parcel of land. The English, unlike their rivals, welcomed people from a variety of nationalities and dissenting sects who came in search of a new life or a safe harbor. And a greater degree of self-government made the English colonies more responsive to new circumstances—if sometimes stalled by controversy.

The compact pattern of English settlement contrasted sharply with the pattern of Spain's far-flung conquests or France's far-reaching trade routes to the interior by way of the St. Lawrence and Mississippi Rivers (discussed in Chapter 4). Geography reinforced England's bent for concentrated occupation and settlement of its colonies. The rivers and bays that indented the coasts served as communication arteries along which colonies first sprang up, but no great river offered a highway to the far interior. About a hundred miles inland in Georgia and the Carolinas, and nearer the coast to the north, the "fall line" of the rivers presented rocky rapids that marked the head of navigation and the end of the coastal plain. About a hundred miles beyond that, and farther back in

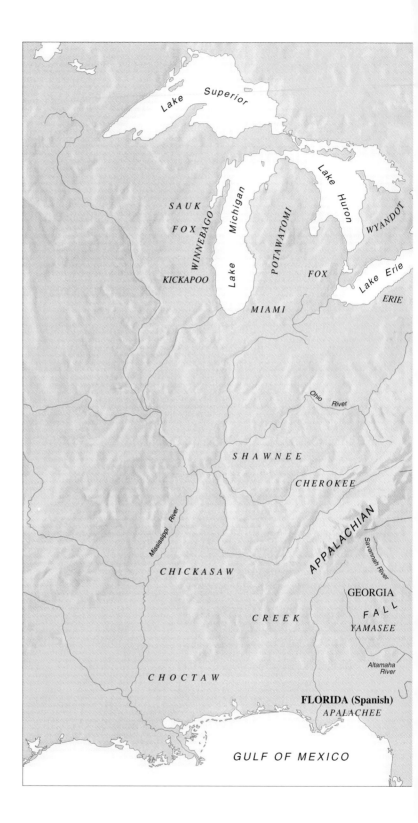

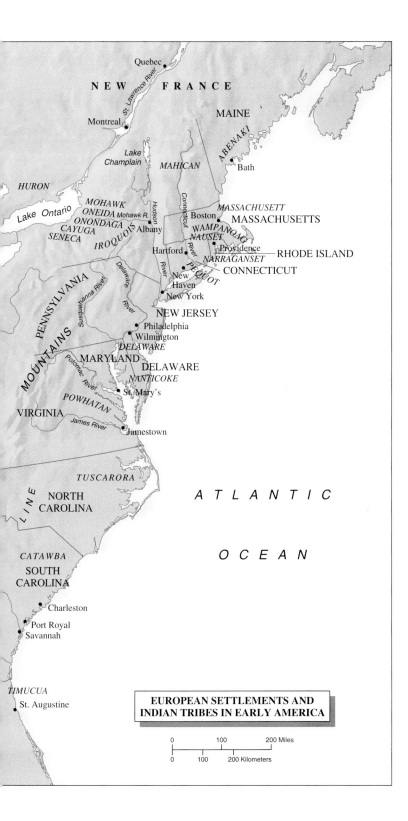

EUROPEAN SETTLEMENTS AND
INDIAN TRIBES IN EARLY AMERICA

NEW FRANCE

Quebec

Montreal

MAINE

Lake
Champlain

HURON

Lake Ontario

MOHAWK
ONEIDA Mohawk R.
ONONDAGA
CAYUGA
SENECA

IROQUOIS

MAHICAN

Bath

ABENAKI

MASSACHUSETT
Boston MASSACHUSETTS
WAMPANOAG
NAUSET

Albany

Hartford

Providence
NARRAGANSET RHODE ISLAND
PEQUOT CONNECTICUT

New
Haven

New York

PENNSYLVANIA

MOUNTAINS

Susquehanna River

Delaware River

NEW JERSEY

Philadelphia
Wilmington
DELAWARE

MARYLAND

Potomac River

NANTICOKE

St. Mary's

DELAWARE

POWHATAN

VIRGINIA

James River

Jamestown

TUSCARORA

LINE

NORTH
CAROLINA

ATLANTIC

OCEAN

CATAWBA

SOUTH
CAROLINA

Charleston

Port Royal
Savannah

TIMUCUA

St. Augustine

Hudson

Connecticut River

St. Lawrence River

0   100   200 Miles

0   100   200 Kilometers

Pennsylvania, stretched the rolling expanse of the Piedmont, literally the foothills. And the final backdrop of English America was the Appalachian Mountain range, some 200 miles from the coast in the south, reaching down to the coast at points in New England, with only one significant break—up the Hudson-Mohawk Valley of New York. For 150 years the farthest outreach of British settlement stopped at the slopes of the mountains. To the east lay the wide expanse of ocean, which served not only as a highway for the transit of ideas and ways of living from Europe to America, but also as a barrier that allowed enough separation for both new and old ideas to evolve in a new environment.

MAKING CONNECTIONS

- What we now know about the early settlements sets the stage for regional differences in social patterns discussed in the next chapter.

- This chapter contained the observation that in founding its American colonies, "the British acted by private investment and with a minimum of royal control." This will change in Chapter 4 as England begins to take control of the American colonies.

- Later relations between colonists and Native Americans, described in Chapter 4, had their roots in the history of these early settlements.

FURTHER READING

Bernard Bailyn's multivolume work *The Peopling of British North America* provides a comprehensive view of migration to the New World. Jack P. Greene provides a brilliant synthesis of British colonization in *Pursuits of Happiness: The Social Development of Early Modern British Colonies and the Formation of American Culture* (1988). The best overview of the colonization of North America in Alan Taylor's *American Colonies* (2001). On the interactions among Indian, European, and African cultures, see Gary Nash's *Red, White, and Black: The Peoples of*

Early America (1982). See Daniel K. Richter's *The Ordeal of the Longhouse: The Peoples of the Iroquois League in the Era of European Colonization* (1992) for a history of the northeastern Iroquois Nation.

Andrew Delbanco's *The Puritan Ordeal* (1989) is a powerful study of the tensions inherent in the Puritan outlook. For information regarding the Puritan settlement of New England, see Virginia Anderson's *New England's Generation: The Great Migration* (1991).

The pattern of settlement in the middle colonies is illuminated in Barry Levy's *Quakers and the American Family: British Settlement in the Delaware Valley* (1988). Settlement of the areas along the South Atlantic is traced in James Horn's *Adapting to a New World: English Society in the Seventeenth-Century Chesapeake* (1994). Robert M. Weir's *Colonial South Carolina* (1983) covers the activities of the Lords Proprietors. For a study of race and the settlement of South Carolina, see Peter Wood's *Black Majority: Negroes in Colonial South Carolina from 1670 through the Stono Rebellion* (1975). A brilliant book on relations between the Catawba Indians and their black and white neighbors is James H. Merrell's *The Indians' New World: Catawbas and Their Neighbors from European Contact through the Era of Removal* (1989).

3 ⌘ COLONIAL WAYS OF LIFE

CHAPTER ORGANIZER

This chapter focuses on:

- the social and economic differences among the southern, middle, and New England colonies.

- how various groups of people of different genders, races, and classes fit into colonial society.

- the impact of the Enlightenment and the Great Awakening on the American colonies.

The process of carving a new civilization out of an abundant yet violent frontier involved a clash of cultures among European, African, and Indian peoples. War, duplicity, displacement, and enslavement were the tragic results. Yet on another level the process of creating a "New World" was largely the story of thousands of diverse folk engaged in the everyday tasks of building homes, planting crops, raising families, enforcing laws, and worshipping their God. Those who colonized America during the seventeenth and eighteenth centuries were part of a massive social migration occurring throughout Europe and Africa. Everywhere, it seemed, people were moving from farms to villages, from villages to cities, and from homelands to colonies. They came not so much from nations as from distinctive locales—the streets of London and other cities in southern and central England, the farms of Yorkshire and the Scottish Highlands, the villages of Germany, Switzerland, and Protestant Ireland, and the savannas and jungles of West Africa. They moved for different reasons. Most were responding to powerful social and economic forces, as rapid population growth and the rise of commercial agriculture squeezed people off the land. Many traveled in search of political security or religious freedom. Africans were captured and moved to new lands against their will.

America's settlers were mostly young (over half were under twenty-five), male, and poor. Almost half were indentured servants or slaves, and during the eighteenth century England would transport some 50,000 convicts to the North American colonies. About a third of the settlers came with their families, but most arrived alone. Once in America, many of them kept moving, trying to take advantage of new opportunities. Whatever their status or ambition, this extraordinary mosaic of ordinary yet adventurous people was primarily responsible for creating America's enduring institutions and values.

THE SHAPE OF EARLY AMERICA

BRITISH FOLKWAYS   The vast majority of early European settlers came from the British Isles. They clustered in four mass migrations from distinct regions over the seventeenth and eighteenth centuries. The first involved some 20,000 Puritans who settled Massachusetts between 1629 and 1641, most of whom hailed from the East Anglian counties east of London. A generation later, a smaller group of wealthy Royalist cavaliers and their indentured servants migrated from southern England to Virginia. These English aristocrats, mostly Anglicans, had few qualms about the introduction of African slavery. The third migratory wave brought some 23,000 Quakers from the North Midlands of England to the Delaware Valley colonies of West Jersey, Pennsylvania, and Delaware. They imported with them a social system that was distinctive for its sense of spiritual equality, suspicion of class distinctions and powerful elites, and a commitment to plain living and high thinking. The fourth and largest surge of colonization occurred between 1717 and 1775 and included hundreds of thousands of Celtic Britons and Scotch-Irish from northern Ireland, the Scottish Lowlands, and the northern counties of England; these were mostly coarse, feisty, clannish folk who settled in the rugged backcountry along the Appalachian Mountains. Generally poorer than their English counterparts, the Scots had more to gain by moving to the New World.

It was long assumed that the strenuous demands of the American frontier environment served as a great "melting pot" that stripped such immigrants of their native identities and melded them into homogeneous Americans. Yet for all of the transforming effects of the New World, disparate British ways of life have persisted to this day. Although most British settlers spoke a common language and shared the Protestant faith, they carried with them—and retained—sharply different cultural attitudes and customs from their home regions. They spoke distinct dialects, cooked different foods, named and raised their children differently, adopted different educational philosophies and attitudes toward time, preferred different architectural styles, engaged in disparate games and forms of recreation, and organized their societies differently.

In gender relations, religious practices, criminal propensities, and dozens of other ways, many American customs today still reflect age-old British customs. Of course, such cultural continuity is not unique to British Americans. Enduring folkways are also evident among the descendants of settlers from Africa, Europe, Latin America, the Middle East, and Asia. Americans thus constitute a mosaic rather than a homogeneous mass, and they share a quite varied social and cultural heritage.

SEABOARD ECOLOGY   One of the cherished legends of American history has it that those settling British America arrived to find an unspoiled wilderness little touched by human activity. But that was not the case. For thousands of years, Indian hunting practices had produced what one scholar has called the "greatest known loss of wild species" in the continent's history. The Indians had burned forests and dense undergrowth in order to provide cropland, to ease travel through hardwood forests, and to make way for grasses, berries, and other forage for the animals they hunted. Indians worked the cleared lands for six to eight years until the nutrients in the soil were depleted, and then they moved on to new areas. This migratory "slash-and-burn" agriculture increased the rate at which plant nutrients were recycled and also allowed more sunlight to reach the forest floor. These conditions in turn created rich soil and ideal grazing grounds for elk, deer, turkey, bear, moose, and beaver. Nutrients from the topsoil also fertilized the streams and helped produce teeming schools of sturgeon, smelt, and small herrings called alewives. Indian farming practices also halted the normal forest succession and, especially in the Southeast, created large stands of longleaf pines, still the most common source of timber in the region.

Equally important in shaping the ecosystem of America was the European attitude toward the environment. Where the Native Americans tended to be migratory, considering land and animals as communal resources to be shared and consumed only as necessary, many European colonizers viewed natural resources as privately owned commodities to be sold for profit. Settlers thus quickly set about evicting Indians, clearing, fencing, improving, and selling land, growing surpluses, and trapping game for commercial use. These practices transformed the seaboard environment. In many places—Plymouth, for instance, or St. Mary's, Maryland—settlers occupied the sites of former Indian towns, and maize, corn, beans, and squash quickly became colonial staples, along with new crops brought from Europe.

In time a more dense population of humans and their domestic animals created a new landscape of fields, meadows, fences, barns, and houses. Such innovations further altered the ecology of the New World environment. Colonists brought with them new domesticated animals—pigs, sheep, cattle, and horses—as well as new weeds and pests such as dandelions, black flies, and cockroaches. Animal crowding forced further deforestation. So, too, did the ravenous demand for timber to construct ships and houses, a demand that devoured many of the white oak, white pine, cedar, and hickory trees in the East.

There followed consequences no one had anticipated. Because cleared and grazed land is warmer, drier, and more compacted, it is more easily subject to flooding and erosion. Foraging cattle, sheep, horses, and pigs gradually changed the distribution of trees, shrubs, and grasses. The transformed landscape made regions such as New England sunnier, windier, and colder than they had been before colonization. And many Indians, far from being passive observers in this frenzy of environmental change, contributed to the process by trading furs for metal or glass trinkets. This ravaged the populations of large mammals that had earlier been central to Indian culture—and to the ecological balance. By 1800 the physical environment of the eastern seaboard had changed markedly from what it had been in 1600.

POPULATION GROWTH   England's first footholds in America were bought at a fearful price. Many settlers died in the first years. But once the brutal seasoning time was past and the colony was on its feet, Virginia and all its successors grew rapidly. After the last major Indian uprising in 1644, Virginia's population quadrupled from about 8,000 to 32,000 over the next thirty years, then more than doubled, to 75,000, by 1704. Throughout the mainland colonies the yearly growth rate during the eighteenth century ran about 3 percent. In 1625 the English colonists numbered little more than 2,000 in Virginia and Plymouth together; by 1700 the population in the colonies was perhaps 250,000, and during the eighteenth century it doubled at least every twenty-five years. By 1750 the number of colonists had passed 1 million; by 1775 it stood at about 2.5 million. In 1700 the English at home outnumbered the colonists by about 20 to 1; by 1775, on the eve of the American Revolution, the ratio had fallen to 3 to 1.

The prodigious increase of colonial population did not go unnoticed. Benjamin Franklin of Pennsylvania, a keen observer of many things, published in 1751 his *Observations Concerning the Increase of Mankind* in which he pointed out two facts of life that distinguished the colonies from Europe: land was plentiful and cheap; labor was scarce and dear. Just the opposite conditions prevailed in the Old World. From this reversal of conditions flowed many if not most of the changes that European culture underwent in the New World—not the least being that good fortune beckoned the enterprising immigrant and induced the settlers to replenish the earth with large families. Where labor was scarce, children could lend a hand, and once they were grown could find new land for themselves if need be. Colonists tended, as a result, to marry and start new families at an earlier age.

BIRTHRATES AND DEATH RATES   Given the better economic prospects in the colonies, a greater proportion of American women married and the birthrate remained much higher than in Europe. Where in England the average age at marriage for women was twenty-five or twenty-six, in America it dropped to twenty or twenty-one. Men also married younger in the colonies than in the Old World. The birthrate

Mr. John Freake, and Mrs. Elizabeth Freake and Baby Mary. Elizabeth married John at age nineteen; Mary, born when Elizabeth was thirty-two, was the Freakes' eighth and last child.

rose accordingly, since those who married earlier had time for about two additional pregnancies during the childbearing years.

Equally responsible for the burgeoning population in the colonies was a much lower death rate in the New World. After the difficult first years of settlement, infants generally had a better chance to reach maturity, and adults had a better chance to reach old age. In seventeenth-century New England, apart from childhood mortality, men could expect to reach seventy and women nearly that age.

This longevity resulted from several factors. Since the land was more bountiful, famine seldom occurred after the first year, and while the winters were more severe than in England, firewood was plentiful. Being younger on the whole—the average age in the new nation in 1790 was sixteen!—Americans were less susceptible to disease than were Europeans. That they were more scattered than in the Old World meant they were also less exposed to disease. This began to change, of course, as population centers grew and trade and travel increased. By the mid–eighteenth century, the colonies were beginning to have levels of contagion much like those in Europe.

The greatest variations on these patterns occurred in the earliest testing times of the southern colonies. During the first century after the Jamestown settlement, until about 1700, a high rate of mortality and a chronic shortage of women meant that the population increase there could be sustained only by immigration. In the southern climate, English settlers contracted malaria, dysentery, and a host of other diseases. The mosquito-infested rice paddies of the Carolina Tidewater were notoriously unhealthy. And ships that docked at the Chesapeake tobacco plantations brought in with their payloads unseen cargoes of smallpox, diphtheria, and other infections. Given the higher mortality rate, families were often broken by the early death of parents. One consequence was to throw children on their own at an earlier age. Another was probably to make the extended family support network, if not the extended household, more important in the South.

SEX RATIOS AND THE FAMILY   Whole communities of religious or ethnic groups migrated more often to the northern colonies than to the southern, bringing more women in their company. There was no mention of any women at all among the first arrivals at Jamestown. Males were most needed in the early years of new colonies. In fact, as a pamphlet promoting opportunities in America stressed, the infant colonies needed "lusty labouring men . . . capable of hard labour, and that can bear and undergo heat and cold," men adept with the "axe and the hoe." Virginia's seventeenth-century sex ratio of two or three white males to each female meant that many men never married, although nearly every adult woman did. Counting only the unmarried, the ratio went to about eight men for every woman. In South Carolina around 1680 the sex ratio stood at about three to one, but since about three-quarters of the women were married, it was something like seven to one for singles.

A population made up largely of bachelors without strong ties to family and to the larger community made for instability of a high order in the first years. And the high mortality rates of the early years further loosened family ties. A majority of the women who arrived in the Chesapeake colonies during the seventeenth century were unmarried indentured servants, most of whom died before the age of fifty. While the first generations in New England proved to be long-lived, and many more children there knew their grandparents than in the motherland, young people in the seventeenth-century South were apt never to see their grandparents, and in fact to lose one or both of their parents before reaching maturity. But after a time of seasoning, immunities built up. Eventually the southern colonies reverted to a more even sex ratio, and family sizes approached those of New England.

Survival was the first necessity, and for the 90 to 95 percent of colonists who farmed, a subsistence or semi-subsistence economy remained the foundation of being. Not only food, but shelter, implements, utensils, furnishings, and clothing had to be made at home from the materials at hand. Indians taught the newcomers many new techniques for hunting, fishing, and foraging, as well as ways to plant corn and tobacco, tan hides, make canoes, and create dyes from trees and other plants. As the primary social and economic unit, the family became a "little commonwealth" which took on functions performed by the community in other times and places. Production, religion, learning, health care, and other activities centered on the home. Fathers taught sons how to farm, hunt, and fish. Mothers taught daughters how to tend to the chickens, the gardens, and the countless household chores that fell to the women of that time.

WOMEN IN THE COLONIES Most colonists brought to America deeply rooted convictions concerning the inferiority of women. As one preacher stressed, "the woman is a weak creature not endowed with like strength and constancy of mind." Their prescribed role in life was clear: to obey and serve their husbands, nurture their children, and endure the taxing labor required to maintain their households. John Winthrop insisted that a "true wife" would find contentment only "in subjection to her husband's authority." His sister, Lucy Winthrop Downing, accepted such a subordinate position. In a letter to her brother, she confessed: "I am but a wife and therefore it is sufficient for me to follow my husband."

Even high-spirited women such as Virginia's Lucy Parke Byrd submitted to their husbands' absolute authority. The imperious patrician William Byrd II managed his wife's estate without consulting her, kept a tenacious grip on his property—even to the point of forbidding his wife to borrow a book from his library without explicit permission—and saw fit to interfere in her own field of domestic management. In his secret diary he recorded their stormy relationship:

> [April 7] I reproached my wife with ordering the old beef to be kept and the fresh beef to be used first, contrary to good management, on which

she was pleased to be very angry . . . then my wife came and begged my pardon and we were friends again. . . .

[April 8] My wife and I had another foolish quarrel about my saying she listened at the top of the stairs . . . she came soon after and begged my pardon.

[April 9] My wife and I had another scold about mending my shoes, but it was soon over by her submission.

Both social custom and legal codes ensured that most women, like Lucy Byrd, remained deferential. In most colonies they could not vote, preach, hold office, attend public schools or colleges, bring lawsuits, make contracts, or own property.

WOMEN'S WORK   In the eighteenth century, "women's work" typically involved activities in the house, garden, and yard. Farm women usually rose at four in the morning and prepared breakfast by five-thirty. They then fed and watered the livestock, awakened the children, churned butter, tended the garden, prepared lunch, played with the children, worked the garden again, cooked dinner, milked the cows, got the children ready

Prudence Punderson's needlework, "The First, Second, and Last Scene of Mortality" (c. 1776), shows the domestic path, from cradle to coffin, followed by most colonial women.

for bed, and cleaned the kitchen before retiring about nine. Women also combed, spun, spooled, wove, and bleached wool for clothing, knitted linen and cotton, hemmed sheets, pieced quilts, made candles and soap, chopped wood, hauled water, mopped floors, and washed clothes. Female indentured servants in the southern colonies commonly worked as field hands, weeding, hoeing, and harvesting.

Despite the conventions that limited women, the scarcity of labor opened opportunities. Quite a few women went into gainful occupations by necessity or choice. In her role as a paid midwife, for example, Martha Ballard, a farm woman in Maine, delivered almost 800 babies. In the towns women commonly served as tavern hostesses and shopkeepers, but occasionally women also worked as doctors, printers, upholsterers, glaziers, painters, silversmiths, tanners, and shipwrights—often, but not always, widows carrying on their husbands' trades. Some managed plantations, again usually carrying on in the absence of husbands.

The New World environment did generate slight improvements in the status of women. The acute shortage of women in the early years made them more highly valued than in Europe, and the Puritan emphasis on well-ordered family life led to laws protecting wives from physical abuse and allowing for divorces. In addition, colonial laws allowed wives greater control over property that they had contributed to a marriage or that was left after a husband's death. But the central notion of female subordination and domesticity remained firmly entrenched in the New World. As a Massachusetts boy maintained in 1662, the superior aspect of life was "masculine and eternal; the feminine inferior and mortal."

SOCIETY AND ECONOMY IN THE SOUTHERN COLONIES

CROPS   The southern colonies had one unique advantage—the climate. They could grow exotic staples (market crops) prized by the mother country. Virginia, as Charles I put it, was "founded upon smoke." By 1619 tobacco production had reached 20,000 pounds, and in the year of the Glorious Revolution, 1688, it was up to 18 million pounds. "In Virginia and Maryland," wrote Governor Leonard Calvert in 1729, "Tobacco as our Staple is our All, and indeed leaves no room for anything else."

After 1690 rice was as much the staple (cash crop) in South Carolina as tobacco in Virginia. The rise and fall of tidewater rivers made the region ideally suited to a crop that required alternate flooding and draining of the fields. Annual rice exports soared from 400,000 pounds in 1700 to 43 million pounds in 1740.

In the 1740s, another exotic staple appeared—indigo, the blue dyestuff that found an eager market in the British clothing industry. An enterprising young woman named Eliza Lucas produced the first crop on her father's Carolina plantation, left in her care when she was only seventeen. She thereby founded a major industry, and as the wife of Charles Pinckney, later brought forth a major family dynasty that flourished in the golden age of Charleston.

Southern pine trees provided harvests of lumber and naval stores. The resin from pine trees could be boiled to make tar, which was in great demand as a way to waterproof ropes and caulk wooden ships. From their early leadership in the production of pine tar, North Carolinians would later earn the nickname of Tar Heels. In the interior, a fur trade flourished, and in the Carolinas, there was a cattle industry that presaged life later on the Great Plains—with cowboys, roundups, brandings, and long drives to market.

English customs records showed that for the years 1698–1717 South Carolina and the Chesapeake colonies enjoyed a favorable balance of trade with England. But the surplus revenues earned on American goods sold to England were more than offset by "invisible" charges: freight payments to shippers, commissions, storage charges, and interest payments to English merchants, insurance premiums, inspection and customs duties, and outlays to purchase indentured servants and slaves. Thus began a pattern that would plague the southern staple-crop system into the twentieth century. Planter investments went into land and slaves while the profitable enterprises of shipping, trade, investment, and manufacture fell under the sway of outsiders.

LAND   Land was plentiful and cheap throughout the colonial period, although many a frontier squatter ignored the formalities of getting a deed. In colonial law, land titles rested ultimately upon grants from the crown, and in colonial practice, the evolution of land policy in the first colony set patterns that were followed everywhere save in New England. In 1618 the Virginia Company, lacking any assets other than land, sold each investor a fifty-acre "share-right" and gave each settler a "headright" for paying his own way or for bringing in others. When Virginia became a royal colony in 1624, the headright system continued to apply, administered by the governor and his council. Lord Baltimore adopted the same practice in Maryland, and successive proprietors in the other southern and middle colonies adopted variations on the plan.

As time passed, certain tracts were put up for sale and throughout the colonies special grants (often sizable) went to persons of rank or persons who had performed some meritorious service, such as fighting Indians. With the right connections, settlers might amass handsome estates and vast speculative tracts in the interior, looking toward future growth and rising land values. But by the early 1700s, acquisition of land was commonly by purchase under more or less regular conditions of survey and sale by the provincial government.

If one distinctive feature of the South's agrarian economy was a good market in England, another was a trend toward large-scale production. Those who planted tobacco soon discovered that it quickly exhausted the soil, thereby giving an advantage to the planter who had extra fields to rotate in beans and corn or to leave fallow. With the increase of the tobacco crop, moreover, a fall in prices meant that economies of scale

An idyllic view of a Tidewater plantation. Note the easy access to oceangoing vessels.

might come into play—the large planter with lower cost per unit might still make a profit. Gradually he would extend his holdings along the riverfronts, and thereby secure the advantage of direct access to the oceangoing vessels that plied the waterways of the Chesapeake, discharging goods from London and taking on hogsheads of tobacco. So easy was the access, in fact, that the Chesapeake colonies never required a city of any size as a center of commerce, and the larger planters functioned as merchants and harbormasters for their neighbors.

LABOR   Voluntary indentured servitude accounted for probably half the white settlers (mostly from England, Ireland, or Germany) in all the colonies outside New England. The name derived from the indenture, or contract, by which a penniless person promised to work for a fixed number of years in return for transportation to the New World. Poverty and disease in British cities prompted many rootless vagabonds and petty criminals to board ship for America. Not all the servants went voluntarily. The London underworld developed a flourishing trade in "kids" and

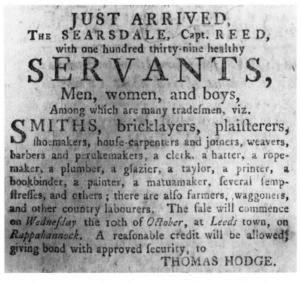

An advertisement from the Virginia Gazette, *October 4, 1779, for indentured servants. These people secured a life in America, but for a steep price. Servants endured years of labor before a contract ended and allowed them their freedom.*

"spirits," who were "kidnapped" or "spirited" into servitude. After 1717, by act of Parliament, convicts guilty of certain crimes could escape the hangman by "transportation" to the colonies.

Once in the colonies, servants contracted with masters. Their rights were limited. They could own property but not engage in trade. Marriage required the master's permission. Runaway servants were hunted down and punished like runaway slaves. Masters could whip servants and extend their indentures for bad behavior. Many servants died from disease or the exhaustion of cultivating tobacco in the broiling sun and thick humidity. In due course, however, usually after four to seven years, the indenture ended and the servant claimed the "freedom dues" set by custom and law—money, tools, clothing, food, and occasionally small tracts of land. Some former servants did very well for themselves. In 1629 seven members of the Virginia legislature were former indentured servants. Others, including Benjamin Franklin's maternal grandmother, married the men who bought their services. Many servants died before completing their indenture, however, and recent evidence suggests that most of those who served their term remained relatively poor thereafter.

SLAVERY   Colonial America was a land of white opportunity and black slavery. Most of the emigrants to America were not British or European, and they did not come willingly. During the eighteenth century, the British colonies imported more than three times as many slaves as free immigrants. Slavery evolved in the Chesapeake after 1619, when a Dutch vessel dropped off twenty Africans in Jamestown. Some of the first Africans were treated as indentured servants, with a limited term. Court records indicate that black and white servants occasionally escaped together. Those few African servants who worked out their term of indenture gained freedom and a fifty-acre parcel of land. They themselves sometimes acquired slaves and white indentured servants. Gradually, however, with rationalizations based on color difference or "heathenism," the practice of hereditary life service for blacks became the custom of the land. By the 1660s, colonial assemblies recognized slavery through laws that later expanded into elaborate and restrictive slave codes.

The sugar islands of the French and British Antilles and the cane fields of Portuguese Brazil had the most voracious appetite for African slaves, using them up in the tropical heat on the average within seven

Rofewell, Aug. 7, 1793.

RAN-AWAY from the fubcri-
ber in *Amelia* county, about the
eighteenth day of *May* laſt, a Negro
Man Slave, named ANTHONY,
about 6 feet and an inch high, formerly the property of Mr. *Nelſon Berke-*
ley, of *Hanover,* and purchaſed by the fubfcriber of Mr.
Michael Hartfield, of *New-Kent* county, where he has
lately been feen. I will give THREE GUINEAS reward to
any perfon who will apprehend the faid flave and deliver
him to me, or Two Guineas to any perfon who ſhall fe-
cure him in any Jail, fo that I get him again.
CHARLES HUDSON.
Amelia, June 21, 1793. (6w)

A notice for a runaway slave in the Virginia Gazette and General Advertiser. *Most of these ads included woodcut illustra-*
tions; here, a runaway is shown being chased by a devil
wielding a pitchfork.

years. By 1675 the English West Indies had over 100,000 slaves, while
the colonies in North America had only about 5,000. But as staple
crops became established on the American continent, and as economic
growth in England slowed the number of white laborers traveling to
America, the demand for slaves grew. As readily available lands diminished, Virginians were less eager to bring in indentured servants who
would lay claim to them at the end of their service. Though British
North America took less than 5 percent of the total slave imports to the
Western Hemisphere during the more than three centuries of that
squalid traffic, it offered better chances for survival if few for human
fulfillment. The natural increase of blacks in America approximated
that of whites by the end of the colonial period. By that time, every fifth
American was either an African or a descendant of one. Slavery was recognized in the laws of all the colonies, but flourished in the Tidewater
South—one colony, South Carolina, had a black majority through most
of the eighteenth century.

AFRICAN ROOTS   Slaves are so often lumped together as a social
group that their great ethnic diversity is overlooked. They came from
lands as remote from each other as Angola and Senegal, on the west

PERCENTAGE OF AFRICAN AMERICANS IN THE TOTAL POPULATION OF THE BRITISH COLONIES, 1660–1780

Year	New England	Middle Colonies	Upper South	Lower South	West Indies
1660	1.7	11.5	3.6	2.0	42.0
1700	1.8	6.8	13.1	17.6	77.7
1740	2.9	7.5	28.3	46.5	88.0
1780	2.0	5.9	38.6	41.2	91.1

Source: U.S. Bureau of the Census, *Historical Statistics of the United States, Colonial Times to 1970* (Washington, D.C.: U.S. Government Printing Office, 1975), 2:1168 (Ser.Z1-19).

coast of Africa, and they spoke Mandingo, Ibo, Kongo, and other languages. Still, the many peoples of Africa did share similar kinship and political systems. Not unlike Native American cultures, African societies were often matrilineal: property and political status descended through the mother rather than the father. When a couple married, the wife did not leave her family; the husband left his family to join that of his bride.

West African tribes were organized hierarchically. Priests and the nobility lorded over the masses of farmers and craftspeople. Below the masses were the slaves, typically war captives, criminals, or debtors. Slaves in Africa, however, did have certain rights. They could marry, be educated, and have children. Their servitude was not permanent, nor were children automatically slaves by virtue of their parentage, as would be the case in North America.

The West African economy centered on hunting, fishing, planting, and animal husbandry. Men and women typically worked alongside one another in the fields. Religious belief served as the spine of West African life. All tribal groups believed in a supreme Creator and an array of lesser gods tied to specific natural forces such as rain, fertility, and animal life. West Africans were pantheistic in that they believed that spirits resided in trees, rocks, and streams. People who died were also subjects of reverence because they served as mediators between the living and the gods.

Africans preyed upon Africans. For centuries, rival tribes had conquered and enslaved one another, and during the seventeenth and eighteenth centuries, African middlemen brought captives to the coast to sell to European slave traders. Once selected and purchased, the slaves were branded with a company mark and packed tightly in slave ships,

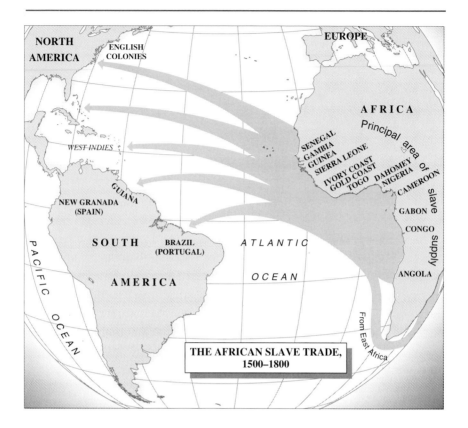

where they endured a four- to six-week Atlantic passage so brutal that one in seven captives died en route. Once in America, they were thrown indiscriminately together and treated like animals. Some slaves rebelled against their new masters, resisting work orders, sabotaging crops and tools, or running away to the frontier. In a few cases they organized rebellions that were ruthlessly suppressed. "You would be surprised at their perseverance," noted one white planter. "They often die before they can be conquered." Captured slaves faced ghastly retribution; many were burned at the stake. After rounding up slaves who participated in the Stono uprising in South Carolina in 1739, enraged planters "Cutt off their heads and set them up at every Mile Post."

SLAVE CULTURE   Slavery in British North America differed greatly from region to region. Africans were a small minority in New England (about 2 percent) and the middle colonies (about 8 percent). Most northern slaves lived in cities. In the South, slaves were far more numerous, and most of them worked on farms and plantations. In 1750 the vast majority of slaves in British America resided in Virginia and Maryland, about 150,000 compared to 60,000 in South Carolina and Georgia and only 33,000 in all of the northern colonies.

With the odds so heavily stacked against resistance, most slaves resigned themselves to their condition. Yet in the process of being forced into lives of bondage, diverse blacks from diverse homelands forged a new identity as African Americans, while at the same time leaving entwined in the fabric of American culture more strands of African heritage than historians and anthropologists can ever disentangle. Among them were new words that entered the language, such as *tabby, tote, cooter, goober, yam,* and *banana,* and the names of the Coosaw, Peedee, and Wando Rivers.

More important were African influences in music, folklore, and religious practices. On one level, slaves used such cultural activities to distract themselves from their servitude; on another level, they used songs, stories, and sermons as coded messages expressing their distaste for masters or overseers. Slave religion, a unique blend of African and Christian beliefs, was frequently practiced in secret. Its fundamental theme was deliverance: God would eventually free them from slavery and open up the gates to Heaven's promised land.

The planters, however, sought to strip slave religion of its liberationist hopes. They insisted that being "born again" had no effect upon their workers' status as slaves. In 1667 the Virginia legislature declared that "the conferring of baptism does not alter the condition of the person as to his bondage or freedom."

Africans brought to America powerful kinship ties. Even though most colonies outlawed slave marriages, many masters realized that slaves would work harder and be more stable if allowed to form families. Though many families were broken up when members were sold, slave culture retained its powerful domestic ties. It also developed gender roles distinct from those of white society. Most slave women were by necessity field workers as well as wives and mothers responsible for household affairs. Since they worked in close proximity to black men, they were treated more equally than most of their white counterparts.

Most of the slaves were fated to become fieldhands, but not all did. Many of those from the lowlands of Africa used their talents as boatmen in the coastal waterways. Some had linguistic skills that made them useful interpreters. Others tended cattle and swine, or hacked

The survival of African culture among American slaves is evident in this late-eighteenth-century painting of a South Carolina plantation. The musical instruments, pottery, and clothing are of African origin, probably Yoruba.

away at the forests and operated sawmills. In a society forced to construct itself, slaves became skilled artisans: blacksmiths, carpenters, coopers, bricklayers, and the like. Some worked as cooks or maids.

Slavery and the growth of a biracial South had economic, political, and cultural effects far into the future, and set America on the way to tragic conflicts. Questions about the beginnings of slavery still have a bearing on the present. Did a deep-rooted color prejudice lead to slavery, for instance, or did the existence of slavery produce the prejudice? Clearly, slavery evolved because of a demand for labor, and the English adopted a trade established by the Portuguese and Spanish more than a century before—the very word "Negro" is Spanish for "black." English settlers often enslaved Indian captives, but they did not bring their European captives into slavery. Color was the crucial difference, or at least the crucial rationalization.

The English associated the color black with darkness and evil; they stamped the different appearance, behavior, and customs of Africans as "savagery." At the very least, such perceptions could soothe the consciences of people who traded in human flesh. On the other hand, most of the qualities that colonial Virginians imputed to blacks to justify slavery were the same qualities that the English assigned to their own poor to explain *their* status: their alleged bent for laziness, improvidence, treachery, and stupidity, among other shortcomings. Similar traits, moreover, were imputed by ancient Jews to the Canaanites and by the Mediterranean peoples of a later date to the Slavic captives sold among them. The names Canaanite and Slav both became synonymous with slavery—the latter lingers in our very word for it. Such expressions would seem to be the product of power relationships and not the other way around. Dominant peoples repeatedly assign ugly traits to those they bring into subjection.

THE GENTRY By the early eighteenth century, Virginia and South Carolina were moving into the golden age of the Tidewater gentry, leaving the more isolated and rustic colony of North Carolina as "a valley of humiliation between two mountains of conceit." The first rude huts of Jamestown had given way to frame and brick houses, but it was only as the seventeenth century yielded to the eighteenth that the stately countryseats in the Georgian, or "colonial," style began to emerge along the banks of the great rivers. In South Carolina the mansions along the Ashley, Cooper, and Wando Rivers boasted spacious gardens and avenues of moss-draped live oaks.

The great houses of the new colonial aristocracy became centers of sumptuous living and legendary hospitality. In their zest for the good

This painting circa 1710 portrays Henry Darnall III, a youth from one of the richest Maryland families, flanked by a black slave. In the background are buildings and gardens that attest to the southern preoccupation with the trappings of English nobility.

life, the planters purchased the latest refinements of London style and fashion, living precariously on credit extended for the next year's crop and the years' crops beyond that. Dependence on outside capital remained a chronic southern problem far beyond the colonial period.

In season the carriages of the Chesapeake elite rolled to the villages of Annapolis and Williamsburg, and the city of Charleston became the center of political life and high fashion. Throughout much of the year, the outdoors beckoned planters to the pleasures of hunting, fishing, and riding. Gambling on horse races, cards, and dice became consuming passions for men and women alike. But a few cultivated high culture. William Byrd II of Westover pursued learning with a passion. He built a library of some 3,600 volumes and often rose early to keep up his Latin, Greek, and Hebrew. The wealthy families commonly sent their sons—and often their daughters— abroad for an education, usually to England, sometimes to France.

RELIGION   After 1642 Virginia Governor William Berkeley decided that the colony was to be Anglican, and he passed laws requiring "all nonconformists . . . to depart the colony with all conveniency." Puritans and

The pulpit of St. James Church, built in the early 1700s in the oldest Anglican parish in South Carolina.

Quakers were hounded out of the colony. By the end of the seventeenth century, Anglicanism predominated in the region, and it proved especially popular among the large landholders. In the early eighteenth century, it became the established (official) church in all the South—and some counties of New York and New Jersey, despite the presence of many dissenters. In the new American environment, however, the Anglican church evolved into something quite unlike the state church of England. The scattered population and the absence of bishops made centralized control difficult.

It has often been said that Americans during the seventeenth century took religion more seriously than at any time since. That may have been true, but it is important to remember how many early Americans were not active communicants. One estimate holds that fewer than one in fifteen residents of the southern colonies were church members. There the tone of religious belief and practice was different from that in Puritan New England or Quaker Pennsylvania. As in England, colonial Anglicans tended to be more conservative, rational, and formal in their forms of worship than their Puritan, Quaker, or Baptist counterparts. Anglicans tended to stress collective rituals over personal religious experience.

SOCIETY AND ECONOMY IN NEW ENGLAND

TOWNSHIPS   In contrast to the seaboard planters who transformed the English manor into the southern plantation, the Puritans transformed the English village into the New England town, although there were several varieties. Land policy in New England had a stronger social and religious purpose than elsewhere. Towns shaped by English precedent and Puritan policy also fitted the environment of a rockbound land, confined by sea and mountains and unfit for large-scale agriculture.

Unlike the pattern of settlement in the southern colonies or in Dutch New York, few New England colonists received huge tracts of land. The standard system was one of township grants to organized groups. A group of settlers, often gathered already into a church, would petition the General Court for a town (what elsewhere was commonly called a "township") and then divide it according to a rough principle of equity—those who invested more, or had larger families or greater status, might receive more land—retaining some pasture and woodland in common and holding some for later arrivals. In some early cases the towns arranged each settler's land in separate strips after the medieval practice, but with time land was commonly divided into separate farms to which landholders would move, away from the close-knit village. Still later, by the early eighteenth century, the colonies used their remaining land as a source of revenue by selling townships to proprietors whose purpose, more often than not, was speculation and resale.

DWELLINGS AND DAILY LIFE   The first colonists in New England arrived to find what one called a "hideous and desolate wilderness, full of wild beasts & wild men." Forced first to live in caves, tents or "English wigwams," they soon built simple, small frame houses clad with hand-split clapboards. The roofs were steeply pitched to reduce the buildup of snow and were covered with thatched grasses or reeds.

By the end of the seventeenth century, most New England homes were plain but sturdy dwellings centered on a fireplace. Some had glass windows brought from England. The interior walls were often plastered and whitewashed, but the exterior boards were rarely painted. It was not until the eighteenth century that most houses were painted, and they were usually a dark "Indian red." New England homes were not commonly painted white until the nineteenth century. The interiors were dark, illuminated only by candles or oil lamps, both of which were expensive; most people usually went to sleep soon after sunset.

Family life revolved around the main room on the ground floor, called the "hall." Here meals would be cooked in a large fireplace. Pots would be suspended on an iron rod over the fire, and food would be served at a table made of rough-hewn planks called "the board." The father was sometimes referred to as the "chair man" because he sat in the only chair (hence the origin of the term "chairman of the board"). The rest of

This frame house, commonly known as a "saltbox house," had two stories in the front, but only one story in back because of its steeply pitched roof. This design prevented the accumulation of snow during New England winters.

the family usually stood to eat or sat on stools or benches. People in colonial times ate with their hands and with wooden spoons. Forks were not introduced until the eighteenth century. The fare was usually corn, boiled meat, and vegetables washed down with beer, cider, rum, or milk. Corn bread was a daily staple, as was cornmeal mush, known as "hasty pudding." Colonists also relished "succotash," an Indian meal of corn and kidney beans cooked in bear grease.

ENTERPRISE   New England farmers faced strenuous challenges. Simply clearing rocks from the glacier-scoured soil might require sixty days of hard labor per acre. The growing season was short, and no profitable crops grew in that harsh climate. The crops and livestock were those familiar to the English countryside: wheat, barley, oats, some cattle, swine, and sheep.

With rich fishing grounds that stretched northward to Newfoundland, it is little wonder that New Englanders turned to the sea for their livelihood. The Chesapeake region afforded a rich harvest of oysters, but New England, by its proximity to waters frequented by cod, mackerel, halibut, and other varieties, became the more important maritime center. Whales, too, abounded in New England waters and supplied oil for lighting and lubrication, as well as ambergris, a waxy substance used in the manufacture of perfumes.

The fisheries, unlike the farms, supplied a staple of export to Europe, while lesser grades of fish went to the West Indies as food for slaves. Fisheries encouraged the development of shipbuilding, and experience at seafaring spurred commerce. This in turn encouraged wider contacts in the Atlantic world and a degree of materialism and cosmopolitanism that clashed with the Puritan credo of plain living and high thinking. In 1714 a worried Puritan deplored the "great extravagance that people are fallen into, far beyond their circumstances, in their purchases, buildings, families, expenses, apparel, generally in the whole way of living."

NEW ENGLAND SHIPBUILDING   The abundant forests of New England represented a source of enormous wealth. Old-growth trees were especially prized by the British government for maritime use as masts and spars. Early on the British government claimed the tallest and straightest American trees, mostly white pines and oaks, for use by the Royal Navy. At the same time, British officials encouraged the colonists to develop their own shipbuilding industry. The New England economy was utterly

Newfoundland fishery, 1705. For centuries, the rich fishing grounds in the eastern waters provided New Englanders with a prosperous industry.

dependent on fishing and maritime commerce, and this placed a premium on the availability of boats and ships—and shipbuilders. In 1641 the Massachusetts General Court declared that shipbuilding "is a business of great importance to the common good" and therefore care must be taken to ensure that boatbuilding was "well performed." American seaports aggressively sought to entice shipwrights to emigrate. In 1637, for example, the town of Salem recruited William Stevens, a skilled London shipwright, by granting him free land "for the building of Ships, provided that it shall be employed for that end." American-built ships quickly became prized by British and European traders for their quality and price. It was much less expensive to purchase American-built ships than to transport American timber to Britain for ship construction, especially since a large ship might require the timber from as many as two thousand trees.

Nearly a third of all British ships were made in the colonies. By the mid-seventeenth century, bustling shipyards had appeared at Boston, Salem, Dorchester, Gloucester, Portsmouth, and many other New England towns where rivers flowed into the ocean and thereby assisted the launching of new ships. By the eighteenth century, Massachusetts was second only to London in the volume of ships produced. Boston alone had fifteen shipyards, and most of the city's skilled workers relied on the shipbuilding trade.

Blessed with abundant timber and access to iron ore in addition to British capital and craftsmen who migrated in droves to New England, colonial shipyards produced large sailing ships destined for Britain, Europe, and Asia as well as hundreds of small sloops and schooners for local fishermen and merchants. Shipbuilding was one of colonial America's first big industries, and it in turn helped nurture many other industries: timber, sawmills, iron foundries, sail lofts, fisheries, and taverns. The availability of "all manner of materials for ship building very cheap" allowed New Englanders to keep freight charges low compared with other trading nations, thus winning the entire West Indian and North American trade with the exception of products only the English could produce.

Thomas Coram was a transplanted English shipwright from England who migrated to Boston because of "the vast planks of oak and fir timber . . . which [he] found abounding" in the area. More than five hundred ships were built at Coram's dockyards between 1697 and 1731. The shipyards were so busy in colonial New England that a person living in the area could not escape "the sound of the ship builder's hammer and the rush of launching vessels."

Constructing a large ship required as many as thirty different skilled trades and two hundred workers. The vessel's hull was laid out by master shipwrights, talented maritime carpenters who used axes and adzes to cut and fit together the pieces to form the keel, or spine of the hull. They then fashioned U-shaped ribs for the hull before enclosing the frame with planking and decking boards that had been prepared by sawyers. Carpenters carefully secured the boards with treenails (pronounced "trunnels"), strong wooden pegs pounded into bored holes. Caulkers made the ship watertight by stuffing the seams with oakum, a loose hemp fiber that was sealed with hot tar.

As the new ship took shape, ropemakers created the ship's extensive rigging. Rope was made by hand. Workers walked backwards away from a spinning wheel twisting handfuls of hemp into a long coil. The workers were called ropewalkers, and the wooden shed where they worked, often a thousand feet long, was called a ropewalk. After the coils of rope were spun, they were dipped in heated tar to preserve them against saltwater rot. Sailmakers, meanwhile, fashioned the sails out of canvas, laying them out in large lofts.

Other craftsmen produced the dozens of other items needed for a sailing vessel: blacksmiths forged iron anchors, chains, hinges, bolts, rudder braces, and circular straps that secured sections of masts together. Blockmakers created the dozens of metalstrapped wooden pulleys need for hoisting sails. Joiners built hatches, ladders, lockers, and furnishings. Painters finished trim and interiors. Ship chandlers provided lamps, oil, and candles. Instrument makers fashioned compasses, chronometers, and sextants to guide the ship.

Such skilled workers were trained in the apprentice-journeyman system then common in England. A master craftsman taught an apprentice the skills of his trade in exchange for wages. After the apprenticeship period, lasting from four to seven years, a young worker would receive a new suit of clothes from the master craftsman and then become a journeyman, literally moving from shop to shop working for wages to hone his skills. Over time, journeymen joined local guilds and became master craftsmen who themselves took on apprentices. In the colonies, the acute demand for skilled laborers and the absence of guilds to regulate work standards and wages by limiting competition resulted in a more flexible labor system. With wages high and land cheap or free, journeymen could often start their own shipyards with a small amount of capital. The workday in a colonial shipyard lasted from dawn to dusk. Laborers were given breaks at 11 A.M. and 4 P.M. for "grog," a heated mixture of rum and water.

It took four to six months to build a major sailing ship. The ship christenings and launchings were festive occasions that attracted large crowds and dignitaries. Shops and schools would often close to enable people to attend. All of the workers joined the celebration. Rhode Island shipbuilders allocated fifty dollars to the master builder of each yard "to be expended in providing an entertainment for the carpenters that worked on the ships." The ceremony would begin with a clergyman blessing the new vessel. Then the ship's owner or a senior member of the crew would "christen" the ship before ropes were cut and blocks removed to allow the hull to slide into the water.

TRADE   By the end of the seventeenth century, the colonies had become part of a great North Atlantic connection, trading not only with the British Isles and the British West Indies, but also—and often illegally—with Spain, France, Portugal, Holland, and their colonies from America to the shores of Africa. Out of necessity the colonists had to import manufactured goods from Britain and Europe: hardware, machinery, paint, instruments of navigation, and various household items. The colonies thus served as an important market for English goods from the mother country. The central problem for the colonies was to find the means of paying for the imports—the eternal problem of the balance of trade.

The mechanism of trade in New England and the middle colonies differed from that of the South in two respects: their lack of staples to exchange for English goods was a relative disadvantage, but the abundance of their own shipping and mercantile enterprise worked in their favor. After 1660, in order to protect English agriculture and fisheries, the English government raised prohibitive duties against certain major colonial exports: fish, flour, wheat, and meat, while leaving the door open to timber, furs, and whale oil, products in great demand in the home country. New York and New England in the years 1698–1717 bought more from England than they sold there, incurring an unfavorable trade balance.

The northern colonies met the problem partly by using their own ships and merchants, thus avoiding the "invisible" charges for trade and transport, and by finding other markets for the staples excluded from England, thus acquiring goods or bullion to pay for imports from the mother country. American lumber and fish therefore went to southern Europe, Madeira, and the Azores for money or in exchange for wine; lumber, rum, and provisions went to Newfoundland; and all of these and more went to the West Indies, which became the most important outlet of all. American merchants could sell fish, bread, flour, corn, pork, bacon, beef, and horses to West Indian planters who specialized in sugarcane. In return they got money, sugar, molasses, rum, indigo, dyewoods, and other products, much of which went eventually to England.

This gave rise to the famous "triangular trade" (more a descriptive convenience than a rigid pattern) in which New Englanders shipped rum to the west coast of Africa and bartered for slaves, took the slaves on the "Middle Passage" to the West Indies, and returned home with various commodities including molasses, from which they manufactured rum. In another version they shipped provisions to the West Indies, carried sugar and molasses to England, and returned with manufactured goods from Europe.

The colonies suffered from a chronic shortage of hard money, which drifted away to pay for imports and shipping charges. Various expedients met the shortage of currency: the use of wampum or commodities, the

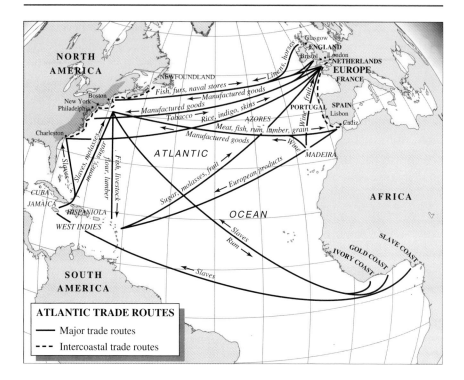

ATLANTIC TRADE ROUTES
— Major trade routes
--- Intercoastal trade routes

monetary value of which colonial governments tried vainly to set by law. Promissory notes of individuals or colonial treasurers often passed as a crude sort of paper money. Most of the colonies at one time or another issued bills of credit, on promise of payment later (hence the dollar "bill"), and most set up land banks that issued paper money for loans to farmers on the security of their lands, which were mortgaged to the banks. Colonial farmers began to recognize that an inflation of paper money led to an inflation of crop prices, and therefore asked for more and more paper money. Thus began in colonial politics what was to become a recurrent issue in later times, the question of currency inflation. Whenever the issue arose, debtors commonly favored growth in the money supply, which would make it easier for them to settle accounts, whereas creditors favored a limited money supply, which would increase the value of their capital. In 1751 Parliament outlawed legal-tender paper money in New England, and in 1764 throughout the colonies.

RELIGION The Puritans had come to America to create pious and prosperous communities, not to tolerate sinfulness in their New Zion.

Yet the picture of the dour Puritan, hostile to anything that gave pleasure, is false. Puritans, especially those of the upper class, wore colorful
clothing, enjoyed secular music, and imbibed prodigious quantities of
rum. "Drink is in itself a good creature of God," said the Reverend Increase Mather, "but the abuse of drink is from Satan." If found incapac-
itated by reason of strong drink, a person was subject to arrest. A Salem
man, for example, was tried for staggering into a house where he "eased
his stomak in the Chimney." Repeated offenders were forced to wear
the letter "D" in public.

Moderation in all things except piety was the Puritan guideline, and it
applied to sexual activity as well. Contrary to prevailing images of Puritan
prudery, they quite openly acknowledged natural human desires. One
minister stressed that intimacy between partners was a necessary component of a successful marriage. Any unwillingness to engage in sexual
intercourse on the part of husband or wife "Denies all reliefe in Wedlock
unto Human necessity: and sends it for supply unto Beastiality." Of
course, sexual activity outside the bounds of marriage was strictly forbidden, but like most social prohibitions it may have provoked transgres-
sion. New England court records are filled with cases of adultery and
fornication. A man found guilty of coitus with an unwed woman could
be jailed, whipped, fined, disenfranchised, and forced to marry the
woman. Women offenders were also jailed and whipped, and in some
cases adulterers were forced to wear the letter "A" in public. In part the
abundance of sex offenses is explained by the disproportionate number
of men in the colonies. Many were unable to find a wife and were therefore tempted to satisfy their sexual desires outside of marriage.

The Puritans who settled Massachusetts, unlike the Separatists of
Plymouth, proposed only to form a purified version of the Anglican
church. They believed that they could remain loyal to the Church of
England, the unity of church and state, and the principle of compulsory
uniformity. But their remoteness from England led them to adopt a congregational form of church government identical with that of the Pilgrim Separatists, and for that matter little different from the practice of
Anglicans in the southern colonies.

In the Puritan version of Calvin's theology, God had voluntarily entered into a covenant, or contract, with people through which they could
secure salvation. By analogy, therefore, an assembly of true Christians
could enter into a church covenant, a voluntary union for the common

worship of God. From this it was a fairly short step to the idea of a voluntary union for purposes of government. The history of New England affords examples of several such limited steps toward constitutional government: the Mayflower Compact, the Cambridge Agreement of John Winthrop and his followers, the Fundamental Orders of Connecticut, and the informal arrangements whereby the Rhode Island settlers governed themselves until they secured a charter in 1663.

The covenant theory contained certain kernels of democracy in both church and state, but democracy was no part of Puritan political thought, which like so much else in Puritan belief began with original sin. Humanity's innate depravity made government necessary. The Puritan was dedicated to seeking not the will of the people but the will of God, and the ultimate source of authority was the Bible. But the Bible had to be explained. Hence, most Puritans deferred to an intellectual elite for a true knowledge of God's will. By law, every town had to support a church through taxes levied on every household. And every community member was required to attend midweek and Sunday religious services. The average New Englander heard 7,000 sermons during a lifetime.

The church exercised a pervasive influence over the life of the New England town, but unlike the Church of England it technically had no political power. Thus while Puritan New England has often been called a theocracy, the church was entirely separated from the state—except that the residents were taxed for its support. And if not all inhabitants were church members, all were nonetheless required to attend church services.

New England Puritans were assailed by doubts, by a fear of falling away from godly living, by the haunting fear that despite their best outward efforts they might not be among God's elect. Add such concerns to the long winters that kept the family cooped up during the dark, cold months, and one has a formula for seething resentments and recriminations that, for the sake of peace in the family, had to be projected outward toward neighbors. The New Englanders of those peaceable kingdoms therefore built a reputation as the most litigious people on the face of God's earth, continually quarreling over property disputes, business dealings, and other issues, and building in the process a flourishing legal profession.

DIVERSITY AND SOCIAL STRAINS   Despite long-enduring myths, New England towns were not always pious, harmonious, and self-sufficient

School Street, Salem, around 1765. The mansion of a wealthy merchant dominates this street scene in Salem, a prosperous port town.

peasant utopias populated by praying Puritans. Many communities were founded not as religious farming utopias but as secular centers of fishing, trade, or commercial agriculture, and the animating concerns of residents in such towns tended to be more entrepreneurial than spiritual. After a Puritan minister delivered his first sermon to a congregation in the fishing port of Marblehead, a crusty fisherman admonished him: "You think you are preaching to the people of the Bay. Our main end was to catch fish." Similar priorities appeared in highly commercialized inland towns such as Springfield, Massachusetts. There, too, material opportunity rather than religious communalism governed individual behavior. Yet such acquisitive individualism, while generating marked social inequalities, was accompanied by growing social stability as an economic elite came to exercise paternalistic control over town affairs.

In many of the godly backwoods communities, social strains increased as time passed, a consequence primarily of population pressure on the land and rising disparities of wealth. "Love your neighbor," said Benjamin Franklin's Poor Richard, "but don't pull down your fence." Initially, among the first settlers, fathers exercised strong authority over sons through their control of the land. They kept the sons and their families in the town, not letting them set up their own households or get title to their farmland until they reached middle age. In New England, as elsewhere, fathers tended to subdivide their land among all the male children. But by the eighteenth century, with land scarcer, the younger sons were either getting control of property early or moving on. Often they were forced out, with family help and blessings, to seek land elsewhere or new kinds of work in the commercial cities along the coast or inland rivers. With the growing pressure on land in the settled regions, poverty and social tension increased in what had once seemed a country of unlimited opportunity.

The emphasis on a direct accountability to God, which lay at the base of all Protestant theology, itself caused a persistent tension and led believers to challenge authority in the name of private conscience. Massachusetts repressed such heresy in the 1630s, but it resurfaced during the 1650s among Quakers and Baptists, and in 1659–1660 the colony hanged four Quakers who persisted in returning after they were expelled. These acts caused such revulsion—and an investigation by the crown—that they were not repeated, although heretics continued to face harassment and persecution.

More damaging to the Puritan utopia was the growing worldliness of New England, which placed growing strains on church discipline. More and more children of the "visible saints" found themselves unable to give the required testimony of regeneration. In 1662 an assembly of ministers at Boston accepted the "Half-Way Covenant," whereby baptized children of church members could be admitted to a "halfway" membership and secure baptism for their own children in turn. Such members, however, could neither vote in church nor take communion. A further blow to Puritan control came with the Massachusetts royal charter of 1691, which required toleration of dissenters and based the right to vote in public elections on property rather than on church membership.

THE DEVIL IN NEW ENGLAND   The strains accompanying Massachusetts's transition from Puritan utopia to royal colony reached an unhappy climax in the witchcraft hysteria at Salem Village (now the town of Danvers) in 1692. Belief in witchcraft was widespread throughout Europe and New England in the seventeenth century. Prior to the dramatic episode in Salem, almost three hundred New Englanders (mostly middle-aged women) had been accused as witches, and more than thirty had been hanged. New England was, in the words of Cotton Mather, "a country . . . extraordinarily alarum'd by the wrath of the Devil."

Still, the outbreak in Salem was distinctive in its scope and intensity. Salem Village was about eight miles from the larger Salem Town, a thriving port. A contentious community made up of independent farm families and people who depended on the commercial activity of the port, Salem Village struggled to free itself from the influence and taxes of Salem proper. The tensions that arose apparently made the residents especially susceptible to the idea that the devil was at work in the village.

During the winter of 1691–1692, several adolescent girls began meeting in the kitchen of the town minister, the Reverend

Three "notorious witches" hanged in Chelmsford, England, 1589. In New England, a century later, more than thirty people were hanged during a period of "witchcraft hysteria."

Samuel Parris. There they gave rapt attention to the voodoo stories told by Tituba, Parris's West Indian slave. As the days passed, the entranced girls began to behave oddly—shouting, barking, groveling, and twitching for no apparent reason. A doctor concluded that the girls were bewitched. When asked who was tormenting them, the girls replied that three women— Tituba, Sarah Good, and Sarah Osborne—were Satan's servants.

Authorities thereupon arrested the three women. At a special hearing before the magistrates, the "afflicted" girls rolled on the floor in convulsive fits as the accused women were questioned. In the midst of the hearing, Tituba shocked listeners by not only confessing to the charge but also divulging the names of many others in the community who she claimed were also performing the devil's work. Soon thereafter, dozens more girls and young women began to experience the same violent contortions. The accusations spread throughout the community. Within a few months, the Salem Village jail was filled with townspeople— men, women, and children—accused of practicing witchcraft.

At the end of May the authorities arrested Martha Carrier. A farmer had testified that several of his cattle suffered "strange deaths" soon after he and Carrier had an argument. Little Phoebe Chandler added that she had been stricken with terrible stomach pains soon after she heard Carrier's voice telling her she was going to be poisoned. Even Carrier's own children testified against her: they reported that their mother had recruited them as witches. But the most damning testimony was provided by several young girls. When they were brought into the hearing room, they began writhing in agony at the sight of Carrier. They claimed that they could see the devil whispering in her ear. Carrier declared that it was "a shameful thing that you should mind these folks that are out of their wits. I am wronged." A few days later she was hanged. Rebecca Nurse, a pious seventy-one-year-old matriarch of a large family went to the gallows in July. George Jacobs, an old man whose servant girl accused him of witchcraft, dismissed the whole chorus of accusers as "bitch witches." He was hanged in August.

But as the net of accusation spread wider, extending far beyond the confines of Salem, leaders of the Massachusetts Bay colony began to worry that the witch-hunts were out of control. The governor intervened when his own wife was accused of serving the devil. He disbanded the special court in Salem and ordered the remaining suspects released. A year after it had begun, the fratricidal event was finally over. Nineteen people (including some men married to women who had been convicted) had been hanged; one man—the stubborn Giles Corey—was pressed to death by heavy stones, and more than one hundred others were jailed. Nearly everybody responsible for the Salem executions later recanted, and nothing quite like it happened in the colonies again.

What explains the witchcraft hysteria at Salem? Some have argued that it may have represented nothing more than a contagious exercise in adolescent imagination intended to enliven the dreary routine of everyday life. Yet it was adults who pressed the formal charges against the accused and provided most of the testimony. This has led some scholars to speculate that long-festering local feuds and property disputes may have triggered the prosecutions.

More recently, historians have focused on the most salient fact about the accused witches: almost all of them were women. Many of the supposed witches, it turns out, had in some way defied the traditional roles assigned to females. Some had engaged in business transactions outside the home; others did not attend church; some were curmudgeons. Most of them were middle-aged or older and without sons or brothers.

They thus stood to inherit property and live as independent women. The notion of autonomous spinsters flew in the face of prevailing social conventions.

Whatever the precise cause, there is little doubt that the witchcraft controversy reflected the peculiar social dynamics of the Salem community. Late in 1692, as the hysteria in Salem subsided, several of the afflicted girls were traveling through nearby Ipswich when they encountered an old woman resting on a bridge. "A witch!" they shouted and began writhing as if possessed. But the people of Ipswich were unimpressed. Passersby showed no interest in the theatrical girls. Unable to generate either sympathy or curiosity, the girls picked themselves up and continued on their way.

SOCIETY AND ECONOMY IN THE MIDDLE COLONIES

AN ECONOMIC MIX   Both geographically and culturally the middle colonies stood between New England and the South, blending their own influences with elements derived from the older regions on either side. In so doing they more completely reflected the diversity of colonial life and more fully foreshadowed the pluralism of the later American nation than the regions on either side. Their crops were those of New England but more bountiful, owing to better land and a longer growing season, and they developed surpluses of foodstuffs for export to the plantations of the South and the West Indies: wheat, barley, oats, and other cereals, flour, and livestock. Three great rivers—the Hudson, Delaware, and Susquehanna—and their tributaries gave the middle colonies ready access to the backcountry and to the fur trade of the interior, where New York and Pennsylvania long enjoyed friendly relations with the Iroquois, Delaware, and other tribes. As a consequence the region's commerce rivaled that of New England, and indeed Philadelphia in time supplanted Boston as the largest city of the colonies.

Land policies in the middle colonies followed the headright system of the South. In New York the early royal governors carried forward, in practice if not in name, the Dutch device of the patroonship, granting to influential favorites vast estates on Long Island and up the Hudson and Mohawk Valleys. These realms most nearly approached the medieval manor. They were self-contained domains farmed by tenants who paid fees to use the landlords' mills, warehouses, smokehouses, and wharfs. But with free land available elsewhere, New York's population languished, and the new waves of immigrants sought the promised land of Pennsylvania.

AN ETHNIC MIX In the makeup of their population the middle colonies stood apart from both the mostly English Puritan settlements and the biracial plantation colonies to the South. In New York and New Jersey, for instance, Dutch culture and language lingered, along with the Dutch Reformed church. Along the Delaware River the few Swedes and Finns, the first settlers, were overwhelmed by the influx of English and Welsh Quakers, followed in turn by the Germans and Scotch-Irish.

The Germans came mainly from the Rhineland, a region devastated by incessant war. (Until German unification in 1871, ethnic Germans—those Europeans speaking German as their native language—lived in a variety of areas and principalities in central Europe.) William Penn's brochures encouraging settlement in Pennsylvania circulated throughout central Europe in German translation, and his promise of religious freedom appealed to persecuted sects, especially the Mennonites, German Baptists whose beliefs resembled those of the Quakers.

In 1683 a group of Mennonites founded Germantown near Philadelphia. They were the vanguard of a swelling migration in the eighteenth century that included Lutherans, Reformed Calvinists, Moravians, Dunkers, and others, a large proportion of whom paid their way as indentured servants, or "redemptioners," as they were commonly called. West of Philadelphia they created a belt of settlement in which the "Pennsylvania Dutch" (a corruption of *Deutsch*, meaning German) predominated, as well as a channel for the dispersion of German populations throughout the colonies.

The more aggressive Scotch-Irish began to arrive later and moved still farther out in the backcountry throughout the eighteenth century. "Scotch-Irish" is an enduring misnomer for Ulster Scots, Presbyterians transplanted from Scotland to confiscated lands in northern Ireland to give that country a more Protestant tone. The Ulster Scots, mostly Presbyterians, fled both from Anglican persecution and from economic disaster

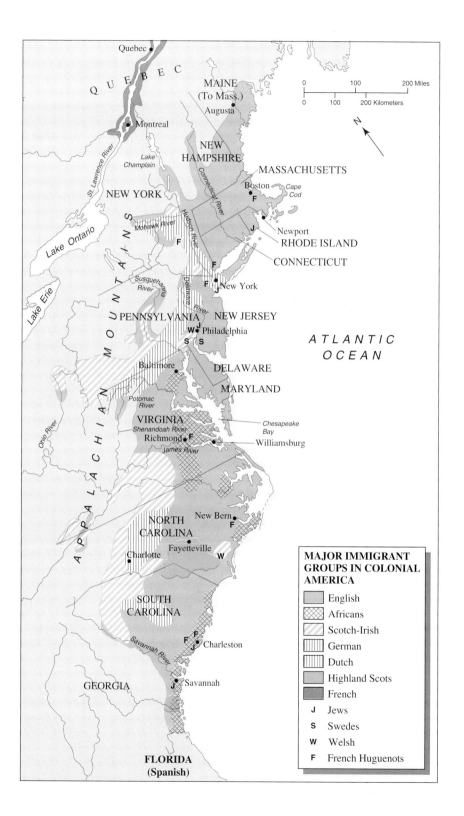

Quebec

QUEBEC

Montreal

St. Lawrence River

Lake Champlain

MAINE
(To Mass.)

Augusta

NEW
HAMPSHIRE

MASSACHUSETTS

NEW YORK

Boston

Cape Cod

F

Lake Ontario

Mohawk River

F

Connecticut River

Hudson River

J

Newport

RHODE ISLAND

CONNECTICUT

Lake Erie

Susquehanna
River

F

Delaware River

F

J

New York

APPALACHIAN MOUNTAINS

PENNSYLVANIA

NEW JERSEY

J

W

Philadelphia

S

S

ATLANTIC
OCEAN

Baltimore

DELAWARE

MARYLAND

Potomac
River

Ohio River

VIRGINIA

Shenandoah River

Richmond

F

James River

Chesapeake
Bay

Williamsburg

New Bern

NORTH
CAROLINA

F

Charlotte

Fayetteville

W

SOUTH
CAROLINA

Savannah River

F

F

Charleston

J

GEORGIA

J

Savannah

FLORIDA
(Spanish)

**MAJOR IMMIGRANT
GROUPS IN COLONIAL
AMERICA**

English

Africans

Scotch-Irish

German

Dutch

Highland Scots

French

J   Jews

S   Swedes

W   Welsh

F   French Huguenots

N

caused by English tariffs. Between 1717 and 1775, over a quarter million of them left northern England, southern Scotland, and northern Ireland for America. They looked mainly to Pennsylvania and the fertile valleys stretching southwestward into Virginia and Carolina.

The Germans and Scotch-Irish became the largest non-English elements in the colonies, but other groups enriched the population in New York and the Quaker colonies. French Huguenots (Calvinists whose religious freedom was revoked in France in 1685), Irish, Welsh, Swiss, Jews, and others. New York had inherited from the Dutch a tradition of toleration that had given the colony a diverse population before the English conquest: French-speaking Walloons and French, Germans, Danes, Portuguese, Spaniards, Italians, Bohemians, Poles, and others, including some New England Puritans. The Protestant Netherlands had given haven to the Sephardic Jews expelled from Spain and Portugal, and enough of them found their way into New Netherland to found a synagogue there.

What could be said of Pennsylvania as a refuge for the persecuted might be said as well of Rhode Island and South Carolina, which practiced a similar religious toleration. Newport and Charleston, like New York and Philadelphia, became centers of minuscule Jewish populations. French Huguenots made their greatest mark on South Carolina, more by their enterprise than by their numbers. A number of Highland Scots came directly from their homeland rather than by way of Ulster, especially after suppression of a rebellion in 1745 on behalf of the Stuart pretender to the throne, "Bonnie Prince Charlie."

The eighteenth century was the great period of expansion and population growth in British North America, and during those years a large increase of the non-English stock took place. A rough estimate of the national origins of the white population as of 1790 found it to be 61 percent English, 14 percent Scottish and Scotch-Irish, 9 percent German, 5 percent Dutch, French, and Swedish, 4 percent Irish, and 7 percent miscellaneous or unassigned. If one adds to the 3,172,444 whites in the 1790 census the 756,770 nonwhites, not even considering uncounted Indians, it seems likely that only about half the populace, and perhaps fewer, could trace their origins to England. Of the black slaves, about 75 percent had been transported from the bend of the African coastline between the Senegal and Niger Rivers; most of the rest came from Congo-Angola.

THE BACKCOUNTRY   Pennsylvania in the eighteenth century became the great distribution point for the diverse ethnic groups of European origin, just as the Chesapeake Bay region and Charleston became the distribution points for African peoples. Before the mid–eighteenth century, settlers in the Pennsylvania backcountry reached the Appalachian Mountain range. Rather than crossing the steep ridges, the Scotch-Irish and Germans filtered southward along what came to be called the Great Philadelphia Road, the primary internal migration route during the colonial period. It headed west from the port city, traversing Chester and Lancaster counties, and turned southwest at Harris's Ferry (now Harrisburg), where it crossed the Susquehanna River. Continuing south across western Maryland, it headed down the Shenandoah Valley of Virginia, and on into the Carolina and Georgia backcountry. Germans were first in the upper Shenandoah Valley, and to the south of them Scotch-Irish filled the lower valley. Migrants continued to move into the Carolina and Georgia backcountry, while others migrated from Charleston.

Along the fringes of the frontier, known as the Piedmont, were commonly found the Scotch-Irish, who had acquired in their homeland and in Ulster a stubborn fighting spirit. They lived in scattered settlements of isolated log cabins. With time, of course, neighborhoods grew up within visiting distance, animal and Indian trails broadened into wagon roads, and crossroads stores became community gathering places where conversation could be lubricated with the whiskey that was abundant on the Scotch-Irish frontier. Government was slow to reach these remote settlements, and the frontier communities were often disorderly.

COLONIAL CITIES

During the seventeenth century the American colonies remained in comparative isolation from one another, evolving subtly distinctive folkways and unfolding separate histories. Boston and New York, Philadelphia and Charleston were more likely to keep in closer touch with London than with each other. The Carolina upcountry had more in common with the Pennsylvania backcountry than either had with the urban cultures of Charleston or Philadelphia. Since commerce was their chief reason for being, colonial cities hugged the coastline or, like Philadelphia, sprang up on rivers where oceangoing vessels could reach them. Never holding more than 10 percent of the colonial population, the large cities exerted a disproportionate influence in commerce, politics, and civilization. By the end of the colonial period, Philadelphia, with some 30,000 people, was the largest city in the colonies and second only to London in the British Empire. New York, with about 25,000, ranked second; Boston numbered 16,000; Charleston, 12,000; and Newport, Rhode Island, 11,000.

THE SOCIAL AND POLITICAL ORDER   The urban social elite was dominated by the merchants who bartered the products of American farms and forests for the molasses and rum of the West Indies, the manufactured goods of Europe, and the slaves of Africa. Their trade in turn stimulated the sail makers, instrument makers, and other craftsmen who supplied vessels leaving port. After the merchants, who constituted the chief urban aristocracy, came a middle class of retailers, innkeepers, and artisans. Almost two-thirds of urban adult male workers were artisans, people who made their living at handicrafts. They included carpenters and coopers (barrel makers), shoemakers and tailors, silversmiths and blacksmiths, sail makers, stonemasons, weavers, and potters. At the bottom of the pecking order were sailors and unskilled workers.

The Rapalje Children *by John Durand, circa 1768. These children of a wealthy Brooklyn merchant wear garb typical of upper-crust urban society.*

Class stratification in the cities became more pronounced as time passed. One study of Boston found that in 1687 the richest 15 percent of the population owned 52 percent of the taxable wealth; by 1771 the top 15 percent owned about 67 percent and the top 5 percent owned some 44 percent of the wealth. In Philadelphia the concentration of wealth was even more pronounced.

Problems created by urban growth are nothing new. Colonial cities were busy, crowded, and dangerous places. They required not only paved streets and lighting but regulations to protect children and animals in the streets from reckless riders. Regulations restrained citizens from tossing their garbage into the streets. Fires that on occasion swept through closely packed buildings led to preventive standards in building codes, restrictions on burning rubbish, and the organization of fire companies. Rising crime and violence required more police protection. And in cities the poor became more visible than in the countryside.

Colonists brought with them the English principle of public responsibility for the indigent. The number of Boston's poor receiving public assistance rose from 500 in 1700 to 4,000 in 1736, New York's from 250 in 1698 to 5,000 in the 1770s. Most of such public assistance went to "outdoor" relief in the form of money, food, clothing, and fuel. Almshouses also appeared in colonial cities to house the destitute.

THE URBAN WEB   Transit within and between cities was difficult at first. The first roads were likely to be Indian trails, which themselves often followed the tracks of bison through the forests. The trails widened with travel, then were made roads by order of provincial and local authorities. Land travel at first had to go by horse or by foot. The first public stagecoach line opened in 1732. From the main ports good roads might reach thirty or forty miles inland, but all were dirt roads subject to washouts and mudholes. Aside from city streets there was not a single hard-surfaced road during the entire colonial period.

Taverns were an important aspect of colonial travel, since movement by night was too risky. By the end of the seventeenth century, there were more taverns in America than any other business. Indeed, they became the most important social institution in the colonies— and the most democratic. By 1690 there were fifty-four taverns in Boston alone, half of them operated by women. In rural areas or along the main roads, the first taverns were simply farmhouses that offered travelers something potent to drink and a bed in a corner or hayloft. In the coastal cities, they tended to be seedy grogshops along the waterfront, catering to sailors and prostitutes, or more elegant establishments in the uptown commercial districts with proper English names such as the Green Dragon, the Black Horse, the Blue Bell, or the Golden Lion.

Like private clubs today, colonial taverns and inns were places to drink, relax, read the newspaper, play cards or billiards, gossip about people or politics, learn news from travelers, or conduct business. Local ordinances regulated the taverns, setting their prices and usually prohibiting them from serving liquor to blacks, Indians, servants, or apprentices.

John Adams recorded in his diary that the crowded Boston taverns produced "diseases, vicious habits, bastards, and legislators." In 1726 a concerned Bostonian wrote a letter to the community declaring that "the abuse of strong Drink is becoming Epidemical among us, and it is very justly Supposed ... that the Multiplication of Taverns has contributed not a little to this Excess of Riot and Debauchery." Despite the objections by some that crowded taverns engendered disease and debauchery, colonial taverns and inns continued to proliferate, and by the mid–eighteenth century they would become the gathering place for protests against British rule.

Taverns served as a collective form of communication; personal communication, however, was more complicated. Postal service through the seventeenth century was almost nonexistent—people entrusted letters to

A tobacconist's trade card from 1770 captures the atmosphere of taverns in the late eighteenth century. Here, men in a Philadelphia tavern share conversation while they drink ale and smoke pipes.

travelers or sea captains. Massachusetts set up a provincial postal system in 1677, and Pennsylvania in 1683. Under a parliamentary law of 1710, the postmaster of London named a deputy in charge of the colonies and a postal system eventually extended the length of the Atlantic seaboard. Benjamin Franklin, who served as deputy postmaster for the colonies from 1753 to 1774, sped up the service with shorter routes and night-traveling post riders, and he increased the volume by inaugurating lower rates.

More reliable mail deliveries gave rise to newspapers in the eighteenth century. Before 1745 twenty-two newspapers had been started, seven in New England, ten in the middle colonies, and five in the South. An important landmark in the progress of freedom of the press was John Peter Zenger's trial for seditious libel for publishing criticisms of New York's governor in his newspaper, the *New York Weekly Journal*. Zenger was imprisoned for ten months and brought to trial in 1735. The established rule in English common law held that one might be punished for criticism that fostered "an ill opinion of the government." The jury's function was only to determine whether the defendant had published the opinion. Zenger's lawyer startled the court with his claim that the editor had published the truth—which the judge ruled an unacceptable defense. The jury, however, agreed with the assertion and held the editor not guilty. The libel law remained standing as before, but editors thereafter were emboldened to criticize officials more freely.

THE ENLIGHTENMENT

DISCOVERING THE LAWS OF NATURE   Through their commercial contacts, newspapers, and other activities, colonial cities became the centers for the dissemination of fashion and ideas. In the world of ideas a new fashion was abroad: the Enlightenment. During the seventeenth century, Europe experienced a scientific revolution in which the ancient view of an earth-centered universe was overthrown by the new heliocentric (sun-centered) system of Polish astronomer Nicolaus Copernicus. A climax to the scientific revolution came with Sir Isaac Newton's *Principia* (*Mathematical Principles of Natural Philosophy*, 1687), which set forth his theory of gravitation. Newton depicted a mechanistic universe moving in accordance with natural laws that could be grasped by human reason and explained by mathematics. He implied that natural laws governed all things—the orbits of the planets and also the orbits of human relations: politics, economics, and society. Reason could make people aware, for instance, that the natural law of supply and demand governed economics or that natural rights to life, liberty, and property determined the limits and functions of government.

Much of enlightened thought could be reconciled with established beliefs—the idea of natural law existed in Christian theology, and religious people could reason that the rational universe of Copernicus and Newton simply demonstrated the glory of God. Yet when people carried Newton's outlook to its ultimate logic, as the Deists did, the idea of natural law reduced God to the position of a remote Creator—as the French *philosophe* Voltaire put it, the master clockmaker who planned the universe and set it in motion. Evil in the world, in this view, resulted not from original sin and innate depravity so much as it did from ignorance, an imperfect understanding of the laws of nature. Humanity, the English philosopher John Locke argued in his *Essay on Human Understanding* (1690), is largely the product of the environment, the mind being a blank tablet on which experience is written. The way to improve both society and human nature was by the application and improvement of Reason—which was the highest Virtue (Enlightenment thinkers often capitalized both words).

THE ENLIGHTENMENT IN AMERICA   However interpreted, such ideas profoundly affected the climate of thought in the eighteenth century. The premises of Newtonian science and the Enlightenment, moreover, fitted the American experience. In the New World people no longer moved solely in the worn grooves of tradition that defined the roles of priest or peasant or noble. The experience of colonial settlement placed a premium on observation, experiment, and the need to think anew. America was therefore receptive to the new science.

John Winthrop, Jr., three times governor of Connecticut, wanted to establish industries and mining in America. These interests led to his work in chemistry and membership in the Royal Society of London. He owned probably the first telescope brought to the colonies. His cousin, John Winthrop IV, was a professional scientist and Harvard professor who introduced to the colonies the study of calculus and ranged over the fields of astronomy, geology, chemistry, and electricity. David Rittenhouse of Philadelphia, a clockmaker, became a self-taught scientist who built probably the first telescope made in America. John Bartram of Philadelphia spent a lifetime traveling and studying American plant life, and gathered in Philadelphia an extensive botanical garden.

FRANKLIN'S INFLUENCE   Benjamin Franklin epitomized the Enlightenment, in the eyes of both Americans and Europeans. Born in Boston in 1706, he was the son of a candle and soap maker. Apprenticed to his older brother, a printer, Franklin left home at the age of seventeen, bound for Philadelphia. There, before he was twenty-four, he owned a print shop, where he edited and published the *Pennsylvania Gazette.* When he was twenty-seven he brought out *Poor Richard's Almanac,* filled with homely maxims on success and happiness. Before he retired from business at the age of forty-two, Franklin, among other achievements, had founded a library, set up a fire company, helped start the academy that became the University of Pennsylvania, and organized a debating club that grew into the American Philosophical Society.

Science was Franklin's passion. His *Experiments and Observations on Electricity* (1751) went through many editions in several languages and established his reputation as a leading thinker and experimenter. His speculations extended widely to the fields of medicine, meteorology, geology, astronomy, physics, and other aspects of science. He invented the Franklin stove, the lightning rod, and a glass harmonica for which Mozart and Beethoven composed. The triumph of this untutored genius confirmed the Enlightenment trust in the powers of Nature and Reason.

Benjamin Franklin as a young man.

EDUCATION IN THE COLONIES   For the colonists at large, education in the traditional ideas and manners of society—even literacy itself—remained primarily the responsibility of family and church. The modern conception of free public education was slow in coming and failed to win universal acceptance until the twentieth century. Yet colonists were concerned from the beginning that steps needed to be taken lest the children of settlers grow up untutored in the wilderness.

Conditions in New England proved most favorable for the establishment of schools. The Puritan emphasis on Scripture reading, which all Protestants shared in some degree, implied an obligation to ensure literacy. And the compact towns of that region made schools more feasible than among the scattered people of the southern colonies. In 1647 the Massachusetts Bay colony enacted the famous "ye olde deluder Satan" Act (designed to thwart the Evil One), which required every town of fifty or more families to set up a grammar school (a Latin school that could prepare a student for college). Although the act was widely evaded, it did signify a serious purpose to promote education.

The Dutch in New Netherland were as interested in education as the New England Puritans. In Pennsylvania the Quakers never heeded William Penn's instructions to establish public schools, but they did finance a number of private schools teaching practical as well as academic subjects. In the southern colonies efforts to establish schools were hampered by the more scattered populations, and in parts of the backcountry by indifference and neglect. Some of the wealthiest planters and merchants of the Tidewater sent their children to England or hired

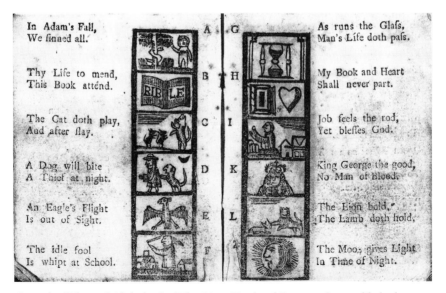

From the "Rhymed Alphabet" of The New England Primer, *first published in America in the 1680s.*

tutors. In some places wealthy patrons or the people collectively managed to raise some kind of support for "old field" schools and academies at the secondary level.

THE GREAT AWAKENING

STIRRINGS   During the early eighteenth century, the new currents of rationalism stimulated by the Enlightenment aroused concerns among orthodox believers in Calvinism. Many people seemed to be drifting away from the old moorings of piety. Despite the belief that the Lord had allowed great Puritan and Quaker merchants of Boston and Philadelphia to prosper, there remained a haunting fear that the devil had lured them into the vain pursuit of worldly gain, deism, and skepticism. And out along the fringes of settlement, many of the colonists were unchurched. On the frontier, people had no minister to preach or administer sacraments or perform marriages. According to some ministers, these pioneers had lapsed into a primitive and sinful life, little different from the "heathen" Indians. By the 1730s, the sense of religious decline provoked a widespread revival of faith, which became known as the Great Awakening. Within a few years, a wave of evangelism would sweep the colonies from one end to the other.

In 1734–1735 a remarkable spiritual revival occurred in the congregation of Jonathan Edwards, a Congregationalist minister in Northampton, in western Massachusetts. One of America's most brilliant philosophers and theologians, Edwards entered Yale in 1716 at age thirteen and was graduated valedictorian four years later. In 1726 Edwards was called to serve the Congregational church in Northampton. There he found the town's spirituality at low ebb. More people frequented taverns than churches, and Christians, he believed, had become preoccupied with making and spending money. Religion had also become too intellectual, thereby losing its emotional force. "Our people," he said, "do not so much need to have their heads stored [with new knowledge] as to have their hearts touched." His own vivid descriptions of the torments of hell and the delights of heaven helped rekindle spiritual fervor among his congregants. By 1735 Edwards could report that "the town seemed to be full of the presence of God; it never was so full of love, nor of joy." To judge the power of the Awakening, he thought, one need only observe

George Whitefield's dramatic eloquence roused American congregants, leading many to experience a religious rebirth.

that "it was no longer the Tavern" that drew local crowds, "but the Minister's House."

About the same time, William Tennent, an Irish-born Presbyterian revivalist, set up a "Log College" in Neshaminy, Pennsylvania, for the education of ministers to serve the Scotch-Irish Presbyterians living around Philadelphia. The true catalyst of the Great Awakening, however, was a twenty-seven-year-old English minister, George Whitefield, whose reputation as a spellbinding evangelist preceded him to the colonies. Congregations were lifeless, he claimed, "because dead men preach to them." Too many ministers were "slothful shepherds and dumb dogs." His objective was to restore the fires of religious fervor to American congregations. In the autumn of 1739 Whitefield arrived in Philadelphia and began preaching to huge crowds. After visiting Georgia, he made a triumphal procession northward to New England, drawing great crowds and releasing "Gales of Heavenly Wind" that blew gusts throughout the colonies.

Possessed of a golden voice, Whitefield enthralled audiences with his unparalleled eloquence. Even the skeptical Ben Franklin, who went to see Whitefield preach in Philadelphia, found himself so carried away that he emptied his pockets into the collection plate. Whitefield urged his listeners to experience a "new birth"—a sudden, emotional moment of conversion and salvation. By the end of his sermon, one listener reported, the entire congregation was "in utmost Confusion, some crying out, some laughing, and Bliss still roaring to them to come to Christ, as they answered, *I will, I will, I'm coming, I'm coming.*"

Jonathan Edwards took advantage of the commotion stirred up by Whitefield to spread his own revival gospel throughout New England. The Awakening reached its peak in 1741, when Edwards delivered his most famous sermon at Enfield, Massachusetts. Entitled "Sinners in the Hands of an Angry God," it represented a devout appeal to repentance.

Edwards reminded the congregation that hell was real and that God's vision was omnipotent, his judgment certain. He noted that God "holds you over the pit of hell, much as one holds a spider, or some loathsome insect, over the fire, abhors you, and is dreadfully provoked . . . he looks upon you as worthy of nothing else, but to be cast into the fire." When he finished, he had to wait several minutes for the congregation to quiet down before leading them in a closing hymn.

Edwards and Whitefield inspired many imitators, some of whom carried evangelism to extremes. Once unleashed, spiritual enthusiasm is hard to control. In many ways the Awakening backfired on those who had intended it to bolster church discipline and social order. Some of the revivalists began to court those at the bottom of the social scale— laborers, seamen, servants, and farm folk. The Reverend James Davenport, for instance, a fiery itinerant New England Congregationalist, set about shouting, raging, and stomping on the devil, beseeching his listeners to renounce the established clergy and become the agents of their own salvation. The churched and unchurched flocked to hear his mesmerizing sermons. Seized by the terror and ecstasy, they groveled on the floor or lay unconscious on the benches, to the chagrin of more decorous churchgoers. One never knew, the more traditional clergymen warned, whence came these enthusiasms—perhaps they were devilish delusions intended to discredit the true faith.

PIETY AND REASON   Everywhere the fragmenting force of the Awakening brought splits, especially in the more Calvinistic churches. Presbyterians divided into the "Old Side" and "New Side"; Congregationalists into "Old Lights" and "New Lights." New England religious life would never be the same. The more traditional clergy were undermined as church members chose sides and either dismissed their ministers or deserted them. Many of the "New Lights" went over to the Baptists, and others flocked to Presbyterian or, later, Methodist groups, which in turn divided and subdivided into new sects.

New England Puritanism disintegrated amid the ecstatic revivals of the Great Awakening. The precarious balance in which the founders had held the elements of emotionalism and reason collapsed. In consequence, New England attracted more and more Baptists, Presbyterians, Anglicans, and other denominations, while the revival frenzy scored its most lasting victories along the frontiers of the middle and southern colonies. In the more sedate churches of Boston, moreover, the principle of rational religion gained the upper hand in a reaction against the excesses of revival emotion. Boston ministers such as Charles Chauncey and Jonathan Mayhew reexamined Calvinist theology and found it too forbidding and irrational that people could be forever damned by predestination.

In reaction to taunts that the "born-again" revivalist ministers lacked learning, the Awakening gave rise to the denominational colleges that became so characteristic of American higher education. The three colleges already in existence had originated from religious motives: Harvard, founded in 1636, because the Puritans dreaded "to leave an illiterate ministry to the church when our present ministers shall lie in the dust"; the College of William and Mary, in 1693, created to strengthen the Anglican ministry; and Yale College, in 1701, set up to educate the Puritans of Connecticut, who felt that Harvard was drifting from the strictest orthodoxy. The College of New Jersey, later Princeton University, was founded by Presbyterians in 1746. In close succession came King's College (1754) in New York, later renamed Columbia University, an Anglican institution; the College of Rhode Island (1764), later called Brown University, Baptist; Queen's College (1766), later known as Rutgers, Dutch Reformed; and Congregationalist Dartmouth (1769), the outgrowth of an earlier school for Indians. Among the colonial colleges, only the University of Pennsylvania, founded as the Philadelphia Academy in 1754, arose from a secular impulse.

The Great Awakening, like the Enlightenment, set in motion powerful currents that still flow in American life. It implanted in American culture the evangelical crusade and the emotional appeal of revivalism. The movement weakened the status of the old-fashioned clergy and encouraged believers to exercise their own judgment, and thereby weakened habits of deference generally. By encouraging the proliferation of denominations, it heightened the need for toleration of dissent. But in some respects the counterpoint between the Awakening and the Enlightenment, between the principles of spirit and reason, led by different roads to similar ends. Both movements emphasized the power and right of individual decision making, and both aroused millennial hopes that America would become the promised land in which people might attain the perfection of piety or reason, if not of both.

MAKING CONNECTIONS

- This chapter contained hints of tensions in colonial Virginia
  society; such tensions would periodically come to a head, as in
  Bacon's Rebellion, discussed in Chapter 2.

- During the imperial crisis of the 1760s and 1770s, the ideas of
  the Great Awakening and especially the Enlightenment helped
  shape the American response to British actions and thereby
  contributed to a revolutionary mentality.

FURTHER READING

The diversity of colonial societies may be seen in David Hackett
Fischer's *Albion's Seed: Four British Folkways in America* (1989). On the
economic development of New England, see Christine Heyrman's *Commerce and Culture: The Maritime Communities of Colonial Massachusetts*
(1984) and Stephen Innes's *Creating the Commonwealth: The Economic
Culture of Puritan New England* (1995). John Frederick Martin's *Profits
in the Wilderness: Entrepreneurship and the Founding of New England
Towns in the Seventeenth Century* (1991) indicates that economic concerns rather than spiritual motives were driving forces in many New
England towns.

Paul S. Boyer and Stephen Nissenbaum's *Salem Possessed* (1974)
connects the notorious witch trials to changes in community structure.
For an interdisciplinary approach, see John Demos's *Entertaining Satan: Witchcraft and the Culture of Early New England* (1982). Bernard
Rosenthal challenges many myths concerning the Salem witch trials in
Salem Story: Reading the Witch Trials of 1692 (1993).

Discussions of women in the New England colonies can be found in
Laurel Ulrich's *Good Wives: Image and Reality in the Lives of Women in
Northern New England, 1650–1750* (1982), Joy Buel and Richard Buel,
Jr.'s *The Way of Duty* (1984), and Carol Karlsen's *The Devil in the Shape
of a Woman: Witchcraft in Colonial New England* (1987). John Demos

describes family life in *A Little Commonwealth: Family Life in Plymouth Colony* (1970).

On New England Indians, see Kathleen Bragdon's *Native People of Southern New England, 1500–1650* (1996). For analyses of Indian wars, see Alfred Cave's *The Pequot War* (1996) and Jill Lepore's *The Name of War: King Philip's War and the Origins of American Identity* (1998). The story of the Iroquois is told well in Daniel Richter's *The Ordeal of the Longhouse: The Peoples of the Iroquois League in the Era of European Colonization* (1992). Indians in the southern colonies are the focus of James Axtell's *The Indians' New South* (1997).

For the social history of the southern colonies, see Allan Kulikoff's *Tobacco and Slaves: The Development of Southern Cultures in the Chesapeake, 1680–1800* (1986) and Kathleen Brown's *Good Wives, Nasty Wenches, and Anxious Patriarchs: Gender, Race, and Power in Colonial Virginia* (1996). Family life along the Chesapeake Bay is described in Gloria L. Main's *Tobacco Colony* (1982) and Daniel B. Smith's *Inside the Great House: Planter Family Life in Eighteenth-Century Chesapeake Society* (1980).

Edmund S. Morgan's *American Slavery, American Freedom: The Ordeal of Colonial Virginia* (1975) examines Virginia's social structure, environment, and labor patterns in a biracial context. On the interaction of the cultures of blacks and whites, see Mechal Sobel's *The World They Made Together: Black and White Values in Eighteenth-Century Virginia* (1987). Black viewpoints are presented in Timothy H. Breen and Stephen Innes's *"Myne Owne Ground": Race and Freedom on Virginia's Eastern Shore, 1640–1676* (1980). David W. Galenson's *White Servitude in Colonial America* (1981) looks at the indentured labor force.

Henry F. May's *The Enlightenment in America* (1976) examines intellectual trends in eighteenth-century America. Lawrence A. Cremin's *American Education: The Colonial Experience, 1607–1783* (1970) surveys educational developments.

On the Great Awakening, see Patricia U. Bonomi's *Under the Cope of Heaven: Religion, Society, and Politics in Colonial America* (1986) and Frank Lambert's *Inventing the "Great Awakening"* (1999). For evangelism in the South, see Christine Heyrman's *Southern Cross: The Beginnings of the Bible Belt* (1997). The political impact of the new religious enthusiasm is shown in Rhys Isaac's *The Transformation of Virginia, 1740–1790* (1982). Patricia J. Tracy's *Jonathan Edwards, Pastor* (1980) stresses the Northampton minister's relations to his community.

4 ⬩ THE IMPERIAL PERSPECTIVE

CHAPTER ORGANIZER

This chapter focuses on:

- England's changing policies in the political and economic administration of the colonies.

- how colonial governments were structured.

- the relations between English colonists and their neighbors in North America: the French, Spanish, and Indians.

*T*he British differed from the Spanish and French in the degree of autonomy they allowed their colonies in the Western Hemisphere. Unlike New France and New Spain, New England was in effect a self-governing community. There was much less control by the mother country, in part because the English were unwilling to incur the expenses of a vast colonial bureaucracy. The constant struggle between Parliament and the Stuart kings prevented England from perfecting either a systematic colonial policy or effective agencies of imperial control. After the Restoration of the Stuart monarchy in 1660, a more comprehensive plan of colonial administration slowly emerged, but even so it lacked coherence and efficiency.

As a result of inefficient—and often lax—colonial administration by the mother country, Americans grew accustomed to loose and often paradoxical imperial policies. For instance, the British government granted home rule to the settlements along the Atlantic coast and then sought to keep them from exercising it. It regarded the English colonists as citizens, but it refused to grant them the privileges of citizenship. It insisted that the settlers contribute to the expense of maintaining the colonies, but it refused to allow them a voice in the shaping of administrative policies. Such inconsistencies made tensions inevitable. By the mid–eighteenth century, when Britain tried to impose on its American colonies tighter controls, it was too late. British Americans had developed a far more powerful sense of their rights than any other colonial people, and they were determined to assert and defend those rights.

ENGLISH ADMINISTRATION OF THE COLONIES

Throughout the colonial period, the king was the source of legal authority in America, and land titles derived ultimately from royal grants. All colonies except Georgia received charters from the king before the Glorious Revolution of 1688, when the crown lost supremacy to Parliament. The colonies therefore continued to stand as "dependencies of the crown," and the important colonial officials held office at the pleasure of the crown. After King George granted a group of investors a charter for the new colony of Georgia in 1732, its status conformed to the established practice.

The king exercised his power through the Privy Council, a body of some thirty to forty advisers appointed by and responsible solely to him, and this group became the first agency of colonial supervision. But the Privy Council was too large and too busy to keep track of daily colonial affairs. So in 1634 King Charles I entrusted colonial affairs to eleven of its members, the Lords Commissioners for Plantations in General, with William Laud, archbishop of Canterbury, as its head. The Laud Commission grew in part out of the troubles following the dissolution of the Virginia Company and in part out of Laud's design to impose political and religious conformity on New England. In 1638 his commission ordered Massachusetts to return its charter and answer charges that colonial officials had violated its provisions. Sir Ferdinando Gorges, appointed governor-general of New England, planned to subdue the region by force if necessary, and might have quashed the Puritan experiment except for the troubles at home that prevented further action. The Civil War in England, which lasted from 1642 to 1649, was followed by Oliver Cromwell's Puritan Commonwealth and Protectorate, and both developments gave the colonies a respite from efforts at royal control.

THE MERCANTILE SYSTEM   Cromwell showed little passion for colonial administration, but he had a lively concern for colonial trade, which had fallen largely to Dutch shipping during the civil war in England. Therefore, in 1651 Parliament adopted a Navigation Act that excluded nearly all foreign shipping from the English and colonial trade. The act required that all goods imported into England or the colonies must arrive on English ships and that the majority of each crew must be English. In all cases colonial ships and crews qualified as English. The act excepted European goods, which might come in ships of the country that produced the goods, but only from the place of origin or the port from which they were usually shipped.

On economic policy, if nothing else, Restoration England under Charles II followed the lead of Cromwell and all the other major European powers of the seventeenth and eighteenth centuries. The new Parliament adopted the mercantile system, or mercantilism, which assumed that the total of the world's gold and silver remained essentially fixed, with only a nation's share in that wealth subject to change. Thus a nation could gain wealth only at the expense of another country—by seizing its gold and silver and dominating its trade. To acquire gold and silver, the government had to direct all economic activities, limiting foreign imports and preserving a favorable balance of trade. This required the government to encourage manufacturers, through subsidies and monopolies if need be. Mercantilism also required a nation to develop and protect its own shipping, and to make use of colonies as sources of raw materials and markets for its finished goods.

The Navigation Act of 1660 gave Cromwell's act of 1651 a new twist. Ships' crews now had to be not just a majority but three-quarters English, and certain specified goods were to be shipped only to England or other English colonies. The list of "enumerated" goods initially included tobacco, cotton, indigo, ginger, dyewoods, and sugar. Rice, hemp, masts, copper ore, and furs, among other items, were later added to the list. Not only did England (and its colonies) become the sole outlet for these colonial exports, but three years later the Navigation Act of 1663 sought to make England the funnel through which all colonial imports had to be routed. The act was sometimes called the Staple Act because it made England the staple (market or trade center) for all goods sent to the colonies. Virtually everything shipped from Europe to America had to stop off in England, be landed, and duty paid on it before reshipment. A third major act rounded out the trade system. The Navigation Act of 1673 (sometimes called the Plantation Duty Act) required that every captain loading enumerated articles give bond to land them in England, or if they were destined for another colony, that he pay on the spot a duty roughly equal to that paid in England.

ENFORCING THE NAVIGATION ACTS The Navigation Acts supplied a convenient rationale for a colonial system: to serve the economic needs of the mother country. Yet enforcement was spotty. During the reign of Charles I a bureaucracy of colonial administrators began to emerge, but it took shape slowly and incompletely. After the Restoration of 1660, supervision of colonial affairs fell once again to the Privy Council, or rather to a succession of its committees. In 1675 Charles II introduced some order into the chaos when, as his father had done before, he designated certain privy councilors the Lords of Trade. The Lords of Trade were to make the colonies abide by the mercantile system and to seek out ways to make them more profitable to England and the crown. To these ends, they served as the clearinghouse for all colonial affairs, building up a bureaucracy of colonial experts. The Lords of Trade named governors, wrote or reviewed the governors' instructions, and handled all reports and correspondence dealing with colonial affairs.

Within five years of the Plantation Duty Act, between 1673 and 1678, collectors of customs appeared in all the colonies, and shortly thereafter a surveyor general of the customs in the American colonies was named. The most notorious of these, insofar as resentful colonists were concerned, was Edward Randolph, the first man to make an entire career in the colonial service and the nemesis of insubordinate colonials for a quarter century.

Randolph arrived at Boston in 1676 to demand that Massachusetts answer complaints that it had usurped the proprietary rights in New Hampshire and Maine. Randolph submitted a report bristling with

This view of eighteenth-century Boston shows the importance of shipping and its regulation in the colonies, especially in Massachusetts Bay.

hostility. The Bay colony had not only ignored royal wishes, it had tolerated violations of the Navigation Acts, refused appeals from its courts to the Privy Council, and had operated a mint in defiance of the king's prerogative. Massachusetts officials had told him, Randolph reported, "that the legislative power is and abides in them solely to act and make laws by virtue" of their charter. The Lords of Trade began legal proceedings against the colonial charter in 1678. Meanwhile, Randolph returned in 1680 to inaugurate the royal colony of New Hampshire, then set up shop as the king's collector of customs in Boston, whence he dispatched repeated accounts of colonial recalcitrance. Eventually, in 1684, the Lords of Trade won a court decision that annulled the charter of Massachusetts. The Puritan utopia was fast becoming a lost cause.

THE DOMINION OF NEW ENGLAND   Temporarily, the government of Massachusetts Bay was placed in the hands of a special royal commission. Then in 1685 Charles II died, to be succeeded by his brother, the duke of York, as James II, the first Catholic sovereign since the death of Queen Mary in 1558. James II asserted his powers more forcefully than his brother had. The new king readily approved a proposal to create a Dominion of New England and to place under its sway all colonies south through New Jersey.

The Dominion was to have a government named by royal authority; a governor and council would rule without any assembly. The royal governor, Sir Edmund Andros, appeared in Boston in 1686 to establish his rule, which he soon extended over Connecticut and Rhode Island, and in 1688 over New York and East and West New Jersey. Andros was a soldier, accustomed to taking—and giving—orders. He seems to have been honest, efficient, and loyal to the crown, but tactless in circumstances that called for the utmost diplomacy—the uprooting of long-established institutions in the face of popular hostility.

A rising resentment greeted Andros's measures, especially in Massachusetts. Taxation was now levied without the consent of the General Court, and when residents of one seaboard town protested against taxation without representation, several of them were imprisoned or fined. Andros suppressed town governments, enforced the trade laws, and subdued smuggling. Most ominous of all, Andros and his lieutenants took over one of the Puritan churches for Anglican worship in Boston. Puritan leaders believed, with good reason, that he was conspiring to break their power and authority.

But the Dominion of New England was scarcely established before the Glorious Revolution of 1688 erupted in England. King James II, like Andros in New England, had aroused resentment by instituting arbitrary measures and openly parading his Catholic faith. The birth of a son, sure to be reared a Catholic, put the opposition on notice that James's system would survive him. The Catholic son, rather than the Protestant daughters, Mary and Anne, would be next in line for the throne. Parliamentary leaders, their patience exhausted, invited Mary and her husband, the Dutch leader, William of Orange, to assume the throne as joint monarchs. James, seeing his support dwindling, fled the country.

King James II (1685–1688).

THE GLORIOUS REVOLUTION IN AMERICA   When news reached Boston that William of Orange had landed in England, Boston staged its own Glorious Revolution, as bloodless as that in England. Andros and his councilors were arrested, and Massachusetts reverted to its former government. In rapid sequence the other colonies that had been absorbed into the Dominion followed suit. All were permitted to retain their former status except Massachusetts and Plymouth which, after some delay, were united under a new charter in 1691 as the royal colony of Massachusetts Bay.

In New York, however, events took a different course. There, Andros's lieutenant-governor was deposed by a German immigrant, Jacob Leisler, who assumed the office of governor pending approval from England. For two years he kept the province under his control with the support of the militia. Finally, in 1691, the king appointed a new governor. When Leisler hesitated to turn over authority, he was charged with treason. Leisler and his son-in-law were hanged on May 16, 1691. Four years too late, in 1695, Parliament exonerated them of all charges. Leisler and anti-Leisler factions would poison the political atmosphere of New York for years to come.

The new British monarchs, William and Mary, made no effort to restore the Dominion of New England. But the crown salvaged a remnant of that design by bringing more colonies under royal control through the appointment of governors in Massachusetts, New York, and Maryland. Maryland, however, reverted to proprietary status in 1715 after the fourth Lord Baltimore became Anglican. Pennsylvania had an even briefer career as a royal colony, 1692–1694, before reverting to Penn's proprietorship. New Jersey became a royal province in 1702, South Carolina in 1719, North Carolina in 1729, and Georgia in 1752.

The Glorious Revolution had significant long-term effects on American history in that the Bill of Rights and the Toleration Act, passed in England in 1689, influenced attitudes and the course of events in the colonies. Even more significant, the overthrow of James II set a precedent for revolution against the monarch. In defense of that action the philosopher John Locke published his *Two Treatises on Government* (1690), which had an enormous impact on political thought in the colonies. The *First Treatise* refuted theories of the divine right of kings. The more important *Second Treatise* set forth Locke's contract theory of government, which claimed that people were endowed with certain natural rights to life, liberty, and property. The need to protect such rights led people to establish governments. Kings were parties to such agreements, and obligated to protect the property and lives of their subjects. When they failed to do so, the people had the right—in extreme cases—to overthrow the monarch and change their government.

The idea that governments emerged by contract out of a primitive state of nature is of course hypothetical, not an account of actual events. But in the American experience governments had actually grown out of contractual arrangements such as Locke described: the Mayflower Compact, the Cambridge Agreement, the Fundamental Orders of Connecticut. The royal charters themselves constituted a sort of contract between the crown and the settlers. Locke's writings understandably appealed to colonial readers, and his philosophy probably had more influence in America than in England.

AN EMERGING COLONIAL SYSTEM   The accession of William and Mary to the English throne provoked a refinement of the existing Navigation Acts. In 1696 two developments created at last the semblance, and to some degree the reality, of a coherent colonial system. First, the Navigation Act of 1696 required colonial governors to enforce the trade laws, allowed customs officials to use "writs of assistance" (general search warrants that did not have to specify the place to be searched), and ordered that accused violators be tried in admiralty courts because colonial juries habitually refused to convict their peers. Admiralty cases were decided by judges whom the governors appointed.

Second, also in 1696, William III created the Lords of Trade and Plantations (the Board of Trade) to take the place of the Lords of Trade. Colonial officials were required to report to the board, and its archives constitute the largest single collection of materials on colonial relations with the mother country from that time on. The Board of Trade investigated the enforcement of the Navigation Acts and recommended ways to limit colonial manufactures and to encourage the production of raw materials. At the board's behest, Parliament enacted a bounty for the production of ship timber, masts, hemp, rice, indigo, and other commodities. The board examined all colonial laws and made recommendations for their disallowance by the crown. In all, 8,563 colonial laws eventually were examined and 469 of them were eliminated.

SALUTARY NEGLECT   From 1696 to 1725 the Board of Trade worked vigorously toward subjecting the colonies to a more efficient royal control. After the death of Queen Anne in 1714, however, its energies waned. The throne went in turn to the Hanoverian monarchs, George I (1714–1727) and George II (1727–1760), German princes who were next in the Protestant line of succession by virtue of descent from James I. Under these monarchs, the cabinet (a kind of executive committee in the Privy Council) emerged as the central agency of administration. Robert Walpole, as first minister (1721–1742), deliberately followed a policy that the philosopher Edmund Burke later called "a wise and salutary neglect." The Board of Trade became chiefly an agency of political patronage, studded with officials who took an interest mainly in their salaries.

THE HABIT OF SELF-GOVERNMENT

Government within the American colonies, like colonial policy, evolved without plan. In broad outline the governor, council, and assembly in each colony corresponded to the king, lords, and commons of the mother country. At the outset, all the colonies except Georgia had begun as projects of trading companies or feudal proprietors holding charters from the crown, but eight colonies eventually relinquished or forfeited their charters and became royal provinces. In these the crown named the governor. In Maryland, Pennsylvania, and Delaware the governor remained the choice of a proprietor, although each had an interim period of royal government. Connecticut and Rhode Island were the last of the corporate colonies; they elected their own governors to the end of the colonial period. In the corporate and proprietary colonies, and in Massachusetts, the charter served as a rough equivalent to a written constitution. Over the years certain anomalies appeared as colonial governments diverged from that of England. On the one hand, the governors retained powers and prerogatives that the king had lost in the course of the seventeenth century. On the other hand, the assemblies acquired powers, particularly with respect to government appointments, that Parliament had yet to gain.

POWERS OF THE GOVERNORS   The crown never vetoed acts of Parliament after 1707, but the colonial governors still held an absolute veto and the crown could disallow (in effect, veto) colonial legislation on advice of the Board of Trade. With respect to the assembly, the governor still had the power to determine when and where it would meet, to prorogue (adjourn or recess) sessions, and to dissolve the assembly for new elections or to postpone elections indefinitely at his pleasure. The crown, however, had to summon Parliament every three years and call elections at least every seven, and could not prorogue sessions. The royal or proprietary governor, moreover, nominated for life appointment the members of his council (except in Massachusetts, where they were chosen by the lower house), and the council functioned as both the upper house of the legislature and the highest court of appeal within the colony. With respect to the judiciary, in all but the charter colonies the governor held the prerogative of creating courts and of naming and dismissing judges, powers explicitly denied the king in England. Over time, however, the colonial assemblies generally made good their claim that courts should be created only by legislative authority, although the crown repeatedly disallowed acts to grant judges life tenure in order to make them more independent.

As chief executive the governor could appoint and remove officials, command the militia and naval forces, and grant pardons. In these respects his authority resembled the crown's, for the king still exercised executive authority and had the power to name administrative officials. This often served as a powerful means of royal influence in Parliament, since the king could appoint members or their friends to lucrative offices. While the arrangement might seem a breeding ground for corruption or tyranny, it was often viewed in the eighteenth century as a stabilizing influence, especially by the king's friends. But it was an influence less and less available to the governors. On the one hand, colonial assemblies nibbled away at their power of appointment; on the other hand, the authorities in England more and more drew the control of colonial patronage into their own hands.

POWERS OF THE ASSEMBLIES   Unlike the governor and council, who were appointed by an outside authority, either king or proprietor, the colonial assembly was elected. Whether called the House of Burgesses (Virginia), of Delegates (Maryland), of Representatives (Massachusetts), or simply "assembly," the lower houses were chosen by popular vote in

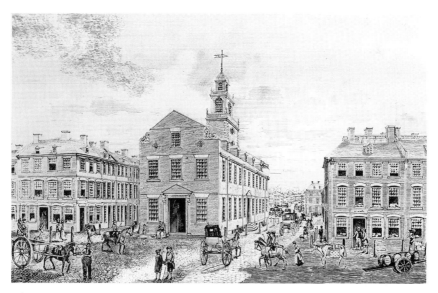

The Boston State House, built in 1713.

counties or towns or, in South Carolina, parishes. Although the English Toleration Act of 1689 did not apply to the colonies, religious tests for voting tended to be abandoned thereafter (the Massachusetts charter of 1691 so specified) and the chief restriction left was a property qualification, based on the notion that only men who held a "stake in society" could vote responsibly. Yet the property qualifications generally set low hurdles in the way of potential voters. Property holding was widespread, and a greater proportion of the population could vote in the colonies than anywhere else in the world of the eighteenth century.

Women, children, Indians, and blacks were excluded from the political process—as a matter of course—and continued to be excluded for the most part into the twentieth century, but the qualifications excluded few adult free white males. Virginia, which at one time permitted all freemen to vote, in the eighteenth century required only the ownership of twenty-five acres of improved land or one hundred acres of wild land, or the ownership of a "house" and part of a lot in town, or a service in a five-year apprenticeship in Williamsburg or Norfolk. Qualifications for membership in the assembly ran somewhat higher, and officeholders tended to come from the more well-to-do—a phenomenon not unknown today—but there were exceptions. One unsympathetic colonist observed in 1744 that the New Jersey assembly "was chiefly composed of me-chanicks and ignorant wretches; obstinate to the last degree."

Colonial politics of the eighteenth century mirrored English politics of the seventeenth. In one case, there had been a tug-of-war between king and Parliament, ending with the supremacy of Parliament, con-firmed by the Glorious Revolution. In the other case, colonial governors were still trying to wield prerogatives that the king had lost in England. The assemblies knew this; they also knew the arguments for the "rights" and "liberties" of the people and their legislative bodies, and against the dangers of despotic power. A further anomaly in the situa-tion was the undefined relationship of the colonies to Parliament. The colonies had been created by authority of the crown and their govern-mental connections ran to the crown, yet Parliament on occasion passed laws that applied to the colonies and were tacitly accepted by the colonies. Colonists became confused: were they governed by Par-liament or the king?

By the early eighteenth century, the assemblies, like Parliament, held two important strands of power—and they were perfectly aware of the parallel. First, they held the power of the purse strings in their right to vote on taxes and expenditures. Second, they held the power to initiate legislation and not merely, as in the early history of some colonies, the right to act on proposals from the governor and council. They used these powers to pull other strands of power into their hands when the chance presented itself. The governor in most colonies was held on a tight leash by the assembly's power to vote annually to adjust salaries.

Assemblies, because they controlled finance, demanded and often got the right to name tax collectors and treasurers. Then they stretched the claim to cover public printers, Indian agents, supervisors of public works and services, and other officers of the government. By specifying how appropriations should be spent, they played an important role even in military affairs and Indian relations, as well as other matters. Indeed, in the choice of certain administrative officers they pushed their power beyond that of Parliament in England, where appointment remained a crown prerogative.

All through the eighteenth century, the assemblies expanded their power and influence, sometimes in conflict with the governors, some-times in harmony with them, and often in the course of routine busi-ness passing laws and setting precedents the collective significance of which neither they nor the imperial authorities fully recognized. Once established, however, these laws and practices became fixed principles, parts of the "constitution" of the colonies. Self-government became first a habit, then a "right."

TROUBLED NEIGHBORS

SPANISH AMERICA IN DECLINE   By the start of the eighteenth century, the Spanish ruled over a huge colonial empire spanning North America. Yet their settlements in the borderlands north of Mexico were a colossal failure when compared to the colonies of the other European powers. In 1821, when Mexico declared its independence from Spain without firing a shot and the Spanish withdrew from North America, the most populated Hispanic settlement, Santa Fe, had only 6,000 residents. The next largest, San Antonio and St. Augustine, totaled only 1,500 each.

The Spanish failed to create thriving North American colonies for several reasons. Perhaps the most obvious was that the region lacked the gold and silver as well as the large native populations that attracted Spanish priorities to Mexico and Peru. In addition, the Spanish were distracted by their need to control the perennial unrest in Mexico among the natives and *mestizos* (people of mixed Indian and European ancestry). Moreover, those Spaniards who led the colonization effort in the borderlands were so preoccupied with military and religious exploitation that they never devoted enough attention to the factors necessary for producing viable settlements with self-sustaining economies. Only rarely, for example, did the Spanish send women to their colonies in North America. They never understood that the main factor in creating successful communities was a thriving market economy. Instead, they concentrated on building missions and forts and looking—in vain—for gold. Where the French and the English built their Indian policies around trading relationships (including firearms), Spain emphasized conversion to Catholicism, forbade manufacturing within the colonies, and strictly limited trade with the natives.

NEW FRANCE   Permanent French settlements in the New World differed considerably from both the Spanish and the English models. The French settlers were predominantly male but much smaller in number

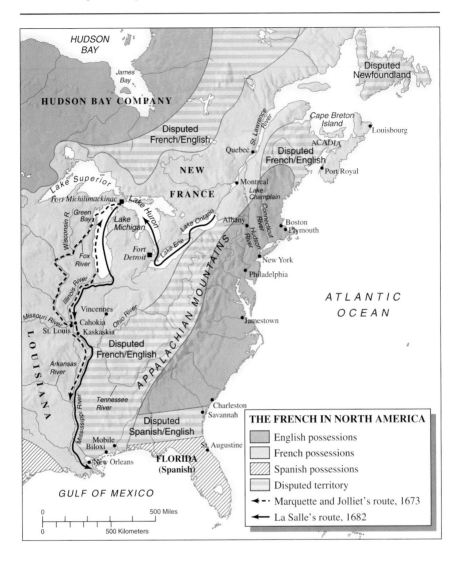

than the English and Spanish settlers. About 40,000 French colonists came to the New World during the seventeenth and eighteenth centuries. The relatively small French population proved to be an advantage in forcing the French to develop cooperative relationships with the Indians. Unlike the English settlers, the French established trading outposts rather than farms, mostly along the St. Lawrence River, on lands not claimed by Indians. They thus did not have to confront initial hostility. In addition, the French served as effective mediators between rival Great Lakes tribes. This diplomatic role gave them much more local authority and influence than their English counterparts, who disdained such mediation.

The heavily outnumbered and disproportionately male French settlers sought to integrate themselves with Indian culture rather than to displace it. Many French traders married Indians and raised mixed families, in the process exchanging languages and customs. The French also encouraged the Indians to embrace Catholicism and hate the English. This more fraternal bond between the French and the Indians proved to be a source of strength in the wars with the English, enabling New France to survive until 1760, despite the lopsided disparity in numbers between the two colonial powers.

French exploration began when Samuel de Champlain landed on the shores of the St. Lawrence River in 1603, and two years later at Port Royal, Acadia (later Nova Scotia). Champlain led another expedition in 1608, during which he founded Quebec, a year after the Jamestown landing. While Acadia remained a remote outpost, New France expanded well beyond Quebec, from which Champlain pushed his explorations up the great river and into the Great Lakes as far as Lake Huron, and southward to the lake that still bears his name. There, in 1609, he joined a band of Huron and Algonquian allies in a fateful encounter, fired his musket into the ranks of their Iroquois foes, and kindled a hatred that pursued New France to the end. The Iroquois stood as a buffer against French designs to move toward the English of the middle colonies and as a constant menace on the flank of the French waterways to the interior. In fact, for over a century, Indians determined the military balance of power within North America. In 1711 the governor-general of New France declared that "the Iroquois are more to be feared than the English colonies."

Until his death in 1635 Champlain governed New France under a trading company whose charter imposed a fatal weakness. The company won a profitable monopoly of the fur trade, but it had to limit the population to French Catholics. Neither the enterprising, seafaring Huguenots (French Protestants) of coastal France nor foreigners of any faith were allowed to populate the country. Great land grants went to persons who promised to bring settlers to work the land under feudal tenure. The colony therefore remained a scattered patchwork of dependent peasants, Jesuit missionaries, priests, soldiers, officials, and *coureurs de bois* (literally, runners of the woods), who ranged the interior in quest of furs.

Samuel de Champlain firing at a group of Mohawks, killing two chiefs (1609).

In 1663 King Louis XIV and his chief minister, Jean Baptiste Colbert, changed New France into a royal colony and pursued a plan of consolidation and stabilization. Colbert dispatched new settlers, including shiploads of young women to lure disbanded soldiers and traders into settled matrimony. He sent out tools and animals for farmers, nets for fishermen, and tried to make New France self-sufficient in foodstuffs. The population grew from about 4,000 in 1665 to about 15,000 in 1690.

FRENCH LOUISIANA   From the Great Lakes French explorers moved southward. In 1673 Louis Jolliet and Père Jacques Marquette, a Jesuit priest, ventured into Lake Michigan, up the Fox River from Green Bay, then down the Wisconsin River to the Mississippi, and on as far as the Arkansas River. Satisfied that the great Mississippi river flowed to the Gulf of Mexico, they turned back for fear of meeting with Spaniards. Nine years later Robert Cavalier, sieur de La Salle, went all the way to the Gulf of Mexico and named the country Louisiana after King Louis XIV of France.

Settlement of the Louisiana country finally began in 1699 when Pierre le Moyne, sieur d'Iberville, landed a colony near Biloxi, Mississippi.

The main settlement then moved to Mobile Bay an;d in 1710 to the present site of Mobile, Alabama. For nearly half a century the driving force in Louisiana was Jean Baptiste le Moyne, sieur de Bienville, a younger brother of Iberville. Bienville arrived with settlers in 1699, when he was only eighteen, and left the colony for the last time in 1743, when he was sixty-two. Sometimes called the "Father of Louisiana," he served periodically as governor and always as adviser during those years. In 1718 he founded New Orleans, which shortly thereafter became the capital. Louisiana, first a royal colony, then a proprietary and then a corporate colony, again became a royal province in 1731.

In contrast to the English colonies, French Louisiana grew haltingly in the first half of the eighteenth century. Its population in 1732 was only 2,000 whites and about 3,800 slaves. The sweltering climate and mosquito-infested environment enticed few settlers. Poorly administered, dependent on imports for its sustenance, and expensive to defend, it continued throughout the century to be a financial liability to the French government. It never became the thriving trade center with the Spanish that its founders had envisioned.

"France in America had two heads," the historian Francis Parkman wrote, "one amid the snows of Canada, the other amid the canebrakes of Louisiana." The French thus had one enormous advantage: access to the great water routes that led to the heartland of the continent. In the Illinois region, scattered settlers began farming the fertile soil, and courageous priests established missions at places such as Terre Haute ("high land") and Des Moines ("some monks"). Because of geography as well as deliberate policy, however, French America remained largely a vast wilderness traversed by a mobile population of traders, trappers, missionaries—and, mainly, Indians. In 1750 when the English colonials numbered about 1.5 million, the total French population was no more than 80,000.

Yet in some ways the French had the edge on the British. They offered European goods to Indians in return for furs, encroached far less upon Indian lands, and so won allies against the English who came to possess the land. French governors could mobilize for action without any worry about quarreling assemblies or ethnic and religious diversity. The British may have had the greater population, but their separate colonies often worked at cross purposes. The middle colonies, for instance, protected by the Iroquois buffer, could afford to ignore the French threat—for a long time at least. Whenever conflict threatened, colonial assemblies seized the moment to extract new concessions from their governors. Colonial merchants, who built up a trade supplying foodstuffs to the French, persisted in smuggling supplies even in wartime.

THE COLONIAL WARS

French and British colonists clashed from the beginning of settlement. The Acadians fought with English settlers in Maine. Only a thin stretch of woods separated New England from Quebec and Montreal, and an English force briefly occupied Quebec from 1629 to 1632. Between New York and Quebec, Lake Champlain supplied an easy water route for invasion in either direction, but the Iroquois stood athwart the path. Farther south, the mountainous wilderness widened into an almost impenetrable buffer. On the northernmost flank, the isolated

A view of Quebec, the spires of its cathedrals and seminaries soaring high (1740s).

Hudson Bay Company offered British competition for the fur trade of the interior, and both countries laid claim to Newfoundland. On the southernmost flank, the British and French jockeyed for position in the Caribbean sugar islands.

But for most of the seventeenth century, the two continental empires developed in relative isolation from each other, and for most of that century the homelands remained at peace with each other. After the Restoration, Charles II and James II pursued a policy of friendship with the French king, Louis XIV. The Glorious Revolution of 1688, however, worked an abrupt reversal in English diplomacy. William III, the new king, as leader of the Dutch Republic had fought a running conflict against the ambitions of Louis XIV. His ascent to the throne brought England almost immediately into a Grand Alliance against Louis in the War of the League of Augsburg, sometimes called the War of the Palatinate and known in the colonies simply as King William's War (1689–1697).

This was the first of four great European and intercolonial wars over the next sixty-four years: the War of the Spanish Succession (Queen Anne's War, 1702–1713), the War of the Austrian Succession (King George's War, 1744–1748), and the Seven Years' War (the French and Indian War, which lasted nine years in America, 1754–1763). In all except the last, the battles in America were but a sideshow to greater battles in Europe, where British policy pivoted on keeping a balance of power against the French. The alliances shifted from one fight to the next, but Britain and France were pitted against each other every time.

Thus for much of the eighteenth century, the colonies were embroiled in wars and rumors of wars. The effect on much of the population was devastating. New England, especially Massachusetts, suffered probably more than the rest, for it was closest to the centers of French population. It is estimated that 900 Boston men (about 2.5 percent of the eligible males) died in the fighting. This meant that the city was faced with assisting a large population of widows and orphans. Even more important, these prolonged conflicts had profound consequences for Britain that later would reshape the contours of its relationship with America. The wars with France led the English government to incur an enormous debt, establish a huge navy and a standing army, and excite a militant sense of nationalism. During the early eighteenth century, these changes in British financial policy and political culture provoked critics in Parliament to charge that traditional liberties were being usurped by a tyrannical central government. After the French and Indian War, American colonists began making the same point.

KING WILLIAM'S WAR   In King William's War, scattered fighting occurred in the Hudson Bay posts, most of which fell to the French, and in Newfoundland, which also fell to a French force. The French aroused their Indian allies to join in raids along the northern frontier. In Massachusetts, Captain William Phips, who was about to become the first royal governor, organized an expedition of American militia that took Acadia. Various expeditions against French Canada failed to coalesce, and the war finally degenerated into a series of frontier raids. It ended ingloriously with the Treaty of Ryswick (1697), which returned the colonies to their prewar status.

QUEEN ANNE'S WAR   Fighting resumed only five years later. The War of the Spanish Succession was known to the colonists as Queen Anne's War. It saw the French and Spanish allied against the English. This time the Iroquois, tired of fighting the French, remained neutral.

An Iroquois warrior in an eighteenth-century French etching.

The brunt of the fighting occurred in New England, South Carolina, and Florida. Between 1706 and 1713, a sporadic border war raged between South Carolina and Spanish Florida, and the English with their Indian allies took the war nearly to St. Augustine.

South Carolina's Indian allies in fact constituted most of a force that responded to North Carolina's call for help in the Tuscarora War (1711–1713). The Tuscaroras, a numerous people who had long led a settled life in the Tidewater, suddenly found their lands invaded in 1709 by German and Swiss settlers. The war began when the Tuscaroras assaulted the new settlements. It ended when slave merchants of South Carolina mobilized their Indian allies, killed about 1,000 Tuscaroras and enslaved another 700. The survivors found refuge in the north, where they became the sixth nation of the Iroquois League.

In New England, the exposed frontier from Maine to Massachusetts suffered repeated raids during Queen Anne's War. In the winter of 1704, French and Indian forces sacked several Massachusetts villages. The settlers were either slaughtered or taken on desperate marches through the snow to captivity among the Indians or the French Canadians.

In the complex Peace of Utrecht (1713), Louis XIV recognized British title to the Hudson Bay, Newfoundland, Acadia (now Nova Scotia), and St. Christopher, as well as the British claim to sovereignty over the Iroquois. (Nobody consulted the Iroquois.) The French renounced any claim to special privileges in the commerce of Spanish or Portuguese America. Spain agreed not to transfer any of its American territory to a third party, and granted to the British the asiento, a contract for supplying Spanish America with 4,800 slaves annually over a period of thirty years. This opened the door for British smuggling, a practice that grew into a major cause of friction and, eventually, of renewed warfare.

In the South, the frontier flared up once more shortly after the war. The former Indian allies, outraged by the continuing advance of British settlement, attacked the Charleston colony. The Yamasee War of 1715 was the southern equivalent of King Philip's War in New England, a desperate struggle that threatened the colony's very existence. Once again, however, the Indians were unable to present a united front. The Cherokees remained neutral for the sake of their fur trade, and the defeated Yamasees retired into Florida, leaving open the country in which the new colony of Georgia appeared eighteen years later.

KING GEORGE'S WAR   The third great international war began in 1739 with a preliminary bout between England and Spain, called the War of Jenkins' Ear in honor of an English seaman who lost an ear to a Spanish soldier and exhibited the shriveled member as part of a campaign to arouse London against Spain's rudeness to smugglers.

The war began with a great British disaster, a grand expedition against Porto Bello in Panama, for which thousands of colonists volunteered and in which many died of yellow fever. One of the survivors, Lawrence Washington of Virginia, memorialized the event by naming his estate Mount Vernon after the ill-starred but popular English admiral in command. Along the southern frontier the new colony of Georgia, less than a decade old, now served its purpose as a military buffer. General James Oglethorpe staged a raid on St. Augustine and later fought off Spanish counterattacks.

In 1744 France entered the war, which merged with another general European conflict, the War of the Austrian Succession, or King George's War in the colonies. Once again border raids flared along the northern frontier. Governor William Shirley of Massachusetts mounted an expedition against French Canada and conquered Fort Louisbourg on Cape Breton after a long siege. It was a costly conquest, but the war ended in stalemate. In the Treaty of Aix-la-Chapelle (1748) the British exchanged Louisbourg for Madras, which the French had taken in India.

Thereafter, the focus of attention turned to the Ohio River Valley. French traders had moved westward to the Great Lakes and down the Mississippi, but the Ohio River, with short portages from Lake Erie to its headwaters, would make a shorter connecting link for French America. During the 1740s, however, fur traders from Virginia and Pennsylvania had also begun to exploit that disputed region. Not far behind were the Pennsylvania and Virginia land speculators. "The English," one French agent warned the Indians, "are much less anxious to take away your peltries than to become masters of your lands." Virginians had organized several land companies, most conspicuously the Ohio Company, to which the king granted 200,000 acres along the upper Ohio in 1749, with a promise of 300,000 more.

The French resolved to act before the British advance became a dagger pointed at the continental heartland. In 1749 French scouts proceeded down the Allegheny and Ohio Rivers to spy out the land, woo the Indians, and bury leaden plates with inscriptions stating the French claim. Engravings hardly made the soil French, but in 1753 a new governor, the Marquis Duquesne, arrived in Canada and set about making good on the claim with a chain of forts in the region.

THE FRENCH AND INDIAN WAR When news of these trespasses reached Williamsburg, the governor sent out an emissary to warn off

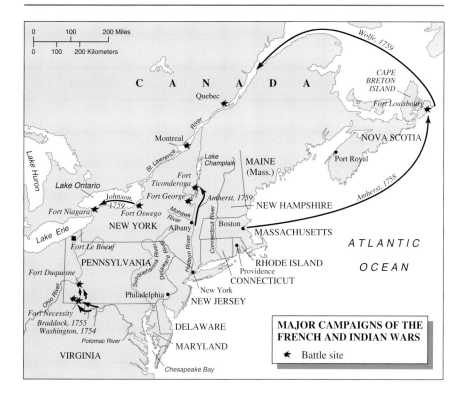

MAJOR CAMPAIGNS OF THE
FRENCH AND INDIAN WARS
★ Battle site

the French. An ambitious young adjutant-general of the Virginia militia, Major George Washington, whose older brothers owned a part of the Ohio Company, volunteered for the mission. With a few companions Washington made his way to Fort Le Boeuf and returned with a polite but firm French refusal. The Virginia governor then sent a small force to erect a fort at the strategic fork where the Allegheny and Mononga-hela Rivers meet to form the great Ohio. No sooner had the English started building than a larger French force appeared, ousted them, and proceeded to build Fort Duquesne (now Pittsburgh) on the same strategic site.

Meanwhile, Washington had been organizing a force of volunteers, and in the spring of 1754 he went out with an advance guard and a few Indian allies. Near Great Meadows in southwestern Pennsylvania they foolishly attacked a French detachment. It marked the first bloodshed of a long—and finally decisive—war that reached far beyond America. Washington retreated with his prisoners and hastily constructed a crude stockade, Fort Necessity, which soon fell under siege by a larger French force from Fort Duquesne. On July 4, 1754, Washington surrendered and was permitted to withdraw with his survivors. With that disaster in the backwoods a great world war had begun, but Washington came out of it with his reputation intact—and he was world famous at the age of twenty-two.

Back in London the Board of Trade already had taken notice of the growing conflict in the backwoods of North America and had called a meeting in Albany, New York, of commissioners from all the colonies as far south as Maryland to confer on precautions. The Albany Congress (June 19 to July 10, 1754), which was meeting when the first shots sounded at Great Meadows, ended with little accomplished. The delegates conferred with Iroquois chieftains and sent them away loaded with gifts in return for some halfhearted promises of support. The congress is remembered mainly for the Plan of Union worked out by a committee under Benjamin Franklin and adopted by unanimous vote of the commissioners. The plan called for a chief executive, a kind of supreme governor to be called the President-General of the United Colonies, appointed and supported by the crown, and a supreme assembly called the Grand Council, with forty-eight members chosen by the colonial assemblies. This federal body would oversee matters of defense, Indian

Benjamin Franklin's symbol of the need to unite the colonies against the French in 1754 would become popular again twenty years later, when the colonies faced a different threat.

relations, and trade and settlement in the West and would levy taxes to support its programs.

It must have been a good plan, Franklin reasoned, since the assemblies thought it gave too much power to the crown and the crown thought it gave too much to the colonies. At any rate the assemblies either rejected or ignored the plan. Only two substantive results came out of the congress. Its idea of a supreme commander for British forces in America was adopted, as was its advice that a New Yorker who was a friend of the Iroquois be made British superintendent of the northern Indians.

In London the government decided to force a showdown in America. In 1755 the British fleet captured Nova Scotia and expelled most of its French population. Some 5,000–7,000 Acadians who refused to take an oath of allegiance to the British crown were scattered through the colonies from Maine to Georgia. Impoverished and homeless, many of them desperately found their way to French Louisiana, where they became the Cajuns (a corruption of "Acadians") whose descendants still preserve elements of the French language along the remote bayous and in many urban centers.

The backwoods, however, became the scene of one British disaster after another over the next three years. In 1755 a new British commander-in-chief, the arrogant and naive General Edward Braddock, arrived in Virginia with two regiments of army regulars. With the addition of some colonial troops, including George Washington as a volunteer staff officer, Braddock hacked a road through the wilderness from the upper Potomac to the vicinity of Fort Duquesne, near present-day Pittsburgh. Hauling heavy artillery to surround the French fort, along with a wagon train of supplies, Braddock's 2,200 men achieved a great feat of military logistics and were on the verge of success when, seven miles from Fort Duquesne, the surrounding woods suddenly came alive with Indians and French soldiers in Indian costume. Beset on three sides by concealed enemies, the British forces panicked and retreated in disarray, abandoning most of their artillery and supplies. Braddock lost his life in the encounter, and his second in command directed the remaining British regulars to the safety of Philadelphia. The French victory demonstrated that backwoods warfare in North America depended on Indian allies and frontier tactics for success.

A WORLD WAR   For two years, war raged along the frontier without becoming the cause of war in Europe. In 1756, however, the colonial war merged with what became the Seven Years' War in Europe. There, Empress Maria Theresa of Austria, still brooding over the loss of territory in the previous conflict, worked a diplomatic revolution by bringing Austria's old enemy France, as well as Russia, into an alliance against Frederick the Great of Prussia. Britain, ever mindful of the European balance of power, now deserted Austria to ally with Frederick. The onset of war brought into office a new British government with the eloquent William Pitt as head of the ministry. Pitt's ability and assurance ("I know that I can save England and no one else can") instilled confidence at home and abroad.

British sea power soon began to cut off French reinforcements and supplies to the New World—and the trading goods with which they bought Indian allies. Pitt improved the British forces, gave command to young men of ability, and carried the battle to the enemy. In 1758 the tides began to turn when Fort Louisbourg fell in Canada. The Iroquois, sensing the turn of fortunes, pressed their dependents, the Delawares, to call off the frontier attacks on English settlements.

In 1759 the war reached its climax in a three-pronged offensive against the French in Canada, along what had become the classic invasion routes: via Niagara, Lake Champlain, and up the St. Lawrence Rivers. On the Niagara expedition the British were joined by a group of Iroquois, and they captured Fort Niagara, which virtually cut the French lifeline to the interior. On Lake Champlain, General Jeffrey Amherst took Fort George and Fort Ticonderoga, then paused to refortify and await reinforcements for an advance northward.

Meanwhile, the most decisive battle was shaping up at Quebec. There, British forces led by General James Wolfe waited out the advance of General Louis Joseph de Montcalm and his French infantry until they were within close range, then loosed a simultaneous volley followed by one more that devastated the French ranks—and ended French power in North America for all time. News of the British victory reached London along with similar reports from India, where English forces had reduced French outposts one by one and established the base for an expanding British control of India.

The war in North America dragged on until 1763, but the rest was a process of mopping up. In the South, where little significant action had occurred, belated hostility flared up between the settlers and the Cherokee nation. A force of British regulars and colonial militia broke

Cherokee resistance in 1761. In the North, just as peace was signed, a chieftain of the Ottawas, Pontiac, conspired to organize all the Indians of the frontier and launched a series of attacks that were not completely suppressed until the end of 1764, after the backwoods had been ablaze for ten years.

In 1760 King George II died, and his grandson ascended to the throne as George III. He resolved to seek peace and forced Pitt out of office. Pitt had wanted to declare war on Spain before the French could bring that other Bourbon monarchy into the conflict. He was forestalled, but Spain belatedly entered in 1761 and during the next year met the same fate as the French: in 1762 British forces took Manila in the Philippines and Havana in Cuba.

THE PEACE OF PARIS   The Peace of Paris of 1763 brought an end to the world war and to French power in North America. Britain took all French North American possessions east of the Mississippi River (except New Orleans) and all of Spanish Florida. The English invited the Spanish settlers to remain and practice their Catholic religion, but few accepted the offer. The Spanish king ordered them to evacuate the

With Quebec in the background, France kneels before a victorious Britain (1763).

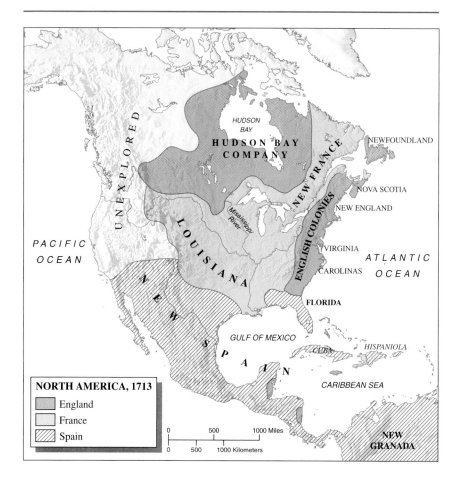

NORTH AMERICA, 1713

England

France

Spain

colony and provided free transportation to Spanish possessions in the Caribbean. Within a year most of the Spaniards sold their property at bargain prices to English speculators and began an exodus to Cuba and Mexico.

In compensation for the loss of Florida, Spain received Louisiana (New Orleans and all French land west of the Mississippi River) from France. Unlike the Spanish in Florida, however, few of the French settlers left Louisiana after 1763. The French government encouraged them to work with their new Spanish governors to create a bulwark against further English expansion. Spain would hold title to Louisiana for nearly four decades, but would never succeed in erasing its French roots. The French-born settlers always outnumbered the Spanish.

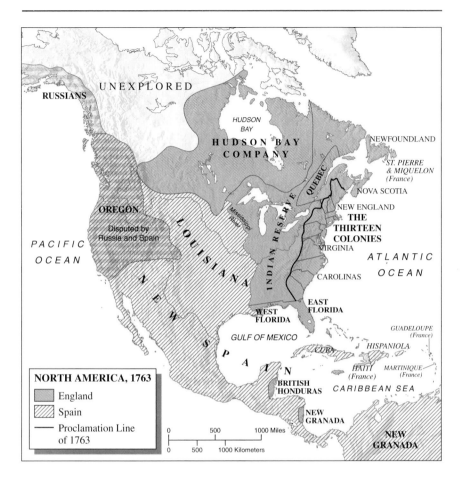

The loss of Louisiana left France with no territory on the continent of North America. In the West Indies, France gave up Tobago, Dominica, Grenada, and St. Vincent. British power reigned supreme over North America east of the Mississippi River.

But a fatal irony would pursue the British victory. In gaining Canada the British government put in motion a train of events that would end twenty years later with the loss of all the rest of British North America. Britain's success against France threatened the Indian tribes of the interior because they had long depended on playing off one European power against the other. Now, with the British dominant on the continent, American settlers were emboldened to encroach even farther into Indian lands. In addition, victory on the battlefields encouraged the British to tighten their imperial control over the American colonists and to demand more financial contributions from America for military defense. Meanwhile, France, humiliated in 1763, thirsted for revenge. In London, Benjamin Franklin, agent for the colony of Pennsylvania (1764–1775), found the French minister inordinately curious about America and suspected him of wanting to ignite the coals of controversy. Less than three years after Franklin left London, and only fifteen years after the conquest of New France, he would be in Paris arranging an alliance on behalf of Britain's rebellious colonists.

MAKING CONNECTIONS

· Although the British victory in the French and Indian War brought the colonies and England closer together in some ways, it was also an important factor in the approach of the American Revolution, as demonstrated in Chapter 5.

· One of the great struggles of the Revolution would be transforming the dependent British colonies described in this chapter into independent American states as described in Chapter 6.

FURTHER READING

The economics motivating colonial policies are covered in John J. McCusker and Russell R. Menard's *The Economy of British America, 1607–1789*, rev. ed. (1991). The problems of colonial customs administration are explored in Michael Kammen's *Empire and Interest: The American Colonies and the Politics of Mercantilism* (1970).

The Andros crisis and related topics are treated in Jack M. Sosin's *English America and the Revolution of 1688* (1982). Stephen S. Webb's *The Governors-General: The English Army and the Definition of the Empire, 1569–1681* (1979) argues that the crown was more concerned with military administration than with commercial regulation, and

Webb's *1676: The End of American Independence* (1984) shows how the Indian wars undermined the autonomy of colonial governments.

The early Indian wars are treated in Jill Lepore's *The Name of War: King Philip's War and the Origins of American Identity* (1998) and Francis Jennings's *The Invasion of America* (1975). See also Jennings's *The Ambiguous Iroquois Empire* (1984) and *Empire of Fortune: Crowns, Colonies, and Tribes in the Seven Years' War in America* (1988), and Richard Aquila's *The Iroquois Restoration: Iroquois Diplomacy on the Colonial Frontier, 1701–1754* (1983). Gregory Evans Dowd describes the unification efforts of Indians east of the Mississippi in A *Spirited Resistance: The North American Indian Struggle for Unity, 1745–1815* (1992).

A good introduction to the imperial phase of the colonial conflicts is Howard H. Peckham's *The Colonial Wars, 1689–1762* (1964). More analytical is Douglas Leach's *Arms for Empire: A Military History of the British Colonies in North America* (1973). Fred Anderson's *Crucible of War: The Seven Years' War and the Fate of Empire in British North America, 1754–1766* (2000) is the best history of the Seven Years' War.

5 ∽ FROM EMPIRE
TO INDEPENDENCE

CHAPTER ORGANIZER

This chapter focuses on:

- the changes in British colonial policy after 1763.

- how the Whig ideology shaped the colonial response to changes in British policy.

- the role of Revolutionary leaders, including Samuel Adams, John Dickinson, Thomas Paine, and Thomas Jefferson.

*S*eldom if ever since the days of Queen Elizabeth had England thrilled with such pride as in the closing years of the Great War for Empire. In 1760 young George III ascended to the throne. Three years later the Peace of Paris confirmed the possession of a great new British empire spanning the globe. Most important, the Peace of Paris effectively ended the French imperial domain in North America. This in turn influenced the future development of the vast region between the Appalachian Mountains and the Mississippi River and from the Gulf of Mexico to Hudson Bay. The maturing mainland colonies began to experience dynamic agricultural and commercial growth that enormously increased their importance to the British economy. Yet the North American colonies remained both extraordinarily diverse in composition and outlook and peculiarly averse to cooperative efforts. That they would manage to unify themselves and declare independence in 1775 was indeed surprising—even to them.

THE HERITAGE OF WAR

In 1763 the colonists shared in the patriotic zeal generated by the great victory over the French. But the moment of euphoria masked festering resentments and new problems that were the heritage of the war. Underneath the pride in the British Empire, an American nationalism was maturing. Colonials were beginning to think and speak of themselves more as Americans than as English or British. With the French out of the way and a vast new land to exploit, they could look to the future with confidence.

Many Americans had a new sense of importance after fighting a vast world war with such success. Some harbored resentment, justified or not, at the haughty air of British soldiers, and many in the early stages of the war had lost their awe of British troops, who were so inept at frontier fighting. Recent studies of the Seven Years' War reveal that many Americans became convinced as well of their moral superiority to their British allies. Ninety percent of the New England provincial soldiers were probably volunteers, and most of them were sons of prosperous and pious farm families. The proportion of volunteers was lower in New York and much lower in Virginia until pay rates and bounties were raised in a successful effort to boost recruitment.

At least one-third of military-age New England males fought in the Seven Years' War. For them, army life was both a revelation and an opportunity. From their isolated farms they converged to form huge army camps—hives of thousands of strangers living in overcrowded and disease-infested conditions. Although they admired the courage and discipline of British redcoats under fire, many New Englanders abhorred the carefree cursing, whoring, and Sabbath breaking they observed among British troops. But most upsetting were the daily "shrieks and cries" resulting from the brutal punishments imposed by the British leaders on their wayward men. Minor offenses might earn hundreds of lashes, and a thousand was the standard punishment for desertion. One American soldier recorded in his diary in 1759 that "there was a man whipped to death belonging to the Light Infantry. They say he had twenty-five lashes after he was dead." The brutalities of British army life thus heightened the New Englanders' sense of their separate identity and of their greater worthiness to be God's chosen people. It also emboldened Americans to defy British rule because the colonists no longer needed protection from the French.

British forces nevertheless had borne the brunt of the war and had won it for the American colonists, who had supplied men and materials, sometimes reluctantly, and who persisted in trading with the enemy. Molasses in the French West Indies, for instance, continued to draw New England ships like flies. The trade was too important for the colonists to give up, but was more than British authorities could tolerate. Along with naval patrols, one important means of disrupting this illegal trade was the use of "writs of assistance," general search warrants that allowed officers to enter any place during daylight hours to seek evidence of illegal trade.

In 1760 Boston merchants hired attorney James Otis to fight the writs in the courts. He lost, but in the process advanced the provocative argument that any act of Parliament that authorized such "instruments of slavery" violated the British constitution and was therefore void. This was a radical idea for its time. Otis sought to overturn a major tenet of the English legal system, namely that acts of Parliament were by their very nature constitutional.

The peace that secured an empire in 1763 also laid upon the British government a burden of new problems. How should the British manage the defense and governance of their new global possessions? What should they do about the American lands inhabited by Indians but coveted by whites? How was the British government to pay for an unprecedented debt built up during the war and bear the new expenses of expanded colonial administration and defense? And—the thorniest problem of all, as it turned out—what role should the colonies play in all this? The problems were of a magnitude and complexity to challenge men of the greatest statemanship and vision, but those qualities were rare among the ministers of George III.

BRITISH POLITICS

In British politics during the late eighteenth century, nearly everybody was a Whig, even King George. Whig had been the name given to those who opposed James II, led the Glorious Revolution of 1688, and secured the Protestant Hanoverian succession in 1714. The Whigs were the champions of individual liberty and parliamentary supremacy, but with the passage of time Whiggism had drifted into complacency. The dominant group of landholding Whig families was concerned mostly with the pursuit of personal gain and with local questions rather than great issues of statecraft. In the absence of party organization, parliamentary politics hinged on factions bound together by personal loyalties, family connections, and local interests, and on the pursuit of royal patronage.

In the administration of government, an inner "cabinet" of the king's ministers had been supplanting the unwieldy Privy Council as the center of power since the Hanoverian succession. The kings still had the prerogative of naming their ministers. They used it to form coalitions of men who controlled enough factions in the House of Commons to command majorities for the government's measures, though the king's ministers were still technically responsible to the king rather than to parliamentary majorities.

Throughout the 1760s, the king turned first to one and then to another leader, ministries came and went, and

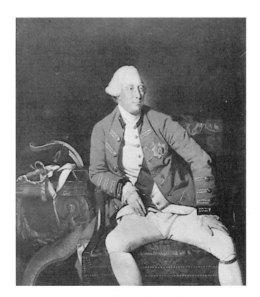

George III, at age thirty-three, the young king of a victorious empire.

the government fell into instability just as the new problems of empire required creative solutions. Ministries rose and fell because somebody offended the king or because somebody's friend failed to get a job. Colonial policy remained marginal to the chief concerns of British politics. The result was inconsistency and vacillation followed by stubborn inflexibility.

WESTERN LANDS

No sooner was peace arranged in 1763 than the problem of the western lands became a governmental crisis. The Indians of the Ohio region, skeptical that their French friends were helpless and fully expecting the reentry of English settlers, grew receptive to the warnings of Pontiac, chief of the Ottawas. In 1763 Pontiac's effort to seize Fort Detroit was betrayed and failed, but the western tribes joined his campaign to reopen frontier warfare. Within a few months, Indians had wiped out every British post in the Ohio region except Fort Detroit and Fort Pitt. A relief force lifted the siege of Fort Pitt, and Pontiac abandoned the attack on Fort Detroit, but the outlying settlements suffered heavy losses before British forces could stop the attacks. Pontiac himself did not agree to peace until 1766.

THE PROCLAMATION OF 1763 To keep the peace on the frontier and to keep earlier promises to the Delawares and Shawnees, the ministers in London postponed further settlement. The immediate need was to stop Pontiac's warriors and reassure the Indians. There were influential fur traders, moreover, who preferred to keep the wilderness as a game preserve. The pressure for expansion into Indian-held territory might ultimately prove irresistible—British and American speculators were already dazzled by the prospects—but there would be no harm in a pause while things settled down and a new policy evolved. The king's ministers therefore brought forward, and the king signed, the Royal Proclamation of 1763. The order drew a Proclamation Line along the crest of the Appalachians beyond which settlers were forbidden to go and colonial governors were forbidden to authorize surveys or issue land grants. It also established the new British colonies of Quebec and East and West Florida, the last two consisting mainly of small settlements at St. Augustine and St. Marks, respectively.

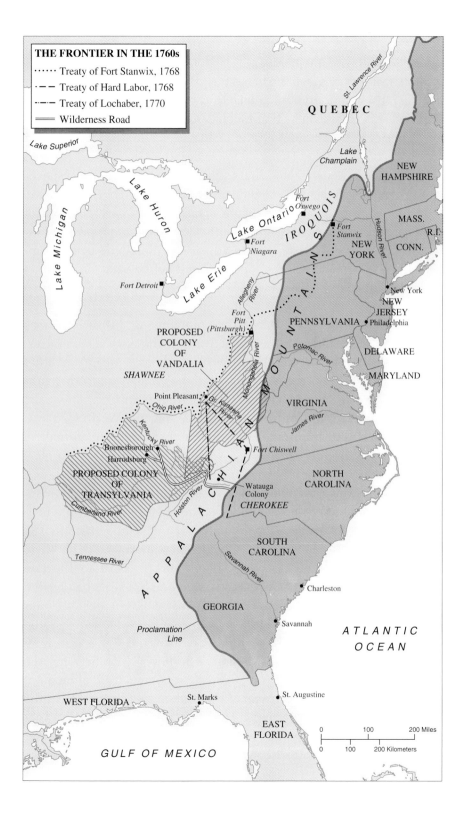

THE FRONTIER IN THE 1760s
······ Treaty of Fort Stanwix, 1768
·—· Treaty of Hard Labor, 1768
·—·— Treaty of Lochaber, 1770
=== Wilderness Road

Lake Superior

QUEBEC

St. Lawrence River

Lake Champlain

NEW HAMPSHIRE

Lake Huron

Lake Michigan

Fort Oswego

IROQUOIS

MASS.

Lake Ontario

Fort Stanwix

R.I.

Fort Niagara

NEW YORK

CONN.

Hudson River

Lake Erie

Fort Detroit

Allegheny River

New York

NEW JERSEY

Fort Pitt (Pittsburgh)

PENNSYLVANIA

Philadelphia

PROPOSED COLONY OF VANDALIA

Monongahela River

Potomac River

DELAWARE

SHAWNEE

MARYLAND

Point Pleasant

Ohio River

Gr. Kanawha River

VIRGINIA

James River

Kentucky River

Boonesborough

Harrodsburg

Fort Chiswell

PROPOSED COLONY OF TRANSYLVANIA

Holston River

Watauga Colony

NORTH CAROLINA

Cumberland River

CHEROKEE

Tennessee River

SOUTH CAROLINA

Savannah River

APPALACHIAN MOUNTAINS

Charleston

GEORGIA

Savannah

ATLANTIC OCEAN

Proclamation Line

WEST FLORIDA

St. Marks

St. Augustine

EAST FLORIDA

GULF OF MEXICO

0   100   200 Miles
0   100   200 Kilometers

The line did not remain intact for long. In 1768 the chief royal agents for Indian affairs negotiated two treaties (Fort Stanwix and Hard Labor) by which the Iroquois and Cherokees gave up their claims to lands in the Ohio region—a strip in western New York, a large area of southwestern Pennsylvania, and between the Ohio and Tennessee Rivers farther south. In 1770, by the Treaty of Lochaber, the Cherokees agreed to move the line below the Ohio River still farther westward. Land speculators, including Benjamin Franklin and a number of British investors, soon formed a syndicate and sought a vast domain covering most of present West Virginia and eastern Kentucky, where they proposed to establish the colony of Vandalia. The British Board of Trade lent its support, but the formalities were not completed before Vandalia vanished in the revolutionary crisis.

SETTLERS PUSH WEST   Defying the prohibitions against intrusions into Indian lands, hardy settlers pushed on over the Appalachian ridges; by 1770 the town of Pittsburgh had twenty log houses. In 1769 another colony was settled on the Watauga River by immigrants from southwestern Virginia, soon joined by settlers from North Carolina. The Watauga colony turned out to be within the limits of North Carolina, but so far removed from other settlements that it became virtually a separate republic under the Watauga Compact of 1772; North Carolina took it into the new district of Washington in 1776.

Another opening developed south of the Ohio River into the "dark and bloody" ground of Kentucky, which had been something of a neutral hunting preserve shared by the northern and southern tribes. The Shawnees, who lived north of the Ohio River, still claimed rights there despite the Iroquois and Cherokee concessions. In 1774 conflicts on the northwestern frontier of Virginia erupted into full-scale battles that forced the Shawnees to surrender their claims.

Judge Richard Henderson of North Carolina formed a plan to settle the area. He organized the Transylvania Company in 1774, and in 1775 bought from the Cherokees a dubious title to the land between the Kentucky and Cumberland Rivers. Next he sent out a band of men under the most famous frontiersman of them all, Daniel Boone, to cut the Wilderness Road from the upper Holston River via the Cumberland Gap in southwestern Virginia on up to the Kentucky River. Along this road settlers moved up to Boonesborough, and Henderson set about organizing a government for his colony of Transylvania. But his claim was weak. Transylvania sent a delegation to the Continental Congress, which refused to receive it, and in 1776 Virginia responded to a petition from the Harrodsburg settlers and organized much of present Kentucky into a county of Virginia.

GRENVILLE AND THE STAMP ACT

GRENVILLE'S COLONIAL POLICY   Just as the Proclamation of 1763 was being drafted, a new British ministry had begun to grapple with the problems of imperial finances. The new first minister and first lord of the Treasury, George Grenville, was much like the king: industrious, honest, and hardheaded. Grenville took for granted the need for redcoats to defend the American frontier, although the colonies had been left mostly to their own devices before 1754. He also wanted to keep a large army (10,000 men) in America to avoid a rapid demobilization that would retire a large number of influential officers and thereby provoke political criticism at home. But he faced sharply rising costs for American frontier defense, on top of an already staggering government debt. During the mid-1760s, the interest payments on the government's debts consumed 60 percent of the annual budgets.

Because there was a large tax burden at home and a much lighter one in the colonies, Grenville reasoned that the prosperous Americans should share the cost of their own defense. He also learned that the royal customs service in America was grossly inefficient. Evasion and corruption were rampant. Grenville issued stern orders to colonial officials to tighten enforcement and ordered the British navy to patrol the coasts for smugglers. In Parliament he secured an Act for the Encouragement of Officers Making Seizures (1763), which set up a new maritime or vice-admiralty court in Halifax (replacing the ineffectual admiralty courts established in 1696) with jurisdiction over all the colonies, a court that had both original and appellate jurisdiction, but had no juries of colonists sympathetic to smugglers. The period of "salutary neglect" in the enforcement of the Navigation Acts was coming to an end, causing great annoyance to American shippers.

The Great Financier, or British Economy for the Years
1763, 1764, 1765. *A cartoon critical of Grenville's tax
policies. America, depicted as an Indian
(at left), groans under the burden of new taxes.*

Strict enforcement of the old Molasses Act of 1733 posed a serious
threat to New England's mercantile prosperity, which in turn created
markets for British goods. The tax on molasses had been set prohibi-
tively high, not for purposes of revenue but to prevent trade with the
French sugar islands. Yet the rum distilleries consumed more molasses
than the British West Indies provided, and as the governor of Massachusetts wrote to the king: "Even illegal trade, where the balance is in
favor of British subjects, makes its final return to Great Britain."
Grenville recognized that the molasses tax, if enforced, would be
ruinous to a major colonial enterprise. So he put through a new Revenue
Act of 1764, commonly known as the Sugar Act, which cut the duty in
half. This, he believed, would reduce the temptation to smuggle or to
bribe the customs officers. In addition the Sugar Act levied new duties
on imports of foreign textiles, wines, coffee, indigo, and sugar. The act,
Grenville estimated, would help defray "the necessary expenses of defending, protecting, and securing, the said colonies and plantations."
For the first time, Parliament had adopted duties (taxes on imports or

exports) frankly designed to raise revenues in the colonies and not merely intended to regulate trade.

Another of Grenville's new regulatory measures had an important impact on the colonies: the Currency Act of 1764. The colonies faced a chronic shortage of money, which kept going out to pay debts in England. To meet the shortage, they issued their own paper money. British creditors, however, feared payment in such a depreciated currency. To alleviate their fears, Grenville prohibited the colonies from printing money. The result was a decline in the value of existing paper money, since nobody was obligated to accept it in payment of debts, even in the colonies. The deflationary impact of the Currency Act, combined with new duties on commodities and stricter enforcement, jolted a colonial economy already suffering a postwar decline.

THE STAMP ACT But Grenville's plan to make Americans pay for British military and commercial expenses remained incomplete: the Sugar Act would defray only a fraction of the cost of maintaining the 10,000 soldiers stationed along the western frontier. He had in mind still another measure to raise money in America, a stamp tax. On February 13, 1765, Parliament created revenue stamps and required that they be purchased and fixed to printed matter and legal documents of all kinds: newspapers, pamphlets, broadsides, almanacs, bonds, leases, deeds, licenses, insurance policies, ship clearances, college diplomas, even dice and playing cards. The requirement would go into effect on November 1, 1765.

That same year Grenville completed his new system of colonial regulations when he put through the Quartering Act. In effect it was yet another tax. The Quartering Act required the colonies to supply British troops with provisions and to provide them with barracks or submit to their use of inns and vacant buildings. It applied to all colonies, but affected mainly New York, headquarters of the British forces.

THE IDEOLOGICAL RESPONSE The cumulative effect of Grenville's measures raised colonial suspicions to a fever. Unwittingly, this plodding minister of a plodding king stirred up a storm of protest and set in motion a profound exploration of English traditions and imperial relations. The radical ideas of the minority "Real Whigs" slowly began to take hold in the colonies. These ideas derived from various sources but above all from John Locke's justification of the Glorious Revolution, his *Two Treatises on Government* (1690). Locke and other "Real Whigs" viewed English history as a struggle by Parliament to preserve life, liberty, and property against royal tyranny.

In 1764 and 1765 the colonists felt that Grenville and Parliament had loosed upon them the very engines of tyranny from which Parliament had rescued England in the seventeenth century. A standing army was the historic ally of despots, and now with the French gone and Pontiac subdued, thousands of British soldiers remained in the colonies. For what purpose—to protect the colonists or to subdue them? It was beginning to seem clear that it was the latter. Among the fundamental rights of English people were trial by jury and the presumption of innocence, but the new vice-admiralty courts excluded juries and put the burden of proof on the defendant. Most important, English citizens had the right to be taxed only by their elected representatives. Parliament claimed that privilege in England, and the colonial assemblies had long exercised it as their most cherished principle in America. Now Parliament was usurping the assemblies' power of the purse strings. This could only lead to tyranny and enslavement.

THE QUESTION OF REPRESENTATION   In a flood of colonial pamphlets, speeches, and resolutions, critics of the Stamp Act repeated a slogan familiar to all Americans: "no taxation without representation," a cry that had been raised years before in response to the Molasses Act of 1733. In 1764 James Otis, now a popular leader in the Massachusetts assembly, set forth the basic argument in a pamphlet, *The Rights of the British Colonists Asserted and Proved.* Grenville had one of his subordinates prepare an answer, which developed the ingenious theory of "virtual representation." If the colonies had no vote in Parliament, his reasoning went, neither did most Englishmen who lived in boroughs that had developed since the last apportionment. Large cities had grown up that had no right to elect a member, while old boroughs with little or no population still returned members. Nevertheless, each member of Parliament represented the interests of the whole country and indeed the whole empire. Charleston, South Carolina, for instance, had fully as much representation as Manchester, England.

Many colonial critics considered "virtual representation" nonsense, justified neither by logic nor by their own experience. In America, to be sure, the apportionment of assemblies failed to keep pace with the westward movement of population, but it was based more nearly on population and—in contrast to British practice—each member was expected to live in the district he represented. In a pamphlet widely circulated during 1765, Daniel Dulany, a young lawyer of Maryland, suggested that even if the theory had any validity for England, where the interests of electors might be closely tied to those of nonelectors, it had none for colonists 3,000 miles away, whose interests differed and whose distance made it impossible for them to influence members of Parliament.

PROTEST IN THE COLONIES   The Stamp Act became the chief target of colonial protest against British greed and arrogance. Unlike the Sugar Act, which affected mainly New England, the Stamp Act burdened all colonists who did any kind of business. And it affected most of all the articulate elements in the community: merchants, planters, lawyers, printer-editors—all strategically placed to influence public opinion.

Through the spring and summer of 1765, colonial resentment boiled over in mass meetings, parades, bonfires, and other demonstrations. The protesters included farmers, artisans, laborers, businessmen, dock workers, and seamen alarmed at the disruption of business. Lawyers, editors, and merchants took the lead or lent support. The militants began to call themselves Sons of Liberty. They met underneath "Liberty Trees"—in Boston a great elm on Hanover Square, in Charleston a live oak.

One day in mid-August, 1765, nearly three months before the effective date of the Stamp Act, an effigy of Boston's stamp agent swung from the Liberty Tree. In the evening a mob carried it through the streets, destroyed the stamp office, and used the wood to burn the effigy. Somewhat later another mob sacked the homes of Lieutenant-Governor Thomas Hutchinson and the local customs officer. Thoroughly shaken, the Boston stamp agent resigned his commission, and stamp agents throughout the colonies were hounded out of office. Loyalists, those colonists supportive of British policies, deplored such riotous violence, arguing that the American rebels were behaving more tyrannically than the British.

By November 1, its effective date, the Stamp Act was a dead letter. Business went on without the stamps. Newspapers appeared with a skull and crossbones in the corner where the stamp belonged. After

In protest of the Stamp Act, which was to take effect the next day, the Pennsylvania Journal *appeared with the skull and crossbones on its masthead.*

passage of the Sugar Act, a movement had begun to boycott British goods rather than pay the import duties. Now colonists adopted nonimportation agreements to exert pressure on British merchants. Americans knew that they had become a major market for British products. By shutting off imports, they could exercise real leverage. Homegrown sage and sassafras took the place of British tea. Homespun garments became the fashion as symbols of colonial defiance. In this regard, the nonimportation movement offered opportunities for women to participate in political agitation.

The widespread protests encouraged colonial unity, as Americans discovered that they had more in common with each other than with London. The Virginia House of Burgesses struck the first blow against the Stamp Act in the Virginia Resolves, a series of resolutions inspired by young Patrick Henry. Virginians, the burgesses declared, were entitled to the rights of Englishmen, and Englishmen could be taxed only by their own representatives. Virginians, moreover, had always been governed by laws passed with their own consent. Newspapers spread the resolutions throughout the colonies, along with even more radical statements that were kept out of the final version of the Resolves and other assemblies hastened to copy Virginia's example.

In 1765, the Massachusetts House of Representatives issued a circular letter inviting the various assemblies to send delegates to confer in New York on appeals for relief from the king and Parliament. Nine responded, and from October 7 to 25, 1765, the Stamp Act Congress of twenty-seven delegates issued expressions of colonial sentiment: a Declaration of the Rights and Grievances of the Colonies, a petition to the king for relief, and a petition to Parliament for repeal of the Stamp Act. The delegates acknowledged that the colonies owed a "due subordination" to Parliament and recognized its right to regulate colonial trade, but they questioned Parliament's right to levy taxes, which were a free gift granted by the people through their representatives. Grenville responded by denouncing the colonists as "ungrateful."

REPEAL OF THE ACT   The storm had scarcely broken before Grenville's ministry was out of office, dismissed not because of the colonial turmoil but because he had fallen out with the king over the appointment of government officials. The king installed a new minister, the marquis of Rockingham, leader of the "Rockingham Whigs," the "Old Whig" faction, which included people who sympathized with the colonists' views. Pressure from British merchants who feared the economic consequences of the nonimportation movement bolstered Rockingham's resolve to repeal the Stamp Act, but he needed to move carefully in order to win a majority. Simple repeal was politically impossible without some affirmation of parliamentary authority. When Parliament assembled early in the year, William Pitt demanded that the Stamp Act be repealed "absolutely, totally, and immediately," but urged that Britain's authority over the colonies "be asserted in as strong terms as possible," except on the point of taxation.

In 1766 Parliament repealed the Stamp Tax, but at the same time passed the Declaratory Act, which asserted the full power of Parliament to make laws binding the colonies "in all cases whatsoever." It was a cunning evasion that made no concession with regard to taxes, but made no mention of them either. It reinforced a distinction between "external" taxes on trade and "internal" taxes within the colonies, a distinction that would have fateful consequences for the future. For the moment, however, the Declaratory Act was a face-saving gesture. Amid the rejoicing and relief on both sides of the Atlantic there were no omens that the quarrel would be reopened within a year. To be sure, the Sugar Act

The Repeal, or the Funeral Procession of Miss America-Stamp *(1766)*. *Grenville carries the dead Stamp Act in its coffin. In the background, trade with America starts up again.*

remained on the books, but Rockingham reduced the molasses tax from threepence to a penny a gallon.

FANNING THE FLAMES

Meanwhile, the king continued to play musical chairs with his ministers. Rockingham fell because he lost the confidence of the king. William Pitt then formed a ministry that included the major factions of Parliament. The ill-matched combination would have been hard to manage even if Pitt had remained in charge, but the old warlord began to slip over the fine line between genius and madness. For a time in 1767 the guiding force in the ministry was the witty and reckless Charles Townshend, chancellor of the Exchequer (Treasury), whose "abilities were superior to those of all men," according to Horace Walpole, "and his judgement below that of any man." The erratic Townshend took advantage of Pitt's mental confusion to re-open the question of colonial taxation. He asserted that "external" taxes were tolerable to the colonies—not that he believed it for a moment.

THE TOWNSHEND ACTS   In 1767 Townshend put his plan through the House of Commons, and a few months later he died, leaving behind a bitter legacy: the Townshend Acts. First, he sought to bring the New York assembly to its senses. That body had defied the Quartering Act and refused to provide beds or supplies for the king's troops. Parliament, at Townshend's behest, suspended all acts of the colonial assembly until it yielded. New York protested but finally caved in, inadvertently confirming the British suspicion that too much indulgence had encouraged colonial bad manners. Townshend followed up with the Revenue Act of 1767, which levied duties ("external taxes") on colonial imports of glass, lead, paint, paper, and tea. Third, he set up a Board of Customs Commissioners at Boston, the colonial headquarters of smuggling. Finally, he reorganized the vice-admiralty courts, providing four in the continental colonies—at Halifax, Boston, Philadelphia, and Charleston.

The Townshend duties did increase government revenues, but the intangible costs were greater. The duties taxed goods exported from England, indirectly hurting British manufacturers, and had to be collected in colonial ports, increasing collection costs. But the higher cost was a new drift into ever-greater conflict. The Revenue Act of 1767 posed a more severe threat to colonial assemblies than Grenville's taxes, for Townshend proposed to apply these revenues to pay governors and other officers and thereby release them from financial dependence on the colonial assemblies.

DICKINSON'S *LETTERS*   The Townshend Acts surprised the colonists, but this time the storm gathered more slowly than it had two years before. Once again citizens resolved to resist, to boycott British goods, to develop their own manufactures. Once again the colonial press spewed out expressions of protest, most notably the essays of John Dickinson, a Philadelphia lawyer who hoped to resolve the dispute by persuasion. Late in 1767 his twelve "Letters of a Pennsylvania Farmer" (as he chose to style himself) began to appear in the *Pennsylvania Chronicle,* from which they were copied in other papers and in pamphlet form. His argument repeated with greater detail and more elegance what the Stamp Act Congress had already said. The colonists held that Parliament might regulate commerce and collect duties incidental to that purpose, but it had no right to levy taxes for *revenue,* whether they were internal or external. Dickinson used the language of moderation throughout. "The cause of Liberty is a cause of too much dignity to be sullied by turbulence and tumult," he argued. The colonial complaints should "speak at the same time the language of affliction and veneration."

SAMUEL ADAMS AND THE SONS OF LIBERTY   But the affliction grew and the veneration waned. British ministers could neither conciliate moderates like Dickinson nor cope with firebrands such as Samuel Adams of Boston, who was now emerging as the supreme genius of revolutionary agitation. Born in 1722, Adams graduated from Harvard and soon thereafter inherited the family brewery, which he quickly ran into bankruptcy. The lure of monetary gain never intoxicated him. His distant cousin John Adams described Sam as a "plain, simple, decent citizen, of middling stature, dress, and manners," who prided himself on his frugality and his distaste for ceremony and display. Politics, not profit, was his abiding passion, and he spent most of his time debating political issues with sailors, roustabouts, and stevedores at local taverns. Adams insisted that Parliament had no right to legislate at all for the colonies, that Massachusetts must return to the spirit of its Puritan founders and defend itself from a new conspiracy against its liberties.

While other men tended their private affairs, Sam Adams was whipping up the Sons of Liberty and organizing protests in the Boston town meeting and the provincial assembly. Early in 1768 he and James Otis formulated a Massachusetts circular letter, which the assembly dispatched to the other colonies. The letter restated the illegality of parliamentary taxation and invited the support of other colonies. In London the earl of Hillsborough, just appointed to the new office of secretary of state for the colonies, only made matters worse. He ordered the Massachusetts assembly to withdraw the Adams-Otis letter. The assembly refused and was dissolved.

Samuel Adams, an organizer of the Sons of Liberty.

In 1769 the Virginia assembly passed a new set of resolves reasserting its exclusive right to tax Virginians and calling upon the colonies to unite in the cause. Virginia's royal governor promptly dissolved the assembly, but the members met independently, dubbed themselves a "convention" after Boston's example, and adopted a new set of nonimportation agreements.

In London, events across the Atlantic still provoked only marginal interest. The king's long effort to reorder British politics to his liking was coming to fulfillment, and that was the big news. In 1769 new elections for Parliament finally produced a majority of the "King's Friends." And George III found a minister to his taste in Frederick, Lord North, the chancellor of the Exchequer who had replaced Townshend. In 1770 the king installed a cabinet of the King's Friends, with North as first minister. North, who venerated the traditions of Parliament, was no stooge for the king, but the two worked in harmony.

THE BOSTON MASSACRE   The impact of colonial boycotts on English commerce had persuaded Lord North to modify the Townshend Acts, just in time to halt a perilous escalation of conflict. The presence of British soldiers in Boston had been a constant provocation. Crowds heckled and ridiculed the red-coated soldiers.

On March 5, 1770, in the square before the customs house, a group of rowdies began taunting and snowballing the British sentry on duty. His call for help brought reinforcements. Then somebody rang the town firebell, drawing a larger crowd to the scene. At their head, or so the story goes, was Crispus Attucks, a runaway mulatto slave who had worked for some years on ships out of Boston. Finally a soldier was knocked down, rose to his feet, and fired into the crowd. When the smoke cleared, five people lay on the ground dead or dying, and eight more were wounded. The cause of colonial resistance now had its first martyrs, and the first to die was Crispus Attucks. Those involved in the shooting were indicted for murder, but they were defended by John Adams, Sam's cousin, who thought they were the victims of circumstance, provoked, he said, by a "motley rabble of saucy boys, negroes and mulattoes, Irish teagues and outlandish Jack tars." All of the British soldiers were acquitted except two, who were convicted of manslaughter and branded on their thumbs.

Paul Revere's partisan engraving of the Boston Massacre.

The so-called Boston Massacre sent shock waves throughout the colonies—and in London. Late in April 1770 Parliament repealed all the Townshend duties save one. The cabinet, by a fateful vote of five to four, had advised keeping the tea tax as a token of parliamentary authority. Colonial diehards insisted that pressure should be kept on British merchants until Parliament gave in altogether, but the nonimportation movement soon faded. Parliament, after all, had given up the substance of the taxes, with one exception, and much of the colonists' tea was smuggled in from Holland anyway.

For two years thereafter, colonial discontent simmered down. The Stamp Act was gone, as were all the Townshend duties except that on tea. But most of the Grenville-Townshend innovations remained in effect: the Sugar Act, the Currency Act, the Quartering Act, the vice-admiralty courts, the Board of Customs Commissioners. The redcoats had left Boston, but they remained nearby, and the British navy still patrolled the coast. Each remained a source of irritation and the cause of occasional incidents. There was still tinder awaiting a spark, and the most rebellious among the colonists promoted continuing conflicts. As

Sam Adams stressed, "Where there is a spark of patriotick fire, we will enkindle it."

DISCONTENT ON THE FRONTIER

Many American colonists had no interest in the disputes over British regulatory policy raging along the seaboard. Parts of the back-country stirred with quarrels that had nothing to do with the Stamp and Townshend Acts. Rival land claims to the east of Lake Champlain pitted New York against New Hampshire, and the Green Mountain Boys led by Ethan Allen against both. Eventually the denizens of the area would set up shop on their own as the state of Vermont, created in 1777 although not recognized as a member of the Union until 1791. In Pennsylvania sporadic quarrels broke out with land claimants who held grants from Virginia and Connecticut, whose boundaries under their charters overlapped those granted to William Penn, or so they claimed.

A more dangerous division in Pennsylvania arose when a group of frontier ruffians took the law into their own hands. Outraged at the lack of frontier protection during Pontiac's rebellion because of pacifist Quaker influence in the Pennsylvania assembly, a group from Paxton, near Harrisburg, called the "Paxton Boys" took revenge by massacring peaceful Conestoga Indians in Lancaster County; then they threatened the so-called Moravian Indians, a group of Christian converts near Bethlehem. When the Indians took refuge in Philadelphia, some 1,500 angry Paxton Boys marched on the capital, where Benjamin Franklin talked the vengeful frontiersmen into returning home by enabling them to present their demands to the governor and the general assembly.

Farther south, frontier folk of South Carolina had similar complaints about the lack of protection against horse thieves, cattle rustlers, and Indians. Backcountry residents organized societies called "Regulators" to administer vigilante justice in the region and refused to pay taxes until they gained effective government. In 1769 the assembly finally set up six new circuit courts in the region, but still did not respond to the backcountry's demand for representation in the legislature.

In North Carolina the protest was less over the lack of government than over the abuses and extortion inflicted by appointees from the eastern part of the colony. Farmers felt especially oppressed at the refusal either to issue paper money or to accept produce in payment of taxes, and in 1766 they organized to resist. Efforts of these Regulators to stop seizures of property and other court proceedings led to more disorders and an enactment of a bill that made the rioters guilty of treason. In the spring of 1771 Governor William Tryon led 1,200 militiamen into the Piedmont center of Regulator activity. There he met and defeated some 2,000 ill-organized Regulators in the Battle of Alamance, in which eight were killed on each side. Tryon's men then ranged through the backcountry, forcing some 6,500 Piedmont settlers to sign an oath of allegiance.

These internal disputes and revolts within the colonies illustrate the fractious diversity of opinion and outlook evident among Americans on the eve of the Revolution. Colonists were of many minds about many things, including British rule. The disputatious frontier in colonial America also helped convince British authorities that the colonies were inherently unstable and that they required firmer oversight, even to the extent of using military force to ensure civil stability.

A WORSENING CRISIS

Two events in 1772 further eroded the colonies' fragile relationship with the mother country. Near Providence, Rhode Island, a British schooner, the *Gaspee,* patrolling for smugglers, accidentally ran aground. A crowd from the town boarded the ship, removed the crew, and set fire to the vessel. A commission of inquiry was formed with authority to hold suspects, but no witnesses could be found. Four days after the burning, on June 13, 1772, Governor Thomas Hutchinson told the Massachusetts assembly that his salary thenceforth would come out of the customs revenues. Soon thereafter word came that judges of the Superior Court would be paid from the same source and no longer be dependent on the assembly for their income. The assembly expressed a fear that this portended "a despotic administration of government."

The existence of the *Gaspee* investigative commission, which bypassed the courts of Rhode Island, and the independent salaries for royal officials in Massachusetts, suggested to the residents of other colonies that the same might be in store for them. The discussion of colonial rights and parliamentary encroachments regained momentum.

Ever the agitator, Sam Adams convinced the Boston town meeting to form a Committee of Correspondence, which issued a statement of rights and grievances and invited other towns to do the same. Committees of Correspondence sprang up across Massachusetts and spread into other colonies. In 1773 the Virginia assembly proposed the formation of such committees on an intercolonial basis, and a network of the committees spread across the colonies, mobilizing public opinion and keeping colonial resentments at a simmer. In unwitting tribute to their effectiveness, a Massachusetts Loyalist called the committees "the foulest, subtlest, and most venomous serpent ever issued from the egg of sedition."

THE BOSTON TEA PARTY   Lord North soon provided the colonists with the occasion to bring resentment from a simmer to a boil. In 1773 he undertook to help some friends bail out the East India Company, which was foundering in a spell of bad business. The company had in its British warehouses some 17 million pounds of tea. Under the Tea Act of 1773 the government would refund the British duty of twelve pence per pound on all that was shipped to the colonies and collect only the existing threepence duty payable at the colonial port. By this arrangement colonists could get tea more cheaply than English buyers could. North, however, miscalculated in assuming that price alone would govern colonial reaction. Even worse, he permitted the East India Company to serve retailers directly through its own agents or consignees, bypassing the wholesalers who had handled it before. Once that kind of monopoly was established, colonial merchants began to wonder, how soon would the precedent apply to other commodities?

The Committees of Correspondence, backed by colonial merchants, alerted people to the new danger. The government, they said, was trying to purchase colonial acquiescence with cheap tea. Before the end of the year, large shipments of tea went out to major colonial ports. After colonial merchants refused to accept the tea, it went back to England. In Charleston it was unloaded into warehouses—and later sold to finance the Revolution.

In Boston, however, Governor Hutchinson and Sam Adams engaged in a test of will. The captains of the ships carrying the tea, alarmed by the radical opposition, proposed to turn back. Hutchinson, who had two sons who stood to profit from the tea, demanded that the tea be landed and the duty paid. On November 30, 1773, the Boston town meeting warned officials not to assist the landing of the tea. But they were legally bound to seize the cargo after twenty days in port, which in this case fell on December 16. On that night in December a group of men, disguised as Mohawk Indians, boarded the three ships and threw the 342 chests of tea overboard—cheered on by a crowd along the shore. Like those who had burned the *Gaspee,* they remained parties unknown—except to hundreds of Bostonians.

Given a more deft response from London, the Boston Tea Party might easily have undermined the radicals' credibility. Many people, especially merchants, were aghast at the wanton destruction of property. A town meeting in Bristol, Massachusetts, condemned the action. Ben Franklin called on his native city to pay for the tea and apologize. But the British authorities had reached the end of their patience. They were now convinced that the very existence of the empire was at stake. The rebels in Boston had instigated what could become a widespread effort to evade royal authority and imperial regulations. A firm response was required. "The colonists must either submit or triumph," George III wrote to Lord North, and North strove to make the king's judgment a self-fulfilling prophecy.

THE COERCIVE ACTS   In 1774 Parliament enacted four measures designed by Lord North to discipline Boston. The Boston Port Act closed the port from June 1, 1774, until the city paid for the lost tea. An Act for the Impartial Administration of Justice let the governor transfer to England the trial of any official accused of committing an offense in the line of duty—no more redcoats would be tried on technicalities. A new Quartering Act directed local authorities to provide lodging for soldiers, in private homes if necessary. Finally, the Massachusetts Government Act made the colony's council and law-enforcement officers all appointive rather than elected; sheriffs would select jurors; and no town meeting could be held without the governor's consent, except for the annual election of town officers. In May, General Thomas Gage replaced Hutchinson as governor and assumed command of British forces. Massachusetts now had a military governor.

These actions were designed to isolate Boston and make an example of the colony. Instead they galvanized colonial resistance. At last, it seemed to the colonists, their worst fears were being confirmed. If

The Able Doctor, or America Swallowing the Bitter Draught. *This 1774 engraving shows Lord North, with the Boston Port Act in his pocket, pouring tea down America's throat. America spits it back.*

these "Intolerable Acts," as the colonists labeled the Coercive Acts, were not resisted, they would eventually be applied to the other colonies.

Further confirmation of British designs came with news of the Quebec Act, passed in June. The act provided that the government to the north in Canada would not have a representative assembly and would be instead led by an appointed governor and council. It also gave a privileged position to the Catholic church. The measure seemed merely another indicator of tyrannical British designs for the rest of the colonies. In addition, colonists pointed out that they had lost many lives in an effort to liberate the trans-Appalachian West from the control of French Catholics. Now the British seemed to be protecting papists at the expense of their own colonists. What was more, the act placed within the boundaries of Quebec the western lands north of the Ohio River, lands that Pennsylvania, Virginia, and Connecticut claimed.

Meanwhile, colonists rallied to the cause of besieged Boston, taking up collections and sending provisions. In Williamsburg, when the Virginia assembly met in May, a young member of the Committee of Correspondence, Thomas Jefferson, proposed to set aside June 1, the effective date of the Boston Port Act, as a day of fasting and prayer in Virginia. The governor immediately dissolved the assembly, whose members retired to the Raleigh Tavern and drew up a resolution for a "Continental Congress" to make representations on behalf of all the colonies. Similar calls were coming from Providence, New York, Philadelphia, and elsewhere, and in June the Massachusetts assembly suggested a meeting in Philadelphia in September. Shortly before George Washington left to represent Virginia at the gathering, he wrote to a friend: "the crisis is arrived when we must assert our rights, or submit to every imposition that can be heaped upon us, till custom and use shall make us as tame and abject slaves, as the blacks we rule over with such arbitrary sway."

THE CONTINENTAL CONGRESS   On September 5, 1774, the First Continental Congress assembled in Philadelphia. There were fifty-five members representing twelve continental colonies, all but Georgia, Quebec, Nova Scotia, and the Floridas. Peyton Randolph of Virginia was elected president and Charles Thomson, "the Sam Adams of Philadelphia," became secretary, but not a member. The Congress agreed to vote by colonies, although Patrick Henry urged the members to vote as individuals on the grounds that they were not Virginians or New Yorkers or whatever, but Americans. In effect, the delegates functioned as a congress of ambassadors, gathered to join forces on common policies and neither to govern nor to rebel but to adopt and issue a series of resolutions and protests.

The Congress gave serious consideration to a plan of union introduced by Joseph Galloway of Pennsylvania. He proposed to set up a central administration of a governor-general appointed by the crown and a grand council chosen by the assemblies to regulate "general affairs." All measures dealing with America would require approval of both this body and Parliament. The plan was defeated by a vote of only six to five. Meanwhile a silversmith from Boston, Paul Revere, had come riding in from Massachusetts with the radical Suffolk Resolves, which the Congress proceeded to endorse. The resolutions declared the Intolerable Acts null and void, urged Massachusetts to arm for defense, and called for economic sanctions against British commerce.

In place of Galloway's plan, the Congress adopted a Declaration of American Rights, which conceded only Parliament's right to regulate commerce and those matters that were strictly imperial affairs. It proclaimed once again the rights of Americans as English citizens, denied Parliament's authority with respect to internal colonial affairs, and proclaimed the right of each colonial assembly to determine the need for British troops within its own province. In addition the Congress sent the king a petition for relief and issued addresses to the people of Great Britain and the colonies.

Finally the Continental Congress adopted the Continental Association of 1774, which recommended that every county, town, and city form committees to enforce a boycott on all British goods. These committees would become the organizational and communications network for the Revolutionary movement, connecting every locality to the leadership. The Continental Association also included provisions for the nonimportation of British goods (implemented in 1774) and the nonexportation of American goods to Britain (to be implemented in 1775 unless colonial grievances were addressed).

In taking its bold stand, the Congress had adopted what later would be called the dominion theory of the British Empire, a theory long implicit in the assemblies' claim to independent authority but more recently formulated in two widely circulated pamphlets by James Wilson of Pennsylvania (*Considerations on the Nature and Extent of the Legislative Authority of the British Parliament*) and Thomas Jefferson of Virginia (*Summary View of the Rights of British America*). Each tract had argued that the colonies were not subject to Parliament but merely to the crown; each colony, like England itself, was a separate realm.

In London the king fumed. He wrote his prime minister that the "New England colonies are in a state of rebellion," and "blows must decide whether they are to be subject to this country or

Forging Fetters for the Americans. *A cartoon attacking British parliamentary measures of 1775 and 1776.*

independent." British critics of the American actions reminded the colonists that Parliament had absolute sovereignty. Power could not be shared. Parliament could not abandon its claim to authority in part without abandoning it altogether.

Parliament declared Massachusetts in rebellion, forbade the New England colonies to trade with any nation outside the empire, and excluded New Englanders from the North Atlantic fisheries. Lord North's Conciliatory Resolution, adopted February 27, 1775, was as far as they would go. Under its terms, Parliament would refrain from any measures but taxes to regulate trade and would grant to each colony the duties collected within its boundaries, provided the colonies would contribute voluntarily to a quota for defense of the empire. It was a formula, said one English skeptic, not for peace but for new quarrels.

SHIFTING AUTHORITY

Events were already moving beyond conciliation. All through late 1774 and early 1775 the defenders of American rights were seizing the initiative. The uncertain and unorganized Loyalists, if they did not submit to nonimportation agreements, found themselves confronted with persuasive committees of "Whigs," with tar and feathers at the ready. The Continental Congress urged each colony to mobilize its militia units. The militia, as much a social as a military organization in the past, now began serious training in formations, tactics, and marksmanship. Royal and proprietary officials were losing control as provincial congresses assumed authority and colonial militias organized, raided military stores, and gathered arms and gunpowder. But British military officials remained smugly confident. Major John Pitcairn wrote home from Boston in 1775: "I am satisfied that one active campaign, a smart action, and burning two or three of their towns, will set everything to rights."

LEXINGTON AND CONCORD Pitcairn soon had his chance. On April 14, 1775, General Thomas Gage, the British commander, received secret orders to suppress the "open rebellion" that existed in the colony. He decided to capture and arrest leaders of the Provincial Congress and to seize the militia's supply depot at Concord, about twenty miles outside of Boston. On the night of April 18, Lieutenant-

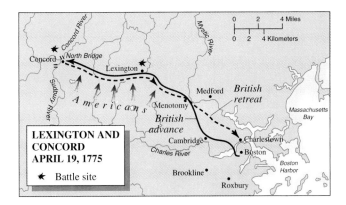

Colonel Francis Smith and Major Pitcairn gathered 700 men on Boston Common and set out by way of Lexington. When local patriots got wind of the plan, Boston's Committee of Safety sent Paul Revere and William Dawes by separate routes on their famous ride to spread the alarm. Revere reached Lexington about midnight and alerted John Hancock and Sam Adams, who were hiding there. Joined by Dawes and Dr. Samuel Prescott, Revere rode on toward Concord. A British patrol intercepted the trio, but Prescott slipped through with the warning.

At dawn on April 19 the British advance guard found Captain John Parker and about seventy Minute Men lined up on the dewy Lexington green. Parker apparently intended only a silent protest, but Major Pitcairn rode onto the green, swung his sword, and yelled: "Disperse, you damned rebels! You dogs, run!" The Americans had already begun quietly backing away when someone fired a shot, whereupon the British soldiers loosed a volley into the Minute Men, then charged them with bayonets, leaving eight dead and ten wounded.

The British officers hastily brought their men under control and led them to Concord. There the Americans already had carried off most of their munitions, but the British destroyed what they could. At Concord's North Bridge the growing American forces inflicted fourteen casualties on a British platoon, and by about noon the British began marching back to Boston. By then, however, the road back had turned into a gauntlet of death as rebels from "every Middlesex village and farm" sniped from behind stone walls, trees, barns, houses, all the way back to Charlestown peninsula. By nightfall the redcoat survivors were safe under the protection of the fleet and army at Boston, having

The Retreat. *An American cartoon showing the retreat of British forces at Lexington and Concord, April 1775.*

suffered over 250 casualties along the way. A British general reported to London that the Americans had earned his respect: "Whoever looks upon them as an irregular mob will find himself much mistaken."

THE SPREADING CONFLICT   The war had begun. When the Second Continental Congress convened at Philadelphia on May 10, 1775, British-held Boston was under siege by Massachusetts militia units. On the very day that Congress met, Fort Ticonderoga in New York fell to a force of Green Mountain Boys under hotheaded Ethan Allen of Vermont and Massachusetts volunteers under Benedict Arnold of Connecticut. Two days later the colonial force took Crown Point, north of Ticonderoga.

The Continental Congress, with no legal authority and no resources, met amid reports of spreading warfare; it had little choice but to assume the de facto role of a revolutionary government. On June 15 it named George Washington general and commander-in-chief of a Continental army. He accepted on the condition that he receive no pay. The Congress fastened on Washington because his service in the French and Indian War made him one of the most experienced officers in America. The fact that he was from influential Virginia heightened his attractiveness. To finance the enterprise the Congress resorted to a familiar colonial expedient, printing paper money.

On June 17, the very day that Washington was commissioned, the colonials and British forces engaged in their first major fight, the Battle of Bunker Hill. While the Congress deliberated, both American and British forces in and around Boston had grown. Militiamen from Rhode Island, Connecticut, and New Hampshire joined in the siege. British reinforcements included three major-generals—Sir William Howe, Sir Henry Clinton, and John Burgoyne. On the day before the battle, American forces fortified the high ground overlooking Boston. Breed's Hill was the battle location, nearer to Boston than Bunker Hill, the site first chosen (and the source of the battle's erroneous name).

The rebels were spoiling for a fight. As Joseph Warren, a dapper Boston physician, put it, "the British say we won't fight; by heavens, I hope I shall die up to my knees in blood!" He soon got his wish. With civilians looking on from rooftops and church steeples, the British launched a conventional frontal assault in the blistering heat, with 2,200 British troops moving in tight formation through tall grass. The Americans, pounded by naval guns, watched from behind their earthworks as the waves of brightly uniformed British troops advanced up the hill. The militiamen waited until the attackers came within fifteen to twenty paces, then loosed a shattering volley. The militiamen cheered as they watched the greatest soldiers in the world retreating in panic.

The Battle of Bunker Hill and the burning of Charlestown peninsula.

Within a half hour, however, the British had reformed and attacked again. Another sheet of flame and lead greeted them, and the vaunted redcoats retreated a second time. Still, the proud British generals were determined not to let such ragtag rustics humiliate them. On the third attempt, when the colonials began to run out of gunpowder and were forced to throw stones, a bayonet charge ousted them. The British took the high ground, but at the cost of 1,054 casualties. Colonial losses were about 400. "A dear bought victory," recorded General Clinton, "another such would have ruined us."

The Battle of Bunker Hill had two profound effects. First, the high number of British casualties made the English generals more cautious in subsequent encounters with the Continental army. Second, Congress recommended after the battle that all able-bodied men enlist in the militia. This tended to divide the male population into Patriot and Loyalist camps. A middle ground was no longer tenable.

In early March 1776, American forces occupied Dorchester Heights to the south of Boston and brought the city under threat of bombardment with cannons and mortars. General William Howe, who had replaced Gage as British commander, retreated by water to Halifax, Nova Scotia. The last British forces, along with fearful American Loyalists, embarked on March 17, 1776. By that time British power had collapsed nearly everywhere, and the British forces faced not the suppression of a rebellion but the reconquest of a continent.

While American forces held Boston under siege, the Continental Congress pursued the dimming hope of a compromise settlement. On July 5 and 6, 1775, the delegates issued two major documents: an appeal to the king known as the Olive Branch Petition, and a Declaration of the Causes and Necessity of Taking Up Arms. The Olive Branch Petition, written by John Dickinson, professed continued loyalty to King George III and begged him to restrain further hostilities pending a reconciliation. The Declaration, also largely Dickinson's work, traced the history of the controversy, denounced the British for the unprovoked assault at Lexington, and rejected independence but affirmed the colonists' purpose to fight for their rights rather than submit to slavery. When the Olive Branch Petition reached London, the outraged king refused even to look at it. On August 22 he declared the American colonists "as open and avowed enemies." The next day he issued a proclamation of rebellion.

Before the end of July 1775 the Congress authorized an attack on British troops in Quebec in the vain hope of rallying support from the French inhabitants in Canada. One force, under Richard Montgomery, advanced by way of Lake Champlain; another, under Benedict Arnold, struggled through the Maine woods. Together they held Quebec under siege from mid-September until their final attack was repulsed on December 30, 1775. Montgomery was killed in the battle and Arnold wounded.

In the South, Virginia's governor raised a Loyalist force, including slaves recruited on promise of freedom, but met defeat in December 1775. In North Carolina, Loyalist Highland Scots, joined by some former Regulators, lost a battle with a Patriot force at Moore's Creek Bridge. The Loyalists had set out for Wilmington to join a British expeditionary force under Lord Cornwallis and Sir Henry Clinton. That plan frustrated, the British commanders decided to attack Charleston instead, but the Patriot militia there had partially finished a palmetto log fort on Sullivan's Island (later named in honor of its commander, Colonel William Moultrie). When the British fleet attacked on June 28, 1776, the spongy palmetto logs absorbed the naval fire, and Fort Moultrie's cannon returned it with devastating effect. The fleet, with over 200 casualties and every ship damaged, was forced to retire. South Carolina honored the palmetto tree by putting it on its state flag.

As the fighting spread north into Canada and south into Virginia and the Carolinas, the Continental Congress assumed more of the functions of government. It appointed commissioners to negotiate treaties of peace with Indian tribes, organized a Post Office Department with Benjamin Franklin as postmaster-general, and authorized formation of a navy and a marine corps.

Still, the delegates continued to hold back from declaring independence. Yet through late 1775 and early 1776 word came of one British action after another that proclaimed rebellion and war. In December 1775 a Prohibitory Act declared the colonies closed to all commerce. The king and cabinet also recruited mercenaries in Europe. Eventually almost 30,000 Germans served, about 17,000 of them from the principality of Hesse-Cassel, and "Hessian" became the name applied to them all. Parliament remained deaf to the warnings of members that the reconquest of America would not only be costly in itself but that the effort might lead to another great war with France and Spain.

COMMON SENSE   In 1776 Thomas Paine's pamphlet *Common Sense* was published anonymously in Philadelphia. Paine had arrived there from England thirteen months before. Coming from a humble Quaker background, Paine had distinguished himself chiefly as a drifter, a failure in marriage and business. At age thirty-seven he set sail for America with a letter of introduction from Benjamin Franklin and the purpose of setting up a school for young ladies. When that did not work out, he moved into the political controversy as a freelance writer, and with *Common Sense* proved himself the consummate Revolutionary rhetorician. Until his pamphlet appeared, the squabble had been mainly with Parliament; few colonists considered independence an option. Paine, however, directly attacked allegiance to the monarchy, which had remained the last frayed connection to Britain, and refocused the hostility previously vented on Parliament. The common sense of the matter, it seemed, was that King George III bore the responsibility for the malevolence toward the colonies. Americans should consult their own interests, abandon George III, and declare their independence: "The blood of the slain, the weeping voice of nature cries, 'TIS TIME TO PART."

INDEPENDENCE

Within three months, more than 150,000 copies of Paine's pamphlet were in circulation, an enormous number for the time. "*Common Sense* is working a powerful change in the minds of men," George Washington said. A visitor to North Carolina's Provincial Congress could "hear nothing praised but *Common Sense* and independence." One by one the provincial governments authorized their delegates in the Continental Congress to take the final step. On June 7 Richard Henry Lee of Virginia moved "that these United Colonies are, and of right ought to be, free and independent states. . . ." Lee's resolution passed on July 2, a date that "will be the most memorable epoch in the history of America," John Adams wrote to his wife, Abigail. The memorable date, however, became July 4, 1776, when the Congress

The Continental Congress votes Independence, July 2, 1776.

adopted Thomas Jefferson's Declaration of Independence, a statement of political philosophy that still retains its dynamic force.

JEFFERSON'S DECLARATION   Although Jefferson is often called the "author" of the Declaration of Independence, he is more accurately termed its draftsman. In June 1776 the Continental Congress appointed a committee of five men—Jefferson, Benjamin Franklin, John Adams, Robert Livingston of New York, and Roger Sherman of Connecticut—to develop a public explanation of the reasons for colonial discontent and to provide a rationale for independence. John Adams convened the committee on June 11. The group asked Adams and Jefferson to produce a first draft, whereupon Adams deferred to Jefferson because of the thirty-three-year-old Virginian's reputation as an eloquent writer.

During two days in mid-June 1776, in his rented lodgings in Philadelphia, Jefferson used a quill pen and a portable desk to write the first statement of American grievances and principles. He later explained that his purpose was "not to find out new principles, or new arguments, never before thought of, not merely to say things which had never been said before; but to place before mankind the common sense of the subject, in terms so plain and firm as to command their assent. . . ." He intended his words to serve as "an expression of the American mind, and to give to that expression the proper tone and spirit called for by the occasion."

Jefferson did not write in a vacuum. Between April and early July 1776, over ninety local "declarations" of independence had already been issued by Massachusetts towns; by militias in New York and Pennsylvania; and by counties, grand juries, and provincial congresses throughout the colonies. During his two-day drafting exercise, Jefferson drew primarily upon two sources: his own draft preamble to the Virginia Constitution written a few weeks earlier, and George Mason's draft of Virginia's Declaration of Rights, which appeared in Philadelphia newspapers in mid-June. It was Mason's text that stimulated many of Jefferson's most famous phrases. Mason had written that "all men are born equally free and independent, and have certain inherent natural Rights, . . . among which are the Enjoyment of Life and Liberty, with the Means of acquiring and possessing Property, and pursuing and obtaining Happiness and Safety."

Jefferson shared his draft with the committee members, and they made several minor revisions to the opening paragraphs and to his listing of the charges against King George III. They then submitted the document to the entire Congress. The legislators turned themselves into a Committee of the Whole to consider the draft. They made eighty-six changes in Jefferson's declaration, including shortening its overall length by one-fourth. Most of the revisions dealt with the section summarizing British colonial policy over the previous fifteen years, but the Congress did see fit to insert two references to God. Jefferson regretted many of the changes, believing his colleagues had "mangled" the document. But overall the legislative editing improved the declaration, making it more concise, accurate, and coherent—and, as a result, more powerful.

The Declaration of Independence constitutes an eloquent restatement of John Locke's contract theory of government—the theory, in Jefferson's words, that governments derived "their just Powers from the consent of the people," who were entitled to "alter or abolish" those that denied their "unalienable rights" to "life, Liberty, and the pursuit of Happiness." The appeal was no longer simply to "the rights of Englishmen" but to the broader "laws of Nature and Nature's God." Parliament, which had no proper authority over the colonies, was never mentioned by name. The enemy was a king who had "combined with others to subject us to a jurisdiction foreign to our constitution, and unacknowledged by our laws. . . ." The document set forth "a history of repeated injuries and usurpations, all having in direct object the establishment of an absolute Tyranny over these States." The "Representatives of the United States of America," therefore, declared the thirteen "United Colonies" to be "Free and Independent States."

"WE ALWAYS HAD GOVERNED OURSELVES" So it had come to this, thirteen years after Britain acquired domination of North America. In explaining the causes of the Revolution, historians have advanced many theories and explanations: excessive trade regulation, the restrictions on settling western lands, the tax burden, the mounting debts to British merchants, the growth of a national consciousness, the lack of representation in Parliament, ideologies of Whiggery and the Enlightenment, the abrupt shift from a mercantile to an "imperial" policy after 1763, class conflict, and revolutionary conspiracy.

Each of them separately and all of them together are subject to challenge, but each contributed something to collective grievances that rose to a climax in a gigantic failure of British statesmanship. A conflict between British sovereignty and American rights had come to a point of confrontation that adroit statesmanship might have avoided, sidestepped, or outflanked. Irresolution and vacillation in the British ministry finally gave way to the stubborn determination to force an issue long permitted to drift. The colonists, conditioned by the Whig interpretation of history, saw these developments as the conspiracy of a corrupted oligarchy—and finally, they decided, of a despotic king—to impose an "absolute Tyranny."

Perhaps the last word on causes of the Revolution should belong to an obscure participant, Levi Preston, a Minute Man from Danvers, Massachusetts. Asked sixty-seven years after Lexington and Concord about British oppressions, he responded, as his young interviewer reported later: " 'What were they? Oppressions? I didn't feel them.' 'What, were you not oppressed by the Stamp Act?' 'I never saw one of those stamps. . . . I am certain I never paid a penny for one of them.' 'Well, what then about the tea-tax?' 'Tea-tax! I never drank a drop of the stuff; the boys threw it all overboard.' 'Well, then, what was the matter? and what did you mean in going to the fight?' 'Young man, what we meant in going for those redcoats was this: we always had governed ourselves, and we always meant to. They didn't mean we should.' "

MAKING CONNECTIONS

- The American revolutionary rhetoric was important not only for fighting the American Revolution; it also provided the framework for the creation of state and national governments after independence had been won. This will be discussed in the next two chapters.

- The section titled "Discontent on the Frontier" showed the tension between people in the more urban eastern areas of several states and those on the western frontier. These same tensions will reappear in several future chapters—for example, in the Federalist/Antifederalist debate over ratification of the Constitution (in Chapter 7).

FURTHER READING

For a narrative survey of the events leading to the Revolution, see Edward Countryman's *The American Revolution* (1985). For the perspective of Great Britain on the imperial conflict, see Ian Christie's *Crisis of Empire* (1966).

The intellectual foundations for revolt are traced in Bernard Bailyn's *The Ideological Origins of the American Revolution* (1967). To understand how these views were connected to organized protest, see Pauline Maier's *From Resistance to Revolution: Colonial Radicals and the Development of American Opposition to Britain, 1765–1776* (1972) and Jon Butler's *Becoming America: The Revolution before 1776* (2000).

A number of books deal with specific events in the chain of crisis. Oliver M. Dickerson's *The Navigation Acts and the American Revolution* (1951) stresses the change from trade regulation to taxation in 1764. Edmund S. Morgan and Helen M. Morgan's *The Stamp Act Crisis* (rev. ed., 1962) gives the colonial perspective on that crucial event. Also valuable are Hiller B. Zobel's *The Boston Massacre* (1970), Benjamin W.

Labaree's *The Boston Tea Party* (1964), and David Ammerman's *In the Common Cause: American Response to the Coercive Acts of 1774* (1974).

Pauline Maier's *American Scripture: Making the Declaration of Independence* (1997) is the best analysis of the framing of that document. For accounts of how the imperial controversy affected individual colonies, see Edward Countryman's *A People in Revolution* (1981), on New York; Richard L. Bushman's *King and People in Provincial Massachusetts* (1985); James H. Hutson's *Pennsylvania Politics, 1746–1770* (1972); Rhys Isaac's *The Transformation of Virgina, 1740–1790* (1982), and A. Roger Ekirch's *"Poor Carolina": Politics and Society in Colonial North Carolina, 1729–1776* (1981).

Events west of the Appalachians are chronicled concisely by Jack M. Sosin in *The Revolutionary Frontier, 1763–1783* (1967). Military affairs in the early phases of the war are handled in John W. Shy's *Toward Lexington: The Role of the British Army in the Coming of the American Revolution* (1965) and in other works listed in Chapter 6.

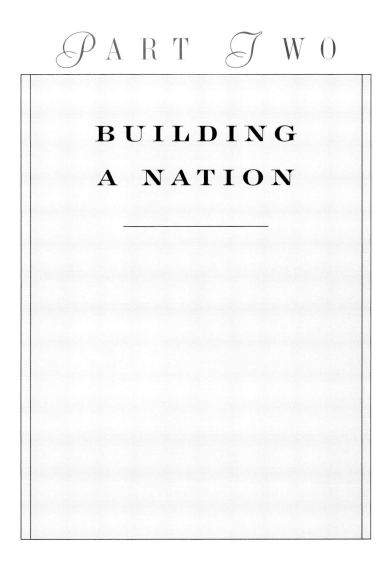

PART TWO

BUILDING
A NATION

The signing of the Declaration of Independence generated great excitement among the rebellious colonists. It was one thing for Patriot leaders to declare American independence from British authority, but it was quite another to win it on the battlefield. Barely a third of the colonists actively supported the Revolution, the political stability of the new nation was uncertain, and George Washington found himself in command of a poorly supplied, inexperienced army.

Yet the Revolutionary movement would persevere and prevail. The skill and fortitude of Washington and his lieutenants enabled the American armies to exploit their geographic advantages. Equally important was the intervention of the French on behalf of the Revolutionary cause. The Franco-American alliance proved to be decisive. After eight years of sporadic fighting and heavy human and financial losses, the British gave up the fight and their American colonies.

Amid the Revolutionary turmoil, the Patriots faced the daunting task of forming new governments for themselves. Their deeply engrained resentment of British imperial rule led them to decentralize power and grant substantial sovereignty to the individual states. As Thomas Jefferson declared, "Virginia, Sir, is my country." Such local ties help explain why the colonists focused their attention on creating new state constitutions rather than a national government. The Articles of Confederation, ratified in 1781, provided only the semblance of national authority. All final power to make and execute laws remained with the states.

After the end of the Revolutionary War in 1783, the flimsy political bonds authorized by the Articles of Confederation proved inadequate to the needs of the new—and expanding—nation. This realization led to the calling of the Constitutional Convention in 1787. The process of drafting and ratifying the new constitution prompted a debate about the relative significance of national power, local control, and individual freedom that has provided the central theme of American political thought ever since.

The American Revolution, however, involved much more than the apportionment of political power. It also unleashed social forces and posed social questions that would help to reshape the very fabric of American culture. What would be the role of women, blacks, and Native Americans in the new republic? How would the contrasting economies of the various regions of the new United States be developed? Who would control and facilitate access to the vast territories to the west of the original thirteen *states? How would the new republic relate to the other nations of the world?*

These controversial questions helped foster the creation of the first national political parties in the United States. During the 1790s, Federalists led by Alexander Hamilton and Republicans led by Thomas Jefferson and James Madison engaged in heated debate about the political and economic future of the new nation. With Jefferson's election as president in 1800, the Republicans gained the upper hand in national politics for the next quarter century. In the process they presided over a maturing American society that aggressively expanded westward at the expense of the Native Americans, ambivalently embraced industrial development, fitfully engaged in a second war with Great Britain, and ominously witnessed a growing sectional controversy over slavery.

6 THE AMERICAN REVOLUTION

CHAPTER ORGANIZER

This chapter focuses on:

- American and British military strategies and the Revolutionary War's major turning points.

- the effect of the war on the home front.

- the American Revolution considered as a "social revolution." in matters of social equality, slavery, the rights of women, and religious freedom.

- the beginnings of a distinctive American culture.

Few foreign observers thought that the upstart American revolutionaries could win a war against the world's greatest empire—and the Americans did lose most of the battles of the Revolution. But they eventually forced the British to sue for peace and grant their independence, an unlikely result that reflects the tenacity of the Patriots as well as the peculiar difficulties facing the British as they tried to conduct a far-flung campaign thousands of miles from home. The costly military commitments they maintained elsewhere around the globe further complicated the British situation.

Fighting in the New World, however, was not an easy task for either side. The Americans had to create a military force capable of opposing the foremost army in the world. Recruiting, supplying, equipping, training and paying soldiers were monumental challenges, especially for a fledgling nation in the midst of forming its first governments. Yet the tenacity of the revolutionaries bore fruit, as war-weariness and political dissension in London hampered British efforts to suppress the rebel forces.

Like all major military events, the Revolution had unexpected consequences affecting political, economic, and social life. It not only secured American independence, generated a new sense of nationalism, and created a unique system of self-governance; it also began a process of societal definition and change that has yet to run its course. The turmoil of Revolution upset traditional class and social relationships and helped transform the lives of people who had long been relegated to the periphery of historical concern—blacks, women, and Indians. In important ways, then, the Revolution was much more than simply a war for independence. It was an engine for political experimentation and social change.

1776: Washington's Narrow Escape

On July 2, 1776, the day that Congress voted for independence, British redcoats landed on the undefended Staten Island across from Manhattan. They were the vanguard of a gigantic effort to reconquer America and the first elements of an enormous force that gathered around New York Harbor over the next month. By mid-August General William Howe, with the support of a fleet under his older brother, Admiral Richard, Lord Howe, had some 32,000 men at his disposal, the largest single force ever mustered by the British in the eighteenth century. Washington transferred most of his men from Boston, but he could gather only about 19,000 militiamen and members of the Continental army. This was too small a force to defend New York, but Congress wanted it held. This forced Washington to expose his men to entrapments from which they escaped more by luck and Howe's caution than by any strategic genius of the American commander. Washington was still learning the art of generalship, and the New York campaign afforded some expensive lessons.

FIGHTING IN NEW YORK AND NEW JERSEY The first conflicts took place on Long Island, where the Americans wanted to hold Brooklyn Heights, from which New York City might be bombarded. By invading and occupying New York, the British hoped to sever New England from the rest of the rebellious colonies. Howe inflicted heavy losses in early battles and forced Washington to evacuate Long Island to reunite

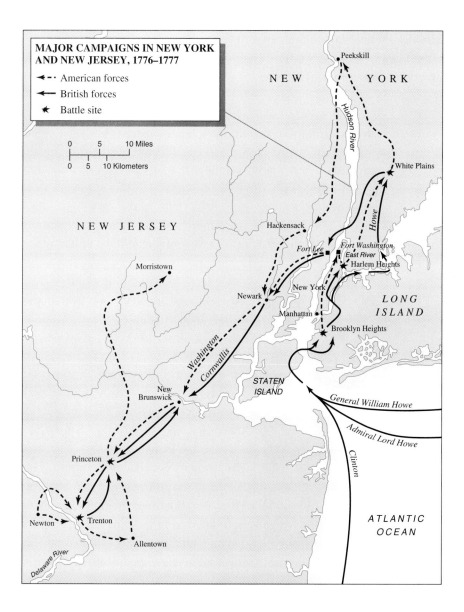

MAJOR CAMPAIGNS IN NEW YORK AND NEW JERSEY, 1776–1777

◄--· American forces
◄— British forces
✷ Battle site

his dangerously divided forces. A timely rainstorm, with strong winds and high tides, enabled the Americans to withdraw to Manhattan under cover of darkness.

Had Howe moved quickly, he could have trapped Washington's army in lower Manhattan. The main American force of 6,000 men, however, withdrew northward to mainland New York, crossed the Hudson River, and then retreated slowly across New Jersey and over the Delaware River into Pennsylvania. In the retreat marched a British volunteer, Thomas Paine. Having opened an eventful year with his inspiring pamphlet *Common Sense,* he now composed *The American Crisis,* in which he penned an immortal line:

> These are the times that try men's souls: The summer soldier and the sunshine patriot will, in this crisis, shrink from the service of his country; but he that stands it NOW deserves the love and thanks of man and woman. Tyranny, like Hell, is not easily conquered. Yet we have this consolation with us, that the harder the conflict, the more glorious the triumph.

The pamphlet, ordered read in the American army camps, bolstered the shaken morale of the Patriots—as events would soon do more decisively.

George Washington at Princeton, *by Charles Willson Peale.*

General Howe, firmly—and luxuriously—based in New York (which the British held throughout the war), established outposts in New Jersey and to the east at Newport, and settled down to wait out the winter. Washington, however, was not yet ready to hibernate. Instead he seized the initiative. On Christmas night 1776, he slipped across the icy Delaware River, with some 2,400 men. Near dawn at Trenton, the Americans surprised a garrison of 1,500 Hessians (German mercenaries) still befuddled from too much holiday rum. It was a total rout from which only 500 royal soldiers escaped death or capture. Only six of Washington's men were wounded, one of whom was Lieutenant James Monroe, the future president. At nearby Princeton on January 3 the Americans repelled three regiments of British redcoats before taking refuge in winter quarters at Morristown, in the hills of northern New Jersey. The campaigns of 1776 had ended, after repeated defeats, with two minor victories that bolstered the Patriot cause. Howe had missed his great chance, indeed several chances, to bring the rebellion to a speedy end. Grumbled one British officer, the Americans had "become a formidable enemy," even though they had yet to win a full-scale conventional battle.

AMERICAN SOCIETY AT WAR

CHOOSING SIDES   Since the end of the French and Indian War, the colonies had required all adult males between the ages of fifteen and sixty to enroll in their local militia company. They attended a monthly drill and turned out on short notice for emergencies. When fighting erupted between the British and American revolutionaries, members of community militias chose sides.

Opinion among the colonists concerning the war divided in three ways: Patriots or Whigs (as the revolutionaries called themselves), Tories (as Patriots called the Loyalists, recalling the die-hard defenders of royal prerogative in England), and an indifferent middle group swayed mostly by the better organized and more energetic radicals. That the Loyalists were numerous is evident from the departure during and after the war of roughly 100,000 of them, or more than 3 percent of the total population. But the Patriots were probably the largest of the three groups. There was a like division in British opinion. The aversion of so many English to the war was one reason for the government's hiring German mercenaries.

Estimating how many Americans remained loyal to Britain was a central concern of English military planners, for they based many of their decisions on such figures. Through most of the war, in New Jersey and in other colonies, the British chased an elusive Tory majority that Loyalists kept telling them was waiting only for British regulars to show the flag. Often they miscalculated. Generally, American Tories were concentrated in the seaport cities, but they came from all walks of life. Governors, judges, and other royal officials were almost all Loyalists; most Anglican ministers also preferred the mother country; colonial merchants might be tugged one way or the other, depending on how much they had benefited or suffered from mercantilist regulation; the great southern planters were swayed one way by dependence on British bounties, another by their debts to British merchants. In the backcountry of New York and the Carolinas, many humble folk rallied to the crown. Where planter aristocrats tended to be Whig, as in North Carolina, backcountry farmers (many of them recently Regulators) leaned to the Tories.

In few places, however, were there enough Tories to assume control without the presence of British troops, and nowhere for very long. Time and again the British forces were frustrated by both the failure of Loyalists to materialize in strength and the collapse of Loyalist militia units once regular detachments pulled out. Even more disheartening was what one British officer called "the licentiousness of the troops, who committed every species of rapine and plunder," and thereby converted potential friends into enemies. British and Hessian regulars, brought up in a hard school of warfare, tended to treat all civilians as hostile.

The inability of the British to use Loyalists effectively as pacification troops led them to abandon areas once they had conquered them. Because Patriot militias quickly returned whenever the British left an area, any Loyalists in the region faced a difficult choice: either accompany the British and leave behind their property or stay and face the wrath of the Patriots. In addition, the British policy of offering slaves their freedom in exchange for their loyalty and service alienated large numbers of neutral or even Tory planters.

The Patriot militia kept springing to life whenever redcoats appeared nearby, and all adult white males, with few exceptions, were obligated under state law to serve when called. With time, even the most apathetic would be pressed into a commitment, if only to turn out for drill. And sooner or later nearly every colonial county experienced military action that would call for armed resistance. The war itself, then, whether through British and Loyalist behavior or the call of the militia, mobilized the apathetic into at least an appearance of support for the American cause. Once made, this commitment was seldom reversed.

MILITIA AND ARMY   American militiamen served two purposes. They constituted a home guard, defending their own communities, and they also helped augment the Continental army. Dressed in hunting shirts

"One of those ubiquitous American frontiersmen-turned-soldier," second from right. Sketches of the American militia by a French soldier at Yorktown.

and armed with muskets, they preferred to ambush their opponents or engage them in hand-to-hand combat rather than fight in traditional formations. They also tended to kill unnecessarily and torture prisoners. To repel an attack, the militia somehow materialized; the danger past, it evaporated, for there were chores to do at home. They "come in, you cannot tell how," George Washington said in exasperation, "go, you cannot tell when, and act you cannot tell where, consume your provisions, exhaust your stores, and leave you at last at a critical moment."

The Continental army, by contrast, was on the whole well trained. Unlike the professional soldiers in the British army, Washington's troops were citizen-soldiers, mostly poor native-born Americans, or immigrants who had been indentured servants or convicts. Many found camp life debilitating and combat horrifying. As General Nathanael Greene, Washington's ablest commander, pointed out, few of the Patriots had ever engaged in mortal combat, and they were hard pressed to "stand the shocking scenes of war, to march over dead men, to hear without concern the groans of the wounded."

Desertions grew as the war dragged on, and the American army fluctuated in size from around 10,000 troops to as high as 20,000 and as low as 5,000. At times Washington could put only 2,000 to 3,000 men in the field. Regiments were organized state by state, and the states were supposed to keep them filled with volunteers, or conscripts if need be, but Washington could never be sure that his requisitions would be met.

PROBLEMS OF FINANCE AND SUPPLY   The Congress found it difficult to supply the army. None of the states provided more than a part of its share, and Congress reluctantly let army agents take supplies directly from farmers in return for certificates promising future payment. Many of the states found a ready source of revenue in the sale of abandoned Loyalist estates. Nevertheless, the Congress and the states fell short of funding the war's cost, and resorted to printing paper money.

Congress did better at providing munitions than other supplies. In 1777 Congress established a government arsenal at Springfield, Massachusetts, and during the war, states offered bounties for the manufacture of guns and powder. Still, most munitions were supplied either by capture during the war or by importation from France, where the government was all too glad to help rebels against its British archenemy.

During the harsh winter at Morristown (1776–1777), George Washington's army nearly disintegrated as enlistments expired and deserters fled the hardships. Only about 1,000 Continentals and a few militiamen stuck it out. With the spring thaw, however, recruits began arriving to claim the bounty of $20 and 100 acres of land offered by Congress to those who would enlist for three years or for the duration of the conflict, if less. With some 9,000 regulars Washington began sparring and feinting with Howe in northern New Jersey. Howe had been making other plans, however, and so had other British officers.

1777: SETBACKS FOR THE BRITISH

Divided counsels, overconfidence, poor communications, and indecision plagued British planning for the campaigns of 1777. After the removal of General Gage during the siege of Boston, "Gentleman Johnny" Burgoyne took command of the northern armies. He proposed to bisect the colonies. His men would advance southward from Canada to the Hudson River while another force moved eastward from Oswego in western New York down the Mohawk River Valley. Howe, meanwhile, would lead a third force up the Hudson River from New York City. Howe in fact had proposed a similar plan, combined with an attack on New England.

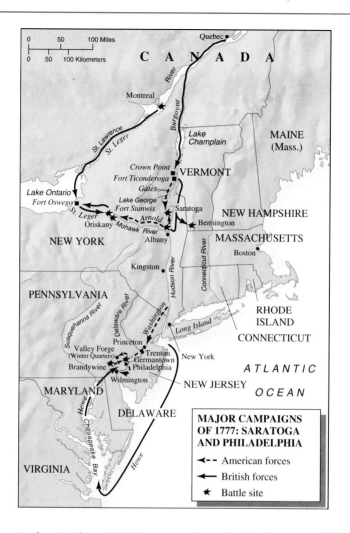

MAJOR CAMPAIGNS
OF 1777: SARATOGA
AND PHILADELPHIA

◄- - American forces

◄— British forces

★ Battle site

Had he stuck to it, he might have cut the colonies in two and delivered them a disheartening blow. But he changed his mind and decided to move against the Patriot capital, Philadelphia, expecting that the Pennsylvania Tories would then rally to the crown and secure the colony.

Washington, sensing Howe's purpose, withdrew most of his men from New Jersey to meet the new threat. At Brandywine Creek, south of Philadelphia, Howe pushed Washington's forces back on September 11, and fifteen days later the British occupied Philadelphia. Washington counterattacked at Germantown on October 4, but reinforcements from Philadelphia under General Lord Cornwallis arrived in time to repulse the attack. Washington retired into winter quarters at Valley

Forge, Pennsylvania, while Howe and his men remained for the winter in the relative comfort of Philadelphia, twenty miles away. Howe's plan had succeeded, up to a point. He had taken Philadelphia—or as Benjamin Franklin put it, Philadelphia took him. But the Tories there proved fewer than he expected, and his decision to move on Philadelphia from the south, by way of Chesapeake Bay, put his forces even farther away from Burgoyne's army. Meanwhile, Burgoyne was stumbling into disaster in the north.

SARATOGA   Burgoyne moved southward from Canada toward Lake Champlain in 1777 with about 7,000 men, his mistress, and a baggage train that included some thirty carts filled with his personal belongings and a large supply of champagne. Such heavily laden forces had a difficult time traversing the wooded and marshy terrain. He sent part of his forces down the St. Lawrence River with Lieutenant-Colonel Barry St. Leger, and at Oswego they were joined by a force of Iroquois allies. This combined force headed east toward Albany.

The vainglorious General John Burgoyne, commander of England's northern forces. Burgoyne and most of his British troops surrendered to the Americans at Saratoga on October 17, 1777.

The American army in the north had dwindled during the winter. When Burgoyne brought his cannon to bear on Fort Ticonderoga, the Continentals prudently abandoned the fort, but with substantial loss of gunpowder and supplies. An angry Congress thereupon fired the American commander and replaced him with Horatio Gates, a favorite of the New Englanders. Fortunately for the American forces, Burgoyne delayed at Ticonderoga, thereby enabling reinforcements to arrive from the south and New England.

The more mobile Americans inflicted two serious reversals on the British forces. At Oriskany, New York, on August 6, 1777, a band of militiamen repulsed an ambush by Tories and Indians under St. Leger, and gained time for General Benedict Arnold to bring a thousand Continentals to the relief of Fort Stanwix. The Indians, convinced they faced an even greater force than they actually did, deserted, and the Mohawk Valley was secured for the Patriot forces. To the east, at Bennington, Vermont (August 16), New England militiamen led by Colonel John Stark decimated a British foraging party. Stark had pledged that morning: "We'll beat them before night, or Molly Stark will be a widow." As American reinforcements continued to gather, and after two other defeats by the Americans, Burgoyne pulled back to Saratoga, where General Horatio Gates's forces surrounded him.

On October 17, 1777, Burgoyne, resplendent in his scarlet, gold, and white uniform, surrendered to the plain, blue-coated Gates, and most of his 5,700 soldiers were imprisoned in Virginia. Gates allowed Burgoyne himself to go home, where he received an icy reception. Gates was ecstatic. He wrote his wife: "If old England is not by this lesson taught humility, then she is an obstinate old slut, bent upon her ruin."

ALLIANCE WITH FRANCE   In early December 1777, news of the American triumph at Saratoga reached London and Paris, where it was celebrated almost as if it were a French victory. The French foreign minister, the comte de Vergennes, had watched the developing Anglo-American crisis with great anticipation and had sent a special agent to Philadelphia to encourage the colonists and hint at French aid.

In 1776 the French had taken their first step toward aiding the colonists, sending fourteen ships with military supplies to America; most of the Continental army's gunpowder in the first years of the war came from this source. The Spanish government added a donation, and soon established its own supply company.

Word of the American victory at Saratoga led to the signing in early 1778 of two treaties: a Treaty of Amity and Commerce, in which France recognized the new United States and offered trade concessions, including important privileges to American shipping, and a Treaty of Alliance. Under the latter both parties agreed, first, that if France entered the war, both countries would fight until American independence was won; second, that neither would conclude a "truce or peace" without "the formal consent of the other first obtained"; and third, that each guaranteed the other's possessions in America "from the present time and forever against all other powers." France further bound itself to seek neither Canada nor other British possessions on the mainland of North America.

By June 1778 British vessels had fired on French ships, and the two nations were at war. In 1779, after extracting French promises to help it regain territories taken by the British in previous wars, Spain entered the war as an ally of France, but not of the United States. In 1780 Britain declared war on the Dutch, who persisted in a profitable trade with the French and Americans. The rebellious farmers at Lexington and Concord had indeed fired the "shot heard round the world." Like Washington's encounter with the French in 1754, it was the start of another world war, and the fighting now spread to the Mediterranean, Africa, India, the West Indies, and the high seas.

1778: BOTH SIDES REGROUP

After Saratoga, Lord North knew that the war was unwinnable, but the king refused to let him either resign or make peace. On March 16, 1778, the House of Commons adopted a program that in effect granted all the American demands prior to independence. Parliament repealed the Townshend tea duty, the Massachusetts Government Act, and the Prohibitory Act, which had closed the colonies to commerce, and sent peace commissioners to Philadelphia to negotiate an end to hostilities. But the American Congress refused to begin any negotiations until Britain recognized American independence or withdrew its forces.

Unbeknownst to the British peace commissioners, the crown had already authorized the evacuation of British troops from Philadelphia, a withdrawal that further weakened what little bargaining power they had. After Saratoga, General Howe had resigned his command and Sir Henry Clinton had replaced him, with orders to pull out of Philadelphia, and if necessary, New York, but to keep Newport. He was to supply troops for an expedition in the South, where the government believed a latent Tory sentiment in the backcountry needed only the British presence for its release. The ministry was right, up to a point, but the sentiment turned out once again, as in other theaters of war, to be weaker than it seemed.

For Washington's army at Valley Forge, the winter of 1777–1778 was a season of suffering far worse than the previous winter at Morristown. The American force, encamped near Philadelphia, endured unrelenting cold, hunger, and disease. Many soldiers deserted or resigned their commissions, leading Washington to warn Congress that unless substantial supplies were forthcoming, the army "must inevitably be reduced to one or other of these three things: starve, dissolve, or disperse." The winter witnessed dissension in Congress and the army. Some critics wanted to make Washington the scapegoat for the Patriots' plight, but there was never any concerted effort to replace him.

Desperate for relief, Washington ordered two of his generals, Nathanael Greene and Henry Lee, to organize foraging expeditions. Their troops crossed the Delaware River into New Jersey and on into Delaware and the eastern shore of Maryland, confiscating horses, cattle, and livestock in exchange for "receipts" to be honored by the Continental Congress. By March the once gaunt troops at Valley Forge saw their strength restored. Their improved health enabled Washington to begin a training program designed to bring unity to his motley array of forces. Because few of the regimental commanders had any formal military training, their troops lacked leadership, discipline, and skill. To remedy this defect, Washington turned to an energetic Prussian soldier of fortune, Frederick William Augustus Henry Ferdinand, baron von Steuben. He used an interpreter and frequent profanity to instruct the troops, teaching them close-order drill, how to march in formations, and how to handle their weapons. By the end of March the ragtag soldiers were beginning to resemble a professional army.

As winter drew to an end the army's morale stiffened when Congress promised extra pay and bonuses after the war. The good news from France helped as well. As General Clinton's British forces withdrew eastward toward New York, Washington pursued them across New Jersey. On June 28 he engaged the British in an indecisive battle at Monmouth Court House. But the Battle of Monmouth was significant for revealing Washington's temper and leadership qualities. In the midst of the fighting, he discovered that his potbellied subordinate, General Charles Lee, was retreating rather than attacking as ordered. Infuriated, Washington swore at Lee "till the leaves shook the trees." Then Washington rallied the troops just in time to stave off defeat. Clinton slipped away into New York while Washington took up a position at White Plains, north of the city. From that time on, the northern theater, scene of the major campaigns and battles in the first years of the war, settled into a long stalemate, interrupted by minor and mostly inconclusive engagements.

ACTIONS ON THE FRONTIER   The one major American success of 1778 occurred far from the New Jersey battlefields. Out to the west the British under Colonel William Hamilton at Forts Niagara and Detroit had incited frontier Tories and Indians to raid western settlements and offered to pay bounties for American scalps. To end such attacks, young George Rogers Clark took 175 frontiersmen on flatboats down the Ohio

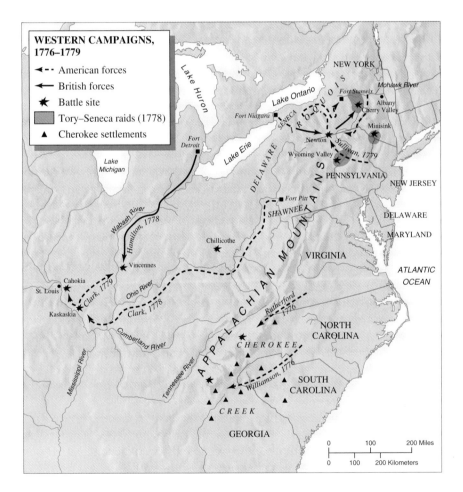

WESTERN CAMPAIGNS, 1776–1779

◀- - American forces
◀— British forces
✴ Battle site
▮ Tory–Seneca raids (1778)
▲ Cherokee settlements

River early in 1778, marched through the woods, and on the evening of July 4 took Kaskaskia (in present-day Illinois) by surprise. The French inhabitants, terrified at first, "fell into transports of joy" at news of the French alliance with the Americans. Then, without bloodshed, Clark took Cahokia (opposite St. Louis), Vincennes, and some minor outposts in what he now called the county of Illinois in the state of Virginia. After the British retook Vincennes, Clark marched his men (almost half French volunteers) through icy rivers and flooded prairies, sometimes in water neck deep, and laid siege to the astonished British garrison. Clark, the hardened woodsman, tomahawked Indian captives in sight of the fort to show that the British afforded them no protection. He spared the British captives when they surrendered, however. Clark is often credited with having conquered the West for the new nation, but there is no evidence that the peace negotiators in 1782 had yet heard of his exploits.

While Clark's captives traveled eastward, a much larger American expedition moved through western Pennsylvania to attack Iroquois strongholds in western New York. There the Tories and Indians had terrorized frontier settlements all through the summer of 1778. Led by the charismatic Mohawk Joseph Brant, the Iroquois killed hundreds of militiamen along the Pennsylvania frontier. In response, Washington dispatched an expedition of 4,000 men under General John Sullivan. At Newton (now Elmira) on August 29, 1779, Sullivan defeated the only serious opposition and proceeded to carry out Washington's instruction that the Iroquois country be not "merely overrun but destroyed." The American force burned about forty Seneca and Cayuga villages together with their orchards and food supplies, leaving many of the Indians

The Mohawk leader Thayendanegea (Joseph Brant), who fought against the Americans in the Revolution. Portrait painted by Gilbert Stuart in 1786.

homeless and without enough provisions to survive. The action broke the power of the Iroquois federation for all time, but it did not completely pacify the frontier. Sporadic encounters with various tribes of the region continued to the end of the war.

In the Kentucky territory, Daniel Boone and his small band of settlers risked constant attack from the Shawnees and their British and Tory allies. During the Revolution, they survived frequent ambushes, at least seven skirmishes, and three pitched battles. In 1778 Boone and some thirty men, aided by their wives and children, held off an assault by more than 400 Indians at Boonesborough. Thereafter, Boone himself was twice shot and twice captured. Indians killed two of his sons, a brother, and two brothers-in-law. His daughter was captured and another brother was wounded four times. Despite such ferocious fighting and dangerous circumstances, the white settlers refused to leave Kentucky.

In early 1776 a delegation of northern Indians—Shawnees, Delawares, and Mohawks—had talked the Cherokees into striking at frontier settlements in Virginia and the Carolinas. Swift retaliation followed as Carolina forces burned Cherokee towns and destroyed corn. By weakening the major Indian tribes along the frontier, the American Revolution, among its other results, cleared the way for rapid settlement of the trans-Appalachian West after the war.

THE WAR IN THE SOUTH

At the end of 1778 the focus of British military efforts shifted suddenly to the south. The whole region from Virginia southward had been free from major action since 1776. Now the British would test King George's belief that a sleeping Tory power in the South needed only the presence of a few redcoats to awaken it. General Clinton decided to take Savannah, Georgia, and roll northeast, gathering momentum from the Loyalist countryside. For a while the idea seemed to work, but it ran afoul of two developments: first, the Loyalist strength was less than estimated; and second, the British forces behaved so harshly that they drove even Loyalists into rebellion.

SAVANNAH AND CHARLESTON   In November 1778 a British force attacked Savannah. The invaders quickly overwhelmed the Patriots, took the town, and brushed aside opposition in the interior. There followed a byplay of thrust and parry between British and South Carolinian forces until the redcoats finally drove toward Charleston, plundering plantation houses along the way.

The seesaw campaign took a major turn when General Clinton accompanied by General Charles Cornwallis brought new naval and land forces southward to join a massive amphibious attack that bottled up American general Benjamin Lincoln on the Charleston peninsula. On May 12, 1780, Lincoln surrendered the city and its 5,500 defenders, the greatest single American loss of the war. At this point Congress, against Washington's advice, turned to the victor of Saratoga, Horatio Gates, to take command and sent him south. Clinton returned to New York and left General Cornwallis in charge of the British troops in the South. Cornwallis led three columns from Charleston to subdue the Carolina interior and surprised Gates's force at Camden, South Carolina, routing his new army, which retreated all the way back to Hillsborough, North Carolina, 160 miles away. It had come to pass as Gates's friend and neighbor Charles Lee had warned after Saratoga: "Beware that your Northern laurels do not turn to Southern willows."

THE CAROLINAS   From the point of view of British imperial goals, the southern colonies were ultimately more important than the northern ones because they produced valuable staple crops such as tobacco, indigo, and naval stores. The war in the Carolinas eventually involved not only opposing British and American armies, but also degenerated into brutal guerrilla-style civil conflicts between local Loyalists and local Patriots. Such infighting brought chaos.

Cornwallis had South Carolina just about under control, but his subordinates Banastre Tarleton and Patrick Ferguson, who mobilized Tory militiamen, overreached themselves in their effort to subdue the Whigs. "Tarleton's Quarter" became an epithet for savagery, because "Bloody Tarleton" gave little quarter to vanquished foes. Ferguson sealed his own doom when he threatened to march over the mountains and hang the leaders of the Watauga country. Instead the feisty "overmountain men" went after Ferguson and, allied with other backcountry Whigs, caught him and his Tories on King's Mountain, just inside South Carolina. There, on October 7, 1780, they routed his force. By then feelings were so strong that American irregulars continued firing on Tories trying to

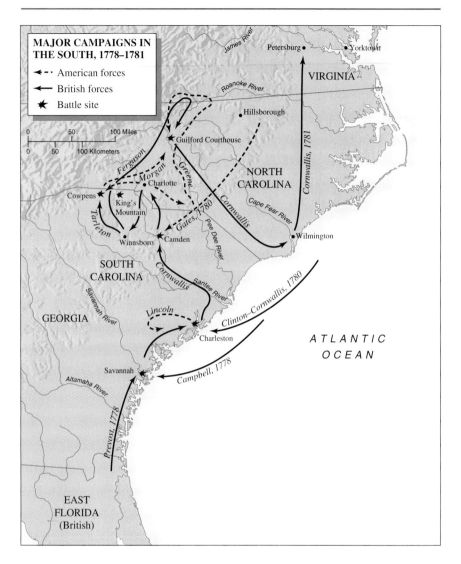

MAJOR CAMPAIGNS IN
THE SOUTH, 1778–1781

◄--- American forces
◄— British forces
★ Battle site

surrender and later inflicted indiscriminate slaughter on Tory prisoners.
King's Mountain was the turning point of the war in the South. By prov-
ing that the British were not invincible, it emboldened small farmers to
join guerrilla bands under partisan leaders such as Francis Marion, "the
Swamp Fox," and Thomas Sumter, "the Gamecock."

While the overmountain men were closing in on Ferguson, Congress
had chosen a new commander for the southern theater, General
Nathanael Greene, the "fighting Quaker" of Rhode Island. A man of infinite patience, skilled at managing men and saving supplies, careful to

avoid needless risks, he was suited to a war of attrition against the British forces. From Charlotte, where he arrived in December 1780, Greene moved his army eastward toward the Pee Dee River. As a diversion he sent General Daniel Morgan with about 700 men on a sweep to the west of Cornwallis's headquarters at Winnsboro.

Taking a position near Cowpens, a cow-grazing area in northern South Carolina, Morgan found himself swamped by militia units joining him faster than he could provide for them. Tarleton caught Morgan and his men on January 17, 1781, with the rain-swollen Broad River at their backs—a position Morgan took deliberately to force the green militiamen to stand and fight. Once the battle was joined, Tarleton mistook a readjustment in the American line for a militia panic, and rushed his men forward, only to be ambushed by Morgan's cavalry. Tarleton escaped, but more than 100 of his men were killed and more than 700 were taken prisoner.

Morgan then fell back into North Carolina, linked up with Greene's main force at Guilford Courthouse (now Greensboro), and then led Cornwallis on a wild goose chase up to the Dan River. Once the Americans had crossed, the British could not follow, for their supplies were running low. Cornwallis was forced to draw back to Hillsborough. When reinforcements from Virginia and the Carolinas arrived, Greene returned to Guilford Courthouse and offered battle on March 15, 1781. Having inflicted heavy losses, the Americans prudently withdrew to fight another day.

Cornwallis marched off toward the coast at Wilmington to lick his wounds and take on new supplies. Greene then resolved to go back into South Carolina in the hope of drawing Cornwallis after him or forcing the British to give up the state. There he joined forces with the local guerrillas, and in a series of brilliant actions kept losing battles while winning the war: "We fight, get beat, rise, and fight again," he said. By September 1781 he had narrowed British control in the Deep South to Charleston and Savannah, although for more than a year longer Whigs and Tories slashed at each other "with savage fury" in the backcountry, where there was "nothing but murder and devastation in every quarter," Greene said.

Meanwhile Cornwallis had headed north away from Greene, reasoning that Virginia must be eliminated as a source of reinforcement before the Carolinas could be subdued. In May 1781 he marched north into Virginia. There, since December 1780, Benedict Arnold, now a *British* general, was engaged in a war of maneuver against American forces. Arnold, until September 1780, had been American commander at West Point. Overweening in ambition, lacking in moral scruples, and a reckless spender on his fashionable wife, Arnold had nursed a grudge against Washington over an official reprimand for his extravagances as commander of reoccupied Philadelphia. Traitors have a price, and Arnold had found his: he had crassly plotted to sell out the West Point garrison to the British, and he even suggested how they might capture George Washington himself. Only the fortuitous capture of the British go-between, Major John André, had ended Arnold's plot. Forewarned that his plan had been discovered, Arnold had joined the British in New York while the Americans hanged André as a spy.

YORKTOWN   When Cornwallis linked up with Arnold at Petersburg, their combined forces rose to 7,200, far more than the small American army there. The arrival of American reinforcements led Cornwallis to pick Yorktown as a defensible site. There appeared to be little reason to worry about a siege, since Washington's main land force seemed preoccupied with attacking New York and the British navy controlled American waters.

To be sure, there was a small American navy, but it was no match for the British fleet. Yet American privateers distracted and wounded the British fleet. Most celebrated were the exploits of Captain John Paul Jones. Off England's coast on September 23, 1779, Jones and his crew won a desperate battle with a British frigate, which the Americans captured and occupied before their own ship sank. This was the occasion for his stirring and oftrepeated response to a British demand for surrender: "I have not yet begun to fight."

Still, such heroics were little more than nuisances to the British. But at a critical point, thanks to the French navy, the British lost control of the Chesapeake waters. Indeed, it is impossible to imagine an American victory in the Revolution without the assistance of the French. As long as the British navy maintained supremacy at sea, the Americans could not hope to force a settlement to their advantage. For three years Washington had waited to get some military benefit from

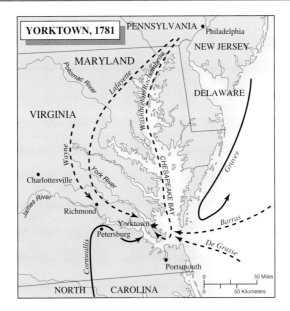

the French alliance. In July 1780 the French had finally landed a force of about 6,000 at Newport, Rhode Island, which the British had given up to concentrate on the South, but the French force had sat there for a year, blockaded by the British fleet.

Then, in 1781, the elements for combined action suddenly fell into place. In May, as Cornwallis moved into Virginia, Washington persuaded the commander of the French army to join forces for an attack on New York. The two armies linked up in July, but before they could strike at New York, word came from the West Indies that Admiral de Grasse was bound for the Chesapeake with his entire French fleet and some 3,000 soldiers. Washington immediately set out toward Yorktown, all the while preserving the semblance of a flank movement against New York. Meanwhile, French ships slipped out of the British barricade at Newport and also headed south toward Chesapeake Bay.

On August 30 de Grasse's fleet reached Yorktown, and he landed his troops to join the American force already watching Cornwallis. On September 6, the day after a British fleet appeared, de Grasse gave battle and forced the British to give up the effort to relieve Cornwallis,

Surrender of Lord Cornwallis. *John Trumbull completed his painting of the pivotal British surrender at Yorktown in 1794.*

whose fate was quickly sealed. De Grasse then sent ships up the Chesapeake to ferry down the allied armies, which brought the total American and French forces to more than 16,000, or better than double the size of Cornwallis's army.

The siege began on September 28. On October 14 two major redoubts guarding the left of the British line fell to French and American attackers, the latter led by Washington's aide Alexander Hamilton. A British counterattack failed to retake them. Later that day a squall forced Cornwallis to abandon a desperate plan to escape across the York River. On October 17, 1781, four years to the day after Saratoga, Cornwallis sued for peace, and on October 19 the British force of more than 7,000 marched out, their colors cased, as the British band played somber tunes along with the English nursery rhyme "The World Turned Upside Down." Cornwallis himself claimed to be too "ill" to appear. His dispatch to his superior was telling: "I have the mortification to inform your Excellency that I have been forced to . . . surrender the troops under my command."

NEGOTIATIONS

Whatever lingering hopes of victory the British may have harbored vanished at Yorktown. "Oh God, it's all over," Lord North groaned at news of the surrender. On February 27, 1782, the House of Commons voted against continuing the war, and on March 5 authorized the crown to make peace. On March 20 Lord North resigned.

The Continental Congress named a five-man commission to negotiate a peace treaty. Only three members of the commission were active, however: John Adams, who was on state business in the Netherlands; John Jay, minister to Spain; and Benjamin Franklin, already in Paris. Franklin and Jay did most of the work.

The French commitment to Spain complicated matters. Spain and the United States were both allied with France, but not with each other. America was bound by its alliance to fight on until the French made peace, and the French were bound to help the Spanish recover Gibraltar from England. Unable to deliver Gibraltar, or so the tough-minded Jay reasoned, the French might try to bargain off American land west of the Appalachians in its place. Fearful that the French were angling for a separate peace with the British, Jay persuaded Franklin to play the same game. Ignoring their instructions to consult fully with the French, they agreed to further talks with the British. On November 30, 1782, the talks produced a preliminary treaty with Great Britain. If it violated the spirit

American Commissioners of the Preliminary Peace Negotiations with Great Britain, *a painting by Benjamin West. From left, John Jay, John Adams, Benjamin Franklin, Henry Laurens, and Franklin's nephew, William Temple Franklin (1782).*

of the alliance, it did not violate the strict letter of the treaty with France, for the French minister was notified the day before it was signed, and final agreement still depended on a Franco-British settlement.

THE PEACE OF PARIS   Early in 1783 France and Spain gave up on Gibraltar and reached an armistice with Britain. The final signing of the Peace of Paris came on September 3, 1783. In accord with the bargain already struck, Great Britain recognized the independence of the United States and agreed to a Mississippi River boundary to the west. Both the northern and southern borders left ambiguities that would require further definition. Florida, as it turned out, passed back to Spain. The British further granted Americans the "liberty" of fishing off Newfoundland and in the St. Lawrence Gulf, and the right to dry their

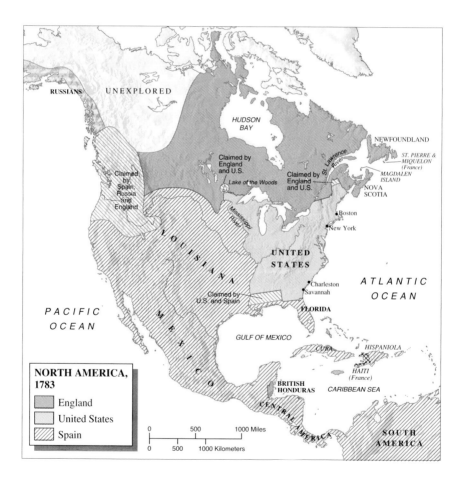

catches on the unsettled Atlantic coast of Canada. On the matter of debts, the best the British could get was a promise that their merchants should "meet with no legal impediment" in seeking to collect money owed them by Americans. And on the tender point of Loyalists whose estates had been confiscated, the negotiators agreed that Congress would "earnestly recommend" to the states the restoration of confiscated property. Each of the last two points was little more than a face-saving gesture for the British.

On November 24 the last British troops left New York City, and on December 4 they evacuated Staten Island and Long Island. That same day Washington took leave of his officers in New York. On December 23 he appeared before the Continental Congress, meeting in Annapolis, Maryland, to resign his commission. Before the end of the next day he was back at Mount Vernon, home in time for Christmas.

THE POLITICAL REVOLUTION

REPUBLICAN IDEOLOGY   The Americans had won their War for Independence. Had they undergone a political revolution as well? Years later, John Adams offered one answer: "The Revolution was effected before the war commenced. The Revolution was in the minds and hearts of the people. . . . This radical change in the principles, opinions, sentiments, and affections of the people, was the real American Revolution."

Yet Adams's observation ignores the fact that the Revolutionary War itself served as the catalyst for a prolonged internal debate about what new forms of government would best serve an independent republic. The conventional British model of mixed government sought to balance monarchy, aristocracy, and the common people and thereby protect individual liberty. Because of the more democratic nature of their society, however, Americans knew that they must derive new political assumptions and institutions. They had no monarchy or aristocracy. Yet how could sovereignty reside in the common people? How could Americans ensure the survival of a republican form of government, long assumed to be the most fragile? The war thus provoked a spate of state constitution-making that remains unique in human history.

A struggle for the rights of English citizens in the colonies became a fight for independence in which those rights found expression in governments that were new, yet deeply rooted in the colonial experience and the prevailing viewpoints of Whiggery and the Enlightenment. With the Loyalists displaced or dispersed, such ideas as the contract theory of government, the sovereignty of the people, the separation of powers, and natural rights found their way into the new frames of government that were devised while the fight went on—amid other urgent business.

The very idea of republican government was a radical departure in that day. A republic, it was presumed, would endure only as long as the majority of the people were virtuous and willingly placed the good of society above the self-interest of individuals. Herein lay the hope and the danger of the new American experiment in popular government: even as leaders enthusiastically fashioned new state constitutions, they feared that their experiments in republicanism would fail because of a lack of civic virtue.

NEW STATE CONSTITUTIONS   Most of the political experimentation between 1776 and 1787 occurred at the state level in the form of written constitutions in which the people are sovereign and delegate limited authority to the government. In addition, the states initiated bills of rights guaranteeing particular individual freedoms, and fashioned procedures for constitutional conventions that have also remained an essential part of the American political system. In sum, the innovations at the state level during the Revolution created a reservoir of ideas and experience that formed the basis for the creation of the federal constitution in 1787.

In 1776 Congress advised the colonies to set up new governments "under the authority of the people." At first the authority of the people was exercised by legislatures, which simply adopted constitutions and implemented them. But they had little more status than ordinary statutory law, it could be argued, since the people had no chance to express their wishes directly. Massachusetts invented what became a standard device for American constitution-making: a body separate from and superior to the legislature to exercise the people's sovereignty. In 1779–1780 Massachusetts elected a special convention, chosen for the specific purpose of making a constitution. The invention of the constitutional convention was an altogether original contribution to the art of government, and one that other states copied. The resultant document went out to the town meetings with the provision that two-thirds or more would have to ratify it, which they did.

The first state constitutions varied mainly in detail. They formed governments much like the colonial governments, with elected governors and senates instead of appointed governors and councils. Generally they embodied a separation of powers (legislative, executive, judicial) as a safeguard against abuses. Most of them also included a bill of rights that protected the time-honored rights of petition, freedom of speech, trial by jury, freedom from self-incrimination, and the like. Most tended to limit the powers of governors and increase the powers of the legislatures, which had led the people in their quarrels with the colonial governors. Pennsylvania went so far as to eliminate the governor and upper house of the legislature altogether. It had an executive council of twelve, including a president, and operated until 1790 with a unicameral legislature limited only by a house of "censors" who reviewed its work every five years.

THE ARTICLES OF CONFEDERATION   The central government, the Continental Congress, exercised governmental powers without any constitutional sanction before March 1781. Plans for a permanent frame of government emerged very early, however. Richard Henry Lee's motion for independence included a call for a plan of confederation. As early as July 1776, a committee headed by John Dickinson produced a draft constitution, the "Articles of Confederation and Perpetual Union." For more than a year Congress debated the articles in between more urgent matters and finally adopted them in November 1777. All states ratified promptly except Maryland, which insisted that the seven states claiming western lands should cede them to the authority of Congress. Maryland did not relent until early 1781, when Virginia gave up its claims under the old colonial charter to the vast region north of the Ohio River. New York had already relinquished a dubious claim based on its "jurisdiction" over the Iroquois, and the other states eventually abandoned their charter claims.

When the Articles of Confederation became effective in March 1781, they did little more than legalize the status quo. "The United States in Congress Assembled" had a multitude of responsibilities but little authority to carry them out. The Congress was intended not as a legislature, nor as a sovereign entity unto itself, but as a collective substitute for the monarch. In essence, it was to be a plural executive rather than a parliamentary body. It had full power over foreign affairs and questions of war and peace; it could decide disputes between the states; it had authority over coinage, postal service, and Indian affairs, and responsibility for the government of the western territories. But it had no courts and no power to enforce its resolutions and ordinances upon either states or individuals. It also had no power to levy taxes, but had to rely on requisitions, which state legislatures could ignore.

The states, after their battles with Parliament, were in no mood for a strong central government. The Congress in fact had less power than the colonists had once accepted in Parliament, since it could not regulate interstate and foreign commerce. For certain important acts, moreover, a "special majority" was required. Nine states had to approve measures dealing with war, treaties, coinage, finances, or the army and navy. Unanimous approval of the states was needed to levy tariffs (often called "duties") on imports. Amendments to the articles also required unanimous ratification by all the states. The Confederation had neither an executive nor a judicial branch; there was no administrative head of government (only the president of the Congress, chosen annually) and no federal courts.

For all its weaknesses, however, the Confederation government represented the most pragmatic structure for the new nation. After all, the Revolution on the battlefields had yet to be won, and America's statesmen could not risk the prolonged and divisive debates over the distribution of power that other forms of government would have provoked.

THE SOCIAL REVOLUTION

Political revolutions easily spawn social revolutions. Just as the Great Awakening brought with it unintended social effects, the turmoil from the Revolution allowed long pent-up frustrations among the lower ranks to find expression. What did the Revolution mean to those workers, servants, farmers, and freed slaves who participated in the Stamp Act demonstrations, supported the boycotts, idolized Tom Paine, and fought with Washington and Greene?

Many laboring folk hoped that the Revolution would remove, not reinforce, the elite's traditional political and social advantages. The more conservative Patriots would have been content to replace royal officials with the rich, the well-born, and the able, and let it go at that. But more radical revolutionaries raised the question not only of home rule but of who should rule at home.

EQUALITY AND ITS LIMITS This spirit of equality found outlet in several directions, one of which was simply a weakening of old habits of deference. A Virginia gentleman told of being in a tavern when a group of farmers came in, spitting and pulling off their muddy boots without regard to the sensibilities of the gentlemen present: "The spirit of independence was converted into equality," he wrote, "and every one who bore arms, esteems himself upon a footing with his neighbors. . . . No doubt each of these men considers himself, in every respect, my equal." No doubt each did.

What was more, participation in the army or militia excited people who had taken little interest in politics before. The new political opportunities afforded by the creation of state governments led more ordinary citizens into participation than ever before. The social base of the new legislatures was thus much broader than that of the old assemblies.

In this watercolor by Benjamin Latrobe, a gentleman plays billiards with artisans, suggesting that "the spirit of independence was converted into equality."

Men fighting for their liberty found it difficult to justify denying other white men the rights of suffrage and representation. The property qualifications for voting, which already admitted an overwhelming majority of white males, were lowered still further. In Pennsylvania, Delaware, North Carolina, Georgia, and Vermont, any male taxpayer could vote, although officeholders usually had to meet higher property requirements. Men who had argued against taxation without representation now questioned the denial of proportionate representation for the backcountry, which generally enlarged its presence in the legislatures. More often than not the political newcomers were men of lesser property and little formal education. All states concentrated much power in a legislature chosen by a wide suffrage, but not even Pennsylvania, which adopted the most radical of the state constitutions, went quite so far as universal male suffrage.

New developments in land tenure that grew out of the Revolution extended the democratic trends of suffrage requirements. Confiscations resulted in the seizure of Tory estates by all the state legislatures. These properties, however, were of small consequence in contrast to the unsettled areas formerly at the disposal of crown and proprietors, now in the hands of popular assemblies. Much of this land was now used for bonuses to veterans of the war. Moreover, western lands, formerly closed by the Proclamation of 1763 and the Quebec Act of 1774, were soon thrown open for settlers.

THE PARADOX OF SLAVERY   The Revolutionary generation of leaders was the first to confront the issue of slavery and to consider abolishing it. The principles of liberty and equality had clear implications for enslaved blacks. Before the Revolution, only Rhode Island, Connecticut, and Pennsylvania had halted the importation of slaves. After independence, all the states except Georgia stopped the traffic, although South Carolina later reopened it.

Black soldiers or sailors were present at most of the major battles, from Lexington to Yorktown; most were on the Loyalist side. The British promised freedom to slaves, as well as indentured servants, who would bear arms for the Loyalist cause. In response, General Washington at the end of 1775 reversed the policy of excluding blacks from American forces—except the few already in militia companies—and Congress quickly approved. Only two states, South Carolina and Georgia, held out completely against the policy, but by a rough estimate few blacks, probably no more than about 5,000, were admitted to the total American forces of about 300,000, and most of those were free blacks from northern states. They served mainly in white units, although Massachusetts did organize two all-black companies, and Rhode Island organized one.

Slaves who served in the cause of independence won their freedom and in some cases land bounties. But the British army, which carried off probably tens of thousands of slaves during the war, was a greater instrument of emancipation than the American forces. Most of the newly freed blacks found their way to Canada or to British colonies in the Caribbean. American Whigs showed no mercy

Elizabeth Freeman, born in Africa around 1742, was sold as a slave to a Massachusetts family. She won her freedom by claiming in court that the "inherent liberty" of all applied to slaves as well.

to blacks who were caught aiding or abetting the British cause. A Charleston mob hanged and then burned Thomas Jeremiah, a free black who was convicted of telling slaves that the British "were come to help the poor Negroes." White Loyalists who were caught stirring up slave militancy were tarred and feathered.

In the northern states, which had fewer slaves than the southern states, the doctrines of liberty led swiftly to emancipation for all either during the fighting or shortly afterward. Vermont's Constitution of 1777 specifically forbade slavery. The Massachusetts Constitution of 1780 proclaimed the "inherent liberty" of all. In 1780 Pennsylvania declared that all children born thereafter to slave mothers would become free at age twenty-eight, after enabling their owners to recover their initial cost. In 1784 Rhode Island provided freedom for all children of slaves born thereafter, at age twenty-one for males, eighteen for females. New York lagged until 1799 in granting freedom to mature slaves born after enactment, but an act of 1817 set July 4, 1827, as the date for emancipation of all remaining slaves.

In the states south of Pennsylvania, emancipation was less popular. Yet even there slaveholders expressed moral qualms. Thomas Jefferson wrote in his *Notes on Virginia* (1785): "Indeed I tremble for my country when I reflect that God is just; that his justice cannot sleep forever." But he, like many other white southerners, could not bring himself to free his slaves. In the southern states, antislavery sentiment went no further than a relaxation of the manumission laws under which owners might free their slaves as individual acts. Some 10,000 slaves in Virginia were manumitted during the 1780s. A much smaller number would be shipped back to Africa during the early nineteenth century. By the outbreak of the Civil War in 1861, approximately half of the blacks living in Maryland were free.

Manumission freed slaves by the action of a white owner. But slaves, especially in the upper South, also earned freedom through their own actions during the Revolutionary era, frequently by running away. They often gravitated to the growing number of African-American communities in the North. Because of emancipation laws in the northern states, and with the formation of free black neighborhoods in the North and in several southern cities, runaways found refuge and the opportunities for new lives. It is estimated that 55,000 slaves fled to freedom during the Revolution.

THE STATUS OF WOMEN The logic of liberty applied to the status of women as much as to that of blacks. Women in the colonies had remained essentially confined to the domestic sphere during the eighteenth century. They could not vote or preach or hold office. Few had access to formal education. Although women could own property and execute contracts, in several colonies married women could not legally own property—even their own clothes—and they had no legal rights over their children. Divorces were extremely difficult to obtain.

Yet the Revolution offered women new opportunities and engendered in many a new outlook. The war drew women at least temporarily into new pursuits. Women supported the armies in various roles, such as handling supplies, serving as couriers, and working as camp followers—cooking, cleaning, and nursing the soldiers. Wives often followed their husbands to camp, and on occasion took their places in the line, as Margaret Corbin did at Fort Washington when her husband fell at his artillery post, or Mary Ludwig Hays (better known as Molly Pitcher) did when her husband collapsed of heat exhaustion. An exceptional case was that of Deborah Sampson, who joined a Massachusetts regiment as "Robert Shurtleff" and served from 1781 to 1783 by the "artful concealment" of her sex.

To be sure, most women retained the domestic outlook that had long been imposed on them by society. But a few free-spirited reformers demanded equal treatment. In an essay entitled "On the Equality of the Sexes," written in 1779 and published in 1790, Judith Sargent Murray of Gloucester, Massachusetts, stressed that women were perfectly capable of excelling outside the domestic sphere.

Early in the Revolutionary struggle, Abigail Adams, one of the most learned, spirited, and independent women of the time, wrote to her husband John: "In the new Code of Laws which I suppose it will be necessary for you to make I desire you would remember the Ladies. . . . Do not put such unlimited power into the hands of the Husbands." Since men were "Naturally Tyrannical," she wrote, "why then, not put it out of the power of the vicious and the Lawless to use us with cruelty and indignity with impunity." Otherwise, "If particular care and attention is not paid to the Ladies we are determined to foment a Rebellion, and will not hold ourselves bound by any Laws in which we have no voice, or Representation."

Frontispiece from Lady's Magazine, *1792. "The Genius of the Ladies Magazine, accompanied by the Genius of Emulation, who carries in her hand a laurel crown, approaches Liberty, and kneeling, presents her with a copy of the Rights of Woman." The* Lady's Magazine *reprinted extensive extracts from Mary Wollstonecraft's* A Vindication of the Rights of Woman *(1792).*

Husband John expressed surprise that women might be discontented, but he clearly knew the privileges enjoyed by males and was determined to retain them: "Depend upon it, we know better than to repeal our Masculine systems." Thomas Jefferson was of one mind with Adams on this matter. When asked about women's voting rights, he replied that "the tender breasts of ladies were not formed for political convulsion."

The legal status of women did not improve dramatically as a result of the Revolutionary ferment. Married women in most of the states still forfeited control of their own property to their husbands, and women gained no permanent political rights. Under the 1776 New Jersey constitution, which neglected to specify an exclusively male franchise because the delegates apparently took the distinction for granted, women who met the property qualifications for voting exercised the right until they were denied access early in the nineteenth century.

FREEDOM OF RELIGION   The Revolution also set in motion a transition from the toleration of religious dissent to a complete freedom of religion in the separation of church and state. The Anglican church, established as the official religion in five colonies and parts of two others, was especially vulnerable because of its association with the crown and because dissenters outnumbered Anglicans in most states except Virginia. And all but Virginia removed tax support for the church before the

The Congregational church developed a national presence in the early nineteenth century, and Lemuel Haynes, depicted here, was its first black preacher.

fighting was over. In 1776 the Virginia Declaration of Rights guaranteed the free exercise of religion, and in 1786 the Virginia Statute of Religious Freedom (written by Thomas Jefferson) declared that "no man shall be compelled to frequent or support any religious worship, place or ministry whatsoever" and "that all men shall be free to profess, and by argument to maintain, their opinions in matters of religion." These statutes and the Revolutionary ideology that justified them helped shape the course that religion would take in the new United States: pluralistic and voluntary rather than state supported and monolithic.

In churches as well as in government, the Revolution set off a period of constitution-making, as some of the first national church bodies emerged. In 1784 the Methodists, who at first were an offshoot of the Anglicans, came together in a general conference at Baltimore under Bishop Francis Asbury. The Anglican church, rechristened Episcopal, gathered in a series of meetings which by 1789 had united the various dioceses in a federal union; in 1789 the Presbyterians also held their first general assembly in Philadelphia. The following year, the Catholic church had its first bishop in the United States when John Carroll was named bishop of Baltimore.

THE EMERGENCE OF AN AMERICAN CULTURE

The Revolution helped generate among some Americans a sense of common nationality. In the First Continental Congress, Patrick Henry asserted that such a sense of identity had come to pass: "The distinctions between Virginians, Pennsylvanians, New Yorkers, and New Englanders are no more. I am not a Virginian but an American."

The concrete experience of the war reinforced the rhetoric. Soldiers who went to fight in other states broadened their horizons. John Marshall, future chief justice, served first in the Virginia militia and then in the Continental army in the Middle States and endured the winter of 1777–1778 at Valley Forge. He later wrote: "I found myself associated with brave men from different states who were risking life and everything valuable in a common cause. I was confirmed in the habit of considering America as my country and Congress as my government." The Revolution thus marked the start of a national consciousness and a national tradition.

A painting by Benjamin West depicting Willam Penn's treaty with the Indians in 1682.

INDEPENDENCE DAY   One of the first ways to forge a national consciousness was through the annual celebration of the new nation's independence from Great Britain. On July 2, 1776, when the Second Continental Congress had resolved "that these United Colonies are, and of right ought to be, free and independent states," John Adams had written his wife Abigail that future generations would remember that date as their "day of deliverance." Adams realized that celebrating the birth of the nation would help to unite a disparate republic. People, he predicted, would celebrate the occasion with "solemn acts of devotion to God Almighty" and with "pomp and parade, with shows, games, sports, guns, bells, bonfires and illuminations [fireworks] from one end of this continent to the other, from this time forward, forever more."

Adams got everything right but the date. Americans fastened not upon July 2 but July 4 as their Independence Day. To be sure, it was on the Fourth that Congress formally adopted the Declaration of Independence and ordered it to be printed and distributed within the states, but America by then had been officially independent for two days.

The Declaration of Independence was not read in public until July 8 and was not copied onto parchment and signed by the delegates until August 2.

As luck would have it, July 4 became Independence Day by accident. In 1777 Congress forgot about any acknowledgment of the first anniversary of independence until July 3, when it was too late to honor July 2. As a consequence, the Fourth won by default.

Independence Day quickly became the most popular and most important public ritual in the United States. Huge numbers of people from all walks of life suspended their normal routines in order to devote a day to parades, formal orations, and fireworks displays. In the process, the infant republic began to create its own myth of national identity that transcended local or regional concerns. "What a day!" exclaimed the editor of the *Southern Patriot* in 1815. "What happiness, what emotion, what virtuous triumph must fill the bosoms of Americans!"

EDUCATION   The most lasting cultural effect of postwar nationalism may well have been its mark on education. In the colonies there had been a total of nine colleges, but once the Revolution was over, eight more sprang up in the 1780s and six in the 1790s. Several of the state constitutions had provisions for state universities. Georgia's was the first chartered, in 1785, but the University of North Carolina (chartered in 1789) was the first to open, in 1795.

Even more important, the Revolution provided the initial impetus for state-supported public school systems. Many of the founders believed that the survival of the new nation depended upon instilling in the public an appreciation for the fragility of republican government and its utter dependence on private and civic virtue. They viewed public schools as the best institutions for such moral and civic development. In such schools, it was hoped, American children not only would become literate but would also learn to choose the public good over all private interests and concerns.

Thomas Jefferson agreed that public education would serve as the very "keystone of our arch of government," and in 1779 he introduced his "Bill for the More General Diffusion of Knowledge" into the Virginia assembly. It included an elaborate plan for the state to fund elementary schools for all free persons, and higher education for the talented, up through a state university. Several years later Samuel Adams proposed the same in Massachusetts. Yet almost every one of these schemes for public schools came to naught. Wealthy critics opposed spending tax money on schools that would mingle their sons "in a vulgar and suspicious communion" with the masses. The spread of public schools would have to wait for a more democratic climate.

Education played an important role in broadening and deepening the sense of nationalism, and no single element was as important, perhaps, as the spelling book, an item of almost universal use. Noah Webster prepared an elementary speller published in 1783. By 1890 more than 60 million copies of his "Blue Back Speller" had been printed, and the book continued to sell well into the twentieth century. In his preface Webster issued a cultural Declaration of Independence: "The country," he wrote, "must, in some future time, be as distinguished by the superiority of her literary improvements, as she already is by the liberality of her civil and ecclesiastical constitutions."

AMERICA'S "DESTINY" American nationalism embodied a stirring idea. This first new nation, unlike the Old World nations of Europe, was not rooted in antiquity. Its people, except for the Indians, had not inhabited it over the centuries, nor was there any notion of a common ethnic descent. "The American national consciousness," one observer wrote, "is not a voice crying out of the depth of the dark past, but is proudly a product of the enlightened present, setting its face resolutely toward the future."

Many people, at least since the time of the Pilgrims, had thought America to be singled out for a special identity, a special mission. Jonathan Edwards said God had chosen America as "the glorious renovator of the world," and still later John Adams proclaimed the opening of America "a grand scheme and design in Providence for the illumination and the emancipation of the slavish part of mankind all over the earth." This sense of mission was neither limited to New England nor rooted solely in Calvinism. From the democratic rhetoric of Thomas Jefferson, to the pragmatism of George Washington, to heady toasts bellowed in South Carolina taverns, patriots everywhere articulated a special American leadership role in human history. The mission was now a call to lead the world toward liberty and equality. Meanwhile, however, Americans had to address more immediate problems created by their new nationhood. The Philadelphia doctor and scientist

Benjamin Rush issued a prophetic statement in 1787: "The American war is over: but this is far from being the case with the American Revolution. On the contrary, but the first act of the great drama is closed."

MAKING CONNECTIONS

- The American Revolution was the starting point for the foreign policy of the United States. Many of the specific foreign concerns that will be discussed in Chapters 8 and 9 sprang from issues directly relating to the Revolution.

- Much of what became Jacksonian Democracy (introduced in Chapter 10) can be traced to social and political movements associated with the American Revolution.

- The Articles of Confederation, the document that established the first national government for the United States, saw the new nation through the Revolution, but within a few years the Articles were discarded in favor of a new government, set forth in the Constitution.

FURTHER READING

The Revolutionary War is the subject of Colin Bonwick's *The American Revolution* (1991), Gordon S. Wood's *The Radicalism of the American Revolution* (1991), and Jeremy Black's *War for America: The Fight for Independence, 1775–1783* (1991). John Ferling's *Setting the World Ablaze: Washington, Adams, Jefferson and the American Revolution* (2000) highlights the role played by key leaders.

On the social history of the Revolutionary War, see John W. Shy's *A People Numerous and Armed* (1976), Charles Royster's *A Revolutionary People at War* (1979), and E. Wayne Carp's *To Starve the Army at Pleasure: Continental Army Adminstration and American Political Culture,*

1775–1783 (1984). Colin G. Calloway tells the neglected story of the Indian experiences in the Revolution in *The American Revolution in Indian Country: Crisis and Diversity in Native American Communities* (1995). The imperial, aristocratic, and racist aspects of the Revolution are detailed in Francis Jennings's *The Creation of America: Through Revolution to Empire* (2000).

Why some Americans remained loyal to the crown is the subject of Robert M. Calhoon's *The Loyalists in Revolutionary America, 1760–1781* (1973) and Mary Beth Norton's *The British-Americans* (1972).

The definitive study of African Americans during the Revolutionary era remains Benjamin Quarles's *The Negro in the American Revolution* (1961). Mary Beth Norton's *Liberty's Daughters* (1980) and Linda K. Kerber's *Women of the Republic* (1980) document the role women played in securing independence. Joy D. Buel and Richard Buel, Jr.'s *The Way of Duty* (1984) shows the impact of the Revolution on one New England family.

The standard introduction to the diplomacy of the Revolutionary era is Jonathan R. Dull's *A Diplomatic History of the American Revolution* (1985).

7  SHAPING A FEDERAL UNION

CHAPTER ORGANIZER

This chapter focuses on:

- the achievements and weaknesses of the Confederation government.

- the issues involved in writing the Constitution.

- the debate over ratifying the Constitution.

*I*n an address to fellow graduates at the Harvard commencement ceremony in 1787, young John Quincy Adams lamented "this critical period" when the country was "groaning under the intolerable burden of . . . accumulated evils." The same phrase, the "critical period," has often been used to label the history of the United States under the Articles of Confederation. Fear of a central authority dominated this period. Yet, while there were weaknesses of the Confederation, there were also major achievements. Moreover, lessons learned under the Confederation would serve well in the formulation of a new Constitution, and in the balancing of central and local authority under that Constitution.

THE CONFEDERATION

The Congress of the Confederation had little governmental authority. "It could ask for money but not compel payment," as one historian wrote, "it could enter into treaties but not enforce their stipulations; it could provide for raising of armies but not fill the ranks; it could borrow money but take no proper measures for repayment; it could advise and recommend but not command." The Congress was virtually helpless to cope with problems of diplomacy and postwar depression that would have challenged the resources of a much stronger government. It was not easy to find men of stature to serve in such a body, and often hard to gather a quorum of those who did. Yet in spite of its handicaps, the Confederation Congress somehow managed to survive and to lay important foundations for the future. It concluded the Peace of Paris in 1783. It created the first executive departments. And it formulated principles of land distribution and territorial government that guided expansion all the way to the Pacific coast.

Throughout most of the War for Independence the Congress remained distrustful of executive power. It assigned administrative duties to its committees and thereby imposed a painful burden on conscientious members. At one time or another John Adams, for instance, served on some eighty committees. In 1781, however, Congress began to set up three departments: Foreign Affairs, Finance, and War. Each was to have a single head responsible to Congress. Given time and stability, Congress and the department heads might have evolved into something like the parliamentary cabinet system. As it turned out, these agencies were the forerunners of the government departments that came into being later under the Constitution.

FINANCE   As yet, however, there was neither president nor prime minister, only the presiding officer of Congress and its secretary, Charles Thomson, who served continuously from 1774 to 1789. The closest thing to an executive head of the Confederation was Robert Morris, who as superintendent of finance in the final years of the war became the most influential figure in the government. He wanted to make both himself and the Confederation more powerful. He envisioned a coherent program of taxation and debt management to make the government financially stable; "a public debt supported by public revenue will prove the strongest cement to keep our confederacy to-gether," he confided to a friend. It would wed to the support of the fed-eral government the powerful influence of the public creditors. Morris therefore welcomed the chance to enlarge the debt by issuing new gov-ernment bonds in settlement of wartime claims. Because of the govern-ment's precarious finances, these securities brought only ten to fifteen cents on the dollar, but with a sounder Treasury—certainly with a tax power—they could be expected to rise in value, creating new capital with which to finance banks and economic development.

In 1781, as part of his plan, Morris secured a congressional charter for the Bank of North America, which would hold government deposits, lend money to the government, and issue bank notes. Though a national bank, it was in part privately owned and was expected to turn a profit for Morris and other shareholders, in addition to performing a public service. But Morris's program depended ultimately on a secure income for the government, and it foundered on the requirement of unanimous state approval for amendments to the Articles of Confederation. Local interests and the fear of a central authority—a fear strengthened by the recent quarrels with king and Parliament—hobbled action.

To carry their point, Morris and his nationalist friends in 1783 risked a dangerous gamble. Washington's army, encamped at Newburgh on the Hudson River, had grown restless in the final winter of the war. Their pay was late as usual, and experience gave them reason to fear that claims to land bounties and life pensions for officers might never be honored once their services were no longer needed. A delegation of offi-cers traveled to Philadelphia with a petition for redress. Soon they found themselves drawn into a scheme to line up the army and public creditors with nationalists in Congress and confront the states with the threat of a coup d'état unless they yielded more power to Congress. Alexander Hamilton, congressman from New York and former aide to General Washington, sought to bring his old commander into the plan.

Washington sympathized with the purpose. If congressional powers were not enlarged, he had told a friend, "the band which at present holds us together, by a very feeble thread, will soon be broken, when an-archy and confusion must ensue." But Washington was just as deeply convinced that a military coup would be both dishonorable and danger-ous. When he learned that some of the plotters had planned an unau-thorized meeting of officers, he confronted the conspirators. Drawing his spectacles from his pocket, he began: "I have grown not only gray but blind in the service of my country." When he had finished his dramatic and emotional address, his officers unanimously adopted resolutions denouncing the recent "infamous propositions," and the so-called Newburgh Conspiracy came to a sudden end.

The Confederation never did put its finances in order. The Continental currency had long since become a byword for worthlessness. It was never redeemed. The debt, domestic and foreign, grew from $11 million to $28 million as Congress paid off citizens' and soldiers' claims. Each year Congress ran a deficit on its operating expenses.

LAND POLICY   The one source from which Congress might hope ultimately to draw an independent income was the sale of western lands. Throughout the Confederation period, however, that income remained more a fleeting promise than an accomplished fact. The Confederation nevertheless dealt more effectively with the western lands than with anything else. There Congress had direct authority, at least on paper. Thinly populated by Indians, French settlers, and a growing number of American squatters, the region north of the Ohio River and west of the Appalachian Mountains had long been the site of overlapping claims by colonies and speculators.

As early as 1779 Congress had made a commitment in principle not to treat the western lands as colonies. The delegates resolved instead that western lands ceded by the states "shall be . . . formed into distinct Republican states," equal in all respects to other states. Between 1784 and 1787, policies for the development of the West emerged in three major ordinances of the Confederation Congress. These documents, which rank among its greatest achievements—and among the most important in American history—set precedents that the United States would follow in its expansion all the way to the Pacific. Thomas Jefferson in fact was prepared to grant self-government to western states at an early stage, when settlers would meet and choose their own officials. Under Jefferson's ordinance of 1784, when the population equaled that of the smallest existing state, the territory would achieve full statehood.

In the Land Ordinance of 1785 the delegates outlined a plan of land surveys and sales that would eventually stamp a rectangular pattern on much of the nation's surface, a pattern still visible from the air in many parts of the country because of the layout of roads and fields. Wherever

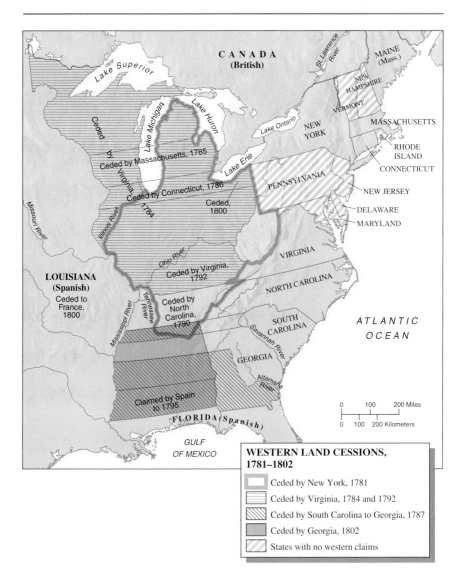

WESTERN LAND CESSIONS, 1781–1802

- Ceded by New York, 1781
- Ceded by Virginia, 1784 and 1792
- Ceded by South Carolina to Georgia, 1787
- Ceded by Georgia, 1802
- States with no western claims

Indian titles had been extinguished, the Northwest was to be surveyed into townships six miles square along east-west and north-south lines. Each township in turn was divided into 36 lots (or sections) one mile square (or 640 acres). The 640-acre sections were to go at auction for no less than $1 per acre, or $640 total. Such terms favored land specu-lators, of course, since few common folk had that much money or were able to work that much land. In later years new land laws would make smaller plots available at lower prices, but in 1785 Congress was faced with an empty Treasury. In each township, however, Congress did reserve the income from the sixteenth section for the support of schools—a significant departure at a time when public schools were rare.

In seven ranges to the west of the Ohio River, an area in which recent treaties had voided Indian titles, surveying began. But before any land sales occurred a group of speculators from New England presented cash-poor Congress with a seductive offer. Organized in Boston, the group took the name of the Ohio Company and sent the Reverend Manasseh Cutler to present their plan. Cutler proved a persuasive lobbyist, and in 1787 Congress voted a grant of 1.5 million acres for about $1 million in certificates of indebtedness to Revolutionary War veterans. The arrangement had the dual merit, Cutler argued, of reducing the debt and encouraging new settlement and sales.

THE NORTHWEST ORDINANCE   Spurred by the plans for land sales and settlement, Congress drafted a more specific frame of territorial government to replace Jefferson's ordinance of 1784. The new plan backed off from Jefferson's recommendation of early self-government. Because of the trouble that might be expected from squatters who were clamoring for free land, the Northwest Ordinance of 1787 required a period of colonial tutelage. At first the territory fell subject to a governor, a secretary, and three judges, all chosen by Congress. Eventually there would be three to five territories in the region, and when any one had 5,000 free male adults it could choose an assembly. Congress then would name a council of five from ten names proposed by the assembly. The governor would have a veto over actions by the territorial assembly, and so would Congress.

The resemblance to the old royal colonies is clear, but there were two significant differences. For one, the Ordinance anticipated statehood when any territory's population reached 60,000. At that point a convention could be called to draft a state constitution and apply to Congress for statehood. For another, it included a Bill of Rights that guaranteed religious freedom, legislative representation in proportion to population, trial by jury, habeas corpus, and the application of common law. Finally, the Ordinance excluded slavery permanently from the Northwest —a proviso Jefferson had failed to get accepted in his ordinance of 1784. This proved a fateful decision. As the progress of emancipation in the existing states gradually freed all slaves above the Mason-Dixon

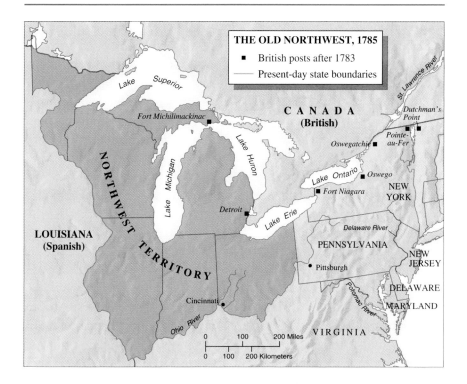

THE OLD NORTHWEST, 1785

■ British posts after 1783
— Present-day state boundaries

Lake Superior

Lake Huron

Lake Michigan

Lake Ontario

Lake Erie

St. Lawrence River

Fort Michilimackinac

CANADA
(British)

Dutchman's Point

Oswegatchie

Pointe-au-Fer

Oswego

Fort Niagara

NEW YORK

Detroit

Delaware River

NORTHWEST

LOUISIANA
(Spanish)

PENNSYLVANIA

NEW JERSEY

Pittsburgh

TERRITORY

DELAWARE
MARYLAND

Cincinnati

Potomac River

Ohio River

VIRGINIA

0   100   200 Miles
0   100   200 Kilometers

line, the Ohio River boundary of the Old Northwest extended the line between freedom and slavery all the way to the Mississippi River.

The Northwest Ordinance had a larger importance beyond establishing a formal procedure for transforming territories into states. It represented a sharp break with the imperialistic assumption behind European expansion into the Western Hemisphere. The new states were to be admitted as equals into the American republic.

The lands south of the Ohio River followed a different line of development. Title to the western lands remained with Georgia, North Carolina, and Virginia for the time being, but settlement proceeded at a far more rapid pace during and after the Revolution, despite the Indians' fierce resentment of encroachments on their hunting grounds. Substantial centers of population grew up around Harrodsburg and Boonesboro in the Kentucky Blue Grass and along the Watauga, Holston, and Cumberland Rivers, as far west as Nashborough (Nashville). In the Old Southwest active movements for statehood arose early. North Carolina tentatively ceded its western claims in 1784, whereupon the Holston settlers formed the short-lived state of Franklin, which became little more than a bone of contention between rival speculators until North Carolina reasserted control in 1789, shortly before the cession of its western lands became final.

Indian claims too were being extinguished. The Iroquois and Cherokees, badly battered during the Revolution, were in no position to resist encroachments. By the Second Treaty of Fort Stanwix (1784), the Iroquois were forced to cede land in western New York and Pennsylvania. In the Treaty of Hopewell (1785), the Cherokees gave up all claims in South Carolina, much of western North Carolina, and large portions of present-day Kentucky and Tennessee. Also in 1785 the major Ohio tribes dropped their claim to most of Ohio, except for a chunk bordering the western part of Lake Erie. The Creeks, pressed by the state of Georgia to cede portions of their lands in 1784–1785, went to war in the summer of 1786 with covert aid from Spanish Florida. When Spanish aid diminished, however, the Creek chief traveled to New York and in 1791 finally struck a bargain that gave the Creeks favorable trade arrangements with the United States but that did not restore the lost lands.

TRADE AND THE ECONOMY   In its economic life, as in planning westward expansion, the young nation dealt vigorously with difficult problems. Congress had little to do with achievements in the economy, but neither could it bear the blame for an acute economic contraction between 1770 and 1790, the result primarily of the war and separation from the British Empire. Although farmers enmeshed in local markets maintained their livelihood during the Revolutionary era, commercial agriculture dependent upon trade with foreign markets suffered a severe downturn. The southern Tidewater saw many slaves carried off by the British. Chesapeake planters also lost their lucrative foreign markets. Tobacco was especially hard hit. The British decision to close its West Indian colonies to American trade devastated what had been a thriving commerce in timber, wheat, and other foodstuffs.

Merchants suffered even more wrenching adjustments than the farmers. Cut out of the British mercantile system, they had to find new outlets for their trade. Circumstances that impoverished some enriched those who financed privateers, supplied the armies on both sides, and hoarded precious goods while demand and prices soared. By the end of the war, a strong sentiment for free trade had developed in both Britain and America. In the memorable year 1776, the Scottish economist Adam Smith brought out *The Wealth of Nations,* a classic manifesto against mercantilism. Some British statesmen embraced the new gospel, but the public and Parliament still clung to the conventions of mercantilism for many years to come.

After the war British trade with America did resume, and American ships were allowed to deliver American products and return to the United States with British goods. American ships could not carry British goods anywhere else, however. The pent-up demand for familiar goods created a vigorous market in exports to America, fueled by British credits and the hard money that had come into America from foreign aid, the expenditures of foreign armies, or wartime trade and privateering. The result was a quick cycle of postwar boom and bust, a buying spree followed by a money shortage and economic troubles that lasted several years.

In colonial days the chronic trade deficit with Britain had been offset by the influx of coins from trade with the West Indies. Now American ships found themselves excluded altogether from the British West Indies. The islands, however, still demanded wheat, fish, lumber, and other

Merchants' Counting House. *Americans involved in overseas trade, such as the merchants depicted here, were sharply affected by the dislocations of war.*

products from the mainland, and American shippers had not lost their talent for smuggling. Already American shippers had begun exploring new outlets, and by 1787 their seaports were flourishing more than ever. Freed from colonial restraints, they now had the run of the seven seas. Trade treaties opened new markets with the Dutch (1782), Swedes (1783), Prussians (1785), and Moroccans (1787), and American shippers found new outlets on their own in Europe, Africa, and Asia. The most spectacular new development, if not the largest, was trade with China. It began in 1784–1785, when the *Empress of China* sailed from New York to Canton and back, around the tip of South America. Profits from its cargo of silks and tea encouraged the outfitting of other ships that carried ginseng root and other American goods to exchange for the luxury goods of East Asia.

By 1790 American commerce and exports had far outrun the trade of the colonies. Merchants had more ships than before the war. Farm exports were twice what they had been. Although most of the exports were the products of forests, fields, and fisheries, during and after the war more Americans had turned to small-scale manufacturing, mainly for domestic markets. By 1787 a summary of major American enterprises included dozens of products from ships and ironwork to shoes, textiles, and soap.

DIPLOMACY   The shortcomings and failures of the Articles of Confederation prompted a growing chorus of complaints. In diplomacy, there remained the nagging problems of relations with Great Britain and Spain, both of which still kept military posts on American soil and conspired with Indians and white settlers in the West. The British, despite the peace treaty of 1783, held on to a string of forts along the Canadian border. From these they kept a hand in the fur trade and a degree of influence with the Indian tribes, whom they were suspected of stirring up to make sporadic attacks on the frontier. They gave as a reason for their continued occupation the failure of Americans to pay their prewar debts to British creditors. According to one Virginian, a common question in his state was: "If we are now to pay the debts due to British merchants, what have we been fighting for all this while?"

Another major irritant was the confiscation of Loyalist property. The peace treaty had encouraged Congress to stop confiscations, to guarantee immunity to Loyalists for twelve months, during which they could return and wind up their affairs, and to recommend that the states give back confiscated property. Persecutions, even lynchings, of Loyalists still occurred until after the end of the war. Some Loyalists returned unmolested, however, and once again took up their lives in their former homes. By the end of 1787, moreover, at the request of Congress, all the states had rescinded the laws that were in conflict with the peace treaty.

With Spain, the chief issues were the southern boundary and the right to navigate the Mississippi River. According to the preliminary treaty with Britain, the United States claimed a line as far south as the 31st parallel; Spain held out for the line running eastward from the mouth of the Yazoo River (at 32°28′N), which it claimed as the traditional boundary. The American treaty with Britain had also specified the right to navigate the Mississippi River to its mouth. Still, the international boundary ran down the middle of the river most of its length, and the Mississippi was entirely within Spanish Louisiana in its lower reaches. The right to navigation was a matter of importance because of the growing settlements in Kentucky and Tennessee, but in 1784 Louisiana's Spanish governor closed the river to American commerce and began to intrigue with the Creeks, Choctaws, Chickasaws, and other Indians of the Southwest against the American settlers and with the settlers against the United States.

THE CONFEDERATION'S PROBLEMS   The problems of trans-Appalachian settlers, however, seemed remote from the everyday concerns of most Americans. What touched them more closely were economic troubles and the currency shortage. Merchants who found themselves excluded from old channels of imperial trade began to agitate for reprisals. State governments, in response, laid special tonnage duties on British vessels and special tariffs on the goods they brought. State action alone, however, failed to work because of lack of uniformity among all the states. British ships could be diverted to states whose duties were less restrictive. The other states tried to meet this problem by taxing British goods that flowed across state lines, creating an impression that states were involved in commercial war with each other. Although these duties seldom affected American goods, there was a clear need, it seemed to commercial interests, for a central power to regulate trade.

Mechanics (skilled workers who made, used, or repaired tools and machines) and artisans (skilled workers who made products) were developing an infant industry. Their products ranged from crude iron nails

American craftsmen, such as this cabinet-maker, favored tariffs against foreign goods that competed with theirs.

to the fine silver bowls of Paul Revere. They wanted to take reprisals against British goods as well as British ships. They sought, and in various degrees obtained from the states, tariffs (taxes) against foreign goods that competed with theirs. The country would be on its way to economic independence, they argued, if only the money that flowed into the country were invested in domestic manufactures instead of being paid out for foreign goods. Nearly all the states gave some preference to American goods, but again the lack of uniformity in their laws put them at cross-purposes, and so urban mechanics along with merchants were drawn into the movement for a stronger central government in the interest of uniform regulation.

The shortage of cash and other economic difficulties gave rise to more immediate demands for paper currency as legal tender, for postponement of tax and debt payments, and for laws to "stay" the foreclosure of mortgages. Farmers who had profited during the war found themselves squeezed afterwards by depressed crop prices and mounting debts while merchants opened up new trade routes. Creditors demanded hard money, but it was in short supply—and paper money was almost nonexistent after the depreciation of the Continental currency. The result was an outcry for relief, and around 1785 the demand for new paper money became the most divisive issue in state politics. Debtors demanded the addition of paper money as a means of easing repayment, and farmers saw issuing paper money as an inflationary way to raise commodity prices.

In 1785–1786 seven states (Pennsylvania, New York, New Jersey, South Carolina, Rhode Island, Georgia, and North Carolina) began issuing paper money. It served in five of these states—Pennsylvania, New York, New Jersey, South Carolina, and Rhode Island—as a means of credit to hard-pressed farmers through state loans on farm mortgages. It was variously used to fund state debts and to pay off the claims of veterans. In spite of the cries of calamity at the time, the money never seriously depreciated in Pennsylvania, New York, and South Carolina. In Rhode Island, however, the debtor party ran wild. In 1786 the Rhode Island legislature issued more paper money than any other state in proportion to population, and declared it legal tender in payment of all debts. Creditors fled the state to avoid being paid in worthless paper.

SHAYS'S REBELLION   Newspapers throughout the country followed the developments in Rhode Island. The little commonwealth, stubbornly independent since the days of Roger Williams, became the prime example of democracy run riot—until its riotous neighbor, Massachusetts, provided the final proof (some said) that the new country was poised on the brink of anarchy: Shays's Rebellion. There, the trouble was not too much paper money but too little, as well as too much taxation.

After 1780, Massachusetts had remained in the grip of a rigidly conservative regime, which levied ever-larger poll and land taxes to pay off a heavy war debt, held mainly by wealthy creditors in Boston. The taxes fell most heavily upon beleaguered farmers and the poor in general. When the Massachusetts legislature adjourned in 1786 without providing either paper money or any other relief from taxes and debts, three western counties erupted into spontaneous revolt.

Armed bands closed the courts and prevented foreclosures. A ragtag "army" of some 1,200 disgruntled farmers under Daniel Shays, a destitute war veteran, advanced upon the federal arsenal at Springfield, Massachusetts, in 1787. Shays and his followers sought a more flexible monetary policy, laws allowing them to use corn and wheat as money, and the right to postpone paying taxes until the depression lifted.

A small militia force, however, scattered the debtor army with a single volley that left four dead. General Benjamin Lincoln, a hero of the Revolution, arrived soon after with reinforcements from Boston and routed the remaining Shaysites. The rebel farmers nevertheless had a victory of sorts. The new state legislature included members sympathetic to the agricultural crisis. They omitted direct taxes the following year, lowered court fees, and exempted clothing, household goods, and tools from the debt process. But a more important consequence was the impetus the rebellion gave to conservatism and nationalism.

Rumors, at times deliberately inflated, greatly exaggerated the extent of this pathetic rebellion of desperate men. The Shaysites were linked to the conniving British and accused of seeking to pillage the wealthy. Panic set in among the republic's elite. In a letter to Thomas Jefferson, Abigail Adams tarred the Shaysites as "Ignorant, restless desperadoes, without conscience or principles . . . mobbish insurgents [who]are for sapping the foundation" of the struggling young government.

Jefferson disagreed. If Adams and others were overly critical of Shays's Rebellion, Jefferson was, if anything, too complacent. From his post in Paris, he wrote to a friend back home: "The tree of liberty must be refreshed from time to time with the blood of patriots and tyrants." Abigail Adams was so infuriated by Jefferson's position that she stopped corresponding with him for months.

CALLS FOR A STRONGER GOVERNMENT   Well before the outbreaks in New England, the advocates of a stronger central authority had come to demand a convention to revise the Articles of Confederation. Self-interest led bankers, merchants, and mechanics to promote a stronger central government as the only alternative to anarchy. Gradually people were losing the fear of a strong central government as they saw evidence that tyranny might come from other quarters, including the common people themselves.

Such developments led many of the Revolutionary leaders to revise their assessment of American character. "We have, probably," concluded George Washington in 1786, "had too good an opinion of human nature in forming our confederation." James Madison decided that people were stretching the meaning of liberty far beyond what he and others had envisioned. He found a "spirit of *locality*" rampant in the state legislature that was destroying the "aggregate interests of the community." Even worse, he saw people taking the law and other people's property into their own hands. Such developments led Madison and others to revise their assumptions about republican virtue. At any given time, they decided, only a distinct minority of citizens could be relied upon to set aside their private interests in favor of the common good. Madison and other so-called Federalists concluded that the new republic must now depend for its success on the constant virtue of the few rather than the public-spiritedness of the many.

In 1785 commissioners from Virginia and Maryland had met at Mount Vernon on George Washington's invitation to promote commerce and economic development and to settle outstanding questions about the navigation of the Potomac and Chesapeake Bay. Washington had a personal interest in the river flowing by his door: it was a potential route to the West, with its upper reaches close to the upper reaches of the Ohio, where his military career had begun thirty years before. The delegates agreed on interstate cooperation, and Maryland suggested a further pact with Pennsylvania and Delaware to encourage water communication between the Chesapeake and the Ohio River; the Virginia legislature agreed, and at Madison's suggestion invited all thirteen states to send delegates for a general discussion of commercial problems. Nine states named representatives, but those from only five appeared at the Annapolis Convention in 1786—neither the New England states nor the Carolinas and Georgia were represented. Apparent failure soon turned into success, however, when the alert Alexander Hamilton, representing New York, presented a resolution for still another convention in Philadelphia to consider all measures necessary "to render the constitution of the Federal Government adequate to the exigencies of the Union."

ADOPTING THE CONSTITUTION

THE CONSTITUTIONAL CONVENTION   After stalling for several months, Congress fell in line in 1787 with a resolution endorsing a convention "for the sole and express purpose of revising the Articles of Confederation." By then five states had already named delegates; before the meeting, called to begin on May 14, 1787, six more states had acted. New Hampshire delayed until June, and its delegates arrived in July. Fearful of consolidated power, tiny Rhode Island kept aloof throughout. (Critics labeled the fractious little state "Rogue Island.") Virginia's Patrick Henry, an implacable foe of centralized government, claimed to "smell a rat" and refused to represent his state. Twenty-nine delegates from nine states began work on May 25. Altogether the state legislatures elected seventy-three men. Fifty-five attended at one time or another, and after four months, thirty-nine signed the Constitution they had drafted.

The durability and flexibility of that document testify to the remarkable quality of the men who made it. The delegates were surprisingly young: forty-two was the average age. Farmers, merchants, lawyers, bankers, many of them were widely read in history, law, and political philosophy. Yet they were also practical men of experience, tested in the fires of the Revolution. Twenty-one had served in the conflict, seven had been

A session of the Constitutional Convention with George Washington presiding.

state governors, most of them had been members of the Continental Congress, and eight had signed the Declaration of Independence.

The magisterial Washington served as presiding officer, but participated little in the debates. Eighty-one-year-old Benjamin Franklin, the oldest delegate, also said little from the floor but did provide a wealth of experience, wit, and common sense behind the scenes. More active in the debates were James Madison, the ablest political philosopher in the group; Massachusetts's dapper Elbridge Gerry, a Harvard graduate who earned the nickname "Old Grumbletonian" because, as John Adams once said, he "opposed everything he did not propose"; George Mason, the irritable author of the Virginia Declaration of Rights and a slave-owning planter with a deep-rooted suspicion of all government; the eloquent, arrogant New York aristocrat Gouverneur Morris, who harbored a venomous contempt for the masses; Scottish-born James Wilson of Pennsylvania, one of the ablest lawyers in the new nation and next in importance at the convention only to Washington and Madison; and Roger Sherman of Connecticut, a self-trained lawyer adept at negotiating compromises. John Adams, like Jefferson, was serving abroad. Also conspicuously absent during most of the Convention was thirty-two-year-old Alexander Hamilton, the staunch nationalist who regretfully went home when the other two New York delegates walked out because of their states'-rights principles.

All the participants acknowledged that Madison emerged as the central figure at the Convention. Small of stature—barely over five feet tall—and frail in health, the thirty-six-year-old Madison was a studious bachelor descended from wealthy slave-owning Virginia planters. He suffered from chronic headaches and was painfully shy. Crowds made him nervous, and he hated to use his high-pitched voice in public, much less in open debate.

But the Princeton graduate possessed a keen, agile mind with a voracious appetite for learning, and the convincing eloquence of his arguments proved to be decisive. "Every person seems to acknowledge his greatness," wrote one delegate. Madison arrived in Philadelphia with trunks full of books and a head full of ideas. He had been preparing for the Convention for months and probably knew more about historic forms of government than any other delegate.

For the most part, the delegates' differences on political philosophy fell within a narrow range. On certain fundamentals they generally agreed: that government derived its just powers from the consent of the people, but that society must be protected from the tyranny of the majority; that the people at large must have a voice in their government, but that checks and balances must be provided to keep any one group from abusing power; that a stronger central authority was essential, but that all power was subject to abuse. They assumed with Madison that even the best people were naturally selfish, and government, therefore, could not be founded altogether upon a trust in goodwill and virtue. Yet by a careful arrangement of checks and balances, by checking power with countervailing power, the Founding Fathers hoped to devise institutions that could constrain individual sinfulness and channel self-interest to benefit the public good.

THE VIRGINIA AND NEW JERSEY PLANS   At the outset the delegates unanimously elected George Washington president of the Convention. One of the first decisions was to meet behind closed doors in order to discourage outside pressures and theatrical speeches to the galleries. The secrecy of the proceedings was remarkably well kept, and knowledge of the debates comes mainly from Madison's extensive notes.

It was Madison, too, who drafted the proposals that set the framework of the discussions. These proposals, which came to be called the "Virginia Plan," embodied a revolutionary idea for the delegates to scrap their instructions to revise the Articles of Confederation and to submit

James Madison was only thirty-six when he assumed a major role in the drafting of the Constitution. This miniature is by Charles Willson Peale (c. 1783).

an entirely new document to the states. The plan proposed separate legislative, executive, and judicial branches, and a truly national government to make laws binding upon individual citizens and upon states as well. Congress would be divided into two houses, a lower one chosen by popular vote and an upper house chosen by the lower house from nominees of the state legislatures. Congress could disallow state laws under the plan and would itself define the extent of its and the states' authority.

On June 15 delegates submitted the "New Jersey Plan," which proposed to keep the existing structure of equal representation of states in a unicameral Congress, but to give it power to levy taxes and regulate commerce and authority to name a plural executive (with no veto) and a Supreme Court.

The different plans presented the Convention with two major issues: whether to amend the Articles of Confederation or draft a new document, and whether to have congressional representation by states or by population. On the first point the Convention voted to work toward a national government as envisioned by the Virginians. Regarding the powers of this government there was little disagreement except in the details. Experience with the Articles had persuaded the delegates that an effective central government, as distinguished from a confederation, needed the power to levy taxes, to regulate commerce, to raise an army and navy, and to make laws binding upon individual citizens. The lessons of the 1780s suggested to them, moreover, that in the interest of order and uniformity the states must be denied certain powers: to issue money, abrogate contracts, make treaties, wage war, and levy tariffs.

But furious disagreements then arose. The first clash in the Convention involved the issue of representation, and it was resolved by the "Great Compromise," sometimes called the "Connecticut Compromise," proposed by Roger Sherman, which gave both groups their way.

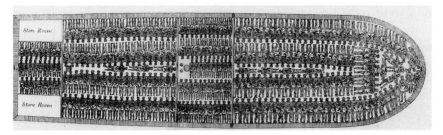

This cross-sectional view of the British slave ship Brookes *shows the abominably crowded conditions the "cargo" endured in the international slave trade.*

The more populous states won apportionment by population in the House of Representatives; the states that sought to protect state power won equality in the Senate, with the vote by individuals and not by states.

An equally contentious struggle ensued between northern and southern delegates over slavery and the regulation of trade, an omen of sectional controversies to come. Slavery, Madison's secretary noted, was a "distracting question" to most of the delegates rather than a compelling moral dilemma. Few if any of the framers of the Constitution even considered the notion of abolition, and they carefully avoided using the term "slavery" in the final document. In this they reflected the prevailing attitudes among white Americans. Most agreed with South Carolina's John Rutledge when he asserted: "Religion and humanity [have] nothing to do with this [slavery] question. Interest alone is the governing principle of nations."

The "interest" of southern delegates, with slaves so numerous in their states, dictated that slaves be counted as part of the population in determining the number of their congressional representatives. Northerners were willing to have slaves counted in deciding each state's share of direct taxes, but not for purposes of representation. On this issue the Confederation Congress had supplied a handy precedent when it sought an amendment to make population rather than land values the standard for fiscal requisitions. The proposed amendment to the Articles would have counted three-fifths of the slaves for this purpose. The delegates, with little dissent, agreed to incorporate the same three-fifths ratio in the new Constitution as a basis for apportioning both representatives and direct taxes.

A more sensitive issue involved an effort to prevent the central government from stopping the transatlantic slave trade. Virginia's George Mason, himself a slave owner, condemned the "infernal traffic," which his state had already outlawed. He argued that the issue concerned "not the importing states alone but the whole union." People in the western territories were "already calling out for slaves for their new lands." He feared that they would "fill the country" with slaves. Such a development would bring forth "the judgment of Heaven" on the country. Southern delegates were quick to challenge Mason's reasoning. They argued that the continued importation of slaves was vital to their states' economies.

To resolve the question, the delegates established a time limit. Congress could not forbid the foreign slave trade before 1808, but it could levy a tax of $10 a head on all slaves imported. In both provisions, a sense of delicacy—and hypocrisy—dictated the use of euphemisms. The Constitution spoke of "free Persons" and "all other persons," of "such persons as any of the States Now existing shall think proper to admit," and of persons "held to Service of Labor." The odious word "slavery" did not appear in the Constitution until the Thirteenth Amendment (1865) abolished it.

If the delegates found the slavery issue distracting, they considered irrelevant any discussion of the legal or political role of women under the new Constitution. The Revolutionary rhetoric of liberty prompted some women to demand political equality. "The men say we have no business" with politics, Eliza Wilkinson of South Carolina observed as the Constitution was being framed, "but I won't have it thought that because we are the weaker sex as to bodily strength we are capable of nothing more than domestic concerns." Her complaint, however, fell on deaf ears. There was never any formal discussion of women's rights at the Convention. The new nationalism still defined politics and government as outside the realm of female endeavor.

The Constitution also said little about the processes of immigration and naturalization, and most of what it said was negative. In Article II, Section 1, it prohibited any future immigrant from becoming president, limiting that office to a "natural born Citizen." In Article I, Sections 2 and 3, respectively, it stipulated that no person could serve in the House of Representatives who had not "been seven Years a Citizen of the United States" or in the Senate who had not "been nine Years a

Citizen." On the matter of defining citizenship, the Constitution gave Congress the authority "to establish an uniform Rule of Naturalization," but offered no further guidance on the matter. As a result, naturalization policy has changed significantly over the years in response to fluctuating social attitudes and political moods. In 1790 the first Congress passed a naturalization law that allowed "free white persons" who had been in the country for as little as two years to be made naturalized citizens in any court. This meant that persons of African descent were denied federal citizenship. It was left to individual states to determine whether free blacks were citizens. And because Indians were not "free white persons," they were also treated as aliens rather than citizens. Not until 1924 would Congress grant citizenship to American Indians.

THE SEPARATION OF POWERS   The details of governmental structure embedded in the Constitution aroused less debate than the basic issues pitting the large against the small states and the northern against the southern states. Existing state constitutions, several of which already separated powers among legislative, executive, and judicial branches, set an example that reinforced the Convention's resolve to disperse power with checks and balances. Although the Founding Fathers hated royal tyranny, most of them also feared the people and favored various mechanisms to check public passions. Some delegates displayed a thumping disdain for any democratizing of the political system. Alexander Hamilton once called the people "a great beast," and Elbridge Gerry asserted that most of the nation's problems "flow from an excess of democracy."

These elitist views were accommodated by the Constitution's mixed legislative system. The lower house was designed to be closest to voters, who elected it every two years. It would be, according to Virginia's George Mason, "the grand repository of the democratic principle of the Government." House members should "sympathize with their constituents, should think as they think, & feel as they feel; and for these purposes should even be residents among them." The upper house, or Senate, its members elected by state legislatures, was intended to be more detached from the voters. Staggered six-year terms prevented the choice of a majority in any given year, and thereby further isolated senators from the passing fancies of public passion.

The decision that a single person be made the chief executive caused the delegates "considerable pause," according to James Madison. George Mason protested that this would create a "fetus of monarchy." Indeed, several of the chief executive's powers actually exceeded those of the British monarch. This was the sharpest departure from the recent experience in state government, where the office of governor had commonly been diluted because of the recent memory of struggles with the colonial executives. The president had a veto over acts of Congress, subject to being overridden by a two-thirds vote in each house, although the royal veto had long since fallen into complete disuse. The president was commander-in-chief of the armed forces and responsible for the execution of the laws. The chief executive could make treaties with the advice and consent of two-thirds of the Senate, and had the power to appoint diplomats, judges, and other officers with the consent of a Senate majority. The president was instructed to report annually on the state of the nation and was authorized to recommend legislation, a provision that presidents eventually would take as a mandate to form and promote extensive programs.

But the president's powers were limited in certain key areas. The chief executive could neither declare war nor make peace; those powers were reserved for Congress. Unlike the British king, moreover, the president could be removed. The House could impeach (indict) the chief executive—and other civil officers—on charges of treason, bribery, or "other high crimes and misdemeanors," and the Senate could remove an impeached president by a two-thirds vote upon conviction. The presiding officer at the trial of a president would be the chief justice, since the usual presiding officer of the Senate (the vice-president) would have a personal stake in the outcome.

The leading nationalists—men like Madison, James Wilson, and Hamilton—wanted to strengthen the independence of the executive by entrusting the choice to popular election. At least in this instance, the nationalists, often accused of being the aristocratic party, favored a bold new departure in democracy. But an elected executive was still too far beyond the American experience. Besides, a national election would have created enormous problems of organization and voter qualification. Wilson suggested instead that the people of each state choose presidential electors equal to the number of their senators and representatives. Others proposed that the legislators make the choice. Finally, the Convention voted to let the legislature decide the method in each state. Before long nearly all the states were choosing the electors by popular vote, and the electors were acting as agents of party will, casting their votes as they had pledged before the election. This method diverged from the original expectation that the electors would deliberate and make their own choices.

On the third branch of government, the judiciary, there was surprisingly little debate. Both the Virginia and New Jersey Plans had called for a Supreme Court, which the Constitution established, providing specifically for a chief justice of the United States and leaving up to Congress the number of other justices. Although the Constitution nowhere authorized the courts to declare laws void when they conflicted with the Constitution, the power of judicial review was implied, and was soon exercised in cases involving both state and federal laws. Article VI declared the federal constitution, federal laws, and treaties to be the "supreme law of the land," state laws or constitutions to the contrary notwithstanding. The advocates of states' rights thought this a victory, since it eliminated the proviso in the Virginia Plan for Congress to settle

Signing the Constitution, September 17, 1787. *Thomas Pritchard Rossiter's painting shows George Washington presiding over what Thomas Jefferson called "an assembly of demi-gods."*

all conflicts with state authority. As it turned out, however, the clause became the basis for an important expansion of judicial review.

While the Constitution extended vast new powers to the national government, the delegates' mistrust of unchecked power is apparent in repeated examples of countervailing forces: the separation of the three branches of government, the president's veto, the congressional power of impeachment and removal, the Senate's power over treaties and appointments, the courts' implied right of judicial review. In addition, the new frame of government specifically forbade Congress to pass bills of attainder (criminal condemnation by legislative act) or ex post facto laws (laws adopted after the event to make past deeds criminal). It also reserved to the states large areas of sovereignty—a reservation soon made explicit by the Tenth Amendment. By dividing sovereignty between the people and the government, the framers of the Constitution provided a distinctive contribution to political theory. That is, by vesting ultimate authority in the people, they divided sovereignty *within* the government. This constituted a dramatic break with the colonial tradition. The British had always insisted that the sovereignty of the king-in-Parliament was indivisible.

The most glaring defect of the Articles of Confederation, the rule of unanimity that defeated every effort to amend them, led the delegates to provide a less forbidding though still difficult method of amending the new Constitution. Amendments could be proposed either by two-thirds vote of each house or by a convention specially called, upon application of two-thirds of the legislatures. Amendments could be ratified by approval of three-fourths of the states acting through their legislatures or special conventions. The national convention has never been used, however, and state conventions have been called only once—to ratify the repeal of the Eighteenth Amendment, which had prohibited alcoholic beverages.

THE FIGHT FOR RATIFICATION   The final article of the Constitution provided that it would become effective upon ratification by nine states (not quite the three-fourths majority required for amendment). After fighting off efforts to censure the Convention for exceeding its authority, the Congress submitted its work to the states on September 28, 1787.

In the ensuing political debate, advocates of the new Constitution, who might properly have been called Nationalists because they preferred a strong central government, assumed the more reassuring name of Federalists. Opponents, who favored a more decentralized federal system, became Antifederalists. The initiative that the Federalists took in assuming their name was characteristic of the whole campaign. They got the jump on their critics. Their leaders had been members of the Convention and were already familiar with the document and the arguments on each point. They were not only better prepared but better organized, and on the whole, made up of the more able leaders in the political community.

Historians have hotly debated the motivation of the advocates of the new Constitution. For more than a century the tendency prevailed to idolize the Founding Fathers. In 1913, however, Charles A. Beard's book *An Economic Interpretation of the Constitution* advanced the shocking thesis that the Philadelphia Convention was made up of men who had a selfish economic interest in the outcome.

Beard argued that the delegates represented an economic elite of speculators in western lands, holders of depreciated government securities, and creditors whose wealth was mostly in "paper": mortgages, stocks, bonds, and the like. The holders of western lands and government bonds would benefit from a stronger government. Creditors generally stood to gain from the prohibitions against state currency issues and against the impairment of contract, provisions clearly aimed at the paper money issues and stay laws that were then effective in many states.

Beard's thesis provided a useful antidote to unquestioning hero worship, and still contains a germ of truth, but he exaggerated. Most of the delegates, according to evidence unavailable to Beard, had no compelling stake in paper wealth, and most were far more involved in landholding. Many prominent nationalists, including the "Father of the Constitution," James Madison, had no western lands, bonds, or much other personal property. Some opponents of the Constitution, on the other hand, held large blocks of land and securities. Economic interests certainly figured in the process, but they functioned in a complex interplay of state, sectional, group, and individual interests that turned largely on how well people had fared under the Confederation.

The most notable aspect of the new American republic was not selfishness but cooperation. The American Revolution led not to general chaos and terror but to "an outbreak of constitution-making." From the 1760s through the 1780s there occurred a prolonged debate over the fundamental issues of government, which in its scope and depth—and in the durability of its outcome—is without parallel.

THE FEDERALIST   Among the supreme legacies of that debate was *The Federalist,* a collection of essays originally published in the New York press between 1787 and 1788. Instigated by Alexander Hamilton, the eighty-five articles published under the name "Publius" included about fifty by Hamilton, thirty by James Madison, and five by John Jay. The authorship of some selections remains in doubt. Written in support of ratification, the essays defended the principle of a supreme national authority, but at the same time sought to reassure doubters that the people and the states had little reason to fear usurpations and tyranny by the new government.

In perhaps the most famous single essay, No. 10, Madison argued that the very size and diversity of the large new country would make it impossible for any single faction to form a majority that could dominate the government. This contradicted prevailing notions of republican forms of government. Republics, the conventional wisdom of the times insisted, could survive only in small, homogeneous countries like Switzerland and the Netherlands. Large republics, on the other hand, would fragment into anarchy and tyranny through the influence of factions. Quite the contrary, Madison insisted. Given a balanced federal polity, a republic could work in large and diverse countries probably better than in smaller nations. "Extend the sphere," he wrote, "and you take in a greater variety of parties and interests; you make it less probable that a majority of the whole will have a common motive to invade the rights of other citizens."

The Federalists insisted that the new union would contribute to prosperity. The Antifederalists, however, talked more of the dangers of power in terms that had become familiar during the long struggles with Parliament and the crown. They noted the absence of a bill of rights protecting the rights of individuals and states. They found the process of ratification highly irregular, as it was—indeed, illegal under the Articles of Confederation. Not only did Patrick Henry refuse to attend the Constitutional Convention, he demanded later (unsuccessfully) that it be investigated as a conspiracy. The Antifederalist leaders—George Mason, Patrick Henry, and Richard Henry Lee of Virginia, George Clinton of New York, Samuel Adams and Elbridge Gerry of Massachusetts, Luther Martin of Maryland—were often men whose careers and reputations had been established well before the Revolution. The Federalist leaders were more likely to be younger men whose careers had begun in the Revolution—men such as Hamilton, Madison, and John Jay.

The disagreement between the two groups, however, was more over means than ends. Both sides, for the most part, agreed that a stronger national authority was needed, and that it required an independent income to function properly. Both were convinced that the people must erect safeguards against tyranny, even the tyranny of the majority. Few of the Constitution's supporters liked it in its entirety, but they felt that it was the best obtainable; few of its opponents found it unacceptable in its entirety. Once the new government had become an accomplished fact, few wanted to undo the work of the Philadelphia convention.

THE DECISION OF THE STATES   Ratification gained momentum before the end of 1787, and several of the smaller states were among the first to act, apparently satisfied that they had gained all the safeguards they could hope for in equality of representation in the Senate. New Jersey and Georgia voted unanimously in favor. Massachusetts, still sharply divided in the aftermath of Shays's Rebellion, was the first state in which the outcome was close. There the Federalists carried the day by winning over

RATIFICATION OF THE CONSTITUTION

Order of Ratification	State	Date of Ratification
1	Delaware	December 7, 1787
2	Pennsylvania	December 12, 1787
3	New Jersey	December 18, 1787
4	Georgia	January 2, 1788
5	Connecticut	January 9, 1788
6	Massachusetts	February 7, 1788
7	Maryland	April 28, 1788
8	South Carolina	May 23, 1788
9	New Hampshire	June 21, 1788
10	Virginia	June 25, 1788
11	New York	July 26, 1788
12	North Carolina	November 21, 1789
13	Rhode Island	May 29, 1790

two hesitant leaders of the popular party. They dangled before John Hancock the possibility of becoming vice-president, and won the acquiescence of Samuel Adams when they agreed to recommend amendments designed to protect human rights, including one that would specifically reserve to the states all powers not granted to the new government. Massachusetts approved by 187 to 168 on February 7, 1788.

New Hampshire was the ninth state to ratify, and the Constitution could now be put into effect, but the union could hardly succeed without the approval of Virginia, the most populous state, or New York, with the third highest population, which occupied a key position geographically. Both states harbored strong opposition groups. In Virginia Patrick Henry became the chief spokesman of backcountry farmers who feared

THE VOTE ON THE CONSTITUTION

Federalist majority

Antifederalist majority

Evenly divided

the powers of the new government, but wavering delegates were won over by the same strategem as in Massachusetts. When it was proposed that the Convention should recommend a bill of rights, Edmund Randolph, who had refused to sign the finished document, announced his conversion to the cause.

Virginia's convention ratified on June 25 by a vote of 89 to 79. In New York, as in New Hampshire, Hamilton and the other Federalists worked for a delay, in the hope that action by New Hampshire and Virginia would persuade the delegates that the new framework would go into effect with or without New York. On July 26, 1788, they carried the day by the closest margin thus far, 30 to 27. North Carolina stubbornly withheld action until amend-

The Tenth Pillar, *an illustration from the* City Gazette *of Charleston that depicts Fame announcing the ratification of the Constitution. This image appeared on July 22, 1788, and the three missing columns represent the three states yet to ratify the Constitution: New York, North Carolina, and Rhode Island.*

ments comprising a bill of rights were actually submitted by Congress. On November 21, 1789, North Carolina joined the new government, which was already under way, 194 to 77. Rhode Island, true to form, continued to hold out, and did not relent until May 29, 1790. Even then the vote was the closest of all, 34 to 32.

Upon notification that New Hampshire had become the ninth state to ratify, the Confederation Congress began to draft plans for an orderly transfer of power. On September 13, 1788, it selected New York City as the seat of the new government and fixed the date for elections. March 4, 1789, was the date set for the meeting of the new Congress. Each state would set the date for electing the first members of Congress. On October 10, 1788, the Confederation Congress transacted its last business and passed into history.

"Our constitution is in actual operation," the elderly Benjamin Franklin wrote to a friend; "everything appears to promise that it will last; but in this world nothing is certain but death and taxes." George Washington

was even more uncertain about the future under the new plan of government. He had told a fellow delegate as the Convention adjourned: "I do
not expect the Constitution to last for more than twenty years."

The Constitution has lasted much longer, of course, and in the process it has provided a model of resilient republican government whose
features have been repeatedly borrowed by other nations through the
years. Yet what makes the American Constitution so distinctive is not
its specific provisions but its remarkable harmony with the particular
"genius of the people" it governs. The Constitution has been neither a
static abstraction nor a "machine that would go of itself," as the poet
James Russell Lowell would later assert. Instead it has provided a flexible system of government that presidents, legislators, judges, and the
people have adjusted to changing social, economic, and political circumstances. In this sense the Founding Fathers not only created "a
more perfect Union" in 1787; they engineered a frame of government
whose resilience has enabled later generations to continue to perfect
their republican experiment. But the framers of the Constitution failed
in one significant respect. In skirting the issue of slavery so as to cement the union, they unknowingly allowed tensions over the "peculiar
institution" to reach the point where there would be no political solution—only civil war.

MAKING CONNECTIONS

- The debate about the nature of the national government and its
  relation to the people and the states reemerged in the Kentucky
  and Virginia Resolutions (Chapter 8), the Hartford Convention
  (Chapter 9), and the Nullification Crisis (Chapter 11).

- Slavery, viewed by the delegates to the Constitutional Convention
  as little more than a "distracting question," soon became a major
  political problem—especially after the Missouri Compromise (in
  Chapter 10).

Further Reading

A good overview of the Confederation period is Richard B. Morris's *The Forging of the Union, 1781–1789* (1987). Another useful analysis of this period is Richard Buel, Jr.'s *Securing the Revolution: Ideology in American Politics, 1789–1815* (1974).

David P. Szatmary's *Shays's Rebellion: The Making of an Agrarian Insurrection* (1980) covers that fateful incident. For a fine account of cultural change during the period, see Joseph J. Ellis's *After the Revolution: Profiles of Early American Culture* (1979).

Excellent treatments of the post-Revolutionary era include Edmund S. Morgan's *Inventing the People* (1988), Michael Kammen's *Sovereignty and Liberty* (1988), and Joyce Appleby's *Inheriting the Revolution* (2000). Among the better collections of essays on the Constitution are *Toward a More Perfect Union* (1988), edited by Neil L. York and *The Framing and Ratification of the Constitution* (1987), edited by Leonard W. Levy and Dennis J. Mahoney.

Bruce Ackerman's *We the People: Foundations* (1990) examines Federalist political principles. For the Bill of Rights that emerged from the ratification struggles, see Robert A. Rutland's *The Birth of the Bill of Rights, 1776–1791* (1955).

8 ⌘ THE FEDERALIST ERA

CHAPTER ORGANIZER

This chapter focuses on:

- the early operation of the new government.

- Alexander Hamilton's Federalist program.

- the beginnings of the first party system (Federalists and Republicans).

- the elements of Federalist foreign policy.

he Constitution called for a powerful central government that would deal effectively with the problems of the vast new nation. But various domestic and foreign crises did not allow an easy transition for the fledgling republic launched so boldly by the revolutionary generation.

A NEW NATION

The framers of the Constitution sought to create a new federal government capable of administering a rapidly expanding territory and population. In 1789 the United States and the western territories covered an area from the Atlantic Ocean to the Mississippi River and included almost 4 million people. This vast new nation harbored distinct regional differences. New England remained a region of small farms and bustling seaports, but it was on the verge of developing a small-scale manufacturing sector. The Middle States boasted the most well-balanced economy, the largest cities, and the most diverse collection of ethnic and religious groups. The South was an agricultural region more ethnically homogeneous and increasingly dependent on slave labor. By 1790 the southern states were exporting as much tobacco as they had been before the Revolution, and new farm commodities such as grains, indigo, and hemp helped diversify the economy. Most important, however, was the surge in cotton production. Between 1790 and 1815, the annual production of cotton rose from less than 3 million pounds to 93 million pounds.

Overall, the United States in 1790 was predominantly a rural society. Eighty percent of households were involved in agricultural production. Only a few cities had more than 5,000 people. The first national census, taken in 1790, reported that there were 750,000 African Americans,

An engraving from the title page of The Universal Asylum and Columbian Magazine, *Philadelphia, 1790. America is represented as a woman laying down her shield to engage in education, art, commerce, and agriculture.*

almost one-fifth of the population. Most of the them lived in the five southernmost states. Less than 10 percent of the blacks lived outside the South. Most African Americans, of course, were slaves, but there were many free blacks as a result of the Revolution. In fact, the proportion of free blacks to slaves was never higher than in 1790.

The 1790 census did not even include the many Indians still living east of the Mississippi River. Most Americans viewed the Native Americans as those peoples whom the Declaration of Independence dismissed as "merciless Indian savages." It is estimated that there were over eighty tribes totaling perhaps as many as 150,000 persons in 1790. In the Old Northwest along the Great Lakes, the British continued to arm the Indians and encouraged them to resist American encroachments. Between 1784 and 1790, Indians killed or captured some 1,500 settlers in Kentucky alone. Such bloodshed generated a ferocious reaction. "The people of Kentucky," observed an official frustrated by his inability to negotiate a treaty between whites and Indians, "will carry on private expeditions against the Indians and kill them whenever they meet them, and I do not believe there is a jury in all Kentucky that will punish a man for it." In the South the five most powerful tribes—the Cherokees, Chickasaws, Choctaws, Creeks, and Seminoles—numbered between 50,000 and 100,000. They steadfastly refused to recognize American authority and used Spanish-supplied weapons to thwart white settlement.

Only about 125,000 whites and blacks lived west of the Appalachian Mountains in 1790. But that was soon to change. The great theme of nineteenth-century American history would be the ceaseless stream of migrants flowing westward from the Atlantic seaboard. By foot, horse, boat, and wagon, pioneers and adventurers headed west. Kentucky, still a part of Virginia but destined for statehood in 1792, harbored 75,000 settlers in 1790. In 1776 there had been only 150 pioneers.

Rapid population growth, cheap land, and new economic opportunities fueled the western migration. Although immigrants contributed significantly to the rising numbers, the extraordinary growth rate resulted primarily from natural increase. The average white woman gave birth to eight children, and the white population doubled approximately once every twenty-two years. This made for a very young population on average. In 1790 almost half of all white Americans were under the age of sixteen.

A NEW GOVERNMENT   The men who drafted the Constitution knew that many questions were left unanswered, and they feared that putting the new frame of government into practice would pose unexpected challenges. On the appointed date, March 4, 1789, the new Congress of the United States, meeting in New York, could muster only eight senators and thirteen representatives. A month passed before both chambers gathered a quorum. Only then could the temporary presiding officer of the Senate count the ballots and certify the foregone conclusion that George Washington, with sixty-nine votes, was the unanimous choice of the electoral college for president. John Adams, with thirty-four votes, the second-highest number, became vice-president.

Washington was a reluctant president. He greeted the news of his election with "a heart filled with distress" because he imagined "the ten thousand embarrassments, perplexities and troubles to which I must again be exposed." He told a friend as he prepared to assume office in New York that he felt like a "culprit who is going to the place of his execution." Yet Washington felt compelled to serve because he had been "summoned by my country." A self-made man with little formal education, he brought to his new office a remarkable capacity for moderation and mediation that helped keep the infant republic from disintegrating.

GOVERNMENTAL STRUCTURE   During the summer of 1789, Congress created executive departments corresponding in each case to those already formed under the Confederation. To head the Department of State, Washington named Thomas Jefferson, recently back from his mission to France. To head the Department of the Treasury, Washington picked his devoted wartime aide Alexander Hamilton, now a prominent lawyer in New York. The new position of attorney-general was occupied by Edmund Randolph, former governor of Virginia.

Almost from the beginning Washington routinely called these men to sit as a group for discussion and advice on matters of policy. This was the origin of the president's cabinet, an advisory body for which the Constitution made no formal provision—except insofar as it provided for the heads of departments. The office of vice-president also took on what would become its typical character. "The Vice-Presidency," John Adams wrote his wife, Abigail, was the most "insignificant office . . . ever . . . contrived."

John Jay as chief justice of the Supreme Court (1794).

The structure of the court system, like that of the executive departments, was left to Congress, except for a chief justice and Supreme Court. Congress determined to set the membership of the highest court at six, the chief justice and five associate justices, and it created thirteen federal district courts. From these, appeals might go to one of three circuit courts, composed of two Supreme Court justices and the district judge, meeting twice a year in each district. Members of the Supreme Court, therefore, became itinerant judges riding the circuit during a good part of the year. All federal cases originated in the district court, and if appealed on issues of procedure or legal interpretation, went to the circuit courts and from there to the Supreme Court.

Washington named John Jay as the first chief justice, and he served until 1795. Born in New York City in 1745, Jay graduated from King's College (now Columbia University). His distinction as a lawyer led New York to send him as its representative to the First and Second Continental Congresses. After serving as president of the Continental Congress in 1779, Jay became the American minister in Spain. While in Europe, he helped John Adams and Benjamin Franklin negotiate the Treaty of Paris in 1783. After the Revolution, Jay served as secretary of foreign affairs. He then joined Madison and Hamilton as coauthor of the *The Federalist* and became one of the most effective champions of the Constitution.

THE BILL OF RIGHTS   In the new House of Representatives, James Madison made a bill of rights a top priority. The lack of such provisions had been one of the Antifederalists' major objections to the Constitution. At first Madison believed that the proposals for a bill of rights were "unnecessary and dangerous." He feared that any list of rights would be incomplete. Madison and other Federalists also worried that specifying such rights might imply the existence of a parallel set of powers never meant to be delegated to the central government. Or, as Alexander Hamilton phrased it in the eighty-fourth paper of *The Federalist*, "Why declare things should not be done which there is no power to do?" Yet the fear of arbitrary federal power would not die. In the end, Madison recognized the need to allay the fears of Antifederalists and to meet the moral obligation imposed by those ratifying conventions that had approved the Constitution with the understanding that amendments would be offered.

Madison viewed a bill of rights as "the most dramatic single gesture of conciliation that could be offered the remaining opponents of the government." Those "opponents" included prominent Virginians George Mason and Richard Henry Lee as well as artisans, small traders, and backcountry farmers who expressed a profound egalitarianism. These "poor and middling" folk were skeptical that even the "best men" were capable of subordinating self-interest to the good of the Republic. They believed that all people were prone to corruption; that no one could be trusted. Therefore, a bill of rights must be added to protect the liberties of all against the encroachments of a few.

The first eight Amendments were modeled after the Virginia Declaration of Rights that George Mason had written in 1776. These provided safeguards for certain rights of individuals: freedom of religion, press, speech, and assembly; the right to keep and bear firearms; the right to refuse to house soldiers in private homes; protection against unreasonable searches and seizures; the right to refuse to testify against oneself; the right to a speedy public trial before an impartial jury and to have legal counsel present; and protection against cruel and unusual punishment.

The Ninth and Tenth Amendments addressed themselves to the demand for specific statements that the enumeration of rights in the Constitution "shall not be construed to deny or disparage others retained by the people" and that "powers not delegated to the United States by the Constitution, nor prohibited by it to the States, are reserved to the States respectively, or to the people." The Tenth Amendment was taken almost verbatim from the Articles of Confederation. The House adopted seventeen amendments in all; the Senate, after conference with the House, adopted twelve; the states in the end voted separately on each proposed amendment and ratified ten, which constitute the Bill of Rights, effective December 15, 1791. The Bill of Rights provided no rights or legal protection to blacks or Indians.

RAISING A REVENUE   Revenue was the new federal government's most critical need. To raise funds, Madison proposed a modest tariff (tax on imports) for revenue only, but the demands of manufacturers in the northern states for higher duties to protect them from foreign competition forced a compromise that imposed higher tariffs on certain listed items. Madison linked the tariff to a proposal for a mercantile system that would levy extra tonnage duties on foreign ships, an especially heavy duty on countries that had no commercial treaty with the United States.

Madison's specific purpose was to wage economic war against Great Britain, which had no such treaty but had more foreign trade with the new nation than any other country. Northern businessmen, however, were in no mood for a renewal of economic pressures, for fear of disrupting the economy. Secretary of the Treasury Hamilton agreed with them. In the end the only discrimination built into the Tonnage Act of 1789 was between American and all foreign ships: American ships paid a duty of 6¢ per ton; American-built but foreign-owned ships paid 30¢; and foreign-built and -owned ships paid 50¢ per ton.

The disagreements created by the trade measures were portents of quarrels yet to come. Should economic policy favor Britain or France? The more persistent question was whether tariff and tonnage duties should penalize farmers in the interest of northern manufacturers and shipowners. By imposing a tax on imports, tariffs and tonnage duties resulted in higher prices on goods bought by Americans, most of whom were tied to the farm economy. This raised a basic and perennial question: Should rural consumers be forced to subsidize the nation's infant manufacturing sector? This issue became a sectional question of South versus North.

HAMILTON'S VISION OF AMERICA

The tariff and tonnage duties, linked as they were to other issues, marked but the beginning of the effort to get the country on a sound fiscal basis. Thirty-four-year-old Alexander Hamilton seized the initiative. The first secretary of the treasury was a protégé of the president. Born out of wedlock on a Caribbean island and deserted by a ne'er-do-well Scottish father, Hamilton was left an orphan at thirteen by the death of his mother. With the help of friends and relatives, he found his way at seventeen to

New York, attended King's College and entered the Revolutionary army, where he became a favorite of George Washington. He studied law, passed the bar examination, established a legal practice in New York, and became a self-made aristocrat, serving as collector of revenues and member of the Confederation Congress. An early convert to nationalism, he had a major role in promoting the Constitutional Convention. Shrewd, energetic, and determined, Hamilton was consumed with ambition. As he recognized at age fourteen, "To confess my weakness, my ambition is prevalent."

Alexander Hamilton, secretary of the treasury from 1789 to 1795.

In a series of classic reports submitted to Congress in the two years from January 1790 to December 1791, Hamilton outlined his program for government finances and the economic development of the United States. The reports were soon adopted, with some alterations in detail but little in substance. The last of the series, the Report on Manufactures, outlined a program of protective tariffs and other governmental supports of business. This eventually would become government policy, despite much brave talk of free enterprise and free trade.

ESTABLISHING THE PUBLIC CREDIT   Hamilton submitted the first and most important of his reports to the House of Representatives in 1790 at the invitation of that body. This First Report on the Public Credit, as it has since been called, made two key recommendations: first, funding of the federal debt at face value, which meant that those citizens holding government bonds could exchange them for new interest-bearing bonds; and second, the federal government's assumption of state debts from the Revolution.

The funding scheme was controversial because many farmers and soldiers in immediate need of money had sold their securities for a fraction of their value to speculators who were eager to buy them up after reading Hamilton's First Report. These common folk argued that they should be reimbursed for their losses; otherwise, the speculators would gain a windfall from the new government's funding of bonds at face value. Hamilton sternly resisted such pleas. The speculators, he argued, had "paid what the commodity was worth in the market, and took the risks." Therefore, they should reap the benefits. In fact, Hamilton insisted, the government should favor the financial community because it represented the bedrock of a successful nation.

The report provoked lengthy debates before its substance was adopted. Then in short order Hamilton authored three more reports: a Second Report on Public Credit, which included a proposal for an excise tax on liquor to aid in raising revenue to cover the nation's debts. Another report recommended a national bank and a national mint—which were established in 1791–1792. Finally, the Report on Manufactures proposed an extensive program of government aid and encouragement to the development of manufacturing enterprises.

Hamilton's program was substantially the one Robert Morris had urged upon the Confederation a decade before, and which Hamilton had strongly endorsed at the time. "A national debt," he had written Morris in 1781, "if it is not excessive, will be to us a national blessing; it will be a powerful cement of our union. It will also create a necessity for keeping up taxation to a degree which without being oppressive, will be a spur to industry." Payment of the national debt, in short, would be not only a point of national honor and sound finance, ensuring the country's credit for the future; it would also be an occasion to assert a federal taxing power and thus instill respect for the authority of the national government. Not least, the plan would win the new government the support of wealthy, influential creditors.

SECTIONAL DIFFERENCES EMERGE Madison, who had been Hamilton's close ally in the movement for a stronger government, broke with him over the matter of a national debt. Madison did not question that the debt should be paid; he was troubled, however, that speculators and "stock-jobbers" would become the chief beneficiaries. That the far greater portion of the debt was owed to northerners than to southerners further troubled him. Madison, whom Hamilton had expected to take the lead for his program in the House, therefore advanced an alternative plan to give a larger share to the first owners than to the later speculators. "Let it be a liberal one in favor of the present holders," Madison conceded. "Let them have the highest price which has prevailed in the market; and let the residue belong to the original sufferers." Madison's opposition touched off a vigorous debate, but Hamilton carried his point by a margin of three to one when the House brought it to a vote.

Madison's opposition to the assumption of state debts got more support, however, and set up a division more clearly along sectional lines. The southern states, with the exception of South Carolina, had whittled down their debts. New England, with the largest unpaid debts, stood to be the greatest beneficiary of the assumption plan. Rather than see Virginia victimized, Madison held out an alternative. Why not, he suggested, have the government assume state debts as they stood in 1783 at the conclusion of the peace? Debates on this point deadlocked the whole question of debt funding and assumption, and Hamilton grew so frustrated with the legislative stalemate that he discussed resigning.

The gridlock finally ended in the summer of 1790 when Jefferson, Hamilton, and Madison agreed to a compromise solution. In return for northern votes in favor of locating the permanent national capital on the Potomac River, Madison pledged to seek enough southern votes to pass the assumption, with the further arrangement that those states with smaller debts would get in effect outright grants from the federal government to equalize the difference. With these arrangements, enough votes were secured to carry Hamilton's funding and assumption schemes. The capital would be moved to Philadelphia for ten years, after which time it would be settled at a Federal City on the Potomac, the site to be chosen by the president.

A NATIONAL BANK   By this vast new financial program, Hamilton had called up from nowhere, as if by magic, a great sum of capital. Having established the public credit, Hamilton moved on to a related measure essential to his vision of national greatness. He called for a national bank, which by issuance of bank notes (paper money) might provide a uniform currency that would address the chronic shortage of gold and silver. Government bonds held by the Bank would back up the value of its new bank notes. The national bank, chartered by Congress, would remain under governmental control, but private investors would supply four-fifths of the $10 million capital and name twenty of the twenty-five directors; the government would provide the other fifth of the capital and name five directors. Government bonds would be received in

The First Bank of the United States in Philadelphia. Proposed by Hamilton, the Bank opened in 1791.

payment for three-fourths of the stock in the Bank, and the other fourth would be payable in gold and silver.

The Bank, Hamilton explained, would serve many purposes. Its notes would provide a stable national currency. Moreover, the Bank would provide a source of capital for loans to fund the development of business and commerce. Bonds, which might otherwise be stowed away in safes, would instead become the basis for a productive capital by backing up bank notes available for loan at low rates of interest, the "natural effect" of which would be "to increase trade and industry." What is more, the existence of the Bank would serve certain housekeeping needs of the government: a safe place to keep its funds, a source of "pecuniary aids" in sudden emergencies, and the ready transfer of funds to and from branch offices through bookkeeping entries rather than shipment of metals.

Once again Madison rose to lead the opposition, arguing that he could find no basis in the Constitution for such a bank. That was enough to raise in President Washington's mind serious doubts as to the constitutionality of the measure, which Congress passed fairly quickly over Madison's objections. Before signing the bill into law, therefore, the president sought the advice of his cabinet, where he found an equal division of opinion. The result was the first great and fundamental debate on constitutional interpretation. Should there be a strict or a broad construction of the document? Were the powers of Congress only those explicitly stated or were others implied? The argument turned chiefly on Article I, Section 8, which authorized Congress to "make all laws which shall be necessary and proper for carrying into execution the foregoing Powers."

Such language left room for disagreement and led to a confrontation between Jefferson and Hamilton. Jefferson pointed to the Tenth Amendment, which reserved to the states and the people powers not delegated to Congress. "To take a single step beyond the boundaries thus specially drawn around the powers of Congress," he wrote, "is to take possession of a boundless field of power, no longer susceptible of any definition." A bank might be a convenient aid to Congress in collecting taxes and regulating the currency, but it was not, as Article I, Section 8, specified, *necessary.*

In a long report to the president, Hamilton countered that the power to charter corporations was included in the sovereignty of any government, whether or not expressly stated. The word "necessary," he explained, often meant no more than "needful, requisite, incidental, useful, or conducive to." And in a classic summary, he expressed his criterion on constitutionality: "This criterion is the *end,* to which the measure relates as a *mean.* If the *end* be clearly comprehended within any of the specified powers, collecting taxes and regulating the currency, and if the measure have an obvious relation to that *end,* and is not forbidden by any particular provision of the Constitution, it may safely be deemed to come within the compass of the national authority."

The president accepted Hamilton's argument and signed the bill. In doing so, he had indeed, in Jefferson's words, opened up "a boundless field of power," which in coming years would lead to a further broadening of implied powers with the approval of the Supreme Court. Under John Marshall, the Court would eventually adopt Hamilton's words almost verbatim. On July 4, 1791, the Bank's stock was put up for sale and sold out within a few hours, with hundreds of buyers turned away.

ENCOURAGING MANUFACTURES   Hamilton's imagination and his ambitions for the new country were not yet exhausted. In the last of his great reports, the Report on Manufactures, he set in place the

*Certificate of the New York Mechanick Society by Abraham Godwin, c. 1785,
which illustrates the growing diversification of labor.*

capstone of his design: the active encouragement of manufacturing to
provide productive uses for the new capital created by his funding, assumption (of state debts), and banking schemes. Hamilton believed
that several advantages would flow from the development of manufactures: the diversification of labor in a country given over too much to
farming; improved productivity through the greater use of machinery;
paid work for those not ordinarily employed outside the home, such as
women and children; the promotion of immigration; a greater scope
for the diversity of talents in business; more ample and various opportunities for entrepreneurial activity; and a better domestic market for
agricultural products.

   To secure his ends, Hamilton proposed to use the means to which
other countries had resorted, and which he summarized: tariffs (taxes)
on foreign goods, or in Hamilton's words, "protecting duties," which in
some cases might be put so high as to deter imports altogether; restraints on the export of raw materials; government-paid bounties

and premiums to encourage certain industries; tariff exemptions for imported raw materials needed for American manufacturing; encouragements to inventions and discoveries; regulations for the inspection of commodities; and finally, the encouragement of improvements in transportation, including the development of roads, canals, and rivers.

Some of Hamilton's tariff proposals were enacted in 1792. Otherwise the program was filed away—but not forgotten. It became an arsenal of arguments for the advocates of manufactures in years to come. Hamilton denied that there was any necessary economic conflict between the northern and southern regions of the Union. If, as seemed likely, the northern and middle states should become the chief scenes of manufacturing, they would create robust markets for agricultural products, some of which the southern states were peculiarly qualified to produce. North and South would both benefit, he argued, as more commerce moved between these regions than across the Atlantic, thus strengthening the Union.

HAMILTON'S ACHIEVEMENT Largely owing to the skillful Hamilton, the Treasury Department began to retire the Revolutionary War debt, and foreign capital began to flow in once again. Prosperity, so elusive in the 1780s, began to flourish once again, although President Washington cautioned against attributing "to the Government what is due only to the goodness of Providence."

Hamilton was inclined toward a truly nationalist outlook, and he focused his energies on the rising power of commercial capitalism. In fact, he would have favored a much stronger central government, including a federal veto on state action, even a constitutional monarchy if that had been practicable.

Hamilton never understood or appreciated the "common folk" of the small villages and farms, the people of the frontier. Along with the planters of the South, such common folk would be at best only indirect beneficiaries of his programs. Below the Potomac River, the Hamiltonian vision excited little enthusiasm except in South Carolina, which had a large state debt to be assumed and a concentration of mercantile interests at Charleston. There were, in short, a vast number of people who were drawn into opposition to Hamilton's new engines of power. In part they were southern, in part backcountry, and in part a politically motivated faction opposing Hamilton in New York.

THE REPUBLICAN ALTERNATIVE

Opposition to the Hamiltonian program provided the seeds of the first national political parties. Hamilton's ideas became the foundation of the party known as the Federalists; Madison and Jefferson became the leaders of those who took the name Republicans and thereby implied that the Federalists really aimed at a monarchy. Neither side in the disagreement over national policy deliberately set out to create a party system. But there were important differences of both philosophy and self-interest that would not subside. At the outset Madison, who had worked with Hamilton to build a national government, assumed leadership of Hamilton's opponents in the Congress. Madison, like Thomas Jefferson, was rooted in Virginia, where opposition to Hamilton's economic policies flourished.

After the compromise that had assured the assumption of state debts, Madison and Jefferson moved into ever more resolute opposition to Hamilton's policies: his effort to place an excise tax on whiskey, which laid a burden especially on the trans-Appalachian farmers, whose livelihood depended on the production and sale of the beverage; his proposal for the national bank; and his Report on Manufactures. As the differences built, hostility between Jefferson and Hamilton grew and festered within the Cabinet, much to the distress of President Washington.

Thomas Jefferson. A portrait by Charles Willson Peale (1791).

Thomas Jefferson, twelve years Hamilton's senior, was in most respects his opposite. Jefferson was an agrarian intellectual, his father a successful surveyor and land speculator, his mother a Randolph, from one of the First Families in Virginia. Jefferson developed a breadth of cultivated interests that ranged widely in science, the arts, and the humanities. Jefferson read or spoke seven languages. He was an architect of distinction (Monticello, the Virginia Capitol, and the

University of Virginia are monuments to his talent), a man who under-stood mathematics and engineering, an inventor, and an agronomist. He knew music and practiced the violin, although some wit said only Patrick Henry played it worse.

Philosophically, Hamilton and Jefferson represented opposite visions of the character of the Union and defined certain fundamental issues of American life that still echo two centuries later. Hamilton foresaw a di-versified capitalistic economy, agriculture balanced by commerce and industry, and was thus the better prophet. Jefferson feared the growth of crowded cities divided into a capitalistic aristocracy on the one hand and a deprived proletariat on the other. Hamilton feared anarchy and loved order; Jefferson feared tyranny and loved liberty.

What Hamilton wanted for his country was a strong central govern-ment actively encouraging capitalistic enterprise. What Jefferson wanted was a decentralized republic made up primarily of small farm-ers: "Those who labor in the earth," he wrote, "are the chosen people of God, if ever he had a chosen people, whose breasts He has made His peculiar deposit for genuine and substantial virtue." Jefferson did not oppose all forms of manufacturing. What he feared was that the unlimited expansion of commerce and industry would produce a growing class of wage laborers who were dependent on others for their livelihood and therefore subject to political manipulation and eco-nomic exploitation.

Where Hamilton was the old-fashioned English Whig, Jefferson, who spent several years in France, was the enlightened *philosophe,* the natural radical and reformer who attacked the aristocratic relics of en-tail and primogeniture in Virginia, opposed an established church, pro-posed an elaborate plan for public schools, prepared a more humane criminal code, and was instrumental in eliminating slavery from the Old Northwest, although he kept the slaves he had inherited. On his tomb were finally recorded the achievements of which he was proudest: author of the Declaration of Independence and the Virginia Statute of Religious Freedom, and founder of the University of Virginia.

In their quarrel, Hamilton came to view Jefferson as the leader of the opposition to his policies. In the summer of 1791 Jefferson and Madison set out on a "botanizing" excursion up the Hudson River in New York. Hamilton and many other Federalists feared that the supposed vacation trip was a cover for consultations with New York political figures who personally and politically opposed Hamilton. While the significance of that single trip was blown out of proportion, there did ultimately arise an informal alliance of Jeffersonian Republicans in the South and New York that would become a constant if sometimes divisive feature of the new party and its successor, the Democratic party.

Still, amid the rising political tensions, there was no opposition to George Washington, who longed to end his exile from Mount Vernon and even began drafting a farewell address, but was urged by both Hamilton and Jefferson to continue in public life. He was the only man who could transcend party differences and hold things together with his unmatched prestige. In 1792 Washington was unanimously reelected.

CRISES FOREIGN AND DOMESTIC

During George Washington's second term, the problems of foreign relations came to center stage, brought there by the consequences of the French Revolution, which had begun during the first months of his presidency. Americans followed the tumultuous events in France with almost universal sympathy, up to a point. By the spring of 1792, though, the French experiment in liberty, equality, and fraternity had transformed itself into a monster. France plunged into war with Austria and Prussia. The Revolution began devouring its own children along with its enemies during the Terror of 1793–1794.

After the execution of King Louis XVI in 1793, Great Britain entered into the coalition of monarchies at war with the French Republic. For the next twenty-two years Britain and France were at war, with only a brief respite, until the final defeat of the French forces under Napoleon in 1815. The European war presented Washington, just beginning his second term, with an awkward decision. By the treaty of 1778, the United States was a perpetual ally of France, obligated to defend her possessions in the West Indies.

But Americans wanted no part of the war. They were determined to maintain their lucrative trade with both sides in the European conflict. Of course, the combatants resented and resisted America's profitable neutrality. For their part, Hamilton and Jefferson found in the neutrality policy one issue on which they could agree. Where they differed was in how best to implement the policy. Hamilton had a simple and direct answer to this problem: declare the French alliance invalid because it was made with a government that no longer existed. Jefferson preferred to delay and use the alliance as a bargaining point with the British. In the end, however, Washington followed the advice of neither. Taking a middle course, on April 22, 1793, the president issued a neutrality proclamation that evaded even the word "neutrality." It simply declared the United States "friendly and impartial toward the belligerent powers" and warned American citizens that "aiding or abetting hostilities" or other un-neutral acts might be prosecuted.

CITIZEN GENÊT   At the same time, Washington accepted Jefferson's argument that the United States should recognize the new French government (becoming the first country to do so) and receive its new ambassador, Citizen Edmond Charles Genêt. Early in 1793 Genêt landed at Charleston, where he immediately organized a Jacobin Club to support that faction of French revolutionaries. Along the route to Philadelphia the enthusiasm of his sympathizers gave Genêt an inflated notion of his potential, not that he needed much encouragement. In Charleston he engaged privateers to capture British ships, and in Philadelphia he continued the process. He intrigued with frontiersmen and land speculators with an eye to an attack on Spanish Florida and Louisiana.

Genêt quickly became an embarrassment even to his Republican friends. Jefferson decided that the French minister had overreached himself when he violated a promise not to outfit a captured British ship as a privateer. Such actions could have provoked a British declaration of war against the United States. When, finally, Genêt threatened in a moment of anger to appeal his cause directly to the American people over the head of their president, the cabinet unanimously agreed that he had to go, and in August 1793 Washington demanded his recall. Meanwhile a new party of radicals had gained power in France and sent over its own minister with a warrant for Genêt's arrest. Instead of returning to Paris to risk the guillotine, Genêt sought asylum in America, married the daughter of New York's governor, settled down as a country gentleman on the Hudson, and died years later an American citizen.

Genêt's foolishness and the growing excesses of the French radicals were fast cooling American support for their revolution. To Hamilton's followers what was occurring in France began to resemble their worst nightmares of democratic anarchy. The French made it hard even for Republicans to retain sympathy, but they swallowed hard and made excuses. "The liberty of the whole earth was depending on the issue of the contest," the genteel Jefferson wrote, "and . . . rather than it should have failed, I would have seen half the earth devastated." Nor did the British make it easy for Federalists to rally to their side. Near the end of 1793 they informed the American government that they intended to occupy their northwestern forts indefinitely and began to seize the cargoes of American ships trading with the French islands.

The French and British causes polarized American opinion. In the contest, it seemed, one either had to be a Republican and support liberty, reason, and France, or become a Federalist and support order, religious faith, and Britain. The division gave rise to some curious loyalties: slaveholding planters joined the cheers for Jacobin radicals who dispossessed aristocrats in France, and supported the protest against British seizures of New England ships; Massachusetts shippers still profited from the British trade and kept quiet. Boston, once a hotbed of revolution, became a bastion of Federalism.

JAY'S TREATY   Early in 1794 the Republican leaders in Congress were gaining support for commercial retaliation to end British trade abuses, when the British gave Washington a timely opening for a settlement. They stopped seizing American ships, and on April 16, 1794, Washington named Chief Justice John Jay as a special envoy to Great Britain. Jay left with instructions to settle all major issues: to get the British out of the northwestern forts, to secure reparations for the losses of American shippers, compensation for slaves carried away in 1783, and a commercial treaty that would legalize American commerce with the British West Indies.

To win his objectives, Jay accepted the British definition of neutral rights: that exports of tar, pitch, and other products needed for naval ships were contraband, that provisions could not go in neutral ships to enemy ports, and the "Rule of 1756," by which trade that was prohibited in peacetime because of mercantilist restrictions could not be opened in wartime. Britain also gained most-favored-nation treatment in American commerce and a promise that French privateers would not be outfitted in American ports. Finally, Jay conceded that the British need not compensate Americans for the slaves who escaped during the

A 1794 watercolor of Fort Detroit, a major center of Indian trade that the British agreed to evacuate in Jay's Treaty.

war and that the old American debts to British merchants would be paid by the American government. In return for these concessions, he won three important points: British evacuation of the northwestern forts by 1796, reparations for the seizures of American ships and cargoes in 1793–1794, and legalization of trade with the British West Indies. But the last of these (Article XII) was so hedged with restrictions that the Senate eventually struck it from the treaty.

Public outrage greeted the terms of the treaty. Even Federalist shippers, ready for settlement on almost any terms, were disappointed at the limitations on their privileges in the West Indies. But much of the outcry was simply expression of disappointment by Republican partisans who sought an escalation of conflict with hated Britain. Some of it was the outrage of Virginia planters at the concession on debts to British merchants and the failure to get reparations for lost slaves. Given the limited enthusiasm of Federalists—Washington himself wrestled with doubts over the treaty—Jay remarked that he could travel across the country by the light of his burning effigies. Yet the Senate debated the treaty in secret, and in the end quiet counsels of moderation prevailed. Without a single vote to spare, Jay's Treaty got the necessary two-thirds majority on June 24, 1795, with Article XII (the provision regarding the West Indies) expunged.

Washington still hesitated but finally signed the treaty as the best he was likely to get. In the House, opponents went so far as to demand that the president produce all papers relevant to the treaty, but the president refused on the grounds that treaty approval was solely the business of the Senate. He thereby set an important precedent of executive privilege (a term not used at the time), and the House finally relented, supplying the money to fund the treaty by a close vote.

THE FRONTIER ERUPTS   Other events also had an important bearing on Jay's Treaty, adding force to the importance of its settlement of the Canadian frontier and strengthening Spain's conviction that it too needed to reach a settlement of long-festering problems along America's southwestern frontier. While Jay was haggling in London, frontier conflict with Indians escalated, with American troops twice crushed by northwestern Indians. At last, Washington named General Wayne, known as "Mad Anthony," to head an expedition into the Northwest Territory. In the fall of 1793 Wayne marched into Indian country with some 2,600 men, built Fort Greenville, and with reinforcements from Kentucky, went on the offensive in 1794.

In August 1794, some 2,000 Shawnee, Ottawa, Chippewa, and Potawatomi warriors, reinforced by some Canadian militia, attacked Wayne's troops at the Battle of Fallen Timbers, but this time the Americans were ready and repulsed them. The Indians suffered heavy losses. American soldiers then destroyed their fields and villages. The Indians

THE TREATY OF GREENVILLE, 1795
Indian cessions

finally agreed to the Treaty of Greenville, signed in August 1795. In the treaty, at the cost of a $10,000 annuity, the United States bought from twelve tribes the rights to the southeastern quarter of the Northwest Territory (now Ohio and Indiana) and enclaves at the sites of Vincennes, Detroit, and Chicago.

THE WHISKEY REBELLION   General Wayne's forces were still mopping up after the Battle of Fallen Timbers when the administration resolved on another show of strength in the backcountry against the so-called Whiskey Rebellion. Alexander Hamilton's excise tax on liquor, levied in 1791, had excited strong feeling among frontier farmers because it taxed their most profitable commodity. During the eighteenth and early nineteenth centuries, nearly all Americans regularly drank alcoholic beverages: beer, hard cider, ale, wine, rum, brandy, or whiskey. In the areas west of the Appalachian Mountains, the primary cash commodity was liquor distilled from grain or fruit. Such emphasis on distillation reflected a practical problem. Many farmers could not afford to transport bulky crops of corn and rye across the mountains or down the Mississippi River to the seaboard markets. Instead, it was much more profitable to distill liquor from the corn and rye, apples and peaches. Unlike grain crops, distilled spirits could be more easily stored, shipped, or sold—at higher profits. A bushel of corn worth 25¢ could yield two and a half gallons of liquor, worth ten times as much.

Western farmers were also suspicious of the new federal government in Philadelphia. The frontiersmen considered the whiskey tax another part of Hamilton's scheme to pick the pockets of the poor to enrich urban speculators. All through the backcountry, from Georgia to Pennsylvania and beyond, the tax provoked resistance and evasion.

In the summer of 1794 the discontent exploded into open rebellion in the four western counties of Pennsylvania, where vigilantes, mostly of Scottish or Irish descent, organized to terrorize revenue officers and taxpayers. They blew up the stills of those who paid the tax, robbed the mails, stopped court proceedings, and threatened an assault on Pittsburgh. On August 7, 1794, President Washington issued a proclamation ordering them home and calling out 12,900 militiamen from Virginia, Maryland, Pennsylvania, and New Jersey. Getting no response from the "Whiskey Boys," he ordered the army to suppress the rebellion.

Washington as commander-in-chief reviews the troops mobilized to quell the Whiskey Rebellion in 1794.

Under the command of General Henry Lee, "a force larger than any Washington had ever commanded" in the Revolution marched out from Harrisburg across the Alleghenies with Alexander Hamilton in their midst, itching to smite the insurgents. But the rebels vanished into the hills, and the troops met with little opposition. By dint of great effort and much marching, they finally rounded up twenty barefoot, ragged prisoners whom they paraded down Market Street in Philadelphia and clapped into prison. Eventually two of these were found guilty of treason, but they were pardoned by Washington on the grounds that one was a "simpleton" and the other "insane." The government had made its point and gained "reputation and strength," according to Hamilton, by suppressing a rebellion that, according to Jefferson, "could never be found." The use of force, however, led many who sympathized with the frontiersmen to become Republicans, who scored heavily in the next Pennsylvania elections. Nor was it the end of whiskey rebellions, which continued in an unending war of wits between moonshiners and revenue officers.

PINCKNEY'S TREATY   While these stirring events were transpiring in Pennsylvania, Spanish intrigues among the Creeks, Choctaws, Chickasaws, and Cherokees in the Southwest were keeping up the

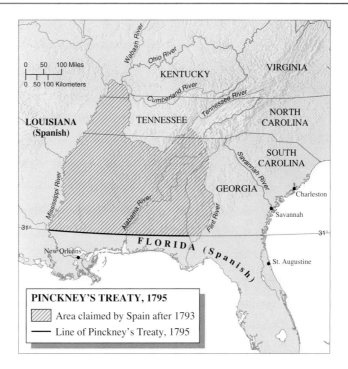

PINCKNEY'S TREATY, 1795
- Area claimed by Spain after 1793
- Line of Pinckney's Treaty, 1795

same turmoil the British had fomented along the Ohio. In Tennessee, settlers reacted by burning and leveling Indian villages. The defeat of their Indian allies, combined with Britain's concessions in the north and worries about possible American intervention in Louisiana, led the Spanish to enter into treaty negotiations with the Americans. United States ambassador Thomas Pinckney won acceptance of a boundary at the 31st parallel, free navigation of the Mississippi River, the right to deposit goods at New Orleans for three years with promise of renewal, a commission to settle American claims against Spain, and a promise on each side to refrain from inciting Indian attacks on the other. Ratification of the Pinckney Treaty ran into no opposition. In fact, it was immensely popular, especially among westerners eager to use the Mississippi River to transport their crops to market.

LAND SETTLEMENT

Now that Jay and Pinckney had settled things with Britain and Spain, and the army in the Northwest and the Tennessee settlers in the

South had smashed the Indians, the West was open for a renewed surge of settlers. New lands, ceded by the Indians in the Treaty of Greenville, revealed Congress once again divided on land policy. There were two basic viewpoints on the matter, one that the public domain should serve mainly as a source of revenue, the other that it was more important to get the new country settled, and this required low land prices. In the long run, the evolution of policy would be from the first toward the second viewpoint, but for the time being the federal government's need for revenue took priority.

LAND POLICY   Opinions on land policy, like other issues, separated Federalists from Republicans. Federalists involved in speculation might prefer lower land prices, but the more influential Federalists like Hamilton and Jay preferred to build the population of the eastern states first, lest the East lose political influence and lose a labor force important to the future growth of manufactures. Men of their persuasion favored high land prices to enrich the Treasury, sale of relatively large parcels of land to speculators rather than small amounts to actual settlers, and the development of compact settlements. Jefferson and Madison were reluctantly prepared to go along for the sake of reducing the national debt, but Jefferson expressed hope for a plan by which the lands could be more readily settled. In any case, he suggested, frontiersmen would do as they had done before: "They will settle the lands in spite of everybody."

For the time, however, Federalist policy prevailed. In the Land Act of 1796 Congress resolved to extend the rectangular surveys ordained in 1785, but it doubled the price to $2 per acre, with only a year in which to complete payment. Half the townships would go in 640-acre sections, making the minimum cost $1,280, and alternate townships would be sold in blocks of eight sections, or 5,120 acres, making the minimum cost $10,240. Either price was well beyond the means of most ordinary settlers, and a bit much even for speculators, who could still pick up state lands at lower prices. By 1800 federal land offices had sold fewer than 50,000 acres under the act. Continuing criticism from the West led to the Land Act of 1800, which reduced the minimum sale to 320 acres and spread the payments over four years. Thus, with a down payment of $160, one could buy a farm. All lands went for the minimum price if they did not sell at auction within three weeks. Under the Land Act of

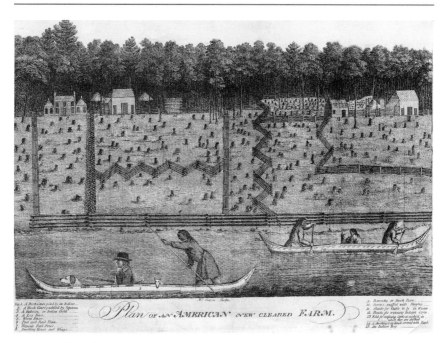

A newly cleared American farm.

1804 the minimum unit was reduced to 160 acres, which became the traditional homestead, and the price per acre went down to $1.64.

THE WILDERNESS TRAIL   The lure of western lands led thousands of settlers to follow Daniel Boone into the territory known as Kentucky or "Kaintuck"—from the Cherokee name Ken-ta-ke ("great meadow"). In the late eighteenth century, Kentucky was a farmer's fantasy and a hunter's paradise, with its fertile soils and abundant forests teeming with buffalo, deer, and wild turkey.

Boone himself was the product of a pioneer background. Born on a small farm in 1734 in central Pennsylvania, the son of hard-working Quakers, he was an experienced farmer, accomplished woodsman, and deadeye marksman by the age of twelve. In 1750 the Boone family moved to western North Carolina. There Daniel emerged as the region's greatest hunter, trading animal skins for salt and other family needs.

After hearing numerous reports about the territory over the mountains, Boone set out alone to find a trail into Kentucky in 1769. Armed

Daniel Boone Escorting Settlers through the Cumberland Gap *by George Caleb Bingham.*

with a long rifle, tomahawk, and hunting knife, dressed in a hunting shirt, deerskin leggings, and moccasins, he found what was called the Warriors Path, a narrow foot trail that buffalo, deer, and Indians had worn along the steep ridges. It took him through the Cumberland Gap. For two years thereafter, Boone explored the region, living off the plentiful game. He returned to North Carolina with exciting stories about the riches of Kentucky.

In 1773 Boone led the first group of settlers through the Appalachian Mountains at Cumberland Gap in southwestern Virginia. Two years later, Boone and thirty woodsmen used axes to widen the Warriors Path into what became known as the Wilderness Road, a passage that more than 300,000 settlers would use over the next twenty-five years. At a point where a branch of the Wilderness Road intersected with the Kentucky River, near what is now Lexington, Boone built a settlement known as Boonesborough in an area called Transylvania.

A steady stream of settlers, mostly Scotch-Irish folk from Pennsylvania, Virginia, and North Carolina, poured into Kentucky during the last quarter of the eighteenth century. Upon their arrival, they typically bought a piece of land from a speculator who preceded them or from a government agent. Many veterans of the Revolutionary War received land grants in Kentucky as compensation for their military service. The pioneers who settled on land that had not been surveyed were called squatters because they had no official title to the land. After the land was surveyed, they were eligible to buy it under rights of ownership called squatters' rights.

The backcountry settlers came on foot or on horseback, often leading a mule or cow that carried their few tools and possessions. On a good day they might cover fifteen miles. Near a creek or spring they would buy a parcel or stake out a claim and mark its boundaries by chopping notches into "witness trees." They then would build a lean-to or half-camp for temporary shelter and clear the land for planting. The larger trees could not be felled with an axe. Instead they were "girdled." A cut would be made around the trunk and the tree would be left to die. Because this often took years, a farmer had to hoe and plant a field filled with stumps and trees.

The pioneers grew melons, beans, turnips, and other vegetables, but corn was the preferred crop because it kept well and had so many uses. Ears were roasted and eaten on the cob, and kernels were ground into meal for making mush, hominy grits, hoecakes and "johnnycakes" (dry biscuits suitable for travelers that were originally called journeycakes). Pigs and cows provided pork and milk, butter and cheese. Many of the frontier families also built crude stills to manufacture a potent whiskey known as "corn likker."

TRANSFER OF POWER

By 1796 President Washington had decided that two terms in office were enough. Tired of the political quarrels and the venom of the partisan press, he was ready to retire once and for all to Mount Vernon. He would leave behind a formidable record of achievement: the organization of a national government with demonstrated power, a secure national credit, the recovery of territory from Britain and Spain, a stable northwestern frontier, and the admission of three new states: Vermont (1791), Kentucky (1792), and Tennessee (1796).

WASHINGTON'S FAREWELL   With the help of John Jay and especially Alexander Hamilton, Washington drafted a valedictory speech to

Mount Vernon, showing the façade facing the Potomac River.

the nation. His farewell address, dated September 17, 1796, called for unity among the American people in backing their new government. Washington decried the spirit of sectionalism. He feared the emergence of regional political parties promoting local interests. In foreign relations, Washington said, America should show "good faith and justice toward all nations" and avoid either "an habitual hatred or an habitual fondness" for other countries. Europe, he noted, "has a set of primary interests which to us have none or a very remote relation. Hence she must be engaged in frequent controversies, the causes of which are essentially foreign to our concerns." The United States should keep clear of those quarrels. It was, moreover, "our true policy to steer clear of permanent alliances with any portion of the foreign world." A key word here is "permanent." Washington opposed permanent arrangements like the one with France, still technically in effect. He specifically advised that "we may safely trust to temporary alliances for extraordinary emergencies." Washington's warning against permanent foreign entanglements thereafter served as a fundamental principle in American foreign policy until the early twentieth century.

THE ELECTION OF 1796   With George Washington out of the race, the United States had its first partisan election for president. The logical choice of the Federalists would have been Washington's protégé Hamilton, the chief architect of their programs. But Hamilton's policies had left scars and made enemies. Nor did he suffer fools gladly, a common affliction of Federalist leaders, including the man on whom the choice fell. In Philadelphia, a caucus of Federalist congressmen chose John Adams as heir apparent, with Thomas Pinckney of South Carolina, fresh from his triumph in Spain, as nominee for vice-president. As expected, the Republicans drafted Thomas Jefferson and added geographical balance to the ticket with Aaron Burr of New York.

The rising strength of the Republicans, fueled by the smoldering resentment toward Jay's Treaty, very nearly swept Jefferson into office, and perhaps would have but for the public appeals of the French ambassador for his election—an action that backfired. Then, despite a Federalist majority among the electors, Alexander Hamilton thought up an impulsive scheme that very nearly threw the election away after all. Thomas Pinckney, Hamilton thought, would be more subject to influence than the strong-minded Adams. He therefore sought to have South Carolina Federalists withhold a few votes from Adams and bring Pinckney in first. The Carolinas more than cooperated—they divided their vote between Pinckney and Jefferson—but New Englanders got wind of the scheme and dropped Pinckney. The upshot of Hamilton's intrigue was to cut Pinckney out of both offices and elect Jefferson vice-president with sixty-eight votes, second to Adams's seventy-one.

THE ADAMS YEARS

John Adams had crafted a distinguished career as a Massachusetts lawyer, a leader in the Revolutionary movement and the Continental Congress, a diplomat in France, Holland, and Britain, and as George Washington's vice-president. His political philosophy fell somewhere between Jefferson's and Hamilton's. He shared neither the one's faith in the common people nor the other's fondness for a financial aristocracy of "paper wealth." He favored the classic mixture of aristocratic, democratic, and monarchical elements, though his use of "monarchical" interchangeably with "executive" exposed him to the attacks of Republicans who saw a monarchist in every Federalist. Yet Adams's fondness for titles and protocol arose from a reasoned purpose, to exploit the human "thirst for distinction." Although he tried to play the role of distinguished executive, he was always haunted by a feeling that he was never properly appreciated—and he may have been right. Yet, on the overriding issue of his administration, war and peace, he kept his head

John Adams.

when others about him were losing theirs—probably at the cost of his reelection.

WAR WITH FRANCE   John Adams faced the daunting task of succeeding the most popular man in America. He also inherited from Washington an undeclared naval war with France, a byproduct of the Jay Treaty. When Jay accepted the British position that food supplies and naval stores—as well as war matériel—were contraband subject to seizure, the French reasoned that American cargoes in the British trade were subject to the same interpretation and loosed their corsairs in the West Indies with even more devastating effect than the British had in 1793–1794. By the time of Adams's inauguration in 1797, the French had plundered some 300 American ships and had broken diplomatic relations. As ambassador to Paris, James Monroe had become so pro-French and so hostile to the Jay Treaty that Washington had felt impelled to remove him for his indiscretions. France then had refused to accept Monroe's replacement, Charles Cotesworth Pinckney (brother of Thomas Pinckney), and ordered him out of the country.

Adams immediately acted to restore relations with France in the face of an outcry for war from the "High Federalists," including Secretary of State Timothy Pickering. Hamilton agreed with Adams on this point and approved his last-ditch effort for a settlement. In 1797 Pinckney returned to Paris with John Marshall (a Virginia Federalist) and Elbridge Gerry (a Massachusetts Republican) for further negotiations. After long, nagging delays, the three commissioners were accosted by three French counterparts (whom Adams labeled X, Y, and Z in his report to Congress), agents of France's unscrupulous foreign minister Charles Maurice de Talleyrand, a past master of the diplomatic shakedown. The three French diplomats delicately let it be known that negotiations could begin only if the Americans paid a bribe of $250,000.

Such bribes were common eighteenth-century diplomatic practice, but Talleyrand's price was high merely for a promise to negotiate. The answer from the American side, according to the commissioners' report, was "no, no, not a sixpence." When the XYZ Affair was reported in Congress and the public press, this was translated into the more stirring slogan: "Millions for defense but not one cent for tribute." Thereafter, the expressions of hostility toward France rose in a crescendo—even the most partisan Republicans were hard put to make any more excuses for the French, and many of them joined a cry for war. Yet Adams resisted a formal declaration of war; the French would have to bear the onus for that. Congress, however, authorized the capture of armed French ships, suspended commerce with France, and renounced the alliance of 1778, which was already a dead letter.

In 1798 George Logan, a Pennsylvania Quaker, visited Paris at his own expense, hoping to head off war. He did secure the release of some American seamen and won assurances that a new American ambassador would be welcomed. The fruit of his mission, otherwise, was passage of the Logan Act (1799), which still forbids private citizens to negotiate with foreign governments without official authorization.

A cartoon indicating the anti-French feeling generated by the XYZ Affair. The three American ministers at left reject the "Paris Monster's" demand for money.

Adams proceeded to strengthen American defenses. An American navy had ceased to exist at the end of the Revolution. No armed ships were available when Algerian brigands began to prey on American commerce in 1794. As a result Congress had authorized the arming of six ships. These were incomplete in 1796 when Washington bought peace with the Algerians, but Congress allowed work on three to continue: the *Constitution,* the *United States,* and the *Constellation,* all completed in 1797. In 1798 Congress authorized a new Department of the Navy. By the end of 1798 the number of naval ships had increased to twenty and by the end of 1799 to thirty-three. But before the end of 1798 an undeclared naval war had begun in the West Indies with the French capture of an American schooner.

While the naval war went on, a new army was authorized in 1798 as a 10,000-man force to serve three years. Adams called Washington from retirement to be its commander, agreeing to Washington's condition that he name his three chief subordinates. Washington sent in the names of Hamilton, Charles C. Pinckney, and Henry Knox. In the old army the three ranked in precisely the opposite order, but Washington insisted that Hamilton be his second in command. Adams relented, but resented the slight to his authority as commander-in-chief. The rift among Federalists thus widened further. Because of Washington's age, the choice meant that Hamilton would command the army in the field, if it ever took the field. But recruitment went slowly until well into 1799, by which time all fear of French invasion was dispelled. Hamilton continued to dream of imperial glory, though, planning the seizure of Louisiana and the Floridas to keep them out of French hands, and even the invasion of South America, but these remained Hamilton's dreams.

Peace overtures began to come from the French by the autumn of 1798, before the naval war was fully under way. Adams decided to act on the information and took it upon himself, without consulting the cabinet, to name the American minister to the Netherlands, William Vans Murray, as special envoy to Paris. The Hamiltonians, infected with a virulent attack of war fever, fought the nomination but finally compromised, in the face of Adams's threat to resign, on a commission of three envoys. After a long delay they left late in 1799 and arrived to find themselves confronting a new government under First Consul Napoleon Bonaparte. By the Convention of 1800, they won the best terms they could from the triumphant Napoleon. In return for giving up all claims of indemnity for American losses, they got official suspension of the 1778 perpetual alliance with France and the end of the quasi war. The Senate ratified, contingent upon outright abrogation of the alliance, and the agreement became effective on December 21, 1801.

THE WAR AT HOME The simmering conflict with France mirrored an ideological war at home between Federalists and Republicans. Already heated partisan politics had begun boiling over during the latter years of Washington's administration. The rhetoric grew so personal that fighting duels became a common way to defend one's honor. Federalists and Republicans saw each other as traitors to the principles of the American Revolution. Jefferson, for example, decided that Alexander Hamilton, George Washington, John Adams, and the Federalists were suppressing individual liberty in order to promote selfish interests. He adamantly opposed Jay's Treaty because it was pro-British and anti-French, and he was disgusted by the army's suppression of the Whiskey Rebellion.

Such volatile issues forced people to take sides, and the Revolutionary generation of leaders, a group that John Adams called the "band of brothers," began to fragment into die-hard factions. Long-standing political friendships disintegrated amid the venomous partisan attacks. Jefferson observed that a "wall of separation" had come to divide the nation's political leaders. "Politics and party hatreds," he told his daughter, "destroy the happiness of every being here."

Jefferson was no innocent in the matter; his no-holds-barred tactics directly contributed to the partisan tensions. As vice-president, he displayed a gracious deviousness. He led the Republican faction opposed to Federalist John Adams, and he actively schemed to embarrass the president. In 1797 Jefferson secretly hired a rogue journalist, James Callender, to produce a scurrilous pamphlet that described President Adams as a deranged monarchist intent upon naming himself king. By the end of the century, Jefferson had become an ardent advocate of polarized party politics: "I hold it as immoral to pursue a middle line, as between parties of Honest men and Rogues, into which every country has divided."

For his part, the combative, vain John Adams refused to align himself with the Federalists, preferring instead to mimic George Washington and retain his independence as chief executive. He was too principled and too prickly to toe a party line. Soon after his election, he invited Jefferson to join with him in creating a bipartisan administration. After all, they had worked well together in the Continental Congress and in France, and they harbored great respect for each other. But after consulting with James Madison, Jefferson refused to accept the new president's offer. Within a year, he and Adams were at each other's throats. Adams expressed regret at losing Jefferson as a friend but "felt obliged to look upon him as a man whose mind is warped by prejudice." He had become "a child and the dupe" of the Republican faction in Congress led by James Madison.

The conflict with France only served to deepen the partisan divide emerging in the young United States. The real purpose of the French crisis all along, the more ardent Republicans suspected, was to provide Federalists with an excuse to put down the domestic opposition. The infamous Alien and Sedition Acts of 1798 lent credence to their suspicions. These four measures, passed in the wave of patriotic war fever, limited freedom of speech and the press and the liberty of aliens. Proposed by Federalists in Congress, they did not originate with Adams but had his blessing. Goaded by his astute wife, Abigail, his primary counselor, Adams signed the controversial statutes and in doing so made the greatest mistake of his presidency. Timothy Pickering, his disloyal secretary of state, claimed that Adams acted without consulting "any member of the government and for a reason truly remarkable—because he knew we should all be opposed to the measure." By succumbing to the partisan hysteria and enacting the vindictive Alien and Sedition Acts, Adams seemed to bear out what Benjamin Franklin had said about him years before: he "means well for his country, is always an honest man, often a wise one, but sometimes and in some things, [he is] absolutely out of his senses."

Three of the four acts reflected hostility to foreigners, especially the French and Irish, a large number of whom had become active Republicans and were suspected of revolutionary intent. The Naturalization Act lengthened from five to fourteen years the residence requirement for citizenship. The Alien Act empowered the president to deport "dangerous" aliens on pain of imprisonment. The Alien Enemy Act authorized the president in time of declared war to expel or imprison enemy aliens at will. Finally, the Sedition Act defined as a high misdemeanor any conspiracy against legal measures of the government, including interference with federal officers and insurrection or riot. What is more, the law forbade writing, publishing, or speaking anything of "a false, scandalous and malicious" nature against the government or any of its officers.

Considering what Federalists and Republicans said about each other, the Sedition Act, applied rigorously, could have caused the imprisonment of nearly the whole government. In practice, however, the purpose was transparently partisan, designed to punish Republicans, whom Federalists could scarcely distinguish from Jacobins and traitors. To be sure, partisan Republican journalists were resorting to scandalous lies and misrepresentations, but so were Federalists; it was a time when both sides seemed afflicted with paranoia. But the fifteen indictments brought under the act, with ten convictions, were all directed at Republicans.

In the very first case one unfortunate was fined $100 for wishing out loud that the wad of a salute cannon might hit President Adams in his rear. The most conspicuous targets of prosecution were Republican editors and a Republican congressman, Matthew Lyon of

Republican representative Matthew Lyon and the Connecticut Federalist Roger Griswald go at each other on the floor of the House (1798). Lyon soon became a target of the Sedition Act.

Vermont, a rough-and-tumble Irishman who published censures of Adams's "continual grasp for power" and "unbounded thirst for ridiculous pomp, foolish adulation, and selfish avarice." For such libels Lyon got four months and a fine of $1,000, but from his cell he continued to write articles and letters for the Republican papers. The few convictions under the act only created martyrs to the cause of freedom of speech and the press, and exposed the vindictiveness of Federalist judges.

Lyon and the others based a defense on the unconstitutionality of the Sedition Act, but Federalist judges were scarcely inclined to entertain such notions. It ran against the Republican grain, anyway, to have federal courts assume the authority to declare laws unconstitutional. To offset the "reign of witches" unleashed by the Alien and Sedition Acts, therefore, Jefferson and Madison conferred and brought forth drafts of what came to be known as the Kentucky and Virginia Resolutions. These passed the legislatures of the two states in 1798, while further Kentucky Resolutions, adopted in 1799, responded to counterresolutions from northern states. These resolutions, much alike in their arguments, denounced the Alien and Sedition Acts as "alarming infractions" of constitutional rights and advanced what came to be known as the state-compact theory. Since the Constitution arose as a compact among the states, the resolutions argued, it followed logically that the states should assume the right to say when Congress had exceeded its powers. The Virginia Resolutions, drafted by Madison, declared that states "have the right and are in duty bound to interpose for arresting the progress of the evil." The second set of Kentucky Resolutions, in restating the states' right to judge violations of the Constitution, added: "That a nullification of those sovereignties, of all unauthorized acts done under color of that instrument, is the rightful remedy."

These doctrines of interposition and nullification, revised and edited by later theorists, were destined to be used for causes unforeseen by the authors of the Kentucky and Virginia Resolutions. (Years later Madison would disclaim the doctrine of nullification as developed by John C. Calhoun, but his own doctrine of "interposition" would resurface as late as the 1950s as a device to oppose racial integration.) At the time, it seems, both men intended the resolutions to serve chiefly as propaganda, the opening guns in the political campaign of 1800. Neither Kentucky nor Virginia took steps to nullify or interpose its authority against enforcement of the Alien and Sedition Acts. Instead both called upon the other states to help them win a repeal. Jefferson counseled against any thought of violence, which was "not the kind of opposition the American people will permit." He assured a fellow Virginian that "the reign of witches" would soon end, that it would be discredited by the arrival of the tax collector more than anything else.

REPUBLICAN VICTORY   As the presidential election of 1800 approached, grievances were mounting against Federalist policies: taxation to support an unneeded army; the Alien and Sedition Acts, which cast the Federalists as anti-liberty; the lingering fears of "monarchism"; the hostilities aroused by Hamilton's programs; the suppression of the Whiskey Rebellion; and Jay's Treaty. When Adams decided for peace in 1800, he probably doomed his one chance for reelection, a wave of patriotic war fever with a united party behind him. His decision gained him much goodwill among the people at large, but left the Hamiltonians unreconciled and his party divided. In 1800 the Federalists summoned enough unity to name as their candidates Adams and Charles C. Pinckney; they agreed to cast all their electoral votes for both. But the Hamiltonians continued to snipe at Adams and his policies, and soon after his renomination Adams removed two of them from his cabinet. Hamilton struck back with a pamphlet questioning Adams's fitness to be president, citing his "disgusting egotism." Intended for private distribution among Federalist leaders, the pamphlet reached the hands of Aaron Burr, who put it in general circulation.

Jefferson and Burr, as the Republican candidates, once again represented the alliance of Virginia and New York. Jefferson, perhaps even more than Adams, became the target of vilification as a supporter of the radical French revolutionaries and an atheist. His election, Americans were warned, would bring "dwellings in flames, hoary hairs bathed in blood, female chastity violated . . . children writhing on the pike and halberd." Jefferson kept quiet, refused to answer the attacks, and directed the campaign by mail from his home at Monticello. He was advanced as the farmers' friend, the champion of states' rights, frugal government, liberty, and peace.

Adams proved more popular than his party, whose candidates generally fared worse than the president, but the Republicans edged him out by seventy-three electoral votes to sixty-five. The decisive states were New York and South Carolina, either of which might have given the victory to Adams. But in New York Burr's organization won control of the legislature, which cast the electoral votes. In South Carolina, Charles Pinckney (cousin to the Federalist Pinckneys) won over the legislature by well-placed promises of Republican patronage. Still, the result was not final, for Jefferson and Burr had tied with seventy-three votes each, and the choice of the president was thrown into the House of Representatives, where Federalist diehards tried vainly to give the election to Burr. This was too much for Hamilton, who opposed Jefferson but held a much lower opinion of Burr. Eventually the deadlock was broken when a confidant of Jefferson assured a Delaware congressman that Jefferson would refrain from wholesale removals of Federalists and uphold the new fiscal system. The representative resolved to vote for Jefferson, and several other Federalists agreed simply to cast blank ballots, permitting Jefferson to win without any of them actually having to vote for him.

Before the Federalists relinquished power to the Jeffersonian Republicans on March 4, 1801, their "lame-duck" Congress passed the

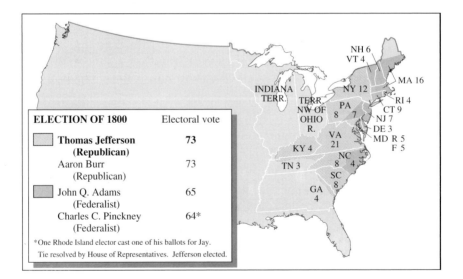

ELECTION OF 1800 Electoral vote

Thomas Jefferson **73**
(Republican)

Aaron Burr 73
(Republican)

John Q. Adams 65
(Federalist)

Charles C. Pinckney 64*
(Federalist)

*One Rhode Island elector cast one of his ballots for Jay.

Tie resolved by House of Representatives. Jefferson elected.

Judiciary Act of 1801. Intended to ensure Federalist control of the judicial system, this act provided that the next vacancy on the Supreme Court should not be filled, created sixteen circuit courts with a new judge for each, and increased the number of attorneys, clerks, and marshals. Before he left office, Adams named John Marshall to the vacant office of chief justice and appointed good Federalists to all the new positions, including forty-two justices of the peace for the new District of Columbia. The Federalists, defeated and destined never to regain national power, had in the words of Jefferson "retired into the judiciary as a stronghold."

The election of 1800 marked a turning point in American political history. It was the first time that one political party, however ungracefully, relinquished power to the opposition party. Jefferson's victory signaled the end of the patrician politics of the past and the emergence of a new, more democratic political system dominated by parties, partisanship, and wider public participation—at least among white men. Before and immediately after independence, politics was popular but not democratic: people took a keen interest in public affairs, but socially prominent families, the "rich, the able, and the well born," dominated political life. However, the fierce political battles of the late 1790s, culminating in Jefferson's election as president in 1800, wrested control of politics from the governing elite and established the right of ordinary people to play an active role in governing the young republic. With the gradual elimination of property qualifications for voting, and the proliferation of newspapers, pamphlets, and other publications, the "public sphere" where political issues were debated and decided expanded enormously in the early nineteenth century.

John Adams regretted the democratization of politics and the rise of fractious partisanship. "Jefferson had a party, Hamilton had a party, but the commonwealth had none," he sighed. The defeated president was so distraught at the turn of events that he decided not to participate in Jefferson's inauguration. Instead he boarded a stagecoach for the 500-mile trip north to his home in Quincy, Massachusetts. He and Jefferson would not communicate for the next twelve years. As John Adams returned to his Massachusetts farm, he reported that he had exchanged "honors and virtue for manure."

MAKING CONNECTIONS

- Thomas Jefferson's Republican philosophy offered a strong alternative to Hamilton's Federalism. As the next chapter shows, however, once the Republicans got into power, they adopted a number of Federalist principles and positions.

- The Bank of the United States and the protective tariff continued to be controversial. The Bank was renewed for another twenty years in 1816, the same year in which the first truly protective tariff was passed (Chapter 10), but in the 1830s the Bank was eliminated, and the tariff became a major source of sectional conflict (Chapter 11).

- The foreign policy crises with England and France described in this chapter will lead to the War of 1812, discussed in Chapter 9.

FURTHER READING

The best introduction to the early Federalists remains John C. Miller's *The Federalist Era, 1789–1800* (1960). Other works analyze the ideological debates among the nation's first leaders. Richard Buel, Jr.'s *Securing the Revolution: Ideology in American Politics, 1789–1815* (1974), Joyce Appleby's *Capitalism and a New Social Order* (1984), Drew McCoy's *The Last of the Fathers: James Madison and the Republican Legacy* (1989), and Stanley Elkins and Eric McKitrick's *The Age of Federalism* (1993) trace the persistence and transformation of ideas first fostered during the Revolutionary crisis.

The 1790s may also be understood through the views and behavior of national leaders. Joseph Ellis's *Founding Brothers: The Revolutionary Generation* (2000) is a superb group study. Also see the following biographies: Richard Brookhiser's *Founding Father: Rediscovering George Washington* (1996) and *Alexander Hamilton, American* (1999), and Joseph Ellis's *Passionate Sage: The Character and Legacy of John Adams*

(1993). For a female perspective, see Phyllis Lee Levin's *Abigail Adams* (1991). The Republican viewpoint is the subject of Lance Banning's *The Jeffersonian Persuasion: Evolution of a Party Ideology* (1978).

Federalist foreign policy is explored in Jerald A. Comb's *The Jay Treaty* (1970) and William C. Stinchcombe's *The XYZ Affair* (1980).

For specific domestic issues, see Thomas Slaughter's *The Whiskey Rebellion: Frontier Epilogue to the American Revolution* (1986) and Harry Ammon's *The Genêt Mission* (1973). The treatment of Indians in the Old Northwest is explored in Richard H. Kohn's *Eagle and Sword: The Federalists and the Creation of the Military Establishment in America, 1783–1802* (1975). For the Alien and Sedition Acts, consult James Morton Smith's *Freedom's Fetters: The Alien and Sedition Laws and American Civil Liberties* (1966).

Several books focus on social issues of the post-Revolutionary period, including *Keepers of the Revolution: New Yorkers at Work in the Early Republic* (1992), edited by Paul A. Gilje and Howard B. Rock, Ronald Schultz's *The Republic of Labor: Philadelphia Artisans and the Politics of Class, 1720–1830* (1993), and Peter Way's *Common Labour: Workers and the Digging of North American Canals, 1780–1860* (1993).

The African-American experience in the Revolutionary era is detailed in Mechal Sobel's *The World They Made Together: Black and White Values in Eighteenth-Century Virginia* (1988) and Gary B. Nash's *Forging Freedom: The Formation of Philadelphia's Black Community, 1720–1840* (1988).

9 ❧ THE EARLY REPUBLIC

*T*he early years of the new republic laid the foundation for the nation's development as the first society in the world organized around the principle of democratic capitalism and its promise of equal opportunity for all—except slaves, Indians, and women. White male Americans in the fifty years after independence were on the move and on the make. Their prospects seemed unlimited, their optimism unrestrained. A dynamic economy in the early stages of the nation's development rewarded those with the freedom to pursue happiness—whether through hard work and technological ingenuity or crass exploitation of others. As John Adams observed, "There is no people on earth so ambitious as the people of America . . . because the lowest can aspire as freely as the highest."

Land sales west of the Appalachian Mountains soared in the early nineteenth century as aspiring farmers shoved Indians aside in order to establish homesteads of their own. Enterprising, mobile, and increasingly diverse in religion and national origin, tens of thousands of ordinary folk uprooted themselves from settled communities and went in search of personal advancement, occupying more territory in a single generation than had been settled in the 150 years of colonial history. Annual sales of western land increased from a hundred thousand acres in the 1790s to half a million after 1800, and farms multiplied at a rate unmatched since the original colonial settlements. "Never again," as historian Joyce Appleby writes, "would so large a portion of the nation live in new settlements." Between 1800 and 1820, the trans-Appalachian population soared from 300,000 to 2,000,000. By 1840, over 40 percent of Americans lived west of the mountains in eight new states that had joined the Union.

The migrants flowed westward in three streams between 1780 and 1830. One ran from the old South—Virginia, Maryland, and the Carolinas—into the newer states of Georgia, Alabama, and Mississippi. Another traversed the Blue Ridge Mountains from Maryland and Virginia, crossing into Kentucky and Tennessee. The third route was in the North, taking New Englanders westward across the Berkshires into New York, Pennsylvania, Ohio, and Michigan. Many of these pioneers stayed only a few years before continuing westward, constantly in search of cheaper and more fertile land.

Of course, many people were not so mobile or even free. Slaves and servants lacked even the minimal resources to redirect their lives. Others were content with the status quo or simply sought to replicate the way of life of their parents. Still others were constrained by domineering fathers who dictated their life choices.

The prevailing spirit of opportunistic independence affected free blacks as well as whites, Indians as well as immigrants. Free blacks were the fastest growing segment of the population during the early nineteenth century. Many slaves gained their freedom during the Revolutionary War, either by escaping, by joining the British forces, or by serving in American units. Every state except South Carolina promised freedom for slaves who fought the British. Afterwards, state after state in the North outlawed slavery, and antislavery societies blossomed, exerting increasing pressure on the South to end the degrading practice. The westward migration of whites brought incessant conflict with Native Americans. Indians fiercely resisted but ultimately succumbed to a federal government and federal army determined to displace them.

Most white Americans, however, were less concerned about Indians and slavery than they were about seizing their own personal opportunities. Politicians chose to suppress the volatile issue of slavery rather than to confront it; their priorities were elsewhere. Westward expansion, economic growth, urban development, and the democratization of politics fostered a pervasive entrepreneurial spirit among the generation of young Americans born after 1776—especially outside the South. In 1790 nine out of ten Americans lived on the land and engaged in what is called household production; their sphere of activity was local. But with each passing year, farmers increasingly focused on producing surplus crops and livestock to be sold in regional markets. Cotton prices soared and in the process the deep South grew ever more committed to a plantation economy dependent on slave labor, New England merchants, and world markets. The burgeoning market economy produced boom and bust cycles, but, overall, the years from 1790 to 1830 were quite prosperous, with young Americans experiencing a "widening scope of opportunity."

The colonial economy had been organized around what Great Britain wanted from its New World possessions. This dependency brought the hated imperial restrictions on manufacturing, commerce, and shipping. With independence, however, Americans could create new industries, pursue new careers, and exploit new markets. It was not simply Alexander Hamilton's financial initiatives and the actions of wealthy investors and speculators that sparked America's dramatic commercial growth in these years. It also resulted from the efforts of ordinary men and women who were willing to take risks, uproot families, use unstable paper money from unregulated local banks, purchase factory-made goods, and tinker with new machines and tools. Free enterprise was the keynote of the era.

While most people continued to wrest their living from the land, a rising number of young adults found employment in new or greatly expanded enterprises: textiles, banking, transport, publishing, retail, teaching, preaching, medicine, law, construction, and engineering. Technological innovations (steam power, power tools, and new modes of transportation) and their social applications (mass communication, turnpikes, postal service, banks, and corporations) fostered an array of new industries and businesses. The emergence of a factory system transformed the nature of work for many Americans. Proud apprentices, journeymen, and master craftsmen who controlled their labor and invested their work with an emphasis on quality rather than quantity resented the proliferation of mills and factories populated by "half-trained" workers dependent on an hourly wage and subject to the sharp fluctuations of the larger economy.

The decentralized agrarian republic of 1776, nestled along the Atlantic seaboard, had become by 1830 a sprawling commercial nation connected by networks of roads and canals and cemented by economic relationships—all animated by a restless spirit of enterprise, experimentation, and expansion.

JEFFERSONIAN SIMPLICITY

On March 4, 1801, Thomas Jefferson, tall and thin, with ill-fitting clothes, red hair, and a ruddy complexion, became the first president to be inaugurated in the new federal city, Washington, District of

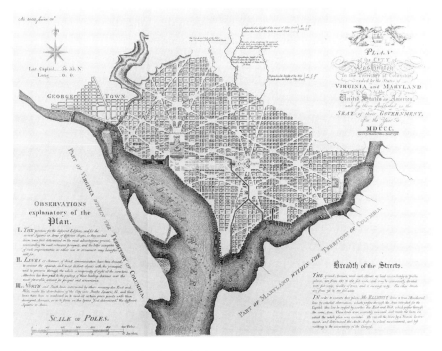

Plan of Washington, D.C., from 1792.

Columbia. Washington was still a motley array of buildings around two centers, Capitol Hill and the Executive Mansion. The Congress, having met in eight different towns and cities since 1774, had at last found a permanent home, but as yet enjoyed few amenities. There were only two places of amusement, one a racetrack, the other a theater filled with "tobacco smoke, whiskey breaths, and other stenches."

Jefferson's informal inauguration befitted the primitive surroundings. The new president left his lodgings and walked down a stump-strewn Pennsylvania Avenue to the unfinished Capitol. He entered the Senate chamber, took the oath from Chief Justice John Marshall, read his inaugural address in a barely audible voice, and returned to his boardinghouse for dinner. A tone of simplicity and conciliation ran through his inaugural address: "We are all Republicans—we are all Federalists. If there be any among us who would wish to dissolve this Union or to change its republican form, let them stand undisturbed as monuments of the safety with which error of opinion may be tolerated where reason is left free to combat it." Jefferson concluded with a summary of the "essential principles" that would guide his administration: "Equal and exact justice to all men . . . ; peace, commerce, and honest friendship with all nations, entangling alliances with none . . . ; freedom of religion; freedom of the press; and freedom of person, under the protection of the habeas corpus; and trial by juries impartially selected. . . . The wisdom of our sages and the blood of our heroes have been devoted to their attainment."

JEFFERSON IN OFFICE

The deliberate display of republican simplicity at Jefferson's inauguration set the style of his administration. He took pains to avoid the occasions of pomp and circumstance that had characterized Federalist administrations and which to his mind suggested the trappings of kingship. Presidential messages went to Congress in writing lest they resemble the parliamentary speech from the throne. The practice also allowed Jefferson, a notoriously bad public speaker, to exploit his skill as a writer.

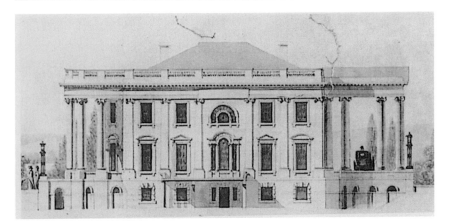

A watercolor of the president's house during Jefferson's term in office. Jefferson called it "big enough for two emperors, one pope, and the grand lama in the bargain."

Jefferson liked to think of his election as the "Revolution of 1800," but the margin had been razor thin, and the policies that he followed were more conciliatory than revolutionary. His overwhelming reelection in 1804 attests to the popularity of his philosophy. Perhaps the most revolutionary thing about Jefferson's presidency was the orderly transfer of power in 1801, an uncommon event in the world of that day. "The changes of administration," a Washington lady wrote in her diary, "which in every age have most generally been epochs of confusion, villainy and bloodshed, in this our happy country take place without any species of distraction, or disorder."

Jefferson placed in policy-making positions men of his own party, and he was the first president to pursue the role of party leader, cultivating congressional support at his dinner parties and otherwise. In the cabinet, the leading figures were Secretary of State James Madison, a longtime neighbor and political ally, and Secretary of the Treasury Albert Gallatin, a Swiss-born Pennsylvania Republican whose financial skills had won him the respect of Federalists. In an effort to cultivate Federalist New England, Jefferson chose men from that region for the positions of attorney-general, secretary of war, and postmaster-general.

In lesser offices, however, Jefferson refrained from wholesale removal of Federalists, preferring to wait until vacancies appeared. But pressure from Republicans forced him to often remove Federalists. In one area, he managed to remove the offices rather than the appointees. In 1802 Congress repealed the Judiciary Act of 1801, and so abolished the circuit judgeships and other offices to which Adams had made his "midnight appointments." A new judiciary act restored to six the number of Supreme Court justices, and set up six circuit courts, each headed by a justice.

MARBURY V. MADISON   John Adams's "midnight appointments" sparked the case of *Marbury* v. *Madison* (1803), the first in which the Supreme Court declared a federal law unconstitutional. The case involved the appointment of William Marbury as justice of the peace in the District of Columbia. Marbury's appointment letter, or commission, signed by President Adams two days before he left office, was still undelivered when Madison took office as secretary of state, and Jefferson directed him to withhold it. Marbury then sued for a court order (a writ of mandamus) directing Madison to deliver his commission.

The Court's unanimous opinion, written by John Marshall, held that Marbury deserved his commission, but then denied that the Court had jurisdiction in the case. Section 13 of the Judiciary Act of 1789, which gave the Court original jurisdiction in mandamus proceedings, was unconstitutional, the Court ruled, because the Constitution specified that the Court should have original jurisdiction only in cases involving ambassadors or states. The Court, therefore, could issue no order in the case. With one bold stroke Marshall had chastised the Jeffersonians while avoiding an awkward confrontation with an administration that might have defied his order. At the same time, he established the precedent that the Court could declare a federal law invalid on the grounds that it violated provisions of the Constitution. The Court's decision, about which Jefferson could do nothing, confirmed his fear of the judges' partisanship, and he resolved to counter their influence. In 1804 Republicans used the impeachment power against two of the most partisan Federalist judges, and succeeded in ousting one of the two, District Judge John Pickering of New Hampshire. Pickering was clearly insane, which was not a high crime or misdemeanor, but he was also given to profane and drunken harangues from the bench, which the Senate quickly decided was an impeachable offense.

DOMESTIC REFORMS   Jefferson's first term was a succession of triumphs in both domestic and foreign affairs. He did not set out to dismantle Alexander Hamilton's economic program. Under Treasury Secretary Gallatin's tutoring, he learned to accept the national bank as an essential convenience, and he did not endorse the Bank's repeal, which more dogmatic Republicans sponsored. It was too late of course to undo Hamilton's funding and debt assumption operations, but none too soon in the opinion of both Jefferson and Gallatin to begin retiring the resultant federal debt. At the same time, Jefferson won the repeal of the whiskey tax and other Federalist excises, much to the relief of backwoods distillers, drinkers, and grain farmers.

Without income from the excise taxes, frugality was all the more necessary to a federal government dependent for revenue chiefly on tariffs and the sale of western lands. Happily for the Treasury, both activities flourished. The European war brought a continually increasing traffic to American shipping and thus tariff revenues to the federal Treasury. At the same time, settlers flocked into the western lands, which were coming more and more within their reach. The admission of Ohio in 1803 increased to seventeen the number of states.

By the "wise and frugal government" promised in the inaugural address, Jefferson and Gallatin reasoned, the United States could live within its income, like a prudent farmer. The basic formula was simple: cut back expenses on the military. A standing army menaced a free society anyway. It therefore should be kept to a minimum and the national defense left, in Jefferson's words, to "a well-disciplined militia, our best

Cincinnati in 1800, twelve years after its founding. Though its population was only about 750, its inhabitants were already promoting Cincinnati as "the metropolis of the north-western territory."

reliance in peace, and for the first moments of war, till regulars may relieve them." The navy, which the Federalists had already reduced after the quasi war with France, ought to be reduced further. Coastal defense, Jefferson argued, should rely on land-based fortifications and a "mosquito fleet" of small gunboats.

In 1807 Jeffersonian reforms culminated with an act that outlawed the foreign slave trade as of January 1, 1808, the earliest date possible under the Constitution. At the time South Carolina was the only state that still permitted the trade, having reopened it in 1803. But for years to come an illegal traffic would continue. By one informal estimate perhaps 300,000 slaves were smuggled into the United States between 1808 and 1861.

THE BARBARY PIRATES   Issues of foreign relations intruded on Jefferson early in his term, when events in the Mediterranean quickly gave him second thoughts about the need for a navy. On the Barbary Coast of North Africa the rulers of Morocco, Algiers, Tunis, and Tripoli had for years practiced piracy and extortion. After the Revolution, American shipping in the Mediterranean became fair game, no longer protected by British payments of tribute. The new American government yielded up protection money too, first to Morocco in 1786, then to the others in the 1790s. In 1801, however, the pasha of Tripoli upped his demands and declared war on the United States by the symbolic gesture of chopping down the flagpole at the United States consulate. Jefferson sent warships to blockade Tripoli.

A wearisome war dragged on until 1805, punctuated in 1804 by the notable exploit of Lieutenant Stephen Decatur, who slipped into Tripoli Harbor by night and set fire to the frigate *Philadelphia,* which had been captured (along with its crew) after it ran aground. The pasha finally settled for $60,000 ransom and released the *Philadelphia*'s crew, whom he had held hostage for more than a year. It was still tribute, but less than the $300,000 the pasha had demanded at first, and much less than the cost of war.

THE LOUISIANA PURCHASE   While the conflict with Barbary pirates continued, events elsewhere led to the greatest single achievement of the Jefferson administration. The Louisiana Purchase of 1803 more than doubled the territory of the United States. It included the entire Mississippi River Valley west of the river itself. Louisiana, settled by the French, had been ceded to Spain in 1763. Since that time the dream of retaking Louisiana had stirred in French minds. In 1800 Napoleon Bonaparte secured its return in exchange for a promise (never fulfilled) to set up a Spanish princess and her husband in Italy as rulers of an enlarged Tuscany. When word of the deal reached Washington in 1801, Jefferson hastened Robert R. Livingston, the new minister to France, on his way. Spain in control of the Mississippi River outlet was bad enough, but Napoleon in control could only mean serious trouble. "The day that France takes possession of New Orleans," Jefferson wrote Livingston, "we must marry ourselves to the British fleet and nation," an unhappy prospect for the French-loving Jefferson.

Negotiations with the French dragged out into 1803, while Spanish forces remained in control in Louisiana, awaiting the arrival of the French. Early that year James Monroe was sent to assist Livingston in Paris. But no sooner had he arrived than Napoleon's minister, Talleyrand, surprised Livingston by asking if the United States would like to buy the whole of the Louisiana territory. Livingston, once he regained his composure, snapped up the offer.

By the treaty of cession, dated April 30, 1803, the United States obtained the Louisiana Territory for about $15 million. The treaty was vague in defining the boundaries of Louisiana. Its language could be stretched to provide a tenuous claim on Texas and a much stronger claim on West Florida, from Baton Rouge on the Mississippi River past Mobile to the Perdido River on the east. When Livingston asked about the boundaries, Talleyrand responded: "I can give you no direction. You have made a noble bargain for yourselves, and I suppose you will make the most of it."

The surprising turn of events had presented Jefferson with a noble bargain, a great new "empire of liberty," but also with a constitutional dilemma. Nowhere did the Constitution mention the purchase of territory. Jefferson at first thought to resolve the matter by offering an amendment, but his advisers argued against delay lest Napoleon change his mind. The power to purchase territory, they reasoned, resided in the power to make treaties. Jefferson relented, trusting, he said, "that the good sense of our country will correct the evil of loose construction when it shall produce ill effects." New England Federalists boggled at the prospect of new states that would probably strengthen the Jeffersonian party, and centered their fire on a proviso that the inhabitants be "incorporated in the Union" as citizens. In a reversal that anticipated many future reversals on constitutional issues, Federalists found themselves arguing strict construction of the Constitution while Republicans brushed aside such scruples in favor of implied power.

The Senate ratified the treaty by an overwhelming vote of 26 to 6, and on December 20, 1803, American officials took formal possession of the sprawling Louisiana territory. For the time being the Spanish kept West Florida, but within a decade that area would be ripe for the plucking. In 1808 Napoleon put his brother on the throne of Spain. With the Spanish colonial administration in disarray, American settlers in 1810 staged a rebellion in Baton Rouge and proclaimed the Republic of West Florida, which was quickly annexed and occupied by the United States as far eastward as the Pearl River. In 1812 the state of Louisiana absorbed the region—still known today as the Florida parishes. In 1813, with Spain itself a battlefield for French and British forces, Americans took over the rest of West Florida, now the Gulf coast of Mississippi and Alabama. Legally, the American government has claimed ever since, all these areas were included in the original Louisiana Purchase.

EXPLORING THE CONTINENT As an amateur scientist long before he was president, Jefferson had nourished an active curiosity about the region west of the Mississippi River, its geography, its flora and fauna, and its prospects for trade and agriculture. In 1803 he asked Congress for $2,500 to send a mapping and scientific expedition to the Far Northwest, beyond the Mississippi River, in what was still foreign territory. Congress approved, and Jefferson assigned as commanders twenty-nine-year-old Meriwether Lewis, the president's private secretary, and another Virginian, William Clark.

In 1804 the "Corps of Discovery," numbering nearly fifty, set out from St. Louis to ascend the Missouri River. Forced to live off the land, they quickly adapted themselves to a new environment. Local Indians introduced them to new clothes made from deer hides and taught them new hunting techniques. Six months later, near the Mandan Sioux

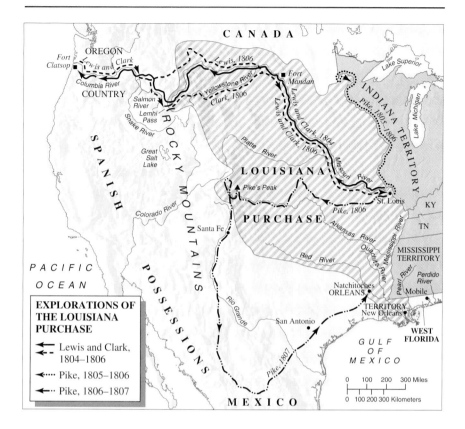

EXPLORATIONS OF THE LOUISIANA PURCHASE

◀— Lewis and Clark, 1804–1806

◀···· Pike, 1805–1806

◀—·· Pike, 1806–1807

villages in what later became North Dakota, they built Fort Mandan and wintered in relative comfort, sending back downriver a barge loaded with specimens such as the prairie dog, previously unknown to science, and the magpie, previously unknown in America.

In the spring Lewis and Clark added to the main party a remarkable Shoshone woman named Sacajawea ("Canoe Launcher"), who proved an enormous help as interpreter with the Indians of the region, and the group set out once again upstream. At the head of the Missouri River they took the north fork, thenceforth the Jefferson River, crossed the Continental Divide at Lemhi Pass, and in dugout canoes descended the Snake and Columbia Rivers to the Pacific. Near the later site of Astoria at the mouth of the Columbia, they built Fort Clatsop, in which they spent another winter. The following spring, they split into two parties, with Lewis heading back by almost the same route, and Clark going by way of the Yellowstone River. They rejoined each other at the juncture of the Missouri and Yellowstone Rivers, returning together to St. Louis in 1806, having been gone nearly two and a half years.

No longer was the Far West unknown country. Although it was nearly a century before a good edition of the *Journals of Lewis and Clark* appeared in print, many of their findings came out piecemeal, including an influential map in 1814. Convinced that they had found a practical route for the China trade, Lewis and Clark were among the last to hold out hope for a water route through the continent. Their reports of friendly Indians and abundant beaver pelts quickly attracted traders and trappers to the region, and also gave the United States a claim to the Oregon country by right of discovery and exploration.

While Lewis and Clark were gone, Jefferson sent Lieutenant Zebulon Pike to find the source of the Mississippi River. He mistakenly picked a tributary, later discoveries showed, but contributed to knowledge of the upper Mississippi River Valley. Then, during 1806–1807, he went out to the headwaters of the Arkansas River as far as Colorado. He discovered Pike's Peak but failed in an attempt to climb it, and made a roundabout return by way of Santa Fe, courtesy of Spanish soldiers who captured his party. Pike's travel account, while less reliable and less full than that of Lewis and Clark, appeared first and gave Americans

Captain Clark and his men shooting bears, from a book of engravings of the Lewis and Clark expedition (c. 1810).

their first overall picture of the Great Plains and Rocky Mountains. It also contributed to the widespread belief that the arid regions of the West constituted a Great American Desert, largely unfit for human habitation.

POLITICAL SCHEMES   Jefferson's policies, including the Louisiana Purchase, brought him almost solid support in the South and West. Even New Englanders were moving to his side. By 1809 John Quincy Adams, the son of the second president, would become a Republican! Die-hard Federalists read the handwriting on the wall. The acquisition of a vast new empire in the West would reduce New England to insignificance in political affairs, and along with it the Federalist cause. Under the leadership of Senator Thomas Pickering, a group of ardent Massachusetts Federalists called the Essex Junto considered seceding from the Union, an idea that would simmer in New England circles for another decade.

Soon they hatched a scheme to link New York with New England and contacted Vice-President Aaron Burr, who had been on the outs with the Jeffersonians. Their plan depended on Burr's election as governor of New York, but in 1804, Burr lost to the regular Republican candidate. The extreme Federalists, it turned out, could not even hold members of their own party to the plan, which Hamilton bitterly opposed on the grounds that Burr was "a dangerous man, and one who ought not to be trusted with the reins of government."

When Hamilton's remarks appeared in the public press, Burr's demand for an explanation led to a duel in 1804 at Weehawken, New Jersey. On a grassy ledge above the Hudson River, Burr shot Hamilton through the heart. Hamilton personally opposed dueling, but his romantic streak and sense of honor compelled him to demonstrate his courage. He went to his death, as his son had done in a similar affair the previous year, determined not to fire at his opponent. Burr had no such scruples. The death of Hamilton ended both Pickering's scheme and Burr's political career—but not his intrigues.

Meanwhile the presidential campaign of 1804 got under way when a congressional caucus of Republicans renominated Jefferson and chose New Yorker George Clinton for vice-president. Opposed by the Federalists Charles C. Pinckney and Rufus King, Jefferson and Clinton won 162 of 176 electoral votes. Jefferson's policy of conciliation had made him a national rather than a sectional candidate.

DIVISIONS IN THE REPUBLICAN PARTY

RANDOLPH AND THE *TERTIUM QUID*   Freed from a strong opposition—Federalists made up only a quarter of the new Congress—the Republican majority began to fragment. John Randolph, initially a loyal Jeffersonian, became the most conspicuous of the dissidents. He was a powerful combination of principle, eccentricity, and rancor. Famous for his venomous assaults delivered in a shrill soprano voice, the Virginian congressman strutted about the House floor with a whip in his hand, a symbol that he flourished best in opposition. Few colleagues had the stomach for his tongue-lashings.

Randolph became the crusty spokesman for a shifting group of "Old Republicans," whose adherence to party principles had rendered them more Jeffersonian than Jefferson himself. Their philosopher was John Taylor of Caroline, Virginia, a planter-pamphleteer whose theories of states' rights and strict construction had little effect at the time but delighted the secessionists of later years. Neither Randolph nor Taylor could accept Jefferson's pragmatic gift for adjusting principle to circumstance.

Randolph first began to smell a rat in the case of the Yazoo Fraud, a land scheme that originated in Georgia but entangled speculators from all over. In 1795 the Georgia legislature had sold to four land companies, in which some of the legislators were involved, 35 million acres in the Yazoo country (Mississippi and Alabama) for $500,000 (little more than a penny an acre). A new legislature rescinded the sale the following year, but not before some of the land claims had been sold to third parties. When Georgia finally ceded its western lands to federal authority in 1802, Jefferson sought a compromise settlement of the claims. But Randolph managed to block passage of the necessary measures and in the ensuing quarrels was removed as Speaker of the House. The snarled Yazoo affair plagued the courts and Congress for another decade. Finally, in the case of *Fletcher* v. *Peck* (1810), Chief Justice Marshall ruled that the original sale, however fraudulent, was a legal contract. Marshall held that the repeal impaired the obligation of contract and was therefore unconstitutional. Final settlement came in 1814 when Congress awarded $4.2 million to the speculators.

Randolph's definitive break with Jefferson came in 1806, when the president sought an appropriation of $2 million for a thinly disguised bribe to the French to win their influence in persuading Spain to yield the Floridas to the United States. "I found I might co-operate or be an honest man—I have therefore opposed and will oppose them," Randolph said. Thereafter he resisted Jefferson's initiatives almost out of reflex. Randolph and his colleagues were sometimes called "Quids," or the *Tertium Quid* (the "third something"), and their dissents gave rise to talk of a third party, neither Republican nor Federalist. But that never happened. Some of the dissenters in 1808 backed James Monroe against James Madison for the presidential succession, but the campaign quickly fizzled. The failure of the Quids would typify the experience of almost all third-party movements thereafter.

THE BURR CONSPIRACY   John Randolph may have become enmeshed in dogma, but Aaron Burr was never one to let principle stand in the way. Sheer brilliance and opportunism carried him to the vice-presidency. He might easily have become heir apparent to Jefferson, but a taste for intrigue was the tragic flaw in his character. Caught up in the dubious schemes of Federalist die-hards in 1800 and again in 1804, he ended his political career once and for all when he killed Alexander Hamilton in a duel. Indicted for murder and heavily in debt, the vice-president fled to Spanish-held Florida. Once the furor subsided, he boldly returned to Washington to preside over the Senate. As long as he stayed out of New York and New Jersey, he was safe.

But Burr focused his attention less on the Senate than on a cock-eyed scheme to carve out a personal empire for himself in the West. What came to be known as the Burr Conspiracy was hatched when Burr met with General James Wilkinson. Just what he and Burr were up to probably will never be known. The most likely explanation is that they conspired to get Louisiana to secede and set up an independent republic. Earlier Burr had solicited

Aaron Burr.

British support for his scheme to separate "the western part of the United States in its whole extent."

Whatever the goal, Burr learned in early 1807 that Jefferson had ordered his arrest. He tried to flee to Florida, but was caught and taken to Richmond for a trial. Charged with treason, Burr was brought for trial before Chief Justice John Marshall. The case revealed both Marshall and Jefferson at their partisan worst, and it established two major constitutional precedents. First, Jefferson ignored a subpoena requiring him to appear in court with certain papers in his possession. He refused, as George Washington had refused, to submit papers to the Congress on grounds that the independence of the executive branch would be compromised if the president were subject to a court writ. The second major precedent was the rigid definition of treason. On this Marshall adopted the strictest of constructions. Treason under the Constitution, he wrote, consists of "levying war against the United States or adhering to their enemies" and requires "two witnesses to the same overt act" for conviction. Since the prosecution failed to produce two witnesses to an overt act of treason by Burr, the jury found him not guilty.

Whether or not Burr escaped his just deserts, Marshall's strict construction of the Constitution protected the United States, as the authors of the Constitution clearly intended, against the capricious judgments of "treason" that governments through the centuries have used to terrorize dissenters. As to Burr, with further charges pending, he skipped bail and took refuge in France, but returned unmolested in 1812 to practice law in New York. He survived to a virile old age. At age eighty, shortly before his death, he was divorced on grounds of adultery.

WAR IN EUROPE

Oppositionists of whatever stripe were more an annoyance than a threat to Jefferson. The more intractable problems of his second term involved the renewal of the European war in 1803, which helped resolve the problem of Louisiana but put more strains on Jefferson's desire to avoid "entangling alliances" and the quarrels of Europe. In 1805 Napoleon's crushing defeat of Russian and Austrian forces at Austerlitz left him in control of western Europe. The same year, Britain's defeat of the French and Spanish fleets in the Battle of Trafalgar secured control of the seas. The war resolved itself into a battle of elephant and whale, Napoleon dominant on land, the British dominant on the water, neither able to strike a decisive blow at the other, and neither restrained by an overly delicate sense of neutral rights or international law.

HARASSMENT BY BRITAIN AND FRANCE   For two years after the renewal of European warfare, American shippers reaped the benefits, taking over trade with the French and Spanish West Indies. But in the case of the *Essex* (1805), a British court ruled that the practice of shipping French and Spanish goods through American ports while on their way elsewhere did not neutralize enemy goods. Such a practice violated the British Rule of 1756, under which trade closed in time of peace remained closed in time of war. Goods shipped in violation of the rule, the British held, were liable to seizure at any point under the doctrine of continuous voyage. In 1807 the commercial provisions of Jay's Treaty expired and James Monroe, ambassador to Great Britain, failed to get a renewal satisfactory to Jefferson. After that, the British interference with American shipping increased, not just to keep supplies from Napoleon's continent but also to hobble competition with British merchant ships.

In a series of Orders in Council adopted in 1806 and 1807, the British ministry set up a "paper blockade" of Europe that barred all trade between England and Europe. Moreover, vessels headed for continental ports were required to get British licenses and were subject to British inspection. It was a "paper blockade" because even the powerful British navy was not large enough to monitor every European port. Napoleon retaliated with his "Continental System," proclaimed in the Berlin Decree of 1806 and the Milan Decree of 1807. In the Berlin Decree, he declared his own paper blockade of the British Isles and barred British ships from ports under French control. In the Milan Decree, he ruled that neutral ships that complied with British regulations were subject to seizure when they reached continental ports. The situation presented American shippers with a dilemma. If they complied with the demands of one side, they were subject to seizure by the other.

The risks were daunting, but the prospects for profits were so great that American shippers ran the risk. For seamen the danger was heightened by a renewal of the practice of impressment. The use of press gangs to kidnap men in British (and colonial) ports was a long-standing

method of recruitment for the British navy. The seizure of British subjects from American vessels became a new source of recruits, justified
on the principle that British subjects remained British subjects for life:
"Once an Englishman, always an Englishman." Mistakes might be made,
of course, since it was sometimes hard to distinguish British subjects
from Americans; indeed a flourishing trade in fake citizenship papers
arose in American ports. Impressment was mostly confined to merchant
vessels, but on at least two occasions before 1807, vessels of the American navy had been stopped on the high seas and seamen removed.

In the summer of 1807, the British frigate *Leopard* accosted an
American naval vessel, the frigate *Chesapeake,* just outside territorial
waters off Norfolk, Virginia. After the *Chesapeake*'s captain refused to
be searched, the *Leopard* opened fire, killing three Americans and
wounding eighteen. The *Chesapeake,* caught unready for battle, was
forced to strike its colors (lowering the flag was a sign of surrender). A
British search party seized four men, one of whom was later hanged for
desertion from the British navy. Soon after the *Chesapeake* limped back
into Norfolk, the *Washington Federalist* editorialized: "We have never,
on any occasion, witnessed . . . such a thirst for revenge. . . ." Public
wrath was so aroused that Jefferson could have had war on the spot.
Had Congress been in session, he might have been forced into war. But
Jefferson, like Adams before him, resisted the war fever and suffered
politically as a result. One Federalist called Jefferson a "dish of skim
milk curdling at the head of our nation."

THE EMBARGO   Jefferson resolved to use public indignation against
the British to promote "peaceable coercion." In 1807, in response to his
request, Congress passed the Embargo Act, which stopped all export of
American goods and prohibited American ships from leaving for foreign
ports. The constitutional basis of the embargo was the power to regulate commerce, which in this case Republicans interpreted broadly as
the power to prohibit commerce.

Jefferson's embargo, however, failed from the beginning because
few Americans were willing to make the necessary sacrifices. The ide-
alistic spirit that had made economic pressures effective in the pre-
Revolutionary crises was lacking. Illegal trade with Britain and France
remained profitable despite the risks, and violation of the embargo
was almost laughably easy. Lax enforcement and loopholes in the act

Preparation for War to Defend Commerce. *In 1806 and 1807 American shipping was caught in the crossfire of war between Britain and France.*

permitted ships to leave port under the pretense of engaging in coastal trade or whaling, or under an amendment passed a few months after the act for the purpose of bringing home American property stored in foreign warehouses. Some 800 ships left on such missions, but few of them returned before the embargo expired. Trade across the Canadian border flourished. As it turned out, France was little hurt by the act. The lack of American cotton hurt some British manufacturers and workers, but they carried little weight with the government, and British shippers benefited. With American ports closed, they found a new trade in Latin American ports thrown open by the colonial authorities when Napoleon occupied the mother countries of Spain and Portugal.

American resistance to the embargo revived the moribund Federalist party in New England, which renewed the charge that Jefferson was in league with the French. At the same time, farmers in the South and West suffered for want of outlets for their grain, cotton, and tobacco. After fifteen months of ineffectiveness, Jefferson finally accepted failure and in 1809 repealed the embargo shortly before he relinquished the "splendid misery" of the presidency.

This 1807 Federalist cartoon compares Washington (left) to Jefferson (right). Washington is flanked by the British lion and the American eagle, while Jefferson is flanked by a snake and a lizard. Below Jefferson are volumes by French philosophers.

In the election of 1808 the succession passed to another Virginian, Secretary of State James Madison. George Clinton was again the candidate for vice-president. The Federalists, backing Charles C. Pinckney and Rufus King of New York, revived enough as a result of the embargo to win 47 votes to Madison's 122.

THE DRIFT TO WAR   Madison's presidency was entangled in foreign affairs from the beginning. Still insisting on neutral rights and freedom of the seas, he pursued Jefferson's policy of "peaceable coercion" by different but no more effective means. In place of the embargo Congress had substituted the Nonintercourse Act, which reopened trade with all countries except France and Great Britain and authorized the president to reopen trade with whichever of these gave up its restrictions. British minister David Erskine assured Madison's secretary of state that Britain would revoke its restrictions in 1809. With that assurance, Madison reopened trade with Britain, but Erskine had acted on his own and the foreign secretary, repudiating his action, recalled him. Nonintercourse resumed, but it proved as ineffective as the embargo. In the vain search for an alternative, Congress in 1810 reversed its ground and adopted a measure introduced by Nathaniel Macon of North Carolina, Macon's Bill Number 2, which reopened trade with the warring powers but provided that, if either dropped its restrictions, nonintercourse would be restored with the other.

This time Napoleon took a turn at trying to bamboozle Madison. Napoleon's foreign minister, the duc de Cadore, informed the American minister in Paris that he had withdrawn the Berlin and Milan Decrees, but the carefully worded Cadore letter had strings attached: revocation of the decrees depended on withdrawal of the British Orders in Council. The strings were plain to see, but either Madison misunderstood or, more likely, went along in hope of putting pressure on the British. The British initially refused to give in, and on June 1, 1812, Madison reluctantly asked Congress for war. On June 16, 1812, however, the British foreign minister, facing economic crisis, announced revocation of the Orders in Council. Britain preferred not to risk war with the United States on top of its war with Napoleon. But on June 18, 1812, the Congress concurred with Madison's request for war without knowing of the British repeal. With more time, with more patience, or with a transatlantic cable, Madison's policy would have been vindicated without resort to war.

THE WAR OF 1812

CAUSES   The main cause of the war—the demand for neutral shipping rights—seems clear enough. Neutral rights dominated Madison's war message and provided the salient reason for a mounting hostility toward the British. Yet the geographical distribution of the congressional vote for war raises a troubling question. The preponderance of the vote for war came from members of Congress representing the farm regions from Pennsylvania southward and westward. The maritime states of New York and New England, the region that bore the brunt of British attacks on American trade, voted against the declaration of war. One explanation for this seeming anomaly is simple enough. The farming regions suffered damage to their markets for grain, cotton, and tobacco, while New England shippers made profits in spite of British restrictions.

Other plausible explanations for the sectional vote, however, include frontier Indian attacks, which were blamed on the British, western land hunger, and the desire for new lands in Canada and the Floridas. Indian troubles were endemic to a rapidly expanding West. Land-hungry settlers and speculators kept moving out ahead of government surveys and sales in search of fertile acres. The constant pressure to open new lands repeatedly forced or persuaded Indians to sign treaties they did not always understand, causing stronger resentment among tribes that were losing more and more of their lands. It was an old story, dating from the Jamestown settlement, but one that took a new turn with the rise of two Shawnee leaders, Tecumseh and his twin brother Tenskwatawa, "the Prophet."

Tecumseh saw with blazing clarity the consequences of Indian disunity. From his base on the Tippecanoe River in northern Indiana, he traveled from Canada to the Gulf of Mexico in his efforts to form a confederation of tribes to defend Indian hunting grounds, insisting that no land cession was valid without the consent of all tribes, since they held the land in common. His brother supplied the inspiration of a religious revival, calling upon the Indians to worship the "Master of Life," to resist the white man's liquor, and lead a simple life within their means. By 1811 Tecumseh had matured his plans and headed south to win the Creeks, Cherokees, Choctaws, and Chickasaws to his cause.

William Henry Harrison, the governor of the Indiana territory, learned of Tecumseh's plans, met with him twice, and pronounced him "one of those uncommon geniuses who spring up occasionally to produce revolutions and overturn the established order of things." In the fall of 1811, Harrison decided that Tecumseh must be stopped. He gathered a thousand troops and advanced on Tecumseh's capital, Prophet's Town, on the Tippecanoe River, while the leader was away. The Indians attacked Harrison's encampment on the Tippecanoe River,

Tecumseh, the Shawnee leader who tried to unite the tribes in defense of their lands. He was killed in 1813 at the Battle of the Thames.

although Tecumseh had warned against any fighting in his absence. The Shawnees lost a bloody engagement that left about a quarter of Harrison's men dead or wounded. Only later did Harrison realize that he had inflicted a defeat on the Indians, who had become so demoralized that many fled to Canada. Harrison then burned their town and destroyed all its supplies. Tecumseh's dreams of an Indian confederacy went up in smoke, and Tecumseh himself fled to British protection in Canada.

The Battle of Tippecanoe reinforced suspicions that the British were inciting the Indians. Actually the incident was mainly Harrison's doing. With little hope of help from war-torn Europe, Canadian authorities had steered a careful course, discouraging warfare but seeking to keep the Indians' friendship and fur trade. To eliminate the Indian menace, American frontiersmen reasoned, they needed to remove its foreign support, and they saw the province of Ontario as a pistol pointing at the United States. Conquest of Canada would accomplish a twofold purpose. It would eliminate British influence among the Indians and open a new empire for land-hungry Americans. It was also the only place, in case of war, where the British were vulnerable to American attack. East Florida, still under Spanish control, posed a similar threat. Spain was too weak or unwilling to prevent sporadic Indian attacks across the frontier. The British were also suspected of smuggling through Florida and intriguing with the Indians on the southwest border.

Such concerns helped generate a war fever. In the Congress that assembled in late 1811, new members from southern and western districts clamored for war in defense of "national honor." Among them were Henry Clay of Kentucky, who became Speaker of the House, Richard M. Johnson of Kentucky, Felix Grundy of Tennessee, and John C. Calhoun of South Carolina. John Randolph of Roanoke christened these "new boys" the "War Hawks." After they entered the House, Randolph said, "We have heard but one word—like the whip-poor-will, but one eternal monotonous tone—Canada! Canada! Canada!"

PREPARATIONS   As it turned out, the War Hawks would get neither Canada nor Florida, for James Madison had carried into war a nation that was ill-prepared both financially and militarily. In 1811, despite earnest pleas from Treasury Secretary Gallatin, Congress had let the twenty-year charter of the Bank of the United States expire. A combination of strict-constructionist Republicans and Anglophobes, who feared the large British interest in the Bank, did it in. Also, many state banks were mismanaged, resulting in deposits lost through bankruptcy. Trade had approached a standstill and tariff revenues had declined. Loans were needed for about two-thirds of the war costs while northeastern opponents to the war were reluctant to lend money.

The military situation was almost as bad. War had been likely for nearly a decade, but Republican austerities had prevented preparations. When the war began the army numbered only 6,700 men, ill trained, poorly equipped, and led by aging officers. Most of the senior officers were veterans of the Revolution. One young Virginia officer named Winfield Scott, destined for military distinction, commented that most of the veteran commanders "had very generally slunk into either sloth, ignorance, or habits of intemperate drinking."

The navy, on the other hand, was in comparatively good shape, with able officers and trained men whose seamanship had been tested in the fighting against France and Tripoli. Its ships were well outfitted and seaworthy—all sixteen of them. In the first year of the war it was the navy that produced the only American victories in isolated duels with

John Bull stung to agony by the *Wasp* and *Hornet, two American ships with early victories in the War of 1812.*

British vessels, but their effect was mainly an occasional lift to morale. Within a year the British had blockaded the American coast, except for New England, where they hoped to cultivate antiwar feeling, and most of the little American fleet was bottled up in port.

THE WAR IN THE NORTH   The only place where the United States could effectively strike at the British was Canada. Madison's best hope was a quick attack on Quebec or Montreal to cut Canada's lifeline, the St. Lawrence River. Instead, the old history of the indecisive colonial wars was repeated, for the last time. Inadequate preparations, poor leadership, untrained troops, and faulty coordination stymied the American armies.

The administration opted for a three-pronged drive against Canada: along the Lake Champlain route toward Montreal, with General Henry Dearborn in command; along the Niagara River, with forces under General Stephen Van Rensselaer; and into Upper Canada (north of Lake Erie) from Detroit, with General William Hull and some 2,000 men. In 1812, Hull marched his men across the Detroit River but was pushed back to Detroit by the British. Sickly and senile, Hull procrastinated in Detroit while his position worsened. The British commander cleverly played upon Hull's worst fears. Gathering what redcoats he could to parade in view of Detroit's defenders, he announced that thousands of Indian allies were at the rear and that once fighting began he would be unable to control them. Fearing massacre, Hull surrendered his entire force.

Along the Niagara front, General Van Rensselaer was more aggressive. An advance party of 600 Americans crossed the Niagara River and worked their way up the bluffs on the Canadian side. The stage was set for a major victory, but the New York militia refused to reinforce Van Rensselaer's men, claiming that their military service did not obligate them to leave the country. They complacently remained on the New York side and watched their outnumbered countrymen fall to a superior force across the river.

On the third front, the old invasion route via Lake Champlain, General Dearborn led his army north from Plattsburgh, New York, toward Montreal. He marched them up to the border, where the militia once again stood on its alleged constitutional rights and refused to cross, and then marched them back to Plattsburgh.

Madison's navy secretary now pushed vigorously for American control of inland waters. At Presque Isle (Erie), Pennsylvania, twenty-eight-year-old Commodore Oliver H. Perry, already a fourteen-year veteran who had seen action against Tripoli, was fetching hardware up from Pittsburgh and building ships from the wilderness lumber. By the end of the summer Perry had superior numbers and set out in search of the British, whom he found at Lake Erie's Put-in-Bay, on September 10, 1813. After completing the preparations for battle, Perry told an aide: "This is the most important day of my life."

It was indeed. Two British warships used their superior weapons to pummel the *Lawrence,* Perry's flagship, at long distance. Blood flowed on the deck so freely that the sailors slipped and fell as they wrestled with the cannon. After four hours of intense shelling, none of the *Lawrence*'s guns was left working, and most of the crew were dead or wounded. The British expected the Americans to turn tail, but Perry

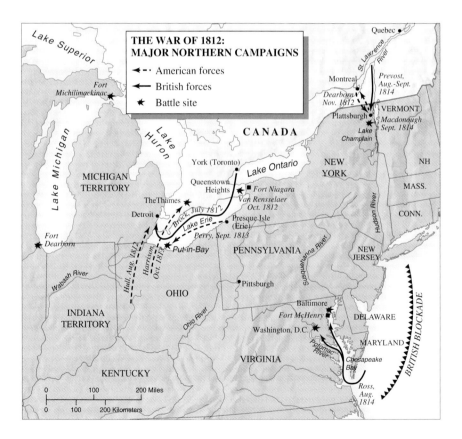

THE WAR OF 1812:
MAJOR NORTHERN CAMPAIGNS

◄-· American forces
◄— British forces
✴ Battle site

refused to quit. He had himself rowed to another vessel, carried the battle to the enemy, and finally accepted surrender of the entire British squadron. Hatless and bloodied, Perry then sent to General William Henry Harrison the long-awaited message: "We have met the enemy and they are ours."

American naval control of waters in the region forced the British to evacuate Upper Canada. They gave up Detroit, and when they took a defensive stand at the Battle of the Thames (October 5), General Harrison inflicted a defeat that eliminated British power in Upper Canada. In the course of the battle Tecumseh fell, and his dream of Indian unity died with him.

THE WAR IN THE SOUTH   In the Southwest, too, the war flared up in 1813. On August 30 the Creeks attacked Fort Mims, on the Alabama River above Mobile, killing almost half the people in the fort. The news found Andrew Jackson home in Tennessee recovering from a street brawl with Thomas Hart Benton, later a senator from Missouri. As major-general of the Tennessee militia, Jackson summoned about 2,000 volunteers and set out on a campaign that utterly crushed the Creek resistance. The decisive battle occurred on March 27, 1814, at the Horseshoe Bend of the Tallapoosa River, in the heart of the upper Creek country. In the Treaty of Fort Jackson, the Creeks ceded two-thirds of their lands to the United States, including part of Georgia and most of Alabama.

Four days after the Battle of Horseshoe Bend, Napoleon's empire collapsed. Now free to deal with America, the British developed a threefold plan of operations for 1814. They would launch a two-pronged invasion of America via Niagara and Lake Champlain to increase the clamor for peace in the Northeast; extend the naval blockade to New England, subjecting coastal towns to raids; and seize New Orleans to cut the Mississippi River, lifeline of the West.

MACDONOUGH'S VICTORY   The main British effort focused on a massive invasion via Lake Champlain. From the north General George Prevost, governor-general of Canada, advanced with the finest army yet assembled on American soil: fifteen regiments of regulars, plus militia and artillerymen, a total of about 15,000. The front was saved only by Prevost's vacillation and the superb ability of Commodore

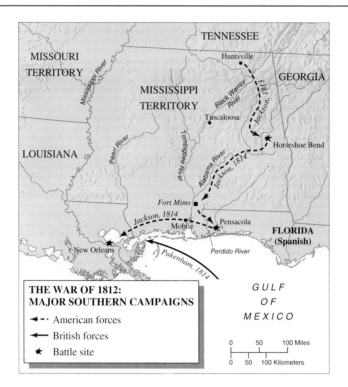

TENNESSEE

MISSOURI
TERRITORY

Huntsville

GEORGIA

Mississippi River

MISSISSIPPI
TERRITORY

Black Warrior River

Jackson, 1813

Jackson, 1814

Tuscaloosa

LOUISIANA

Pearl River

Tombigbee River

Alabama River

Horseshoe Bend

Fort Mims

Jackson, 1814

Mobile

Pensacola

FLORIDA
(Spanish)

New Orleans

Pakenham, 1814

Perdido River

GULF
OF
MEXICO

**THE WAR OF 1812:
MAJOR SOUTHERN CAMPAIGNS**

◀--· American forces

◀— British forces

★ Battle site

0   50   100 Miles

0   50   100 Kilometers

Thomas Macdonough, commander of the American naval squadron
on Lake Champlain. A land assault might have taken Plattsburgh and
forced Macdonough out of his protected position nearby, but England's
army bogged down while its flotilla engaged Macdonough in a deadly
battle.

The British concentrated their superior firepower on Macdonough's
ship, the *Saratoga*. With his starboard battery disabled, Macdonough
executed a daring maneuver known as "winding ship." He turned the
Saratoga around while at anchor and brought its undamaged side into
action with devastating effect. The *Saratoga* had to be scuttled, but
the battle ended with the entire British flotilla either destroyed or
captured.

FIGHTING IN THE CHESAPEAKE   Meanwhile, however, American
forces suffered the most humiliating experience of the war, the capture and burning of Washington, D.C. With attention focused on the
Canadian front, the Chesapeake Bay offered the British a number of

inviting targets, including Baltimore, now the fourth-largest city in America. A British force landed without opposition in 1814 at Benedict, Maryland, and headed for Washington, forty miles away. To defend the capital the Americans had a force of about 7,000, including only a few hundred regulars and 400 sailors. At Bladensburg, Maryland, the American militia melted away in the face of the smaller British force.

The British marched unopposed into Washington, where British officers ate a meal prepared for President and Mrs. Madison, who had joined the other refugees in Virginia. The British then burned the White House, the Capitol, and most other government buildings. A tornado the next day compounded the damage, but a violent thunderstorm dampened both the fires and the enthusiasm of the British forces, who left to prepare a new assault on Baltimore.

The attack on Baltimore was a different story. With some 13,000 men, chiefly militia, American forces fortified the heights behind the city. About 1,000 men held Fort McHenry, on an island in the harbor. When the British came into sight of the city, they halted in the face of American defenses. All through the following night the fleet bombarded Fort McHenry to no avail, and the invaders abandoned the attack. Francis Scott Key, a Washington lawyer, watched the siege from a vessel in the harbor. The sight of the flag still in place at dawn inspired him to draft the verses of "The Star-Spangled Banner." Later revised and set to the tune of an English drinking song, it eventually became the national anthem.

THE BATTLE OF NEW ORLEANS   The British failure at Baltimore followed by three days their failure on Lake Champlain, yet their offensive against New Orleans had yet to run its course. Along the Gulf coast Andrew Jackson had been busy shoring up the defenses of Mobile and New Orleans. Without authorization, he invaded Spanish Florida and took Pensacola to end British intrigues there. Back in Louisiana, he began to erect defenses on the approaches to New Orleans, anticipating a British approach by the interior to pick up Indian support and control the Mississippi River. Instead the British fleet, with some 8,000 European veterans under General Sir Edward Pakenham, took up positions on a level plain on the banks of the Mississippi River, just south of New Orleans.

Andrew Jackson's defeat of the British at New Orleans, January 1815.

Pakenham's painfully careful approach—he waited until all his artillery was available—gave Jackson time to build earthworks bolstered by cotton bales. It was an almost invulnerable position, but Pakenham, contemptuous of Jackson's force of frontier militiamen, Creole aristocrats, free blacks, and pirates, rashly ordered his veterans forward in a frontal assault at dawn on January 8, 1815. His redcoats ran into a murderous hail of artillery shells and deadly rifle fire. Before the British withdrew, about 2,000 had been wounded or killed, including Pakenham himself, whose body, pickled in a barrel of rum, was returned to the ship where his wife awaited news of the battle.

The Battle of New Orleans occurred after a peace treaty had already been signed in Europe. But this is not to say that it was an anticlimax or that it had no effect on the outcome of the war, for the treaty was yet to be ratified and the British might have exploited the possession of New Orleans had they won it. The battle did assure ratification of the treaty as it stood, and both governments acted quickly.

THE TREATY OF GHENT   Peace efforts had begun in 1812 even before hostilities got under way. The British, after all, had repealed their Orders in Council two days before the declaration of war and confidently expected at least an armistice. Secretary of State James Monroe, however, told the British that they would have to give up the outrage of impressment as well. Meanwhile Czar Alexander of Russia offered to mediate the dispute, hoping to relieve the pressure on Great Britain, his ally against France. Madison sent Albert Gallatin and James Bayard to join John Quincy Adams, American ambassador to Russia, in St. Petersburg. They arrived in 1813, but the czar was at the war front, and they waited impatiently for six months. At that point, the British refused Russia's mediation and instead offered to negotiate directly. Madison then appointed Henry Clay and Jonathan Russell to join the other three commissioners in talks that finally got under way in the Flemish city of Ghent in August.

In contrast to the array of talent gathered in the American contingent, the British diplomats were nonentities, really messengers acting for the Foreign Office, which was more concerned with the effort to remake the map of Europe at the Congress of Vienna. The Americans had more leeway to use their own judgment, and sharp disagreements developed that had to be patched up by Albert Gallatin. The sober Adams and the hard-drinking, poker-playing Clay, especially, rubbed each other the wrong way. The American delegates at first were instructed to demand that the British abandon impressment and paper blockades, and to get payments for seizures of American ships. The British opened the discussions with demands for territory in New York and Maine, removal of American warships from the Great Lakes, an autonomous Indian buffer state in the Northwest, access to the Mississippi River, and abandonment of American fishing rights off Labrador and Newfoundland. If the British insisted on such a position, the Americans informed them, the negotiations would be at an end.

But the British were stalling, awaiting news of victories to strengthen their hand. The news of American victory on Lake Champlain arrived in October and weakened the British resolve. Their will to fight was further eroded by a continuing power struggle at the Congress of Vienna, by the eagerness of British merchants to renew trade with America, and by the war-weariness of a tax-burdened public. The British finally decided that the American war was not worth the cost. One by one demands were dropped on both sides until the envoys agreed to end the war, return the prisoners, restore the previous boundaries, and settle nothing else. The questions of fisheries and disputed boundaries were referred to commissions for future settlement. The Treaty of Ghent was signed on Christmas Eve of 1814.

THE HARTFORD CONVENTION   While the diplomats converged on a peace settlement, an entirely different kind of meeting took place in Hartford, Connecticut. An ill-fated affair, the Hartford Convention represented the climax of New England's disaffection with "Mr. Madison's war." New England had managed to keep aloof from the war and extract a profit from illegal trading and privateering. New England shippers monopolized the import trade and took advantage of the chance to engage in smuggling with the enemy. After the fall of Napoleon, however, the British extended their blockade to New England, occupied Maine, and conducted several raids along the coast. Even Boston seemed threatened. Instead of rallying to the American flag, however, Federalists in the Massachusetts legislature on October 5, 1814, voted for a convention of New England states to plan independent action.

On December 15 the Hartford Convention assembled with delegates chosen by the legislatures of Massachusetts, Rhode Island, and Connecticut, with two delegates from Vermont and one from New Hampshire: twenty-two in all. The convention included an extreme group, Timothy Pickering's "Essex Junto," who were prepared to secede from the Union, but it was controlled by a more moderate group led by Harrison Gray Otis, who wanted only a protest in language reminiscent of Madison's Virginia Resolutions of 1798. As the ultimate remedy for their grievances, they proposed seven constitutional amendments designed to limit Republican influence: abolishing the counting of slaves in apportioning state representation in Congress, requiring a two-thirds vote to declare war or admit new states, prohibiting embargoes lasting more than sixty days, excluding the foreign-born from federal offices, limiting the president to one term, and forbidding successive presidents from the same state.

Their call for a later convention in Boston carried the unmistakable threat of secession if the demands were ignored. Yet the threat quickly evaporated. When messengers from Hartford reached Washington, they found the battered capital celebrating the good news from Ghent and New Orleans. The consequence was a fatal blow to the Federalist party, which never recovered from the stigma of disloyalty stamped on it by the Hartford Convention.

THE WAR'S AFTERMATH   For all the fumbling ineptitude with which the War of 1812 was fought, it generated an intense feeling of patriotism.

We Owe Allegiance to No Crown.
*The War of 1812 generated a new
feeling of nationalism.*

Despite the standoff with which it ended at Ghent, the American public nourished a sense of victory, courtesy of Andrew Jackson and his
men at New Orleans as well as the heroic exploits of American frigates
in their duels with British ships. Under Republican leadership, the nation had survived a "Second War of Independence" against the greatest
power on earth, and emerged with new symbols of nationhood and a
new gallery of heroes. The war also launched the United States toward
economic independence, as the interruption of trade encouraged the
growth of American manufactures. After forty years of independence, it
dawned on the world that the new American republic might be here to
stay, and that it might be something more than a pawn in European
power games.

As if to underline the point, Congress authorized a quick, decisive blow
at the pirates of the Barbary Coast. During the War of 1812 they had
again set about plundering American ships. On March 3, 1815, little more
than two weeks after the Senate ratified the Treaty of Ghent, Congress
sent Captain Stephen Decatur with ten vessels to the Mediterranean. He
first seized two Algerian ships and then sailed boldly into the harbor of
Algiers. On June 30, 1815, the dey of Algiers agreed to cease molesting
American ships and to give up all American prisoners. Decatur's show
of force induced similar treaties from Tunis and Tripoli. This time there
was no tribute; this time, for a change, the Barbary pirates paid for the

damage they had done. This time victory put an end to the piracy and extortion in that quarter, permanently.

One of the strangest results of the War of 1812 and its aftermath was a reversal of roles by the Republicans and Federalists. Out of the wartime experience the Republicans had learned some lessons in nationalism. Certain needs and inadequacies revealed by the war had "Federalized" Madison, or "re-Federalized" this Father of the Constitution. Perhaps, he reasoned, a peacetime army and navy were necessary. The lack of a national bank had added to the problems of financing the war. Now Madison wanted it back. The rise of new industries during the war led to a clamor for increased tariffs on imports to protect the infant American companies from foreign competition. Madison went along. The problems of overland transportation in the West had revealed the need for internal improvements. Madison agreed, but on that point kept his constitutional scruples. He wanted a constitutional amendment. So while Madison embraced nationalism and broad construction of the Constitution, the Federalists took up the Jeffersonians' position of states' rights and strict construction. It was the first great reversal of roles in constitutional interpretation. It would not be the last.

MAKING CONNECTIONS

- Jefferson's embargo and the War of 1812 encouraged the beginnings of manufacturing in the United States, an important subject in Chapter 12.

- The Federalist party collapsed because of its opposition to the War of 1812. But as the next chapter shows, Republicans did not prosper as much as might have been expected in the absence of political opposition.

- The American success in the War of 1812 (a moral victory at best) led to a tremendous sense of national pride and unity, a spirit analyzed in the next chapter.

FURTHER READING

Marshall Smelser's *The Democratic Republic, 1801–1815* (1968) presents an overview of the Republican administrations. The standard biography of Jefferson is Joseph J. Ellis's *American Sphinx: The Character of Thomas Jefferson* (1997). On the life of Jefferson's friend and successor, see Drew R. McCoy's *The Last of the Fathers: James Madison and the Republican Legacy* (1989). Joyce Appleby's *Capitalism and a New Social Order* (1984) minimizes the impact of republican ideology.

Linda K. Kerber's *Federalists in Dissent: Imagery and Ideology in Jeffersonian America* (1970) explores the Federalists while out of power. The concept of judicial review and the courts can be studied in Richard E. Ellis's *The Jeffersonian Crisis* (1971). On John Marshall, see G. Edward White's *The Marshall Court and Cultural Change, 1815–1835* (1991). Milton Lomask's two-volume *Aaron Burr: The Years from Princeton to Vice President, 1756–1805* (1979) and *The Conspiracy and the Years of Exile, 1805–1836* (1982) trace the career of that remarkable American.

For the Louisiana Purchase, consult Alexander De Conde's *This Affair of Louisiana* (1976). For a captivating account of the Lewis and Clark expedition, see Stephen Ambrose's *Undaunted Courage: Meriwether Lewis, Thomas Jefferson and the Opening of the American West* (1996). Bernard W. Sheehan's *Seeds of Extinction* (1973) is more analytical about the Jeffersonians' Indian policy and opening of the West.

Burton Spivak's *Jefferson's English Crisis: Commerce, the Embargo, and the Republican Revolution* (1979) discusses Anglo-American relations during Jefferson's administration; Clifford L. Egan's *Neither Peace nor War* (1983) covers Franco-American relations. An excellent revisionist treatment of the events that brought on war in 1812 is J. C. A. Stagg's *Mr. Madison's War* (1983). The war itself is the focus of Donald R. Hickey's *The War of 1812: A Forgotten Conflict* (1989). See also David Curtis Skaggs and Gerard T. Altoff's *A Signal Victory: The Lake Erie Campaign, 1812–1813* (1997).

PART THREE

AN EXPANSIVE NATION

Americans during the early nineteenth century formed a relentless migratory stream that spilled over the Appalachian Mountains, spanned the Mississippi River, and in the 1840s, reached the Pacific Ocean. Wagons, canals, flatboats, steamboats, and eventually railroads helped expedite the westward migration. The feverish expansion of the United States into new western territories brought Americans into conflict with Native Americans, Mexicans, and the British. Only a few people, however, expressed moral reservations about displacing others. Most Americans believed it was the "manifest destiny" of the United States to spread across the entire continent—at whatever cost and at whomever's expense. Americans generally believed that they enjoyed the blessing of Providence in their efforts to consolidate the entire continent under their control.

While most Americans continued to earn their living from the soil, textile mills and manufacturing plants began to dot the landscape and transform the nature of work and the pace of life. By mid-century the United States was emerging as one of the world's major industrial powers. In addition, the lure of cheap land and plentiful jobs, as well as the promise of political equality and religious freedom, attracted hundreds of thousands of immigrants from Europe. These newcomers, mostly from Germany and Ireland, faced ethnic prejudices, religious persecution, and language barriers that made assimilation into American culture all the more difficult.

All these developments gave to American life in the second quarter of the nineteenth century a dynamic and fluid quality. The United States, said the philosopher-poet Ralph Waldo Emerson, was "a country of beginnings, of projects, of designs, of expectations." A restless optimism characterized the period. People of lowly social status who heretofore had accepted their lot in life now strove to climb the social ladder and enter the political arena. The patrician republic espoused by Jefferson and Madison gave way to the frontier democracy promoted by the Jacksonians. Americans were no longer content to be governed by a small, benevolent aristocracy of talent and wealth. They began to demand—and obtain—government of, by, and for the people.

The fertile economic environment during the antebellum era helped foster the egalitarian idea that individuals (except African Americans, Native Americans, and women) should have an equal opportunity to better themselves and should be granted political rights and privileges. In America, observed a journalist in 1844, "One has as good a chance as another according to his talents, prudence, and personal exertions."

The exuberant individualism embodied in such mythic expressions of economic equality and political democracy also spilled over into the cultural arena during the first half of the nineteenth century. The so-called romantic movement applied democratic ideals to philosophy, religion, literature, and the fine arts. In New England, Ralph Waldo Emerson and Henry David Thoreau joined other transcendentalists in espousing a radical individualism. Other reformers were motivated more by a sense of spiritual mission than democratic individualism. Reformers sought to introduce public-supported schools, abolish slavery, promote temperance, and improve the lot of the disabled, insane, and imprisoned. Their efforts helped ameliorate some of the problems created by the frenetic pace of economic growth and territorial expansion. But the reformers made little headway against slavery. It would take a brutal civil war to dislodge America's "peculiar institution."

10 ℰ NATIONALISM AND SECTIONALISM

CHAPTER ORGANIZER

This chapter focuses on:

- the elements of the "Era of Good Feelings."

- how economic policies, diplomacy, and judicial decisions reflected the nationalism of these years.

- the various issues that promoted sectionalism.

- the fate of the Republican party after the collapse of the Federalists.

*A*mid the jubilation after the War of 1812 Americans began to transform their young nation. Hundreds of thousands of people began to stream westward at the same time that what had been a largely local economy was being transformed into a national market. The dispersion of plantation slavery and the cotton culture into the Old Southwest—Georgia, Alabama, Mississippi, Louisiana, and Texas—disrupted family ties and transformed social life. In the North and West, meanwhile, a dynamic urban middle class began to emerge and grow within towns and cities. Such dramatic changes prompted vigorous political debates over economic policies, transportation improvements, and the extension of slavery into the new territories. In the process the nation began to divide into three powerful regional blocs—North, South, and West—whose shifting alliances shaped the political landscape until the Civil War.

ECONOMIC NATIONALISM

Immediately after the War of 1812, Americans experienced a new surge of nationalism. The young United States was growing from a loose confederation of territories into a fully functioning nation-state that spanned almost an entire continent. An abnormal economic prosperity after the war fed a feeling of well-being and enhanced the prestige of the national government. Jefferson's embargo ironically had given impulse to the factories that he abhorred. The idea spread that the country needed a more balanced economy of farming, commerce, and manufacturing. After a generation of war, shortages of farm products in Europe forced up the prices of American products and stimulated agricultural expansion, indeed, a wild speculation in farmlands. Southern cotton, tobacco, and rice came to account for

The Union Manufactories of Maryland in Patapsco Falls, Baltimore County, c. 1815. *A textile mill begun during the embargo of 1807; by 1825 the Union Manufactories would employ over 600 people.*

about two-thirds of American exports. At the same time, the postwar market was flooded with cheap English goods that planters and farmers could buy. The new American manufacturers would seek protection from this foreign competition.

President Madison, in his first annual message to Congress after the war, recommended several steps toward strengthening the government: better fortifications, a permanent army and a strong navy, a new national bank, effective protection of new industries, a system of canals and roads for commercial and military use, and to top it off, a great national university. "The Republicans have out-Federalized Federalism," one New Englander remarked. Congress responded by authorizing a standing army of 10,000 and strengthening the navy as well.

THE BANK OF THE UNITED STATES The trinity of economic nationalism—proposals for a second national bank, protective tariff, and internal improvements—inspired the greatest controversies. After the first national bank expired in 1811, the country had fallen into a financial muddle. State-chartered banks mushroomed with little or no control, and their bank notes (paper money) flooded the channels of commerce with currency of uncertain value. Because hard money had been so short during the war, many state banks had suspended specie (gold or silver) payments in redemption of their notes, thereby depressing their value. The absence of a central bank had been a source of financial embarrassment to the government, which had neither a ready means of floating loans nor a way of transferring funds across the country.

Madison and most younger Republicans salved their constitutional scruples about a national bank with a dash of pragmatism. The issue, Madison said, had been decided "by repeated recognitions . . . of the validity of such an institution in acts of the legislative, executive, and judicial branches of the Government, accompanied by . . . a concurrence of the general will of the nation." In 1816 Congress adopted over the protest of Old Republicans provision for a new Bank of the United States (B.U.S.), which would be located in Philadelphia. Once again the charter ran for twenty years, and the federal government owned a fifth of the stock and named five of the twenty-five directors, with the Bank serving as the government depository for federal funds. Its bank notes were accepted in payments to the government. In return for its privileges the Bank had to take care of the government's funds without charge, lend the government $5 million on demand, and pay the government a cash bonus of $1.5 million.

The debate on the Bank, then and later, was colorful and bitter, and it helped to set the pattern of regional alignment for most other economic issues. Missouri senator Thomas Hart Benton predicted that the currency-short western towns would be at the mercy of a centralized eastern bank. "They may be devoured by it any moment! They are in the jaws of the monster! A lump of butter in the mouth of a dog! One gulp, one swallow, and all is gone!"

The debate over the B.U.S. was also noteworthy because of the leading roles played by the great triumvirate of John C. Calhoun of South Carolina, Henry Clay of Kentucky, and Daniel Webster of New Hampshire, later of Massachusetts. Calhoun, still in his youthful phase as a War Hawk nationalist, introduced the measure and pushed it through, justifying its constitutionality by citing the congressional power to regulate the currency. Clay, who had helped to kill Hamilton's bank in 1811, now confessed that he had failed to foresee the evils that resulted, and asserted that circumstances had made the Bank indispensable. Webster, on the other hand, led the opposition of the New England Federalists, who did not want the banking center moved from Boston to Philadelphia. Later, after he moved from New Hampshire to Massachusetts, Webster would return to Congress as the champion of a much stronger national power, while events would carry Calhoun in the other direction.

A PROTECTIVE TARIFF   The shift of capital from commerce to manufactures, begun during the embargo of 1807, had speeded up during the war. Peace in 1815 brought a sudden renewal of cheap British imports and generated pleas for the protection of infant American industries. The self-interest of the manufacturers, who as yet had little political impact, was reinforced by a patriotic desire for economic independence from Britain. New England shippers and southern farmers opposed tariffs, but both sections had sizable minorities who believed that the promotion of industry through tariffs enhanced both sectional and national welfare.

The Tariff of 1816, the first intended more for the protection of industry against foreign competition than for revenue, easily passed in Congress. The South and New England both split their votes, with

New England supporting the tariff and the South opposing it, and the Middle States and Old Northwest cast only five negative votes altogether. Nathaniel Macon of North Carolina opposed the tariff and defended the Old Republican doctrine of strict construction. The power to protect industry, Macon said, like the power to establish a bank, rested on the idea that there were implied powers embedded in the Constitution; Macon worried that such implied powers might one day be used to abolish slavery. The minority of southerners who voted for the tariff, led by Calhoun, did so because they hoped that the South might itself become a manufacturing center. South Carolina was then developing a few textile mills. According to the census of 1810, the southern states had approximately as many manufacturers as New England. Within a few years, however, New England moved well ahead of the South, and Calhoun went over to Macon's views against protection. The tariff then became a sectional issue, with manufacturers, wool processors, and food, sugar, and hemp growers favoring higher tariffs, while cotton planters and shipping interests favored lower duties.

INTERNAL IMPROVEMENTS   The third major issue of the time involved internal improvements: the building of roads and the development of water transportation. The war had highlighted the shortcomings of existing facilities. Troop movements through the western wilderness proved very difficult, and settlers found that unless they located near

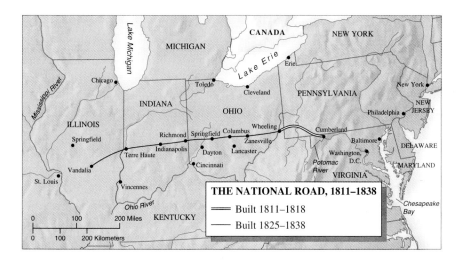

THE NATIONAL ROAD, 1811–1838

═══ Built 1811–1818

──── Built 1825–1838

navigable waters, they were cut off from trade and limited to a frontier subsistence.

The federal government had entered the field of internal improvements under Jefferson. He and both of his successors recommended an amendment to give the federal government undisputed power in the field. But lacking that, the constitutional grounds for federal action rested mainly on provision for national defense and expansion of the postal system. In 1803, when Ohio became a state, Congress decreed that 5 percent of the proceeds from land sales in the state would go to building a National Road from the Atlantic coast into Ohio and beyond as the territory developed. In 1806 Jefferson signed a measure for a survey, and construction of the National Road began in 1811.

Originally called the Cumberland Road, it was the first federally financed interstate road network. By 1818 it was open from Cumberland, Maryland, to Wheeling on the Ohio River. By 1838 the road extended all the way to Vandalia, Illinois. By reducing transportation costs and opening up new markets, the National Road and other privately financed turnpikes helped accelerate the commercialization of agriculture.

In 1817 John C. Calhoun put through the House a bill to place in a fund for internal improvements the $1.5 million bonus the Bank of the United States had paid for its charter, as well as all future dividends on the government's bank stock. Opposition centered in New England and the South, which expected to gain least, and support came largely from the West, which badly needed good roads. On his last day in office Madison vetoed the bill. While sympathetic to its purpose, he could not overcome his "insuperable difficulty . . . in reconciling the bill with the Constitution" and suggested instead a constitutional amendment. Internal improvements remained for another hundred years, with few exceptions, the responsibility of states and private enterprise. The federal government did not enter the field on a large scale until passage of the Federal Highways Act of 1916.

"Good Feelings"

JAMES MONROE As James Madison approached the end of a turbulent tenure, he, like Jefferson, turned to a fellow Virginian, another secretary of state, as his successor: James Monroe. In the Republican caucus Monroe won the nomination, then overwhelmed his Federalist opponent, Rufus King of New York, 183 to 34 in the electoral college. The "Virginia dynasty" continued. Like three of the four presidents before him, Monroe was a Virginia planter, but with a difference: he came from the small-planter group. At the outbreak of the Revolution he was just beginning college at William and Mary. He joined the army at the age of sixteen, fought with Washington at Trenton, and later studied law with Jefferson.

James Monroe, portrayed as he entered the presidency in 1816.

Monroe never displayed the depth of his Republican predecessors in scholarship or political theory, but what he lacked in intellect he made up for in dedication to public service. His soul, Jefferson said, if turned inside out, would be found spotless. Monroe served in the Virginia assembly, as governor of the state, in the Confederation Congress and United States Senate, and as minister to Paris, London, and Madrid. Under Madison, he had been secretary of state, and twice doubled as secretary of war. Tall, rawboned Monroe, with his powdered wig, cocked hat, and knee breeches, was the last of the Revolutionary generation to serve in the White House and the last president to dress in the old style.

Firmly grounded in Republican principles, Monroe failed to keep up with the onrush of the new nationalism. He accepted as accomplished fact the Bank and the protective tariff, but during his tenure there was no further extension of economic nationalism. Indeed, there was a minor setback. He permitted the National (or Cumberland) Road to be carried forward, but in his veto of the Cumberland Road Bill (1822) he denied the authority of Congress to collect tolls to pay for its repair and maintenance. Like Jefferson and Madison, he also urged a constitutional amendment to remove all doubt about federal authority in the field of internal improvements.

Whatever his limitations, Monroe surrounded himself with some of the ablest young Republican leaders. John Quincy Adams became secretary of state. William Crawford of Georgia continued as secretary of the treasury. John C. Calhoun headed the War Department after Henry Clay refused the job in order to stay on as Speaker of the House. The new administration found the country in a state of well-being: America was at peace and the economy was flourishing. Soon after his 1817 inauguration, Monroe embarked on a goodwill tour of New England. In Boston, lately a hotbed of wartime dissent, a Federalist paper commented on the president's visit under the heading "Era of Good Feelings." The label became a popular catchphrase for Monroe's administration, and one that historians seized upon later. Like many a maxim, it conveys just enough truth to be sadly misleading. A resurgence of factionalism and sectionalism erupted just as the postwar prosperity collapsed in the Panic of 1819. The "Era of Good Feelings" was very brief.

For two years, however, general harmony reigned, and even when the country's troubles returned, little of the blame fell on Monroe. In 1820 he was reelected without opposition. The Federalists were too weak to put up a candidate. Monroe won all the electoral votes except for three abstentions and one vote from New Hampshire for John Quincy Adams. The Republican party was dominant—for the moment. In fact, it was about to follow the Federalists into oblivion. Amid the general political contentment of the era, the first party system was fading away, but rivals for the succession soon commenced the process of forming new parties.

IMPROVING RELATIONS WITH BRITAIN   Adding to the prevailing contentment after the war was a growing rapprochement with the recent enemy. American shippers resumed trade with Britain (and India). The Treaty of Ghent had left unsettled a number of minor disputes, but subsequently two important compacts—the Rush-Bagot Agreement of 1817 and the Convention of 1818—removed several potential causes of irritation. In the first, resulting from an exchange of notes between Acting Secretary of State Richard Rush and British minister Charles Bagot, the threat of naval competition on the Great Lakes vanished with an arrangement to limit forces there to several federal ships collecting customs duties. Although the exchange made no reference to the land boundary between the United States and

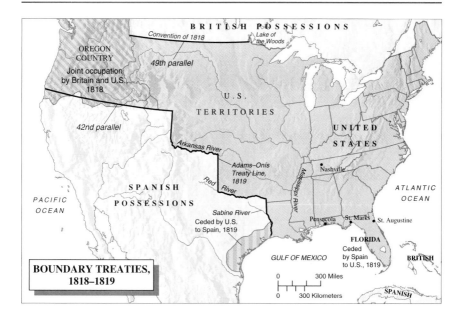

BOUNDARY TREATIES, 1818–1819

Canada, its spirit gave rise to the tradition of an unfortified border, the longest in the world.

The Convention of 1818 covered three major points. The northern limit of the Louisiana Purchase was settled by extending the national boundary along the 49th parallel west from Lake of the Woods in Minnesota to the crest of the Rocky Mountains. West of that point the Oregon Country would be open to joint occupation by the British and Americans, but the boundary remained unsettled. The right of Americans to fish off Newfoundland and Labrador, granted in 1783, was acknowledged once again.

The chief remaining problem was Britain's exclusion of American ships from the West Indies in order to reserve that lucrative trade for British ships. This remained a chronic irritant, and the United States retaliated with several measures. Under a Navigation Act of 1817, importation of West Indian produce was restricted to American vessels or vessels belonging to West Indian merchants. In 1818 American ports were closed to all British vessels arriving from a colony that was legally closed to vessels of the United States. In 1820 Monroe approved an act of Congress that specified total non-intercourse—with British vessels, with all British colonies in the Americas, and even in goods taken to England and reexported. The rapprochement with Britain therefore fell short of perfection.

EXTENSION OF BOUNDARIES   The year 1819 was one of the more fateful years in American history. Controversial efforts to expand American territory, a sharp financial panic, a tense debate over the extension of slavery, and several landmark Supreme Court cases combined to bring an unsettling end to the "Era of Good Feelings." The new nationalism reached a climax with the acquisition of Florida and the extension of America's southwestern boundary to the Pacific, but nationalism quickly began to run afoul of domestic crosscurrents that would submerge the country in sectional squabbles.

In the calculations of global power, it was perhaps long since reckoned that Florida would someday pass to the United States. Spanish sovereignty was more a technicality than an actuality, and extended little beyond St. Augustine on the east coast and Pensacola and St. Marks on the Gulf. The province had been a thorn in the side of the United States during the recent war as a center of British intrigue, a haven for Creek refugees, who were beginning to take the name Seminole ("runaway" or "separatist"), and a harbor for runaway slaves and criminals. Florida also stood athwart the outlets of several important rivers flowing to the Gulf.

Spain, once dominant in the Americas, was now a declining power unable to enforce its obligations under the Pinckney Treaty of 1795 to pacify the frontiers. In 1816 American forces clashed with a group of escaped slaves who had taken over a British fort on the Appalachicola River. Seminoles were soon fighting white settlers in the area, and in 1817 Americans burned a Seminole border settlement, killed five of its inhabitants, and dispersed the rest across the border into Florida.

Portrait of an escaped slave who lived with the Seminoles in Florida.

At this point Secretary of War Calhoun authorized a campaign against the Seminoles, and he summoned General Andrew Jackson from Nashville to take command. Jackson's orders allowed him to pursue the offenders into Spanish territory, but not to attack any Spanish post. A frustrated Jackson pledged to President Monroe that if the United States wanted Florida, he could wind up the whole controversy in sixty days.

When it came to Spaniards or Indians, few white Tennesseans—and certainly not Andrew Jackson—were likely to bother with technicalities. Jackson pushed eastward through Florida, reinforced by Tennessee volunteers and a party of friendly Creeks, taking a Spanish post and skirmishing with the Seminoles, destroying their settlements. Jackson hanged two

Andrew Jackson, victor at the Battle of New Orleans, Indian fighter, and future president.

of their leaders. He then turned west and seized Pensacola and returned home to Nashville. The whole episode had taken about four months; the Florida panhandle was in American hands by 1818.

The news of Jackson's exploits aroused anger in Madrid and concern in Washington. Spain demanded the return of its territory, and the punishment of Jackson, but Spain's impotence was plain for all to see. Monroe's cabinet was at first prepared to disavow Jackson's action, especially his direct attack on Spanish posts. Calhoun, as secretary of war, was inclined, at least officially, to discipline Jackson for disregard of orders—a stand that caused bad blood between the two men later—but privately confessed a certain pleasure at the outcome. In any case a man as popular as Jackson was almost invulnerable. And he had one important friend, Secretary of State John Quincy Adams, who realized that Jackson had strengthened his hand in negotiations already under way with the Spanish minister. American forces withdrew from Florida, but negotiations resumed with the knowledge that the United States could retake Florida at any time.

With the fate of Florida a foregone conclusion, Adams now turned his eye on a larger purpose, a definition of the western boundary of the Louisiana Purchase and—his boldest stroke—extension of a boundary to the Pacific coast. In lengthy negotiations, Adams gradually gave ground on claims to Texas, but stuck to his demand for a transcontinental line. Agreement finally came early in 1819. Spain ceded all of Florida in return for American assumption of private American claims against Spain up to $5 million. The western boundary of the Louisiana Purchase would run along the Sabine River and then in stair-step fashion up to the Red River, along the Red, and up to the Arkansas River. From the source of the Arkansas it would go north to the 42nd parallel and thence west to the Pacific coast. A dispute over land claims held up ratification for another two years, but those claims were revoked and final ratifications were exchanged in 1821. Florida became an American territory, and its first governor was briefly Andrew Jackson. In 1845 Florida achieved statehood.

CRISES AND COMPROMISES

THE PANIC OF 1819   Adams's Transcontinental Treaty was a triumph of foreign policy and the climactic event of the postwar nationalism. Even before it was signed in 1819, however, two thunderclaps signaled the end of the brief "Era of Good Feelings" and gave warning of stormy weather ahead: the financial Panic of 1819 and the controversy over statehood for Missouri. The occasion for the panic was the sudden collapse of cotton prices in the English market. At one point in 1818 cotton had soared to 32½¢ per pound. The pressure of high prices forced British textile mills to turn away from American sources to cheaper East Indian cotton, and by 1819 cotton averaged only 14.3¢ per pound at New Orleans. The price collapse set off a decline in the demand for other American goods and suddenly revealed the fragility of the prosperity that had begun after the War of 1812.

Since 1815 a speculative bubble had grown, with expectations that economic expansion would go on forever. But American industry struggled to find markets for its goods. Even the Tariff of 1816 had not been enough to eliminate British competition. What was more, businessmen, farmers, and land speculators had inflated the bubble with a volatile expansion of credit. The sources of this credit were both government and banks. Under the Land Act of 1800 the government extended four years' credit to those who bought western lands. After 1804 one could buy as little as 160 acres at a minimum price of $1.64 per acre (although in auctions the best lands went for more). In many cases speculators took up large tracts, paying only one-fourth down, and then sold them to settlers with the understanding that the settlers would pay the remaining installments. With the collapse of crop prices, and then of land values, both speculators and settlers saw their incomes plummet.

The reckless practices of state banks compounded the inflation of credit. To enlarge their loans they issued more bank notes than they could redeem. Even the Second Bank of the United States, which was supposed to introduce some order to the financial arena, got caught up in the mania. Its first president yielded to the contagion of get-rich-quick fever that was sweeping the country. The proliferation of branches, combined with little supervision from Philadelphia, carried the Bank into the same reckless extension of loans that state banks had pursued. In 1819, just as alert businessmen began to take alarm, a case of extensive fraud and embezzlement in the Baltimore branch of the B.U.S. came to light. The disclosure prompted the appointment of Langdon Cheves, former congressman from South Carolina, as the Bank's president and the establishment of a sounder policy.

Cheves reduced salaries and other costs, postponed dividends, restrained the extension of credit, and presented for redemption the state bank notes that came in, thereby forcing the state-chartered banks to keep specie reserves. Cheves rescued the Bank from near-ruin, but only by putting heavy pressure on state banks. State banks in turn put pressure on their debtors, who found it harder to renew old loans or get new ones. In 1823, his job completed, Cheves relinquished his position to Nicholas Biddle of Philadelphia. The Cheves policies were the result rather than the cause of the Panic, but they pinched debtors, who found it all the more difficult to meet their obligations. Hard times lasted about three years, and the Bank took much of the blame in the popular mind. The Panic passed, but resentment of the Bank lingered in the South and the West.

THE MISSOURI COMPROMISE   Just as the Panic spread over the country, another cloud appeared on the horizon, the onset of a fierce sectional controversy over slavery. By 1819 the country had an equal number of slave and free states, eleven of each. The line between them was defined by the southern and western boundaries of Pennsylvania and the Ohio River. Although slavery still lingered in some places north of the line, it was on the way to extinction there. Beyond the Mississippi River, however, no move had been made to extend the dividing line across the Louisiana

Henry Clay.

Purchase territory, where slavery had existed from the days when France and Spain had colonized the area. At the time the Missouri Territory embraced all of the Louisiana Purchase except the state of Louisiana (1812) and the Arkansas Territory (1819). In the westward rush of population, the old French town of St. Louis became the funnel through which settlers pushed on beyond the Mississippi. These were largely settlers from the South who brought their slaves with them.

In 1819 the House of Representatives was asked to approve legislation enabling Missouri to draft a state constitution, its population having passed the minimum of 60,000. At that point Representative James Tallmadge, Jr., a New York congressman, introduced a resolution prohibiting the further introduction of slaves into Missouri, which already had some 10,000 slaves, and providing freedom at age twenty-five for those born after the territory's admission as a state. After brief but fiery exchanges, the House passed the amendment on an almost strictly sectional vote. The Senate rejected it by a similar tally, but with several northerners joining in the opposition. With population at the time growing faster in the North, a balance between the two sections could be held only in the Senate. In the House, slave states had 81 votes while free states had 105; a balance was unlikely ever to be restored in the House.

Maine's application for statehood made it easier to arrive at an agreement. Since colonial times Maine had been the northern province of Massachusetts. The Senate linked its request for separate statehood with Missouri's and voted to admit Maine as a free state and Missouri as a slave state, thus maintaining the balance between free and slave states in the Senate. An Illinois senator further extended the compromise by an amendment to exclude slavery from the rest of the Louisiana Purchase north of 36°30', Missouri's southern border. Slavery thus would continue in the Arkansas Territory and in the state of Missouri,

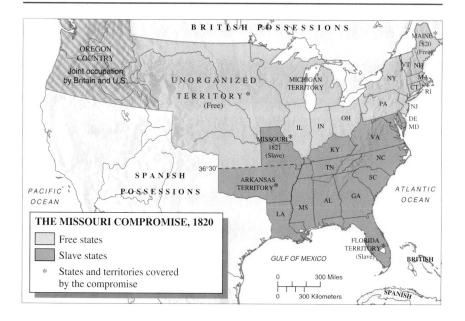

THE MISSOURI COMPROMISE, 1820

☐ Free states

■ Slave states

* States and territories covered by the compromise

and be excluded from the remainder of the area. But that was country that Zebulon Pike's reports had persuaded the public was the Great American Desert, unlikely ever to be settled. For this reason the arrangement seemed to be a victory for the slave states. By a very close vote it passed the House on March 2, 1820.

Then another problem arose. The proslavery elements that dominated Missouri's constitutional convention inserted in the proposed new state constitution a proviso excluding free blacks and mulattoes from the state. This clearly violated the requirement of Article IV, Section 2, of the Constitution: "The Citizens of each State shall be entitled to all Privileges and Immunities of Citizens in the Several States." Free blacks were citizens of many states, including the slave states of North Carolina and Tennessee where, until the mid-1830s, they also voted.

The renewed controversy threatened final approval of Missouri's admission until Henry Clay formulated a "Second Missouri Compromise." Admission of Missouri as a state depended on assurance from the Missouri legislature that it would never construe the offending clause in such a way as to sanction denial of privileges that citizens held under the Constitution. It was one of the more artless dodges in American history, for it required the legislature to affirm that the state constitution did not mean what it clearly said, but the compromise worked. The Missouri legislature duly adopted the pledge, while denying that the legislature had any power to bind the people of the state. On August 10, 1821, President Monroe proclaimed the admission of Missouri as the twenty-fourth state. For the moment, the controversy subsided. "But this momentous question," the aging Thomas Jefferson wrote to a friend after the first compromise, "like a firebell in the night awakened and filled me with terror. I considered it at once as the knell of the Union."

JUDICIAL NATIONALISM

JOHN MARSHALL, CHIEF JUSTICE   Meanwhile nationalism still flourished in the Supreme Court, where Chief Justice John Marshall preserved Hamiltonian Federalism for yet another generation. Marshall, a survivor of the Revolution and a distant cousin of Thomas Jefferson, established the power of the Supreme Court by his force of mind and crystalline logic.

During Marshall's early years on the Court (altogether he served thirty-four years), he affirmed the principle of judicial review. In *Marbury* v. *Madison* (1803) and *Fletcher* v. *Peck* (1810), the Court first struck down a federal law and then a state law as unconstitutional. In the cases of *Martin* v. *Hunter's Lessee* (1816) and *Cohens* v. *Virginia* (1821), the Court assumed the right to take appeals from state courts on the grounds that the Constitution, laws, and treaties of the United States could be kept uniformly the supreme law of the land only if the Court could review decisions of state courts. In the first case, the Court overruled Virginia's confiscation of Loyalist property, because this

Chief Justice John Marshall, pillar of judicial nationalism.

violated treaties with Great Britain; in the second, it upheld Virginia's right to forbid the sale of lottery tickets.

PROTECTING CONTRACT RIGHTS   In the fateful year 1819, Marshall and the Court made two more decisions of major importance in checking the states and building the power of the central government: *Dartmouth College v. Woodward* and *McCulloch v. Maryland*. The Dartmouth College case involved an attempt by the New Hampshire legislature to alter a provision in Dartmouth's charter, under which the college's trustees became a self-perpetuating board. In 1816 the state's Republican legislature, offended by this relic of monarchy and even more by the Federalist majority on the board, placed Dartmouth under a new board named by the governor. The original trustees sued, lost in the state courts, but with Daniel Webster as counsel won on appeal to the Supreme Court. The charter, Marshall said for the Court, was a valid contract that the legislature had impaired, an act forbidden by the Constitution. This implied a new and enlarged definition of *contract* that seemed to put private corporations beyond the reach of the states that chartered them. But thereafter states commonly wrote into charters and general laws of incorporation provisions making them subject to modification. Such provisions were then part of the "contract."

STRENGTHENING THE FEDERAL GOVERNMENT   Marshall's single most important interpretation of the constitutional system appeared in the case of *McCulloch v. Maryland*. McCulloch, a clerk in the Baltimore branch of the Bank of the United States, failed to affix state revenue stamps to bank notes as required by a Maryland law taxing the notes. Indicted by the state, McCulloch, acting for the Bank, appealed to the Supreme Court, which handed down a unanimous judgment upholding the power of Congress to charter the Bank and denying any right of the state to tax the Bank. In a lengthy opinion Marshall rejected Maryland's argument that the federal government was the creature of sovereign states. Instead, he argued, it arose directly from the people acting through the conventions that ratified the Constitution. While sovereignty was divided between the states and the national government, the latter, "though limited in its powers, is supreme within its sphere of action."

Marshall then went on to endorse the doctrine of the federal government having implied constitutional powers. The "necessary and proper" clause, he argued, did not mean "absolutely indispensable." The test of constitutionality was in his view a practical one: "Let the end be legitimate, let it be within the scope of the Constitution, and all means which are appropriate, which are plainly adapted to that end, which are not prohibited, but consistent with the letter and spirit of the Constitution, are constitutional."

Maryland's effort to tax the national bank conflicted with the supreme law of the land. One great principle that "entirely pervades the Constitution," Marshall wrote, was "that the Constitution and the laws made in pursuance thereof are supreme: that they control the Constitution and laws of the respective states, and cannot be controlled by them." The effort by a state to tax a federal bank therefore was unconstitutional, for the "power to tax involves the power to destroy"—which was precisely what the legislatures of Maryland and several other states had in mind with respect to the Bank.

REGULATING INTERSTATE COMMERCE   Marshall's last great decision, *Gibbons* v. *Ogden* (1824), established national supremacy in regulating interstate commerce. In 1808 Robert Fulton and Robert Livingston, who pioneered commercial use of the steamboat, won from the New York legislature the exclusive right to operate steamboats on the state's waters. From them in turn Aaron Ogden received exclusive right to navigation across the Hudson River between New York and New Jersey. Thomas Gibbons, however, operated a coastal trade under a federal license and came into competition with Ogden. On behalf of a unanimous Court, Marshall ruled that the monopoly granted by the state conflicted with the federal Coasting Act under which Gibbons operated. Congressional power to regulate commerce, the Court said, "like all others vested in Congress, is complete in itself, may be exercised to its utmost extent, and acknowledges no limitations other than are prescribed in the Constitution."

The opinion stopped just short of stating an exclusive federal power over commerce, and later cases would clarify the point that states had a concurrent jurisdiction so long as it did not come into conflict with federal action. For many years there was in fact little federal regulation of commerce, so that in striking down the monopoly created by the state Marshall had opened the way to extensive development of steamboat

Deck Life on the *Paragon*, 1811–1812. *The* Paragon, *"a whole floating town," was the third steamboat operated on the Hudson by Robert Fulton and Robert R. Livingston.*

navigation and, soon afterward, steam railroads. Economic expansion often depended on judicial nationalism.

NATIONALIST DIPLOMACY

THE NORTHWEST   In foreign affairs, too, nationalism continued to be an effective force. Within two years after final approval of John Quincy Adams's Transcontinental Treaty, the secretary of state was able to draw another important transcontinental line. In 1819 Spain had abandoned its claim to the Oregon Country above the 42nd parallel. Russia, however, had claims along the Pacific coast as well. In 1741 Vitus Bering, in the employ of Russia, had explored the strait that now bears his name, and in 1799 the Russian-American Company had been formed to exploit the resources of Alaska. In 1821 the Russian czar claimed the Pacific coast as far south as 51°, which in the American view lay within the Oregon Country.

In 1823 Secretary of State John Quincy Adams contested "the right of Russia to any territorial establishment on this continent." The American government, he informed the Russian minister, assumed the principle "that the American continents are no longer subjects for any new European colonial establishments." His protest resulted in a treaty signed in 1824 whereby Russia, which had more pressing concerns in Europe, accepted the line of 54°40′ as the southern boundary of its claim. In 1825 a similar agreement between Russia and Britain gave the Oregon Country clearly defined boundaries, although it was still subject to joint occupation by the United States and Great Britain under their agreement of 1818. In 1827 both countries agreed to extend indefinitely the provision for joint occupation, subject to termination by either power.

THE MONROE DOCTRINE   Adams's disapproval of further colonization also had clear implications for Latin America. One consequence of the Napoleonic Wars and French occupation of Spain and Portugal had been a series of wars of liberation in Latin America. Within little more than a decade after the flag of rebellion was first raised in 1811, Spain had lost almost its entire empire in the Americas. All that was left were the islands of Cuba, Puerto Rico, and Santo Domingo. The only other European possessions in the Americas, 330 years after Columbus, were Russian Alaska, British Canada, British Honduras, and Dutch, French, and British Guiana.

In 1823 rumors began to circulate that France wanted to restore the Spanish king's power over Spain's American empire. Monroe and Secretary of War Calhoun were alarmed at the possibility, although John Quincy Adams took the more realistic view that such action was unlikely. British foreign minister George Canning told the American minister to London that the two countries should jointly oppose any incursions by France or Spain in the Western Hemisphere.

Monroe at first agreed, with the support of his sage advisers Jefferson and Madison. Adams, however, urged upon Monroe and the cabinet the independent course of proclaiming a unilateral policy against the restoration of Spain's colonies. "It would be more candid," Adams said, "as well as more dignified, to avow our principles explicitly to Russia and France, than to come in as a cockboat in the wake of the British man-of-war." Adams knew that the British navy would stop any action by the Quadruple Alliance in Latin America, and he suspected that the

Alliance had no real intention to intervene anyway. The British, moreover, wanted the United States to agree not to acquire any more Spanish territory, including Cuba, Texas, or California, but Adams preferred to avoid such a commitment.

Monroe incorporated the substance of Adams's views in his annual message to Congress in 1823. The Monroe Doctrine, as it was later called, comprised four major points: (1) that "the American continents . . . are henceforth not to be considered as subjects for future colonization by any European powers"; (2) the political system of European powers was different from that of the United States, which would "consider any attempt on their part to extend their system to any portion of this hemisphere as dangerous to our peace and safety"; (3) the United States would not interfere with existing European colonies; and (4) the United States would keep out of the internal affairs of European nations and their wars.

At the time the statement drew little attention either in the United States or abroad. The Monroe Doctrine, not even so called until 1852, became one of the cherished principles of American foreign policy, but for the time being it slipped into obscurity for want of any occasion to invoke it. In spite of Adams's affirmation, the United States came in as a cockboat in the wake of the British man-of-war after all, for the effectiveness of the doctrine depended on British naval supremacy. The doctrine had no standing in international law. It was merely a statement of intent by an American president to the Congress, and did not even draw enough interest at the time for European powers to renounce it.

ONE-PARTY POLITICS

Almost from the start of Monroe's second term the jockeying for the presidential succession had begun. Three members of Monroe's cabinet were active candidates: Secretary of War John Calhoun, Secretary of the Treasury William Crawford, and Secretary of State John Quincy Adams. Henry Clay, longtime Speaker of the House, also hungered after the office. And on the fringes of the Washington scene a new force appeared in the person of Andrew Jackson, the scourge of the British, Spaniards, Creeks, and Seminoles, the epitome of what every frontiersman admired, who was elected a senator from Tennessee in

1823. All were Republicans, for again no Federalist stood a chance, but they were competing in a new political world, complicated by the cross-currents of nationalism and sectionalism. With only one party there was in effect no party, for there existed no generally accepted method for choosing a "regular" candidate.

PRESIDENTIAL NOMINATIONS Selection of presidential candidates by congressional caucus, already under attack in 1816, had disappeared in the wave of unanimity that reelected Monroe in 1820 without the formality of a nomination. The friends of Crawford sought in vain to breathe life back into "King Caucus," but only a minority of congressmen appeared in answer to the call. They duly named Crawford for president, but the endorsement was so weak as to be more a handicap than an advantage. Crawford was in fact the logical successor to the Virginia dynasty, a native of the state though a resident of Georgia. He had flirted with nationalism, but swung back to states' rights and strict construction, and assumed leadership of a faction, called the Radicals, that included Old Republicans and those who distrusted the nationalism of Adams and Calhoun. Crawford's candidacy floundered from the beginning, for the candidate had been stricken in 1823 by some unknown disease that left him half-paralyzed and half-blind. His friends protested that he would soon be well, but he never did fully recover.

Long before the Crawford caucus met in early 1824, indeed for two years before, the country had broken out in a rash of presidential endorsements by state legislatures and public meetings. In 1822 the Tennessee legislature named Andrew Jackson. In 1824 a mass meeting of Pennsylvanians added their endorsement. Jackson, who had previously kept silent, responded that while the presidency should not be sought, it should not be declined. The same meeting named Calhoun for vice-president, and Calhoun accepted. The youngest of the candidates, he was content to take second place and bide his time. Meanwhile, the Kentucky legislature had named its favorite son, Henry Clay, in 1822. The Massachusetts legislature named John Quincy Adams in 1824.

Of the four candidates, only two had clearly defined programs, and the outcome was an early lesson in the danger of being committed on the issues too soon. Crawford's friends emphasized his devotion to states' rights and strict construction. Clay, on the other hand, took his stand for the "American System": he favored the national bank, the protective

The presidential "race" of 1824, with Adams, Crawford, and Jackson striding to the finish line on the left and Clay lagging behind on the far right.

tariff, and a national program of internal improvements to bind the country together and build its economy. Adams was close to Clay, openly dedicated to internal improvements but less strongly committed to the tariff. Jackson, where issues were concerned, carefully avoided commitment so as to capitalize on his popularity as the hero of the Battle of New Orleans.

THE "CORRUPT BARGAIN" The 1824 election turned on personalities and sectional allegiance more than on issues. Adams, the only northern candidate, carried New England, the former bastion of Federalism, and most of New York's electoral votes. Clay took Kentucky, Ohio, and Missouri. Crawford carried Virginia, Georgia, and Delaware. Jackson swept the Southeast, plus Illinois and Indiana, and, with Calhoun's support, the Carolinas, Pennsylvania, Maryland, and New Jersey. All candidates got scattered votes elsewhere. In New York, where Clay was strong, his supporters were outmaneuvered by the Adams forces in the legislature, which still chose the presidential electors.

The result was inconclusive in both the electoral vote and the popular vote, wherever the state legislature permitted the choice of electors by the people. In the electoral college Jackson had 99 votes, Adams 84, Crawford 41, Clay 37. In the popular vote the trend ran about the same: Jackson

154,000, Adams 109,000, Crawford 47,000, and Clay 47,000. Whatever might have been said about the outcome, one thing seemed apparent. It was a defeat for Clay's American System: New England and New York opposed him on internal improvements, the South and Southwest on the protective tariff. Sectionalism had defeated the national program.

Yet the advocate of the American System now assumed the role of president-maker, as the election was thrown into the House of Representatives, where Speaker Clay's influence was decisive. Clay had little trouble in choosing, since he regarded Jackson as unfit for the office. "I cannot believe," he muttered, "that killing 2,500 Englishmen at New Orleans qualifies for the various, difficult and complicated duties of the Chief Magistracy." He eventually threw his support to Adams. The final vote in the House, which was by state, carried Adams to victory with thirteen votes to Jackson's seven and Crawford's four.

It was a costly victory, for the result united Adams's foes and crippled his administration before it got under way. There is no evidence that Adams entered into any bargain with Clay to win his support. Still the charge was widely believed after Adams made Clay his secretary of state, and thus put him in the office from which three successive presidents had risen. Adams's Puritan conscience could never quite overcome a sense of guilt at the maneuverings that were necessary to gain his election, but a "corrupt bargain" was too much out of character for credence. Yet credence it had with a large number of people, and on that cry a campaign to elect Jackson next time was launched almost immediately after the 1824 decision. The Crawford people, including Martin Van Buren, the "Little Magician" of New York politics, soon moved into the Jackson camp. So too did the new vice-president, John Calhoun of South Carolina, who ran on both the Adams and the Jackson tickets but favored the general from Tennessee.

JOHN Q. ADAMS'S PRESIDENCY   John Quincy Adams was one of the ablest men, hardest workers, and finest intellects ever to enter the White House. Yet he lacked the common touch and the politician's gift for maneuver. A stubborn man who saw two brothers and two sons die from alcoholism, he suffered from chronic bouts of depression that provoked in him a grim self-righteousness and self-pity, self-doubts, and self-loathing, qualities that did not endear him to fellow politicians.

His idealism also irritated the party faithful. He refused to play the game of patronage, arguing that it would be dishonorable to dismiss "able and faithful political opponents to provide for my own partisans." In four years he removed only twelve officeholders. His first annual message to Congress included a grandiose blueprint for national development, set forth in such a blunt way that it became a disaster of political ineptitude.

In the boldness and magnitude of its conception, the Adams plan outdid those of both Hamilton and Clay. The central government, the president proposed, should promote internal improvements, set up a national university, finance

John Quincy Adams, a brilliant man but ineffective leader.

scientific explorations, build astronomical observatories, and create a new Department of the Interior. To refrain from using broad federal powers, Adams insisted, "would be treachery to the most sacred of trusts."

Whatever grandeur of conception the message to Congress had, it was obscured by an unhappy choice of language. For the son of John Adams to cite the example "of the nations of Europe and of their rulers" was downright suicidal. At one fell swoop he had revived all the Republican suspicions of the Adamses and served to define a new party system. The minority who cast their lot with Adams and Clay were turning into National-Republicans; the opposition, the growing party of Jacksonians, were the Democratic-Republicans, who would eventually drop the name Republican and become Democrats.

Adams's headstrong plunge into nationalism and his refusal to play the game of politics condemned his administration to utter frustration. Congress ignored his domestic proposals, and in foreign affairs the triumphs that he had scored as secretary of state had no sequels. The climactic effort to discredit Adams came on the tariff issue. The

Panic of 1819 had provoked calls for a higher tariff in 1820, but the effort failed by one vote in the Senate. In 1824 the advocates of protection renewed the effort, with greater success. The Tariff of 1824 favored the Middle Atlantic and New England manufacturers with higher duties on woolens, cotton, iron, and other finished goods. Clay's Kentucky won a tariff on hemp, and a tariff on raw wool brought the wool-growing interests to the support of the measure. Additional revenues were provided by duties on sugar, molasses, coffee, and salt. The tariff on raw wool was in obvious conflict with that on manufactured woolens, but the two groups got together and reached an agreement.

At this point Jackson's supporters saw a chance to advance their candidate through an awkward scheme hatched by John Calhoun. The plan was to present a bill with such outrageously high tariffs on raw materials that the manufacturers of the East would join the commercial interests there, and, with the votes of the agricultural South and Southwest, defeat the measure. In the process Jackson men in the Northeast could take credit for supporting the tariff, and Jackson men, wherever it fitted their interests, could take credit for opposing it— while Jackson himself remained in the background. Virginia's John Randolph saw through the ruse. The bill, he asserted, "referred to manufactures of no sort or kind, but the manufacture of a President of the United States."

The complicated scheme helped elect Jackson, but in the process Calhoun became a victim of his own scheming. The high tariffs ended up becoming law. Calhoun calculated neither upon the defection of Van Buren, who supported a crucial amendment to satisfy the woolens manufacturers, nor upon the growing strength of manufacturing interests in New England. Daniel Webster, now a senator from Massachusetts, explained that he was ready to deny all he had said against the tariff because New England had built up her manufactures on the understanding that the protective tariff was a settled policy.

When the tariff bill passed on May 11, 1828, it was Calhoun's turn to explain his newfound opposition to the gospel of protection, and nothing so well illustrates the flexibility of constitutional principles as the switch in positions by Webster and Calhoun. Back in South Carolina, Calhoun prepared the *South Carolina Exposition and Protest* (1828), which was issued anonymously along with a series of resolutions by the

Jackson is to be President, and you will be HANGED. *This anti-Jackson cartoon, published during the 1828 campaign, shows him as a frontier ruffian.*

South Carolina legislature. In that document Calhoun declared that a state could nullify an act of Congress that it found unconstitutional.

JACKSON SWEEPS IN   Thus far the stage was set for the election of 1828, which might more truly be called a revolution than that of 1800. But if the issues of the day had anything to do with the election, they were hardly visible in the campaign, in which politicians on both sides reached depths of scurrilousness that had not been plumbed since 1800. Jackson was denounced as a hot-tempered and ignorant barbarian, co-conspirator with Aaron Burr, a participant in repeated duels and frontier brawls, a man whose fame rested on his reputation as a killer. In addition, his enemies dredged up the old story that Jackson had lived in adultery with his wife Rachel before they had been legally married; in fact they had lived together for two years in the mistaken belief that her divorce from a former husband was final. As soon as the official divorce had come through, Jackson and Rachel had been remarried.

The Jacksonians, however, got in their licks against Adams, condemning him as a man who had lived his adult life on the public treasury, who had been corrupted by foreigners in the courts of Europe, and who had al-legedly delivered up an American girl to serve the lust of Czar Alexander I while serving as minister to Russia. They called him a gambler and a spend-thrift for having bought a billiard table and a chess set for the White House, and a puritanical hypocrite for despising the common people and warning

Congress to ignore the will of its constituents. He had finally reached the presidency, the Jacksonians claimed, by a corrupt bargain with Henry Clay.

In the campaign of 1828 Jackson held most of the advantages. As a military victor he projected patriotism. As a son of the West and a fabled Indian fighter he was a hero in the frontier states. As a farmer, lawyer, and slaveholder, he had the trust of southern planters. Debtors and local bankers who hated the national bank turned to Jackson. In addition, his vagueness on the issues protected him from attack by various interest groups. Not least of all, Jackson benefited from a spirit of democracy in which the common folk were no longer satisfied to look to their betters for leadership, as they had done in the eighteenth century. It had become politically fatal to be labeled an aristocrat. Jackson's coalition now included even a seasoning of young Federalists eager to shed the stigma of aristocracy and get on in the world.

Since the Revolution and especially since 1800, white male suffrage had been gaining ground. The traditional story has been that a surge of Jacksonian Democracy came out of the West like a great wave, supported mainly by small farmers, leading the way for the East. But there were other forces working in the older states toward a wider franchise: the Revolutionary doctrine of equality, and the feeling on the parts of the workers, artisans, and small merchants of the towns, as well as small farmers and landed gentry, that a democratic ballot provided a means to combat the rising commercial and manufacturing interests. From the beginning Pennsylvania had opened the ballot box to all adult males who paid taxes; by 1790 Georgia and New Hampshire had similar arrangements. Vermont, in 1791, became the first state with universal manhood suffrage, having first adopted it in 1777. Kentucky, admitted in 1792, became the second. Tennessee (1796) had only a light taxpaying qualification. New Jersey in 1807, and

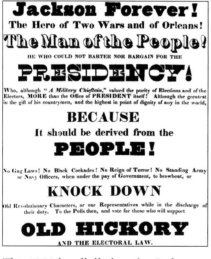

This 1828 handbill identifies Jackson, "The Man of the People," with the democratic impulse of the time.

Maryland and South Carolina in 1810, abolished property and taxpaying requirements, and the new states of the West after 1815 came in with either white manhood suffrage or a low taxpaying requirement. Connecticut (1818), Massachusetts (1821), and New York (1821) all abolished their property requirements.

Along with the broadening of the suffrage went a liberalization of other features of government. Representation was reapportioned more nearly in line with population. An increasing number of officials, even judges, were named by popular vote. Final disestablishment of the Congregational church in New England came in Vermont (1807), New Hampshire (1817), Connecticut (1818), Maine (1820), and Massachusetts (1834). In 1824 six state legislatures still chose the presidential electors. By 1828 the popular vote prevailed in all but South Carolina and Delaware, and by 1832 in all but South Carolina.

The spread of the suffrage brought a new type of politician to the fore: the man who had special appeal to the masses or knew how to organize the people for political purposes, and who became a vocal advocate of the people's right to rule. Jackson fitted the ideal of this new political world, a

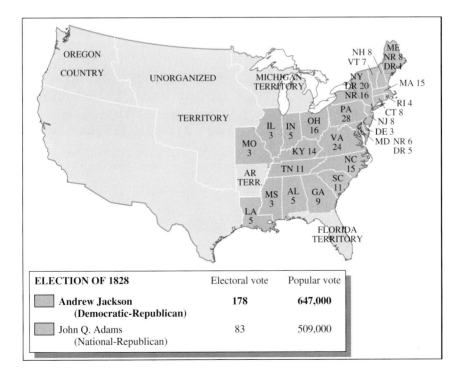

ELECTION OF 1828	Electoral vote	Popular vote
Andrew Jackson (Democratic-Republican)	178	647,000
John Q. Adams (National-Republican)	83	509,000

leader sprung from the people rather than an aristocratic leader, a frontiersman of humble origin who had scrambled up the political ladder by will and tenacity. "Adams can write," went one of the campaign slogans, "Jackson can fight." He could write too, but he once said that he had no respect for a man who could think of only one way to spell a word.

When the 1828 returns came in, Jackson won by a comfortable margin. The electoral vote was 178 to 83, and the popular vote was about 647,000 to 509,000 (the figures vary). Adams won all of New England, (except for one of Maine's nine electoral votes), sixteen of the thirty-six from New York, and six of the eleven from Maryland. All the rest belonged to Jackson.

MAKING CONNECTIONS

- Thomas Jefferson referred to the Missouri Compromise as "a firebell in the night." He was right. The controversy over the expansion of slavery, introduced here, will reappear in Chapter 14, in the discussion of Texas and the Mexican War.

- John Quincy Adams's National-Republicans, who could trace some of their ideology back to the Federalists, will be at the core of the Whig coalition that opposes Jackson in Chapter 11.

- Several of the issues on which the nation united during the "Era of Good Feelings"—the Bank and the protective tariff, for example—will become much more divisive, as discussed in the next chapter.

FURTHER READING

The standard overview of the "Era of Good Feelings" remains George Dangerfield's *The Awakening of American Nationalism, 1815–1828* (1965). A classic overview of the economic trends of the period is Douglas C. North's *The Economic Growth of the United States, 1790–1860*

(1961). An excellent synthesis of the era is Charles Sellers's *The Market Revolution* (1991).

On diplomatic relations during James Monroe's presidency, see Williams Earl Weeks's *John Quincy Adams and American Global Empire* (1992). For relations after 1812, see Ernest R. May's *The Making of the Monroe Doctrine* (1976).

Background on Andrew Jackson can be obtained from works cited in Chapter 11. The campaign that brought Jackson to the White House is analyzed in Robert V. Remini's *The Election of Andrew Jackson* (1963).

11 ⟡ THE JACKSONIAN IMPULSE

CHAPTER ORGANIZER

This chapter focuses on:

- the social and political context of the Jackson and Van Buren administrations.

- Andrew Jackson's attitudes and actions concerning the tariff (and nullification), Indian policy, and the Bank of the United States.

- the rise of a new party system (Democrats and Whigs).

*T*he election of Andrew Jackson initiated a new era in American politics and social development. He was the first president not to come from a prominent colonial family. As a self-made soldier, politician, and land speculator from the backcountry, he symbolized the changing social scene. The nation he prepared to govern was vastly different from that led by Washington and Jefferson. In 1828 the United States boasted twenty-four states and nearly 13 million people, many of them recent arrivals from Germany and Ireland. The national population was growing at a phenomenal rate, doubling every twenty-three years. An incredible surge in foreign demand for cotton and other goods, along with British investment in American enterprises, helped fuel a revolution in transportation and an economic boom. Textile mills sprouted like mushrooms across the New England countryside, their ravenous spinning looms fed by cotton grown in the newly cultivated lands of Alabama and Mississippi. This fluid new economic environment fostered a mad scramble for material gain and political advantage. People of all backgrounds engaged in a frenzied effort to acquire wealth and thereby gain social status and prestige.

The Jacksonians sought to democratize economic opportunity and political participation. Yet to call the Jacksonian era the "age of the common man," as many historians have done, is misleading. While political participation increased during the Jacksonian era, most of the common folk remained *common* folk. The period never produced true economic and social equality. Power and privilege, for the most part, remained in the hands of an "uncommon" elite of powerful men. Jacksonians in power proved to be as opportunistic and manipulative as the patricians they displaced. And they never embraced the principle of material equality. "Distinctions in society will always exist under every just government," Andrew Jackson observed. "Equality of talents, or education, or of wealth cannot be produced by human institutions." He and other Jacksonians wanted every American to have an equal chance to compete in the economic marketplace and political arena, but they never sanctioned equality of results. "True republicanism," one commentator declared, "requires that every man shall have an equal chance—that every man shall be free to become as unequal as he can." But in the afterglow of Jackson's election victory, few observers troubled with such distinctions. It was time to celebrate the commoner's ascension to the presidency.

SETTING THE STAGE

INAUGURATION   Inauguration day, March 4, 1829, was balmy after a bitterly cold winter. When Andrew Jackson, a sixty-one-year-old widower, emerged from his lodgings, dressed in black out of respect to his late wife Rachel, who had died in December, a great crowd filled both the east and west slopes of Capitol Hill. The new president, plagued by a persistent cough and severe headaches, delivered his inaugural address

All Creation Going to the White House. *The scene following Jackson's inauguration as president, according to satirist Robert Cruikshank.*

in a voice so low that few in the crowd of 15,000 spectators could hear it. It mattered little, for Jackson's advisers had eliminated anything that might give offense. On the major issues of the tariff, internal improvements, and the Bank of the United States, Jackson remained vague. Only a few points foreshadowed policies that he would pursue: he favored retirement of the national debt, a proper regard for states' rights, a "just" policy toward Indians, and rotation in federal offices, which he pronounced "a leading principle in the republican creed"—a principle his enemies would dub the "spoils system."

After his speech Jackson mounted his horse and rode to the White House, where a reception was scheduled for all who chose to come. The boisterous party that followed evoked the climate of turmoil that seemed always to surround Jackson. The revelers pushed into the White House, surged through the rooms, broke dishes, leaped onto the furniture—all in an effort to shake the president's hand or at least get a glimpse of him. To one observer, "the reign of 'King Mob' seemed triumphant."

Jackson's father had died before he was born, and his mother scratched out a meager living as a housekeeper before dying of cholera when Andrew was 15. Jackson grew to be proud, gritty, short-tempered, and a good hater. During the Revolution, when he was a young boy, two of his brothers were killed by redcoats, and the young Jackson suffered a scar from a British officer's saber that he carried with him for life. He also carried with him the conviction that it was not enough for a man to be right; he had to be tough as well, a quality that inspired his soldiers to nickname him "Old Hickory." During a duel with a man reputed to be the best shot in Tennessee, Jackson nevertheless let his opponent fire first. For his gallantry Jackson received a bullet wedged next to his heart. But he straightened himself, patiently took aim, and killed his aghast foe. "I should have hit him," Jackson claimed, "if he had shot me through the brain."

APPOINTMENTS AND POLITICAL RIVALRIES Jackson believed that a man should serve a term in government, then return to the status of private citizen, for officeholders who stayed too long grew corrupt. And democracy, he argued, "is promoted by party appointments by newly elected officials." Jackson hardly foresaw how these principles would work out in practice, and it would be misleading to link him too closely with what came to be called the "spoils system." He in fact behaved with great moderation compared to the politicians of New York and Pennsylvania, where the spoils of office nourished extensive political machines. During his first year in office Jackson replaced only about 9 percent of the appointed officials in the federal government, and during his entire term fewer than 20 percent.

Jackson's administration was from the outset a house divided between the partisans of Secretary of State Martin Van Buren of New York and those of Vice-President John C. Calhoun of South Carolina. Much of the political history of the next few years would turn upon the rivalry of the two, as each man jockeyed for position as Jackson's successor. It soon became clear that Van Buren held most of the advantages, foremost among them his skill at timing and tactics. Jackson, new to political administration, leaned heavily on him for advice and for help in soothing the ruffled feathers of rejected office seekers. Van Buren had perhaps more skill at maneuvering than Calhoun, and certainly more freedom to maneuver, because his home base of New York was more secure politically than Calhoun's base in South Carolina.

But Calhoun, a man of towering intellect, humorless outlook, and apostolic zeal, could not be taken lightly. A visitor remarked after a three-hour discussion with the bushy-browed Calhoun, "I hate a man who makes me think so much . . . and I hate a man who makes me feel my own inferiority." Since returning from Washington to his South Carolina plantation in 1825, Calhoun had nurtured his crops and his ardent love for his native region. Now as vice-president he was determined to defend southern interests against the worrisome advance of northern industrialism and abolitionism.

THE EATON AFFAIR   In his battle with Calhoun over political power, Van Buren had luck on his side. Fate handed him a trump card: the succulent scandal of the Peggy Eaton affair. The daughter of an Irish tavern owner, Margaret "Peggy" Eaton was a vivacious widow whose husband had supposedly committed suicide upon learning of her affair with Tennessee senator John Eaton. Her marriage to Eaton, three months before he became Jackson's secretary of war, had scarcely made a virtuous woman of her in the eye of the proper ladies of Washington. Floride Calhoun, the vice-president's wife, especially objected to Peggy Eaton's lowly origins and unsavory past. She pointedly snubbed her, and other cabinet wives followed suit.

Peggy's plight reminded Jackson of the gossip that had pursued his own Rachel, and he pronounced Peggy "chaste as a virgin." To a friend he wrote: "I did not come here to make a Cabinet for the Ladies of this place, but for the Nation." His cabinet members, however, were unable to cure their wives of what Van Buren dubbed "the Eaton Malaria." Van Buren, though, was a widower, and therefore free to lavish on poor Peggy all the attention that Jackson thought was her due. The amused John Quincy Adams looked on from afar and noted in his diary that Van Buren had become the leader of the party of the frail sisterhood. Mrs. Eaton herself finally wilted under the chill and withdrew from society. The outraged Jackson came to link Calhoun with what he called a conspiracy against her and drew even closer to Van Buren.

INTERNAL IMPROVEMENTS   While Washington social life weathered the chilly winter of 1829–1830, Van Buren delivered some additional blows to Calhoun. It was easy to bring Jackson into opposition to internal improvements and thus to federal programs with which Calhoun had long been identified. Jackson did not oppose road building per se, but he had the same constitutional scruples as Madison and Monroe about federal aid being used to fund local projects. In 1830 the Maysville Road

Bill, passed by Congress, offered Jackson a happy chance for a dual thrust at both Calhoun and Henry Clay. The bill authorized the government to buy stock in a road from Maysville to Clay's hometown of Lexington. The road lay entirely within the state of Kentucky, and though part of a larger scheme to link up with the National Road via Cincinnati, it could be viewed as a purely local undertaking. On that ground Jackson vetoed the bill as unconstitutional, to widespread popular acclaim.

Yet while Jackson continued to oppose federal aid to local projects, he supported interstate projects such as the National Road, as well as road building in the territories, and river and harbor bills, the "pork barrels" from which every congressman tried to pluck a morsel for his district. Even so, Jackson's attitude toward the Maysville Road set an

King Andrew the First. *Opponents considered Jackson's Maysville veto an abuse of power. This cartoon shows King Andrew Jackson trampling on the Constitution, internal improvements, and the Bank of the United States.*

important precedent, on the eve of the railroad age, for limiting federal initiative in internal improvements. Railroads would be built altogether by state and private capital at least until 1850.

NULLIFICATION

CALHOUN'S THEORY   There is a fine irony to John Calhoun's plight in the Jackson administration, for the South Carolinian was now in midpassage from his early phase as a War Hawk nationalist to his later phase as a states'-rights sectionalist. Conditions in his home state had brought on this change. Suffering from agricultural depression, South Carolina lost almost 70,000 people to emigration during the 1820s and was fated to lose nearly twice that number in the 1830s. Most

South Carolinians blamed the protective tariff for raising the price of manufactured goods. Insofar as tariffs discouraged the sale of foreign goods in the United States, they reduced the ability of British and French traders to acquire the American money and bills of exchange with which to buy southern cotton. This worsened already existing problems of low cotton prices and exhausted lands. Compounding the South Carolinians' malaise was growing anger over the North's criticism of slavery. Hardly had the country emerged from the Missouri controversy when Charleston, South Carolina, was thrown into panic by the Denmark Vesey slave insurrection of 1822, though the Vesey plot was put down before it got very far.

The unexpected passage of the Tariff of 1828 (called the "Tariff of Abominations" by its critics) left Calhoun no choice but to join those in opposition or give up his home base. Calhoun's *South Carolina Exposition and Protest* (1828), written in opposition to that tariff, actually had been an effort to check the most extreme states'-rights advocates with finespun theory in which nullification stopped short of secession from the Union. The unsigned statement accompanied resolutions of the South Carolina legislature protesting the tariff and urging its repeal. Calhoun, it was clear, had not entirely abandoned his earlier nationalism. He wanted to preserve the Union by protecting the minority rights that the agricultural and slaveholding South claimed. The fine balance he struck between states' rights and central authority was actually not as far removed from Jackson's own philosophy as it might seem, but growing tension between the two men would complicate the issue. The flinty Jackson, in addition, was determined to draw the line at any defiance of federal law.

John C. Calhoun.

Nor would Calhoun's theory permit any state to take up such defiance lightly. His concept of nullification or interposition, whereby a state could interpose state authority and in effect repeal a federal law, would follow that by which the original thirteen states had ratified the Constitution. A special state convention, like the ratifying conventions embodying the sovereign power of the people, could declare a federal law null and void within the state's borders because it violated the Constitution, the original compact among the states. One of two outcomes would then be possible. Either the federal government would have to abandon the law, or it would have to get a constitutional amendment removing all doubt as to its validity. The immediate issue was the constitutionality of a tariff designed mainly to protect American industries against foreign competition. The South Carolinians argued that the Constitution authorized tariffs for revenue only.

THE WEBSTER-HAYNE DEBATE   South Carolina leaders had proclaimed their dislike for the tariff, but they had postponed any action against its enforcement, awaiting with hope the election of 1828 in which antitariff Calhoun was the Jacksonian candidate for vicepresident. There the issue stood until 1830, when the great Webster-Hayne debate sharpened the lines between states' rights and the Union.

The immediate occasion for the debate, however, was the question of public lands. The federal government still owned immense tracts of unsettled land, and what to do with them set off an intense sectional debate. Late in 1829 Senator Samuel A. Foot of Connecticut, an otherwise obscure figure, proposed that the federal government restrict land sales in the West. When the Foot Resolution came before the Senate in 1830, Thomas Hart Benton of Missouri denounced it as a sectional attack designed to hamstring the settlement of the West so that the East might maintain its supply of cheap factory labor. Robert Y. Hayne of South Carolina took Benton's side. Hayne saw in the issue a chance to strengthen the alliance of South and West reflected in the vote for Jackson. Perhaps by supporting a policy of cheap lands in the West, the southerners could gain western support for lower tariffs. The government, said Hayne, endangered the Union by imposing any policy that would cause a hardship on one section to the benefit of another. The use of public lands as a source of revenue to the central government would create "a fund for corruption—fatal to the sovereignty and independence of the states."

Daniel Webster of Massachusetts rose to defend the East. Possessed of a thunderous voice and a theatrical flair, Webster was widely recognized as the nation's foremost orator and lawyer. With the gallery hushed, Webster denied that the East had ever shown a restrictive policy toward the West.

The eloquent Massachusetts senator Daniel Webster stands to rebut the argument for nullification in the Webster-Hayne debate.

He then rebuked those southerners who disparaged the Union. Webster had adroitly lured Hayne into defending states' rights and upholding the doctrine of nullification instead of pursuing a coalition with the West.

Hayne took the bait. Himself an accomplished speaker, he launched into a defense of the *South Carolina Exposition,* appealed to the example of the Virginia and Kentucky Resolutions of 1798, and called attention to the Hartford Convention, in which New Englanders had taken much the same position against majority measures as South Carolina did. The Union constituted a compact of the states, he argued, and the federal government, which was their "agent," could not be the judge of its own powers, else its powers would be unlimited. Rather, the states remained free to judge when their agent had overstepped the bounds of its constitutional authority. The right of state interposition was "as full and complete as it was before the Constitution was formed."

In rebuttal to the state-compact theory, Webster defined a nationalistic view of the Constitution. From the beginning, he asserted, the American Revolution had been a crusade of the united colonies rather than of each separately. True sovereignty resided in the people as a whole, for whom both federal and state governments acted as agents in their respective spheres. If a single state could nullify a law of the general government, then the Union would be a "rope of sand," a practical absurdity. A state could neither nullify a federal law nor secede from the Union. The practical outcome of nullification would be a confrontation leading to civil war.

Hayne may have had the better of the argument historically in advancing the state-compact theory, but the Senate galleries and much of the country at large thrilled to the eloquence of "the God-like Daniel." Webster's closing statement became an American classic, reprinted in school texts and committed to memory by schoolchild orators: "Liberty and Union, now and forever, one and inseparable." In the practical world of coalition politics Webster had the better argument, for the Union and majority rule meant more to westerners, including Jackson, than the abstractions of state sovereignty and nullification. As for the public lands, the Foot Resolution was soon defeated anyway. And whatever one might argue about the origins of the Union, its evolution would more and more validate Webster's position.

THE RIFT WITH CALHOUN As yet, however, Jackson had not spoken out on the issue. Like Calhoun, he was a slaveholder, albeit a westerner, and might be expected to sympathize with South Carolina, his native state. Soon all doubt was removed, at least on the point of nullification. On April 13, 1830, the Jefferson Day Dinner was held in Washington to honor the birthday of the former president. It was a party affair, but the Calhounites controlled the arrangements with an eye to advancing their own doctrine. Jackson and Van Buren were invited as a matter of course, and the two agreed that Jackson should present a toast proclaiming his opposition to nullification. When his turn came, after twenty-four toasts, many of them extolling states' rights, Jackson raised his glass, pointedly stared at Calhoun, and announced: "Our Union—It must be preserved!" Calhoun, who followed, tried quickly to retrieve the situation with a toast to "The Union, next to our liberty most dear! May we all remember that it can only be preserved by respecting the rights of the States and distributing equally the benefit and the burden of the Union!" But Jackson had set off a bombshell that exploded the plans of the states'-righters.

Nearly a month afterward a final nail was driven into the coffin of Calhoun's presidential ambitions. On May 12, 1830, Jackson first saw a letter containing final confirmation of reports that had been reaching him

The Rats Leaving a Falling House. *During his first term Jackson was beset by dissension within his administration. Here "public confidence in the stability and harmony of this administration" is toppling.*

of Calhoun's stand in 1818, when as secretary of war he had proposed to discipline Jackson for his Florida invasion. A tense correspondence between Jackson and Calhoun followed, and ended with a curt note from Jackson cutting it off. "Understanding you now," Jackson wrote two weeks later, "no further communication with you on this subject is necessary."

The growing rift between the two proud men prompted Jackson to remove all Calhoun partisans from the cabinet. Before the end of the summer of 1831, the president had a new cabinet entirely loyal to him. He then named Van Buren, who had resigned from the cabinet, minister to Great Britain, and Van Buren departed for London. Van Buren's friends now urged Jackson to repudiate his previous intention of serving only one term. It might be hard, they felt, to get the nomination in 1832 for the New Yorker, who had been charged with intrigues against Calhoun, and the still-popular Carolinian might yet carry off the prize.

Jackson relented and in the fall of 1831 announced his readiness for one more term, with the idea of returning Van Buren from London in time to win the presidency in 1836. But in 1832, when the Senate reconvened, Van Buren's enemies opposed his appointment as minister to England, and gave Calhoun, as vice-president, a chance to reject the nomination by a tie-breaking vote. "It will kill him, sir, kill him dead," Calhoun told Senator Thomas Hart Benton. Benton disagreed: "You have broken a minister, and elected a Vice-President." So, it turned out, he had. Calhoun's vote against Van Buren provoked popular sympathy for the New Yorker, who returned from London and would soon be nominated to succeed Calhoun.

Now that his presidential hopes were blasted, Calhoun assumed public leadership of the South Carolina nullificationists. They thought that, despite Jackson's gestures, tariff rates remained too high and represented an unconstitutional tax designed to enrich the industrial North at the expense of the agricultural South. Jackson accepted the principle of using tariffs to protect new American industries from foreign competition. Nevertheless, he had called upon Congress in 1829 to reduce tariffs on goods "which cannot come in competition with our own products." Late in the spring of 1830 Congress lowered duties on consumer products such as tea, coffee, salt, and molasses. That and the Maysville veto, coming at about the same time, mollified a few South Carolinians, but nullifiers regarded the two actions as "nothing but sugar plums to pacify children." By the end of 1831 Jackson was calling for further reductions to take the wind out of the nullificationists' sails, and the Tariff of 1832, pushed through by John Quincy Adams (back in Washington as a congressman), cut rates again. But tariffs on cottons, woolens, and iron remained high.

THE SOUTH CAROLINA ORDINANCE   South Carolinians, living in the only state where slaves were a majority of the population, feared that the federal authority to impose tariffs might eventually be used to end slavery. In the state elections of 1832, attention centered on the nullification issue. The nullificationists took the initiative in organization and agitation, and the Unionist party was left with a distinguished leadership but only small support. A special session of the legislature called for the election of a state convention, which overwhelmingly adopted an ordinance of nullification that repudiated the tariff acts of 1828 and 1832 and forbade collection of the duties in the state after February 1, 1833. The reassembled legislature then provided that any citizen whose property was seized by federal authorities for failure to pay the duty could get a state court order to recover twice its value. The legislature also chose Robert Hayne as governor and elected Calhoun to succeed him as senator. Calhoun promptly resigned as vice-president in order to defend nullification on the Senate floor.

JACKSON'S FIRM RESPONSE   In the crisis South Carolina found itself standing alone, despite the sympathy expressed elsewhere. Jackson's response was measured but not rash—at least not in public. In private he threatened to hang Calhoun and all other traitors—and later expressed regret that he had failed to hang at least Calhoun. In his annual message on December 4, 1832, Jackson announced his firm intention to enforce the tariff, but once again urged Congress to lower the rates. On December 10 Jackson followed up with his Nullification Proclamation, which characterized the doctrine of nullification as an "impractical absurdity." He appealed to the people of his native state not to follow false leaders: "The laws of the United States must be executed. . . . Those who told you that you might peaceably prevent their execution, deceived you; they could not have been deceived themselves. . . . Their object is disunion. But be not deceived by names. Disunion by armed force is treason."

CLAY'S COMPROMISE Jackson sent federal soldiers and ships to Charleston. The nullifiers mobilized the state militia while unionists in the state organized a volunteer force. In 1833 the president requested from Congress a "Force Bill" specifically authorizing him to use the army to compel compliance with federal law in South Carolina. Under existing legislation he already had such authority, but this affirmation would strengthen his hand. At the same time he supported a bill in Congress that would have lowered tariff duties substantially within two years.

The nullifiers postponed enforcement of their ordinances in anticipation of a compromise. Passage of the compromise bill depended on the support of Henry Clay, who finally yielded to those urging him to save the day. On February 12, 1833, he brought forth a plan to reduce the tariff gradually until 1842, by which time the rate on cotton would be cut in half. It was less than South Carolina would have preferred, but it got the nullifiers out of the corner into which they had painted themselves.

On March 1, 1833, Congress passed the compromise tariff and the Force Bill, and the next day Jackson signed both. The South Carolina convention then met and rescinded its nullification of the tariff acts. In a face-saving gesture, it then nullified the Force Bill, for which Jackson no longer had any need. Both sides were able to claim victory. Jackson had upheld the supremacy of the Union, and South Carolina had secured a reduction of the tariff. Calhoun, worn out by the controversy, returned to his plantation. "The struggle, so far from being over," he ominously wrote, "is not more than fairly commenced."

JACKSON'S INDIAN POLICY

During the 1820s and 1830s the United States was fast becoming a multicultural nation of peoples from many different countries. Most whites, however, were openly racist in their treatment of blacks and Indians. As economic growth reinforced the institution of slavery and accelerated westward expansion, policy makers struggled to preserve white racial homogeneity and hegemony. "Next to the case of the black race within our bosom," declared former president James Madison, "that of the red [race] on our borders is the problem most baffling to the policy of our country."

Andrew Jackson, however, saw nothing baffling about Indian policy. His attitude toward Indians was the typically western one, that the Native Americans were barbarians and better off out of the way. At the Battle of Horseshoe Bend in Alabama in 1814, General Jackson's federal troops had massacred nearly 900 Creeks. Jackson and most Americans on the frontier despised and feared Indians—and vice versa. Jackson believed that a "just, humane, liberal policy toward Indians" dictated moving all of them onto the plains west of the Mississippi River, to the "Great American Desert," which white settlers would never covet, since it was fit mainly for horned toads and rattlesnakes.

INDIAN REMOVAL   In response to a request by Jackson, Congress in 1830 approved the Indian Removal Act. It authorized the president to give Indians federal land in the West in exchange for the land they occupied in the East and South. By 1835 Jackson was able to announce that the policy had been carried out or was in process of completion for all but a handful of Indians. Some 46,000 people were relocated at government expense. The policy was effected with remarkable speed, but even that was too slow for state authorities in the South and Southwest. Unlike the Ohio River Valley and the Great Lakes region, where the flow of white settlement had constantly pushed the Indians westward before it, in the Old Southwest settlement moved across Kentucky and Tennessee and down the Mississippi, surrounding the Creeks, Choctaws, Chickasaws, Seminoles, and Cherokees. These tribes had over the years taken on many of the features of white society. The Cherokees even had such products of "white civilization" as a constitution, a written language, and black slaves.

Most of the northern tribes were too weak to resist the offers of Indian commissioners who, if necessary, used bribery and alcohol to woo the chiefs, and there was, on the whole, remarkably little resistance. In Illinois and Wisconsin Territory an armed clash erupted in 1832, which came to be known as the Black Hawk War, when the Sauk and Fox under Chief Black Hawk sought to reoccupy some lands they had abandoned in the previous year. Facing famine and hostile Sioux west of the Mississippi, they were simply seeking a place to raise a corn crop. The Illinois militia mobilized to expel them, chased them into Wisconsin Territory, and massacred women and children as they tried to escape across the Mississippi. The Black Hawk War came to be remembered later, however, less because of the atrocities inflicted on the Indians than because the participants included two native Kentuckians later pitted against each other: Lieutenant Jefferson Davis of the regular army and Captain Abraham Lincoln of the Illinois volunteers.

In the South two nations, the Seminoles and Cherokees, put up a stubborn resistance to the federal removal policy. The Seminoles of Florida fought a protracted guerrilla war in the Everglades from 1835 to 1842. But their resistance waned after 1837, when their leader, Osceola, was seized by treachery under a flag of truce, imprisoned, and left to die at Fort Moultrie near Charleston Harbor. After 1842 only a few hundred Seminoles remained, hiding out in the swamps. Most of the rest had been banished to the West.

THE CHEROKEES' TRAIL OF TEARS The Cherokees had by the end of the eighteenth century fallen back into the mountains of northern Georgia and western North Carolina, onto land guaranteed to them in 1791 by treaty with the United States. But when Georgia ceded its western lands in 1802, it did so on the ambiguous condition that the United States extinguish all Indian titles within the state "as early as the same can be obtained on reasonable terms." In 1827 the Cherokees, relying on their treaty rights, adopted a constitution in which they declared pointedly that they were not subject to any other state or nation. In 1828 Georgia responded by declaring that after June 1, 1830, the authority of state law would extend over the Cherokees living within the boundaries of the state.

The discovery of gold in 1829 whetted the whites' appetite for Cherokee lands and brought bands of rough prospectors into the country. The Cherokees sought relief in the Supreme Court, but in *Cherokee Nation* v. *Georgia* (1831) John Marshall ruled that the Court lacked jurisdiction because the Cherokees were a "domestic dependent nation" rather than a foreign state in the meaning of the Constitution. Marshall added, however, that the Cherokees had "an unquestionable right" to their lands "until title should be extinguished by voluntary cession to the United States." In 1830 a Georgia law had required whites in the territory to get licenses authorizing their residence there, and to take an oath of allegiance to the state. Two New England missionaries among the Indi-

Elias Boudinot, editor of the Cherokee Phoenix, *signed the Indian removal treaty in 1835 and was subsequently murdered.*

ans refused and were sentenced to four years at hard labor. On appeal their case reached the Supreme Court as *Worcester* v. *Georgia* (1832), and the Court held that the Cherokee Nation was "a distinct political community" within which Georgia law had no force. The Georgia law was therefore unconstitutional.

Six years earlier Georgia had faced down President John Quincy Adams when he tried to protect the rights of the Creeks. Now Georgia faced down the Supreme Court with the tacit consent of another president. Jackson did nothing to enforce the Court's decision. In the circumstances there was nothing for the Cherokees to do but give in and sign a treaty, which they did in 1835. They gave up their lands in the Southeast in exchange for tracts in the Indian Territory west of Arkansas, $5 million from the federal government, and expenses for transportation.

By 1838 some 17,000 Cherokees had departed on the "Trail of Tears" westward, following the Choctaws, Chickasaws, Creeks, and Seminoles on an 800-mile journey marked by the cruelty and neglect of soldiers and private contractors, and scorn and pilferage by whites along the way. A few held out in the mountains and acquired title to federal lands in North Carolina; thenceforth they were the "Eastern Band" of

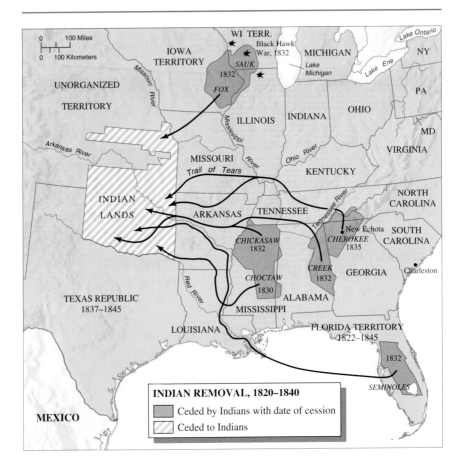

INDIAN REMOVAL, 1820–1840

Ceded by Indians with date of cession

Ceded to Indians

the Cherokees. Some Seminoles were able to hide out in the Everglades, and a few of the others remained scattered in the Southeast, especially mixed-blood Creeks who could pass for white. Only 8,000 of the exiles survived the forced march to Oklahoma.

THE BANK CONTROVERSY

THE BANK'S OPPONENTS The overriding national issue in the campaign of 1832 was neither Jackson's Indian policy nor South Carolina's obsession with the tariff. It was the question of rechartering the Bank of the United States (B.U.S.). On the Bank issue, as on others, Jackson had made no public commitment, but his personal opposition to the Bank was already formed. Jackson had absorbed the western attitude of hostility toward the Bank after the Panic of 1819, and held to a conviction that it was unconstitutional no matter what Chief Justice John Marshall had said in *McCulloch v. Maryland*. Banks in general had fed a speculative mania, and Jackson, suspicious of all banks, preferred a hard-money policy.

Under the management of Nicholas Biddle, the Bank of the United States had prospered and grown. The Bank had facilitated business expansion and supplied a stable currency by forcing the 464 state banks to keep a specie reserve (gold or silver) on hand to back their paper currency. The Bank also acted as the collecting and disbursing agent for the federal government, which held one-fifth of the Bank's $35 million capital stock. From the start, this combination of private and public functions caused problems for the B.U.S. As the government's revenues soared, the Bank became the most powerful lending institution in the country, a central bank, in effect, whose huge size enabled it to determine the amount of available credit for the nation.

Arrayed against the Bank were powerful enemies: some of the state and local banks that had been forced to reduce their volume of paper money, debtor groups that suffered from the reduction, and businessmen and speculators "on the make," who wanted easier credit. States'-rights groups questioned the Bank's constitutionality, though Calhoun, who had sponsored the original charter and valued the Bank's function of regulating the currency, was not among them. Financiers on New York's Wall Street resented the supremacy of the Bank on Philadelphia's Chestnut Street.

Many westerners and workingmen, like Jackson, felt in their bones that the Bank was, in Thomas Hart Benton's word, a "Monster," a monopoly controlled by a wealthy few with power that was irreconcilable with a democracy. "I think it right to be perfectly frank with you," Jackson told Biddle in 1829, "I do not dislike your Bank any more than all banks." Jackson was perhaps right in his instinct that the Bank lodged too much power in private hands, but mistaken in his understanding of the Bank's policies. By issuing paper money of its own, the Bank provided a stable and uniform currency for the expanding economy as well as a mechanism to control the pace of growth.

Biddle at first tried to conciliate Jackson by appointing a number of Jackson men to branch offices of the Bank. In his first annual message (1829), however, Jackson questioned the Bank's constitutionality and asserted (whatever the evidence to the contrary) that it had failed to maintain a sound and uniform currency. Jackson talked of a compromise, perhaps a bank completely owned by the government with its operations confined chiefly to government deposits, its profits payable to the government, and its authority to set up branches in any state, dependent on the state's wishes. But Jackson would never commit himself on the precise terms of compromise. The defense of the Bank was left up to Biddle.

BIDDLE'S RECHARTER EFFORT   The Bank's twenty-year charter would run through 1836, but Biddle could not afford the uncertainty of waiting until then for a renewal. He pondered whether to force the issue of recharter before the election of 1832 or after. On this point, leaders of the National-Republicans, especially Henry Clay and Daniel Webster (who was legal counsel to the Bank as well as a senator), argued that the time to move was before the election. Clay, already the candidate of the National-Republicans, proposed to make the Bank the central election issue. Friends of the Bank held a majority in Congress, and Jackson would risk loss of support in the election if he vetoed a

Jackson battling the hydra-headed Bank of the United States.

renewal. But they failed to grasp the depth of prejudice against the Bank, and succeeded mainly in handing to Jackson a popular issue on the eve of the election. "The Bank," Jackson told Martin Van Buren in May 1832, "is trying to kill me. But I will kill it."

Both houses passed the recharter by comfortable margins, but without the two-thirds majority needed to override a veto. On July 10, 1832, Jackson vetoed the bill, sending it back to Congress with a ringing denunciation of monopoly and special privilege. Jackson argued that the Bank was unconstitutional, whatever the Court and Congress said. "The opinion of the judges has no more authority over Congress than the opinion of Congress had over the judges, and on that point the President is independent of both." Besides, there were substantive objections aside from the question of constitutionality. Foreign stockholders in the Bank had an undue influence. The Bank had shown favors to members of Congress and exercised an improper power over state banks. The bill, he argued, demonstrated that "Many of our rich men have not been content with equal protection and equal benefits, but have besought us to make them richer by act of Congress." An effort to overrule the veto failed in the Senate, thus setting the stage for a nationwide financial crisis.

CAMPAIGN INNOVATIONS   The year 1832 witnessed another presidential election. For the first time a third party entered the field. The Anti-Masonic party was, like the Bank of the United States, the object of strong emotions then sweeping the nation. The group had grown out of popular hostility toward the Masonic order, members of which were suspected of having kidnapped and murdered a New Yorker for revealing the "secrets" of his lodge. Opposition to a fraternal order was hardly the foundation on which to build a lasting political party, but the Anti-Masonic party had three important "firsts" to its credit: in addition to being the first third party, it was the first party to hold a national nominating convention and the first to announce a platform, all of which it accomplished in 1831 when it nominated William Wirt of Maryland for president.

The major parties followed its example by holding national conventions of their own. In December 1831 the delegates of the National-Republican party assembled in Baltimore to nominate Henry Clay for president. Jackson endorsed the idea of a nominating convention for

George Caleb Bingham's Verdict of the People *depicts the increasingly democratic politics of the early to mid–nineteenth century.*

the Democratic party (the name "Republican" was now formally dropped) to demonstrate popular support for its candidates. To that purpose the convention, also meeting at Baltimore, adopted the two-thirds rule for nomination (which prevailed until 1936, when it became a simple majority), and then named Martin Van Buren as Jackson's running mate. The Democrats, unlike the other two parties, adopted no formal platform at their first convention, and relied to a substantial degree on hoopla and the personal popularity of the president to carry their cause.

The outcome was an overwhelming endorsement of Jackson in the electoral college by 219 votes to 49 for Clay, and a less overwhelming but solid victory in the popular vote, by 688,000 to 530,000. William Wirt carried only Vermont, with several electoral votes. South Carolina, preparing for nullification and unable to stomach either Jackson or Clay, delivered its eleven votes to Governor John Floyd of Virginia.

REMOVAL OF GOVERNMENT DEPOSITS   Jackson interpreted his election as a mandate to further weaken the Bank. He asked Congress to investigate the safety of government deposits in the Bank, since one of the current rumors told of empty vaults, carefully concealed. After a committee had checked, the Calhoun and Clay forces in the House of Representatives passed a resolution affirming that government deposits were safe and could be continued. The resolution passed on March 2, 1833, by chance the same day that Jackson signed the compromise tariff and the Force Bill. With the nullification issue out of the way, however, Jackson was free to wage his unrelenting war on the Bank, that "hydra of corruption," which still had nearly four years to run on its charter. Despite the House study and resolution, Jackson now resolved to remove all government deposits from the Bank.

When Secretary of the Treasury Louis McLane opposed removal of the government deposits and suggested a new and modified version of the Bank, Jackson again shook up his cabinet. In the reshuffling, Attorney-General Roger Taney moved to the Treasury Department, where he gladly complied with the presidential wishes, which corresponded to his own views.

Taney continued to draw on governmental accounts with Biddle's bank, and to deposit all new federal receipts in state banks. By the end of 1833 there were twenty-three state banks that had the benefit of federal deposits, "pet banks" as they came to be called. Transferring the government's deposits was a highly questionable action under the law, and the Senate voted to censure Jackson for his actions. Biddle refused to surrender. "This worthy President," he declared, "thinks that because he has scalped Indians and imprisoned Judges he is to have his way with the Bank. He is mistaken." Biddle ordered that the B.U.S. curtail loans throughout the nation and demand the immediate redemption of state bank notes in gold or silver as fast as possible. He sought to bring the economy to a halt, create a sharp depression, and reveal to the nation the importance of maintaining the Bank. By 1834 the tightness of credit was creating complaints of business distress, which was probably exaggerated by both sides in the Bank controversy for political effect: Biddle to show the evil consequences of the withdrawal of deposits, Jacksonians to show how Biddle abused his power.

Biddle's contraction policy unwittingly unleashed, however, a speculative binge encouraged by the deposit of government funds in the pet

The Downfall of Mother Bank. *In this pro-Jackson cartoon, the Bank crumbles and Jackson's opponents flee in the face of the heroic president's removal of government deposits.*

state banks. With the restraint of Biddle's bank removed, the state banks gave full rein to their wildcat tendencies. New banks mushroomed, printing bank notes with abandon for the purpose of lending to speculators. Sales of public lands rose from 4 million acres in 1834 to 15 million in 1835 and to 20 million in 1836. At the same time, the states plunged heavily into debt to finance the building of roads and canals, inspired by the success of New York's Erie Canal. By 1837 total state indebtedness had soared to $170 million, a very large sum for that time. The supreme irony of Jackson's war on the Bank was that it sparked the speculative mania that he most feared.

FISCAL MEASURES   The surge of cheap money reached its greatest extent in 1836, when events combined suddenly to deflate it. Most important among these were the Distribution Act and the Specie Circular. Distribution of the government's surplus funds to the states had long been a pet project of Henry Clay. One of its purposes was to eliminate the federal surplus, thus removing one argument for cutting the tariff. Much of the surplus, however, resulted from the "land office business" in western real estate, and was therefore in the form of bank notes that had been issued to speculators. Many westerners thought that the solution to the surplus was simply to lower the price of land; southerners preferred to lower the tariff—but such action would now upset the compromise achieved in the Tariff of 1833. For a time the annual surpluses could be applied to paying off the government debt, but the debt, reduced to $7 million by 1832, was entirely paid off by 1835.

Still the federal surplus continued to mount. Clay again proposed distribution, but Jackson had constitutional scruples about the process. Finally, a compromise was worked out whereby the government would distribute most of the surplus as loans to the states. To satisfy Jackson's scruples the funds were technically "deposits," but in reality they were never demanded back. Distribution was to be in proportion to each state's representation in the two houses of Congress, and was to be paid out in quarterly installments, beginning in 1837.

The Specie Circular, issued by the secretary of the treasury at Jackson's order, applied the president's hard-money conviction to the sale of public lands. According to his order, the government would accept only gold or silver in payment for land. The purposes declared in the circular were to "repress frauds," to withhold support "from the monopoly of the public lands in the hands of speculators and capitalists," and to discourage the "ruinous extension" of bank notes and credit.

Irony dogged Jackson to the end on this matter. Since few actual settlers could get their hands on gold or silver, they were now left all the more at the mercy of speculators for land purchases. Both the Distribution Act and the Specie Circular put many state banks in a precarious plight. The distribution of the surplus to the state governments resulted in federal funds being withdrawn from the state banks. In turn, the state banks had to require many borrowers to pay back their loans immediately in order to make the transfer of federal funds to the state governments. This caused greater disarray among the already chaotic state banking community. At the same time, the new requirement that only hard money be accepted for federal land purchases put an added strain on the supplies of gold and silver.

BOOM AND BUST   But the boom and bust cycle of the 1830s had causes larger even than Andrew Jackson, causes that were beyond his control. The inflation of mid-decade was rooted not so much in a prodigal expansion of bank notes, as it seemed at the time, but in an increase of gold and silver payments from England and France, and especially from Mexico, for investment and for the purchase of American cotton and other products. At the same time, British credits enabled Americans to buy British goods without having to export gold or silver. Meanwhile, the flow of hard cash to China, where silver had been much prized, decreased. The Chinese now took in payment for their goods British credits, which they could in turn use to cover rapidly increasing imports of opium from British India.

Contrary to appearances, therefore, the reserves of gold and silver in American banks kept pace with the increase of bank notes, despite reckless behavior on the part of some banks. But by 1836 a tighter British economy caused a decline in British investments and in British demand for American cotton just when the new western lands were creating a rapid increase in cotton supply. Fortunately for Jackson, the Panic of 1837 did not erupt until he was out of the White House and safely back at the Hermitage, his plantation near Nashville, Tennessee. His successor would serve as the scapegoat.

In May 1837 New York banks suspended gold and silver payments on their bank notes, and fears of bankruptcy set off runs on banks around the country, many of which were soon overextended. A brief recovery followed in 1838, stimulated in part by a bad wheat harvest in England, which forced the British to buy American wheat. But by 1839 that stimulus had passed. The same year a bumper cotton crop overloaded the market, and a collapse of cotton prices set off a depression from which the economy did not fully recover until the mid-1840s.

VAN BUREN AND THE NEW PARTY SYSTEM

THE WHIG COALITION   Before the depression set in, however, the Jacksonian Democrats reaped a political bonanza. Jackson had slain the dual monsters of nullification and the Bank, and the people loved him for it. The hard times following the contraction of the economy turned people against Biddle and the B.U.S., but not against Jackson, the professed friend of "the people" against the "selfish" interests of financiers and speculators. But his opponents began in 1834 to pull together a new coalition of diverse elements united chiefly by their hostility to Jackson.

The imperious demeanor of the feisty champion of democracy had given rise to the name of "King Andrew I." His followers therefore were "Tories," supporters of the king, and his opponents became "Whigs," a name that linked them to the patriots of the American Revolution.

The diverse coalition making up the Whigs clustered around its center, the National-Republican party of John Quincy Adams, Henry Clay, and Daniel Webster. Into the combination came remnants of the Anti-Masonic and Democratic parties who for one reason or another were alienated by Jackson's stands on the Bank or states' rights. Of the forty-one Democrats in Congress who had voted to recharter the Bank, twenty-eight joined the Whigs by 1836.

Whiggery always had about it an atmosphere of social conservatism and superiority. The core Whigs were the supporters of the charismatic Henry Clay and his "American System." In the South the Whigs enjoyed the support of the urban banking and commercial interests, as well as their planter associates, owners of most of the slaves in the region. In the West, farmers who valued internal improvements joined the Whig ranks. Most states'-rights supporters eventually dropped away, and by the early 1840s the Whigs were becoming more clearly the party of Henry Clay's nationalism, even in the South. Unlike the Democrats, who attracted Catholics from Germany and Ireland, Whigs tended to be native-born and British-American evangelical Protestants—Presbyterians, Baptists, and Congregationalists—who were active in promoting social reforms such as abolitionism and temperance.

THE ELECTION OF 1836   By the presidential election of 1836 a new two-party system was emerging out of the Jackson and anti-Jackson forces, a system that would remain in fairly even balance for twenty years. In 1835, eighteen months before the election, the Democrats held their second national convention and nominated Jackson's hand-picked successor, Vice-President Martin Van Buren. The Whig coalition, united chiefly in its opposition to Jackson, held no convention but adopted a strategy of multiple candidacies, hoping to throw the election into the House of Representatives.

The result was a free-for-all reminiscent of 1824, except that this time one candidate stood apart from the rest. It was Van Buren against the field. The Whigs put up three favorite sons: Daniel Webster, named

Martin Van Buren, the "Little Magician."

by the Massachusetts legislature; Hugh Lawson White, chosen by anti-Jackson Democrats in the Tennessee legislature; and William Henry Harrison of Indiana, nominated by a predominantly Anti-Masonic convention in Harrisburg, Pennsylvania. In the South the Whigs made heavy inroads on the Democratic vote by arguing that Van Buren would be soft on anti-slavery advocates and that the South could trust only a southerner—that is, White—as president. In the popular vote Van Buren outdistanced the entire Whig field, with 765,000 votes to 740,000 votes for the Whigs, most of which were cast for Harrison. Van Buren had 170 electoral votes, Harrison 73, White 26, and Webster 14.

Martin Van Buren, the eighth president, was the first of Dutch ancestry. The son of a tavernkeeper in Kinderhook, New York, he had been schooled in a local academy, read law, and entered politics. Although he kept up a limited legal practice, he had been for most of his adult life a professional politician, so skilled in the arts of organization and manipulation that he came to be known as the "Little Magician." In 1824 he supported Crawford, then switched to Jackson in 1828, but continued to look to the Old Republicans of Virginia as the southern anchor of his support. After a brief tenure as governor of New York, he resigned to join the cabinet, and because of Jackson's favor became vice-president.

THE PANIC OF 1837   Van Buren owed much of his success to good luck. But once he had climbed to the top of the greased pole, luck suddenly deserted him. Van Buren had inherited a financial panic. An already precarious economy was tipped over into crisis by depression in England, which resulted in a drop in the price of American cotton, and caused English banks and investors to cut back their commitments in the New World and to refuse extensions of loans. This was a particularly hard blow, because much of America's economic expansion depended on European—and mainly English—investment capital. On top of everything else, in 1836 there had been a failure of the wheat crop, the export of which in good years helped offset the drain of payments abroad. As creditors hastened to foreclose, the inflationary spiral went into reverse. States curtailed ambitious plans for roads and canals, and in many cases felt impelled to repudiate their debts. In the crunch, a good many of the wildcat banks succumbed, and the federal government itself lost some $9 million it had deposited in pet banks.

The working classes, as always, were particularly hard hit during the economic slump, and they largely had to fend for themselves. By the fall of 1837, one-third of the workforce was jobless, and those still fortunate enough to have jobs saw their wages cut by 30 to 50 percent within two years. At the same time, prices for food and clothing soared. As winter approached in 1837, a journalist reported that in New York City there were 200,000 people "in utter and hopeless distress with no means of surviving the winter but those provided by charity." There was no government aid; churches and voluntary societies were the major sources of support for the indigent.

Van Buren's advisers and supporters were inclined to blame the depression on speculators and bankers, but at the same time to expect

The Times. *This anti-Jacksonian cartoon depicts the effects of the depression of 1837: a panic at a state bank, beggars in the street.*

that the evildoers would get what they deserved in a healthy shakeout that would bring the economy back to stability. Van Buren did not believe that he or the government had any responsibility to rescue hard-pressed farmers or businessmen or to provide public relief. He did feel obliged to keep the government itself in a healthy financial situation, however. To that end he called a special session of Congress in 1837, which quickly voted to postpone indefinitely the distribution of the surplus because of a probable upcoming deficit, and also approved an issue of Treasury notes to cover immediate expenses.

AN INDEPENDENT TREASURY   Van Buren believed that the government should cease risking its deposits in shaky state banks and set up an Independent Treasury. Under this plan the government would keep its funds in its own vaults and do business entirely in hard money. The Independent Treasury Act provoked opposition from a combination of Whigs and conservative Democrats who feared deflation. It took Van Buren several years of maneuvering to get what he wanted. Calhoun signaled a return to the Democratic fold, after several years of flirting with the Whigs, when he came out for the Independent Treasury Act. Van Buren gained western support by backing a more liberal land policy. Congress finally passed the Independent Treasury Act on July 4, 1840. Although it lasted little more than a year before the Whigs repealed it in 1841, it would be restored in 1846.

The drawn-out struggle over the Treasury was only one of several squabbles that kept Washington preoccupied through the Van Buren years. A flood of petitions for Congress to abolish slavery and the slave trade in the District of Columbia brought on tumultuous debate, especially in the House of Representatives. Border incidents growing out of a Canadian insurrection in 1837 and a dispute over the Maine boundary kept British-American animosity at a simmer, but General Winfield Scott, the president's ace troubleshooter, managed to keep the hotheads in check along the border. The spreading malaise of the time was rooted in the depressed condition of the economy, which lasted through Van Buren's entire term. Fairly or not, the administration became the target of growing discontent. The president won renomination easily enough, but could not get the Democratic convention to agree on his vice-presidential choice, which the convention left up to the Democratic electors.

THE "LOG CABIN AND HARD CIDER" CAMPAIGN   The Whigs got an early start on their campaign when they met at Harrisburg, Pennsylvania, on December 4, 1839, to choose a candidate. Henry Clay expected 1840 to be his year and had soft-pedaled talk of his American System in the interest of building broader support. Although he led on the first ballot, the convention sought a Whiggish Jackson, as it were, a military hero who could enter the race with few known political convictions or enemies. One possibility was Winfield Scott, but the delegates finally turned to William Henry Harrison. His credentials were impressive: victor at the Battle of Tippecanoe against the Shawnees in 1811, former governor of the Indiana Territory, briefly congressman and senator from Ohio, more briefly minister to Colombia. Another advantage of Harrison's was that the Anti-Masons liked him. To rally their states'-rights wing, the Whigs chose for vice-president John Tyler of Virginia, a close friend of Clay.

The Whigs had no platform. That would have risked dividing a coalition united chiefly by opposition to the Democrats. But they had a catchy slogan, "Tippecanoe and Tyler too." And they soon had a rousing campaign theme, which a Democratic paper unwittingly supplied them when the *Baltimore Republican* declared sardonically "that upon condition of his receiving a pension of $2,000 and a barrel of cider, General Harrison would no doubt consent to withdraw his pretensions, and spend his days in a log cabin on the banks of the Ohio." The Whigs seized upon the cider and log cabin symbols to depict Harrison as a simple man sprung from the people. Actually, he sprang from one of the first families of Virginia and lived in a large farmhouse.

The Whig "Log Cabin and Hard Cider" campaign featured portable log cabins rolling through the streets along with barrels of cider. All the devices of hoopla were mobilized: placards, emblems, campaign buttons, floats, effigies, great rallies, and a campaign newspaper, *The Log Cabin*. Building on the example of the Jacksonians' campaign to discredit John Quincy Adams, the Whigs pictured Van Buren, who unlike Harrison really did come from humble origins, as an aristocrat living in luxury at "the Palace."

"We have taught them to conquer us!" the *Democratic Review* lamented. The Whig party had not only learned its lessons well, it had learned to improve on its teachers in the art of campaigning. "Van! Van! Is a Used-up Man!" went one of the campaign refrains, and down he

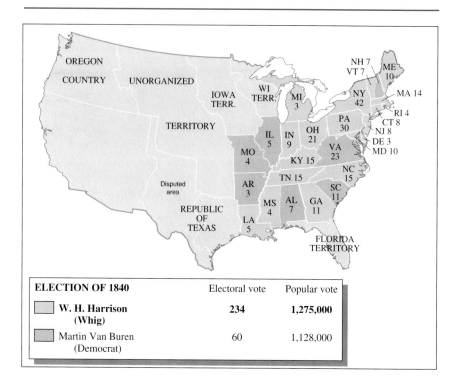

ELECTION OF 1840	Electoral vote	Popular vote
W. H. Harrison (Whig)	**234**	**1,275,000**
Martin Van Buren (Democrat)	60	1,128,000

went by the thumping margin of 234 votes to 60 in the electoral college. In the popular vote it was closer: 1,275,000 for Harrison; 1,128,000 for Van Buren.

ASSESSING THE JACKSON YEARS

The Whigs may have won in 1840, but the Jacksonian impulse had permanently altered American politics. By 1840 both parties were organized down to the precinct level, and the proportion of adult white males who voted in the presidential election tripled, from 26 percent in 1824 to 78 percent in 1840. That much is beyond dispute, but the phenomenon of Jackson, the heroic symbol for an age, continues to spark historical debate.

The earliest historians of the Jackson era belonged largely to an eastern elite nurtured in a "Whiggish" culture, men who could never quite forgive Jackson for the spoils system, which in their view excluded the fittest from office. A later school of "progressive" historians depicted

Jackson as the leader of a vast democratic movement that welled up in the West and mobilized a farmer-labor alliance to sweep the "Monster" Bank into the dustbin of history. Some historians have recently focused attention on local power struggles in which the great national debates of the time often seemed empty rhetoric or at most snares to catch the voters. One view of Jackson makes him out to be essentially a frontier opportunist for whom democracy "was good talk with which to win the favor of the people."

Most recently, scholars highlight that "Jacksonian Democracy" was for white males only; it did not apply to blacks, Indians, or women. These revisionist historians also stress that greater participation in politics was much more of a northern than a southern development. As late as 1857, for example, North Carolina's fifty-acre property requirement for voting disenfranchised almost half the state's voters.

Yet there seems little question that, whatever else Jackson and his supporters had in mind, they followed an ideal of republican virtue, of returning to the Jeffersonian vision of the Old Republic in which government would play as limited a role as possible. In the Jacksonian view the alliance of government and business was always an invitation to special favors and an eternal source of corruption. The national bank was the epitome of such evil. The right policy for government, at the national level in particular, was to refrain from granting special privileges and to let free competition in the marketplace regulate the economy.

In the bustling world of the nineteenth century, however, the idea of a return to agrarian simplicity was a futile exercise in nostalgia. Instead, free enterprise policies opened the way for a host of aspiring entrepreneurs eager to replace the established economic elite with a new order of free enterprise capitalism. And in fact there was no great conflict in the Jacksonian mentality between the farmer or planter who delved in the soil and the independent speculator and entrepreneur who grew wealthy by other means. Jackson himself was all these things. What the Jacksonian mentality could not foresee was the degree to which, in a growing country, unrestrained enterprise could lead to new centers of economic power largely independent of governmental regulation. But history is forever pursued by unintended consequences. Here the ultimate irony would be that the laissez-faire rationale for republican simplicity eventually became the justification for the growth of unregulated corporate powers far greater than any ever wielded by Biddle's bank.

> **MAKING CONNECTIONS**
>
> • This chapter analyzed the political side of "Jacksonian Democracy." Chapter 12 concludes with an assessment of the accuracy of that term from social and economic perspectives.
>
> • John C. Calhoun, Henry Clay, and Daniel Webster, three of the statesmen described in this chapter, continued for many years to be the major spokesmen for their positions. The last great debate for the three, over the Compromise of 1850, is discussed in Chapter 16.

FURTHER READING

A recent survey of events covered in the chapter is Daniel Feller's *The Jacksonian Promise: America, 1815–1840* (1995). A more political focus can be found in Harry L. Watson's *Liberty and Power: The Politics of Jacksonian America* (1990).

A still-valuable standard introduction to the development of political parties of the 1830s is Richard P. McCormick's *The Second Party System* (1966). For an outstanding analysis of women in New York City during the Jacksonian period, see Christine Stansell's *City of Women: Sex and Class in New York, 1789–1860* (1986). In *Chants Democratic: New York City and the Rise of the American Working Class, 1788–1850* (1984), Sean Wilentz analyzes the social basis of working-class politics. The best biography of Jackson remains Robert V. Remini's three-volume work: *Andrew Jackson: The Course of American Empire, 1767–1821* (1977), *Andrew Jackson: The Course of American Freedom, 1822–1832* (1981), and *Andrew Jackson: The Course of American Democracy, 1833–1845* (1984). On Jackson's successor, consult John Niven's *Martin Van Buren: The Romantic Age of American Politics* (1983). Studies of other major figures of the period include John Niven's *John C. Calhoun and the Price of Union* (1988), Merrill Peterson's *The Great Triumvirate: Webster, Clay, and Calhoun* (1987), and

Robert Remini's *Henry Clay: Statesman for the Union* (1992) and *Daniel Webster: The Man and His Time* (1997).

The political philosophies of Jackson's opponents are treated in Michael Holt's *The Rise and Fall of the Whig Party* (1999) and Harry Watson's *Andrew Jackson versus Henry Clay* (1998).

Two studies of the impact of the Bank controversy are William G. Shade's *Banks or No Banks: The Money Question in the Western States, 1832–1865* (1972) and James R. Sharp's *The Jacksonians versus the Banks: Politics in the States after the Panic of 1837* (1970).

The outstanding book on the nullification issue remains William W. Freehling's *Prelude to Civil War: The Nullification Controversy in South Carolina, 1816–1836* (1966). John M. Belohlavek's *"Let the Eagle Soar!": The Foreign Policy of Andrew Jackson* (1985) is a thorough study of Jacksonian diplomacy. Ronald N. Satz's *American Indian Policy in the Jacksonian Era* (1974) surveys the relocation policy.

12   THE DYNAMICS OF GROWTH

CHAPTER ORGANIZER

This chapter focuses on:

- the expansion of agriculture, industry, and transportation.

- patterns of immigration at mid-century.

- the status of labor unions.

The Jacksonian-era political debate between democratic and elitist elements was rooted in a profound transformation of American social and economic life. Between 1815 and 1850, the United States expanded all the way to the Pacific coast. An industrial revolution in the Northeast began to reshape the contours of the economy and propel an unrelenting process of urbanization. In the West an agricultural empire began to emerge based upon the foundation of corn, wheat, and cattle. In the South cotton became king, and its reign came to depend on the expanding institution of slavery. At the same time, innovations in transportation—larger horse-drawn wagons called Conestogas, canals, steamboats, and railroads—conquered time and space and knit together a national market for goods and services. An economy based primarily on small-scale farming and local commerce matured into a far-flung capitalist marketplace entwined with world markets. These economic developments in turn generated changes in every other area of American life, from politics to the legal system, from the family to social values, from work to recreation.

AGRICULTURE AND THE NATIONAL ECONOMY

The first stage of industrialization brought with it an expansive commercial and urban outlook that by the end of the century would supplant the agrarian philosophy espoused by Thomas Jefferson and many others. "We are greatly, I was about to say fearfully, growing," John C. Calhoun told his congressional colleagues in 1816, and many other statesmen shared his ambivalent outlook. Would the republic retain its virtue and cohesion amid the turmoil of chaotic commercial development? In the brief period of good feelings after the War of 1812, however, such a troublesome question was easily brushed aside. Economic opportunities seemed available to Americans everywhere, and nowhere more than in Calhoun's native South Carolina. The reason was cotton, the new staple crop of the South, which was spreading from South Carolina and Georgia into the new lands of Mississippi, Alabama, Louisiana, and Arkansas.

COTTON   Cotton had been used from ancient times, but the industrial revolution and its spread of textile mills created a rapidly growing market for the fluffy fiber. Cotton had remained for many years rare and expensive because of the need for hand labor to separate the lint from the tenacious seeds. But by the mid-1780s in coastal Georgia and South Carolina a long-fiber Sea Island cotton was being grown commercially that could easily be separated from its shiny black seeds by squeezing it through rollers. Sea Island cotton, however, like the rice and indigo of the colonial Tidewater, was not suited to the soil and climate of the upcountry. And the green seed of the upland cotton clung to the lint so stubbornly that the rollers crushed the seed and spoiled the fiber. One person working all day could manage to separate barely a pound by hand. Cotton could not yet be king until a better way was found to separate the tenacious seeds from the fiber.

The rising cotton kingdom of the lower South was born at a plantation called Mulberry Hill in coastal Georgia, the home of Catharine Greene, widow of the Revolutionary War hero Nathanael Greene. At Mulberry

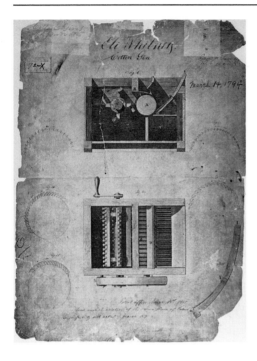

Eli Whitney's drawing of a cotton gin, which accompanied his 1794 federal patent application, shows the side and the top of the machine and the saw teeth that separate the seeds from the cotton fiber.

Hill, discussion often turned to the promising new crop and to speculation about better ways to remove the seeds. In 1792, on the way to a job as a tutor in South Carolina, young Eli Whitney, recently graduated from Yale, visited fellow graduate Phineas Miller, who was overseer at Mulberry Hill. Catharine Greene noticed her visitor's mechanical aptitude, which had been nurtured in boyhood by the needs of a Massachusetts farm. When she suggested that young Whitney devise a mechanism for removing the seed from upland cotton, he mulled it over and solved the problem in ten days. In the spring of 1793, his job as a tutor quickly forgotten, Whitney had a working model of a cotton gin (short for engine). With it one person could separate fifty times as much cotton as could be done by hand. The device was an "absurdly simple contrivance," too much so as it turned out. A simple description was all any skilled worker needed to make a copy, and by the time Whitney and Miller had secured a patent in 1794, a number of copies were already in use. As a consequence, the two men were never able to make good on the promise of riches that the gin offered, and spent most of their modest gains in expensive lawsuits.

Although Whitney realized little profit from his idea, he had unwittingly begun a revolution. Green-seed cotton first engulfed the up-country hills of

South Carolina and Georgia, and after the War of 1812 migrated into the former Creek, Choctaw, and Chickasaw lands to the west. Cotton production soared, and in the process planters found a new and profitable use for slavery. Planters migrated westward with their gangs of workers in tow, and a lucrative trade began to develop in the sale of slaves from the coastal South to the West. The cotton culture became a way of life that tied the Old Southwest to the coastal Southeast in a common interest.

Not the least of the cotton gin's revolutionary consequences, although less apparent at first, was that cotton became almost immediately a major export commodity. Cotton exports averaged about $9 million in value from 1803 to 1807, about 22 percent of the value of all exports; from 1815 to 1819 they averaged over $23 million, or 39 percent of the total; and from the mid-1830s to 1860 they accounted for more than half the value of all exports in the nation. The South supplied the North both raw materials and markets for manufactures. Income from the North's role in handling the cotton trade then provided surpluses for capital investment.

FARMING THE WEST   The westward flow of planters and their slaves to Alabama and Mississippi during these flush times mirrored another migration through the Ohio Valley and the Great Lakes region, where the Indians had been steadily pushed westward. "Old America seems to be breaking up and moving westward," an English traveler observed in 1817 as he watched the migrants make their way along westward roads in Pennsylvania. Family groups, stages, light wagons, and riders on horseback made up "a scene of bustle and business, extending over three hundred miles, which is truly wonderful." In 1800 some 387,000 settlers were counted west of the Atlantic states; by 1810, 1,338,000 lived over the mountains; by 1820, 2,419,000. By 1860 more than half the nation's population resided in trans-Appalachia, and the restless movement had long since spilled across the Mississippi and touched the shores of the Pacific.

North of the expanding cotton belt in the Gulf states, the fertile woodland soils, riverside bottom lands, and black loam of the prairies drew farmers from the rocky lands of New England and the exhausted soils of the Southeast. A new land law of 1820, passed after the Panic of 1819, eliminated the credit provisions of the 1800 act but reduced the minimum price from $1.64 to $1.25 per acre and the minimum plot from 160 to 80 acres. The settler could get a farm for as little as $100,

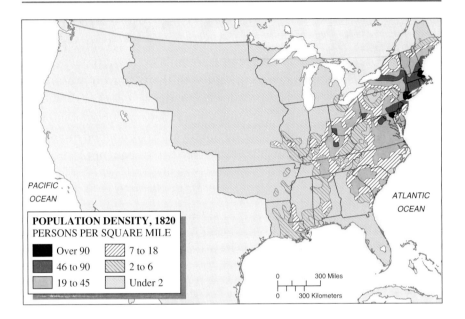

POPULATION DENSITY, 1820
PERSONS PER SQUARE MILE

- Over 90
- 46 to 90
- 19 to 45
- 7 to 18
- 2 to 6
- Under 2

PACIFIC OCEAN

ATLANTIC OCEAN

0   300 Miles

0   300 Kilometers

and over the years the proliferation of state banks made it possible to continue buying on credit. Even that was not enough for westerners, who began a long—and eventually victorious—agitation for further relaxation of the land laws. They favored preemption, the right of squatters to purchase land at the minimum price, and graduation, the progressive reduction of the price on lands that did not sell.

Congress eventually responded with two new land bills. Under the Preemption Act of 1830, a renewable law made permanent in the Preemption Act of 1841, squatters could stake out claims ahead of the land surveys and later get 160 acres at the minimum price of $1.25 per acre. In effect the law recognized a practice enforced more often than not by frontier vigilantes. Under the Graduation Act of 1854, which Senator Thomas Hart Benton had promoted since the 1820s, prices of unsold lands were to go down in stages until the lands could sell for 12½¢ per acre after thirty years.

The process of settling new lands followed the old pattern of clearing trees, grubbing out the stumps and underbrush, and settling down at first to a crude subsistence. The development of effective iron plows greatly eased the backbreaking job of breaking up the soil. As early as 1797 an American inventor had secured a patent on an iron plow, but a superstition that iron poisoned the soil prevented much use until after 1819,

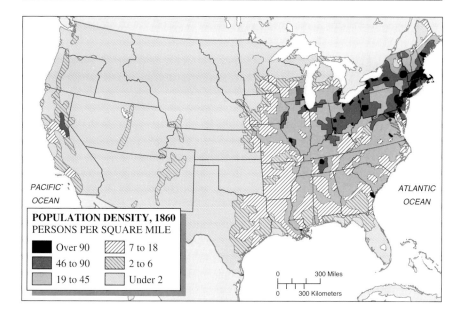

POPULATION DENSITY, 1860
PERSONS PER SQUARE MILE

- Over 90
- 46 to 90
- 19 to 45
- 7 to 18
- 2 to 6
- Under 2

PACIFIC
OCEAN

ATLANTIC
OCEAN

0   300 Miles

0   300 Kilometers

when Jethro Wood of New York developed an improved version with separate parts that could be replaced without buying a whole new plow. The
prejudice against iron suddenly vanished, and the demand for plows grew
so fast that Wood, like Whitney, could not supply the need and spent
much of his remaining fifteen years fighting against patent infringements.
The iron plow was a special godsend to those farmers who first ventured
into the sticky black loams of the treeless prairies of the Midwest. Further improvements would follow, including John Deere's steel plow
(1837) and the chilled-iron and steel plow of John Oliver (1855).

By the 1840s new mechanical seeders replaced the need to sow
seed by hand. Even more important, twenty-two-year-old Cyrus Hall
McCormick of Virginia invented a primitive grain reaper in 1831, a development as significant to the agricultural economy of the Old Northwest
as the cotton gin was to the South. After tinkering with his machine for
almost a decade, McCormick began selling them by the dozens. In
1847 he moved to Chicago, to be closer to the agricultural heartland,
and built a manufacturing plant for his reapers and mowers. Within a
few years he had sold thousands of new machines, transforming the
scale of American agriculture. Using a hand-operated sickle, a farmer
could harvest half an acre of wheat a day; with a McCormick reaper two
people could work twelve acres a day.

McCormick's Reaping Machine. *This illustration appeared in the catalogue of the Great Exhibition at the Crystal Palace in London, 1851. The plow eased the transformation of rough plains into fertile farm land, and the reaping machine accelerated farm production.*

McCormick's success attracted other manufacturers and inventors, and soon there were mechanical threshers to separate the grains of wheat from the straw. Farming remained, as it still is, a precarious vocation, subject to the whims of climate, the assault of insects, and the fluctuations of foreign markets, but by the 1850s it had become a major commercial activity. As the volume of agricultural products soared, prices dropped, income rose, and the standard of living for many farm families in the Old Northwest improved.

Transportation and the National Economy

NEW ROADS   Transportation improvements helped spur the development of a national market. As settlers moved west, there developed a stronger demand for better roads. In 1795 the Wilderness Road, along the trail blazed by Daniel Boone twenty years before, was opened to covered-wagon and stagecoach traffic, thereby easing the route through the Cumberland Gap into Kentucky and along the Knoxville and Old Walton Roads, completed the same year, into Tennessee. Even so, travel was difficult at best. Stagecoaches crammed with as many as a dozen people crept along at four miles per hour. One early stage rider said he alternately walked and rode and "though the pain of riding exceeded the fatigue of walking, yet . . . it refreshed us by varying the weariness of our bodies." South of these roads there were no such major highways. South Carolinians and Georgians pushed westward on whatever trails or rutted roads had appeared.

To the northeast a movement for graded and paved roads (macadamized with crushed stones packed down) gathered momentum after completion of the Philadelphia-Lancaster Turnpike in 1794 (the term derives from a pole or pike at the tollgate, turned to admit the traffic). By 1821 some 4,000 miles of turnpikes had been completed, mainly connecting eastern cities. Western traffic moved along the Frederick Turnpike to Cumberland and thence along the National Road, to Wheeling on the Ohio River in 1818, then to Columbus in the Northwest Territory and on to Vandalia, Illinois, by about mid-century. This 600-mile road passed through an eighty-foot-wide clearing. The road itself was twenty feet wide.

WATER TRANSPORT   Once turnpike travelers had reached the Ohio River, they could float westward in comparative comfort. At Pittsburgh, Wheeling, and other points the emigrants could buy flatboats. At the destination the boat could be used again or sold for lumber. In the early 1820s an estimated 3,000 flatboats went down the Ohio every year, and

Steamers at the levee at St. Paul, Minnesota, 1859.

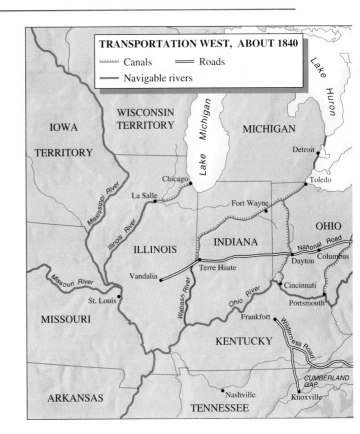

TRANSPORTATION WEST, ABOUT 1840

for many years after that the flatboat remained the chief conveyance for heavy traffic downstream.

By the early 1820s the turnpike boom was giving way to new developments in water transportation: the river steamboat and the canal barge, which carried bulk commodities far more cheaply than did covered wagons on the National Road. As early as 1787 one inventor had launched a steamboat on the Delaware River, but no commercially successful steamboat appeared until Robert Fulton and Robert R. Livingston sent the *Clermont* up the Hudson River to Albany in 1807. Thereafter, the use of the steamboat spread rapidly to other eastern rivers and to the Ohio and Mississippi, opening nearly half a continent to water traffic.

By 1836, 361 steamboats navigated the western waters, reaching ever farther up the tributaries that connected to the Mississippi. By the 1840s, shallow-draft, steam-powered ships that traveled *on* rather than *in* the water became the basis of the rivermen's boast that the boats

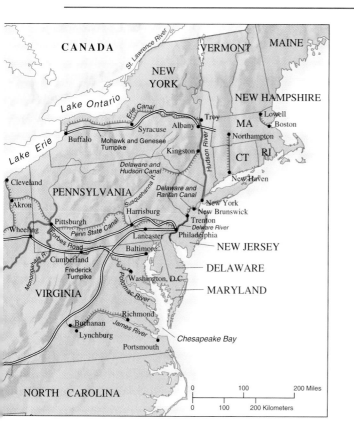

were "so built that when the river is low and the sandbars come out for air, the first mate can tap a keg of beer and run the boat four miles on the suds." These boats ventured into far reaches of the Mississippi River Valley, up such rivers as the Wabash, the Monongahela, the Cumberland, the Tennessee, the Missouri, and the Arkansas.

The durable flatboat, however, still carried to market most of the western wheat, corn, flour, meal, bacon, ham, pork, whiskey, soap and candles (the byproducts of slaughterhouses), lead from Missouri, copper from Michigan, wood from the Rockies, and ironwork from Pittsburgh. But the steamboat, by bringing two-way traffic to the Mississippi River Valley, created a continental market and an agricultural empire that became the new breadbasket of America. Farming became even more a commercial activity producing surpluses for the livestock and commodities markets. Along with the new farmers came promoters, speculators, and land boomers. Villages at strategic trading points along the streams evolved into centers of commerce and urban life. The port of New Orleans grew in the 1830s and 1840s to lead all others in exports.

But by then the Erie Canal was drawing eastward much of the trade that once went down to the Gulf, and this would have major economic and political consequences, tying together the West and East while further isolating the Deep South. In 1817 the New York legislature endorsed Governor De Witt Clinton's dream of connecting the Hudson River with Lake Erie. Eight years later, in 1825, the canal was open for its entire 360 miles from Albany to Buffalo; branches soon put most of the state within reach of the canal.

The Erie Canal was an engineering marvel. The longest canal in the world, it traversed rivers and valleys, forests and marshes. It reduced travel time from New York City to Buffalo from twenty days to six, and the cost of moving a ton of freight plummeted from $100 to $5. After 1828 the Delaware and Hudson Canal linked New York with the anthracite fields of northeastern Pennsylvania. The speedy success of the New York system inspired a mania for canals that lasted more than a decade and resulted in the completion of about 3,000 miles of waterways

Junction of the Erie and Northern Canals, *an aquatint by John Hill, 1830–1832.*

by 1837. But no canal ever matched the spectacular success of the Erie, which rendered the entire Great Lakes region an economic tributary to the port of New York. With the further development of canals spanning Ohio and Indiana from north to south, much of the upper Ohio River Valley also came within the economic sphere of New York.

RAILROADS   The Panic of 1837 and the subsequent depression cooled the canal fever. Some states that had borrowed heavily to finance canals had to repudiate their debts. The holders of repudiated bonds had no recourse. Meanwhile, a new and more versatile form of transportation was gaining on the canal: the railroad. Vehicles that ran on iron rails had long been in use, especially in mining, but now came a tremendous innovation—the use of steam power—as the steam locomotive followed soon after the steamboat. As early as 1814 the first practical steam locomotive was built in England. In 1825, the year the Erie Canal was completed, the world's first commercial steam railway began operations in England. By the 1820s the port cities of Baltimore, Charleston, and Boston were alive with schemes to connect the hinterlands by rail.

On July 4, 1828, Baltimore got the jump on other cities when Charles Carroll, the last surviving signer of the Declaration of Independence, laid the first stone in the roadbed of the Baltimore and Ohio (B&O) Railroad. Four years later the roadbed reached seventy-three miles west of Baltimore. By 1840 the railroads, with a total of 3,328 miles, had outdistanced the canals by just two miles. Over the next twenty years, though, railroads grew nearly tenfold to cover 30,626 miles; more than two-thirds of this total was built in the 1850s.

The railroad was responsible for a tremendous increase in the size of American cities. Rail lines were laid out to connect cities with one another; the small towns and villages were bypassed. By 1853 New York had connections all the way to Chicago, and in two years to St. Louis. Farther south, the rail network still had many gaps in 1860. By 1857 Charleston, Savannah, and Norfolk connected by way of lines into Chattanooga and thence along a single line to Memphis, the only southern route that connected the east coast and the Mississippi River.

Travel on the early railroads was a risky venture. Iron straps on top of wooden rails, for instance, tended to work loose and curl up into "snakesheads" that sometimes pierced railway coaches. Wood was used

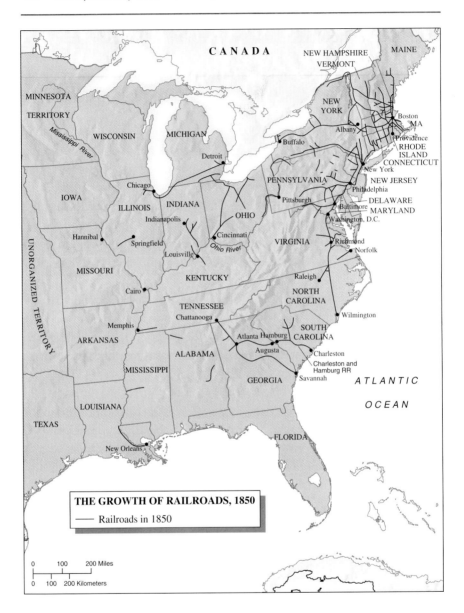

THE GROWTH OF RAILROADS, 1850

— Railroads in 1850

for fuel, and the sparks often caused fires along the way or damaged passengers' clothing. Land travel, whether by stagecoach or train, was a jerky, bumpy, wearying ordeal.

Water travel, where available, offered far more comfort, but railroads gained supremacy over other forms of transport because of their economy, speed, and reliability. They averaged ten miles per hour, more than twice

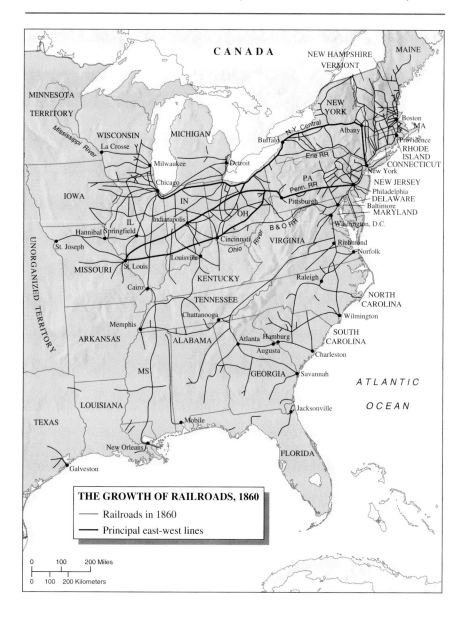

THE GROWTH OF RAILROADS, 1860

— Railroads in 1860

— Principal east-west lines

0   100   200 Miles

0   100   200 Kilometers

as fast as stagecoaches and four times as fast as water travel. By 1859, railroads had reduced the cost of transportation services by $150 million to $175 million, accounting for a saving that amounted to some 4 percent of the gross national product. By 1890, the saving would increase to almost 15 percent. Railroads provided indirect benefits by encouraging new settlement and the expansion of farming. During the antebellum period, the reduced costs brought on by the railroads aided the expansion of farming more than manufacturing, since manufacturers in the Northeast, especially New England, had better access to water transportation. The railroads' demand for iron and equipment of various kinds, however, did provide an enormous market for the industries that made these capital goods. And the ability of railroads to operate year round in all kinds of weather gave them an advantage in carrying finished goods, too.

OCEAN TRANSPORT   For oceangoing traffic, the start of service on regular schedules was the most important change of the early 1800s. In the first week of 1818 ships of the Black Ball Line inaugurated weekly transatlantic service between New York and Liverpool. Beginning with four ships in all, the Black Ball Line thereafter had one ship leaving each port monthly at an announced time. With the economic recovery in 1822, the packet business grew in a rush. By 1845 some fifty-two transatlantic shipping lines were based in New York City, with three regular sailings per week. Many others ran in the coastwise trade, to Charleston, Savannah, New Orleans, and elsewhere.

The same year, 1845, witnessed a great innovation with the launching of the first clipper ship, the *Rainbow*. Built for speed, the sleek clippers were the nineteenth-century equivalent of the supersonic jetliner. They doubled the speed of the older merchant vessels, and trading companies rushed to purchase them. Long and lean, with taller masts and more sails, they cut dashing figures during their brief but colorful career, which lasted less than two decades. What provoked the clipper boom was the lure of Chinese tea, a drink long coveted in America but in scarce supply. The tea leaves were a perishable commodity that had to reach market quickly, and the new clipper ships made this possible. Even more important, the discovery of California gold in 1848 lured thousands of prospectors and entrepreneurs from the Atlantic seaboard. These new settlers generated an urgent demand for goods, and the clippers met the need. In 1854 the *Flying Cloud* took eighty-nine days and eight hours to make the distance from New York to San Francisco. But clippers, while fast, lacked ample cargo space, and after the Civil War they would give way to the steamship.

THE ROLE OF GOVERNMENT   The dramatic transportation improvements of the antebellum era were the product of both state government

Clipper ship at the New York docks, 1840s.

and private initiatives, sometimes undertaken jointly and sometimes separately. After the Panic of 1837, however, the states left railroad development mainly to private corporations. Still, several southern and western states built their own lines, and most states granted generous tax concessions to railroad companies.

The federal government helped too, despite the constitutional scruples of some against direct involvement in internal improvements. The government bought stock in turnpike and canal companies, and after the success of the Erie Canal, extended land grants to several western states for the support of canal projects. Congress provided for railroad surveys by government engineers, and reduced the tariff duties on iron used in railroad construction. In 1850 Senator Stephen A. Douglas of Illinois and others prevailed on Congress to extend a major land grant to support a north-south line connecting Chicago with Mobile, Alabama. Grants of three square miles for each mile of railroad subsidized the building of the Illinois Central and the Mobile and Ohio Railroads. Regarded at the time as a special case, the 1850 grant set a precedent for other bounties that totaled about 20 million acres by 1860—a small amount compared to the grants for transcontinental lines in the Civil War decade.

A COMMUNICATIONS REVOLUTION

During the first half of the nineteenth century, the transportation revolution helped spark dramatic improvements in communications across the expanding nation. At the beginning of the century, it took days—often weeks—for news to travel along the Atlantic seaboard. For example, after George Washington died in 1799 in Arlington, Virginia, the news of his death did not appear in New York City newspapers until a week later. Naturally, news took even longer to travel to and from Europe. On December 24, 1814, the United States and Great Britain met in Belgium to sign the peace treaty ending the War of 1812. Yet two weeks later, on January 8, 1815, the Battle of New Orleans occurred. Both armies were oblivious to the cease-fire that had already been declared. It took forty-nine days for news of the peace treaty to reach New York City from Europe.

The speed of communications accelerated greatly as the nineteenth century unfolded. The construction of turnpikes, canals, and railroads, and the development of steamships and the telegraph generated a communications revolution. By 1829 it was possible to "convey" Andrew Jackson's inaugural address from Washington, D.C., to New York City in sixteen hours. It took six days to reach New Orleans. Mail began to be delivered by "express," a system in which riders could get fresh horses at a sequence of relay stations. Still, even with such advances, the states and territories west of the Appalachian Mountains struggled to get timely deliveries and news.

TECHNOLOGY IN AMERICA   Americans became famous for their "practical" inventiveness. In 1814 Dr. Jacob Bigelow, a Harvard botanist, began to lecture on "The Elements of Technology," a word he did much to popularize. In his book of the same title he argued that technology constituted the chief superiority of moderns over the ancients, effecting profound changes in ways of living.

One of the most striking examples of the connection between pure research and innovation was in the work of Joseph Henry, a Princeton physicist. His research in electromagnetism provided the basis for Samuel F. B. Morse's invention of the telegraph and for electrical motors later on. In 1846 Henry became head of the new Smithsonian Institution, founded with a bequest from the Englishman James

Smithson "for the increase and diffusion of knowledge." The year 1846 also saw the founding of the American Association for the Advancement of Science.

It would be difficult to exaggerate the importance of science and technology in changing the ways people live and work. All aspects of life—the social, cultural, economic, and political—were and are shaped by it. To cite but a few examples: improved transportation and a spreading market economy combined with innovations in canning and refrigeration to provide people a more healthy and varied diet. Fruit and vegetables, heretofore available only during harvest season, could be shipped in much of the year. Scientific breeding of cattle helped make meat and milk more abundant.

Technological advances also helped improve living conditions: houses were larger, better heated, and better illuminated. Although working-class residences had few creature comforts, the affluent were able to afford indoor plumbing, central heating, gas lighting, bathtubs, iceboxes, and sewing machines. Even the lower classes were able to afford new coal-burning cast-iron cooking stoves that facilitated the preparation of more varied meals and improved heating. The first sewer systems began to help rid city streets of human and animal waste, while underground water lines enabled fire companies to use hydrants rather than bucket brigades. Machine-made clothes fit better and were cheaper than homespun; newspapers and magazines were more abundant and afford-able, as were clocks and watches. Invention often brought about com-pletely new enterprises, the steamboat and the railroad being the most spectacular, without which the pace of development would have been slowed immeasurably.

A spate of inventions in the 1840s generated dramatic changes in American life. In 1844 Charles Goodyear patented a process for vul-canizing rubber, which made it stronger and more elastic. In 1846 Elias Howe invented the sewing machine, soon improved by Isaac Merritt Singer. The sewing machine, incidentally, actually slowed the progress of the factory. Since it was adapted to use in the home, it gave the "putting-out" system a new lease on life in the clothing industry.

In 1844 the first intercity telegraph message was transmitted from Baltimore to Washington on the device Samuel Morse had invented back in 1832. The telegraph may have triggered more social changes than any other invention. Until it appeared, communications were conveyed by boat, train, horseback, or on foot. With the telegraph, people could learn of events and exchange messages instantaneously. The telegraph was slow to catch on at first, but by the mid-1850s the American Telegraph Company and the Western Union Company had consolidated national networks. In 1861, seventeen years after the first demonstration, connections were completed to San Francisco, and an entire continent had been wired for instant communication.

The Growth of Industry

While the South and West developed the agricultural basis for a national economy, the Northeast was engineering an industrial revolution. Technology in the form of the cotton gin, the harvester, and improvements in transportation had quickened agricultural development and to some extent decided its direction. But technology altered the economic landscape even more profoundly by giving rise to the factory system.

EARLY TEXTILE MANUFACTURES   At the end of the colonial period, manufacturing remained in the household or handicraft stage of development, or at most the "putting-out" stage, in which the merchant capitalist would distribute raw materials (say, leather patterns for shoes) to be worked up at home, then collected and sold. Farm families themselves had to produce much of what they needed in the way of crude implements, shoes, and clothing, and in their simple workshops inventive genius was sometimes nurtured. The transition from such home production to the factory was slow, but one for which a base had been laid before 1815.

In the eighteenth century Great Britain had jumped out to a long head start in industrial production. The foundations of Britain's advantage were the invention of the steam engine in 1705 and its improvement by James Watt in 1765; and a series of inventions that mechanized the production of textiles. Britain carefully guarded its hard-won secrets, forbidding the export of machines or descriptions of them, even restricting the departure of informed mechanics. But the secrets could not be kept. In 1789 Samuel Slater arrived in America from England with the plan of a water-powered spinning machine in his head. He contracted with an enterprising merchant-manufacturer in Rhode Island to

New England Factory Village, *1830. Mills and factories gradually transformed the New England landscape in the early nineteenth century.*

build a mill in Pawtucket, and in this little mill, completed in 1790, nine children turned out a satisfactory cotton yarn, which was then worked up by the putting-out system.

The progress of textile production was slow and faltering until Thomas Jefferson's embargo in 1807 stimulated domestic production. Policies adopted during the War of 1812 restricted imports and encouraged the merchant capitalists of New England to switch their resources into manufacturing. New England, it happened, had the distinct advantage of its many rivers that provided waterpower and water transportation. By 1815 textile mills numbered in the hundreds. A flood of British imports after the War of 1812 dealt a temporary setback to the infant industry, but the foundations of textile manufacture were laid, and they spurred the growth of garment trades and a machine-tool industry to build and service the mills.

THE LOWELL SYSTEM The factory system sprang full-blown upon the American scene at Waltham, Massachusetts, in 1813, in the plant of the Boston Manufacturing Company, formed by the Boston Associates, including Francis Cabot Lowell. Their plant was the first factory in

Merrimack Mills and Boarding Houses, *1848, in Lowell, Massachusetts.*

which the processes of spinning and weaving by power machinery were brought under one roof, mechanizing every process—from raw material to finished cloth. In 1822 the Boston Associates developed a new water-powered center at a village, renamed Lowell, along the Merrimack River. At this "Manchester of America" the Merrimack Manufacturing Company developed a new plant similar to the Waltham mill. Companies organized on the Waltham plan produced by 1850 a fifth of the nation's total output of cotton cloth. The chief features of this plan were large capital investment, the concentration of all processes in one plant under unified management, and specialization in a relatively coarse cloth requiring minimal skill by the workers.

The founders of the enterprise sought to establish at Lowell an industrial center compatible with republican values of plain living and high thinking. During the early decades of the nineteenth century, Thomas Jefferson and others had claimed that urban-industrial development threatened a republican form of government rooted in self-reliant agrarianism. Sensitive to this view, Lowell's owners insisted that they could design model, red-brick factory centers and communities that would strengthen rather than corrupt the social fabric. To avoid the drab, crowded, and wretched life of English mill villages, they located American mills in the countryside and established an ambitious program of paternal supervision for the workers.

The operators in the Lowell factories were mostly young women from New England farm families. Employers preferred women because of their dexterity in operating machines and their willingness to work for wages lower than those paid to men. Moreover, by the 1820s there was a surplus of females in the region because so many men had migrated westward in search of cheap land and new economic opportunities. As many of the household goods produced by daughters gave way to the "store-bought" goods of a market economy, young farm women faced diminishing prospects for employment as well as for marriage. The chance to escape the routine of farm life and to earn cash money to help the family or improve their own circumstances also drew many women workers to the Lowell mills. As one female mill worker explained, she was working because of "a father's debts . . . to be paid, an aged mother to be supported, a brother's ambition to be aided."

In the early 1820s a steady stream of single women began flocking toward Lowell and the other mill towns cropping up across the region. To reassure worried parents, the mill owners promised to provide the "Lowell girls" with tolerable work, prepared meals, secure and comfortable boardinghouses, moral discipline, and a variety of educational and cultural opportunities.

Initially the "Lowell idea" worked pretty much according to plan. Visitors commented on the well-designed mills with their lecture halls and libraries. The laborers appeared "healthy and happy." The women workers lived in dormitories staffed by matronly supervisors who enforced mandatory church attendance, temperance regulations, and curfews. Despite their thirteen-hour day and six-day workweek tending the knitting looms, some of the women found the time and energy to form study groups, publish a literary magazine, and attend lectures by Ralph Waldo Emerson and other luminaries of the era. But Lowell soon lost its innocence as it experienced mushrooming growth. By 1840 there were thirty-two mills and factories in operation, and the blissful rural town had become a bustling, grimy, bleak industrial city.

Other factory centers began sprouting up across New England, displacing forests and farms and engulfing villages, filling the air with smoke, noise, and stench. Between 1820 and 1840 the number of Americans

Women Workers inside a Textile Mill. *Although mill work once provided women with an opportunity for independence and education, conditions soon deteriorated as profits took precedence over the workers.*

engaged in manufactures increased eightfold, and the number of city dwellers more than doubled. Booming growth transformed the Lowell experiment in industrial republicanism. By 1846 a concerned worker told those young farm women thinking about taking a job in a factory that they would do well not to leave their "homes in the country. It will be better for you to stay at home on your fathers' farms than to run the risk of being ruined in a manufacturing village."

During the 1830s, as textile prices and mill wages dropped, relations between workers and managers deteriorated. A new generation of owners and foremen began stressing efficiency and profit margins over community values. They worked people and machines at a faster pace. The women organized strikes to protest deteriorating working conditions. In 1834, for instance, they unsuccessfully "turned out" (struck) against the mills after learning of a sharp cut in their wages.

The "Lowell girls" drew attention less because they were typical than because they were special. An increasingly common pattern for industry was the family system, sometimes called the Rhode Island or Fall River system, which prevailed in textile companies outside of northern New England. The Rhode Island factories, which relied on waterpower, often were built in unpopulated areas, and part of their construction included tenements or mill villages. Whole families might be hired, the men for heavy labor, the women and children for the lighter work. Like the Lowell model, the Rhode Island system promoted paternalism. Employers dominated the life of the mill villages. The employees worked from sunup to sunset, and longer in winter—a sixty-eight- to seventy-two-hour week. Such hours were common on the farms of the time, but in textile mills the work was more intense and offered no seasonal letup.

INDUSTRY AND CITIES The rapid growth of commerce and industry spurred a rapid growth of cities. Using the census definition of "urban" as places with 8,000 inhabitants or more, the proportion of urban population grew from 3 percent in 1790 to 16 percent in 1860. Because of their strategic locations, the four great Atlantic seaports of New York, Philadelphia, Baltimore, and Boston remained the largest cities. New Orleans became the nation's fifth-largest city from the time of the Louisiana Purchase. Its focus on cotton exports, to the neglect of imports, however, eventually caused it to lag behind its eastern competitors. New York outpaced all its competitors and the nation as a whole in its population growth. By 1860 it was the first American city to reach a

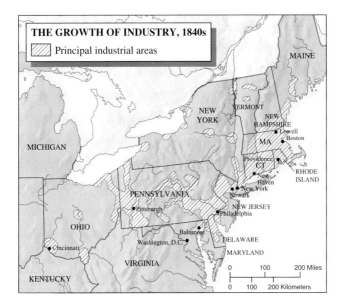

THE GROWTH OF INDUSTRY, 1840s
Principal industrial areas

Broadway and Canal Street, New York City, 1836. *New York's economy and industry and those of many cities rapidly grew before the 1840s.*

population of more than a million, largely because of its superior harbor and its unique access to commerce.

Pittsburgh, at the head of the Ohio River, was already a center of iron production by 1800, and Cincinnati, at the mouth of the Little Miami River, soon surpassed all other meatpacking centers. Louisville, because it stood at the falls of the Ohio River, became an important trading center and remained so after the short Louisville and Portland Canal bypassed the falls in 1830. On the Great Lakes the leading cities also stood at important breaking points in water transportation: Buffalo, Cleveland, Detroit, Chicago, and Milwaukee. Chicago was well located to become a hub of both water and rail transportation on into the trans-Mississippi West. During the 1830s St. Louis tripled in size mainly because most of the trans-Mississippi fur trade was funneled down the Missouri River. By 1860 St. Louis and Chicago were positioned to challenge Boston and Baltimore for third and fourth places.

Before 1840 commerce dominated the activities of major cities, but early industry often created new concentrations of population at places convenient to waterpower or raw materials. During the 1840s and 1850s, however, the stationary steam engine and declining transportation costs offset the advantages of locations near waterpower and resources, and the attractions of older cities were enhanced: pools of experienced labor,

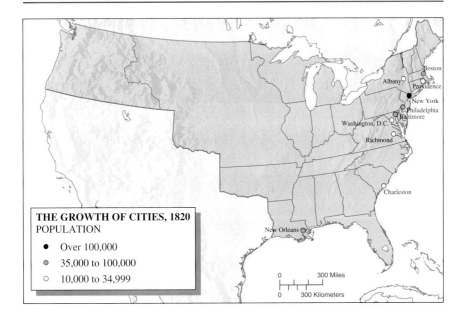

THE GROWTH OF CITIES, 1820
POPULATION
- ● Over 100,000
- ◉ 35,000 to 100,000
- ○ 10,000 to 34,999

capital, warehousing and trading services, access to information, the savings of bulk purchasing and handling, and the many amenities of city life. Urbanization thus was both a consequence of economic growth and a positive force in its promotion.

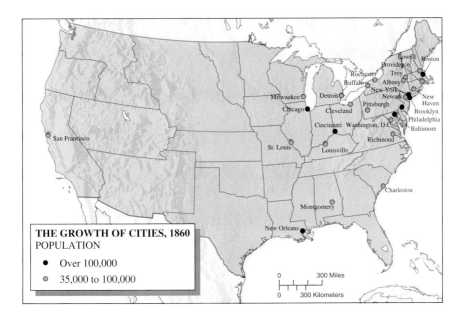

THE GROWTH OF CITIES, 1860
POPULATION
- ● Over 100,000
- ◉ 35,000 to 100,000

THE POPULAR CULTURE

During the colonial era, Americans had little time for play or amusement. Their priority was sheer survival, and most worked from dawn to dusk, six days a week. In rural areas free time was often spent in communal activities such as barn raisings and corn-husking parties, shooting matches and foot races, while on the seacoast people sailed and fished. In colonial cities people attended balls, sleigh rides, picnics, and played "parlor games" at home—billiards, cards, and chess.

By the early nineteenth century, however, a more urban society could indulge in more diverse forms of recreation. As more people moved into cities in the first half of the nineteenth century, they began to create a distinctive urban culture. Laborers and shopkeepers sought new forms of leisure and entertainment as pleasant diversions from their long workdays.

URBAN RECREATION   Social drinking was pervasive during the first half of the nineteenth century. In 1829 the secretary of war estimated that three-quarters of the nation's laborers drank at least four ounces of "hard liquor" daily. The drinking of distilled spirits highlighted virtually every social event or public occasion. Barn raisings, corn huskings, quilting parties, militia musters, church socials, court sessions, holidays, and political gatherings all featured liquor, cider, or beer.

This drinking culture cut across all regions, races, and classes. Among the lustiest drinkers were stage drivers, trappers, lumberjacks, riverboatmen, and canal builders—restless, rootless men who lived alone in unstructured settings. The thousands of laborers engaged in the construction of canals and railroads, mines and factories, lived in crude shelters for a few weeks or months and then moved on to the next work site. For these transient workers, social drinking was a means of passing the time in places where they had no family, friends, or other roots. College students were also notoriously heavy imbibers. One Dartmouth student told the college president "that the least quantity he would put up with . . . was from two to three pints daily." Part of the appeal of alcoholic beverages was their relatively low cost when compared to tea, coffee, or milk. Water was frowned upon because it offered no "food value." Whatever the reason, alcoholic beverages had become by the 1830s the primary social lubricant. Taverns and social or sporting

Bare Knuckles. *Blood sports emerged as popular entertainment in the cities for men of all social classes.*

clubs in the burgeoning cities served as the nexus of recreation and leisure.

So-called blood sports were also a popular form of amusement. Cockfighting and dogfighting at saloons attracted excited crowds and frenzied betting. Prizefighting (also known as boxing) eventually displaced the animal contests. Imported from Britain, boxing proved popular with all social classes. The early contestants tended to be Irish or English immigrants, often sponsored by a neighborhood fire company, fraternal association, or street gang.

In the antebellum era, boxers fought with bare knuckles, and the results were brutal. A match ended only when a contestant could not continue. One such bout in 1842 lasted 119 rounds and ended when one fighter died in his corner. Such deaths prompted clergymen to condemn prizefighting, and several cities outlawed the practice, only to see it reappear as an underground activity.

THE PERFORMING ARTS   The most popular form of indoor entertainment was the theater. During the first half of the nineteenth century, people of all classes flocked to opera houses and theaters to watch a wide spectrum of performances: Shakespeare's tragedies, "blood and thunder" melodramas, comedies, minstrels, operas, magic shows, acrobatic troupes, and local pageants.

The audiences were predominantly young and middle-aged men. "Respectable" women rarely attended because of the boisterous atmosphere and the prevailing cult of domesticity that kept women in the home. Behavior in antebellum theaters was raucous and at times disorderly. Patrons were participants as well as spectators. Audiences cheered the heroes and heroines and hissed the villains. If an actor did not meet expectations, audiences would hurl curses, nuts, eggs, fruit, shoes, or chairs.

MINSTREL SHOWS   The 1830s witnessed the emergence of the first uniquely American form of mass entertainment: the blackface minstrel show. Rooted in an old tradition of folk theatricals, the minstrel shows featured white performers made up as blacks. "Minstrelsy" drew upon African-American subjects and reinforced prevailing racial stereotypes. It featured banjo and fiddle music, "shuffle" dances, and low-brow humor. Between the 1830s and 1870s, the minstrel shows were immensely popular throughout the nation, especially among northern working-class ethnics and southern whites.

The two most famous minstrel performers were George Washington Dixon, who invented a character named "Zip Coon," and Thomas "Daddy" Rice, who popularized a song-and-dance routine called "Jump Jim Crow." Wearing ragged clothes, Rice would perform a shuffle dance while singing, "I jump 'jis so / An' ev'y time I turn about I jump Jim Crow." Rice claimed that the inspiration for his act was an old Louisville slave belonging to Jim Crow whom he saw entertaining other workers at a livery stable.

The most popular minstrel songs were written by a young composer named Stephen Foster. Born in Pittsburgh on July 4, 1826, Foster was a self-taught musician who could pick up any tune by ear. In 1846 he composed a song named "Oh! Susanna." It immediately became a national favorite, and by 1849 there were fifteen different editions of the sheet music in print. The popularity of "Oh! Susanna" catapulted Foster into the national limelight, and he followed it with equally popular tunes such as "Massa's in de Cold, Cold Ground," "Old Folks at Home" (popularly known as "Way Down upon the Suwannee River"), "Old Black Joe," and "My Old Kentucky Home," all of which perpetuated the sentimental myth of contented slaves, and none of which used actual African-American melodies.

Minstrel Show at the American Theater in New York City, 1833. *Thomas "Daddy" Rice performing in blackface as Jim Crow imitated African-American songs and dances. Minstrel shows enjoyed national popularity but reinforced racial stereotypes.*

Although antebellum minstrel shows usually portrayed slaves as loyal and happy and caricatured free blacks in the North as superstitious buffoons who preferred slavery to freedom, minstrelsy represented more than an expression of virulent racism and white exploitation of black culture; it also provided a medium for the expression of authentic African-American forms of dance and music.

IMMIGRATION

Throughout the nineteenth century, land in America remained plentiful and relatively cheap, while labor was scarce and relatively dear. The United States thus remained a strong magnet for immigrants, offering them chances to take up farms in the country or jobs in the cities. Glowing reports from early arrivals who made good reinforced romantic views of American opportunity and freedom. "Tell Miriam," one immigrant wrote back, "there is no sending children to bed without supper, or husbands to work without dinner in their bags." A German immigrant in Missouri applauded America's "absence of overbearing soldiers, haughty clergymen, and inquisitive tax collectors." In 1834 an English immigrant reported that America is ideal "for a poor man that is industrious, for he has to want for nothing."

During the forty years from the outbreak of the Revolution until the end of the War of 1812, immigration had slowed to a trickle. The French Revolution and the Napoleonic Wars restricted travel from Europe until 1815. Thereafter, however, the numbers of new arrivals rose steadily: 10,199 in 1825; 23,322 in 1830; 84,066 in 1840. After 1845 the tempo picked up rapidly. During the 1830s, total arrivals had numbered fewer than 600,000. In the 1840s almost three times as many, or 1.7 million, emigrated, and during the 1850s 2.6 million more came. The years from 1845 to 1854 saw the greatest proportionate influx of immigrants in American history, 2.4 million, or about 14.5 percent of the total population in 1845.

During the early 1800s most European immigrants entered the United States through the Port of New York. As many as forty ships a day would discharge passengers at wharves, and the newcomers would immediately have to fend for themselves in their alien environment. Before long, thieves, thugs, and wily con men began preying upon the new arrivals. The infectious diseases that many of the immigrants brought with them also aroused popular concern. In 1855 the problems associated with the immigrants' arrival in America provoked the New York state legislature to lease Castle Garden, at the southern tip of Manhattan, for use as an immigration receiving center. Inside the depot, clerks would record the names, nationalities, and destinations of the new arrivals, physicians would give them a cursory physical exam, and labor bureau representatives would assist them in seeking jobs.

THE IRISH   In 1860 America's population was 31 million, with more than one of every eight foreign-born. The largest groups among them were 1.6 million Irish, 1.2 million Germans, and 588,000 British (mostly English). What caused so many Irish to flee their homeland in the nineteenth century was the onset of a prolonged depression that brought immense social hardship. The most densely populated country in Europe, Ireland was so ravaged by the economic collapse that in rural areas the average age at death declined to nineteen.

After an epidemic of potato rot in 1845 brought famine to rural Ireland that killed more than a million peasants, the flow of Irish immigrants to

Canada and the United States rose to a flood. Buoyed by the promise of a better life in America, the immigrants braved the Atlantic crossing in crowded and unsanitary conditions. Thousands died of dysentery, typhus, and malnutrition during the six-week ocean crossing on what came to be called "coffin ships." In 1847 alone, 40,000 Irish perished at sea.

In 1847 Irish arrivals in America numbered above 100,000, and Irish immigration stayed above that level for eight years, reaching a peak of 221,000 in 1851. By 1850 the Irish constituted 43 percent of the foreign-born population in the United States. Unlike the German immigrants, who were predominantly male, the Irish newcomers were more evenly apportioned by sex; in fact a slight majority of them were women, most of them single young adults. Most of the Irish arrivals had been tenant farmers, but their rural sufferings left them little taste for farm work and little money to buy land in America. Great numbers of the men hired on with construction gangs building the canals and railways. Others worked in iron foundries, steel mills, warehouses, and shipyards. Many Irish women found jobs as domestic servants, laundresses, or textile mill workers in New England. In 1845 the Irish constituted only 8 percent of the workforce in the Lowell mills; by 1860 they made up 50 percent. Although there were substantial Irish communities in New Orleans, Vicksburg, and Memphis, relatively few immigrants during the Jacksonian era found their way into the South, where land was expensive and industries scarce. The widespread use of slaves also left few opportunities in the region for free manual laborers.

Too poor to move inland, most of the destitute Irish congregated in the eastern cities, in or near their port of entry. By the 1850s the Irish made up over half the populations of Boston and New York City, and they were almost as prominent in Philadelphia. Irish newcomers crowded into filthy, poorly ventilated tenements, plagued by high rates of crime, infectious disease, prostitution, alcoholism, and infant mortality. The archbishop of New York City at mid-century described the Irish as "the poorest and most wretched population that can be found in the world."

But many enterprising Irish immigrants forged remarkable success stories. Twenty years after arriving in New York, Alexander T. Stewart became the owner of America's largest department store and thereafter accumulated vast real-estate holdings in Manhattan. Michael Cudahy, who began work in a Milwaukee meatpacking business at age fourteen,

In 1847, nearly 214,000 Irish emigrated to the United States and Canada aboard ships of the White Star Line and other companies. Thirty percent of these immigrants died on board, despite company promises of "unusually spacious, well lighted, ventilated, and warmed" steerage accommodations.

became head of the Cudahy Packing Company and developed the process for the summer curing of meats under refrigeration. Dublin-born Victor Herbert emerged as one of America's most revered composers, and Irish dancers and playwrights came to dominate the American stage. Irishmen were equally successful in the boxing arena and on the baseball diamond.

These accomplishments did little to quell the acute anti-Irish sentiments prevalent in nineteenth-century America. Irish immigrants confronted demeaning stereotypes and intense anti-Catholic prejudices. The Irish were stereotyped as ignorant, filthy, clannish folk incapable of assimilation. Many employers posted "No Irish Need Apply" signs. But Irish Americans could be equally contemptuous of other groups, such as free African Americans who competed with them for low-status jobs. In 1850 the *New York Tribune* expressed concern that the Irish, having themselves escaped from "a galling, degrading bondage" in their homeland, typically voted against any proposal for equal rights for the Negro and frequently arrived at the polls shouting, "Down with the Nagurs! Let them go back to Africa, where they belong." For their part, many African Americans viewed the Irish with equal disdain. In 1850 a slave expressed a common sentiment: "My Master is a great tyrant, he treats me badly as if I were a common Irishman."

In part because of the hostility they faced, the Irish communities in American cities retained much of their ethnic and cultural identity. Neighborhood newspapers, churches, political groups, saloons, volunteer fire companies, and fraternal associations such as the Friendly Sons of St. Patrick bolstered a sense of community. Especially popular were Irish militia companies with colorful names: the Jasper Greens, Napper Tandy Light Artillery, and Irish Rifles. The Hibernian Society and the Shamrock Society aided Irish immigrants, and Irish newspapers such as the *Boston Pilot* remain in circulation today.

After becoming naturalized citizens, the Irish formed powerful blocs of voters. Drawn mainly to the party of Andrew Jackson, they set a crucial pattern of identification with the Democrats that other ethnic groups by and large followed. In Jackson the Irish immigrants found a hero. Himself the son of Irish colonists, he was also popular for having defeated the hated British at New Orleans. In addition, the Irish loathing of aristocracy, which they associated with British rule, attracted them to a politician and a party claiming to represent "the common man." Although property requirements initially kept most Irish Americans from voting, a New York state law extended the franchise in 1821, and five years later the state removed the property qualification altogether. In 1828 masses of Irish voters made the difference in the election between Jackson and John Quincy Adams. One newspaper expressed alarm at this new force in politics: "It was emphatically an Irish triumph. The foreigners have carried the day." Although women, African Americans, and Native Americans still could not vote, the Irish newcomers were able to use the franchise to exert a remarkable political influence.

Perhaps the greatest collective achievement of the Irish immigrants was stimulating the growth of the Catholic church in the United States. Years of persecution had instilled in Irish Catholics a fierce loyalty to the doctrines of the church as "the supreme authority over all the affairs of the world." Such passionate attachment to Catholicism generated both community cohesion among Irish Americans and fears of Romanism among American Protestants. By 1860 Catholics had become the largest single denomination in the United States.

THE GERMANS   During the eighteenth century, Germans had responded to William Penn's offer of religious freedom and cheap, fertile land by coming in large numbers to America. As a consequence, when a new wave of German migration formed in the 1830s, there were still large enclaves of Germans in Pennsylvania and Ohio who had preserved their language and cultures.

The new wave of German migration peaked in 1854, just a few years after the crest of Irish arrivals, when 215,000 Germans disembarked in American ports. These immigrants included a large number of learned, cultured professional people—doctors, lawyers, teachers, engineers— some of them refugees from the failed German revolutions of 1830 and 1848. In addition to an array of political opinions ranging from laissez-faire conservatism to Marxism, the Germans brought with them a variety of religious preferences. A third of the new arrivals were Catholic, most were Protestants (usually Lutherans), and a significant number were Jewish or freethinking atheists or agnostics. By the end of the century, some 250,000 German Jews had emigrated to America.

Unlike the Irish, the Germans settled more in rural areas than cities, and they included many independent farmers, skilled workers, and shopkeepers who arrived with some means to get themselves established in skilled jobs or on the land. More so than the Irish, they migrated in families and groups rather than as individuals, and this clannish quality helped them better sustain elements of German language and culture in their New World environment. More of them also tended to return to

German Beer Garden, New York, 1825. *German immigrants settled their own communities and retained traditions from their homeland.*

their native country. About 14 percent of the Germans eventually went back to their homeland, compared to 9 percent of the Irish.

Among the German immigrants who prospered in the New World were Ferdinand Schmacher, who began peddling oatmeal in glass jars in Ohio and eventually formed the Quaker Oats Company; Heinrich Steinweg, a piano maker from Lower Saxony, who in America changed his name to Steinway and became famous for the quality of his pianos; and Levi Strauss, a Jewish tailor who followed the gold rushers to California and began making long-wearing work pants that later were dubbed blue jeans or Levi's. Major centers of German settlement developed in Missouri and southwestern Illinois (around St. Louis), in Texas (near San Antonio), in Ohio, and in Wisconsin (especially around Milwaukee). The larger German communities developed traditions of bounteous food, beer, and music, along with German *Turnvereine* (gymnastic societies), sharp-shooter clubs, fire engine companies, and kindergartens.

THE BRITISH, SCANDINAVIANS, AND CHINESE British immigrants continued to arrive in the United States in large numbers during the first half of the nineteenth century. They included large numbers of professionals, independent farmers, and skilled workers. Some British workers, such as Samuel Slater, helped transmit the technology of British factories into the United States. Two other groups that began to arrive in some number during the 1840s and 1850s were just the vanguard of greater numbers to come. Annual arrivals from Scandinavia did not exceed 1,000 until 1843, but by 1860 a total of 72,600 Scandinavians lived in America. The Norwegians and Swedes gravitated to Wisconsin and Minnesota, where the climate and woodlands reminded them of home. By the 1850s, the sudden development of California was bringing in Chinese who, like the Irish in the East, did the heavy work of construction. Infinitesimal in numbers until 1854, the Chinese in America numbered 35,500 by 1860.

NATIVISM Not all Americans welcomed the flood of immigrants. Many natives resented the newcomers with their unknown languages and mysterious customs. The flood of Irish and German Catholics aroused Protestant hostility to "popery." A militant Protestantism growing out of the evangelical revivals in the early nineteenth century fueled the anti-Catholic hysteria. There were also fears of political radicalism among the Germans and of voting blocs among the Irish, but above all hovered the menace of unfamiliar religious practices. Catholic authoritarianism was widely perceived as a threat to hard-won liberties, religious and political.

In 1834 a series of anti-Catholic sermons by Lyman Beecher, a popular Congregationalist minister who served as president of Lane Seminary in Cincinnati, provoked a mob to attack and burn the Ursuline Convent in Charlestown, Massachusetts. In 1844 armed clashes between Protestants and Catholics in Philadelphia ended with about 20 killed and 100 injured. Sporadically, the nativist spirit took organized form in groups that claimed to prove their patriotism by hating foreigners and Catholics.

As early as 1837 a Native American Association was formed in Washington D.C., but the most significant such group was the Order of the Star Spangled Banner, founded in New York City in 1849. Within a few years this group had grown into a formidable third party. In 1854 delegates from thirteen states gathered to form the American party, which had the trappings of a secret fraternal order. Members pledged never to vote for any foreign-born or Catholic candidate. When asked

A Know-Nothing cartoon showing the Catholic church attempting to control American religious and political life through Irish immigration.

about the organization, they were to say "I know nothing." In popular parlance the American party became the Know-Nothing party. For a season it seemed that the American party might achieve major-party status. In state and local campaigns during 1854 the Know-Nothings carried one election after another. They swept the Massachusetts legislature, winning all but two seats in the lower house. That fall they elected more than forty congressmen. For a while the Know-Nothings threatened to control New England, New York, and Maryland, and showed strength elsewhere, but the anti-Catholic movement subsided when slavery became the focal issue of the 1850s.

The Know-Nothings demanded the exclusion of immigrants and Catholics from public office and the extension of the period for naturalization (citizenship) from five to twenty-one years, but the party never gathered the political strength to effect such legislation. Nor did Congress act during the period to restrict immigration in any way. The first federal law on immigration, passed in 1819, enacted only safety and health regulations regarding supplies and the number of passengers on immigrant ships. This and subsequent acts designed to protect immigrants from overcrowding and unsanitary conditions were, however, poorly enforced.

ORGANIZED LABOR

Skilled workers in American cities before and after the Revolution were called artisans, craftsmen, or mechanics. They made or repaired shoes, hats, saddles, ironware, silverware, jewelry, glass, ships, ropes, furniture, tools, weapons, and an array of wooden products. Printers published books, pamphlets, and newspapers. These skilled workers operated within a "guild system," a centuries-old economic and social structure developed in medieval Europe. At the top of the hierarchy was the master craftsman who owned his own business and spent much of his time dealing with customers, ordering supplies, keeping the books, and managing the journeymen and apprentices who worked alongside him. Journeymen were skilled workers paid by the hour or by the number of items produced. They had started their careers as young apprentices indentured to the master craftsmen for three to seven years as they learned the "art and mystery" of their work. Apprentices were provided

The Cabinetmaker, *an image of labor from* The Book of Trades, *1807.*

room and board along with their training. Between the ages of eighteen and twenty-one, the apprentice was promoted to journeyman status and given a set of tools and clothes as symbols of his new position as an independent artisan entitled to his own wages.

The daily routine of these urban workers engaged in the "finishing trades" was a mixture of labor, recreation, and fellowship. Their workday began at around 6 A.M. At 8:30 they would take a break to eat pastries. At 11 another break would feature a dram of beer or sugared rum. The workers ate their lunch around 1 P.M. and then took another break in late afternoon. During their breaks they would engage in animated discussions of political issues, social trends, and an array of other topics and ideas. One visitor said that these conversations buzzed with opinions on "political, social, and religious reform." Artisans took great pride in the quality of their work and in their philosophy of labor. A New England cooper (barrel maker) praised the willingness of skilled laborers to be content with a "middling" income: he and his self-reliant colleagues occupied a "condition below the dissipation of wealth and above the solicitude of necessity."

The widespread promotion of free enterprise among free laborers, however, was not open-ended. Several of the skilled trades, especially shoemakers and printers, formed their own professional associations to help regulate pay and working conditions as well as to control the number of tradesmen. Like medieval guilds organized by particular trades, the trade associations were local societies intended to promote the interests of the members. The trade groups pressured politicians for tariffs protecting them from foreign imports, provided insurance benefits, and drafted regulations to improve working conditions, ensure quality control, and provide equitable treatment of apprentices and journeymen. In addition, they sought to control the total number of tradesmen so as to maintain wage levels. The New York shoemakers, for instance, complained about employers taking on too many apprentices, insisting that "two was as many as one man can do justice by."

The use of slaves as skilled workers also caused great controversy. White journeymen in the South complained about competing with slave labor. Other artisans refused to take advantage of slave labor. The Baltimore Carpenters' Society, for example, admitted as members only those employers who refused to use slave labor.

During the 1820s and 1830s, artisans who emphasized quality and craftsmanship for a custom trade found it hard to meet the low prices created by the new factories and mass-production workshops. At this time, few workers belonged to unions, but a growing fear that they were losing status led artisans of the major cities into intense activity in labor politics and unions.

EARLY UNIONS   Early labor unions faced serious legal obstacles. Unions were prosecuted as unlawful conspiracies. In 1806, for instance, Philadelphia shoemakers were found guilty of a "combination to raise their wages." The decision broke the union. Such precedents were used for many years to hamstring labor organizations until the Massachusetts Supreme Court made a landmark ruling in the case of *Commonwealth v. Hunt* (1842). In this case the court ruled that forming a trade union was not in itself illegal, nor was a demand that employers hire only members of the union. The Court also declared that workers could strike if an employer hired nonunion laborers.

Until the 1820s, labor organizations took the form of local trade unions, confined to one city and one craft. During the ten years from 1827 to 1837, organization on a larger scale began to take hold. In 1834 the National Trades' Union was set up to federate the city societies. At the same time national craft unions were established by the shoemakers, printers, combmakers, carpenters, and hand-loom weavers, but

The Shoemaker *from* The Book of Trades, *1807. When bootmakers and shoemakers in Philadelphia went on strike in 1806, a court found them guilty of a "conspiracy to raise their wages."*

all the national groups and most of the local ones vanished in the economic collapse of 1837.

LABOR POLITICS   With the widespread removal of property qualifications for voting, labor politics flourished briefly during the Jacksonian era, especially in Philadelphia. A Working Men's party, formed there in 1828, gained the balance of power in the city council that fall. This success inspired other Working Men's parties in New York, Boston, and about fifteen states. The Working Men's parties were broad reformist groups devoted to the interests of labor, but they faded quickly. The inexperience of labor politicians left the parties prey to manipulation by political professionals. In addition, some of their issues were co-opted by the major parties. Labor parties also proved vulnerable to attack on grounds of extreme radicalism or dilettantism.

Once the labor parties had faded, many of their supporters found their way into a radical wing of the Jacksonian Democrats. This faction became the Equal Rights party and in 1835 acquired the name "Locofocos" when their opponents from New York City's regular Democratic organization, Tammany Hall, turned off the gas lights at one of their meetings and the Equal Rights supporters produced candles, lighting them with the new friction matches known as Locofocos. The Locofocos soon faded as a separate group, but they endured as a radical faction within the Democratic party.

While the labor parties elected few candidates, they did succeed in drawing notice to their demands, many of which attracted the support of middle-class reformers. Above all they promoted free public education and the abolition of imprisonment for debt, causes that won widespread popular support. The labor parties and unions actively promoted the ten-hour workday to prevent employers from abusing workers. In 1836 President Jackson established the ten-hour workday at the Philadelphia Navy Yard in response to a strike, and in 1840 President Van Buren extended the limit to all government offices and projects. In private jobs the ten-hour workday became increasingly common, although by no means universal, before 1860. Other reforms put forward by the Working Men's parties included mechanics' lien laws, to protect workers against nonpayment of wages; reform of a militia system that allowed the rich to escape service with fines but forced the poor to face jail terms; the abolition of "licensed monopolies," especially banks;

measures to ensure hard money and to protect workers against inflated bank-note currency; measures to restrict competition from prison labor; and the abolition of child labor.

LABOR AND REFORM   After the financial panic of 1837, the nascent labor movement went into decline, and during the 1840s, the focus of its radical spirit turned toward the promotion of cooperative societies. During the 1830s, there had been sporadic efforts to provide self-employment through producers' cooperatives, but the movement began to catch on after the iron molders of Cincinnati set up a successful shop in 1848. Soon the tailors of Boston had a cooperative workshop that employed thirty to forty men. New York was an especially strong center of such activity, with cooperatives among tailors, shirtmakers, bakers, shoemakers, and carpenters. Consumer cooperatives became much more vigorous and involved more people. The New England Protective Union, formed in 1845, organized a central purchasing agency for co-op stores.

Most people were drawn to the producers' and consumers' movement for practical reasons: to reduce their dependence on employers or to reduce the cost of purchases. After peaking in the early 1850s, however, the cooperatives went into decline. The high mobility of Americans and the heterogeneous character of the population as immigration increased created unfavorable conditions. Insufficient capital and weak, inexperienced management also plagued the cooperative movement.

THE REVIVAL OF UNIONS   Unions began to revive with improved business conditions in the early 1840s. Still, the unions remained local and weak. Often they came and went with a single strike. The greatest single labor dispute before the Civil War came on February 22, 1860, when shoemakers at Lynn and Natick, Massachusetts, walked out for higher wages. Before the strike ended, it had spread through New England, involving perhaps twenty-five towns and 20,000 workers. The strike stood out also because the workers won. Most of the employers agreed to wage increases, and some also agreed to recognize the union as a bargaining agent.

By the mid–nineteenth century, the labor union movement was maturing. Workers began to emphasize the importance of union recognition and regular collective-bargaining agreements. They also shared a growing sense of solidarity. In 1852 the National Typographical Union revived the effort to organize skilled crafts on a national scale. Others followed, and by 1860 about twenty such organizations had appeared, although none was strong enough as yet to do much more than hold national conventions and pass resolutions.

THE RISE OF THE PROFESSIONS

The dramatic social changes of the first half of the nineteenth century opened up an array of new professions for Americans to pursue. Bustling new towns required new services—retail stores, printing shops, post offices, newspapers, schools, banks, law firms, doctors' offices, and others—which created high-status jobs that had never existed in large numbers before. By definition, professional workers are those who have specialized knowledge and skills that ordinary people lack. To be a professional in Jacksonian America, to be a self-governing individual exercising trained judgment in an open society, was the epitome of the democratic ideal, an ideal that rewarded hard work, ambition, and merit.

The workforce was broadened and diversified by the rapid expansion of new communities, public schools, and institutions of higher learning; the emergence of a national market-economy; and the growing sophistication of American life and society fostered by new technologies. In the process, expertise garnered special prestige. In 1849 Henry Day delivered a lecture entitled "The Professions" at Case Western Medical School. He declared that the most important social functions in modern life were the professional skills. In fact, Day claimed, American society had become utterly dependent on "professional services."

TEACHING   Teaching was one of the fastest growing vocations in the antebellum period. Public schools initially preferred men over women in the hiring of teachers, usually hiring them at age seventeen or eighteen. The pay was so low that few stayed in the profession their entire careers, but for many educated, restless young adults, teaching was a convenient first job that offered independence and stature, as well as an alternative to the rural isolation of farming. New Englander Bronson Alcott remembered being attracted to teaching by "a curiosity to see beyond the limits of my paternal home and become acquainted with the great world." Church groups and civic leaders started private academies or seminaries for girls. Initially viewed as finishing schools for young women, they soon added courses in the liberal arts: philosophy, literature, Latin, and Greek.

LAW, MEDICINE, AND ENGINEERING   Teaching was a common stepping-stone for men who became lawyers. In the decades after the Revolution, young men, often hastily or superficially trained, swelled the ranks of the legal profession. They typically would teach a year or two before clerking for a veteran attorney who would train them in the law in exchange for their labors. The quality of such on-the-job training varied greatly from office to office. The absence of formal standards for legal training and the scarcity of law schools help explain why there were so many attorneys in the antebellum period. In 1820 eleven out of the twenty-four states required no specific length or type of study for aspiring lawyers. By 1851 the ideal of equal access to the professions led the Indiana state legislature to specify in its new constitution that "Every person of good moral character, being a voter, shall be entitled to admission to practice law in all courts of justice." And lawyers often pursued other careers as well—in journalism, banking, and especially politics. The prominent clergyman Lyman Beecher complained that lawyers had displaced ministers as the nation's leading public spokesmen.

Like attorneys, physicians in the early republic often had little formal academic training. Healers of every stripe and motivation assumed the title of *doctor* and established medical practices without regulation. Most of them were self-taught or learned their profession by assisting a doctor for several years, occasionally supplementing such internships with a few classes at the handful of new medical schools that in 1817 graduated a total of only 225 students. That same year there were almost 10,000 physicians in the nation. By 1860 there were 60,000 self-styled physicians, and quackery was abundant. Only a couple of states saw fit to regulate the medical profession. The president of the new American Medical Association, formed in 1847, admitted that the process of becoming a physician across the country had become haphazard and lax, "corrupt and degenerate." As a result, the medical profession had lost its social stature and public confidence.

Yet despite their relative lack of first-rate medical education, American physicians were responsible for many breakthroughs in treating a variety of illness.

The physical and industrial expansion of the United States during the first half of the nineteenth century gave rise to the profession of engineering, a field that has since become the single largest professional occupation for men in the United States. Specialized expertise was required for the building of canals and railroads, the development of machine tools and steam engines, and the construction of roads and bridges. Beginning in the 1820s, Americans gained access to technical knowledge in mechanics' institutes, scientific libraries, and special schools that sprouted up across the young nation. Rensselaer Polytechnic Institute was founded in Troy, New York, in 1824 to teach the "applications of science to the common purposes of life." The already existing Franklin Institute of Philadelphia shifted its emphasis in the 1830s to mechanical engineering. By the outbreak of the Civil War, engineering had become one of the largest professions in the nation.

WOMEN'S WORK   Women during the first half of the nineteenth century still worked primarily in the home. The prevailing assumption was that women by nature were most suited to marriage, motherhood, and the accompanying domestic duties. The only professions readily available to women were nursing (often midwifery, the delivery of babies) and teaching, both of which were extensions of the domestic roles of health care and child care. Teaching and nursing brought relatively lower status and pay than the male-dominated professions.

Many middle-class and affluent women spent their time outside the home engaged in religious and benevolent work. They were unstinting volunteers in churches and reform societies. A very few women, however, courageously pursued careers in male-dominated professions. Harriet Hunt of Boston was a teacher who, after nursing her sister through a serious illness, set up shop in 1835 as a self-taught physician and persisted in medical practice although twice rejected for admission by Harvard Medical School. Elizabeth Blackwell of Ohio managed to gain admission into Geneva Medical College in western New York, despite the disapproval of the faculty. When she walked into her first class, "a hush fell upon the class as if each member had been struck with paralysis." Blackwell had the last laugh when she finished at the head of her class in 1849, but thereafter the medical school refused to admit any more women. Blackwell went on to found the New York Infirmary for Women and Children and later had a long career as a professor of gynecology at the London School of Medicine for Women.

JACKSONIAN INEQUALITY

During the years before the Civil War, the United States had begun to develop a distinctive urban working class, most conspicuously in the factories and the ranks of unskilled workers, often including many Irish or German immigrants. More and more journeymen, aware that they were likely to remain lifelong wage earners, joined unions to protect their interests. But the American legend of "rags to riches," the image of the self-made man, was a durable myth. Speaking to the Senate in 1832, Kentucky's Henry Clay claimed that almost all the successful factory owners he knew were "enterprising self-made men, who have whatever wealth they possess by patient and diligent labor." The legend had just enough basis in fact to gain credence. John Jacob Astor, the wealthiest man in America, worth more than $20 million at his death in 1848, came of humble if not exactly destitute origins. Son of a minor official in Germany, he arrived in 1784 with little or nothing, made a fortune first on the western fur trade, then parlayed that into a large fortune in New York real estate. But his and similar cases were more exceptional than common.

Research by social historians on the rich in major eastern cities shows that while men of moderate means could sometimes run their inheritances into fortunes by good management and prudent speculation, those who started out poor and uneducated seldom made it to the top. In 1828 the top 1 percent of New York's families (owning $34,000 or more) held 40 percent of the wealth, and the top 4 percent held 76 percent. Similar circumstances prevailed in Philadelphia, Boston, and other cities.

A supreme irony of the times was that "the age of the common man," "the age of Jacksonian Democracy," seems actually to have been an age of growing economic and social inequality. Why this happened is difficult to say, except that the boundless wealth of the untapped frontier narrowed as the land was occupied and claims on various entrepreneurial opportunities were staked out. Such developments took place in New

England towns even before the end of the seventeenth century. But despite growing social distinctions, it seems likely that the white population of America, at least, was better off than the general run of European peoples. New frontiers, both geographical and technological, raised the level of material well-being for all. And religious as well as political freedoms continued to attract people eager for liberty in a new land.

MAKING CONNECTIONS

- Eli Whitney's invention of the cotton gin had a profound effect on southern economic and social development. Chapter 15 describes the economy and society of the Old South in greater detail.

- The westward migration traced in this chapter will increase tremendously in the 1840s, a trend discussed in Chapter 14.

- As this chapter demonstrated, the birth and expansion of railroads in the first half of the nineteenth century were an important part of "The Dynamics of Growth." Chapter 16 shows how a proposal for the first transcontinental railroad had an unexpected side effect: it intensified the debate over the spread of slavery westward.

FURTHER READING

On economic development in the nation's early decades, see Stuart W. Bruchey's *Enterprise: The Dynamic Economy of a Free People* (1990). The classic study of transportation and economic growth is George R. Taylor's *The Transportation Revolution, 1815–1860* (1951). A fresh view is provided in Sarah H. Gordon's *Passage to Union: How the Railroads Transformed American Life, 1829–1929* (1997). On the Erie Canal, see

Carol Sheriff's *The Artificial River: The Erie Canal and the Paradox of Progress* (1996).

The impact of technology is traced in David J. Jeremy's *Transatlantic Industrial Revolution: The Diffusion of Textile Technologies between Britain and America, 1790–1830s* (1981) and John L. Larson's *Internal Improvement: National Public Works and the Promise of Popular Government in the Early United States* (2001).

Paul Johnson's *A Shopkeeper's Millennium: Society and Revivals in Rochester, New York, 1815–1837* (1978) studies the role religion played in the emerging industrial order. The attitude of the worker during this time of transition is surveyed in Edward E. Pessen's *Most Uncommon Jacksonians: The Radical Leaders of the Early Labor Movement* (1967). Detailed case studies of working communities include Anthony F. C. Wallace's *Rockdale: The Growth of an American Village in the Early Industrial Revolution* (1978); Thomas Dublin's *Women at Work: The Transformation of Work and Community in Lowell, Massachusetts, 1826–1860* (1979); and Sean Wilentz's *Chants Democratic* (1984), on New York City. Walter Licht's *Working for the Railroad: The Organization of Work in the Nineteenth Century* (1983) is rich in detail.

For a fine treatment of urbanization, see Charles N. Glaab and A. Theodore Brown's *A History of Urban America* (1976). On immigration, see Michael Coffey and Terry Golway, *The Irish in America* (1997).

13. AN AMERICAN RENAISSANCE: RELIGION, ROMANTICISM, AND REFORM

CHAPTER ORGANIZER

This chapter focuses on:

- the rise of new religious movements.

- the development of a distinctive American literary culture.

- the variety of social reform movements.

The American novelist Nathaniel Hawthorne once lamented the difficulty of writing a novel "about a country where there is no shadow, no antiquity, no mystery, no picturesque and gloomy wrong." Unlike nations of the Old World, steeped in history and romance, the United States was an infant nation swaddled in the rational ideas of the Enlightenment. Those ideas, most vividly set forth in Thomas Jefferson's Declaration of Independence, had in turn a universal application that would influence religion, literature, and various social reform movements.

RATIONAL RELIGION

In the eyes of many if not most American citizens, the United States had a mission to stand as an example to the world of republican virtue, much as John Winthrop's "city upon a hill" had once stood as an example of an ideal Christian community to erring humanity. The concept of America as having a special mission in fact still carried spiritual overtones, for the religious fervor quickened in the Great Awakening had reinforced the idea of national purpose. This infused the national character with an element of perfectionism—and an element of impatience when reality fell short of expectations. The combination of religious belief and social idealism brought major reforms and advances in human rights. It also brought disappointments that at times festered into cynicism and alienation.

DEISM   The currents of the Enlightenment and the Great Awakening, now mingling, now parting, flowed on into the nineteenth century and in different ways eroded the remnants of Calvinist orthodoxy. As time passed, the image of a just but stern God promising predestined hellfire and damnation gave way to a more optimistic religious outlook. Enlightenment rationalism increasingly stressed humankind's inherent goodness rather than depravity, and it encouraged a belief in social progress and the promise of individual perfectibility.

Many leaders of the Revolutionary War era, such as Thomas Jefferson and Benjamin Franklin, became deists, even while nominally attached to existent churches. Deism, which arose in eighteenth-century Europe, carried the logic of Sir Isaac Newton's image of the world as a smoothly operating machine to its logical conclusion. The God of the deist had planned the universe, built it, set it in motion, and then left it to its own fate. By the use of reason people might grasp the natural laws governing the universe. Deists rejected the belief that every statement in the Bible was literally true. They were skeptical of miracles and questioned the divinity of Jesus. Deists also defended free speech and freedom from religious coercion of all sorts.

Orthodox believers could hardly distinguish such doctrine from atheism, but Enlightenment rationalism soon began to make deep inroads into American Protestantism. The old Puritan churches around Boston proved most vulnerable to logic of Enlightenment rationalism. Boston's progress—or some would say degeneration—from Puritanism to prosperity had persuaded many affluent families that they were anything but sinners in the hands of an angry God. Drawn toward more consoling and less strenuous doctrines, some went back to the traditional rites of the Episcopal church. More of them simply dropped or qualified their adherence to Calvinism while remaining in the Congregational churches.

UNITARIANISM AND UNIVERSALISM   By the end of the eighteenth century, many New Englanders were drifting into Unitarianism, a belief that emphasized the oneness and benevolence of God, the inherent goodness of humankind, and the primacy of reason and conscience over established creeds and confessions. People were not inherently depraved, Unitarians stressed; they were capable of doing tremendous good, and *all* were eligible for salvation. Boston was very much the center of the movement, and it flourished chiefly within Congregational churches. During the early nineteenth century, more and more liberal churches adopted the name of Unitarian.

William Ellery Channing of Boston's Federal Street Church emerged as the most inspiring Unitarian leader. "I am surer that my rational nature is from God," he said, "than that any book is an expression of his will." The American Unitarian Association in 1826 had 125 churches (all but 5 of them in Massachusetts). That same year, when the Presbyterian minister Lyman Beecher moved to Boston, he deplored the inroads made by the new rationalist faith: "All the literary men of Massachusetts were Unitarian; all the trustees and professors of Harvard College were Unitarian; all the elite of wealth and fashion crowded Unitarian churches."

A parallel anti-Calvinist movement, Universalism, attracted a different social group: working-class people of more humble status. In 1779 John Murray founded the first Universalist church at Gloucester, Massachusetts. In 1794 a Universalist convention in Philadelphia organized the sect. Universalism stressed the salvation of all men and women, not just a predestined few. God, they taught, was too merciful to condemn anyone to eternal punishment. "Thus, the Unitarians and Universalists were in fundamental agreement," wrote one historian of religion, "the Universalists holding that God was too good to damn man; the Unitarians insisting that man was too good to be damned." Although both sects remained relatively small, they exercised a powerful influence over intellectual life, especially in New England.

THE SECOND GREAT AWAKENING

By the end of the eighteenth century, Enlightenment secularism had made deep inroads into American thought. Yet for all the impact of rationalism, Americans remained a profoundly religious people—as they have ever since. There was, the perceptive French visitor Alexis de Tocqueville observed, "no country in the world where the Christian religion retains a greater influence over the souls of men than in America." Around 1800, however, fears that secularism was taking root sparked a revival that soon grew into a Second Awakening.

An early revivalist leader, Timothy Dwight, became president of Yale College in 1795 and struggled to purify a place which, in Lyman Beecher's words, had turned into "a hotbed of infidelity." Like his grandfather, Jonathan Edwards, Dwight helped launch a series of revivals that swept the student body and spread to all of New England as well.

REVIVALS ON THE FRONTIER In its frontier phase the Second Awakening, like the first, generated great excitement and strange manifestations. It gave birth, moreover, to a new institution, the camp meeting, in which the fires of faith were repeatedly rekindled. Itinerant preachers found ready audiences among lonely frontier folk hungry for spiritual intensity and a sense of community. Women especially flocked to the revivals and sustained religious life on the frontier. In the backwoods and in small rural hamlets, the traveling revival was as welcome an event as the traveling circus.

Among the established sects, the Presbyterians were entrenched among the Scotch-Irish from Pennsylvania to Georgia. They gained further from the Plan of Union worked out in 1801 with the Congregationalists of Connecticut and later with other states. Since the two groups agreed on doctrine and differed mainly on the form of church government, they were able to form unified congregations and call a minister from either church. The result through much of the Old Northwest was that New Englanders became Presbyterians by way of the "Presbygational" churches.

The Baptists embraced a simplicity of doctrine and organization that appealed especially to the common people of the frontier. Their theology was grounded in the infallibility of the Bible and the recognition of humankind's innate depravity. But they replaced the Calvinist notion of predestination with the concept of universal redemption and highlighted the ritual of adult baptism. They also stressed the equality of all before God, regardless of wealth, social standing, or educational training. Since each congregation was its own highest authority, a frontier church need appeal to no hierarchy before setting up shop and calling a minister or naming one of its own. Sometimes whole congregations moved across the mountains as a body. As Theodore Roosevelt later described it: "Baptist preachers lived and worked exactly as their flocks. . . . they cleared the ground, split rails, planted corn, and raised hogs on equal terms with their parishioners."

The Methodists, who shared with Baptists an emphasis on salvation by free will, established a much more centralized church structure. They also developed the most effective evangelical method of

A lithograph of a religious camp meeting from 1849, in which the men and the women can be seen sitting in separate sections.

all: the minister on horseback who sought out people in the most remote areas with the message of salvation as a gift free for the taking.
The "circuit rider" system began with Francis Asbury, a tireless
British-born revivalist who scoured the trans-Appalachian frontier for
lost souls, traversing fifteen states, preaching some 25,000 sermons
while defying hostile Indians and suffering through harsh winters. Asbury established a mobile evangelism perfectly suited to the frontier
environment and the new democratic age.

Peter Cartwright emerged as the most successful Methodist "circuit
rider," and he grew justly famous for his highly charged sermons. He
recalled stopping at a decaying Baptist church in frontier Kentucky:
"While I was preaching, the power of God fell on the assembly, and
there was an awful shaking among the dry bones. Several fell to the
floor and cried for mercy. . . . I believe if I had opened the doors of the
Church then, all of them would have joined the Methodist Church."
Cartwright typified the Methodist disdain for an educated clergy, at one
point arguing that it was "the illiterate Methodist preachers [who] actually set the world on fire." Frontier folk, he stressed, "wanted a preacher
who could mount a stump, a block, or old log" and arouse the "hearts and
consciences of the people." They did not need or want a learned clergy
delivering formal—and dull—sermons. By the 1840s the Methodists had
grown into the largest Protestant church in the country.

The Great Revival spread quickly through the West and into more
settled regions back East. Camp meetings were held typically in late
summer or fall, when farm work slackened. People came from far and
wide, camping in wagons, tents, or crude shacks. Blacks, whether slave
or free, were allowed to set up their own adjacent camp revivals. The
largest camp meetings tended to be ecumenical affairs, with Baptist,
Methodist, and Presbyterian ministers working as a team.

The crowds often numbered in the thousands, and the unrestrained
atmosphere made for chaos. If a particular hymn or sermon excited
someone, they would cry, shout, dance, or repeat the phrase. One visitor at a Kentucky camp revival described it as a "scene of confusion
that could scarce be put into human language." He noted that no
fewer than seven ministers at one time were scattered among the
thousands of faithful, all preaching at the top of their lungs. Mass excitement swept up even the most skeptical onlookers, and infusions of
the spirit moved participants to strange manifestations. Some went

into trances; others contracted the "jerks," laughed the "holy laugh," babbled in unknown tongues, or got down on all fours and barked like dogs to "tree the Devil."

But to dwell on the bizarre aspects of the camp meetings would be to distort an institution that offered a redemptive social outlet to isolated rural folk. This was especially true for women, for whom the camp meetings provided an alternative to the rigors and loneliness of frontier domesticity. Camp meetings also brought a more settled community life through the churches they spawned, and they helped spread a more democratic faith among the frontier people.

THE "BURNED-OVER DISTRICT"   Regions swept by such revival fevers might be compared to forests devastated by fire. Western New York, in fact, experienced such intense levels of evangelical activity that it was labeled the "Burned-Over District." Lyman Beecher called the Awakening of 1831 "the greatest work of God, and the greatest revival of religion, that the world has ever seen."

The most successful evangelist in the "Burned-Over District" was a lawyer named Charles Grandison Finney. In 1839 he preached for six months in Rochester and helped generate 100,000 conversions. Finney wrestled with an age-old question that had plagued Protestantism for centuries: What role can the individual play in earning salvation? Orthodox Calvinists had long argued that people could neither earn nor choose salvation on their own accord. Grace was a gift of God, a predetermined decision incapable of human understanding or control. In contrast, Finney insisted that the only thing preventing conversion was the individual. And what most often discouraged individual conversion was the terrifying loneliness of the decision. Finney transformed revivals into collective conversion experiences in which spectacular public events displaced private communion, and the unregenerate were brought into intense public contact with praying Christians.

Finney compared his methods to those of politicians who used advertising and showmanship to get attention. "New measures are necessary from time to time to awaken attention and bring the gospel to bear on the public mind." To those who challenged such calculated use of emotion Finney had a frank answer: "The results justify my methods." He carried the methods of the frontier revival into the cities of the East and as far as Great Britain. His gospel combined faith and good works: one led to the other. "All sin consists in selfishness," he said, "and all holiness or virtue, in disinterested benevolence." In 1835 Finney took the chair of theology in the new Oberlin College, founded by pious New Englanders in Ohio's Western Reserve. Later he served as its president. From the start Oberlin radiated a spirit of reform predicated on faith; it was the first college in America to admit either women or blacks, and it was a hotbed of antislavery agitation.

THE MORMONS   The Burned-Over District gave rise to several new religious movements, of which the most important was the Church of Jesus Christ of Latter-day Saints, or the Mormons. The founder, Joseph Smith, Jr., born in Vermont, was the child of wandering parents who finally settled in the village of Palmyra, New York. In 1820 the fourteen-year-old Smith had a vision of "two Personages, whose brightness and glory defy all description." They identified themselves as the Savior and God the Father and cautioned him that all existing religious denominations were false. About three years later, Smith claimed, an angel led the seventeen-year-old to a hill near his father's farm in upstate New York where he found the Book of Mormon engraved on golden tablets in a language he called "reformed Egyptian." Four years later, he rendered into English what he claimed to be a lost section of the Bible. This was the story of ancient Hebrews who had inhabited the New World and to whom Jesus had made an appearance.

The Mormon Temple in Nauvoo, Illinois, c. 1840.

On the basis of this revelation, the charismatic Smith began forming his own church in 1830, and within a few years he had gathered converts by the thousands, most of them New

England small farmers who had migrated to western New York. They found in Mormonism the promise of a pure kingdom of Christ in America and an alternative to the social turmoil and the degrading materialism of the era. In their search for a refuge from persecution, the Mormons moved from New York to Kirtland, Ohio, where Smith was tarred and feathered, then to several places in Missouri, and finally in 1839 to Commerce, Illinois, along the Mississippi River, which they renamed Nauvoo. There they settled and grew rapidly for some five years. In 1844 a crisis arose when dissidents accused Smith of practicing polygamy. Non-Mormons in the neighboring counties attacked Nauvoo, and Smith and his brother Hyrum were arrested. On June 27, 1844, an anti-Mormon lynch mob stormed the feebly defended jail and shot both Joseph and Hyrum Smith.

In Brigham Young, the remarkable successor to Joseph Smith, the Mormons found a leader of uncommon qualities: strong-minded, intelligent, and decisive, but also stern and authoritarian. After the murder of Smith, Young patched up an unsure peace with the neighbors by promising an early exodus from Nauvoo. Before the year was out, Young had chosen a new land near the Great Salt Lake in Utah, then part of Mexico, guarded by mountains to the east and north, deserts to the west and south, yet itself fed by mountain streams. Despite its isolation, it was close enough to the Oregon Trail for the Mormon "saints" to prosper by trade with passing "gentiles."

The Mormon trek was better organized and less burdensome than most of the overland migrations of the time. Early in 1846 a small band of courageous believers crossed the frozen Mississippi River into Iowa to set up the Camp of Israel, the first in a string of way stations along the route. By the fall of 1846, in wagons and on foot, all 15,000 of the migrants had reached the prepared winter quarters on the Missouri River, where they paused until the first bands set out the next spring for the Promised Land.

The first arrivals at Salt Lake in 1847 found only "a broad and barren plain hemmed in by mountains . . . the paradise of the lizard, the cricket and the rattlesnake." Young tapped the ground with his cane and announced that their new holy city would be built on the spot, "laid out perfectly square, north and south, east and west." By the end of 1848, the Mormons had developed an efficient irrigation system, and over the next decade, they brought about the greening of the

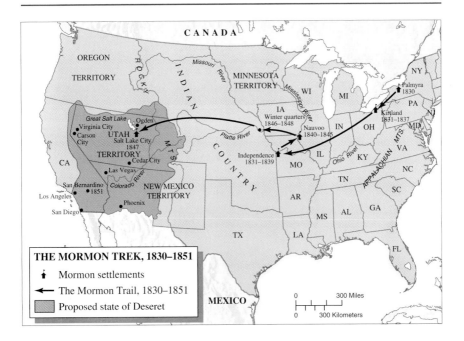

desert. The Mormons had scarcely arrived when their land became part of the United States. They organized at first their own state of Deseret (meaning "land of the honey bee," according to Young) with ambitious boundaries that reached the Pacific in southern California. But the Utah Territory, which Congress created, afforded them almost the same control, with Governor Young the chief political and theocratic authority. By 1869 some 80,000 Mormons had settled in Utah. Today there are 9 million Mormons, and it is the fastest growing religion in the world.

ROMANTICISM IN AMERICA

The revival of emotional piety during the early 1800s represented a widespread tendency throughout the Western world to accentuate the stirrings of the spirit over the dry logic of reason and the allure of material gain. Another great victory of heart over head was the romantic movement in thought, literature, and the arts. By the 1780s, a revolt was brewing in Europe against the well-ordered world

Kaaterskill Falls, 1825, *by Thomas Cole.*

of the Enlightened thinkers. Were there not, after all, more things in this world than reason and logic could box up and explain: moods, impressions, and feelings; mysterious, unknown, and half-seen things? Americans also took readily to the romantics' emphasis on individualism, idealizing now the virtues of common people, now the idea of original or creative genius in the artist, the author, or the great personality.

The German philosopher Immanuel Kant gave the worldwide romantic movement a summary definition in the title of his *Critique of Pure Reason* (1781), an influential book that emphasized the limits of human science and reason in explaining the universe. People have innate conceptions of conscience and beauty, the romantics believed, and religious impulses too strong to be dismissed as illusions. In those areas in which science could neither prove nor disprove concepts, people were justified in having faith. The impact of such ideas elevated intuitive knowledge at the expense of rational knowledge.

TRANSCENDENTALISM   The most intense expression of such romantic ideals was the transcendentalist movement of New England, which drew its name from its emphasis on those things that transcended (or rose above) the limits of reason. Transcendentalism, said one of its apostles, meant an interest in areas "a little beyond" the scope of reason. If transcendentalism drew much of its inspiration from Kant, it was also rooted in New England Puritanism, to which it owed a pervasive moralism. It also had a close affinity with the Quaker doctrine of the inner light. The inner light, a gift from God's grace, was transformed into intuition, a faculty of the mind.

An element of mysticism had always lurked in Puritanism, even if viewed as a heresy—Anne Hutchinson, for instance, had been banished for claiming direct revelations from God. The reassertion of mysticism had something in common, too, with the meditative religions of Asia— with which New England now had a flourishing trade. Transcendentalists steeped themselves in the teachings of the Buddha, the Mohammedan Sufis, the Upanishads, and the Bhagavad Gita.

In 1836 an informal discussion group named the Transcendental Club began to meet at the homes of members in Boston and Concord, Massachusetts. It was a loose association of diverse individualists. The club included liberal clergymen such as Theodore Parker, George Ripley, and James Freeman Clarke; writers such as Henry Thoreau, Bronson Alcott, Nathaniel Hawthorne, and Orestes Brownson; and learned women such as Elizabeth and Sophia Peabody and Margaret Fuller. Fuller edited the group's quarterly review, *The Dial* (1840–1844), for two years before the duty fell to Ralph Waldo Emerson, soon to become the acknowledged high priest of transcendentalism.

EMERSON More than any other person, Emerson spread the transcendentalist gospel. Sprung from a line of New England ministers, he set out to be a Unitarian parson, then quit the "cold and cheerless" denomination before he was thirty. After travel to Europe, where he met England's greatest writers, Emerson settled in Concord to take up the life

Ralph Waldo Emerson.

of an essayist, poet, and popular speaker on the lecture circuit, preaching the good news of optimism, self-reliance, and the individual's unlimited potential. Having found pure reason "cold as a cucumber" and discovered that the "ideal is truer than the actual," he was determined to *transcend* the limitations of inherited conventions and of rationalism in order to penetrate the inner recesses of the self.

Emerson's lectures and writings express the core of the transcendentalist worldview. His notable lecture, "The American Scholar," delivered at Harvard in 1837, urged young Americans to put aside their awe of European culture and explore their own new world. It was "our intellectual Declaration of Independence," said one observer.

Emerson's essay on "Self-Reliance" (1841) has a timeless appeal to youth with its message of individualism and the cultivation of one's personality. Like most of Emerson's writings, it is crammed with pungent quotations:

> Whoso would be a man, must be a nonconformist. . . . Nothing is at last sacred but the integrity of your own mind. . . . It is easy in the world to live after the world's opinion; it is easy in solitude to live after our own; but the great man is he who in the midst of a crowd keeps with perfect sweetness the independence of solitude. . . . A foolish consistency is the hobgoblin of little minds, adored by little statesmen and philosophers and divines. . . . Speak what you think now in hard words and tomorrow speak what tomorrow thinks in hard words again, though it contradict everything you said today. . . . To be great is to be misunderstood.

THOREAU Emerson's young friend and Concord neighbor, Henry David Thoreau, practiced the reflective self-reliance that Emerson preached. "I like people who can do things," Emerson stressed, and Thoreau, fourteen years his junior, could do many things well—carpentry, masonry, painting, surveying, sailing, gardening. The philosophical son of a pencil-maker father and domineering, abolitionist mother, Thoreau displayed a sense of uncompromising integrity, outdoor vigor, and tart individuality that Emerson found captivating. "If a man does not keep pace with his companions," Thoreau wrote, "perhaps it is because he hears a different drummer."

Thoreau himself marched to a different drummer all his life. After Harvard, where he exhausted the resources of the library in gargantuan bouts of reading, and after a brief stint as a teacher in which he got in trouble for refusing to cane students, Thoreau settled down to eke out a living by making pencils with his father. But he made frequent escapes to drink in the beauties of nature. He showed no interest in the contemporary scramble for wealth. It too often corrupted the pursuit of happiness. "The mass of men," he wrote, "lead lives of quiet desperation."

Determined himself to practice plain living and high thinking, Thoreau boarded with the Emersons for a time and then embarked on an experiment in self-reliance. On July 4, 1845, he took to the woods to live in a cabin he had built on Emerson's land beside Walden Pond. He

Henry David Thoreau, author of the American classics Walden *and "Civil Disobedience."*

wanted to see how far he could free himself from the complexities and hypocrisies of modern commercial life, and to devote his time to observation, reflection, and writing. His purpose was not to lead a hermit's life. He frequently walked the mile or so to town to dine with his friends, and he often welcomed guests at his cabin. "I went to the woods because I wished to live deliberately," he wrote in *Walden, or Life in the Woods* (1854), "and not, when I came to die, discover that I had not lived."

While Thoreau was at Walden Pond, the Mexican War erupted. Believing it an unjust war to advance the cause of slavery, he refused to pay his state poll tax as a gesture of opposition, for which he was put in jail (for only one night; an aunt paid the tax). The incident was so trivial as to be almost comic, but out of it grew the classic essay "Civil Disobedience" (1849), which was later to influence the passive-resistance movements of Mahatma Gandhi in India and Martin Luther King, Jr., in the American South. "If the law is of such a nature that it requires you to be an agent of injustice to another," Thoreau wrote, "then, I say, break the law. . . ."

The broadening ripples of influence more than a century after Thoreau's death show the impact a contemplative person can have on the world of action. Thoreau and the transcendentalists supplied the force of an animating idea: people must follow their consciences. Though these thinkers attracted only a small following among the public in their own time, they inspired reform movements and were the quickening force for a generation of writers that produced the first great classic age of American literature.

The Flowering of American Literature

The half-decade of 1850–1855 witnessed an outpouring of great literature. It saw the publication of *Representative Men* by Emerson, *Walden* by Thoreau, *The Scarlet Letter* and *The House of the Seven Gables* by Nathaniel Hawthorne, *Moby-Dick* by Herman Melville, and *Leaves of Grass* by Walt Whitman. As a noted literary critic wrote, "You might search all the rest of American literature without being able to collect a group of books equal to these in imaginative quality."

HAWTHORNE   Nathaniel Hawthorne, the supreme writer of the New England group, never shared the sunny optimism of his neighbors or their perfectionist belief in reform. A sometime resident of Concord, Massachusetts, but a native and longtime inhabitant of Salem, he was haunted by the knowledge of evil bequeathed to him by his Puritan forebears—one of whom had been a judge at the Salem witchcraft trials. After college, he worked in obscurity in Salem, gradually began to sell a few stories, and finally earned a degree of fame with his collection of *Twice-Told Tales* (1837). In these, as in most of his later work, he presented powerful moral allegories. His central themes examined sin and its consequences: pride and selfishness, secret guilt, and the impossibility of rooting sin out of the human soul.

DICKINSON   The flowering of New England literature featured, too, a foursome of poets who shaped the American imagination in a day when poetry was still accessible to a wide public: Henry Wadsworth Longfellow, John Greenleaf Whittier, Oliver Wendell Holmes, Sr., and James Russell Lowell. A fifth poet, Emily Dickinson, the most original and powerful of the lot, remained a white-gowned recluse in her second-story bedroom in Amherst, Massachusetts. As she once prophetically wrote, "Success is counted sweetest / By those who ne'er succeed." Only two of her almost 1,800 poems were published (anonymously) before her death in 1886, and the full corpus of her work remained unknown for years thereafter. Born in Amherst in 1830, the child of a prominent, stern father and gentle mother, she received a first-rate secondary education and then attended the new Mount Holyoke Female Seminary. Neither she nor her sister married, and they both lived out their lives in their parents' home.

Emily Dickinson.

Perhaps it was Emily's severe eye trouble during the 1860s that induced her solitary withdrawal from the larger society; perhaps it was the aching despair generated by her unrequited love for a married minister. Whatever the reason, her intense isolation led her to focus her writings on her own shifting psychological state. Her themes were elemental: life, death, fear, loneliness, nature, and, above all, God, a "Force illegible," a "distant, stately lover."

IRVING AND COOPER   A noted British critic asked in 1820: "In the four quarters of the Globe, who reads an American book?" Quoted out of context, the question rubbed Americans the wrong way, but the critic, an admirer of American institutions, foresaw a future flowering in the new country. He did not have long to wait, for within a year Washington Irving's *The Sketch Book* (1820) and James Fenimore Cooper's *The Spy* (1821) were drawing wide notice in Britain as well as in America.

Irving in fact stood as a central figure in the American literary world from the time of his satirical *Diedrich Knickerbocker's A History of New York* (1809) until his death fifty years later. He showed that an American could, after all, make a career of literature. During those years a flood of histories, biographies, essays, and stories poured from his pen. Irving was the first American writer to show that authentic American themes could draw a wide audience. Yet, as Herman Melville later noted, he was less a creative genius than an adept imitator. Even the most "American" of his stories, "Rip Van Winkle" and "The Legend of Sleepy Hollow," drew heavily on German folk tales.

Cooper, a country gentleman, got his start as a writer on a bet with his wife that he could write a better novel than one they had just read. In *The Pioneers* (1823), Cooper introduced Natty Bumppo, an eighteenth-century frontiersman destined to be the hero of five novels collectively labeled *The Leather-Stocking Tales.* Natty Bumppo, a crack shot also known as Hawkeye, and his Indian friend Chingachgook, the epitome of the "noble savage," took their place among the most unforgettable heroes of American literature. Cooper's tales of man pitted against nature in the backwoods, of hairbreadth escapes and gallant rescues, were the first successful romances of frontier life, and they served as models for the later cowboy novels and movies set in the Far West.

POE AND THE SOUTH   By the 1830s and 1840s, new major talents had come on the scene. Edgar Allan Poe, born in Boston but reared in Virginia, was a literary genius and probably the most important American writer of the times. The tormented, heavy-drinking Poe was a master of Gothic horror in the short story and the inventor of the detective story and its major conventions. He judged prose by its ability to provoke emotional tension, and since he considered fear to be the most powerful emotion, he focused his efforts on making the grotesque and supernatural seem disturbingly real to his readers. Anyone who has read "The Tell-Tale Heart" or "The Pit and the Pendulum" can testify to his success.

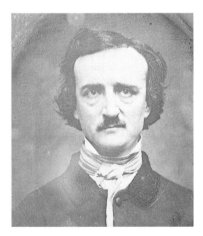

Edgar Allan Poe, perhaps the most inventive American writer of the period.

Among southern authors, William Gilmore Simms best exemplified the genteel man of letters. Editor and writer in many genres, he wrote poems, novels, histories, biographies, essays, short stories, and drama. The peak of his achievement was in two novels published in 1835: *The Yemassee,* a story of Indian war in

1715, and *The Partisan,* first of seven novels about the Revolution in South Carolina. In his own time, Simms was the preeminent southern author and something of a national figure, but he finally dissipated his energies in politics and the defense of slavery. He went down steadily in critical esteem, and most critics would agree with his own epitaph, that he had "left all his better works undone."

MELVILLE   Herman Melville was a New Yorker whose reputation went into a decline after his initial successes. In the twentieth century Melville's reputation was dramatically revived, elevating him into the literary pantheon occupied by the finest American authors. Born of distinguished ancestry on both sides, Melville suffered a sharp reversal of fortunes when his father died a bankrupt. After taking various odd jobs, he shipped out as a seaman at age twenty. Some time later, after eighteen months aboard a whaler, he arrived in the South Seas and jumped ship with a companion in the Marquesas Islands. After several weeks spent with a friendly tribe in the valley of the Typees, he signed on to an Australian whaler, jumped ship again in Tahiti, and finally returned home as a seaman aboard a frigate of the United States Navy. An embroidered

Whaling Ship "Maria," *c. 1850. Harpooning whales, as described by Herman Melville in* Moby-Dick.

account of his exotic adventures in *Typee* (1846) became an instant popular success, which he repeated in *Omoo* (1847), based on his stay in Tahiti.

So many readers took his accounts as fictional (as in part they were) that Melville was inspired to write novels of nautical adventures, and he produced one of the world's great novels in *Moby-Dick* (1851). In the story of Captain Ahab and his obsessive quest for the white whale that had caused the loss of his leg, Melville explored the darker recesses of the soul just as his good friend Hawthorne had done. The book was aimed at two audiences. On one level it was a ripping good yarn of adventure on the high seas. But on another level it explored philosophical and psychological realms: Ahab's single-minded mission to slay the evildoer turned the captain himself into a monster of destruction who sacrificed his ship, his crew, and himself to his folly, leaving as the one survivor the narrator of the story. Unhappily, neither the public nor the critics at the time accepted the novel on either level. After that Melville's career wound down into futility. He supported himself for years with a job in the New York Custom House and turned to poetry, much of which, especially the Civil War *Battle-Pieces* (1866), gained acclaim in later years.

WHITMAN   The most provocative American writer during the antebellum period was Walt Whitman, a vibrant personality who disdained inherited conventions and artistic traditions. There was something elemental in Whitman's character, something bountiful and generous and compelling—even his faults and inconsistencies were ample. Born on a Long Island farm, he moved with his family to Brooklyn and from the age of twelve worked mainly as a handyman and journalist, frequently taking the ferry across the river to booming, bustling Manhattan. The city fascinated him, and he gorged himself on the urban spectacle—shipyards, crowds, factories, shop windows. From such material he drew his editorial opinions and poetic inspiration, but he remained relatively obscure until the first edition of *Leaves of Grass* (1855) caught the eye and aroused the ire of readers. Emerson found it "the most extraordinary piece of wit and wisdom that America has yet contributed," but more conventional critics shuddered at Whitman's explicit sexual references and groused at his indifference to rhyme and meter as well as his buoyant egotism.

The jaunty Whitman, however, refused to conform to genteel notions of art, and he spent most of his career working on his gargantuan *Leaves of Grass,* enlarging and reshaping it in successive editions. The growth of the book he identified with the growth of the country. While he celebrated America, Whitman also set out to "celebrate myself and sing myself." To his generation he was a startling figure with his frank sexual references and homoerotic overtones. He also stood out from the pack of fellow writers in rejecting the idea that a woman's proper sphere was in a supportive and dependent role. Thoreau described Whitman as "the greatest democrat the world has seen."

THE POPULAR PRESS   The renaissance in literature coincided with a massive expansion in the popular press during the first half of the nineteenth century. The steam-driven Napier press, introduced from England in 1825, could print 4,000 sheets of newsprint in an hour. Richard Hoe of New York improved on it, inventing in 1847 the Hoe rotary press, which printed 20,000 sheets an hour. Like many advances in technology, this was a mixed blessing. The high cost of such a press made it harder for a person of small means to break into publishing. On the other hand it expedited production of cheap newspapers, magazines, and books.

Politics in an Oyster House, *1848, by Richard Caton Woodville, depicting a newspaper-reader engaged in eager discussion.*

The availability of daily newspapers costing only a penny each transformed daily reading into a form of popular entertainment. Newspaper circulation skyrocketed in every city. The "penny dailies," explained one editor, "are to be found in every street, lane, and alley; in every hotel, tavern, countinghouse, [and] shop."

The United States had more newspapers than any nation in the world. It needed them to forge a network of communications across the expanding republic. As readership soared, the content of newspapers expanded beyond political news and commentary to include social gossip, sports, and sensational crime and accident reports. The *New York Sun,* in 1833 the first successful penny daily, and others like it often ignored the merely important in favor of scandals and sensations, true or false. James Gordon Bennett, a native of Scotland, perfected this sensational style in the *New York Herald,* which he founded in 1835. His innovations drew readers by the thousands: the first Wall Street column, the first society page (which satirized the well-to-do until it proved more gainful to show readers their names in print), pictorial news, telegraphic news, and great initiative in getting scoops. Eventually, however, the *Herald* suffered from dwelling too much on crime, sex, and depravity in general.

The chief beneficiary of a rising revulsion against the gutter press was the *New York Tribune,* founded as a Whig forum in 1841. Horace Greeley, who became the most important journalist of the era, announced that it would be a cheap but decent paper avoiding the "matters which have been allowed to disgrace the columns of our leading Penny Papers." And despite occasional lapses, Greeley's "Great Moral Organ" typically amused its readers with wholesome human-interest stories. Greeley also won a varied following by plugging the reforms of the day. Socialism, land reform, feminism, abolitionism, temperance, the protective tariff, internal improvements, improved methods of agriculture, vegetarianism, spiritualism, trade unions—all got a share of attention. For a generation the *Tribune* was probably the most influential paper in the country. By 1860 its weekly edition had a national circulation of 200,000.

Meanwhile, the number of newspapers around the country grew from about 1,200 in 1833 to some 3,000 in 1860. The proliferation of newspapers was largely a northern and western phenomenon. Literacy rates in the South lagged behind the rest of the country. Before any state had even been formed in the Northwest Territory, for example, the region boasted thirteen newspapers while at the same time North Carolina had only four.

Magazines found a growing market too. *Niles' Weekly Register* (1811–1849) of Baltimore and Washington, founded by the printer Hezekiah Niles, featured accurate and unbiased coverage of public events—all of which make it a basic source for historians. The *North American Review* of Boston (1815–1940) was a favorite among scholarly readers. Its editor adorned the journal with materials on American history and biography. It also featured coverage of European literature.

Harper's Magazine (1850–present), originally the organ of the publishers Harper and Brothers, pirated the output of popular English writers in the absence of an international copyright agreement. Gradually, however, faced with an outcry against the practice, *Harper's* began paying for fresh contributions and published original material by American authors. *Frank Leslie's Illustrated Newspaper* (1855–1922) in New York used large and striking pictures to illustrate its material. *Leslie's* and a vigorous competitor of somewhat higher quality, *Harper's Illustrated Weekly* (1857–1916), appeared in time to provide a thoroughgoing pictorial record of the Civil War.

EDUCATION

A literate and well-informed citizenry, equipped with knowledge not only for gaining a vocation but also for promoting self-government and self-culture, was one of the animating ideals of the early Republic. Literacy in Jacksonian America was surprisingly widespread, given the condition of public education. By 1840, according to census data, some 78 percent of the total population and 91 percent of the white population could read and write. Ever since the colonial period, in fact, Americans had had the highest literacy rate in the Western world. Most children learned to read in church or private "dame" schools, from formal tutors, or from their families. By 1830, no state had a school system in the modern sense, although Massachusetts had for nearly two centuries required towns to maintain schools. Some major cities had the resources to develop school systems on their own. For instance, the Public School Society of New York, established in 1805, built a model system of free schools in the city, with state aid after 1815.

A scattered rural population, however, did not lend itself so readily to the development of public schools. In 1860, for instance, Louisiana had a population density of 11 per square mile and Virginia 14, while Massachusetts had 127. In many parts of the country, as in South Carolina after 1811, the state provided some aid to schools for children of indigent parents, but such institutions were normally stigmatized as "pauper schools."

EARLY PUBLIC SCHOOLS By the 1830s the demand for public schools peaked. Reformers argued that republican government presupposed a literate and informed electorate. Workers also wanted free schools to give their children an equal chance to pursue the American dream. In 1830 the Working Men's party of Philadelphia called for "a system of education that shall embrace equally all the children of the state, of every rank and condition." Education, it was argued, would improve manners and at the same time lessen crime and poverty.

Horace Mann of Massachusetts led the early drive for statewide school systems. Trained as a lawyer, he sponsored the creation of a state board of education, which he then served as secretary. Mann went on to sponsor many reforms in Massachusetts, including the first state-supported "normal school" for the training of teachers, a state association of teachers, and a minimum school year of six months. He repeatedly promoted the public school system as the way to social stability and equal opportunity. It had never happened, he argued, and never could happen, that an educated people could be permanently poor. "Education then, beyond all other devices of human origin, is a great equalizer of the conditions of men—the balance wheel of the social machinery."

In the South, North Carolina led the way toward state-supported education. By 1860, North Carolina enrolled more than two-thirds of its white school-age population for an average term of four months, kept so low because of the need in a rural state for children to do farm work. But the educational pattern in the South continued to reflect the aristocratic pretensions of the region: the South had a higher percentage of college students than any other region, but a lower percentage of public school students. And the South had some 500,000 white illiterates, more than half the total number in the country.

For all the effort to establish state-supported schools, conditions for public education were seldom ideal. Funds were insufficient for buildings, books, and equipment; teachers were poorly paid, and often poorly prepared.

Most students going beyond the elementary grades went to private academies, often subsidized by church and public funds. Such schools, begun in colonial days, multiplied until there were in 1850 more than 6,000 of them. In 1821 the Boston English High School opened as the first free public secondary school, set up mainly for students not going on to college. By a law of 1827 Massachusetts required a high school in every town of 500; in towns of 4,000 or more the school had to offer Latin, Greek, rhetoric, and other college preparatory courses. Public high schools became well established only after the Civil War. In 1860 there were barely 300 in the whole country.

POPULAR EDUCATION   Beyond the schools there grew up many societies and institutes to inform the general public: mechanics' and workingmen's "institutes," "young men's associations," "debating societies," "literary societies," and such. Outstanding in the field was the Franklin Institute, founded at Philadelphia in 1824 to inform the public mainly in the fields of science and industry. Some cities offered evening classes to those who could not attend day schools. The most widespread and effective means of popular education, however, was the lyceum movement, which shared knowledge through public lectures. Professional agencies provided speakers and performers of all kinds, in literature, science, music, humor, travel, and other fields.

Akin to the lyceum movement and ultimately reaching more people was the development of public libraries. Benjamin Franklin's Philadelphia Library Company (1731) had given impulse to the growth of subscription or association libraries. In 1803 Salisbury, Connecticut, opened a free library for children and in 1833 Peterborough, New Hampshire, established a tax-supported library open to all. The opening of the Boston Public Library in 1851 was a turning point. For the first time, the common people had ready access to an extensive collection of books. By 1860 there were approximately 10,000 public libraries (not all completely free) housing some 8 million volumes.

HIGHER EDUCATION   The post-Revolutionary proliferation of colleges continued after 1800 with the spread of small church schools and state universities. Nine colleges had been founded in the colonial period,

Greek Class at the Western Reserve Eclectic Institute at Hiram, Ohio, 1853. *At front right are the young James A. Garfield and his future wife, Lucretia Randolph.*

all of which survived; but not many of the fifty that sprang up between 1776 and 1800 lasted. Of the seventy-eight colleges and universities in 1840, fully thirty-five had been founded after 1830, almost all attached to religious denominations. A post-Revolutionary movement for state-supported universities flourished in those southern states that had had no colonial university. Federal policy abetted the spread of universities into the West. When Congress granted statehood to Ohio in 1803, it set aside two townships for the support of a state university and kept up that policy in other new states.

The coexistence of state and religious schools, however, provoked conflicts over funding and curriculum. Beset by the need for funds, as colleges usually were, denominational schools often competed with tax-supported schools. Regarding curricula, many of the church schools emphasized theology at the expense of science and the humanities. On the other hand, America's development required broader access to education and programs geared to vocations. The University of Virginia, "Mr. Jefferson's University," founded in 1819, introduced a curriculum modeled after Jefferson's view that education ought to combine pure knowledge with "all the branches of science useful *to us,* and *at this day."* The model influenced the other new state universities of the South and West.

Technical education grew slowly. The United States Military Academy at West Point, founded in 1802, and the Naval Academy at Annapolis, opened in 1845, trained a limited number of engineers. More young men learned technical skills through practical experience with railroad and canal companies, and apprenticeship to experienced technologists. The president of Brown University remarked that there were no colleges to provide "the agriculturalist, the manufacturer, the mechanic, and the merchant with any kind of professional preparation."

Elementary education for girls met with general acceptance, but training beyond that level did not. Most people viewed higher education as unsuited to a woman's destiny in life. Some did argue that education would produce better wives and mothers, but few were ready yet

The George Barrell Emerson School, Boston, *c. 1850. Although higher education for women initially met with some resistance, female seminaries like this one were started in the 1820s and 1830s and taught women mathematics, physics, and history, as well as music, art, and the social graces.*

to demand equality on principle. Progress began with the academies, some of which taught boys and girls alike. Good "female seminaries" like those founded by Emma Willard at Troy, New York (1824), and by Mary Lyon at Mount Holyoke, Massachusetts (1836), prepared the way for women's colleges. Many of them, in fact, grew into such colleges. The curricula in female seminaries usually differed from the courses in men's schools, giving more attention to the social amenities and such "embellishments" as music and art. Vassar, opened at Poughkeepsie, New York, in 1865, is usually credited with being the first women's college to give priority to academic standards. In general the West gave the greatest impetus to coeducation, with state universities in the lead. But once admitted, women students remained in a subordinate status. At Oberlin College in Ohio, for instance, they were expected to clean male students' rooms and were not allowed to speak in class or recite at graduation exercises. Coeducation did not mean equality.

ANTEBELLUM REFORM

The United States in the antebellum period was awash in reform movements. The urge to eradicate evil had its roots in the widespread American sense of spiritual zeal and moral mission, which in turn drew upon rising faith in human perfectibility. Few areas of life escaped the attention of the reformers: They tackled such issues as observance of the Sabbath, dueling, crime and punishment, the hours and conditions of work, poverty, vice, care of the handicapped, pacifism, foreign missions, temperance, women's rights, and the abolition of slavery. Some crusaders challenged a host of evils; others focused on pet causes. One Massachusetts reformer, for example, insisted that "a vegetable diet lies at the basis of all reforms."

TEMPERANCE   The temperance crusade was perhaps the most widespread of all. The census of 1810 reported some 14,000 distilleries producing 25 million gallons of alcoholic spirits each year. William Cobbett, an English reformer who traveled in the United States, noted in 1819 that one could "go into hardly any man's house without being asked to drink wine or spirits, even *in the morning*."

The temperance movement rested on a number of arguments. First and foremost was the religious concern that "soldiers of the cross" should lead blameless lives. The bad effects of distilled beverages on body and mind were noted by the respected physician Benjamin Rush as early as 1784. The dynamic new economy, with factories and railroads moving on strict schedules, made tippling by the labor force a far more dangerous problem than it had been in a simpler economy. Humanitarians also emphasized the relations between drinking and poverty. Much of the movement's propaganda focused on the sufferings of innocent mothers and children. "Drink," said a pamphlet from the

A Temperance Banner, c. 1850, depicting a young man being tempted by a woman who has given him a glass of wine.

Sons of Temperance, "is the prolific source (directly or indirectly) of nearly all the ills that afflict the human family."

In 1826 a group of ministers in Boston organized the American Society for the Promotion of Temperance. The society worked through lecturers, press campaigns, prize essay contests, and the formation of local and state societies. A favorite device was to ask each person who took the pledge to put by his or her signature a T for Total Abstinence. With that a new word entered the language: "teetotaler."

In 1833 the society called a national convention in Philadelphia, where the American Temperance Union was formed. The convention revealed internal tensions, however: Was the goal moderation or total abstinence, and if the latter, abstinence merely from liquor or also from wine, cider, and beer? Should activists work by persuasion or by legislation? Like nearly every movement of the day, temperance had a wing of purist absolutists. They would brook no compromise with Demon Rum and carried the day with a resolution that the liquor traffic was morally wrong and ought to be prohibited by law. The union, at its spring convention in 1836, called for abstinence from all alcoholic beverages—a costly victory that caused moderates to abstain from the temperance movement instead.

The demand for the prohibition of alcoholic beverages led in the 1830s and thereafter to experiments with more stringent regulations and local option laws. In 1838 Massachusetts forbade the sale of spirits in lots of less than fifteen gallons, thereby cutting off sales in taverns and to the poor—who could not handle it as well as their betters, or so their betters thought. After repeal of the law in 1840, prohibitionists in Massachusetts turned to the towns, about a hundred of which were dry by 1845. In 1839 Mississippi restricted sales to no less than a gallon, but the movement went little further in the South. In 1846 Maine enacted a law against sales of less than twenty-eight gallons; five years later Maine forbade the manufacture or sale of *any* intoxicants. By 1855 thirteen states had such laws. Rum-soaked New England had gone legally dry, along with New York and parts of the Midwest. But most of the laws were poorly drafted and vulnerable to court challenge. Within a few years they survived only in northern New England. Still, between 1830 and 1860, the temperance agitation drastically reduced Americans' per-capita consumption of alcohol.

PRISONS AND ASYLUMS   The Romantic era's liberal belief that people were innately good and capable of improvement brought major changes in the treatment of prisoners, the disabled, and dependent children. Public institutions arose dedicated to the treatment and cure of social ills. Earlier these had been "places of last resort," David Rothman wrote in *The Discovery of the Asylum.* Now they "became places of first resort, the preferred solution to the problems of poverty, crime, delinquency, and insanity." Removed from society, the theory went, the needy and deviant could be made whole again. Unhappily, this ideal kept running up against the dictates of convenience and economy. The institutions had a way of turning into breeding grounds of brutality and neglect.

In the colonial period prisons were usually places for brief confinement before punishment, which was either death or some kind of pain or humiliation: whipping, mutilation, confinement in stocks, branding, and the like. A new attitude began to emerge after the Revolution. American reformers argued against the harshness of the penal code and asserted that the certainty of punishment was more important than its severity. Society, moreover, would benefit more from the prevention than the punishment of crime.

Gradually the idea of the penitentiary developed. It would be a place where the guilty experienced penitence and underwent rehabilitation, not just punishment. An early model of the new system, widely copied, was the Auburn Penitentiary, commissioned by New York in 1816. The prisoners at Auburn had separate cells and gathered for meals and group labor. Discipline was severe. The men were marched out in lockstep and never put face to face or allowed to talk. But prisoners were at least reasonably secure from abuse by other prisoners. The system, its advocates argued, had a beneficial effect on the prisoners and saved money since the workshops supplied prison needs and produced goods for sale at a profit. By 1840 there were twelve prisons of the Auburn type.

It was still more common, and the persistent curse of prisons, however, for inmates to be thrown together willy-nilly. In an earlier day of corporal punishments, jails housed mainly debtors. But as practices changed, debtors found themselves housed with convicts. Without provision for food, furniture, or fuel, the debtors would have expired but for charity. The absurdity of the system was so obvious that the tardiness of reform seems strange. New York in 1817 made $25 the minimum for which one could be imprisoned, but no state eliminated the practice altogether until Kentucky acted in 1821. Other states gradually fell in line, but it was still more than three decades before debtors' prisons became a thing of the past.

The reform impulse also found outlet in the care of the insane. The Pennsylvania Hospital (1752), one of the first in the country, had a provision in its charter that it should care for "lunaticks," but before 1800 few hospitals provided care for the mentally ill. The insane were usually confined at home with hired keepers or in jails and almshouses. In the years after 1815, however, asylums that housed the disturbed separately from criminals began to appear.

The most important figure in arousing the public conscience to the plight of these unfortunates was Dorothea Lynde Dix. A pious, withdrawn, almost saintly Boston schoolteacher, she was called upon to instruct a Sunday-school class at the East Cambridge House of Correction in 1841. There she found a roomful of insane persons completely neglected and left without heat on a cold March day. Her conscience provoked, she then commenced a two-year investigation of jails and almshouses in Massachusetts. In a report to the state legislature in 1843, she reported on "the *present* state of insane persons confined within the Commonwealth, in *cages, closets, cellars, stalls, pens! Chained, naked, beaten with rods, and lashed into obedience!*" Keepers of the institutions dismissed her charges as "slanderous lies," but she won the support of leading reformers. From Massachusetts, she carried her campaign throughout the country and abroad. By 1860 she had persuaded twenty states to heed her advice. Dorothea Dix helped transform social attitudes toward mental illness.

WOMEN'S RIGHTS   While Dorothea Dix stood out as an example of the opportunity reform gave middle-class women to enter public life, Catharine Beecher, a leader in the education movement and founder of women's schools in Connecticut and Ohio, published a guide prescribing the domestic sphere for women. *A Treatise on Domestic Economy* (1841) became the leading handbook of what historians have labeled the "cult of domesticity." While Beecher upheld high standards in women's education, she also accepted the prevailing view that the "woman's sphere" was the home and argued that young women should be trained in the domestic arts. Her guide, designed for use also as a textbook, led prospective wives and mothers through the endless rounds from Monday washing to Saturday baking, with instructions on health, food, clothing, cleanliness, care of servants and children, gardening, and hundreds of other household details. Such duties, Beecher emphasized, should never be taken as "petty, trivial or unworthy" since "no statesman . . . had more frequent calls for wisdom, firmness, tact, discrimination, prudence, and versatility of talent."

The social custom of assigning the sexes different roles, of course, was not new. In earlier agrarian societies, gender-based functions were closely tied to the household and often overlapped. As the more complex economy of the nineteenth century matured, economic production came to be increasingly separated from the home, and the home in turn became a refuge from the outside world, with separate and distinctive functions for men and women. Some have argued that the home became a trap for women, a prison that hindered fulfillment. But others have noted that it often gave women a sphere of independence in which they might

The American Woman's Home, *1869. This is an illustrated page from Catharine Beecher's book. Although Beecher believed in the importance of educating women, she argued that women should remain in the home and be skilled in the domestic arts of cooking, cleaning, and child rearing.*

exercise a degree of initiative and leadership. The so-called cult of domesticity idealized a woman's moral role in civilizing husband and family.

The official status of women during this period remained much as it had been in the colonial era. Women were barred from the ministry and most other professions. Higher education was not available. Women could not serve on juries. Nor could they vote. A wife had no control of her property or even of her children. A wife could not make a will, sign a contract, or bring suit in court without her husband's permission. Her legal status was like that of a minor, a slave, or a free black.

Gradually, however, women began to protest their status, and men began to listen. The organized movement for women's rights had its origins in 1840, when the American antislavery movement split over the question of women's right to participate. American women decided then that they needed to organize on behalf of their own emancipation too.

In 1848 two prominent moral reformers and advocates of women's rights, Lucretia Mott, a Philadelphia Quaker, and Elizabeth Cady Stanton, a graduate of Troy Seminary who refused to be merely "a household drudge," called a convention to discuss "the social, civil, and religious condition and rights of women."

The hastily organized Seneca Falls Convention, the first of its kind, issued on July 19, 1848, a clever paraphrase of Jefferson's Declaration of Independence. Called the Declaration of Sentiments, it was mainly the work of Stanton. The document proclaimed the self-evident truth that "all men and women are created equal," and the attendant resolutions said that all laws that placed women "in a position inferior to that of men, are contrary to the great precept of nature, and therefore of no force or authority." Such language was too strong for most of the thousand delegates, and only about a third of them signed it. Ruffled male editors lampooned the women activists as being "love-starved spinsters" and "petticoat rebels." Yet the Seneca Falls gathering represented an important first step in the evolving campaign for women's rights.

From 1850 until the Civil War, the women's rights leaders held annual conventions and carried on a program of organizing, lecturing, and petitioning. The movement had to struggle in the face of meager funds and antifeminist women and men. Its success resulted from the work of a few undaunted women who refused to be cowed by the odds against them. Susan B. Anthony, already active in temperance and antislavery groups, joined the crusade in the 1850s. At age seventeen she had angrily noted, "What an absurd notion that women have not intellectual and moral faculties sufficient for anything else but domestic concerns!" Unlike Stanton and Mott, Anthony was unmarried and therefore able to devote most of her attention to the women's crusade. As one observer put it, Stanton "forged the thunderbolts and Miss Anthony hurled them." Both were young when the movement started and both lived into the twentieth century, focusing after the Civil War on demands for women's suffrage. Many of the feminists like Elizabeth Stanton, Lucretia Mott, and Lucy Stone had supportive husbands, and the movement won prominent male champions such as Ralph Waldo Emerson, Walt Whitman, William Ellery Channing, and William Lloyd Garrison.

Elizabeth Cady Stanton (left) and Susan B. Anthony (right). Stanton "forged the thunderbolts and Miss Anthony hurled them."

The fruits of the movement ripened slowly. Women did not gain the ballot, but there were some legal gains. The state of Mississippi was in 1839 the first to grant married women control over their property; by the 1860s eleven more states had such laws. Still, the only jobs open to educated women in any numbers were nursing and teaching, both of which extended the domestic roles of health care and nurture into the world outside. Both brought relatively lower status and pay than "man's work" despite the skills, training, and responsibility involved. Against the odds, a hardy band of women carved out professional careers.

UTOPIAN COMMUNITIES Amid the pervasive climate of reform during the Jacksonian era, the quest for utopia flourished. Plans for ideal communities had long been an American passion, at least since the Puritans set out to build a wilderness Zion. The visionary communes of the nineteenth century often had purely economic and social objectives, but those rooted in religion proved most durable.

More than a hundred utopian communities sprang up between 1800 and 1900. Those founded by the Shakers, officially the United Society of Believers in Christ's Second Appearing, proved to be long-lasting. Ann Lee Stanley (Mother Ann) reached New York State with eight followers in 1774. Believing religious fervor a sign of inspiration from the Holy Ghost, Mother Ann and her followers had strange fits in which they saw visions and prophesied. These manifestations later evolved into a ritual dance—hence the name Shakers. Shaker doctrine held God to be a dual personality: in Christ the masculine side was manifested, in Mother Ann the feminine element. Mother Ann preached celibacy to prepare Shakers for the perfection that was promised them in Heaven. The church would first gather in the elect, and eventually in the spirit world convert and save all humankind.

Mother Ann died in 1784, but the group found new leaders. From the first community at Mount Lebanon, New York, the movement spread to new colonies in New England, and soon afterward into Ohio and Kentucky. By 1830 about twenty groups were flourishing. In Shaker communities all property was held in common. Governance of the colonies was concentrated in the hands of select groups chosen by the ministry, or "Head of Influence" at Mount Lebanon. To outsiders this might seem almost despotic, but the Shakers emphasized equality of labor and reward, and members were free to leave at will. The Shakers' farms

Shaker Dance. *The Shakers, who were officially named the United Society of Believers in Christ's Second Appearing, participated in ritual dances, as shown in this illustration.*

were among the leading sources of garden seed and medicinal herbs, and many of their manufactures, including clothing, household items, and especially furniture, were prized for their simple beauty. By the mid–twentieth century, however, few members remained alive; they had reached the peak of activity in the years 1830–1860.

John Humphrey Noyes, founder of the Oneida Community, had a quite different model of the ideal community. He was the son of a Vermont congressman. Educated at Dartmouth and then Yale Divinity School, he discovered true religion at one of Charles G. Finney's revivals and entered the ministry. He was forced out, however, when he concluded that with true conversion came perfection and a complete release from sin. In 1836 he gathered a group of "Perfectionists" around his home in Putney, Vermont. Ten years later Noyes announced a new doctrine of "complex marriage," which meant that every man in the community was married to every woman and vice versa. "In a holy community," he claimed, "there is no more reason why sexual intercourse should be restrained by law, than why eating and drinking should be." Authorities thought otherwise, and Noyes was arrested for practicing his "free love" theology. He fled to New York and in 1848 established the Oneida Community, which numbered more than 200 by 1851.

The communal group eked out a living with farming and logging until the mid-1850s, when the inventor of a new steel animal trap joined the community. Oneida traps were soon known as the best in the country. The community then branched out into sewing silk, canning fruits, and making silver spoons. The spoons were so popular that, with the addition of knives and forks, tableware became the Oneida specialty. In 1879, however, the community faced a crisis when Noyes fled to Canada to avoid prosecution for adultery. The members then abandoned universal marriage, and in 1881 decided to convert into a joint-stock company, the Oneida Community, Ltd., which remains today a successful flatware company.

In contrast to these religious-based communities, Robert Owen's New Harmony was based on a secular principle. A British capitalist who worried about the degrading social effects of the factory system, Owen built a model factory town, supported labor legislation, and set forth a scheme for a model community in his pamphlet *A New View of Society* (1813). Later he bought the town of Harmony, Indiana, and promptly christened it New Harmony.

In 1825 a varied group of about 900 colonists gathered in New Harmony for a period of transition from Owen's ownership to the new system of cooperation. After only nine months' trial, Owen turned over management of the colony to a town meeting of all residents and a council of town officers. The high proportion of learned participants generated a certain intellectual electricity about the place. For a time it looked like a brilliant success, but New Harmony soon fell into discord. Every idealist wanted his or her own patented plan put into practice. In 1827 Owen returned from a visit to England to find New Harmony insolvent. The following year he dissolved the project and sold or leased the lands on good terms, in many cases to the settlers. All that remained he turned over to his sons, who stayed and became American citizens.

Brook Farm was surely the most celebrated of all the utopian communities because it had the support of Ralph Waldo Emerson, Margaret Fuller, and countless other well-known literary figures of New England. Nathaniel Hawthorne, a member, later memorialized the failure of Brook Farm in his novel *The Blithedale Romance* (1852). George Ripley, a Unitarian minister and transcendentalist, conceived of Brook Farm as a kind of early-day "think tank," combining high thinking and plain living. The place survived, however, mainly because of an excellent community school that drew tuition-paying students from outside. In 1846

Brook Farm's main building burned down, and the community spirit expired in the embers.

Utopian communities, with few exceptions, quickly ran out of steam. Soon after Hawthorne left Brook Farm he wrote: "It already looks like a dream behind me." His life there was "an unnatural and unsuitable, and therefore an unreal one." Such experiments, performed in relative isolation, had little effect on the real world outside, where reformers wrestled with the sins of the multitudes. Among all the targets of reformers' wrath, one great evil would finally take precedence over the others—human bondage. The paradox of American slavery coupled with American freedom, of "the world's fairest hope linked with man's foulest crime," in Herman Melville's words, would inspire the climactic crusade of the age, abolitionism, one that would ultimately move to the center of the political stage and sweep the nation into an epic struggle.

MAKING CONNECTIONS

- The antislavery campaign, especially its abolitionist aspect, was related to the reform movements in this chapter. It is discussed following the section on slavery in Chapter 15.

- Chapter 17 shows how the Civil War had a significant impact on the status of women in American society, a continuation of a theme discussed here.

FURTHER READING

Russel B. Nye's *Society and Culture in America, 1830–1860* (1974) provides a wide-ranging survey. On the reform impulse, consult Ronald G. Walter's *American Reformers, 1815–1860* (1978). Revivalist religion is treated in Nathan O. Hatch's *The Democratization of American Christianity* (1989), and Christine Heyrman's *Southern*

Cross: The Beginnings of the Bible Belt (1997). On the Mormons, see Leonard J. Arrington's *Brigham Young: American Moses* (1985).

The best introduction to transcendentalist thought is Paul Boller's *American Transcendentalism, 1830–1860* (1974). Several good works describe various aspects of the antebellum reform movement. For temperance, see W. J. Rorabaugh's *The Alcoholic Republic: An American Tradition* (1979) and Barbara Leslie Epstein's *The Politics of Domesticity: Women, Evangelism, and Temperance in Nineteenth-Century America* (1981). Stephen Nissenbaum's *Sex, Diet, and Debility in Jacksonian America* (1980) looks at health reform. On prison reform and other humanitarian projects, see David J. Rothman's *The Discovery of the Asylum* (1971), and Thomas J. Brown's biography, *Dorothea Dix: New England Reformer* (1998). Lawrence A. Cremin's *American Education: The National Experience, 1783–1876* (1980) traces early school reform.

On women during the antebellum period, see Nancy F. Cott's *The Bonds of Womanhood: "Woman's Sphere" in New England, 1780–1835* (1977) and Ellen C. DuBois's *Feminism and Suffrage: The Emergence of an Independent Women's Movement in America, 1848–1869* (1978).

Michael Fellman's *The Unbounded Frame: Freedom and Community in Nineteenth-Century American Utopianism* (1973) surveys the utopian movements.

14 ∽ MANIFEST DESTINY

CHAPTER ORGANIZER

This chapter focuses on:

- national politics in the 1840s.

- the factors leading to westward migrations and the conditions faced by western settlers.

- the causes, course, and consequences of the Mexican War.

*D*uring the 1840s the westering impulse, the quest for a better chance and more living room, continued to excite the American imagination. "If hell lay to the west," one pioneer declared, "Americans would cross heaven to get there." Millions of Americans were willing to cross the Mississippi River and experience unrelenting hardships in order to conquer new frontiers and fulfill their "providential destiny" to subdue the entire continent. By 1860 some 4.3 million people had settled in the trans-Mississippi West.

Of course, most of these settlers and adventurers sought to exploit the many economic opportunities afforded by the new lands. Trappers and farmers, miners and merchants, hunters, ranchers, teachers, domestics, and prostitutes, among others, headed west seeking their fortunes. Others sought religious freedom or new converts to Christianity. Whatever the reason, the pioneers formed an unceasing migratory stream flowing across the Great Plains and the Rocky Mountains. The Indian and Mexican inhabitants of the region soon found themselves swept aside by successive waves of American settlement. In 1858 President James Buchanan could report that the nation was bound east and west "by a chain of Americans which can never be broken."

THE TYLER YEARS

When William Henry Harrison took office in 1841, elected like Jackson mainly on the strength of his military record and his lack of a public stand on key issues, the Whig leaders expected him to be a figurehead, a tool in the hands of Daniel Webster and Henry Clay. Webster became secretary of state. Clay, who preferred to stay in the Senate, tried to fill the cabinet with his friends. Within a few days of the inauguration, signs of strain appeared between Harrison and Clay, whose disappointment at missing the nomination had made him peevish. At one point, an exasperated Harrison exploded: "Mr. Clay, you forget that I am the President." But the quarrel never had a chance to develop, for Harrison served the shortest term of any president—after the longest inaugural address. At the inauguration, held on a chilly, rainy day, he caught cold after delivering a two-hour speech. On April 4, 1841, exactly one month after the inauguration, he died of pneumonia at age sixty-eight.

Thus John Tyler of Virginia, the first vice-president to succeed on the death of a president, served practically all of Harrison's term. And if there was ambiguity about where Harrison stood, there was none about Tyler's convictions. At age fifty-one, the thin, fragile Virginian was the youngest president to date, but he already had a long career behind him as legislator, governor, congressman, and senator, and his opinions on all the important issues had been forcefully stated and were widely known. Although officially a Whig, at an earlier time he might have been called an Old Republican; he was stubbornly opposed to everything associated with Clay's American System—protective tariffs, a national bank, and internal improvements at national expense—and in favor of strict construction and states' rights.

When asked about the concept of nationalism, Tyler replied that he had "no such word in my political vocabulary." Originally a Democrat, he had broken with the party over Andrew Jackson's denial of a state's right to nullify federal laws and Jackson's imperious use of executive authority. In 1840 Tyler had been chosen to "balance" the Whig ticket, with no expectation that he would wield power. Acid-tongued John Quincy Adams said that Tyler was "a political sectarian of the slave-driving, Virginian, Jeffersonian school, principled against all improvement, with all the interests and passions and vices of slavery rooted in his moral and political constitution."

DOMESTIC AFFAIRS   Given more finesse on Henry Clay's part, he might have bridged the divisions among the Whigs over financial issues. But for once, driven by disappointment and ambition, the "Great Compromiser" lost his instinct for compromise. When Congress met in special session in 1841, Clay introduced a series of resolutions designed to supply the platform that the party had evaded in the previous election. The chief points were repeal of the Independent Treasury Act, establishment of a Third Bank of the United States, distribution to the states of proceeds from federal land sales, and a higher tariff. Clay then set out to push his program through Congress. "Tyler dares not resist me. I will drive him before me," he said.

Tyler, it turned out, was not easily driven. Although he agreed to allow the repeal of the Independent Treasury Act and signed a higher tariff bill in 1842, Tyler vetoed Clay's bill for a new national bank. This provoked Tyler's entire cabinet, with the exception of Secretary of State Daniel Webster, to resign. Tyler replaced the five defectors with anti-Jackson Democrats like himself who had become Whigs. Irate congressional Whigs expelled him from the party, and Democrats viewed him as an untrustworthy "renegade." By 1842 Clay's legislative program was in ruins. Yet by opposing Clay and the Whigs, Tyler had become a president without a party.

FOREIGN AFFAIRS   In foreign relations, tensions with Great Britain distracted Tyler's attention. In 1841 British ships patrolling off the coast of Africa threatened to board and search vessels flying the American flag to see if they carried slaves. The American government refused to accept such enforcement. Relations were further strained late in 1841 when American slaves on the *Creole,* bound from Hampton Roads, Virginia, to New Orleans, mutinied and sailed into Nassau, where the

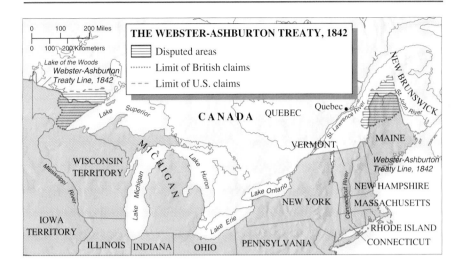

THE WEBSTER-ASHBURTON TREATY, 1842

Disputed areas
.... Limit of British claims
– – – Limit of U.S. claims

British set them free. Secretary of State Webster demanded that the slaves be returned as American property, but the British refused.

Fortunately at this point a new British ministry decided to accept Webster's overtures for negotiations and sent Lord Ashburton to Washington, D.C. The Maine boundary was settled in what Webster later called "the battle of the maps." Webster settled for about seven-twelfths of the contested lands along the Maine boundary, and except for Oregon, which remained under joint occupation, he settled the other border disputes by accepting the existing line between the Connecticut and St. Lawrence Rivers, and by compromising on the line between Lake Superior and Lake of the Woods. The Webster-Ashburton Treaty (1842) also provided for joint patrols off Africa to suppress the slave trade.

THE WESTERN FRONTIER

In the early 1840s, the American people were no more stirred by the quarrels of Tyler and Clay over issues such as the banking system and tariff policy than students of history would be at a later date. What aroused public interest was the mounting evidence that the "empire of freedom" was hurdling the barriers of the "Great American Desert" and the Rocky Mountains, reaching out toward the Pacific coast. In 1845, a New York newspaper editor and Democratic party propagandist named John O'Sullivan gave a name to this aggressive spirit of expansion. "Our manifest destiny," he wrote, "is to overspread the continent allotted by Providence for the free development of our yearly multiplying millions." God, in other words, felt that the United States should extend from the Atlantic to the Pacific—and beyond. At its best this much-trumpeted notion of "Manifest Destiny" offered a moral justification for American expansion, a prescription for what an enlarged United States could and should be. At its worst it was a cluster of flimsy rationalizations for naked greed and imperial ambition. Whatever the case, hundreds of thousands of people began streaming into the Far West in the aftermath of the Panic of 1837 and the prolonged economic depression.

WESTERN INDIANS   The territory across the Mississippi River was a new environment as well as a new culture. The Great Plains and the Far West were already occupied by Indians and Mexicans, peoples who had lived in the region for centuries and had established their own distinctive customs and ways of life. Historians estimate that over 325,000 Indians inhabited the Southwest, the Great Plains, California, and the Pacific Northwest in 1840, when the great migration of white settlers began to pour into the region. These Native Americans often competed with and warred against each other. They were divided into more than 200 different tribes, each with its own language, religion, economic base, kinship practices, and system of governance. Some were primarily farmers; others were nomadic hunters who preyed upon game animals as well as other Indians.

Some twenty-three tribes resided in the Great Plains, a vast grassland stretching from the Mississippi River west to the Rocky Mountains and from Canada to Mexico. This region had been virtually devoid of a human presence until the Spaniards introduced the horse and gun in the late sixteenth century. Prior to the advent of horses, Indians relied upon dogs as their beast of burden. A horse could carry seven times as much weight as a dog. Even more important, the horse dramatically increased the mobility of the Plains Indians, enabling them to leave their villages and follow the great buffalo herds. They used buffalo meat for food and transformed the skins into clothing, bedding, and teepee coverings. The bones and horns served as tools and utensils. Even buffalo manure could be dried and used for fuel.

Buffalo Lancing in the Snow Drifts, *c. 1860s. This painting by George Catlin shows the Sioux hunting buffalo.*

Plains Indians such as the Arapaho, Blackfoot, Cheyenne, Kiowa, and Sioux were horse-borne nomads; they moved across the grasslands, carrying their teepees with them. Disputes over buffalo and hunting grounds provoked clashes between rival tribes, which helps explain the cult of the warrior among the Plains Indians. Scalping or killing an enemy would earn praise from elders and feathers for their ceremonial headdresses. The most revered chiefs were allowed to wear eagle-feather warbonnets. Yet chiefs exercised only modest authority over their followers. As Chief Low Horn, a Blackfoot, explained, the chiefs "could not restrain their young men . . . their young men were wild, and ambitious, in their turn to be braves and chiefs. They wanted by some brave act to win the favor of their young women, and bring scalps and horses to show their prowess."

Several quite different Indian tribes lived to the south and west of the Plains Indians. In the arid region including what is today Arizona, New Mexico, and southern Utah were the peaceful Pueblo tribes—Acoma, Hopi, Laguna, Taos, Zia, Zuni. They were sophisticated farmers who lived in adobe villages along rivers that irrigated their crops of corn, beans, and squash. Their rivals were the Apache and Navajo, warlike hunters who roamed the countryside in small bands and preyed upon the Pueblos. They, in turn, were periodically harassed by their powerful enemies, the Comanches.

To the north, in the Great Basin between the Rocky Mountains and the Sierra Nevada range, Indians such as the Paiutes and Gosiutes struggled to survive in the harsh, arid region of what is today Nevada, Utah, and eastern California. They traveled in family groups and subsisted on berries, pine nuts, insects, and rodents. West of the mountains, along the California coast, the Indians lived in small villages. They gathered wild plants and acorns and were quite adept at fishing in the rivers and bays. More than 100,000 Indians lived in coastal California in the 1840s.

The Indian tribes living along the northwest Pacific coast—the Nisqually, Spokane, Yakima, Chinook, Klamath, and Nez Percé (pierced noses)—enjoyed the most abundant natural resources and the most temperate climate. The ocean and rivers provided bountiful supplies of seafood—whales, seals, salmon, crabs. The lush forests just east of the coast harbored game, berries, and nuts. And the majestic stands of fir, redwood, and cedar offered wood for cooking and shelter.

All these Indian tribes eventually felt the unrelenting pressure of white expansion and conquest. Because Indian life on the Plains depended on the buffalo, the influx of white settlers posed a direct threat to their cultural survival. When federal officials could not coerce, cajole, or confuse Indian leaders into selling title to their tribal lands, fighting ensued. And after the discovery of gold in California in 1848, the tidal wave of white expansion flowed all the way to the west coast.

In 1851 U.S. officials invited the Indian tribes from the northern Plains to a conference held in a grassy valley along the North Platte River, near Ft. Laramie in what is now southeastern Wyoming. Almost 10,000 Indians—men, women, and children—attended the treaty council. What made the huge gathering even more remarkable is that so many of the tribes were at war with one another. After nearly three weeks of heated discussions and after bestowing on the chiefs a mountain of gifts, federal negotiators and tribal leaders agreed to what became known as the Ft. Laramie Treaty. The American government promised to provide an annual cash payment to the Indians as compensation for the damages caused by wagon trains traversing their hunting grounds. In exchange, the Indians agreed to stop harassing white caravans, to allow federal forts to be built, and to confine themselves to a specified area "of limited extent and well-defined boundaries."

As the first comprehensive treaty with the Plains Indians, this agreement foreshadowed the "reservation" concept of Indian management. Several tribes, however, refused to accept the treaty provisions. The most powerful tribe, the Lakota Sioux, reluctantly signed the agreement but thereafter failed to abide by its restrictions. "You have split my lands and I don't like it," declared Black Hawk, a Sioux chief at Ft. Laramie. "These lands once belonged to the Kiowas and the Crows, but we whipped these nations out of them, and in this we did what the white men do when they want the lands of the Indians."

THE SPANISH WEST AND MEXICAN REVOLUTION As American settlers moved westward, they also encountered Spanish-speaking peoples. Many whites were as contemptuous of the Hispanic peoples as they were of Indians. Senator Lewis Cass, the expansionist from Michigan, expressed the sentiment of many Americans during a debate over the annexation of New Mexico. "We do not want the people of Mexico," he declared, "either as citizens or as subjects. All we want is a portion of territory." He viewed Mexicans as ignorant, indolent, and conniving. The vast majority of the Spanish-speaking people in what is today the American Southwest resided in New Mexico. Most of these were of mixed Indian and Spanish blood and were poor ranch hands or small farmers and herders.

The Spanish had been less successful in colonizing Arizona and Texas than they had been in New Mexico and Florida. The Yuma and Apache Indians in Arizona and the Comanches and Apaches in Texas thwarted efforts to establish Catholic missions. After years of fruitless missionary efforts among the Pueblo Indians, one Spaniard complained that "most" of them "have never forsaken idolatry, and they appear to be Christians more by force than to be Indians who are reduced to the Holy Faith." By 1790, the Hispanic population in Texas numbered only 2,510 while in New Mexico it exceeded 20,000.

In 1807 French forces occupied Spain and imprisoned the king. This created both consternation and confusion throughout Spain's colonial possessions, including Mexico. Miguel Hidalgo y Costilla, a *creole* (Europeans born in the New World) Mexican priest, took advantage of the fluid situation to organize a revolt of Indians and *mestizos* (people of mixed Indian and white ancestry) against Spanish rule in Mexico. But

Church interior, Las Trampas, New Mexico, constructed around 1760.

the poorly organized uprising failed miserably. In 1811 Spanish troops captured Hidalgo and executed him. Other Mexicans, however, continued to yearn for independence. In 1820, Mexican creoles again tried to liberate themselves from Spanish authority. By then, the Spanish forces in Mexico had lost much of their cohesion and dedication. Facing a growing revolt, the last Spanish officials withdrew from Mexico in 1821, and it became an independent nation.

Mexican independence unleashed tremors throughout the Southwest. In New Mexico and Arizona, American fur traders streamed into the region and developed a lucrative commerce in beaver pelts. Wagon trains carrying American settlers began to make their way from St. Louis along the Santa Fe Trail. In California, American entrepreneurs flooded into the now-Mexican province and soon became a powerful force for change; by 1848 Americans made up half of the non-Indian population. In Texas, American adventurers decided to promote their own independence from a newly independent—and chaotic—Mexican government. Suddenly, it seemed, the Southwest was a ripe new frontier for American exploitation and settlement.

THE ROCKY MOUNTAINS AND OREGON COUNTRY The Northwest consisted of the Nebraska, Washington, and Oregon Territories. Fur traders were especially drawn to the Missouri River with its many tributaries. By the mid-1820s, there developed the "rendezvous system," in which trappers, traders, and Indians from all over the Rocky Mountain country gathered annually at some designated place, usually in or near the Grand Tetons, in order to trade pelts and hides. But by 1840 the great days of the western fur trade were over. The streams no longer teemed with beavers.

During the 1820s and 1830s, the fur trade had sired a uniquely reckless breed of "mountain men" who deserted civilization for the pursuit of the beaver and reverted to a primitive existence in the wilderness. The rugged trappers lived sometimes in splendid isolation, sometimes in the shelter of primitive forts, and sometimes among Indians. They were the first to find their way around in the Rocky Mountains, and they pioneered the trails over which settlers by the 1840s were beginning to flood the Oregon Country and trickle across the border into California.

Beyond the mountains, the Oregon Country stretched from the 42nd parallel north to 54°40′, between which Spain and Russia had given up their rights, leaving Great Britain and the United States as the only claimants. Under the Convention of 1818, the two countries had agreed to "joint occupation." Until the 1830s, however, joint occupation had been a legal technicality, because the only American presence was the occasional mountain man who wandered into the Pacific slope or the infrequent trading vessel from Boston, Salem, or New York.

George Caleb Bingham's Fur Traders Descending the Missouri, 1845.

Word of Oregon's fertile soil, plentiful rainfall, and magnificent forests gradually spread eastward. By the late 1830s, in the midst of economic hard times after the Panic of 1837, a trickle of emigrants was flowing along the Oregon Trail. Soon, "Oregon Fever" swept the nation. In 1841 and 1842 the first sizable wagon trains made the trip, and in 1843 the movement became a mass migration. "The Oregon fever has broke out," wrote a settler in 1843, "and is now raging like any other contagion." By 1845 there were about 5,000 settlers in the Willamette Valley of Oregon.

CALIFORNIA   California was also an alluring attraction for new settlers and entrepreneurs. It first felt the influence of European culture in 1769, when Spain grew concerned about Russian fur and seal traders moving south along the Pacific coast from their base in Alaska. To thwart Russian intentions, Spain sent a naval expedition to explore and settle the region. The Spanish discovered San Francisco Bay and constructed *presidios* (military garrisons) at San Diego and Monterey. Even more important, Franciscan friars led by Junipero Serra established a mission at San Diego.

Over the next fifty years Franciscans built twenty more missions, spaced a day's journey apart along the coast from San Diego to San Francisco. There they converted Indians and established thriving agricultural estates. The mission-centered culture created by the Hispanics settlers who migrated to California from Mexico was quite different from the patterns of conquest and settlement in Texas and New Mexico. In those more settled regions, the original missions were converted into secular parishes, and the property was divided among the Indians. In California the missions were much larger, more influential, and longer-lasting.

Franciscan missionaries, aided by Spanish soldiers, gathered most of the coastal Indian population in California under their control. They viewed the Indians as ignorant and indolent heathens living in a "free and undisciplined" society. The friars were determined to convert them to Catholicism and make them useful members of the Spanish Empire. Viewing the missions as crucial outposts of their empire, the Spanish government provided military support, annual cash grants, and supplies from Mexico. The Franciscan friars enticed the local Indians into the adobe-walled, tile-roofed missions by offering them gifts or impressing them with their "magical" religious rituals. Once inside the missions, the Indians were baptized into the Catholic faith, taught the Spanish language, and stripped of their Indian heritage. The number of "mission Indians" more than doubled between 1776 and 1784. The mission Indians were forced to wear Spanish clothes, memorize a catechism, abandon their native rituals, and obey the friars. Soldiers living in the mission enforced the will of the friars.

LABOR IN THE MISSIONS The California mission served multiple roles. It was a church, fortress, home, town, farm, and imperial agent. The missions were economic as well as religious and cultural institutions; they quickly became substantial agricultural enterprises. Missions produced crops, livestock, clothing, and household goods, both for profit and to supply the neighboring *presidios* (forts). Indians

Sketch of the Order of San Francisco in the former Mission of Santa Barbara, from a collection of reminiscences by Edward Vischer of California under Spain and Mexico.

provided the labor for the missions. The Franciscans viewed regimented Indian labor as more than a practical necessity: in their view disciplined work was a morally enriching responsibility essential to transforming unproductive Indians into industrious Christians.

The daily routine in the missions began at dawn with the ringing of a bell, which summoned the community to prayer. Work began an hour later and did not end until an hour before sunset. Indians worked at the missions six days a week. They did not work on Sundays and religious holidays. Instead of wages, the Indians received clothing, food, housing, and religious instruction. Children and the elderly were expected to work. Most male Indians performed manual labor in the fields. Some were trained in special skills such as masonry, carpentry, or leatherwork. Women performed domestic chores such as cooking, sewing, cleaning, and shucking corn. During harvest season, everyone was expected to help in the fields.

The Franciscans used overwhelming force to maintain the labor system in the missions. Yet most missions experienced periodic Indian revolts. Rebellious Indians were whipped or imprisoned. Soldiers hunted down runaways. Mission Indians died at an alarming rate. One Franciscan friar reported that "of every four Indian children born, three die in their first or second year, while those who survive do not reach the age of twenty-five." Infectious disease was the primary threat, but the grueling labor regimen took a high toll as well. The Indian population along the California coast declined from 72,000 in 1769 to 18,000 by 1821. Saving souls cost many lives.

EARLY DEVELOPMENT IN CALIFORNIA   For all of its rich natural resources, California remained thinly populated by Indians and mission friars well into the nineteenth century. It was a simple, almost feudal, agrarian society, without schools, industry, or defenses. In 1821, when Mexico wrested its independence from Spain, Californians took comfort in the fact that Mexico City was so far away that it would exercise little effective control over its farthest state. During the next two decades, Californians, including many recent American arrivals, staged ten revolts against the governors dispatched to lord over them.

Yet Mexican rule did produce a dramatic change in California history. In 1824, Mexico passed a colonization act that granted hundreds of huge "rancho" estates to Mexican settlers. With free labor extracted from Indians, who were treated like slaves, the *rancheros* lived a life of self-indulgent luxury and ease, roaming their lands, gambling, horse-racing, bull-baiting, and dancing. These freebooting *rancheros* soon cast covetous eyes on the vast estates controlled by the Franciscan missions. In 1833–1834, they convinced the Mexican government to confiscate the California missions, exile the Franciscan friars, release the Indians from church control, and make the mission lands available to new settlement. Within a few years, some 700 huge new rancho grants of 4,500 to 50,000 acres were issued along the coast from San Diego to San Francisco. Organized like feudal estates, these California ranches resembled southern plantations. But the death rate for Indian workers was twice as high as that of slaves in the Deep South.

Few accounts of life in California, however, took note of the brutalities inflicted on the Indians. Instead they portrayed the region as a proverbial land of milk and honey, ripe for development. Such a natural paradise could not long remain a secret. By the late 1820s, American trappers wandered in from time to time, and American ships began to enter the "hide and tallow" trade. The ranchos of California produced cowhide and beef tallow in large quantity, and both products enjoyed a brisk demand, cowhides mainly for shoes and the tallow chiefly for candles.

By the mid-1830s, shippers began setting up representatives in California to buy the hides and store them until a company ship arrived. One of these agents, Thomas O. Larkin at Monterey, would play

Sutter's Fort, renamed Fort Sacramento during the Mexican War.

a leading role in the American acquisition of California. Larkin stuck pretty much to his trade, operating a retail business on the side, while others branched out and struck it rich in ranching. The most noteworthy of the traders, however, was not American, but Swiss. John A. Sutter had abandoned his Swiss family in order to avoid arrest for bankruptcy. He found his way to California via Oregon, Hawaii, and Alaska, Santa Fe, and Missouri. In Monterey he persuaded the Mexican governor to give him land on which to plant a colony of Swiss émigrés.

At the juncture of the Sacramento and American Rivers (later the site of Sacramento) Sutter built an enormous enclosure that guarded an entire village of settlers and shops. At New Helvetia (Americans called it Sutter's Fort), completed in 1843, no Swiss colony materialized, but the baronial estate, worked by local Indians, became the mecca for Americans bent on settling the Sacramento country. It stood at the end of what became the most traveled route through the Sierras, the California Trail, which forked off the Oregon Trail and led through the mountains near Lake Tahoe. By the start of 1846 there were perhaps 800 Americans in California, along with some 8,000–12,000 Californios (settlers of Spanish descent).

MOVING WEST

Most of the western pioneers during the second quarter of the nineteenth century were American-born whites from the upper South and Midwest. A few blacks joined in the migration. One settler remembered seeing "a Negro woman . . . trampling along through heat and dust, carrying a cast-iron black stove on her head, with her provisions and a blanket piled on top . . . bravely pushing on for California." Although some emigrants traveled by sea to California, most went overland. Between 1841 and 1867, some 350,000 men, women, and children made the arduous trek to California or Oregon, while hundreds of thousands of others settled along the way in Colorado, Texas, Arkansas, and other areas. Americans of diverse ethnic origin and religious persuasion moved westward, and their encounters with the people they found there made for a volatile mix.

THE SANTA FE TRAIL   After gaining its independence in 1821, the new government of Mexico was much more interested in trade with Americans than Spain had been. In Spanish-controlled Santa Fe, in fact, all commerce with the United States had been banned. After 1821, however, trade flourished. Hundreds of entrepreneurs made the thousand-mile trek from St. Louis to Santa Fe, forging a route that became known as the Santa Fe Trail. These American traders braved deserts, mountains, and the threat of Indian attacks. Soon, Mexican traders began leading caravans east to Missouri. By the 1830s, there was so much commercial activity between Mexico and St. Louis that the Mexican silver peso became the primary medium of exchange in Missouri.

As they streamed into Santa Fe, American traders discovered the weakness of Mexico's control over its northern borderlands, and the Americans developed contempt for the "mongrel" population of the region. From the 1820s on, however, that population had begun to include a few Americans who lingered in Santa Fe or Taos, using them as jumping-off points for hunting and trapping expeditions northward and westward.

The traders along the Santa Fe Trail pioneered more than a new trail. They showed that heavy wagons could cross the plains and the mountains, and they developed the technique of organized caravans for common protection.

THE OVERLAND TRAIL   As on the Santa Fe Trail, people bound for Oregon and California traveled in caravans of wagons. But on the Overland Trail (also known as the Oregon Trail), most of the people were settlers rather than traders. They traveled mostly in family groups and came from all over the United States. The wagon trains followed the trail west from Independence, Missouri, along the North Platte River into what is now Wyoming, through South Pass down to Fort Bridger (abode of a celebrated mountain man, Jim Bridger), then down the Snake River to the Columbia River, and along the Columbia to their goal in the fertile Willamette Valley. They usually left Missouri in late spring, completing the grueling 2,000-mile trek in six months. Traveling in ox-drawn, canvas-covered wagons nicknamed "prairie schooners," they jostled their way across the dusty or muddy trails and traversed rugged mountains at the rate of twelve to fifteen miles per day. By 1845, some 5,000 people were making the arduous journey annually. The discovery of gold in California in 1848 brought some 30,000 pioneers along the Oregon Trail in 1849. By 1850, the peak year of travel along the trail, the number had risen to 55,000.

Contrary to popular myth, the Indians rarely attacked wagon trains. Less than 4 percent of the fatalities associated with the Overland Trail experience were the result of Indian attacks. More often, the Indians either allowed the settlers to pass through their tribal lands unmolested or demanded payment. Many wagon trains never encountered a single Indian, and others received generous aid from Indians who served as guides, advisers, or traders. The Indians, one woman pioneer noted, "proved better than represented." To be sure, as the number of pioneers increased dramatically during the 1850s, tensions between overlanders and Indians increased, but never to the degree portrayed in Western novels and films.

Still, the journey west was incredibly difficult. Few who embarked on their western quest were adequately prepared for the ordeals they were to face. The diary of Amelia Knight, who set out for Oregon in 1853 with her husband and their seven children, reveals the mortal threats along the trail: "Chatfield quite sick with scarlet fever. A calf took sick and died before breakfast. Lost one of our oxen; he dropped dead in the yoke. I could hardly help shedding tears. Yesterday my eighth child was born." Cholera claimed many lives. On average there was one grave every eighty yards along the trail between the Missouri River and the Willamette Valley. Some 20,000 pioneers died in all.

The never-ending routine of necessary chores and grinding physical labor on the Overland Trail took its toll on once-buoyant spirits. This

Gathering Buffalo Chips. *Women on the Overland Trail not only had to cook and wash and take care of their children but also had to gather dried buffalo dung for fuel as their wagons crossed the treeless plains.*

was especially true for women, whose labors went on day and night. Uprooting their families and journeying west placed a distinctive burden on wives and mothers accustomed to the comforts of middle-class domesticity. The hardships of trail life shattered the conventional notion of the settled home as the family's moral center and nursery.

Initially, the pioneers along the Overland Trail adopted the same division of labor used back East. Women cooked, washed, sewed, and monitored the children while men drove the wagons, tended the horses and cattle, and handled the heavy labor. But the unique demands of the trail soon dissolved such neat distinctions and posed new tasks. Women found themselves gathering buffalo dung for fuel, pitching in to help dislodge a wagon mired in mud, helping to construct a makeshift bridge, or participating in a variety of other "unladylike" activities. Yet only rarely did menfolk assume conventional female roles. Most of the older women strove to keep distinct the traditional boundaries between men's and women's work, and quarrels frequently erupted. One woman reported that there was "not a little fighting" in their group, "invariably the outcome of disputes over divisions of labor."

The hard labor of the trail understandably provoked tensions within families and powerful yearnings for home. Many a tired pioneer could identify with the following comment in a girl's journal: "Poor Ma said only this morning, 'Oh, I wish we had never started.' She looks so sorrowful and dejected." Another woman wondered "what had possessed my husband, anyway, that he should have thought of bringing us away out through this God forsaken country." Some turned back, but most continued on. And once in Oregon or California they set about establishing stable communities. Noted one settler:

> Friday, October 27.—Arrived at Oregon City at the falls of the Willamette.
> Saturday, October 28.—Went to work.

THE DONNER PARTY   The most tragic story along the Overland Trail involved the party led by George Donner, a prosperous sixty-two-year old farmer from Illinois, who led his family and a train of other settlers along the Oregon Trail in 1846. They made every mistake possible. They started too late in the year, overloaded their wagons, and took a foolish shortcut to California across the Wasatch Mountains in the Utah Territory. In the Wasatch, the Donner party was joined by another group of thirteen pioneers, bringing the total to eighty-seven. Finding themselves lost on their "shortcut," they had to backtrack before finally finding their way across the Wasatch and into the desert leading to the Great Salt Lake. Crossing the desert exacted a terrible toll. They lost over 100 oxen and were forced to abandon several wagons and their precious supplies. Tempers flared as the tired and hungry travelers trudged on. One leader of the party killed a young teamster and was expelled, leaving his wife and children behind.

By the time the Donner party reached Truckee Pass, the last mountain barrier before reaching the Sacramento Valley, the group had grown surly. They knew that they must cross the pass before the next major snowfall hemmed them in, but they were too late. A two-week-long snowfall trapped them in two separate camps. By December eighty-one settlers, half of them children, were marooned, and there was only enough meat to last through the end of the month. Seventeen of the strongest members decided to cross the pass on their own, only to be trapped by more snow on the western slope. Two members died of exposure and starvation. Just before he died, Billy Graves urged his daughters to eat his body. The daughters were appalled by the prospect of cannibalism, but a day later they saw no other choice. The group struggled on, and, when two more died, they, too, were consumed. Only seven lived to reach the Sacramento Valley.

Four search parties were then dispatched to save the rest of the Donner party. Back at the main camps at Alder Creek and Truckee Lake, the survivors slaughtered and ate the last of the livestock, then proceeded to boil hides and bones. When the rescue party finally reached them, they discovered a grisly scene. Thirteen people had died, and cannibalism had become so commonplace that one pioneer noted casually in his diary that "Mrs. Murphy said here yesterday that she thought she would commence on Milt and eat him." As the rescuers led the forty-seven survivors over the pass, George Donner, so weakened that he was unable to walk, stayed behind to die. His wife chose to remain with him.

THE PATHFINDER: JOHN FRÉMONT   Despite the hardships and dangers of the overland crossing, the Far West proved an irresistible attraction. The premier press agent for California, and the Far West generally, was John Charles Frémont, "the Pathfinder"—who mainly "found" paths that the mountain men showed him. Born in Savannah, Georgia, and raised in the South, he had a relentless love of the outdoors and an exuberant, self-promoting personality. Frémont studied at the College of Charleston before being commissioned a second lieutenant in the United States Topographical Corps in 1838. In the early 1840s his new father-in-law, Missouri senator Thomas Hart Benton, arranged the explorations toward Oregon that made Frémont famous. In 1842 he mapped the Oregon Trail—and met Christopher "Kit" Carson, one of the most knowledgeable of the mountain men, who became his frequent associate. In 1843–1844 Frémont,

John Charles Frémont, the Pathfinder.

typically clad in deerskin shirt, blue army trousers, and moccasins, went on to Oregon, then swept down the eastern slopes of the Sierra Nevada Mountains, headed southward through the central valley of California, bypassed the mountains in the south, and returned via Great Salt Lake. His reports on both expeditions, published together in 1845, gained a wide circulation and helped excite the interest of easterners.

TALKS TO ANNEX CALIFORNIA American presidents, beginning with Andrew Jackson, tried to acquire at least northern California, down to San Francisco Bay, by purchase from Mexico. Jackson reasoned that as a free state California could balance the future admission of Texas as a slave state. But Jackson's agent had to be recalled after a clumsy effort to bribe Mexican officials. Tyler's minister to Mexico resumed talks, but they ended abruptly after a bloodless comic-opera conquest of Monterey by the commander of the American Pacific Fleet, who had heard a false rumor of war.

Rumors flourished that the British and French were scheming to grab California, though neither government actually had such intentions. Political conditions in Mexico left the remote territory in near anarchy much of the time, as governors came and went in rapid succession. Amid the chaos many Californios reasoned that they would be better off if they cut ties to Mexico altogether. Some favored an independent state, perhaps under French or British protection. A larger group, led by a Sonoma cattleman, admired the balance of central and local authority in the United States and felt their interests might best be served by American annexation. By the time the Americans were ready to fire the spark of rebellion in California, there was little will in Mexico to resist.

ANNEXING TEXAS

AMERICAN SETTLEMENTS America's lust for new land was most clearly at work in the most accessible of all the Mexican borderlands, Texas. More Americans resided there than in all the other coveted regions combined. In fact, by the 1830s Texas was rapidly turning into an American province, for Mexico welcomed American settlers there as a means of stabilizing the border.

First and foremost among the promoters of Anglo-American settlement was Stephen F. Austin, a Missouri resident who gained from Mexico a huge land grant originally given to his father by Spanish authorities. Before Mexican independence from Spain was fully won, he had started a colony on the lower Brazos River late in 1821, and by 1824 more than 2,000 hardy souls had settled on his lands. In 1825, under a National Colonization Law, the state of Coahuila-Texas offered large tracts to *empresarios,* large ranchers, who promised to sponsor immigrants. Most of the newcomers were southern farmers drawn to rich new cotton lands going for only a few cents an acre. As a young woman settler recalled, "I was a young thing then, but 5 months married, my husband . . . failed in Tennessee. . . . I was ready to go anywhere . . . freely consented. . . . Texas fever rose then . . . there we must go. There without much reflection, we did go." By 1830 the coastal region of eastern Texas had about 20,000 white settlers and 1,000 black slaves brought in to work the cotton.

At that point the Mexican government grew alarmed at the flood of strangers engulfing the province, and it forbade further immigration. But illegal American immigrants moved across the long border as easily as illegal Mexican immigrants would later cross over in the other direction. By 1835 the American population had grown to around 30,000, about ten times the number of Mexicans in Texas. Friction mounted in 1832 and 1833 as Americans organized conventions to demand a state of their own. Instead of granting the request, General Santa Anna, who had seized power in Mexico, dissolved the national congress late in 1834, abolished the federal system, and became dictator of a centralized state. Texans feared the Mexicans intended to free "our slaves and to make slaves of us." They rose in rebellion and summoned a convention which, like the earlier Continental Congress, adopted a "Declaration of Causes" for taking up arms. On March 2, 1836, the Texans declared their independence as Santa Anna approached with an army to suppress them.

INDEPENDENCE FROM MEXICO At San Antonio the Mexican army assaulted a small garrison holed up behind the adobe walls of an abandoned mission, the Alamo. Led by Colonel William B. Travis, a hot-tempered Mississippi lawyer, the troops included not only Texan militiamen but also American volunteers, the most celebrated of whom was

Sam Houston.

Davy Crockett, the Tennessee frontiersman who had fought Indians under Andrew Jackson and then served as a congressman. Full of bounce and brag, he was thoroughly expert at killing. As he once told his men, "Pierce the heart of the enemy as you would a feller that spit in your face, knocked down your wife, burnt up your houses, and called your dog a skunk! Cram his pesky carcass full of thunder and lightning like a stuffed sassidge . . . and bite his nose off into the bargain."

On February 23, 1836, Santa Anna demanded that the 189 defenders at the Alamo surrender. They answered with a cannon shot. The 5,000 Mexicans then launched a series of frontal assaults. For twelve days they were repulsed with fearful losses. Then, on March 6, the defenders of the Alamo were awakened by the sound of Mexican bugles playing the dreaded "Deguello" ("no mercy to the defenders"). Soon thereafter Santa Anna's men attacked from every side. They were twice repulsed, but on the third try, the Mexicans broke through the battered north wall and swarmed through the breach. Colonel Travis was killed by a bullet to the forehead. Davy Crockett and the other frontiersmen used their muskets as clubs, but they too were slain. The notorious slave smuggler, Indian fighter, and inventor of the Bowie knife, Jim Bowie, his pistols emptied, his famous knife bloodied, and his body riddled by Mexican bullets, lay dead on his cot.

Santa Anna ordered the wounded Americans put to death and their bodies burned with the rest. The only survivors were sixteen women, children, and servants. It was a complete victory for the Mexicans, but a costly one. The defenders of the Alamo gave their lives at the cost of 1,544 Mexicans, and their heroic stand inspired the rest of Texas to fanatical resistance. While Santa Anna dictated a glorious victory declaration, his aide wrote in his diary: "One more such 'glorious victory' and we are finished."

The commander-in-chief of the Texas forces was Sam Houston, a Tennessee frontiersman who had learned war under the tutelage of

Andrew Jackson at Horseshoe Bend, had later represented the Nashville district in Congress, and had moved to Texas only three years before. Houston beat a strategic retreat eastward, gathering reinforcements as he went, including volunteer recruits from the United States. Just west of the San Jacinto River he finally paused near the site of the city that later bore his name, and on April 21, 1836, surprised a Mexican encampment there. The Texans charged, yelling "Remember the Alamo," overwhelmed the Mexican force within fifteen minutes, and took Santa Anna prisoner. The Mexican dictator bought his freedom by signing a treaty recognizing Texan independence, with the Rio Grande as the boundary. The Mexican Congress repudiated the treaty, and never officially recognized the loss of its northern province, but the war was at an end.

THE MOVE FOR ANNEXATION The Lone Star Republic then drafted a constitution that legalized slavery and banned free blacks, made Sam Houston its first president, and voted for annexation to the United States. Houston's old friend Andrew Jackson was still president, but even Old Hickory could be discreet when delicacy demanded it. The addition of a new slave state threatened a serious sectional quarrel that might endanger the election of Martin Van Buren, his hand-picked successor. Worse than that, it raised the specter of war with Mexico. Jackson delayed official recognition of the Texas Republic until his last day in office. Van Buren shied away from the issue of annexation during his entire term as president.

Rebuffed in Washington, Texans turned their thoughts to a separate destiny. Under President Mirabeau Bonaparte Lamar, elected in 1838, they began to talk of expanding to the Pacific as a new nation that would rival the United States. France and Britain extended formal recognition to the new Texas Republic and began to develop trade relations. Meanwhile, thousands of Americans poured into the Republic of Texas. The population grew from 40,000 in 1836 to 150,000 in 1845. Many were attracted by the low land prices. And most brought with them a desire to join the United States.

Most Texans had never abandoned their hopes of annexation to the United States either. Reports of growing British influence in Texas created anxieties in the United States government and among southern slaveholders, who became the chief advocates of annexation. Secret negotiations with Texas began in 1843, and that April John C. Calhoun, Tyler's secretary of state, completed a treaty that went to the Senate for ratification.

Calhoun chose this moment also to send the British minister a letter instructing him on the blessings of slavery and stating that annexation of Texas was needed to foil the British abolitionists. Publication of the note fostered the claim that annexation was planned less in the national interest than to promote the expansion of slavery. It was so worded, one observer wrote Jackson, as to "drive off every northern man from the support of the measure." Sectional division, plus fear of a war with Mexico, contributed to the Senate's overwhelming rejection of the treaty. Solid Whig opposition was the most important factor behind its defeat.

POLK'S PRESIDENCY

THE ELECTION OF 1844   Prudent leaders in both political parties had hoped to keep the divisive issue of Texas out of the 1844 presidential campaign. Henry Clay and Martin Van Buren, the leading candidates, had reached the same conclusion about proslavery Texas: when the treaty was submitted to the Senate, they both wrote letters opposing annexation because it might spark civil war. Both letters, dated three days apart, appeared in separate Washington newspapers on April 27, 1844. Clay's "Raleigh letter" (written while he was on a southern tour) added that annexation was "dangerous to the integrity of the Union . . . and not called for by any general expression of public opinion." The outcome of the Whig convention in Baltimore seemed to bear out his view. Party leaders showed no qualms about Clay's stance. The convention nominated him unanimously, and the Whig platform omitted any reference to Texas.

The Democratic convention was a different story. Van Buren's southern supporters, including Jackson, abandoned him because of his opposition to Texas annexation. With the convention deadlocked, expansionists, including Andrew Jackson, brought forward James K. Polk, former Speaker of the House and governor of Tennessee. On the ninth ballot he became the first "dark horse" candidate to win a major-party nomination. The party platform embraced territorial expansion, and to win support in the North and West as well as in the South, it linked the questions of Oregon and Texas, calling for "the reoccupation of Oregon and the reannexation of Texas."

The Democratic combination of southern and western expansionism offered a winning strategy that was so popular that it forced Clay to alter his position, now saying that he had "no personal objection to the annexation of Texas" if it could be achieved "without dishonor, without war, with the common consent of the Union, and upon just and fair terms." His explanation seemed clear enough, but prudence was no match for spread-eagle oratory and the emotional pull of Manifest Destiny. The net result of Clay's stand was to turn more antislavery votes to the Liberty party, which increased its count from about 7,000 in 1840 to more than 62,000 in 1844. In the western counties of New York, the Liberty party drew enough votes away from the Whigs to give the state to Polk. Had he carried New York, Clay would have won the election by seven electoral votes. Instead, Polk won a narrow plurality of 38,000 popular votes nationwide (the first president since John Quincy Adams to win without a majority) but a clear majority of the electoral college, 170 to 105.

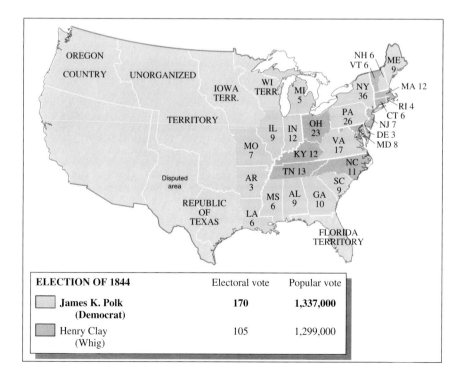

ELECTION OF 1844	Electoral vote	Popular vote
James K. Polk (Democrat)	170	1,337,000
Henry Clay (Whig)	105	1,299,000

Born near Charlotte, North Carolina, trained in mathematics and the classics at the University of North Carolina, Polk had moved to Tennessee as a young man. A successful lawyer and planter, he had entered politics early, served fourteen years in Congress (four as Speaker of the House) and two as governor of Tennessee. Young Hickory, as his partisans liked to call him, was a short, slender man with a shock of long, grizzled hair and a seemingly permanent grimace. He had none of Jackson's charisma, but shared Jackson's opposition to a national bank and other Whig economic policies. He worked so hard during four years in the White House that his health deteriorated, and he died just three months after leaving office.

POLK'S PROGRAM   In domestic affairs "Young Hickory" Polk hewed to the principle of the old hero, but the new Jacksonians subtly reflected the growing influence of the slaveholding South within the party. Abolitionism, Polk warned, could destroy the Union. Antislavery northerners had already begun to drift away from the Democratic party, which they complained was coming to represent the slaveholding interest.

Polk's major objectives were tariff reduction, reestablishment of the Independent Treasury, settlement of the Oregon boundary dispute with Britain, and the acquisition of California from Mexico. He gained them all. The Walker Tariff of 1846, in keeping with Democratic tradition, reduced the tariff rates. In the same year Polk persuaded Congress to restore the Independent Treasury, which the Whigs had eliminated. Twice Polk vetoed internal-improvements bills. In each case his blows to the American System of Henry Clay's Whigs satisfied the urges of the slaveholding South, but at the cost of annoying northerners who wanted higher tariffs and westerners who needed internal improvements.

THE STATE OF TEXAS   Polk's chief concern was geographic expansion. He privately vowed to acquire California, and New Mexico as well, preferably by purchase. The acquisition of slaveholding Texas was already under way when Polk took office. In his final months in office President Tyler, taking Polk's election as a mandate to act, asked Congress to accomplish annexation by joint resolution, which required only a simple majority in each house and avoided the two-thirds Senate

The devil advising Polk to pursue 54°40′ even if "you deluge your country with seas of blood, produce a servile insurrection, and dislocate every joint of this happy and prosperous union."

vote needed to ratify a treaty. Congress had read the election returns too, and after a bitter debate over slavery, the resolution passed by votes of 27 to 25 in the Senate and 120 to 98 in the House. Tyler signed the resolution on March 1, 1845, offering to admit Texas to statehood. A Texas convention accepted the offer, and the voters of Texas ratified the action. The new state formally entered the Union on December 29, 1845. Mexico was furious and dispatched troops to the Rio Grande border.

OREGON   Meanwhile, the Oregon boundary issue heated up as expansionists aggressively insisted that Polk abandon previous offers to settle with Britain on the 49th parallel and stand by the platform pledge to take all of Oregon. The expansionists were prepared to risk war with Britain while relations with Mexico were simultaneously moving toward the breaking point. "All of Oregon or none," the expansionists cried. In his inaugural address, Polk claimed that the American title to Oregon was "clear and unquestionable," but privately he favored a prudent compromise. War with Mexico was brewing; the territory up to 54°40′ seemed of less importance than Puget Sound or the ports of California, on which the British also were thought to have an eye.

Fortunately for Polk, the British government had no enthusiasm for war over that remote wilderness at the cost of profitable trade relations with the United States. From the British viewpoint, the only land in dispute all along had been between the 49th parallel and the Columbia River. But now the fur trade of the region was a dying industry. In 1846 the British government submitted a draft treaty to extend the border along the 49th parallel and through the main channel south of Vancouver Island and to keep the right to navigate all of the Columbia River. On June 15 Secretary of State James Buchanan and British minister Pakenham signed it, and three days later it was ratified in the Senate. The only opposition came from a group of expansionists representing the Old Northwest who wanted more. Most of the country was satisfied. Southerners cared less about Oregon than about Texas, and northern business interests valued British trade more than they valued Oregon. Besides, the country was already at war with Mexico.

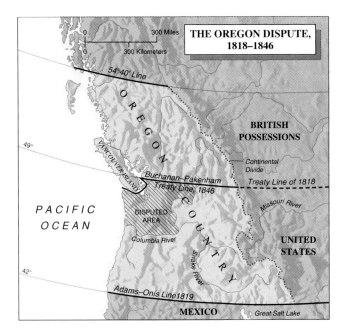

THE MEXICAN WAR

THE OUTBREAK OF WAR   On March 6, 1845, two days after Polk took office, the Mexican ambassador broke off relations and left for home to protest the American annexation of Texas. When an effort at negotiation failed, Polk focused his efforts on unilateral initiatives. Already he was fostering American intrigues against Mexican authority in California. He wrote Consul Thomas O. Larkin in Monterey that he would make no effort to induce California into the Union, but "if the people should desire to unite their destiny with ours, they would be received as brethren." Larkin, who could take a hint, began to line up Americans and sympathetic Californios. Meanwhile Polk ordered American troops under General Zachary Taylor to take up positions on the Rio Grande in the new state of Texas. These positions lay in territory that was doubly disputed: Mexico recognized neither the American annexation of Texas nor the Rio Grande boundary.

The last hope for peace died when John Slidell, sent to Mexico City to negotiate a settlement, finally gave up on his mission in March 1846. Polk then resolved that he could achieve his purposes only by force. He won cabinet approval of a war message to Congress. That very evening, May 9, the news arrived that Mexicans had earlier attacked American soldiers north of the Rio Grande. Eleven Americans were killed, five wounded, and the remainder taken prisoner. Polk's provocative scheme had worked.

In his war message Polk could now take the high ground that a declaration of war would be a response to Mexican aggression, a recognition that war had been forced upon the United States. Mexico, he claimed, "has invaded our territory, and shed American blood upon the American soil." Congress quickly passed the war resolution, and Polk signed the declaration of war on May 13, 1846. But support for the war was guarded. The House authorized a call for 50,000 volunteers and a war appropriation of $10 million, but sixty-seven Whigs voted against that measure, a sign of rising opposition to the war, especially in the North, where people assumed that Polk wanted a war in order to acquire more slave territory.

OPPOSITION TO THE WAR   In the Mississippi Valley, where expansion fever ran high, the war was immensely popular. In New England, however, there was less enthusiasm for "Mr. Polk's War." Whig opinion ranged from lukewarm to hostile. Congressman John Quincy Adams, who voted against participation, called it "a most unrighteous war." An obscure congressman from Illinois named Abraham Lincoln, upon taking his seat in 1847, began introducing "spot resolutions," calling on Polk to name the spot where American blood had been shed on American soil, implying that American troops may, in fact, have been in Mexico when fired upon.

Many New Englanders denounced the war as the work of proslavery southerners seeking new territories. But before the war ended some antislavery men had a change of heart about the war. Mexican territory seemed so unsuited to slave-based agriculture that they endorsed expansion in hope of enlarging the area of free soil. The lure of more land exerted a potent influence even on those who opposed the war.

PREPARING FOR BATTLE   Both the United States and Mexico approached the war ill prepared. American policy had been incredibly reckless, risking war with both Britain and Mexico while doing nothing to strengthen the armed forces until war came. At the outset of war, the regular army numbered barely over 7,000, in contrast to the Mexican force of 32,000. Before the war ended, the American force grew to 104,000, of whom about 31,000 were regular army troops and marines. Most of the new troops were six- and twelve-month state volunteers from the West. The volunteer militia companies, often filled with frontier toughs, lacked uniforms, standard equipment, and discipline. Repeatedly, despite the best efforts of the commanding generals, these undisciplined forces engaged in plunder, rape, and murder.

Nevertheless, being used to a rough-and-tumble life, the motley American troops outmatched larger Mexican forces, which had their own problems with training, discipline, morale, and munitions. Many of the Mexicans were pressed into service or recruited from prisons, and they made less than enthusiastic fighters. Mexican artillery pieces were generally obsolete, and the powder was so faulty that American soldiers could often dodge cannonballs that fell short and bounced ineffectively along the ground.

The United States entered the war without even a tentative plan of action, and politics complicated things. Polk sought to manage every detail of the conflict. What Polk wanted, Thomas Hart Benton wrote later, was "a small war, just large enough to require a treaty of peace, and not large enough to make military reputations, dangerous for the presidency." Winfield Scott, general-in-chief of the army, was a politically ambitious Whig. Nevertheless Polk named him at first to take charge of the Rio Grande front. When Scott quarreled with Polk's secretary of war, however, the exasperated president withdrew the appointment.

There now seemed a better choice for commander. General Zachary Taylor's men had scored two victories over Mexican forces north of the Rio Grande, at Palo Alto (May 8) and Resaca de la Palma (May 9). On May 18 Taylor crossed the river and occupied Matamoros, which a demoralized and bloodied Mexican army had abandoned. These quick victories brought Taylor instant popularity, and the president responded willingly to the demand that he be made commander for the conquest of Mexico. "Old Rough and Ready" Taylor impressed Polk as less of a political threat than Scott. Without a major battle, he had achieved Polk's main objective, the conquest of Mexico's northern provinces.

ANNEXATION OF CALIFORNIA   Along the Pacific coast, conquest was under way before definite news of the Mexican War arrived. Near the end of 1845, John C. Frémont brought out a band of sixty frontiersmen, ostensibly on another exploration of California and Oregon. When the Mexican commandant at Monterey ordered him out of the Salinas Valley, Frémont at first dug in his heels and refused to go, but he soon changed his mind and headed for Oregon. In 1846 he and his men again moved south, this time into the Sacramento Valley. Americans in the area fell upon Sonoma on June 14, proclaimed the "Republic of California," and hoisted the hastily designed Bear Flag, a grizzly bear and star painted on white cloth—a version of which became the state flag.

But the Bear Flag Republic lasted only a month. In July John D. Sloat, the commodore of the Pacific Fleet, having heard of the outbreak of hostilities with Mexico, sent a party ashore to raise the American flag and proclaim California a part of the United States. Most Californians of whatever origin welcomed a change that promised order in preference to the confusion of the Bear Flag Republic.

Before the end of July a new commodore, Robert F. Stockton, began preparations to move against Mexican forces in southern California. Stockton's forces occupied Santa Barbara and Los Angeles. By mid-August

The Battle of the Plains of Mesa took place just before American forces entered Los Angeles. This sketch was made at the scene.

Mexican resistance had dissipated. On August 17 Stockton declared himself governor, with Frémont as military commander in the north. At the same time, another expedition was closing on Santa Fe. On August 18 Colonel Stephen Kearny and 1,600 men entered Santa Fe. After setting up a civilian governor, Kearny divided his remaining force, leading 300 men west toward California.

In southern California, where most of the poorer Mexicans and Mexicanized Indians resented American rule, a rebellion broke out. By the end of October, the rebels had ousted the token American force in southern California. Kearny walked right into this rebel zone when he arrived. At San Diego he met up with Stockton and joined him in the reconquest of southern California, which they achieved after two brief clashes when they entered Los Angeles on January 10, 1847. Rebel forces capitulated three days later.

TAYLOR'S BATTLES   Both California and New Mexico had been taken before General Zachary Taylor fought his first major battle in northern Mexico. Having waited for more men and munitions, he finally moved out of his Matamoros base in September 1846 and assaulted the fortified city of Monterrey, which he took after a five-day siege. Polk, however, was none too happy with the easy terms of surrender to which Taylor agreed, or with Taylor's growing popularity. The whole episode merely confirmed the president's impression that Taylor was too passive to be trusted further with the major campaign. Besides, his victories, if flawed, were leading to talk of Taylor as the next Whig candidate for president.

Yet Polk's grand strategy was itself flawed. Having never seen the Mexican desert, he wrongly assumed that Taylor's men could live off the country and need not depend on resupply. Polk therefore misunderstood the general's reluctance to strike out across several hundred miles of barren land just north of Mexico City. On another point the president was simply duped. The old dictator General Antonio Lopez de Santa Anna, forced out in 1844, got word to Polk from his exile in Cuba that in return for the right considerations he could bring about a settlement of the war. Polk in turn assured the Mexican leader that the

THE MEXICAN WAR:
MAJOR CAMPAIGNS

◄- U.S. forces ◄— Mexican forces

★ Battle site

--- Line set by Treaty of
Guadalupe Hidalgo, 1848

American government would pay well for any territory taken through a settlement. In August 1846, Santa Anna was permitted to pass through the American blockade into Vera Cruz. Soon he was again in command of the Mexican army and then was named president once more. Polk's intrigue unintentionally put perhaps the ablest Mexican general back in command of the enemy army, where he busily organized his forces to strike at Taylor.

By then another American front had been opened, and Taylor was ordered to wait in place. In October 1846 Polk and his cabinet decided to move against Mexico City by way of Vera Cruz. Polk named Winfield Scott to the field command. Taylor, miffed at his reduction to a minor role, disobeyed orders and advanced beyond Saltillo. There, near the hacienda of Buena Vista, Santa Anna met Taylor's untested volunteers with a large but ill-trained and tired army. The Mexican general invited the outnumbered Americans to surrender. "Tell him to go to hell," Taylor replied. In the hard-fought Battle of Buena Vista (February 22–23, 1847), Taylor's son-in-law, Colonel Jefferson Davis, the future president of the Confederacy, led a regiment that broke up a Mexican cavalry charge. Neither side could claim victory. It was the last major action on the northern front, and Taylor was granted leave to return home.

SCOTT'S TRIUMPH   Meanwhile, the long-planned assault on the enemy capital had begun on March 9, 1847, when Winfield Scott's army landed on the beaches south of Vera Cruz. It was the first major amphibious operation by American military forces, and was carried out without loss. Vera Cruz surrendered on March 27 after a week-long siege. Scott then set out on the route taken by Cortés more than 300 years before. Santa Anna tried to set a trap for him at the mountain pass of Cerro Gordo, but Scott's men took more than 3,000 prisoners.

On May 15 Scott's men entered Puebla, the second-largest Mexican city. There Scott lost about a third of his army because men whose twelve-month enlistments had expired felt free to go home, leaving Scott with about 7,000 troops in all. There was nothing to do but hang on until reinforcements and new supplies came up from the coast. Finally, after three months, with his numbers almost doubled, Scott set out on August 7 through the mountain passes into the valley of Mexico, cutting his supply line to the coast.

Scott directed a brilliant flanking operation around the lakes and marshes that guarded the eastern approaches to Mexico City. After a series of battles in which they overwhelmed Mexican defenses, American forces entered Mexico City on September 13, 1847. At the National Palace a battalion of marines raised the American flag and occupied the "halls of Montezuma." News of the victory led some expansionists to new heights of land lust. Editor John L. O'Sullivan, who coined the term "Manifest Destiny," shouted, "More, More, More! Why not take all of Mexico?"

THE TREATY OF GUADALUPE HIDALGO   After the fall of the capital, Santa Anna resigned and a month later left the country. Meanwhile Polk had appointed as chief peace negotiator Nicholas P. Trist, chief clerk of the State Department and a Virginia Democrat of impeccably partisan credentials. Formal talks got under way on January 2, 1848, at the village of Guadalupe Hidalgo just outside the capital, and dragged on through the month. By the Treaty of Guadalupe Hidalgo, signed on February 2, 1848, Mexico gave up all claims to Texas above the Rio Grande and ceded California and New Mexico to the United States. In return the United States agreed to pay Mexico $15 million and assume the claims of American citizens against Mexico up to a total of $3.25 million.

Polk submitted the treaty to the Senate. A growing movement to annex all of Mexico briefly excited the president, but as Polk confided to his diary, rejecting the treaty would be too risky. If he should reject a treaty made in accord with his own original terms in order to gain more territory, "the probability is that Congress would not grant either men or money to prosecute the war." In that case he might eventually have to withdraw the army and lose everything. The treaty went to the Senate, which ratified it on March 10, 1848. By the end of July, the last remaining American soldiers had left Mexico.

THE WAR'S LEGACIES   The seventeen-month-long Mexican War had cost the United States 1,721 killed, 4,102 wounded, and far more—11,155—dead of disease, mostly dysentery and chronic diarrhea ("Montezuma's revenge"). It remains the deadliest war in American military history in terms of the percentage of combatants killed. Out of every 1,000 soldiers in Mexico, some 110 died. The next highest death rate would be in the Civil War, with 65 out of every 1,000 participants.

As a result of the Mexican War, the United States acquired more than 500,000 square miles of territory (more than a million counting Texas), including the great Pacific harbors of San Diego, Monterey, and San Francisco. Except for a small addition made by the Gadsden Purchase of 1853, these annexations rounded out the continental United States.

Several important "firsts" are associated with the Mexican War: the first successful offensive American war, the first occupation of an enemy capital, the first in which martial law was declared on foreign soil, the first in which West Point graduates played a major role, and the first reported by modern war correspondents. It was also the first significant combat experience for a group of junior officers who would later serve as leading generals during the Civil War: Robert E. Lee, Ulysses S. Grant, Thomas "Stonewall" Jackson, George B. McClellan, George Meade, and others.

Initially, the victory in Mexico provoked a surge of national pride. American triumphs "must elevate the *true* self-respect of the American people," Walt Whitman exclaimed. Others were not so sure. Ralph Waldo Emerson rejected war "as a means of achieving America's destiny," but he then accepted the annexation of new territory by force with the explanation that "most of the great results of history are brought about by discreditable means."

As the years passed, the Mexican War was increasingly seen as a war of conquest provoked by a president bent on expansion. For a brief season, the glory of conquest added luster to the names of Zachary Taylor and Winfield Scott. Despite Polk's best efforts, he had manufactured the next, and last, two Whig candidates for president. One of them, Taylor, would replace him in the White House, with the storm of sectional conflict already on the horizon.

The acquisition of Oregon, Texas, and California, and the new Southwest, made the United States a transcontinental nation. Extending authority over these vast new lands greatly expanded the scope of the federal government. In 1849, for example, Congress created the Department of the Interior to supervise the distribution of land, the creation of new territories and states, and the "protection" of the Indians and their lands. President Polk naively assumed that the dramatic expansion of American territory to the Pacific would strengthen "the bonds of Union." He was wrong. No sooner was Texas annexed than a violent debate erupted about the extension of slavery into the new territories. That debate would culminate in a civil war that would nearly destroy the Union.

MAKING CONNECTIONS

- This chapter opened with the brief administration of William Henry Harrison, the first Whig president. The collapse of the Whig party is detailed in Chapter 16.

- The West developed quickly after the expansionist policies of the 1840s. Chapter 19 takes the story to the 1890s.

- This chapter ended by noting how expansionism fueled a "debate [that] would culminate in a civil war that would nearly destroy the Union." Chapter 16's discussion of "The Crisis of Union" traces the relationship between the Mexican War and the Civil War more explicitly.

FURTHER READING

For background on Whig programs and ideas, see Michael Holt's *The Rise and Fall of the American Whig Party* (1999). Several works help interpret the expansionist impulse. Frederick Merk's *Manifest Destiny and Mission in American History* (1963) remains a classic. A more recent treatment of expansionist ideology is Thomas R. Hietala's *Manifest Design: Anxious Aggrandizement in Late Jacksonian America* (1985).

The best survey of western expansion is Richard White's *"It's Your Misfortune and None of My Own": A New History of the American West* (1991). Robert M. Utley's *A Life Wild and Perilous: Mountain Men and the Paths to the Pacific* (1997) tells the dramatic story of the rugged pathfinders who found corridors over the Rocky Mountains. The movement of settlers to the West is ably documented in John Mack Faragher's *Women and Men on the Overland Trail* (1979) and David Dary's *The Santa Fe Trail* (2002). The best account of the California gold rush is Malcolm J. Rohrbough's *Days of Gold: The California Gold Rush and the American Nation* (1997).

Gene M. Brack's *Mexico Views Manifest Destiny, 1821–1846* (1975) takes Mexico's viewpoint on American designs on the West. On James K. Polk, see John H. Schroeder's *Mr. Polk's War* (1973). The best survey of the military conflict is John S. D. Eisenhower's *So Far from God: The U.S. War with Mexico, 1846–1848* (1989). An excellent analysis of the diplomatic aspects of Mexican-American relations is David M. Pletcher's *The Diplomacy of Annexation: Texas, Oregon, and the Mexican War* (1973).

PART FOUR

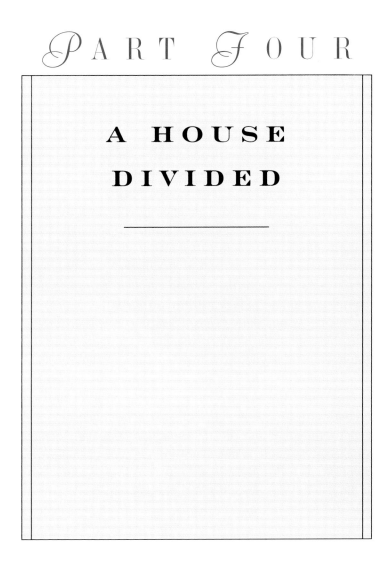

A HOUSE
DIVIDED

Of all the regions of the United States during the first half of the nine-
teenth century, the South was the most distinctive. Southern society re-
mained fundamentally rural and agricultural long after the rest of the
nation embraced the urban industrial revolution. Likewise, the southern
elite's tenacious desire to preserve and expand the institution of slavery
muted social reform impulses in the South and ignited a prolonged politi-
cal controversy that would end in civil war.

The rapid, relentless settlement of the western territories set in motion a
ferocious competition between North and South for political influence in
the burgeoning West. Would the new states in the West be "slave" or
"free"? The issue of allowing slavery into the new territories involved more
than humanitarian concern for the plight of enslaved blacks. By the
1840s, North and South had developed quite different economic interests.
The North wanted high tariffs on imported manufactures to "protect" its
infant industries from foreign competition. Southerners, on the other
hand, favored free trade because they wanted to import British goods in
exchange for the cotton they provided British textile mills.

A series of political compromises glossed over the fundamental differ-
ences between the regions during the first half of the nineteenth century.
But abolitionists refused to give up their crusade against slavery. More-
over, a new generation of politicians emerged in the 1850s, leaders from
both North and South who were less willing to seek political compro-
mises. The continuing debate over allowing slavery into the new western
territories kept sectional tensions at a fever pitch. By the time Abraham
Lincoln was elected in 1860, many Americans had decided that the na-
tion could not survive half-slave and half-free; something had to give.

In a last-ditch effort to preserve the institution of slavery, eleven south-
ern states seceded from the Union and created a separate Confederate na-
tion. This, in turn, prompted northerners such as Lincoln to support a
civil war to preserve the Union. No one realized in 1861 how prolonged
and costly the war between the states would become. Over 630,000 sol-
diers and sailors died of wounds or disease. The colossal carnage caused
even the most seasoned observers to blanch in disbelief. As President Lin-
coln confessed in his second inaugural address, no one expected the war to
become so "fundamental and astonishing."

Nor did people envision how sweeping the war's effects would be on the
future of the country. The northern victory in 1865 restored the Union
and in the process helped to accelerate America's transformation into a

modern nation-state. National power and a national consciousness began to displace the sectional emphases of the antebellum era. A Republican-led Congress pushed through federal legislation to foster industrial and commercial development and western expansion. In the process, the United States began to leave behind the Jeffersonian dream of a decentralized agrarian republic.

The Civil War also ended slavery. Yet the actual status of the freed blacks remained precarious. How would they fare in a society built on slavery maintained by racism? In 1865 the daughter of a Georgia planter expressed her concern about such issues when she wrote in her diary that "there are sad changes in store for both races. I wonder the Yankees do not shudder to behold their work" ahead in trying to "reconstruct" the defeated South.

The former slaves found themselves legally free, but most were without property, homes, education, or training. Although the Fourteenth Amendment (1867) set forth guarantees for the civil rights of African Americans and the Fifteenth Amendment (1870) provided that black males could vote, local authorities found ingenious—and often violent—ways to avoid the spirit and letter of these new laws.

The restoration of the former Confederate states to the Union did not come easily. Much bitterness and resistance remained among the vanquished. Although Confederate leaders were initially disenfranchised, they continued to exercise considerable authority in political and economic matters. Indeed, in 1877 the last federal troops were removed from the occupied South, and former Confederates declared themselves "redeemed" from the stain of occupation. By the end of the nineteenth century, most states of the former Confederacy had devised a system of legal discrimination that re-created many aspects of slavery.

15 — THE OLD SOUTH

CHAPTER ORGANIZER

This chapter focuses on:

- industry and agriculture in the Old South.

- southern society. black and white.

- the antislavery movement and southern reactions to it.

southerners, a North Carolina editor once wrote, are "a mythological people, created half out of dream and half out of slander, who live in a still legendary land." Most Americans, including southerners themselves, harbor a cluster of myths and stereotypes about the South. Perhaps the most enduring myths come from classic movies such as *Gone With the Wind.* The South portrayed in such Hollywood productions was a stable agrarian society led by paternalistic white planters and their families, who lived in white-columned mansions and represented a "natural" aristocracy of virtue and talent within their communities. In these accounts, southerners were kind to their slaves and devoted to the rural values of independence and chivalric honor celebrated by Thomas Jefferson.

By contrast, a much darker myth about the Old South emerged from abolitionist pamphlets and Harriet Beecher Stowe's best-selling novel, *Uncle Tom's Cabin.* These exposés of southern culture portrayed the planters as arrogant aristocrats who raped slave women, brutalized slave workers, and lorded over their communities with haughty disdain for the rights and needs of others. They bred slaves like cattle, broke up slave families, and sold slaves "down the river" to certain death in the Louisiana sugar mills and rice plantations.

Such contrasting myths die hard, in large part because each is rooted in reality. Nonetheless, efforts to get at what really set the Old South apart from the rest of the nation generally pivot on two lines of thought: the impact of environment (climate and geography) and the effects of human decisions and actions. The South's warm, humid climate was ideal for the cultivation of commercial crops such as tobacco, cotton, rice, and sugarcane. The growth of such lucrative cash crops helped foster the plantation system and slavery. In the end, these developments brought the sectional conflict over the extension of slavery and the civil war that shook the foundations of the Old South.

DISTINCTIVENESS OF THE OLD SOUTH

While geography was and is a key determinant of southern folkways, many observers found the origins of southern distinctiveness in the institution of slavery. The resolve of slaveholders to retain control of their socioeconomic order created a sense of racial unity that bridged class divisions among whites. Yet, the biracial character of the population exercised an even greater influence over southern culture. In shaping patterns of speech and folklore, of music, religion, literature, and recreation, black southerners immeasurably influenced and enriched the region's development.

The South differed from other sections of the country, too, in its high proportion of native population, both white and black. Despite a great diversity of origins in the colonial population, the South drew few immigrants after the Revolution. One reason was that the main shipping lines went to northern ports; another, that the prospect of competing with slave labor deterred immigrants. After the Missouri Controversy of 1819–1821, the South became more and more a conscious minority region, its population growth lagging behind that of other sections, its "peculiar institution" of slavery more and more an isolated and odious

Slave quarters on a South Carolina plantation.

thing in Western civilization. Attitudes of defensiveness strongly affected its churches. The religious culture of the white South retreated from the liberalism of the Revolutionary War era into a brittle orthodoxy, which provided one line of defense against new doctrines of any kind, while black southerners found in a similar religious culture a refuge from their hardships, a promise of release on some future day of Jubilee.

The South also differed from the rest of the nation in its architecture; its penchant for fighting, for guns, and for the military; and its country-gentleman ideal. The preponderance of farming remained a distinctive regional characteristic, whether pictured as the Jeffersonian small farmer living by the sweat of his brow or the lordly planter dispatching his slave gangs. But in the end what made the South distinctive was its people's belief, and other people's belief, that the region *was* distinctive.

STAPLE CROPS   The idea of the Cotton Kingdom is itself something of a mythic stereotype. Although cotton was the most important of the staple, or market, crops, it was a latecomer. Tobacco, the first staple crop, had earlier been the mainstay of Virginia and Maryland, and common in North Carolina. After the Revolution, pioneers carried it over the mountains into Kentucky and as far as Missouri. Indigo, an important crop in colonial South Carolina, vanished with the loss of British

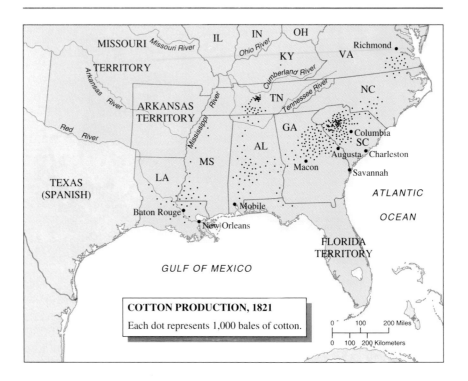

COTTON PRODUCTION, 1821

Each dot represents 1,000 bales of cotton.

bounties for this source of a valuable blue dye, but rice growing continued in a coastal strip that lapped over into North Carolina and Georgia.
Rice growing was limited to the Tidewater because it required frequent
flooding and draining of the fields. Since rice growing required substantial capital for floodgates, ditches, and machinery, the plantations that
grew rice were large and relatively few in number.

Sugar, like rice, required heavy capital investment in machinery to
grind the cane, and was limited to the Deep South because the cane
was susceptible to frost. Since sugar needed the prop of a protective
tariff to enable it to compete with foreign suppliers, it produced the
anomaly in southern politics of pro-tariff congressmen from Louisiana.
Hemp had something of the same effect in the Kentucky Blue Grass region and northwestern Missouri. Both flax and hemp were important to
backcountry farmers at the end of the colonial era. Homespun clothing
was most apt to be linsey-woolsey, a combination of linen and wool. But
flax never developed more than a limited commercial market, and that
mostly for linseed oil. Hemp, on the other hand, developed commercial
possibilities in rope and cotton baling cloth, and canvas for sails.

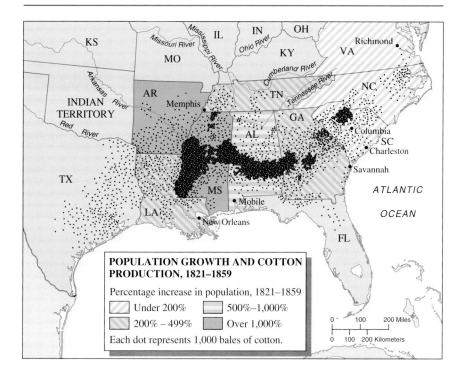

POPULATION GROWTH AND COTTON
PRODUCTION, 1821–1859

Percentage increase in population, 1821–1859

Under 200%   500%–1,000%

200% – 499%   Over 1,000%

Each dot represents 1,000 bales of cotton.

Cotton, the last of the major staple crops, eventually outpaced all the others put together. At the end of the War of 1812, annual cotton production was estimated at less than 150,000 bales; in 1860 it was reported at 4 million. Two things accounted for the dramatic growth: the voracious market for American cotton in British and French textiles, and the cultivation of new lands in the Southwest. Much of the story of the southern people—white and black—from 1820 to 1860 was their movement from Virginia and the Carolinas to fertile cotton lands farther west. By 1860 the center of the cotton belt stretched from eastern North Carolina through the fertile Alabama-Mississippi black belts (so called for the color of the soil), on to Texas, and up the Mississippi Valley as far as southern Illinois. Cotton prices fell sharply after the Panic of 1837, and remained below 10¢ a pound through most of the 1840s, but they advanced above 10¢ late in 1855 and stayed there until 1860, reaching 15¢ in 1857.

AGRICULTURAL DIVERSITY   The focus on cotton and the other cash crops has obscured the degree to which the South fed itself from its own fields. With 30 percent of the country's land mass in 1860, and 39 percent of its population, the slave states produced 52 percent of the nation's corn, 29 percent of the wheat, 19 percent of the oats, 19 percent of the rye, 10 percent of the white potatoes, and 94 percent of the sweet potatoes. The upper South in many areas practiced general farming in much the same way as the Northwest. Cyrus McCormick first tested his mechanical harvester in the wheatfields of Virginia. Corn grew throughout the South, but went less into the market than into local consumption, as feed and fodder, as hoecake and grits.

Livestock added to the diversity of the farm economy. In 1860 the South had half of the nation's cattle, over 60 percent of the swine, nearly 45 percent of the horses, 52 percent of the oxen, 90 percent of the mules, and nearly 33 percent of the sheep, the last mostly in the upper South. Plantations and farms commonly raised livestock for home consumption.

Yet the story of the southern economy was hardly one of unbroken prosperity. The South's staple crops quickly exhausted the soil. In low-country South Carolina, Senator Robert Y. Hayne spoke of "Fields abandoned; and hospitable mansions of our fathers deserted." The older farming lands had trouble competing with the newer soils farther west. But lands in the Old Southwest too began to show wear and tear. By 1855 an Alabama senator noted: "Our small planters, after taking

Planting sweet potatoes on the Hopkinson plantation, Edisto Island, South Carolina, April 1862.

the cream off their lands . . . are going further west and south in search of other virgin lands which they may and will despoil and impoverish in like manner."

So the Southeast and then the Old Southwest faced a growing sense of economic crisis as the nineteenth century advanced. Proposals to deal with the crisis followed two lines. Some argued for agricultural reform and others for diversification through industry and trade. Edmund Ruffin of Virginia stands out as perhaps the greatest of the reformers. After studying the chemistry of soils, he reasoned that most exhausted fields of the upper South were too acidic. He discovered that marl from a seashell deposit in eastern Virginia could restore the fields' fertility. Ruffin published the results in his *Essay on Calcareous Manures* (1832). Such publications and farm magazines in general, however, reached but a minority of farmers, mostly the larger and more successful planters.

MANUFACTURING AND TRADE   By 1840 many thoughtful southerners concluded that the region desperately needed to develop its own manufacturing and trade. The cotton growing mania had led the South to become increasingly dependent on northern manufacturing and trade. Cotton and tobacco were exported mainly in northern vessels. Southerners also relied on merchants in the North for imported goods. The South became a kind of colonial dependency of the North. The merchants of northern cities, a southerner said, "export our . . . valuable productions, and import our articles of consumption and from this agency they derive a profit which has enriched them . . . at our expense."

Along with the call for direct trade in southern ships went a movement for a more diversified economy, for native industries to balance agriculture and trade. Southern publicists called attention to the section's great resources: its raw materials, labor supply, waterpower, wood and coal, and markets. In Richmond, Virginia, the Tredegar Iron Works grew into the most important single manufacturing enterprise in the Old South. It used mostly slave labor to produce cannon, shot, and shell, axes, saws, bridge materials, boilers, and steam engines, including locomotives.

Daniel Pratt of Alabama built Prattville, which grew into a model of diversified industry. Prattville ultimately had a gristmill, a shingle mill, a carriage factory, foundries, a tin mill, and a blacksmith shop. Pratt then

The Tredegar Iron Works in Richmond, Virginia.

launched into the iron business and coal mining, while on the side experimenting with vineyards and vegetable farming. He used both black and white labor, but his approach was paternalistic. Profits from his company store went into churches, schools, a library, an art gallery, and a printing establishment—and into handsome dividends.

Pratt and others directed a program of industrial development that gathered momentum in the 1850s, and in its extent and diversity belied the common image of a strictly agricultural South. Yet despite such efforts the region still lagged well behind the North in its industrial development and commercial network.

ECONOMIC DEVELOPMENT   During the antebellum years, there were two major explanations generally put forward for the lag in southern industrial development. First, blacks were presumed unsuited to factory work. Second, the ruling elite of the Old South developed a lordly disdain for industrial production. A certain aristocratic prestige derived from owning land and slaves. But any argument that black labor was incompatible with industry simply flew in the face of the evidence, since factory owners bought or hired slave operators for just about every kind of manufacture. Given the opportunity, a number of blacks displayed managerial skills as overseers.

One should not take at face value the legendary indifference of aristocratic planters to profits. More often than not the successful planter was a hard-driving newcomer bent on maximizing profits. While the profitability of slavery has been a long-standing subject of controversy, in recent years economic historians have concluded that slaves on the average supplied about a 10 percent return on their cost. Then, as now, this was an enticing profit margin. By a strictly economic calculation, slaves and cotton lands were the most profitable investments available at the time in the South. Some slaveholders, particularly in the newer cotton lands of the old Southwest, were incredibly rich.

WHITE SOCIETY IN THE SOUTH

If an understanding of the Old South must begin with a knowledge of social myths, it must end with a sense of tragedy. White southerners had won short-term gains at the costs of both long-term development and moral isolation in the eyes of the world. The concentration on agriculture and slaves, and the paucity of cities and immigrants, deprived the South of the most dynamic sources of innovation. The slaveholding South hitched its wagon not to a star, but to the (largely British) demand for cotton, which had not slackened from the start of the industrial revolution. During the late 1850s, it seemed that southern agricultural prosperity would never end. The South, "safely entrenched behind her cotton bags . . . can defy the world—for the civilized world depends on the cotton of the South," said a Vicksburg newspaper in 1860. "No power on earth dares to make war upon it," said James H. Hammond of South Carolina. "Cotton is king." What southern boosters could not perceive was what they could least afford: an imminent slackening of the cotton market. The heyday of expansion in British textiles ended by 1860, but by then the Deep South was locked into cotton production for generations to come.

THE PLANTERS Although there were only a few great plantations, they set the tone of southern economic and social life. What distinguished the plantation from the farm, in addition to its size, was the use of a large labor force, under separate control and supervision, to grow primarily staple crops (cotton, rice, tobacco, and sugarcane) for profit. A clear-cut distinction between management and labor set the planter apart from the small slaveholder, who often worked side by side with his or her slaves at the same tasks.

If, to be called a planter, one had to own 20 slaves, only 1 out of every 30 whites in the South in 1860 was a planter. Fewer than 11,000 owned 50 or more slaves, and only 2,300 owned over 100. The census noted

King Cotton Captured, *an engraving showing cotton being trafficked in Louisiana.*

only 11 planters with 500 slaves and just 1 with as many as 1,000. Yet this privileged elite tended to think of its class interest as the interest of the entire South, and to perceive themselves as community leaders and "natural aristocrats." The planter group, making up under 4 percent of the adult white males in the South, owned more than half the slaves, produced most of the cotton, tobacco, and hemp, and all of the sugar and rice. The number of slaveholders was only 383,637, out of a total white population of 8 million. But assuming that each family numbered five people, the whites with some proprietary interest in slavery came to 1.9 million, or roughly one-fourth of the white population. While the preponderance of southern whites belonged to the small farmer class, they tended to defer to the large planters. After all, many small farmers aspired to become planters themselves.

Often the planter did live in the splendor that legend attributed to him, with the wealth and leisure to cultivate the arts of hospitality, good manners, learning, and politics. More often the scene was less charming. Some of the mansions on closer inspection turned out to be modest houses with false fronts. The planter commonly had less leisure than legend would suggest, for he in fact managed a large enterprise. At the same time he often served as the patron to whom workers appealed the actions of their foremen. The quality of life for the slaves was governed far more by the attitude of the master than by the formal slave codes, which were seldom strictly enforced except in times of trouble.

THE PLANTATION MISTRESS The mistress of the plantation, like the master, seldom led a life of idle leisure. Like all farm women, she worked hard. She supervised the domestic household in the same way the planter took care of the business, overseeing food, linens, house-cleaning, the care of the sick, and a hundred other details. Mary Boykin Chesnut of South Carolina complained that "there is no slave like a wife." The wives of all but the most wealthy planters were expected to supervise all the domestic activities of the household and manage the slaves to boot. The son of a Tennessee slaveholder remembered that his mother and grandmother were "the busiest women I ever saw."

White women living within a slave-owning culture also confronted a double standard in terms of moral and sexual behavior. While they were expected to behave as chaste exemplars of Christian piety and sexual discretion, their husbands, brothers, and sons followed an unwritten rule of self-indulgent hedonism. "God forgive us," Mary Chesnut wrote in her diary, "but ours is a monstrous system. Like the patriarchs of old, our men live all in one house with their wives and their concubines; and the mulattoes one sees in every family partly resemble the white children. Any lady is ready to tell you who is the father of all the mulatto children in everybody's household but her own. Those, she seems to think, drop from the clouds." Such a double standard both illustrated and reinforced the arrogant authoritarianism displayed by many male planters. Yet for all of their complaints and burdens, few plantation mistresses engaged in public criticism of the prevailing social order and racist climate.

THE MIDDLE CLASS Overseers on the largest plantations generally came from the middle class of small farmers or skilled workers, or were younger sons of planters. Most aspired to become slaveholders themselves, but others were constantly on the move in search of better positions. Their interests did not always coincide with the long-term interests of the planter. "Overseers are not interested in raising negro children, or meat, in improving land, or improving productive qualities of seed or animals," a Mississippi planter complained. "Many of them do not care whether property has depreciated or improved, so they make a crop to boast of." Occasionally there were black overseers, but the highest management position to which a slave could aspire was usually that of "driver," placed in charge of a small group of slaves with the duty of getting them to work without creating dissension.

The most numerous white southerners were the small farmers (yeomen), those who lived with their families in modest two-room cabins rather than columned mansions. They raised a few hogs and chickens, grew some corn and cotton, and traded with neighbors more than stores. The men in the family focused their energies on outdoor labors. Women also worked in the fields during harvest time, but most of their days were spent attending to domestic chores. Many of these "middling" farmers owned a handful of slaves, but most owned none. The most prosperous of these small farm families generally lived in the mountain-sheltered valleys from the Shenandoah of Virginia down to northern Alabama, areas with rich soil but without ready access to markets, and so less suitable for staple crops or slave labor. But most of the South's small farms were located in the midst of the plantation economy.

In North Carolina in 1860, for instance, 70 percent of the farmers held less than 100 acres, and they were scattered throughout the state. These and other southern farmers were typically mobile folk, willing to pull up stakes and move west or southwest in pursuit of better land. They tended to be fiercely independent and suspicious of government authority, and they overwhelmingly identified with the party of Andrew Jackson and the spiritual fervor of evangelical Protestantism. Even though only a minority of the middle-class farmers owned slaves, most of them supported the slave system. They feared that the slaves, if freed, would compete with them for land, and they also enjoyed the privileged status that racially based slavery afforded them. As one farmer told a northern traveler, "Now suppose they [the slaves] was free. You see they'd all think themselves as good as we." Such sentiments pervaded the border states as well as the Deep South.

THE "POOR WHITES"   Visitors in the Old South often had trouble telling yeomen apart from the true "poor whites," a degraded class relegated to the least desirable land, living on the fringes of polite society. The "poor whites" were characterized by a pronounced lankness and sallowness, given over to hunting and fishing, to hound dogs and moonshine whiskey.

Speculation had it that the "poor whites" were descended from indentured servants or convicts transported to the colonies, or that they were the weakest of the frontier population, forced to take refuge in the sand land, the pine barrens, and the swamps after having been pushed aside by the more enterprising and successful. But the problem was less hereditary than environmental, the consequence of infections and dietary deficiencies that gave rise to a trilogy of "lazy diseases": hookworm, malaria, and pellagra, all of which produced an overpowering lethargy. Many poor whites displayed a morbid craving to chew clay, from which they got the name "dirt eaters"; the cause was a dietary deficiency, although a folklore grew up about the nutritional and medicinal qualities of certain clays. Around 1900 modern medicine discovered the causes and cures for these diseases. By 1930 they had practically disappeared, taking with them many stereotypes of poor whites.

HONOR AND VIOLENCE IN THE OLD SOUTH From colonial times, most southern white males prided themselves on adhering to a moral code centered on a prickly sense of honor. Such a preoccupation with masculine honor was common among Germanic and Celtic peoples (Scottish, Irish, Scotch-Irish, Cornish, and Welsh) from whom most white southerners were descended. It flourished in hierarchical rural societies where face-to-face relations governed social manners.

The dominant ethical code for the southern white elite derived from Protestant religion, classical philosophy, and medieval chivalry, and it depended upon a rigidly hierarchical social system, where one's status was defined by those above and below. Its elements included a combative sensitivity to slights; loyalty to family, locality, state, and region; deference to elders and social "betters"; and an almost theatrical hospitality. It manifested itself in a fierce defense of female purity, a propensity to magnify personal insults into capital offenses, and in public statements such as the following toast proposed by a South Carolina politician: "*The Palmetto State:* Her sons bold and chivalrous in war, mild and persuasive in peace, their spirits flushed with resentment for wrong."

This caricature of prominent Whig newspaper editor James Watson Webb appeared after he provoked a duel between two congressmen in 1838. He is shown armed with a sword cane, a musket, a knife, and several pistols, while being trailed by a turkey representing his arrogance.

Southern white women played an important role in the culture of honor; they were the object of masculine chivalry and the subjects of male rule. The southern "lady" was placed on a pedestal celebrating domestic devotion. While men cultivated and defended their *honor*, women paraded and protected their *virtue*. The southern lady presided over the morals and manners of the household—while readily submitting to patriarchal authority. A southern lady, according to the prevailing standard, was to remain sexually pure, spiritually pious, and domestically submissive—all the while she managed the household efficiently.

The preoccupation of southern white men with a sense of honor steeped in violence found outlets in several popular rituals. Like their Scotch-Irish and English ancestors, white southerners loved to hunt, ride, and gamble—over cards, dice, horse racing, and cockfighting. All such activities provided arenas for masculine camaraderie as well as competition. In some respects southern society itself revolved around such public recreation. During horse race week in Charleston, South Carolina, for instance, courts, schools, and shops shut down so as to enable all to participate.

Southern men of all social classes were preoccupied with an often reckless manliness. As a northern traveler observed, "the central trait of the 'chivalrous southerner' is an intense respect for virility." The duel constituted the ultimate public expression of personal honor and manly courage. Although not confined to the South, dueling was much more common there than in the rest of the young nation, a fact that gave rise to the observation that southerners would be polite until they were angry enough to kill you. Dueling was outlawed in the northern states after Aaron Burr killed Alexander Hamilton in 1804, and a number of southern states and counties banned the practice as well—but the prohibition was rarely enforced.

Amid the fiery political debates over nullification, abolitionism, or the fate of slavery in the territories during the antebellum era, clashing opinions often provoked duels. In Virginia, a state senator and a state representative killed each other in a duel. Many of the most prominent southern leaders engaged in duels—congressmen, senators, governors, editors, and planters. The roster of participants included Andrew Jackson, Henry Clay, Sam Houston, Jefferson Davis, William Crawford, John Randolph, and Albert Sidney Johnston.

So many duels and deaths occurred in the South that "anti-dueling societies" emerged to lobby against the social ritual. Most states outlawed the practice, but to little avail. Judges were reluctant to punish their fellow "gentlemen" for upholding their honor. In many cases, duelists simply agreed to stage their contest in an adjoining state. It was not until after the Civil War that dueling fell into widespread disgrace and began a rapid decline. Humorist Mark Twain deserves the last word: "I thoroughly disapprove of duels. If a man should challenge me, I would take him kindly and forgivingly by the hand and lead him to a quiet place and kill him."

BLACK SOCIETY IN THE SOUTH

Slavery was one of the fastest growing elements of American life during the first half of the nineteenth century. In 1790 there were fewer than 700,000 slaves in the United States. By 1830 there were more than 2 million, and by 1860 there were almost 4 million. Although they all shared the injustices of white racism, African Americans had diverse experiences in the United States, depending upon their geographic location and the nature of their working and living conditions.

"FREE PERSONS OF COLOR" Not all blacks were slaves. In the Old South, "free persons of color" occupied an uncertain status, balanced somewhere between slavery and freedom, subject to legal restrictions not imposed on whites. Over the years, some slaves were able to purchase

Yarrow Mamout was an African Muslim who was sold into slavery, purchased his freedom, acquired property, and settled in Georgetown (now part of Washington, D.C.). Charles Willson Peale executed this portrait of Mamout in 1819, when Mamout was over 100 years old.

their freedom, while some gained freedom as a reward for service in wars. Others were simply freed by conscientious masters, either in their wills or during their lifetimes. By 1860 there were 260,000 free blacks in the slave states.

The free persons of color included a large number of mulattoes, people of mixed racial ancestry. The census of 1860 reported 412,000 persons of mixed racial ancestry in the United States, or about 10 percent of the black population, probably a drastic undercount. In urban centers like Charleston and especially New Orleans, "colored" society became virtually a third caste, a new people who occupied a status somewhere between black and white. Some mulattoes built substantial fortunes and even became slaveholders. They often operated inns serving a white clientele. Jehu Jones, for instance, was the "colored" proprietor of one of Charleston's best hotels. In Louisiana a mulatto, Cyprien Ricard, bought an estate that had ninety-one slaves for $250,000. In Natchez, William Johnson, son of a white father and mulatto mother, operated three barbershops and owned 1,500 acres of land and several slaves.

William Ellison, a freed slave of partial white ancestry who lived in Stateburg, South Carolina, prospered as a cotton-gin maker. In 1816, at the age of twenty-six, he purchased his own freedom from his white master (who may have been his father). By the start of the Civil War, he had become the wealthiest free black in South Carolina, owner of a thriving business, an 800-acre plantation, and some sixty slaves. As a member of Charleston's "brown aristocracy," he looked down upon black people. During the Civil War, Ellison supported the Confederacy.

Black slaveholders, however, were a tiny minority. The 1830 census revealed that only 3,775 free blacks, about 2 percent of the total free black population, owned 12,760 slaves. Although most of these black slave owners were in the South, some also lived in Rhode Island, Connecticut, Illinois, New Jersey, New York, and the border states. Some blacks owned slaves for humanitarian purposes. One minister, for instance, bought slaves and then enabled them to purchase their freedom from him on easy terms. Most often, black slaveholders were free blacks who bought their own family members with the express purpose of later freeing them.

This badge, issued in Charleston, South Carolina, was worn by a free black so he would not be mistaken for someone's property.

THE TRADE IN SLAVES From the first census in 1790 to the eighth in 1860, the number of slaves had grown from 698,000 to almost 4 million. The rise in the slave population occurred mainly through a natural increase, the rate of which was very close to that of whites at the time. When the African slave trade was outlawed in 1808, it seemed to many a step toward the extinction of slavery, but the expansion of the cotton economy, with its voracious appetite for manual workers, soon created such a vested interest in slaves as to dash such hopes. Shutting off the import of slaves only added to the value of those already present.

The rise in the cash value of slaves brought better treatment. Valuable slaves, like valuable livestock, justified at least minimal standards of care. "Massa was purty good," one ex-slave recalled later. "He treated us jus' 'bout like you would a good mule." Another said his master "fed us reg'lar on good, 'stantial food, jus' like you'd tend to you hoss, if you had a real good one." Some owners hired wage laborers, often Irish immigrants, for ditching and other dangerous work rather than risk the lives of the more valuable slaves.

The end of the foreign slave trade gave rise to a flourishing domestic trade, with slaves moving mainly from the used-up lands of the Southeast into the booming new country of the Old Southwest. The slave trade peaked just before 1837, then slacked off, first because of depression, then because agricultural reform and recovery renewed the demand for slaves in the upper South. Many slaves moved south and west with their owners,

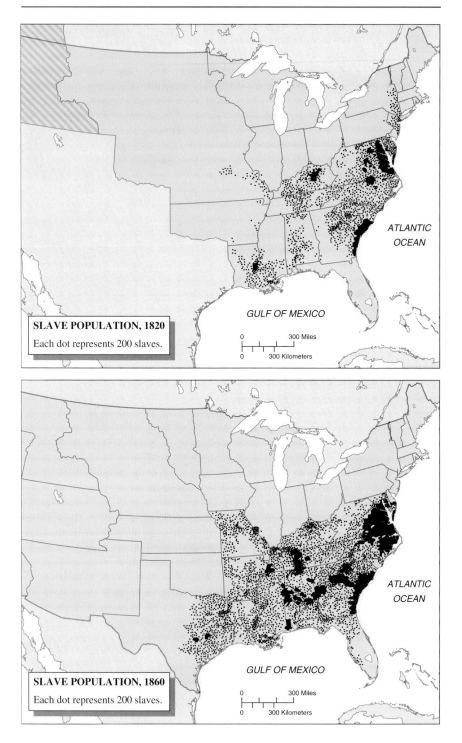

SLAVE POPULATION, 1820

Each dot represents 200 slaves.

ATLANTIC OCEAN

GULF OF MEXICO

0   300 Miles

0   300 Kilometers

SLAVE POPULATION, 1860

Each dot represents 200 slaves.

ATLANTIC OCEAN

GULF OF MEXICO

0   300 Miles

0   300 Kilometers

but there also developed an organized business with brokers, slave pens, and auctioneers. The worst aspect of the slave trade was the breakup of families. Only Louisiana and Alabama (from 1852) forbade separating a child under ten from its mother, and no state forbade separation of husband from wife. Many such sales are matters of record, and although the total number is controversial, it took only a few to damage the morale of all.

PLANTATION SLAVERY   Most slaves labored on plantations. The preferred jobs were those of household servants and skilled workers, including blacksmiths and carpenters. Others might get special assignments as boatmen or cooks. Fieldhands were usually housed in one- or two-room wooden shacks with dirt floors, some without windows. A set of clothes was distributed twice a year, but shoes were generally provided only in winter. On larger plantations there was sometimes an infirmary and regular sick call, but most planters resorted to doctors mainly in cases of severe sickness. Based on detailed records from eleven plantations in the lower South during the antebellum era, scholars have calculated that more than half of all slave babies died in the first year of life, a mortality rate more than twice that of whites.

Fieldhands worked long hours from dawn to dusk. The difference between a good owner and a bad one, according to one ex-slave, was the difference between one who did not "whip too much" and one who "whipped till he's bloodied you and blistered you." Over 50,000 slaves a year escaped. Those not caught often headed for Mexico or the northern states or Canada.

THE EXPERIENCE OF SLAVE WOMEN   Although black males and females often performed similar labors, they did not experience slavery in the same way. Slaveholders had different expectations for the men and women they controlled. During the colonial period, male slaves vastly outnumbered females. By the mid–eighteenth century, however, the gender ratio had come into balance. Once slave owners realized how profitable a fertile female slave could be over time, giving birth every two-and-a-half years to a child who could be sold, they began to encourage reproduction through a variety of incentives. Pregnant slaves were given less work to do and more food. Some plantation owners rewarded new slave mothers with dresses and silver dollars.

The offices of Price, Birch & Co., dealers in slaves, Alexandria, Virginia.

But if motherhood endowed slave women with stature and bene-fits, it also entailed exhausting demands. Within days after childbirth, the slave mother was put to work spinning, weaving, or sewing. A few weeks thereafter, mothers were sent back to the fields. Slave women were expected to do "man's work" outside. They cut trees, hauled logs, plowed fields with mules, dug ditches, spread fertilizer, slaugh-tered and dressed animals, hoed corn, and picked cotton. As a slave who escaped reported, "Women who do outdoor work are used as bad as men."

Once slave women passed their childbearing years, around the age of forty, their workload increased. Slave owners put middle-aged women to work full-time in the fields or performing other outdoor labor. Breast-feeding mothers were often forced to take their babies to the fields with them. A former slave on a Georgia plantation remembered that "women with little babies would have to go to work in de mornings with the rest, come back, nurse their children and go back to the field, stay two or three hours and go a nurse the chillun again, go back to the field and stay till night." On larger plantations, elderly slave women, called "grannies," kept the children during the day while their mothers worked outside. Slave women of all ages usually worked in sex-segregated gangs which enabled them to form close bonds with one another. To enslaved

Americans, developing a sense of community and camaraderie meant emotional and psychological survival.

Unlike male slaves, black girls and women faced the constant threat of sexual abuse by their owners. Sometimes a white master or overseer would rape women in the fields or in cabins. Sometimes the owner would lock a woman in a cabin with a male slave whose task was to impregnate her. Female slaves responded to such sexual abuse in different ways. Some of them seduced masters away from their wives. Others fiercely resisted sexual advances, and they were usually whipped or even killed for their disobedience. Some slave women killed their unwanted babies rather than see them grow up in slavery. Others were able to gather identity and status from the mulatto children they produced.

Female slaves had fewer opportunities than males to escape. In North Carolina during the 1850s, less than 20 percent of runaway slaves were female. Women tended to lack the physical strength and endurance required to run away and stay ahead of relentless pursuers. An even greater impediment to escape was a mother's responsibility to her children. A few slave women did escape, but most of them had to learn to cope and resist within the confines of captivity. For them, resistance to slavery took forms other than flight. Some female slaves engaged in truancy, hiding for several days at a time. Many slave women feigned illness to avoid work. Others sabotaged food or crops or stole from owners. Several slave women started fires. A few actually killed their masters, most often by poison.

CELIA   Occasionally a single historical incident involving ordinary people can illustrate the web of laws and customs within a society. Such is the case with the story of a teenaged slave girl named Celia. In 1850, fourteen-year-old Celia was purchased by Robert Newsom, a prosperous, respected Missouri farmer who owned six slaves, all males except for Celia.

Newsom told his daughters that he bought Celia to work as their domestic servant. In fact, however, the recently widowed Newsom wanted a sexual slave. After purchasing Celia, he raped the girl while driving her back to his farm. For the next five years Newsom treated Celia as his mistress, even building her a brick cabin fifty yards from the main house. During that time she gave birth to two children, presumably his offspring. By 1855 Celia had fallen in love with another slave, George, who demanded that she "quit the old man." Desperate for relief from her tormentor, Celia appealed to Newsom's two grown daughters, but they either could not or would not provide any assistance.

Soon thereafter, on June 23, 1855, the sixty-five-year-old Newsom entered Celia's cabin, ignored her impassioned appeals, and kept advancing until she struck and killed him with a large stick. When family members and neighbors realized that Newsom had disappeared, they questioned George, who eventually pointed to Celia. She finally confessed, but refused to implicate George or anyone else in Newsom's death.

Celia was not allowed to testify at her trial because she was a slave. Her attorneys, all of them slave owners, argued that the right of white women to defend themselves against sexual assault should be extended to slaves as well. The prevailing public opinion in the slave states, however, stressed that the white rape of a slave was not a crime. At worst, it was trespassing. But Newsom could not be accused of trespassing upon his own property, so the judge and jury, all white males, agreed with prevailing sentiment; they pronounced Celia guilty. On December 21, 1855, after two months of trials and futile appeals, Celia was hanged.

The grim story of Celia's brief life and abusive condition highlights the skewed power structure in southern society before the Civil War. Celia bore the double burden of being a slave and a young woman living within a male-dominated society.

SLAVE REBELLIONS   Organized slave resistance was rare in the face of overwhelming white authority and firepower. In the nineteenth century only three major slave insurrections were attempted, and two of those were betrayed before they got under way. In 1800 a slave named Gabriel on a plantation near Richmond hatched a plot involving perhaps a thousand others to seize key points in Richmond and start a general slaughter of whites. Twenty-five of the slave conspirators were executed and ten others deported to the West Indies.

The Denmark Vesey plot in Charleston, discovered in 1822, was believed to be a plan of a free black to assault the white population, seize ships in the harbor, burn the city, and head for Santo Domingo. It never got off the ground. Instead, thirty-five supposed slave rebels were executed and thirty-four deported.

Only the Nat Turner insurrection of 1831 in rural Southampton County, Virginia, got beyond the planning stage. Turner, a black overseer, was also a self-anointed religious exhorter who professed a divine mission in leading a slave rebellion. The revolt began when a small group of slaves killed the adults and children in Turner's master's household and set off down the road repeating the process at other farmhouses, where other slaves joined in. Before it ended at least fifty-five whites were killed. The militia killed large numbers of slaves indiscriminately in the process of putting down the rebels. Seventeen slaves were hanged.

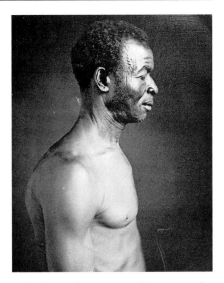

Jack (Driver), Guinea. Plantation of B. F. Taylor, Esq. Columbia, S.C., 1850.

Most slaves, however, did not openly rebel or run away. Instead, they more often retaliated against oppression by malingering or by outright sabotage. Yet there were constraints on such behavior, for laborers would likely eat better on a prosperous plantation than on one they had reduced to poverty. And the shrewdest slaveholders knew that they would more likely benefit from holding out rewards than from inflicting pain. Plantations based on the profit motive fostered between slaves and owners mutual dependency as well as natural antagonism. And in an agrarian society where personal relations counted for much, blacks could win concessions that moderated the harshness of slavery, permitting them a certain degree of individual and community development.

FORGING THE SLAVE COMMUNITY   To generalize about slavery is to miss elements of diversity from place to place and from time to time. The experience could be as varied as people are. Slaves were certainly victims, but to stop with so obvious a perception would be to miss an important story of endurance and achievement. If ever there was a melting pot in American history, the most effective may have been that in which Africans from a variety of ethnic, linguistic, and tribal origins fused into a new community and a new culture as African Americans.

Members of the slave community were bound together in helping one another, which in turn created a sense of cohesion and pride. Slave culture incorporated many African elements, especially in areas with few whites. Among the Gullah blacks of the South Carolina and Georgia coast, a researcher found as late as the 1940s more than 4,000 words still in use from the languages of twenty-one African tribes. Elements of African cultures have thus survived, adapted, and interacted with other cultures with which they came in contact.

SLAVE RELIGION AND FOLKLORE Among the most important manifestations of slave culture was its dynamic religion, a mixture of African and Christian elements. In religion slaves found both balm for the soul and release for their emotions. Most Africans brought with them to the Americas a concept of a Creator, or Supreme God, whom they could recognize in Jehovah, and lesser gods whom they might identify with Christ, the Holy Ghost, and the saints, thereby reconciling their earlier beliefs with the new Christian religion. Alongside the church they maintained beliefs in spirits (many of them benign), magic, and conjuring. Belief in magic is in fact a common human response to conditions of danger or helplessness.

Slaves found great comfort in the church. Masters sought to instill lessons of Christian humility and obedience, but blacks could identify their plight with that of the Israelites in Egypt or of the God who suffered as they did. And the ultimate hope of a better world gave solace in this one. Some owners encouraged religious meetings among their slaves, many of them believing that a Christian slave would be a better slave. "Church was what they called it," one former slave remembered, "but all that [white] preacher talked about was for us slaves to obey our masters and not to lie and steal."

Such a manipulated Christianity alienated many slaves, and most sought to create a genuine faith that spoke to their own spiritual and human needs. This required many of them to worship in secret, stealing away from their quarters to hold "bush meetings." A slave preacher explained that the "way in which we worshiped is almost indescribable. The singing helped provoke a certain ecstasy of emotion, clapping of hands, tossing of heads, which would continue without cessation about half an hour. The old house partook of the ecstasy; it rang with their jubilant shouts, and shook in all its joints."

Slaves found the Bible edifying in its tributes to the poor and oppressed, and they embraced its promise of salvation through Jesus. Likewise, the lyrics in religious "spirituals" helped slaves endure the strain of field labor and provided them with a musical code with which to express their own desire for freedom on earth. The articulate former slave Frederick Douglass stressed that "slaves sing most when they are most unhappy," and spirituals offered them deliverance from their worldly woes.

African cultural forms influenced a music of great rhythmic complexity, forms of dance and body language, spirituals and secular songs, and folk tales. Among oppressed peoples humor often becomes a means of psychological release, and there was a lively humor in the West African "trickster tales" of rabbits, tortoises, or Anansi the spider—relatively weak creatures who outwitted stronger animals. African-American folklore tended to be realistic in its images of wish fulfillment. Until after emancipation there were few stories of superhuman heroes, except for tales about captive Africans who escaped slavery by flying back home across the ocean.

THE SLAVE FAMILY Slave marriages had no legal status, but slave owners generally seem to have accepted marriage as a stabilizing influence on the plantation. Sometimes they performed marriages themselves or had a minister celebrate a formal wedding. Whatever the formalities, the norm for the slave community as for the white was the nuclear family of parents and children, with the father regarded as head of the family. Most slave children were socialized into their culture through the nuclear family, which afforded some degree of independence from white influence.

Childhood was short for slaves. They were forced to grow up fast. As early as five or six years of age, slave children were given work assignments. They collected trash and kindling, picked cotton, scared away crows, weeded, and ran errands. One observer noted that this "army of juveniles are in full training to take the places" of adult workers. By age ten they were full-time field hands. Children were often sold to new masters. In Missouri a female slave saw six of her seven children, ages one to eleven, all sold to six separate masters and separated from her.

Several generations of a family raised in slavery. Plantation of J. J. Smith, Beaufort, South Carolina, 1862.

THE CULTURE OF THE SOUTHERN FRONTIER

There was substantial social and cultural diversity within the South during the three decades before the Civil War. The region known as the Old Southwest, for example, is perhaps the least well known. It included the states and territories west of the Georgia border—Alabama, Mississippi, Louisiana, Texas, and Arkansas—as well as the frontier areas in Tennessee, Kentucky, and Florida.

Largely unsettled until the 1820s, this region bridged the South and the West, exhibiting characteristics of both areas. Raw and dynamic, filled with dangers, uncertainties, and opportunities, it served as a powerful magnet, luring thousands of settlers from Virginia and the Carolinas when the seaboard economy faltered during the 1820s and 1830s. By the 1830s, the bulk of cotton production was occurring in the lower South. The migrating southerners carved out farms, built churches, raised towns, and eventually brought culture and order to a raw frontier. As they took up new lives and occupations, southern pioneers transplanted many practices and institutions from the coastal states. But they also fashioned a distinct new set of cultural values and social customs.

THE DECISION TO MIGRATE   Young white men aspiring to be planters, usually in their twenties, responded to the siren call of fertile soil in the Old Southwest. By the late 1820s, the agricultural economy of the upper South suffered from depressed commodity prices and soil exhaustion. Large farm families, especially, struggled to provide each child with sufficient land and resources to subsist and maintain the family legacy. Thus, the dwindling economic opportunities available in the Carolinas and Virginia as well as restrictive kinship ties led many to migrate to the Old Southwest. As one young pioneer explained, he did not want to "creep and crawl in North Carolina like a poor sloth" when he could amass a fortune in the Old Southwest. Like their northern counterparts, restless southern sons of the planter and professional elite wanted to make it on their own, to be "self-made men," economically self-reliant and socially independent.

Women were underrepresented among migrants to the Old South- west. Few were interested in relocating to a disease-ridden, violent, and primitive territory. The new region did not offer them indepen- dence or adventure. In general, women regretted more than men the loss of kinship ties that migration would entail. To them a stable fam- ily life was more important than the prospect of material gain. As a Carolina woman prepared to depart for Alabama, she confided to a friend that "you *cannot* imagine the state of despair that I am in." An- other said that "my heart bleeds within me" at the thought of the "many tender cords [of kinship] that are now severed forever." Others feared that life on the frontier would produce a "dissipation" of morals. They heard vivid stories of lawlessness, drunkenness, gam- bling, and miscegenation.

Slaves had many of the same reservations about moving west. Almost a million captive blacks were taken to the Southwest during the antebel- lum era, most of them making the journey in the 1830s. Like the white women, they feared the harsh working conditions and torpid heat and humidity of the Southwest. They also were despondent at the breaking up of their family ties. When one young slave girl left Virginia for the Southwest, her mother ran after the wagon, eventually fell down, and rolled "over on de groun' jes' acryin'." She never saw her daughter again.

JOURNEY AND SETTLEMENT   Most of the migrants to the Southwest headed for the fertile lands of Alabama, Mississippi, and central Tennessee. The typical trek was about 500 miles. Along rough roads and trails, the pioneers averaged fifteen miles per day, occasionally staying overnight in taverns, more often camping in the open air. At times the route was clogged with people. One traveler said that often he would see "an uninterrupted line of walkers, wagons, and carriages." Slaves traveled on foot, tied or chained together. Many drowned while fording rivers; others died from disease.

Once in the Southwest, the pioneers bought land that had been appropriated from the Indians. Parcels of 640 acres sold for as little as $2 an acre. Land in Alabama's fertile black belt brought higher prices. As cotton prices soared in the 1830s, aspiring planters bought as much land and as many slaves as possible. As a result, the average size of farms and plantations in the Southwest was larger than that in the Carolinas and Virginia.

But the Southwest was much more unhealthy than the Carolina Piedmont. The hot climate, contaminated water, and poor sanitation spawned an epidemic of diseases. Malaria was especially common. Women and slaves also found their harsh new surroundings uninviting. Life in tents and rude log cabins made many newcomers yearn for the material comforts they had left behind. A male settler reported that "all the men is very well pleased but the women is not very satisfied."

A MASCULINE CULTURE   The southern frontier environment provoked important changes in sex roles, and relations between men and women became even more inequitable. Young adult males indulged themselves in activities that would have generated disapproval in the more settled seaboard society. They drank, gambled, fought, and indulged their sexual desires. In 1834 a South Carolina migrant urged his brother to move west and join him because "you can live like a fighting cock with us."

Alcohol consumption hit new heights in the Old Southwest. Most plantations had their own stills to manufacture whiskey, and alcoholism ravaged frontier families. Violence was also commonplace. A Virginian who settled in Mississippi fought in fourteen duels and killed ten men in the process. The frequency of fights, stabbings, shootings, and murders shocked visitors. So, too, did the propensity of white men to take sexual advantage of slave women. An Alabama woman married to a lawyer and politician was outraged by the "beastly passions" of the white men who fathered slave children and then sold them like livestock. She also recorded in her diary instances of men regularly beating their wives. Wives, it seems, had little choice but to endure such mistreatment because, as one woman wrote about a friend whose husband abused her, she was "wholly dependent upon his care."

ANTISLAVERY MOVEMENTS

EARLY OPPOSITION TO SLAVERY   Scattered criticism of slavery developed in the North and South in the decades after the Revolution, but the first organized emancipation movement appeared with the formation of the American Colonization Society in 1817. The society proposed to return freed slaves to Africa. Its supporters included such prominent figures as James Madison, James Monroe, Henry Clay, John Marshall, and Daniel Webster, and it appealed to diverse opinions. Some backed it as an antislavery group, while others saw it as a way to bolster slavery by getting rid of potentially troublesome free blacks. Leaders of the free black community denounced it from the start. America, they stressed, was now their native land.

Nevertheless, in 1821, agents of the society acquired from local chieftains in West Africa a parcel of land that became the nucleus of a new country. In 1822 the first freed slaves arrived there, and twenty-five years later the society relinquished control to the independent republic of Liberia. But given its uncertain purpose, the colonization movement received only meager support from either antislavery or proslavery elements. In all, up to 1860 only about 15,000 blacks migrated to Africa, approximately 12,000 with the help of the Colonization Society. The number was infinitesimal compared to the number of slave births.

FROM GRADUALISM TO ABOLITIONISM   Meanwhile, in the early 1830s, the antislavery movement took a new departure. Its initial efforts to promote a gradual end to slavery through prohibiting it in the territories and encouraging manumission gave way to demands for immediate abolition everywhere. In 1831, William Lloyd Garrison began

William Lloyd Garrison.

publication in Boston of a new anti-slavery newspaper, *The Liberator*. Garrison, who rose from poverty in Newburyport, Massachusetts, had been apprenticed to a newspaper-man and had edited a number of antislavery papers, but he grew impatient with the strategy of moderation. In the first issue of *The Liberator*, he renounced "the popular but pernicious doctrine of gradual emancipation" and vowed: "I will be as harsh as truth, and as uncompromising as justice."

Garrison's combative language and incendiary militancy provoked outraged retorts from slaveholders. Their angry defense gave *The Liberator* more exposure than anything the newspaper actually said. In the South, literate blacks would more likely encounter Garrison's ideas in the local papers than in the few copies of *The Liberator* that found their way to them. Slaveholders' outrage mounted higher after the Nat Turner insurrection in August 1831. Garrison, they assumed, bore a large part of the responsibility for the affair, but there is no evidence that Nat Turner had ever heard of him, and Garrison said that he had not a single subscriber in the South at the time. What is more, however violent his language, Garrison was a pacifist, opposed to the use of violence.

During the 1830s Garrison became the nation's most fervent, principled, and unyielding foe of slavery. In 1832 he and his followers set up the New England Anti-Slavery Society. The following year, two wealthy New York merchants, Arthur and Lewis Tappan, founded the American Anti-Slavery Society, with the help of Garrison and others. They hoped to exploit the publicity gained by the British antislavery movement, which that same year had induced Parliament to end slavery, with compensation to slaveholders, throughout the British Empire.

The American Anti-Slavery Society sought to convince people "that Slaveholding is a heinous crime in the sight of God, and that the duty, safety, and best interests of all concerned, require its *immediate abandonment*, without expatriation." The society went beyond the issue of emancipation to argue that blacks should "share an equality with the whites, of civil and religious privileges." The group issued a barrage of propaganda for its cause, including periodicals, tracts, agents, lecturers, organizers, and fund-raisers.

THE MOVEMENT SPLITS   As the antislavery movement spread, debates over tactics intensified. The Garrisonians, mainly New Englanders, were radicals who felt that American society had been corrupted from top to bottom and needed universal reform. Garrison embraced just about every important reform movement of the day: antislavery, temperance, pacifism, and women's rights. Deeply affected by the perfectionism of the times, he refused to compromise principle for expediency, to sacrifice one reform for another. Abolition was not enough. He opposed colonization of freed slaves and championed equal social and legal rights for blacks. He broke with the organized church, which to his mind was in league with slavery. The federal government was all the more so. The Constitution, he said, was "a covenant with death and an agreement with hell." Garrison therefore refused to vote.

Other reformers were less dogmatic. They saw American society as fundamentally sound and concentrated their attention on purging it of slavery. Garrison struck them as an impractical fanatic. A showdown came in 1840 on the issue of women's rights. Women had joined the abolition movement from the start, but largely in groups without men. The activities of the Grimké sisters brought the issue of women's rights to center stage.

Sarah and Angelina Grimké, daughters of a prominent South Carolina slaveowning family, had broken with their parents and moved north to embrace Quakerism, antislavery, feminism, and other reforms. Their publications included Angelina's *Appeal to the Christian Women of the South* (1836), calling on southern women to speak and act against slavery, and Sarah's *Letter on the Equality of the Sexes and the Condition of Women* (1838). Having attended Theodore Weld's school for antislavery apostles in New York (Angelina later married Theodore), they set out speaking first to women in New England and eventually to audiences of both men and women.

Such behavior inspired the Congregational clergy of Massachusetts to chastise the Grimké sisters for engaging in unfeminine activity. The chairman of the Connecticut Anti-Slavery Society declared: "No woman shall speak or vote where I am a moderator." Catharine Beecher reminded the activist sisters that women occupied "a subordinate relation in society to the other sex" and should therefore limit their activities to the "domestic and social circle." Angelina Grimké stoutly rejected such conventional arguments. "It is a woman's right," she insisted, "to have a voice in all laws and regulations by which she is to be governed, whether in church or in state."

The debate over the role of women in the antislavery movement crackled and simmered until it finally exploded in 1840. At the Anti-Slavery Society's meeting, the Garrisonians insisted on the right of women to participate equally in the organization, and carried their point. They did not commit the group to women's rights in any other way, however. Contrary opinion, mainly from the Tappans' New York group, ranged from outright antifeminism to simple fear of scattering shots over too many reforms. The New Yorkers broke away to form the American and Foreign Anti-Slavery Society.

BLACK ANTISLAVERY ACTIVITY   White antislavery men also balked at granting full recognition to black abolitionists of either sex. Often blindly patronizing, white abolitionists expected free blacks to take a back seat in the movement. Most blacks became exasperated at such discrimination. Despite the invitation to form separate groups, black leaders were active in the white societies from the beginning. Three attended the organizational meeting of the American Anti-Slavery Society in 1833, and some became outstanding agents for the movement, notably the former slaves who could speak from firsthand experience. Garrison pronounced such men as Henry Bibb and William Wells Brown, both escapees from Kentucky, and Frederick Douglass, who fled Maryland, "the best qualified to address the public on the subject of slavery."

Douglass, blessed with an imposing frame and a simple eloquence, became the best-known black man in America. "I appear before the immense assembly this evening as a thief and a robber," he told a Massachusetts group in 1842. "I stole this head, these limbs, this body from my master, and ran off with them." Fearful of capture after publishing his *Narrative of the Life of Frederick Douglass* (1845), he left for an extended lecture tour of the British Isles and returned two years later with enough money to purchase his freedom. He then started an abolitionist newspaper for blacks, the *North Star*, in Rochester, New York.

Douglass's *Narrative* was but the best known among hundreds of such accounts. Escapees often made it out on their own—Douglass borrowed a pass from a free black seaman—but many were aided by the Underground Railroad, which grew into a vast system to conceal runaways and spirit them to freedom, often over the Canadian border. Levi Coffin, a North Carolina Quaker who moved to Cincinnati and did help many fugitives, was the reputed president. Actually, there seems to have been more spontaneity than system about the matter, and blacks contributed more than was credited in the legend. A few intrepid refugees actually ventured back into slave states to organize escapes. Harriet Tubman, the most celebrated, went back nineteen times.

Equally courageous was the articulate black female abolitionist Sojourner Truth. Born in New York in 1797, the daughter of slaves, she was given the name Isabella. She renamed herself in 1843 after experiencing a mystical conversation with God, who told her "to travel up and down the land" preaching the sins of slavery. She did just that, crisscrossing the country during the 1840s and 1850s, exhorting audiences about abolitionism and women's rights. Having been a slave until freed by a New York law in 1828, Sojourner Truth was able to speak with added conviction and knowledge about the evils of the "peculiar institution" and the inequality of women. As she told a gathering of the Ohio Women's

Frederick Douglass (left) *and Sojourner Truth* (right) *were both leading abolitionists.*

Rights Convention in 1851, "I have plowed, and planted, and gathered into barns, and no man could head me—and ar'n't I a woman? I have borne thirteen children, and seen 'em mos' all sold off into slavery, and when I cried out with a mother's grief, none but Jesus heard—and ar'n't I a woman?"

Through such compelling testimony, Sojourner Truth demonstrated the powerful intersection of abolitionism and women's rights agitation, and in the process she tapped the distinctive energies that women brought to reformist causes. "If the first woman God ever made was strong enough to turn the world upside down all alone," she concluded her address to the Ohio gathering, "these women together ought to be able to turn it back, and get it right side up again!"

REACTIONS TO ANTISLAVERY   Even in the North, Truth, Garrison, Douglass, and other abolitionists had to face down hostile crowds who disliked blacks or found antislavery agitation bad for business. In 1837 a mob in Alton, Illinois, killed the antislavery editor Elijah P. Lovejoy, giving the movement a martyr to both abolition and freedom of the press.

In the 1830s abolitionism took a political turn, focusing at first on the Congress. One shrewd strategy was to deluge Congress with petitions for abolition in the District of Columbia. Most such petitions were presented by former president John Quincy Adams, elected to the House from Massachusetts in 1830. In 1836, however, the House adopted a rule to lay abolition petitions automatically on the table, in effect ignoring them. Adams, "Old Man Eloquent," stubbornly fought this "gag rule" as a violation of the First Amendment, and hounded its supporters until the gag rule was finally repealed in 1844.

Meanwhile, in 1840, the year of the schism in the antislavery movement, a small group of abolitionists called a national convention in Albany, New York, and launched the Liberty party with James G. Birney, onetime slaveholder of Alabama and Kentucky, as its candidate for president. Birney, converted to the cause by Theodore Weld, had tried without success to publish an antislavery paper in Danville, Kentucky. He then moved to Ohio and in 1837 became executive secretary of the American Anti-Slavery Society. In the 1840 election he polled only 7,000 votes, but in 1844 his total rose to 60,000, and from that time forth an antislavery party contested every national election until Abraham Lincoln won the presidency in 1860.

THE DEFENSE OF SLAVERY   Birney was but one among a number of southerners propelled north during the 1830s by the South's growing hostility to emancipationist ideas. The antislavery movement in the upper South had its last stand in 1831–1832 when the Virginia legislature debated a plan of gradual emancipation and colonization, then rejected it by a vote of 73 to 58. Thereafter, leaders of southern thought worked out an elaborate intellectual defense of slavery, presenting it as a positive good.

The evangelical Christian churches, which had widely condemned slavery at one time, gradually turned proslavery, at least in the South. Ministers of all denominations joined in the argument. Had not the patriarchs of the Old Testament held people in bondage? Had not Saint Paul advised servants to obey their masters and told a fugitive servant to return to his master? And had not Jesus remained silent on the subject, at least so far as the Gospels reported his words? In 1843–1844 disputes over slavery split two great denominations along sectional lines and led to the formation of the Southern Baptist Convention and the Methodist Episcopal Church, South. Presbyterians, the only other major denomination to split, did not divide until the Civil War.

A more fundamental feature of the proslavery argument stressed an intrinsic inferiority of blacks. Other arguments took a more "practical" view of slavery. Not only was slavery profitable, it was a matter of social necessity. Thomas Jefferson, for instance, in his *Notes on Virginia* (1785), had argued that emancipated slaves and whites could not live together without risk of race war growing out of the recollection of past injustices. What is more, it seemed clear to some that blacks could not be expected to work under conditions of freedom. They were too shiftless and improvident, the argument went, and in freedom would be a danger to themselves as well as to others. White workers, on the other hand, feared their competition for their jobs.

A new argument on behalf of slavery arose in the late 1850s. Virginian George Fitzhugh and others began to defend slavery as being better for the workers, since it provided them with security in sickness and old age, unlike the "wage slavery" of northern industry, which exploited workers for profit and then cast them away. Within one generation, such ideas had triumphed in the white South over the post-Revolutionary apology for slavery as an evil bequeathed by the forefathers. Opponents of the orthodox faith in slavery as a positive good were either silenced or exiled. Freedom of thought in the Old South had become a victim of the region's growing obsession with the preservation and expansion of slavery.

MAKING CONNECTIONS

- The abolition movement never represented the majority of northerners. As Chapter 16 shows, however, by the end of the 1850s most voters in the North could support the idea of limiting the expansion of slavery westward, if not the abolition of it in the southern states.

- The Civil War brought great changes to southerners, both black and white. Chapter 17 describes the effect of the war on southern society.

- There are striking contrasts between the Old South of this chapter and the New South of Chapter 19.

FURTHER READING

Those interested in the problem of discerning myth and reality in the southern experience should consult William R. Taylor's *Cavalier and Yankee: The Old South and American National Character* (1961). Two recent efforts to understand the mind of the Old South and its defense of slavery are Eugene D. Genovese's *The Slaveholders' Dilemma: Freedom and Progress in Southern Conservative Thought, 1820–1860* (1992) and Eric H. Walther's *The Fire-Eaters* (1992).

Contrasting analyses of the plantation system are Eugene D. Genovese's *The World the Slaveholders Made* (1969) and Gavin Wright's *The Political Economy of the Cotton South* (1978). Stephanie McCurry's *Masters of Small Worlds: Yeoman Households, Gender Relations, and the Political Culture of the Antebellum South Carolina Low Country* (1995) greatly enriches our understanding of households, religion, and political culture.

Other essential works on southern culture and society include Bertram Wyatt-Brown's *Honor and Violence in the Old South* (1986), Elizabeth Fox-Genovese's *Within the Plantation Household: Black and White Women of the Old South* (1988), Catherine Clinton's *The Plantation Mistress: Woman's World in the Old South* (1982), Joan Cashin's *A Family Venture: Men and Women on the Southern Frontier* (1991), and Theodore Rosengarten's *Tombee: Portrait of a Cotton Planter* (1987).

William J. Cooper, Jr.'s *Liberty and Slavery: Southern Politics to 1860* (1983) and Robert F. Durden's *The Self-Inflicted Wound* (1985) cover southern politics of the era. For a look at the role of religion in southern political life, see Mitchell Snay's *Gospel of Disunion: Religion and Separatism in the Antebellum South* (1993).

A provocative discussion of the psychology of black slavery can be found in Stanley M. Elkins's *Slavery: A Problem in American Institutional and Intellectual Life* (3rd ed., 1976). John W. Blassingame's *The Slave Community: Plantation Life in the Antebellum South* (2nd ed., 1979), Eugene D. Genovese's *Roll, Jordan, Roll: The World the Slaves Made* (1974), and Herbert G. Gutman's *The Black Family in Slavery and Freedom, 1750–1925* (1976) all stress the theme of a persisting and identifiable slave culture. On the question of slavery's profitability, see Robert W. Fogel and Stanley L. Engerman's *Time on the Cross: The Economics of Negro Slavery* (2 vols., 1974).

Other works on slavery include Lawrence W. Levine's *Black Culture and Black Consciousness: Afro-American Folk Thought from Slavery to Freedom* (1977), Albert J. Raboteau's *Slave Religion: The "Invisible Institution" in the Antebellum South* (1978), Dorothy Sterling's *We Are Your Sisters* (1984), Deborah Gray White's *Ar'n't I a Woman? Female Slaves in the Plantation South* (1985), and Joel Williamson's *The Crucible of Race* (1985). Charles Joyner's *Down by the Riverside* (1984) offers a vivid reconstruction of one slave community.

Useful surveys of abolitionism include Ronald G. Walters's *The Antislavery Appeal: American Abolitionism after 1830* (1976), James B. Stewart's *Holy Warriors: The Abolitionists and American Slavery* (1976), and Julie Jeffrey's *The Great Silent Army of Abolitionism: Ordinary Women in the Abolitionist Movement* (1998). For the proslavery argument as it developed in the South, see Larry Tise's *Proslavery: A History of the Defense of Slavery in America, 1701–1840* (1988) and James Oakes's *The Ruling Race: A History of American Slaveholders* (1982). The problems southerners had in justifying slavery are explored in Drew G. Faust's *A Sacred Circle: The Dilemma of the Intellectual in the Old South, 1840–1860* (1977) and Kenneth S. Greenberg's *Masters and Statesmen: The Political Culture of American Slavery* (1985).

16 ❧ THE CRISIS OF UNION

CHAPTER ORGANIZER

This chapter focuses on:

- the politicization of slavery.

- how the Compromise of 1850 and the Kansas-Nebraska Act reflected sectional tensions.

- the rise of a third generation party system: Republicans and Democrats.

- the specific events that led to the secession of the southern states.

*J*ohn C. Calhoun and Ralph Waldo Emerson had little in common, but both men sensed in the Mexican War the omens of a greater disaster. Mexico was "the forbidden fruit; the penalty of eating it would be to subject our institutions to political death," Calhoun warned. "The United States will conquer Mexico," Emerson conceded, "but it will be as the man swallows the arsenic. . . . Mexico will poison us." Wars, as both men knew, have a way of corrupting ideals and breeding new wars, often in unforeseen ways. Like Britain's conquest of New France, America's winning of the Southwest gave rise in turn to quarrels over newly acquired lands. In each case the quarrels set in motion a series of disputes: Britain's eighteenth-century crisis of empire had its counterpart in America's nineteenth-century crisis of union.

SLAVERY IN THE TERRITORIES

THE WILMOT PROVISO The Mexican War was less than three months old when the seeds of a new conflict began to sprout. On August 8, 1846, a freshman Democrat from Pennsylvania, David Wilmot, delivered a provocative speech to the House of Representatives. He favored territorial expansion, Wilmot explained, even the annexation of Texas as a slave state. But slavery had come to an end in Mexico, and if new territory should be acquired, "God forbid that we should be the means of planting this institution upon it." Drawing upon the words of the Northwest Ordinance, he proposed that in lands acquired from Mexico, "neither slavery nor involuntary servitude shall ever exist in any part of said territory."

The Wilmot Proviso was never a law, but it politicized the debate over slavery once and for all. For a generation, since the Missouri controversy of 1819–1821, the issue had been lurking in the wings. Now, for the next two decades, the question would never be far from center stage. The House adopted the Wilmot Proviso, but the Senate balked. When Congress reconvened in December 1846, Polk prevailed on Wilmot to withhold his amendment, but by then others were ready to take up the cause. When a New York congressman revived the proviso, he signaled a revolt by the Van Burenites in concert with the antislavery forces of the North. Once again the House approved the amendment; again the Senate refused. In one form or another, however, Wilmot's idea kept cropping up. Abraham Lincoln later recalled that during one term as congressman, 1847–1849, he voted for it "as good as forty times."

John Calhoun meanwhile devised a thesis to counter the proviso, and he set it before the Senate in four resolutions on February 19, 1847. The Calhoun Resolutions, which never came to a vote, argued that since the territories were the common possession of the states, Congress had no right to prevent any citizen from taking slaves into them. To do so would violate the Fifth Amendment, which forbids Congress from depriving any person of life, liberty, or property without due process of law, and slaves were property. By this clever stroke of logic, Calhoun took that basic guarantee of liberty, the Bill of Rights, and turned it into a basic guarantee of slavery. The irony was not lost on his critics, but the point became established southern dogma—echoed by his colleagues and formally endorsed by the Virginia legislature.

Senator Thomas Hart Benton of Missouri, himself a slaveholder but also a Jacksonian nationalist, found in Calhoun's resolutions a set of abstractions "leading to no result." Wilmot and Calhoun between them, he said, had fashioned a pair of shears. Neither blade alone would cut very well, but joined together they could sever the ties of union.

POPULAR SOVEREIGNTY   Many others, like Benton, refused to be polarized, seeking to bypass the brewing conflict. President Polk was among the first to suggest extending the Missouri Compromise dividing free and slave territory at latitude 36°30′all the way to the Pacific. Senator Lewis Cass of Michigan suggested that the citizens of a territory "regulate their own internal concerns in their own way," like the citizens of a state. Such an approach would combine the merits of expediency and democracy. It would take the issue out of the national arena and put it in the hands of those directly affected.

Popular sovereignty, or squatter sovereignty, as the idea was also called, had much to commend it. Without directly challenging the slaveholders' access to the new lands, it promised to open them quickly to non-slaveholding farmers who would almost surely dominate the territories. With this tacit understanding, the idea prospered in Cass's Old Northwest, where Stephen A. Douglas of Illinois and other prominent Democrats soon endorsed it.

When the Mexican War ended in 1848, the question of slavery in the new territories was no longer hypothetical—unless one reasoned, as many did, that their arid climate excluded plantation crops and therefore excluded slavery. For Calhoun, that was beside the point, since the right to carry slaves into the territories was inviolable. In fact, there is little reason in retrospect to credit the argument that slavery had reached its natural limits of expansion. Slavery had been adapted to occupations other than plantation agriculture. Besides, on irrigated lands, cotton later became a staple crop of the Southwest.

Nobody doubted that Oregon would become a free soil territory, but it too was drawn into the growing controversy. Territorial status, pending since 1846, was delayed for Oregon because its provisional government had excluded slavery. To concede that provision would imply an authority drawn from the powers of Congress, since a territory was created by Congress. After much wrangling, an exhausted Congress let Oregon organize without slavery, but postponed decision on the Southwest. Polk signed the bill on the principle that Oregon was north of 36°30′.

Polk had promised to serve only one term; exhausted and having accomplished his major goals, he refused to run again in 1848. At the Democratic convention Lewis Cass won the presidential nomination, but the party refused to endorse the "squatter sovereignty" plan. Instead it simply denied the power of Congress to interfere with slavery in the states and criticized all efforts to bring the question before Congress. The Whigs devised an even more artful shift. Once again, as in 1840, they passed over their party leader, Henry Clay, for a general, Zachary Taylor, whose fame and popularity had grown since the Battle of Buena Vista. He was a resident of Louisiana who owned more than 100 slaves, an apolitical figure who had never voted in a national election. Once again, as in 1840, the party adopted no platform at all.

THE FREE-SOIL COALITION   But the antislavery impulse was not easily squelched. Wilmot had raised a standard to which a broad coalition could rally. People who shied away from abolitionism could readily endorse the exclusion of slavery from the territories. The Northwest Ordinance and the Missouri Compromise supplied honored precedents. By doing so, moreover, one could strike a blow for liberty without caring about slavery itself, or about the slaves. One might simply want free soil for white farmers, while keeping the unwelcome blacks far away in the South, where they belonged. Free soil, therefore, rather than abolition, became the rallying point—and also the name of a new party.

Three major groups entered the free-soil coalition: rebellious Democrats, antislavery Whigs, and members of the Liberty party, which dated from 1840. Disaffection among the Democrats centered in New York, where the Van Burenite "Barnburners" seized upon the free-soil issue as a moral imperative. Free-soil principles among the Whigs centered in Massachusetts, where a group of "Conscience" Whigs battled the "Cotton" Whigs. The latter, according to Charles Sumner, belonged to a coalition of northern businessmen and southern planters, "the lords of the lash and the lords of the loom." Conscience Whigs rejected the slaveholding nominee of their party, Zachary Taylor.

In 1848 these groups—Van Buren Democrats, Conscience Whigs, and Liberty party followers—organized the Free Soil party in a convention at Buffalo, New York, and nominated Martin Van Buren for president. The Free Soil party platform pledged the government to abolish slavery whenever such action became constitutional, but the party's main principle was the Wilmot Proviso, and it entered the campaign with the catchy slogan of "free soil, free speech, free labor, and free men."

The impact of the new party on the election was mixed. The Free Soilers split the Democratic vote enough to throw New York to Taylor, and the Whig vote enough to give Ohio to Lewis Cass, but Van Buren's total of 291,000 votes was far below the popular totals of 1,361,000 for Taylor and 1,222,000 for Cass. Taylor won with 163 to 127 electoral votes, and both major parties retained a national following. Taylor took eight slave states and seven free; Cass just the opposite, seven slave and eight free.

THE CALIFORNIA GOLD RUSH   Meanwhile a new dimension had been introduced into the vexing question of the new territories. On January 24, 1848, gold was discovered in the California territory. The

California News, *by William Sidney Mount, 1850. During the California gold rush, San Francisco quickly became a cosmopolitan city as the population increased almost fifty-fold in a few months.*

word spread quickly, and President Polk's celebration of the discovery in his last annual message, on December 5, 1848, turned the gold fever into a worldwide epidemic.

The California gold rush constituted the greatest mass migration in American history. During 1849 some 80,000 gold seekers reached California, half of them Americans, and by 1854, the number would top 300,000. The "Forty-niners" included people from every social class and from every state and territory, as well as slaves brought by their owners. Most went overland; the rest boarded ship and went by way of Panama or Cape Horn.

After touring the gold region, the territorial governor reported that the influx of newcomers had "entirely changed the character of Upper California." The influx quickly reduced the 14,000 Mexicans to a minority, and sporadic conflicts with the Indians of the Sierra Nevada foothills decimated the native peoples. In 1850 Americans accounted for 68 percent of the population, but there was also a cosmopolitan array of "Sydney Ducks" from Australia, "Kanakas" from Hawaii, "Limies" from London, "Paddies" from Ireland, "Coolies" from China, and "Keskydees" from France (who were always asking "Qu'est-ce qu'il dit?"—"What did he say?").

THE MINING FRONTIER Unlike the land-hungry pioneers who traversed the overland trails, the miners were mostly unmarried young men representing a wide spectrum of ethnic and cultural backgrounds. Few miners were interested in permanent settlement. They wanted to strike it rich and return home. The mining camps in California valleys, canyons, and along creek beds thus sprang up like mushrooms and disappeared almost as rapidly. As soon as rumors of a new strike made the rounds, miners converged on the area, joined soon thereafter by a hodgepodge of merchants and camp followers. Then, when no more gold was found, they picked up and moved on.

The mining shantytowns were disorderly, unsanitary, and often lawless communities; vigilante justice prevailed and leisure time revolved around saloons and gambling halls. One newcomer reported that "in the short space of twenty-four days, we have had murders, fearful accidents, bloody deaths, a mob, whippings, a hanging, an attempt at suicide, and a fatal duel." Within six months of arriving in California in 1849, one in every five of the gold seekers was dead. The gold fields and

Gold Miners, *c. 1850. Daguerreotype of miners panning for gold at their claim.*

mining towns were so dangerous that insurance companies refused to provide coverage. The town of Marysville had seventeen murders in one week. Everyone carried weapons—usually pistols or bowie knives. Suicides were common, and disease was rampant. Cholera and scurvy plagued every camp. With so many uprooted young men thrown together with criminals and vice peddlers, the primary forms of entertainment were gambling and alcohol.

Women were as rare in the mining camps as liquor was abundant. In 1850 less than 8 percent of California's total population was female, and even fewer women hazarded life in the mining camps. Those who did could demand quite a premium for their work as cooks, laundresses, entertainers, and prostitutes. Women from back East who rarely had a suitor suddenly found themselves smothered with attention in the mining country. A female immigrant noted that she had "men come forty miles over the mountains, just to look at me, and I never was called a handsome woman, in my best days, even by my most ardent admirers."

In the polyglot mining camps, white Americans often looked with disdain upon the Hispanics and Chinese, who were most often employed as wage laborers to help in the panning process, separating gold from sand and gravel. But the white Americans focused their contempt on the Indians. In the mining culture it was not a crime to kill Indians or work them to death. American miners tried several times to outlaw foreigners in the mining country but had to settle for a tax on foreign miners that was applied to Mexicans in express violation of the treaty ending the Mexican War.

CALIFORNIA STATEHOOD   As civic leaders emerged within the burgeoning California population, they grew increasingly frustrated by the inability of military authorities to maintain law and order. In this context the new president, Zachary Taylor, thought he saw an ideal opportunity to use California statehood as a lever to end the stalemate in Congress caused by the slavery issue.

Born in Virginia and raised in Kentucky, Taylor had been a soldier most of his adult life. Constantly on the move, he had acquired a home in Louisiana and a plantation in Mississippi. Southern Whigs had rallied to his support, expecting him to uphold the cause of slavery. Instead he turned out to be a southern man with Union principles, who had no more use for Calhoun's proslavery abstractions than Jackson had for his nullification doctrine. Innocent of politics Taylor might be, but "Old Rough and Ready" had the practical mind of the soldier he was. Slavery should be upheld where it existed, he felt, but he had little patience with abstract theories about slavery in territories where it probably could not exist. Why not make California and New Mexico into free states immediately, he reasoned, and bypass the whole issue?

But the Californians, in need of organized government, were already ahead of him. By December 1849, without consulting Congress, California had a free-state government in operation. New Mexico responded more slowly, but by 1850 Americans there had adopted another free-state constitution. The Mormons around Salt Lake, meanwhile, drafted a basic law for the state of Deseret, which embraced most of the Mexican cession, including a slice of the coast from Los Angeles to San Diego. In Taylor's annual message on December 4, 1849, he endorsed immediate statehood for California and enjoined Congress to avoid injecting slavery into the issue of statehood. The new Congress, however, was in no mood for simple solutions.

The Compromise of 1850

The spotlight fell on the Senate, where a stellar cast enacted one of the great dramas of American politics, the Compromise of 1850: the triumvirate of Henry Clay, John Calhoun, and Daniel Webster, with a supporting cast that included William Seward, Stephen A. Douglas, Jefferson Davis, and Thomas Hart Benton. Seventy-three-year-old Henry Clay once again took the role of "Great Compromiser," which he had played in the Missouri and nullification controversies.

THE GREAT DEBATE   In January 1850 Clay presented a package of eight resolutions that wrapped up solutions to all the disputed issues. He proposed to (1) admit California as a free state, (2) organize the remainder territories of the Southwest without restriction as to slavery, (3) deny Texas its extreme claim to much of New Mexico territory, (4) compensate Texas for this by assuming the preannexation Texas debt, (5) uphold slavery in the District of Columbia, but (6) abolish the slave trade across its boundaries, (7) adopt a more effective fugitive slave act, and (8) deny congressional authority to interfere with the interstate slave trade. His proposals, in substance, became the Compromise of 1850, but only after a prolonged debate, the most celebrated, if not the greatest, in the annals of Congress—and the final great debate for Calhoun, Clay, and Webster.

On February 5–6 Clay summoned all his eloquence in a defense of the proposed settlement. In the interest of "peace, concord and harmony," he called for an end to "passion, passion—party, party—and intemperance." Otherwise, continued sectional bickering would lead to a "furious, bloody, implacable, exterminating" civil war. To avoid such a catastrophe, he stressed, California should be admitted as a free state on the terms that its own people had approved.

The debate continued sporadically through February, with Sam Houston rising to the support of Clay's compromise, and Mississippi's Jefferson Davis defending the slavery cause on every point. President Taylor believed that slavery in the South could best be protected if southerners avoided injecting the issue into the dispute over new territories. Unlike Calhoun, he did not believe the new western territories were suitable for slave-based agriculture. Because in his mind the issue of bringing slaves into the territories was moot, he continued to urge the Congress to admit California and New Mexico without reference to slavery. But few others embraced such a simple solution. In fact, a rising chorus of southern leaders threatened to secede if slaves were not allowed into California.

On March 4 Calhoun left his sickbed to sit in the Senate chamber, a gaunt figure with his cloak draped about his shoulders, as a colleague read his speech. "I have, Senators, believed from the first that the agitation of the subject of slavery would, if not prevented by some timely and effective measure, end in disunion," said Calhoun. Neither Clay's compromise nor Taylor's efforts would serve the Union. The South needed simply an acceptance of its rights: equality in the territories, the return of fugitive slaves, and some guarantee of "an equilibrium between the sections." The last, while not spelled out in the speech, referred to Calhoun's notion of a "concurrent majority" by which each section could gain security through a veto power, perhaps through a dual executive.

Three days later Calhoun returned to hear Daniel Webster. The "Godlike Daniel" no longer possessed the thunderous voice of his youth, nor did his shrinking frame project its once magisterial aura, but he remained a formidable presence. He chose as his central theme the preservation of the Union: "I wish to speak today, not as a Massachusetts man, not as a Northern man, but as an American. . . . I speak today for the preservation of the Union. Hear me for my cause." The extent of slavery was already determined, he insisted, by the Northwest Ordinance, by the Missouri Compromise, and in the new lands by the law of nature. The Wilmot Proviso was superfluous: "I would not take pains to reaffirm an ordinance of nature nor to re-enact the will of God." Both sections, to be sure, had legitimate grievances: on the one hand, the excesses of "infernal fanatics and abolitionists" in the North; and on the other hand, southern efforts to expand slavery and heap southern slurs on northern workingmen. But "Secession! Peaceable secession! Sir, your eyes and mine are never destined to see that miracle." Instead of looking into such "caverns of darkness," let "men enjoy the fresh air of liberty and union. Let them look to a more hopeful future."

The March 7 speech was a supreme gesture of conciliation, and Webster had knowingly brought down a storm upon his head. New England antislavery leaders lambasted this new "Benedict Arnold" who had betrayed his region. On March 11 William Seward, freshman Whig senator from New York, gave the antislavery reply to Webster. As the confidant of Taylor, he might have been expected to defend the president's program.

Instead he declared that compromise with slavery was "radically wrong and essentially vicious." There was, he said, "a higher law than the Constitution" that demanded the abolition of slavery.

In mid-April a select Committee of Thirteen bundled Clay's suggestions (insofar as they concerned the Mexican cession) into one comprehensive bill, which the committee reported to the Senate early in May. The measure was quickly dubbed the "Omnibus Bill" because it resembled the contemporary vehicle that carried many riders. Taylor continued to oppose Clay's compromise, and their feud threatened to split the Whig party wide open. Another crisis loomed when word came near the end of June that New Mexico was applying for statehood, with Taylor's support, and with boundaries that conflicted with the Texas claim to the east bank of the Rio Grande.

TOWARD A COMPROMISE On July 4, 1850, friends of the Union staged a grand rally at the base of the unfinished Washington Monument. Taylor went to hear the speeches, lingering in the hot sun. Five days later he died of cholera morbus, a gastrointestinal affliction possibly caused by tainted food or water and exacerbated by the hot summer weather. The outcome of the sectional quarrel, had he lived, probably would have been different; whether for better or worse one cannot know.

Taylor's sudden death, however, strengthened the chances of compromise. The soldier in the White House was followed by a politician, Millard Fillmore. The son of a poor farmer in upper New York, Fillmore had come up through the school of hard knocks. Largely self-educated, he had made his own way in the profession of law and the rough-and-tumble world of New York politics. Experience had taught him caution, which some interpreted as indecision, but he had made up his mind to support Clay's compromise and had so informed Taylor. It was a

Millard Fillmore, whose support of the Compromise of 1850 helped the Union muddle through the crisis.

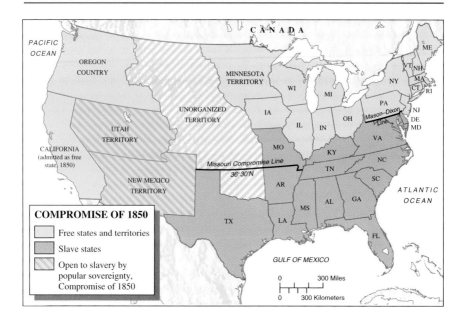

strange switch. Taylor, the Louisiana slaveholder, had been ready to make war on his native region; Fillmore, who southerners thought was antislavery, was ready to make peace.

At this point young Senator Stephen A. Douglas of Illinois, a rising star of the Democratic party, rescued Clay's faltering compromise. Short and stocky, brash and brilliant, Douglas was known as the "Little Giant." His strategy was in fact the same one that Clay had used to pass the Missouri Compromise thirty years before. Reasoning that nearly everybody objected to one or another provision of the Omnibus Bill, Douglas worked on the principle of breaking it up into six (later five) separate measures. Few members were prepared to vote for all of them, but from different elements Douglas hoped to mobilize a majority for each.

It worked. By September 20, President Fillmore had signed the last of the five measures into law. The Union had muddled through, and the settlement went down in history as the Compromise of 1850. For the time it defused an explosive situation and settled each of the major points at issue.

First, California entered the Union as a free state, ending forever the old balance of free and slave states. *Second,* the Texas and New Mexico Act made New Mexico a territory and set the Texas boundary at its present location. In return for giving up its claims east of the Rio Grande, Texas was paid $10 million, which secured payment of the Texas debt. *Third,* the Utah Act set up another territory. The territorial act in each case omitted reference to slavery except to give the territorial legislature authority over "all rightful subjects of legislation" with provision for appeal to federal courts. For the sake of agreement, the deliberate ambiguity of the statement was its merit. Northern congressmen could assume that territorial legislatures might act to exclude slavery on the unstated principle of popular sovereignty. Southern congressmen assumed that they could not.

Fourth, a new Fugitive Slave Act put the matter wholly under federal jurisdiction and stacked the cards in favor of slave-catchers. *Fifth,* as a gesture to antislavery forces, the slave trade, but not slavery itself, was abolished in the District of Columbia. The spectacle of chained-together slaves passing through the streets of the capital was brought to an end.

Millard Fillmore pronounced the five measures making up the Compromise of 1850 "a final settlement." Still, doubts lingered that either North or South could be reconciled to the measures permanently. In the South the disputes of 1846–1850 had transformed the abstract doctrine of secession into a movement animated by such "fire-eaters" as Robert Barnwell Rhett of South Carolina, William Lowndes Yancey of Alabama, and Edmund Ruffin of Virginia.

But once the furies aroused by the Wilmot Proviso were spent, the compromise left little on which to focus a proslavery agitation. The state of California was an accomplished fact, and, ironically, tended to elect proslavery men to Congress. New Mexico and Utah were far away, and in any case at least hypothetically open to slavery. Both in fact adopted slave codes, but the census of 1860 reported no slaves in New Mexico and only twenty-nine in Utah. The Fugitive Slave Act was something else again. It was the one clear-cut victory for the cause of slavery, but would the North enforce it?

THE FUGITIVE SLAVE ACT Southern insistence on the Fugitive Slave Act had presented abolitionists with an emotional new focus for agitation. The Fugitive Slave Act did more than strengthen the hand of slave-catchers; it offered a strong temptation to kidnap free blacks. The law denied alleged fugitives a jury trial and provided that special commissioners got a fee of $10 when they certified delivery of an alleged

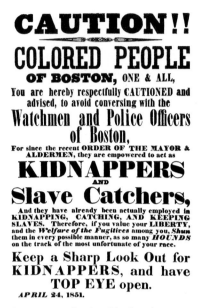

CAUTION!!

COLORED PEOPLE

OF BOSTON, ONE & ALL,

You are hereby respectfully CAUTIONED and advised, to avoid conversing with the

Watchmen and Police Officers of Boston,

For since the recent ORDER OF THE MAYOR & ALDERMEN, they are empowered to act as

KIDNAPPERS

AND

Slave Catchers,

And they have already been actually employed in KIDNAPPING, CATCHING, AND KEEPING SLAVES. Therefore, if you value your LIBERTY, and the *Welfare of the Fugitives* among you, *Shun* them in every possible manner, as so many *HOUNDS* on the track of the most unfortunate of your race.

Keep a Sharp Look Out for KIDNAPPERS, and have TOP EYE open.

APRIL 24, 1851.

A notice to the free blacks of Boston to avoid the "watchmen and police officers" who "are empowered to act as kidnappers and slave catchers," 1851.

slave but only $5 when they refused certification. In addition federal marshals could require citizens to help in enforcement; violators could be imprisoned for up to six months and fined $1,000.

"This filthy enactment was made in the nineteenth century, by people who could read and write," Ralph Waldo Emerson marveled in his journal. He advised neighbors to break the new law "on the earliest occasion." The occasion soon arose in many places. In Detroit only military force stopped the rescue of an alleged fugitive by an outraged mob in October 1850.

There were relatively few such incidents, however. In the first six years of the fugitive act, only three fugitives were forcibly rescued from the slave-catchers. On the other hand, probably fewer than 200 were returned to bondage during the same years. The Fugitive Slave Act had the tremendous effect of widening and deepening the antislavery impulse in the North.

UNCLE TOM'S CABIN   Antislavery forces found their most persuasive appeal not in the Fugitive Slave Act but in the fictional drama of Harriet Beecher Stowe's *Uncle Tom's Cabin* (1852), a combination of unlikely saints and sinners, stereotypes, and melodramatic escapades—and a smashing commercial success. The long-suffering Uncle Tom, the villainous Simon Legree, the angelic Eva, the desperate Eliza taking her child to freedom across the icy Ohio River—all became stock characters of the American imagination. Slavery, seen through Stowe's eyes, subjected its victims either to callous brutality or, at the hands of spendthrift masters, to the indignity of bankruptcy. It took time for the novel to work its effect on public opinion, however. Neither abolitionists nor fire-eaters fought for their sections at the time. The country was enjoying a surge of prosperity, and the course of the presidential campaign in 1852 reflected a common desire to lay sectional quarrels to rest.

THE ELECTION OF 1852 The Democrats chose Franklin Pierce of New Hampshire as their presidential candidate. The platform pledged the Democrats to "abide by and adhere to a faithful execution of the acts known as the Compromise measures." The candidates and the platform generated a surprising reconciliation of the party's factions. Pierce rallied both the southern rights' men and the Van Burenite Democrats. The Free Soilers, as a consequence, mustered only 156,000 votes for John P. Hale in contrast to the 291,000 they tallied for Van Buren in 1848.

"The Greatest Book of the Age." Uncle Tom's Cabin, *as this advertisement indicates, was a tremendous commercial success.*

The Whigs were less fortunate. They repudiated the lackluster Fillmore, who had faithfully supported the Compromise, and once again tried to exploit martial glory. It took fifty-three ballots, but the convention finally chose General Winfield Scott, the hero of Mexico City, a native of Virginia backed mainly by northern Whigs. The convention dutifully endorsed the Compromise, but with some opposition from the North. Scott, an able army commander but politically inept, had gained a reputation for antislavery and nativism, alienating German and Irish ethnic voters. In the end Scott carried only Tennessee, Kentucky, Massachusetts, and Vermont. Pierce overwhelmed him in the electoral college 254 to 42, although the popular vote was close: 1.6 million to 1.4 million.

Pierce, an undistinguished but handsome and engaging figure, a former congressman, senator, and soldier in Mexico, was, like Polk, touted as another "Young Hickory." But the youngest president was unable to unite the warring factions of his party. After the election Pierce wrote a poignant letter to his wife in which he expressed his frustration at the prospect of keeping North and South together. "I can do no right," he sighed. "What am I to do, wife? Stand by me." By the end of Pierce's first year in office, the leaders of his own party had decided he was a failure. By trying to be all things to all people, Pierce looked more and more like a "Northern man with Southern principles."

FOREIGN ADVENTURES

CUBA Foreign diversions now distracted attention from domestic quarrels. Cuba, one of Spain's earliest and one of its last possessions in the New World, continued to be an object of American desire. In the early 1850s a crisis arose over expeditions launched against Cuba from American soil. Spanish authorities retaliated against these provocations by harassing American ships. In 1854 the Cuban crisis expired with the issuance of the Ostend Manifesto. That year the Pierce administration instructed Pierre Soulé, the American minister in Madrid, to offer $130 million for Cuba, which Spain peremptorily spurned. Soulé then joined the American ministers to France and Britain in drafting the Ostend Manifesto. It declared that if Spain, "actuated by stubborn pride and a false sense of honor refused to sell," then the United States must ask itself, "does Cuba, in the possession of Spain, seriously endanger our internal peace and existence of our cherished Union?" If so, "then, by every law, human and divine, we shall be justified in wresting it from Spain. . . ." Publication of the supposedly confidential dispatch left the administration no choice but to disavow what northern opinion widely regarded as a "slaveholders' plot."

DIPLOMATIC GAINS IN THE PACIFIC In the Pacific, American diplomacy scored some important achievements. American trade with China dated from 1785, but was allowed only through the port of Canton. In 1844 the United States and China signed the Treaty of Wanghsia, which opened four ports, including Shanghai, to American trade. The Treaty of Tientsin (1858) opened eleven more ports and granted Americans the right to travel and trade throughout China. American Protestant missionaries also developed a keen interest in

China. About fifty were already there by 1855, and for nearly a century China remained the most active mission field for Americans.

Japan meanwhile had remained for two centuries closed to American trade. Moreover, American whalers wrecked on the shores of Japan had been forbidden to leave the country. Mainly in their interest President Fillmore entrusted a special Japanese expedition to Commodore Matthew Perry, who arrived in Tokyo in 1853. Negotiations led to the Treaty of Kanagawa (1854). Japan agreed to an American consulate, promised good treatment to castaways, and permitted visits in certain ports for supplies and repairs. Broader commercial relations

A Japanese woodcut by Hiroshige Utagawa depicting Commodore Perry's steamship.

came after the first American envoy, Townsend Harris, negotiated the Harris Convention of 1858, which opened five ports to American trade.

THE KANSAS-NEBRASKA CRISIS

American commercial interests in Asia helped spark a growing interest in a transcontinental railroad line connecting the eastern seaboard with the Pacific coast. During the 1850s, the only land added to the United States was a barren stretch of some 30,000 square miles south of the Gila River in present New Mexico and Arizona. This Gadsden Purchase of 1853, in which the United States paid Mexico $10 million, was made to acquire land offering a likely route for a Pacific railroad. The idea of building a railroad linking together the new continental domain of the United States, though a great national goal, reignited sectional rivalries and reopened the slavery issue. Among the many transcontinental routes projected, the four most important were the northern route from Milwaukee to the Columbia River, a central route

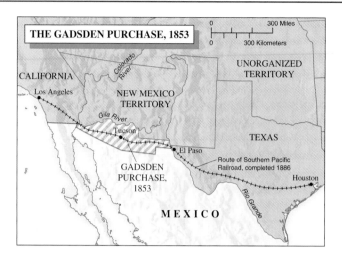

from St. Louis to San Francisco, another from Memphis to Los Angeles, and a more southerly route from Houston to Los Angeles via the Gadsden Purchase.

DOUGLAS'S PROPOSAL In 1852 and 1853 Congress debated and dropped several likely proposals for a transcontinental rail line. For various reasons, including terrain, climate, and sectional interest, Secretary of War Jefferson Davis favored the southern route and encouraged the Gadsden Purchase. Any other route, moreover, would go through the Indian country which stretched from Texas to the Canadian border.

Senator Stephen A. Douglas of Illinois had an even better idea: he thought that Chicago should be the railroad's eastern terminus. Since 1845, therefore, Douglas and others had offered bills for a new territory west of Missouri and Iowa, bearing the Indian name Nebraska. In 1854, as chairman of the committee on territories, Senator Douglas reported yet another Nebraska bill, which became the Kansas-Nebraska Act. Unlike the others this one included the entire unorganized portion of the Louisiana Purchase to the Canadian border. Political necessity then began to transform his proposal from a railroad bill to a proslavery bill. To carry his point, Douglas needed the support of southerners, and to win that support he needed to make some concession on slavery in the new territories. This he did by writing the principle of popular sovereignty into the bill, allowing voters in each territory to decide themselves whether to allow slavery.

It was a clever dodge, since the Missouri Compromise would still exclude slaves until the territorial government had made a decision. Southerners quickly spotted the barrier, and Douglas as quickly made two more concessions. He supported an amendment for repeal of the Missouri Compromise insofar as it excluded slavery north of 36°30′, and he then agreed to organize two territories, Kansas, west of Missouri; and Nebraska, west of Iowa and Minnesota.

Stephen Douglas.

Douglas's motives are unclear. Railroads were surely foremost in his mind, but he was influenced also by the desire to win support for his bill in the South, by the hope that popular sovereignty would quiet the slavery issue and open the Northwest, or by a chance to split the Whigs. But he had blundered, had damaged his presidential chances, and had set his country on the road to civil war. The tragic flaw in his plan was his failure to appreciate the depth of antislavery feelings. Douglas himself preferred that the territories become free. Their climate and geography excluded plantation agriculture, he reasoned, and he could not comprehend how people could get so wrought up over abstract rights to take their slaves into the territories. Yet he had in fact opened the possibility that slavery might gain a foothold in Kansas.

Douglas's proposal to repeal the Missouri Compromise was less than a week old before six antislavery congressmen published a protest, the "Appeal of the Independent Democrats." Their moral indignation quickly spread among those who opposed Douglas. The document arraigned his bill "as a gross violation of a sacred pledge," and as "part and parcel of an atrocious plot" to create "a dreary region of despotism, inhabited by masters and slaves." They called upon their fellow citizens to protest against this "atrocious crime."

Across the North, editorials, sermons, speeches, and petitions echoed this indignation. What had been radical opinion was fast becoming the common view of people in the North. But Douglas had the votes for his Kansas-Nebraska Act, and, once committed, he forced the issue with

THE KANSAS-NEBRASKA ACT, 1854

Free states and territories

Slave states

Open to slavery by popular sovereignty, Compromise of 1850

Open to slavery by popular sovereignty, Kansas-Nebraska Act, 1854

BLEEDING KANSAS

tireless energy. President Pierce impulsively added his support. Southerners lined up behind Douglas, with notable exceptions such as Texas senator Sam Houston, who denounced the Act's violation of two solemn compacts: the Missouri Compromise and the confirmation of the territory to the Indians "as long as grass shall grow and water run." He was not the only one concerned about the Indians, however. Federal agents were already busy hoodwinking or bullying Indians into relinquishing their land claims. Douglas and Pierce whipped reluctant Democrats into line (though about half the northern Democrats refused to yield), pushing the Kansas-Nebraska bill to final passage by 37 to 14 in the Senate and 113 to 100 in the House.

Very well, many in the North reasoned, if the Missouri Compromise was not a sacred pledge, then neither was the Fugitive Slave Act. On June 2 Boston witnessed the most dramatic demonstration against the act. After several attempts had failed to rescue a fugitive slave named

Anthony Burns, a force of soldiers and marines dispatched by President Pierce marched him to a waiting ship through streets lined with people shouting "Kidnappers!" Burns was the last southern slave to be returned from Boston, and was himself soon freed through purchase by the black community of Boston. New Englanders blamed Pierce for this sorry episode. One sent a letter to the White House that read: "To the chief slave-catcher of the United States. You damned, infernal scoundrel, if only I had you here in Boston, I would murder you!"

THE EMERGENCE OF THE REPUBLICAN PARTY   What John Calhoun had called the cords holding the Union together had already begun to fray. The national church organizations of Baptists and Methodists, for instance, had split over slavery by 1845. The national parties, were beginning to buckle under the strain of slavery. The Democrats managed to postpone disruption for yet a while, but their congressional delegation lost heavily in the North, enhancing the influence of the southern wing.

The strain of the Kansas-Nebraska Act, however, soon destroyed the Whig party. Southern Whigs now tended to abstain from voting, while Northern Whigs moved toward two new parties. One was the new American (Know-Nothing) party, which had raised the banner of native Americanism and the hope of serving the patriotic cause of Union. More Northern Whigs joined with independent Democrats and Free Soilers in spontaneous antislavery coalitions with a confusing array of names, including "Anti-Nebraska," "Fusion," and "People's party." These coalitions finally united in 1854 under the name "Republican."

"BLEEDING" KANSAS   After passage of the Kansas-Nebraska Act, attention swung to the plains of Kansas, where opposing elements gathered to stage a rehearsal for civil war. All agreed that Nebraska would be a free state, but Kansas soon exposed the potential for mischief in popular sovereignty. The ambiguity of the law, useful to Douglas in getting it passed, only added to the chaos. The people of Kansas were "perfectly free to form and regulate their domestic institutions in their own way, subject only to the Constitution." That in itself invited conflicting interpretations, but the law was completely silent as to the time of decision, adding to each side's sense of urgency about getting control of the territory.

The settlement of Kansas therefore differed from the usual pioneering efforts. Groups sprang up North and South to hurry right-minded settlers westward. Most of the settlers were from Missouri and surrounding states. Although few of them owned slaves, they were not sympathetic to militant abolitionism. Racism was prevalent even among non-slaveholding whites. Many of the Kansas settlers wanted to keep all blacks, slave or free, out of the territory. "I kem [*sic*] to Kansas to live in a free state," declared a minister, "and I don't want niggers a-trampin' over my grave." By 1860, there were only 627 African Americans in the territory.

When Kansas's first governor arrived in 1854, he found several thousand settlers already there. He ordered a census and scheduled an election for a territorial legislature in 1855. When the election took place, several thousand "Border Ruffians" crossed over from Missouri, illegally swept the polls for proslavery forces, and vowed to kill every "God-damned abolitionist in the Territory." The governor denounced the vote as a fraud, but did nothing to alter the results, for fear of being killed. The legislature expelled the few antislavery members, adopted a drastic slave code, and made it a capital offense to aid a fugitive slave and a felony even to question the legality of slavery in the territory.

Free-state advocates rejected this "bogus" government and moved directly toward application for statehood. In 1855 a constitutional convention, the product of an extralegal election, met in Topeka, drafted a state constitution excluding both slavery and free blacks from Kansas, and applied for admission to the Union. By 1856 a free-state "governor" and "legislature" were functioning in Topeka; thus there were now two illegal governments in the territory. The prospect of getting any government to command general authority in Kansas seemed dim, and both sides began to arm.

Finally, confrontation began to slip into conflict. In May 1856, a proslavery mob entered the free-state town of Lawrence and destroyed newspaper presses, set fire to the free-state governor's private home, stole property that was not nailed down, and trained five cannon on the Free State Hotel, demolishing it.

The "sack of Lawrence" resulted in just one casualty, but the excitement aroused a fanatical Kansas Free Soiler named John Brown, who had a history of mental instability. Two days after the sack of Lawrence, Brown set out with four sons and three other men toward Pottawatomie

This illustration on a sheet music cover for an antislavery song portrays the burning of the Free State Hotel in Lawrence, Kansas, by a proslavery mob in 1856.

Creek, site of a proslavery settlement, where they dragged five men from their houses and hacked them to death in front of their screaming families, ostensibly as revenge for the deaths of free-state men.

The Pottawatomie Massacre (May 24–25, 1856) set off a guerrilla war in the Kansas territory that lasted through the fall. On August 30, Missouri ruffians raided the free-state settlement at Osawatomie. They looted the houses, burned them to the ground, and shot John Brown's son Frederick through the heart. The elder Brown, who barely escaped, looked back at the site being devastated by "Satan's legions," and muttered, "God sees it." He then swore to his surviving sons and followers: "I have only a short time to live—only one death to die, and I will die fighting for this cause." Three years later he would do just that, in a futile uprising that would inflame sentiment in the North and South. Altogether, by the end of 1856, Kansas lost about 200 killed and $2 million in property destroyed during the territorial civil war.

VIOLENCE IN THE SENATE   Violence in Kansas spilled over into Congress. On May 22, 1856, the day after the sack of Lawrence, two days before the Pottawatomie Massacre, a sudden flash of violence on the Senate floor electrified the whole country. Just two days earlier,

Senator Charles Sumner of Massachusetts had delivered an inflammatory speech on "The Crime against Kansas." Sumner, elected five years earlier by a coalition of Free Soilers and Democrats, was a brilliant orator with a sharp tongue. An unyielding foe of slavery, he had no tolerance for opinions different from his own.

His two-day speech, delivered all from memory, was an exercise in studied insult. The proslavery Missourians who crossed into Kansas, Sumner charged, were "hirelings picked from the drunken spew and vomit of an uneasy civilization." Their treatment of Kansas was "the rape of a virgin territory," he said, "and it may be clearly traced to a depraved longing for a new slave State, the hideous offspring of such a crime. . . ." Sumner singled out elderly Senator Andrew Pickens Butler of South Carolina for censure. Butler, Sumner charged, had "chosen a mistress . . . who . . . though polluted in the sight of the world, is chaste in his sight—I mean the harlot, Slavery."

Sumner's rudeness might well have backfired had it not been for Butler's cousin Preston S. Brooks, a fiery-tempered congressman from South Carolina. For two days Brooks brooded over the insult to his relative, knowing that Sumner would refuse a challenge to a duel. On May 22 he found Sumner writing at his Senate desk after an adjournment, accused

"Bully" Brooks's attack on Charles Sumner. The incident worsened the strains on the Union.

him of libel against South Carolina and Butler, and commenced beating him about the head with a cane while stunned colleagues looked on. Sumner, struggling to rise, wrenched the desk from the floor and collapsed. Brooks kept beating the unconscious Sumner until his cane broke.

Brooks had satisfied his rage, but in doing so had created a martyr for the antislavery cause. Like so many other men in those years, he betrayed the zealot's gift for snatching defeat from the jaws of victory. For two and a half years Sumner's empty seat was a solemn reminder of the violence done to him. When the House censured Brooks, he resigned, only to return after being triumphantly reelected. His southern admirers presented him with new canes. The editor of the Richmond *Enquirer* urged Brooks to cane Sumner again: "These vulgar abolitionists in the Senate . . . must be lashed into submission." Northerners who never would have said what Sumner said now hastened to his defense. The news of Sumner's beating drove John Brown "crazy," his eldest son remembered, *"crazy."* People on each side, appalled at the behavior of the other, decided that North and South had developed into different civilizations with incompatible standards of honor. "I do not see," Ralph Waldo Emerson confessed, "how a barbarous community and a civilized community can constitute one state. We must either get rid of slavery, or get rid of freedom."

SECTIONAL POLITICS Within the span of five days in May of 1856, "Bleeding Kansas," "Bleeding Sumner," and "Bully Brooks" had set the tone for another presidential year. The major parties could no longer evade the slavery issue. Already in February it had split the infant American party wide open. Southern delegates, with help from New York, killed a resolution to restore the Missouri Compromise, and nominated Millard Fillmore for president. Later, what was left of the Whig party endorsed him as well.

At its first national convention the new Republican party passed over its leading figure, William H. Seward, who was awaiting a better chance in 1860. Following the Whig tradition, they sought out a military hero, John C. Frémont, the "Pathfinder" and leader in the conquest of California. The Republican platform owed much to the Whigs too. It favored a transcontinental railroad and, in general, more internal improvements. It condemned the repeal of the Missouri Compromise, the Democratic policy of territorial expansion, and "those twin relics of barbarism— Polygamy and Slavery." The campaign slogan echoed that of the Free

Soilers: "Free soil, free speech, and Frémont." It was the first time a major party platform had taken a stand against slavery.

The Democrats, meeting two weeks earlier in June, had rejected Pierce, the hapless victim of so much turmoil. Douglas too was left out because of the damage done by his Kansas-Nebraska Act. The party therefore turned to James Buchanan of Pennsylvania, who had long sought the nomination. The party and its candidate nevertheless hewed to Pierce's policies. The Democratic platform endorsed the Kansas-Nebraska Act and stressed that Congress should not interfere with slavery in either states or territories. The party reached out to its newly acquired ethnic voters by condemning nativism and endorsing religious liberty.

The campaign of 1856 resolved itself into a sectional contest in which parties vied for northern or southern votes. The Republicans had few southern supporters, and only a handful in the border states, where fears of disunion held many Whigs in line. Buchanan thus went into the campaign as the candidate of the only remaining national party. Frémont

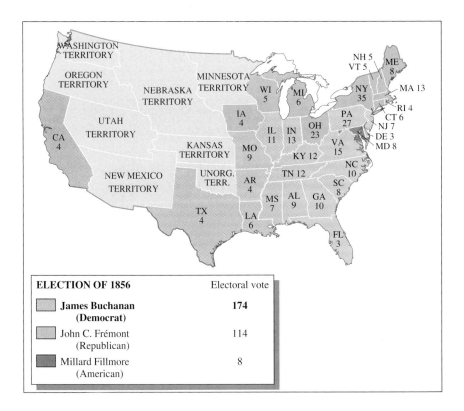

ELECTION OF 1856	Electoral vote
James Buchanan (Democrat)	**174**
John C. Frémont (Republican)	114
Millard Fillmore (American)	8

swept the northernmost states with 114 electoral votes, but Buchanan added five free states—Pennsylvania, New Jersey, Illinois, Indiana, and California—to his southern majority for a total of 174.

Buchanan, the only unmarried president, brought to the White House a portfolio of impressive achievements in politics and diplomacy. His career went back to 1815, when he started as a Federalist legislator in Pennsylvania before switching to Andrew Jackson's party in the 1820s. He had been in Congress for over twenty years, minister to Russia and Britain, and Polk's secretary of state in between. His long quest for the presidency had been built on a southern alliance, and his political debts reinforced his belief that saving the Union depended on concessions to the slave South. Republicans charged that he lacked the backbone to stand up to the southerners who dominated the Democratic majorities in Congress. His choice of four slave-state and only three free-state men for his cabinet seemed another bad omen.

The Deepening Sectional Crisis

During James Buchanan's first six months in office in 1857, he encountered the Dred Scott decision, new troubles in Kansas, and a business panic. These and other challenges proved his undoing.

THE DRED SCOTT CASE   On March 6, 1857, two days after Buchanan's inauguration, the Supreme Court rendered a decision in the long-pending case of *Dred Scott* v. *Sandford*. Dred Scott, born a slave in Virginia about 1800, had been taken to St. Louis in 1830 and sold to an army surgeon, who took him as body servant to Illinois, then to the Wisconsin Territory (later Minnesota), and finally returned him to St. Louis in 1842. While in the Wisconsin Territory, Scott met and married Harriet Robinson, and they eventually had two daughters.

After his master's death in 1843 Scott had tried to buy his freedom. In 1846, Harriet Scott convinced Dred to file suit in Missouri courts claiming that residence in Illinois and the Wisconsin Territory had made him free. A jury decided in his favor, but the state supreme court ruled against him. When the case rose on appeal to the Supreme Court, the country anxiously awaited its opinion on whether freedom once granted could be lost by returning to a slave state.

Chief Justice Roger B. Taney, who played a critical role in the Supreme Court's decision on the Dred Scott case, which fanned the flames of discord.

Each of the nine justices filed a separate opinion, except one who concurred with Chief Justice Roger B. Taney of Maryland. By different lines of reasoning, seven justices ruled that Scott remained a slave. The aging Taney, whose opinion represented the Court, ruled that Scott lacked legal standing because he lacked citizenship. Taney argued that one became a federal citizen either by birth or by naturalization, which ruled out any former slave. He then mistakenly argued that no state had ever accorded citizenship to blacks. At the time the Constitution was adopted, Taney further said, blacks "had for more than a century been regarded as . . . so far inferior, that they had no rights which the white man was bound to respect."

Taney declared that Scott's residency in a free state had not freed him, since, in line with precedent, the decision of the state court governed. This left the question of residency in a free territory. On this point Taney argued that the Missouri Compromise had deprived citizens of property in slaves, an action "not warranted by the constitution." He strongly implied, but never said explicitly, that the compromise had violated the due-process clause of the Fifth Amendment, as John C. Calhoun had earlier argued.

The upshot was that the Supreme Court had declared an act of Congress unconstitutional for the first time since *Marbury* v. *Madison* (1803), and a major act for the first time ever. Congress had repealed the Missouri Compromise in the Kansas-Nebraska Act three years earlier, but the Dred Scott decision now challenged popular sovereignty. If Congress itself could not exclude slavery from a territory, then presumably neither could a territorial government created by act of Congress.

By this decision the Supreme Court had tried to settle a question that Congress had dodged ever since the Wilmot Proviso surfaced. But far from settling it, it had only fanned the flames of dissension. Little wonder that Republicans protested: the Court had declared their anti-slavery program unconstitutional. It had also reinforced the suspicion that the slavocracy was hatching a conspiracy. Were not all but one of the justices who joined Taney southerners? And had not Buchanan chatted with the chief justice at the inauguration and then urged the people to accept the early decision as a final settlement, "Whatever this may be"? (Actually, Buchanan already knew the outcome because two other justices had informed him in private letters.) Besides, if Dred Scott were not a citizen and had no standing in court, there was no case before it. The majority ruling was an *obiter dictum*—a statement not essential to deciding the case and therefore not binding, "entitled to just so much moral weight as would be the judgment of a majority of those congregated in any Washington bar-room."

Proslavery elements, of course, greeted the Court's opinion as binding. Now the fire-eaters among them were emboldened to yet another demand. It was not enough to deny Congress the right to interfere with slavery in the territories; Congress had an obligation to protect the property of slaveholders, making a federal slave code the next step. The idea, first broached by Alabama Democrats in the "Alabama Platform" of 1848, soon became orthodox southern doctrine.

THE LECOMPTON CONSTITUTION   Out in Kansas, meanwhile, the struggle continued. Just before Buchanan's inauguration the proslavery legislature called for an election of delegates to a constitutional convention. Since no provision was made for a referendum on the constitution, however, the governor vetoed the measure and the legislature overrode his veto. The Kansas governor resigned on the day Buchanan took office, and the new president replaced him with Robert J. Walker. A native Pennsylvanian who had made a political career in Mississippi and a former member of Polk's cabinet, Walker had greater prestige than his predecessors, and he put the Union above slavery. In Kansas he scented a chance to advance the cause of both the Union and his party. Under popular sovereignty, fair elections would produce a state that would be both free and Democratic.

Walker arrived in 1857, and with Buchanan's approval, pledged to the free-state Kansans that the new constitution would be submitted to a fair vote. But in spite of his pleas, he arrived too late to persuade free-state men to vote for convention delegates in elections they were sure had been rigged against them. Later, however, Walker did persuade the free-state leaders to vote in the election of a new territorial legislature.

As a result a polarity arose between an antislavery legislature and a proslavery constitutional convention. The convention, meeting at Lecompton, drew up a constitution under which Kansas would become a slave state. A referendum on the document was cunningly contrived so that voters could not vote against the proposed constitution. They could only accept it "with slavery" or "with no slavery," and even the latter meant that slaveowners already in Kansas would "in no measure be interfered with." The vote was set for December 21, 1857, with rules and officials chosen by the convention.

Although Kansas had only about 200 slaves at the time, free-state men boycotted the election on the claim that it too was rigged. At this point President Buchanan took a fateful step. Influenced by southern advisers and politically dependent upon southern congressmen, he decided to renege on his pledge to Governor Walker and support the action of the Lecompton Convention. Walker resigned, and the election went according to form: 6,226 for the constitution with slavery, 569 for the constitution without slavery. Meanwhile, the acting governor had convened the antislavery legislature, which called for another election to vote the Lecompton constitution up or down. Most of the proslavery settlers boycotted this election, and the result on January 4, 1858, was overwhelming: 10,226 against the constitution, 138 for the constitution with slavery, 24 for the constitution without slavery.

The combined results suggested a clear majority against slavery, but Buchanan stuck to his support of the Lecompton constitution, driving another wedge into the Democratic party. Senator Douglas, up for re-election, could not afford to run as a champion of Lecompton. He broke dramatically with the president in a tense confrontation, but Buchanan persisted in trying to drive Lecompton "naked" through the Congress. In the Senate, administration forces held firm, and in 1858 Lecompton was passed. In the House, enough anti-Lecompton Democrats combined to put through an amendment for a new and carefully supervised popular vote in Kansas. Enough senators went along to permit passage of the House bill. Southerners were confident the vote would favor slavery, because to reject slavery the voters would have to reject the constitution, which would postpone statehood until the population reached 90,000. On August 2, 1858, Kansas voters nevertheless rejected Lecompton by 11,300 to 1,788. With that vote, Kansas, now firmly in the hands of its antislavery legislature, largely ended its role in the sectional controversy.

THE PANIC OF 1857   The third crisis of Buchanan's first half year in office, a financial crisis, broke in August 1857. It was brought on by a reduction in demand for American grain caused by the end of the Crimean War (1854–1856), a surge in manufacturing that outran the growth of markets, and the continued weakness and confusion of the state bank-note system. Failure of the Ohio Life Insurance and Trust Company on August 24, 1857, precipitated the panic, which was followed by a depression from which the country did not emerge until 1859.

Everything in those years seemed to get drawn into the vortex of sectional conflict, and business troubles were no exception. Northern businessmen tended to blame the depression on the Democratic Tariff

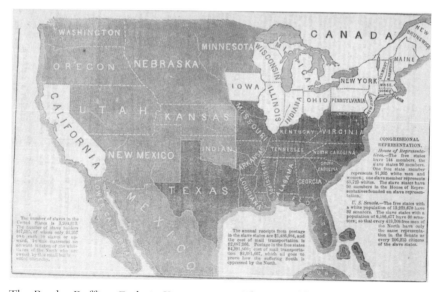

The Border Ruffian Code in Kansas, 1856. This pamphlet published by Horace Greeley's New York Tribune *features a map of the country carved into slave states (dark), free states (white), and those caught in middle (gray). It attempts to "prove how the suffering South is oppressed by the North."*

of 1857, which had set rates on imports at their lowest level since 1816. The agricultural South weathered the crisis better than the North. Cotton prices fell, but slowly, and world markets for cotton quickly recovered. The result was an exalted notion of King Cotton's importance to the world, and apparent confirmation of the growing argument that the southern system of slave-based agriculture was superior to the free-labor system of the North.

DOUGLAS VS. LINCOLN   Amid the recriminations over the Dred Scott decision, Kansas, and the depression, the center could not hold. The Lecompton battle put severe strains on the most substantial cord of union that was left, the Democratic party. To many, Douglas seemed the best hope for unity and union, one of the few remaining Democratic leaders with support in both North and South. But now Douglas was being whipsawed between the extremes. Kansas-Nebraska had cast him in the role of "doughface," a southern sympathizer. His opposition to Lecompton, the fraudulent fruit of popular sovereignty, however, had alienated him from Buchanan's southern junta. But for all his flexibility and opportunism, Douglas had convinced himself that popular sovereignty was a point of principle, a bulwark of democracy and local self-government. In 1858 he faced reelection to the Senate against the opposition of Buchanan Democrats and Republicans. The year 1860 would give him a chance for the presidency, but first he had to secure his home base in Illinois.

To oppose him, Illinois Republicans named Abraham Lincoln of Springfield, the lanky, rawboned former Whig state legislator and one-term congressman, a moderately prosperous small-town lawyer. Lincoln's early life had been the hardscrabble existence of the frontier farm. Born in a Kentucky log cabin in 1809, raised on farms in Indiana and Illinois, the young Lincoln had the wit and will to rise above his coarse beginnings. With less than twelve months of sporadic schooling he learned to read, studied such books as came to hand, and eventually developed a prose style as muscular as the man himself. He worked at various farm tasks, operated a ferry, and made two trips down to New Orleans as a flatboatman. Striking out on his own, he managed a general store in New Salem, Illinois, learned surveying, served in the Black Hawk War (1832), won election to the legislature in 1834 at the age of twenty-five, read law, and was admitted to the bar in 1836.

Lincoln abhorred slavery but was no abolitionist. He did not believe the two races could coexist as equals. But he did oppose any further extension of slavery into new territories, assuming that over time it would die a "natural death." Slavery, he said in the 1840s, was a vexing but "minor question on its way to extinction." Lincoln stayed in the Illinois legislature until 1842, and in 1846 won a term in Congress. After a single term he retired from active politics to cultivate his law practice in Springfield.

In 1854 the Kansas-Nebraska debate drew Lincoln back into the political arena. When Douglas appeared in Springfield to defend popular sovereignty, Lincoln countered from the same platform. In Peoria he preached an old but oft-neglected doctrine: hate the sin but not the sinner.

> When Southern people tell us they are no more responsible for the origin of slavery, than we, I acknowledge the fact. When it is said that the institution exists; and that it is very difficult to get rid of it, in any satisfactory way, I can understand and appreciate the saying. . . .
>
> But all this, to my judgment, furnishes no more excuses for permitting slavery to go into our own free territory, than it would for reviving the African slave trade by law.

At first Lincoln held back from the rapidly growing Republican party, but in 1856 he joined it and gave some fifty speeches for the Frémont ticket in Illinois and nearby states. By 1858 he was the obvious choice to oppose Douglas for the Senate seat. Lincoln resorted to the classic ploy of the underdog: he challenged the favorite to debate him. Douglas had little relish for drawing attention to his opponent, but agreed to meet him in seven places around the state.

Thus the legendary Lincoln-Douglas debates took place, from August 21 to October 15, 1858. As they mounted the platform, the two men could not have presented a more striking contrast. Lincoln was well over six feet tall, sinewy, and craggy-featured, with a singularly long neck and deep-set, brooding, eyes. Unassuming in manner, dressed in homely, well-worn clothes, and walking with a shambling gait, he lightened his essentially serious demeanor with a refreshing sense of humor. To sympathetic observers he conveyed an air of simplicity, sincerity, and common sense. Douglas, on the other hand, was short, rotund, stern, and cocky, attired in the finest custom-tailored suits. A man of considerable abilities and even greater ambition, he strutted to the platform with the pugnacious air of a predestined champion.

At the time and since, much attention focused on the second debate, at Freeport, where Lincoln asked Douglas how he could reconcile popular sovereignty with the Dred Scott ruling that citizens had the right to carry slaves into any territory. Douglas's answer, thenceforth known as the Freeport Doctrine, was to state the obvious. Whatever the Supreme Court might say about slavery, it could not exist anywhere unless supported by local police regulations.

Douglas tried to set some traps of his own. Douglas intimated that Lincoln belonged to the fanatical sect of abolitionists who advocated racial equality. The question was a hot potato, which Lincoln handled with caution. There was "A physical difference between the white and black races" that would "forever forbid the two races living together on terms of social and political equality," he said. But Lincoln insisted that blacks did have an "equal" right to freedom and the fruits of their labor. But the basic difference between the two men, Lincoln insisted, lay in Douglas's professed indifference to the moral question of slavery.

If Lincoln had the better of the argument, at least in the long view, Douglas had the better of the election. Still, according to the Constitution, the voters actually had to choose a legislature, which would then elect the senator. Lincoln men won the larger total vote, but its distribution gave Douglas the legislature, 54 to 41. As the returns trickled in from the fall elections in 1858—there was still no common election date—they recorded one loss after another for Buchanan men. When the elections were over, the administration had lost control of the House. But the new Congress would not meet in regular session until late 1859.

JOHN BROWN'S RAID   The gradual return of prosperity in 1859 offered hope that the sectional storms of the 1850s might yet pass. But the slavery issue still haunted the public mind. In October 1859 John Brown once again surfaced, this time in the East. Since the Pottawatomie Massacre in 1856, he had led a furtive existence, engaging in fund-raising and occasional bushwhacking. His commitment to abolish the "wicked curse of slavery," meanwhile, had intensified to a fever pitch. Self-righteous and demanding, he was driven by a sense of crusading zeal. His penetrating gray eyes, flowing beard, and religious certainty evoked images of a vengeful Abraham and struck fear into supporters and opponents alike.

On October 16, 1859, Brown launched his supreme gesture. From a Maryland farm he crossed the Potomac River with about twenty men, including five blacks, and under cover of darkness occupied the federal arsenal in Harper's Ferry, Virginia (now West Virginia). He planned to arm the many slaves he assumed would flock to his cause, set up a black stronghold in the mountains of western Virginia, and provide a nucleus of support for slave insurrections across the South.

What Brown actually did was to take the arsenal by surprise, seize a few hostages, and hole up in the

John Brown.

fire-engine house until he was surrounded by militiamen and townspeople. The next morning Brown sent his son Watson and another supporter out under a white flag, but the enraged crowd shot them both. Intermittent shooting continued, and another Brown son was wounded. He begged his father to kill him so as to end his suffering, but the righteous Brown lashed out: "If you must die, die like a man." A few minutes later the son was dead.

That night Lieutenant-Colonel Robert E. Lee, U.S. Cavalry, arrived with his aide, Lieutenant J. E. B. Stuart, and a force of marines. The following morning, on October 18, Stuart and his troops broke down the barricaded doors and rushed into the fire-engine house. A young lieutenant found Brown kneeling with his rifle cocked. Before Brown could fire, however, the marine plunged his dress sword into him with such force that the blade bent back double. He then used the hilt to beat Brown unconscious. By then the siege was over. Altogether Brown's men killed four people (including one marine) and wounded nine. Of their own force, ten died (including two of Brown's sons), seven were captured, and five escaped.

Brown, who survived the siege, was quickly tried for treason and conspiracy to incite insurrection, convicted on October 31, and hanged on December 2. Six others died on the gallows later. If Brown had failed in his purpose—whatever it was—he had achieved two things. He had become a martyr for the antislavery cause, and he had set off panic throughout the slaveholding South. At his sentencing he delivered one of the classic American speeches: "Now, if it is deemed necessary that I should forfeit my life for the furtherance of the ends of justice, and mingle my blood further with the blood of my children and with the blood of millions in this slave country whose rights are disregarded by wicked, cruel, and unjust enactments, I say, let it be done."

When Brown, still unflinching, met his end, there were solemn observances in the North. "That new saint," Ralph Waldo Emerson said, "will make the gallows as glorious as the cross." William Lloyd Garrison, the lifelong pacifist, now wished "success to every slave insurrection at the South and in every slave country." By far the gravest effect of Brown's raid was to leave proslavery southerners in no mood to distinguish between John Brown and the Republican party. All through the fall and winter of 1859–1860, rumors of abolitionist conspiracy and slave insurrection swept the region. Every northern visitor, commercial traveler, or schoolteacher came under suspicion, and many were driven out. "We regard every man in our midst an enemy to the institutions of the South," said the *Atlanta Confederacy*, "who does not boldly declare that he believes African slavery to be a social, moral, and political blessing."

The Center Comes Apart

THE DEMOCRATS DIVIDE   Thus amid emotional hysteria and impossible demands the nation ushered in the year of another presidential election, destined to be the most fateful in its history. Four years earlier, in a moment of euphoria, the Democrats had settled on Charleston, South Carolina, as the site for their 1860 convention. Charleston was a hotbed of extremist pro-slavery sentiment, and the city lacked adequate accommodations for the crowds. South Carolina itself had chosen a remarkably moderate delegation, but the radical southern rights' men held the upper hand in the delegations from the Gulf states.

Douglas's supporters reaffirmed the platform of 1856, which simply promised congressional noninterference with slavery. Southern firebrands, however, were now demanding federal protection for slavery in the territories. Buchanan supporters, hoping to stop Douglas, encouraged

PROGRESSIVE DEMOCRACY—PROSPECT OF A SMASH UP.

Prospect of a Smash Up. *This 1860 cartoon shows the Democratic party—the last remaining national party—about to be split by sectional differences and the onrushing Republicans led by Lincoln.*

the strategy. The platform debate reached a heady climax when the Alabama extremist William Yancey informed the northern Democrats that their error had been the failure to defend slavery as a positive good. An Ohio senator offered a blunt reply: "Gentlemen of the South," he said, "you mistake us—you mistake us. We will not do it."

When the southern planks lost, Alabama's delegates walked out of the convention, followed by those representing the other Gulf states, Georgia, South Carolina (except for two stubborn upcountry Unionists), and parts of the delegations from Arkansas and Delaware. The convention then decided to leave the overwrought atmosphere of Charleston and reassemble in Baltimore on June 18. The Baltimore convention finally nominated Douglas on the 1856 platform. The Charleston seceders met first in Richmond, then in Baltimore, where they adopted the slave-code platform defeated in Charleston, and named Vice-President John C. Breckinridge of Kentucky for president. Thus another cord of union had snapped: the last remaining national party had fragmented.

LINCOLN'S ELECTION The Republicans meanwhile gathered in Chicago. There everything suddenly came together for "Honest Abe" Lincoln, the uncommon common man. Lincoln had emerged in the national view during his senatorial campaign two years before, and had since taken a stance designed to make him available for the nomination. He was strong enough on the containment of slavery to satisfy the abolitionists, yet moderate enough to seem less threatening than they were. In 1860 he had gone East to address an audience of influential Republicans at the Cooper Union in New York City, where he emphasized his view of slavery "as an evil, not to be extended, but to be tolerated and protected only because of and so far as its actual presence among us makes that toleration and protection a necessity."

At the Chicago Republican convention, New York's William H. Seward was the early leader among the presidential nominees, but he had been tagged, perhaps wrongly, as an extremist for his earlier statements about an "irrepressible conflict" over slavery. On the first ballot Lincoln finished in second place. On the next ballot he drew almost even with Seward, and when he came within one and a half votes of a majority on the third count, Ohio quickly switched four votes to put him over the top.

The Republican party platform denounced John Brown's raid as "among the gravest of crimes," and promised "the right of each state to order and control its own domestic institutions." The party reaffirmed its resistance to the extension of slavery and, in an effort to gain broader support, endorsed a higher protective tariff for manufacturers, free homesteads for farmers, a more liberal naturalization law for immigrants, and internal improvements, including a transcontinental railroad. With this platform, Republicans made a strong appeal to eastern businessmen, western farmers, and the large immigrant population.

Both major conventions revealed that opinion tended to become more radical in the upper North and Deep South. Attitude followed latitude. In the border states a sense of moderation aroused the die-hard Whigs to

Abraham Lincoln, Republican candidate for president, June 1860.

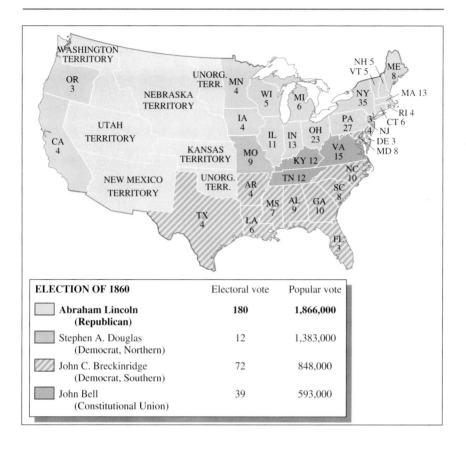

ELECTION OF 1860	Electoral vote	Popular vote
Abraham Lincoln (Republican)	**180**	**1,866,000**
Stephen A. Douglas (Democrat, Northern)	12	1,383,000
John C. Breckinridge (Democrat, Southern)	72	848,000
John Bell (Constitutional Union)	39	593,000

make one more try at reconciliation. Meeting in Baltimore a week before the Republicans met in Chicago, they reorganized into the Constitutional Union party and named John Bell of Tennessee for president. Their only platform was "the Constitution of the Country, the Union of the States, and the Enforcement of the Laws."

Of the four candidates, not one generated a national following, and the campaign evolved into a choice between Lincoln and Douglas in the North, Breckinridge and Bell in the South. One consequence of these separate campaigns was that each section gained a false impression of the other. The South never learned to distinguish Lincoln from the radicals; the North, especially Lincoln, failed to gauge the force of southern intransigence. He stubbornly refused to offer the South assurances or to clarify his position, which he said was a matter of public record.

The one man who tried to break through the veil that was falling between the North and South was Douglas, who tried to mount a national campaign. Only forty-seven, but weakened by excessive drink, ill health, and disappointments, he wore himself out in one final glorious campaign. Early in October 1860, at Cedar Rapids, Iowa, he learned of Republican state victories in Pennsylvania and Indiana. "Mr. Lincoln is the next President," he said. "We must try to save the Union. I will go South." Down through the hostile areas of Tennessee, Georgia, and Alabama Douglas carried appeals on behalf of the Union. "I do not believe that every Breckinridge man is a disunionist," he said, "but I do believe that every disunionist is a Breckinridge man." He was in Mobile when the election came.

By midnight of November 6, Lincoln's victory was clear. In the final count he had about 39 percent of the total popular vote, but a clear majority with 180 votes in the electoral college. He carried every one of the eighteen free states, and by a margin enough to elect him even if the votes for the other candidates had been combined. Among all the candidates, only Douglas had electoral votes from both slave and free states, but his total of 12 was but a pitiful remnant of Democratic Unionism. Bell took Virginia, Kentucky, and Tennessee for 39 votes, and Breckinridge swept the other slave states to come in second with 72.

SECESSION OF THE DEEP SOUTH   Soon after the election, South Carolina held a special election to choose delegates to a convention. In Charleston on December 20, 1860, the convention unanimously endorsed an Ordinance of Secession, declaring the state's ratification of the Constitution repealed and the union with other states dissolved. A Declaration of the Causes of Secession reviewed the threats to slavery, and asserted that a purely sectional party (Republican) had elected to the presidency a man "whose opinions and purposes are hostile to slavery," who had declared "Government cannot endure permanently half slave, half free," and that slavery "is in the course of ultimate extinction."

By February 1, 1861, Mississippi, Florida, Alabama, Georgia, Louisiana, and Texas had declared themselves out of the Union. On February 4, a convention of the seven states met in Montgomery, Alabama; on February 7, they adopted a provisional constitution for the Confederate States of America, and two days later they elected Jefferson Davis as president. He was inaugurated February 18, with Alexander Stephens of Georgia as vice-president.

In all seven states of the southernmost tier, a solid majority had voted for secessionist delegates, but their combined vote would not have been a majority of the presidential vote in November. What happened, it seemed, was what often happens in revolutionary situations: a determined and decisive minority acted quickly in an emotionally charged climate and carried out its program against a confused and indecisive opposition. Trying to decide whether or not a majority of the whites actually favored secession probably is beside the point—a majority were vulnerable to the decisive action of the secessionists.

A handbill announcing South Carolina's secession from the Union.

BUCHANAN'S WAITING GAME History is full of might-have-beens. A bold stroke, even a bold statement, by the lame-duck president at this point might have changed things. But James Buchanan lacked boldness. Besides, a bold stroke might simply have hastened the conflict. No bold stroke came from Lincoln either, nor would he consult with the Buchanan administration during the long months before his inauguration on March 4. He inclined all too strongly to the belief that secession was just another bluff and kept his public silence.

In his annual message on December 3, Buchanan criticized northern agitators for trying to interfere with "slavery in the southern states." He then declared that secession was illegal, but that he lacked authority to coerce a state back into the Union. "Seldom have we known so strong an argument come to so lame and impotent a conclusion," the *Cincinnati Enquirer* editorialized. There was, however, a hidden weapon in the president's reaffirmation of a duty to "take care that the laws be faithfully executed" insofar as he was able. If the president could enforce the law upon all citizens, he would have no need to "coerce" a state. Indeed his position became the policy of the Lincoln administration, which fought a war on the theory that individuals but not states as such were in rebellion.

Buchanan held firmly to his resolve, with some slight stiffening by the end of December 1860, when secession became a fact, but he refrained from taking provocative actions. As the secessionists seized federal property, arsenals, and forts, this policy soon meant holding to isolated positions at Fort Pickens in Pensacola Harbor, some remote islands off southern Florida, and Fort Sumter in Charleston Harbor.

On the day after Christmas the small garrison at Fort Moultrie had been moved into the nearly completed Fort Sumter by Major Robert Anderson, a Kentucky Unionist. South Carolina secessionists exploded at this "provocative" act, and commissioners of the newly "independent" state demanded withdrawal of all federal forces. They had overplayed their hand. Buchanan sharply rejected the South Carolina ultimatum to withdraw. He dispatched a steamer, *Star of the West*, to Fort Sumter with reinforcements and provisions. As the ship approached Charleston Harbor, batteries at Fort Moultrie and Morris Island opened fire and drove it away on January 9. It was in fact an act of war, but Buchanan chose to ignore the challenge. He decided instead to hunker down and ride out the remaining weeks of his term, hoping against hope that one of several compromise efforts would yet prove fruitful.

LAST EFFORTS AT COMPROMISE   Forlorn efforts at compromise continued in Congress until the dawn of inauguration day. On December 18 Senator John J. Crittenden of Kentucky had proposed a series of amendments and resolutions that allowed for slavery in the territories south of 36°30′and guaranteed to maintain slavery where it already existed.

Meanwhile a peace conference met at Willard's Hotel in Washington, D.C., in February 1861. Twenty-one states sent delegates and former president John Tyler presided, but the convention's proposal, substantially the same as the Crittenden Compromise, failed to win the support of either house of Congress. The only compromise proposal that met with any success was an amendment guaranteeing slavery where it existed. Many Republicans, including Lincoln, were prepared to go that far to save the Union, but they were unwilling to repudiate their stand against slavery in the territories. As it happened, after passing the House, the amendment passed the Senate without a vote to spare, by 24 to 12, on the dawn of inauguration day. It would have become the Thirteenth Amendment, with the first use of the word "slavery" in the Constitution, but the states never ratified it. When a Thirteenth Amendment was ratified in 1865, it did not guarantee slavery—it abolished slavery.

MAKING CONNECTIONS

- Through the 1850s, most of the debate over slavery concerned the expansion of slavery into the territories; with Lincoln's Emancipation Proclamation, discussed in the next chapter, the issue shifted to slavery itself.

- Many of the Radical Republicans who designed Reconstruction (Chapter 18) had been antislavery Republicans before the war.

- The proposed transcontinental railroad that brought about the Kansas-Nebraska crisis would finally be completed in 1869 (Chapter 20).

FURTHER READING

The best surveys of the forces and events leading to the Civil War include James M. McPherson's *Battle Cry of Freedom: The Civil War Era* (1988), Stephen B. Oates and Buz Wyeth's *The Approaching Fury: Voices of the Storm, 1820–1861* (1997), Bruce Levine's *Half Slave and Half Free: The Roots of the Civil War* (1992), and David M. Potter's *The Impending Crisis 1848–1861* (1976). The most recent narrative of the political debate leading to secession is Michael A. Morrison's *Slavery and the American West: The Eclipse of Manifest Destiny and the Coming of the Civil War* (1997).

Mark Stegmaier's *Texas, New Mexico, and the Compromise of 1850: Boundary Dispute and Sectional Crisis* (1996) probes that crucial dispute while Michael F. Holt's *The Political Crisis of the 1850s* (1978) traces the demise of the Whigs. Eric Foner shows how events and ideas combined in the formation of a new political party in *Free Soil, Free Labor, Free Men: The Ideology of the Republican Party before the Civil War* (1970). A more straightforward study of the rise of the Republicans is William E. Gienapp's *The Origins of the Republican Party, 1852–1856* (1987). The economic, social, and political crises of 1857 are examined in Kenneth Stampp's *America in 1857: A Nation on the Brink* (1990).

Robert W. Johannsen's *Stephen A. Douglas* (1973) analyzes the issue of popular sovereignty. A more national perspective is provided in James A. Rawley's *Race and Politics: "Bleeding Kansas" and the Coming of the Civil War* (1969). On the role of John Brown in the sectional crisis, see Stephen B. Oates's *To Purge This Land with Blood: A Biography of John Brown* (2nd ed., 1984). An excellent study of the South's journey to secession is William Freehling's *The Road to Disunion* (1990).

On Lincoln's role in the coming crisis of war, see Don E. Fehrenbacher's *Prelude to Greatness* (1962). Harry V. Jaffa's *Crisis of the House Divided* (1959) details the Lincoln-Douglas debates, and Maury Klein's *Days of Defiance: Sumter, Secession, and the Coming of the Civil War* (1997) treats the Fort Sumter controversy. An excellent collection of interpretive essays is *Why the War Came* (1996), edited by Gabor S. Boritt.

17 ↶ THE WAR OF THE UNION

During the four long months between his election and inauguration, Abraham Lincoln said little about future policies and less about past positions. "If I thought a repetition would do any good I would make it," he wrote to an editor in St. Louis. "But my judgment is it would do positive harm. The secessionists per se, believing they had alarmed me, would clamor all the louder." So he stayed in Springfield until mid-February 1861, biding his time. He then boarded a train for a long, roundabout trip, and began to drop some hints to audiences along the way. To the New Jersey legislature, which responded with prolonged cheering, he said: "The man does not live who is more devoted to peace than I am. . . . But it may be necessary to put the foot down." At the end of the journey, reluctantly yielding to rumors of plots against his life, he passed unnoticed on a night train through Baltimore and slipped into Washington, D. C. before daybreak on February 23.

End of the Waiting Game

At the end of 1860, as the possibility of civil war captured the attention of a divided nation, no one imagined that a conflict of horrendous scope and intensity awaited them. On both sides, people believed that the fighting would be a lark, that it would be over in little more than a month, and that their daily lives would go on as usual.

LINCOLN'S INAUGURATION In his inaugural address, Lincoln repeated his pledge not "to interfere with the institution of slavery in the States where it exists. I believe I have no lawful right to do so, and I have no inclination to do so." But the immediate question had shifted from slavery to secession, and most of the speech emphasized Lincoln's view that "the Union of these States is perpetual." The Union, he asserted, preceded the Constitution itself, dating from the Articles of Association in 1774. It was "matured and continued" by the Declaration of Independence and the Articles of Confederation. Yet even if the United States were only a contractual association, "no State upon its own mere motion can lawfully get out of the Union." Lincoln promised to hold areas belonging to the federal government, collect taxes, and deliver the mails unless repelled, but beyond that "there will be no invasion, no using of force against or among the people anywhere." In the final paragraph of the speech, Lincoln offered an eloquent appeal for regional harmony:

> I am loath to close. We are not enemies, but friends. We must not be enemies. Though passion may have strained, it must not break our bonds of affection. The mystic chords of memory, stretching from every battlefield and patriot grave to every living heart and hearthstone all over this broad land, will yet swell the chorus of the Union, when again touched, as surely they will be, by the better angels of our nature.

Lincoln not only entered office amid the gravest crisis yet faced by a president, but he also faced unusual problems of transition. Republicans, in power for the first time, crowded Washington, hungry for office. Four of the seven new cabinet members had been rivals for the presidency: William H. Seward at the State Department, Salmon P. Chase at the Treasury Department, Simon Cameron at the War Department, and

Edward Bates as attorney-general. Four were former Democrats and three were former Whigs. They formed a group of better-than-average ability, though most were so strong-minded they thought themselves better qualified to lead than Lincoln. Only later did they acknowledge with Seward that "he is the best man among us."

THE FALL OF FORT SUMTER   For the time being, Lincoln's combination of firmness and moderation differed little in effect from his predecessor's stance. Harsh judgments of Buchanan's waiting game overlook the fact that Lincoln kept it going. Indeed, his only other choices were to accept secession as an accomplished fact or to use force right away. On the day after he took office, however, word arrived from Charleston that time was running out. Major Robert Anderson, in charge of federal forces at Fort Sumter, had supplies for a month to six weeks, and Confederates were encircling the fort with a "ring of fire."

Events moved quickly to a climax in the next two weeks. On April 4, 1861, Lincoln decided to resupply the sixty-nine men at Fort Sumter. Two days later, he notified the governor of South Carolina that "an attempt will be made to supply Fort Sumter with provisions only. . . ." On April 9, President Jefferson Davis and his cabinet in Montgomery, Alabama, decided against permitting Lincoln to resupply Fort Sumter.

On April 11, Confederate general Pierre G. T. Beauregard, a dapper Creole from Louisiana who had taught artillery to Anderson at West Point, demanded a speedy surrender of the federal garrison. Major Anderson refused, but he said his supplies would be used up in three more days. With the relief ships approaching, Anderson received an ultimatum to yield. He again refused, and at 4:30 A.M. on April 12 the shelling of Fort Sumter began. After more than thirty hours, his ammunition exhausted, Anderson lowered the flag. Although over 3,000 shells hit the fort, the only fatalities were two men killed in an explosion during a final salute to the colors, the first in a melancholy train of war dead.

The guns of Charleston signaled the end of the waiting game. "So Civil War is inaugurated at last," observed New York lawyer George Templeton Strong. "God defend the right." Equally committed was South Carolina's Mary Chesnut: "Woe to those who began this war if they were not in bitter earnest." On the day after Anderson's surrender, Lincoln called upon the loyal states to supply 75,000 militiamen to subdue a rebellion "too powerful to be suppressed by the ordinary course of judicial proceedings." Volunteers rallied around the flag at the recruiting stations. On April 19, Lincoln proclaimed a blockade of southern ports which, as the Supreme Court later ruled, confirmed the existence of war.

TAKING SIDES   Lincoln's war proclamation swept four more states into the Confederacy. Virginia acted first. Its convention passed an Ordinance of Secession on April 17. The Confederate Congress then chose Richmond, Virginia, as its new capital, and the government moved there in June. Three other states followed Virginia in little over a month: Arkansas on May 6, Tennessee on May 7, and North Carolina on May 20. All four of the holdout states, especially Tennessee and Virginia, had areas (mainly in the mountains) where slaves were scarce and where Union support ran strong. In Tennessee the mountain counties would supply more volunteers to the Union than to the Confederate cause. Unionists in western Virginia, bolstered by a Federal army from Ohio under General George B. McClellan, contrived a loyal government

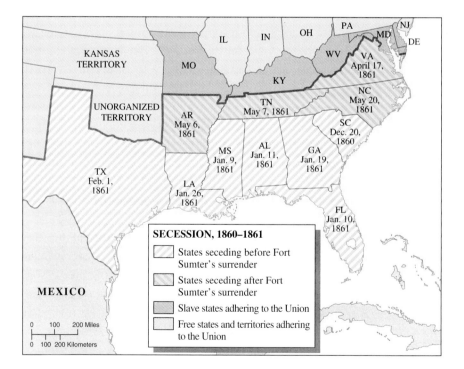

of Virginia that formed a new state. In 1863 Congress admitted West Virginia to the Union with a constitution that provided for gradual emancipation of the few slaves there.

Of the other slave states, Delaware remained firmly in the Union, but Maryland, Kentucky, and Missouri went through bitter struggles for control. The secession of Maryland would have isolated Washington, D.C. within the Confederacy. In fact Baltimore's mayor did cut all connections to the capital. A mob attacked the Sixth Massachusetts Regiment on its way through Baltimore and killed four. To hold the state Lincoln took drastic measures of dubious legality: he suspended the writ of habeas corpus (under which judges could require arresting officers to produce their prisoners and justify their arrest) and rounded up pro-Confederate leaders and threw them in jail. The fall elections ended the threat of Maryland's secession by returning a solidly Unionist majority in the state.

Kentucky, native state of both Lincoln and Jefferson Davis, harbored divided loyalties. But spring elections for a state convention returned a thumping Unionist majority, and the state legislature proclaimed Kentucky's fragile neutrality lasted until September 3, when a Confederate force occupied several towns. General Ulysses S. Grant then moved Union soldiers into Paducah. Thereafter, Kentucky, though divided in allegiance, for the most part remained with the Union. It joined the Confederacy, some have said, only after the war.

Lincoln's effort to hold a middle course in Missouri ran afoul of the maneuvers of less patient men in the state. Unionists there had a numerical advantage, but there were many Confederate sympathizers. For a time the state, like Kentucky, kept an uneasy peace. But elections for a convention brought an overwhelming Union victory, while a pro-Confederate militia under the state governor began to gather near St. Louis. In the city Unionist forces rallied, and on May 10 they surprised and disarmed the rebel militia at its camp. They pursued the pro-Confederate forces into the southwestern part of the state, and after a temporary setback on August 10, the Unionists pushed the Confederates back again, finally breaking their resistance at the Battle of Pea Ridge (March 6–8, 1862), just over the state line in Arkansas. Thereafter border warfare continued in Missouri, pitting against each other rival bands of gunslingers who kept up their feuding and banditry for years after the war was over.

CHOOSING SIDES   Robert E. Lee epitomized the agonizing choice facing many residents of the border states. Son of "Lighthorse Harry" Lee, a Revolutionary War hero, and married to a descendant of Martha Washington, Lee had served in the United States Army for thirty years. When Fort Sumter was attacked, he was summoned by General Winfield Scott, another Virginian, and offered command of the Federal forces. After a sleepless night pacing the floor, Lee told Scott that he could not go against his "country," meaning Virginia. Although Lee failed to "see the good of secession," he could not "raise my hand against my birthplace, my home, my children." Lee resigned his army commission, retired to his estate, and soon answered a call to the Virginia—later the Confederate—service.

Many southerners made great sacrifices to remain loyal to the Union. Some left their native region once the fighting began. Others who remained in the South found ways to support the Union. In every Confederate state except South Carolina, whole regiments were organized to fight for the Union. Some 100,000 men from the southern states fought against the Confederacy. One out of every five soldiers from Arkansas killed in the war fought for the Union side. Of course, some of these southern "Tories" changed sides out of expediency rather than loyalty. Confederate soldiers who had been captured occasionally chose to switch sides and serve on the Indian frontier rather than remain in prison.

Others, however, never embraced the Confederate cause. Many of the loyalists were Irish or German immigrants who had no love for slavery or the planter elite. In the Fredericksburg–San Antonio region of Texas, German Americans opposed secession and the war once fighting erupted. The Confederate state government declared six counties in open rebellion in 1862 and sent in troops to suppress Union sentiment. Any German who criticized the Rebel cause was hanged, shot, or whipped. Confederate cavalry units caught one group of Germans trying to escape to Mexico and killed thirty-four of them. In south Texas almost a thousand Texas-Mexicans fought against Confederate troops. Northwest Arkansas was also a Unionist stronghold. In late 1861, Confederate forces executed several members of the Arkansas Peace Society because they opposed secession and the war. Other members were forced to join the Confederate army. Whatever their motives, these and other southern loyalists played a significant role in helping the Union cause.

THE BALANCE OF FORCE

Shrouded in an ever-thickening mist of larger-than-life mythology, the Union triumph in the Civil War has acquired the mantle of inevitability. The Confederacy's fight for independence, on the other hand, has taken on the aura of a romantic lost cause, doomed from the start by the region's sparse industrial development, smaller pool of able-bodied men, paucity of capital resources and warships, and spotty transportation network.

But in 1861 the military situation seemed by no means so clearcut. For all of the South's obvious disadvantages, it initially enjoyed a captive labor force and the benefits of fighting a defensive campaign on familiar territory. Jefferson Davis and other Confederate leaders were genuinely confident that their cause would prevail on the battlefield. The outcome of the Civil War was not inevitable: it was determined as much by human decisions and human willpower as by physical resources.

Union soldiers photographed at Harper's Ferry, Virginia, in 1862. Neither side in the Civil War was prepared for the magnitude of this first of "modern" wars.

ECONOMIC ADVANTAGES   The South seceded in part out of a growing awareness of its minority status in the nation; a balance sheet of the
sections in 1860 shows the accuracy of that perception. The Union held
twenty-three states, including four border slave states, while the Confederacy had eleven. Ignoring conflicts of allegiance within various states,
which might roughly cancel each other out, the population count was
about 22 million in the Union to 9 million in the Confederacy, and about
4 million of the latter were slaves. The Union therefore had an edge of
about four to one in potential human resources. To help redress the imbalance, the Confederacy mobilized 80 percent or more of its military-
age white males, and a third of them would die during the prolonged war.

An even greater advantage for the North was its industrial development. The states that joined the Confederacy produced just 7 percent
of the nation's manufactures on the eve of the war. What made the
disparity even greater was that little of this was in heavy industry. The
only iron foundry of any size in the Confederacy was the Tredegar Iron
Works in Richmond, which had long supplied the United States Army.
Tredegar's existence strengthened the Confederacy's will to defend its
capital. Yet the Union states, in addition to making most of the country's
shoes, textiles, and iron products, turned out 97 percent of the firearms
and 96 percent of the railroad equipment. They had most of the trained
mechanics, most of the shipping and mercantile firms, and the bulk of
the banking and financial resources.

Even in farm production the northern states overshadowed the rural
South, for most of the North's population was still rooted in the soil.
The Confederacy produced enough foodstuffs to meet minimal needs,
but the disruption of transport caused shortages in many places. The
North, meanwhile, produced a surplus of wheat for export at a time
when drought and crop failures in Europe created a critical demand.
King Wheat supplanted King Cotton as the nation's main export, becoming the chief means of acquiring foreign money and bills of exchange to pay for imports from abroad.

The North's advantage in transport weighed heavily as the war went on.
The Union had more wagons, horses, and ships than the Confederacy,
and an impressive edge in railroads. The Confederacy had only one
east-west rail connection, between Memphis and Chattanooga. The latter was an important rail hub with connections via Knoxville into Virginia
and down through Atlanta to Charleston and Savannah. But the North

The Watervliet Arsenal in New York. The North had an advantage in industrial development and turned out most of the nation's firearms in its foundries.

already had an extensive railroad network. Three major lines gave western farmers an outlet to the eastern seaboard and greatly lessened their former dependence on the Mississippi River.

MILITARY ADVANTAGES   Against the weight of such odds the wonder is that the Confederacy managed to survive for four years. Yet at the start certain factors evened the odds. The most important of these was geography: the Confederates could fight a defensive war on their own territory. In addition, the South had more experienced military leaders. A number of circumstances had given rise to a strong military tradition in the South: frequent campaigns against the Indians, the fear of slave insurrection, and a history of expansionism. Military careers had prestige, and military schools multiplied in the antebellum years, the most notable being The Citadel and Virginia Military Institute. West Point itself drew many southerners, producing an army corps dominated by men from the region. By the end of the war, however, the Union had developed better commanders.

At the start of the war, Union seapower relied on about 90 ships, though only 42 were in active service and most were at distant stations. But under the able guidance of Secretary Gideon Welles, the Union navy eventually grew to 650 vessels of all types. It never completely sealed off the South, but it made it very difficult to enter or leave southern ports. On the inland waters navy gunboats and transports played an even more direct role in securing the Union's control of the Mississippi River and its larger tributaries, which provided easy routes into the center of the Confederacy.

THE WAR'S EARLY COURSE

After the fall of Fort Sumter, partisans on both sides hoped that the war might end with one sudden bold stroke, the capture of Washington or the fall of Richmond. Strategic thought at the time remained under the spell of Napoleon, holding that wars would turn on one climactic battle in which a huge force, massed against an enemy's point of weakness, would demoralize its armies and break its will to resist. Such ideas had been instilled in a generation of West Point cadets, but these lessons neglected the massive losses Napoleon had suffered, losses that finally turned his victories into defeat.

General Winfield Scott, the seventy-five-year-old commander of the Union army, envisioned a long war. He proposed to use the navy to blockade the long Atlantic and Gulf coastlines, and then to divide and subdivide the Confederacy by pushing southward along the main water routes: the Mississippi, Tennessee, and Cumberland Rivers. As word leaked out of Scott's plans, the newspapers impatiently criticized his "Anaconda" strategy, which they judged far too slow, indicative of the commander's old age and caution. The public and many generals on both sides began the war in the belief that victory could be achieved quickly and decisively, without the need for Scott's long-term strategy.

BULL RUN   Nowhere was this naive optimism more clearly displayed than at the first Battle of Bull Run (or Manassas)*. An eager public pressured both sides to strike quickly and decisively. Jefferson Davis allowed the battle-hungry General P. G. T. Beauregard to hurry the

---

*The Federals most often named battles for natural features, the Confederates for nearby towns, thus Bull Run (Manassas), Antietam (Sharpsburg), Stone's River (Murfreesboro), and the like.

main Confederate army to the railroad center at Manassas Junction, Virginia, about twenty-five miles west of Washington. Lincoln decided that General Irvin McDowell's hastily assembled army of some 37,000 might overrun the outnumbered Confederates and quickly march on to Richmond, the Confederate capital. There was a festive mood as hundreds of civilians rode out from Washington to picnic and watch the entertaining spectacle of a one-battle war. Instead they witnessed a bloody, chaotic catastrophe.

It was a hot, dry day on July 21, 1861, when McDowell's raw recruits encountered Beauregard's army dug in behind a meandering little stream called Bull Run. The two generals, who had been classmates at West Point, adopted markedly similar plans—each would try to turn the other's left flank. The Federals almost achieved their purpose early in the afternoon, but Confederate reinforcements led by General Joseph E. Johnston poured in to check the Union offensive. Amid the fury, a South Carolina officer rallied his men by pointing to Thomas Jackson's brigade of Virginians: "Look, there is Jackson with his Virginians, standing like a stone wall." The reference thereafter served as Jackson's nickname.

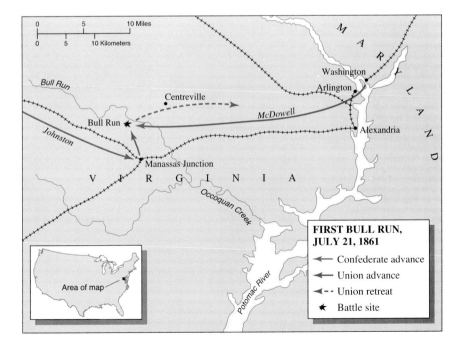

FIRST BULL RUN, JULY 21, 1861

After McDowell's last assault had faltered, his army's frantic retreat turned into a panic as fleeing soldiers and terrified civilians clogged the Washington road. An Ohio congressman and several colleagues tried to rally the frenzied soldiers. "We called them cowards, denounced them in the most offensive terms, pulled out our heavy revolvers and threatened to shoot them, but in vain; a cruel, crazy, mad, hopeless panic possessed them."

Stonewall Jackson had hoped to pursue the fleeing Federals into Washington. "We must give them no time to think," he stressed in a letter to his wife. "We must bewilder them and keep them bewildered. Our fighting must be sharp, impetuous, continuous. We cannot stand a long war." But the Confederates were about as disorganized and exhausted by the battle as the Yankees were, and they failed to give chase. It would have been futile anyway, for the next day a summer downpour turned roads into quagmires.

The Battle of Bull Run was a sobering experience for both sides. Much of the romance—the splendid uniforms, bright flags, rousing songs—gave way to the agonizing realization that this would be a long, mean, and costly struggle. *Harper's Weekly* bluntly warned: "From the fearful day at Bull Run dates war. Not polite war, not incredulous war, but war that breaks hearts and blights homes." The sobering Union defeat "will teach us in the first place . . . that this war must be prosecuted on scientific principles."

THE WAR'S EARLY PHASE   The Battle of Bull Run demonstrated that the war would not be decided with one sudden stroke. General Winfield Scott had predicted as much, and now Lincoln fell back upon Scott's three-pronged "Anaconda" strategy. It called first for the Army of the Potomac to defend Washington and exert constant pressure on the Confederate capital at Richmond. At the same time, the navy would blockade the southern coast and dry up the Confederacy's access to foreign goods and weapons. The final component of the plan would divide the Confederacy by invading the South along the main water routes: the Mississippi, Tennessee, and Cumberland Rivers. This strategy would slowly entwine and crush the southern resistance.

The Confederate strategy was simpler. If the Union forces could be stalemated, Jefferson Davis and others hoped, then the British or French might be convinced to join their cause, or perhaps public sentiment in the North would force Lincoln to seek a negotiated settlement. So at the same time that armies were forming in the South, Confederate diplomats were seeking assistance in London and Paris, and Confederate sympathizers in the North were urging an end to the North's war effort.

NAVAL ACTIONS   After Bull Run, and for the rest of 1861 into early 1862, the most important military actions involved naval war and blockade. The one great threat to the Union navy's blockade of southern ports proved to be short-lived. The Confederates in Norfolk fashioned an ironclad ship from an abandoned Union steam frigate, the *Merrimack*. Rechristened the *Virginia,* it ventured out on March 8, 1862, and wrought havoc among Union ships. But as luck would have it, a new Union ironclad, the *Monitor,* arrived from New York in time to engage the *Virginia* on the next day. They fought to a draw and the *Virginia* returned to port, where the Confederates destroyed it when they had to give up Norfolk soon afterward.

Gradually the Union tightened its grip on the South. In late 1861 a Federal flotilla appeared at Port Royal, South Carolina, pounded the fortifications into submission, and seized the port and nearby sea islands. At Fortress Monroe, Virginia, Union forces held the tip of the peninsula between the James and York Rivers, the scene of much colonial and revolutionary history. The navy extended its bases farther down the Carolina coast in the late summer and fall of 1862. Union troops then captured Hatteras Inlet on the Outer Banks of North Carolina in August, a foothold soon extended to Roanoke Island and New Bern on the mainland. From there the navy's progress extended southward along the Georgia-Florida coast. The Federals first laid siege to Charleston; by 1863 Fort Sumter and the city itself had come under bombardment. In the spring of 1862 Admiral David Farragut forced open the lower Mississippi near its mouth and surprised the defenders of New Orleans. Farragut won a surrender on May 1, then moved quickly to take Baton Rouge in the same way.

FORMING ARMIES   Once the fighting began, the Federal Congress authorized a call for 500,000 more men, and after the Battle of Bull Run added another 500,000. By the end of 1861, the first half million had enlisted. This pell-mell mobilization left the army with a large

An engraving of the recruiting office in City Hall Park, New York. The sign lists the money offered by the office: $677 to new recruits, $777 to veteran soldiers, and $15 to anyone who brings in a recruit.

number of "political" officers, commissioned by state governors or elected by the recruits.

The nineteenth-century army often organized its units along community and ethnic lines. The Union army, for example, included a Scandinavian regiment (the 15th Wisconsin Infantry), a Scottish Highlander unit (the 79th New York Infantry), a French regiment (the 55th New York Infantry), and a mixed unit of Poles, Hungarians, Germans, Spanish, and Italians (the 39th New York Infantry).

In the Confederacy, the first mass enlistment put a great strain on limited means. In March Jefferson Davis was empowered to call 100,000 twelve-month volunteers and to employ state militia up to six months. In May, once the fighting had started, he was authorized to raise up to 400,000 three-year volunteers "without the delay of a formal call upon the respective states." Thus by early 1862, most of the veteran Confederate soldiers were nearing the end of their enlistments without having encountered much significant action. They were also resisting the incentives of bonuses and furloughs for reenlistment. The Confederate government thus turned to conscription. By an act passed on April

16, 1862, all white male citizens, eighteen to thirty-five, were declared members of the army for three years, and those already in service were required to serve out three years. In 1862 the upper age was raised to forty-five, and in 1864 the age limits were further extended to cover all from seventeen to fifty, with those under eighteen and over forty-five reserved for state defense.

The conscription law, however, included two loopholes. First, a draftee might escape service either by providing an able-bodied substitute not of draft age or by paying $500 in cash. Second, exemptions, designed to protect key civilian work, were subject to abuse by men seeking "bombproof" jobs. Exemption of state officials, for example, was flagrantly abused by the governors of Georgia and North Carolina, who were in charge of defining the vital jobs. The exclusion of teachers with twenty pupils inspired a sudden educational renaissance, and the exemption of one white man for each plantation with twenty or more slaves led to bitter complaints about "a rich man's war and a poor man's fight."

The Union took nearly another year to force men into service. In 1863 the government began to draft men aged twenty to forty-five. Exemptions were granted to specified federal and state officeholders and to others on medical or compassionate grounds. For $300, one could avoid service. In both the North and the South, conscription spurred men to volunteer, either to collect bounties or to avoid the disgrace of being drafted.

The draft flouted an American tradition of voluntary service and was widely held to be arbitrary and unconstitutional. In the South the draft also violated states' rights by requiring the exercise of a central power. It might have worked better had it operated through the states, some of which had set up their own drafts to meet the calls of President Davis. The governor of Georgia, who had one of the best records for raising troops at first, turned into a bitter critic of the draft, pronouncing it unconstitutional and trying to obstruct its enforcement. Few of the other governors gave it unqualified support, and Vice-President Alexander Stephens remained opposed to it throughout the war.

Widespread public opposition to the draft impeded its enforcement both in the North and in the South. In New York City, the announcement of a draft lottery on July 11, 1863, incited a week of rioting in which roving bands of working-class toughs, many of them Irish Catholic immigrants, took control of the streets. Although provoked by feelings that the draft loopholes catered to the wealthy, the riots also exposed emerging racial and ethnic tensions. The mobs assaulted conscription offices, factories, docks, and the homes of prominent Republicans. But they directed their wrath most furiously at blacks. They blamed blacks for causing the war and for threatening to take their own unskilled jobs. A white abolitionist watched in horror from her window as the rioters fell upon the city's black neighborhoods:

> A child of 3 years of age was thrown from a 4th story window and instantly killed. A woman one hour after her confinement was set upon and beaten with her tender babe in her arms. . . . Children were torn from their mother's embrace and their brains blown out in the very face of the afflicted mother. Men were burnt by slow fires.

The violence ran completely out of control; over a hundred people were killed before five regiments of battle-weary soldiers brought from Gettysburg restored order.

THE WEST AND THE CIVIL WAR During the Civil War, western settlement continued unabated. New discoveries of gold and silver along the eastern slopes of the Sierra Nevada Mountains and in Montana and Colorado lured thousands of prospectors and their suppliers. New transportation and communication networks emerged to serve the growing population in the West. Telegraph lines sprouted above the plains, and stagecoach lines fanned out to serve the new communities. Dakota, Colorado, and Nevada gained territorial status in 1861, Idaho and Arizona in 1863, and Montana in 1864. Silver-rich Nevada gained statehood in 1864.

With the firing on Fort Sumter, many of the regular army units assigned to frontier outposts in the West began to head east to meet the Confederate threat. In Texas, the Indian Territory (Oklahoma), and southern New Mexico, Union soldiers left altogether. Elsewhere they left behind skeleton units. Texas was the only western state to join the Confederacy. For the most part, the federal government maintained its control of the other western territories during the war.

But it was not easy. Fighting in Kansas and the Indian Territory was widespread and furious. By 1862 Lincoln was forced to dispatch new volunteer units to the West. He had two primary concerns: to protect the shipments of gold and silver and to win over western political support for the war and his presidency.

The most intense fighting in the West during the Civil War occurred along the Kansas-Missouri border. There the disputes between proslavery and antislavery settlers of the 1850s turned into brutal guerrilla warfare. The most prominent pro-Confederate leader in the area was William Quantrill. He and his proslavery followers, mostly teenagers, fought under a black flag, meaning that they gave no quarter. In destroying Lawrence, Kansas, in 1863, Quantrill ordered his forces to "kill every male and burn every house." By the end of the day, 182 boys and men had been killed. Their opponents—the Jayhawkers—responded in kind. They tortured and hanged pro-Confederate prisoners, burned houses, and destroyed livestock.

Many Indian tribes found themselves caught up in the Civil War. Indian regiments fought on both sides, and in Oklahoma they fought against each other. Indians among the Five Civilized Tribes owned black slaves and felt a natural bond with southern whites. Oklahoma's proximity to Texas also influenced the Choctaws and Chickasaws to support the Confederacy. The Cherokees, Creeks, and Seminoles were more divided in their loyalties. For these tribes, the Civil War served as a wedge that fractured their unity. The Cherokees, for example, split in two, some supporting the Union and others supporting the South.

ACTIONS IN THE WESTERN THEATER   Little happened of military significance in the Eastern Theater (east of the Appalachians) before May 1862. On the other hand, the Western Theater (from the mountains to the Mississippi River) flared up with several encounters and an important penetration of the Confederate states. In western Kentucky, Confederate general Albert Sidney Johnston had perhaps 40,000 men stretched over some 150 miles.

Early in 1862 General Ulysses S. Grant made the first Union thrust against the weak center of Johnston's overextended lines. Moving out of Cairo, Illinois, and Paducah, Kentucky, with a gunboat flotilla, he swung southward up the Tennessee River toward Fort Henry. After a pounding from the Union gunboats, Fort Henry fell on February 6. Grant then moved quickly overland to attack nearby Fort Donelson. On February 16 it gave up with some 12,000 men. Grant's terms, "unconditional surrender," and his quick success sent a thrill through the Union.

Ulysses S. "Unconditional Surrender" Grant had not only opened a water route to Nashville, but had thrust his forces between the two strongholds of the western Confederates. Johnston therefore had to give up his foothold in Kentucky and abandon Nashville to Don Carlos Buell's Army of the Ohio (February 25) in order to reunite his forces at Corinth, Mississippi, along the Memphis and Chattanooga Railroad.

SHILOH   After suffering defeats in Kentucky and Tennessee, Confederate general Albert Sidney Johnston regrouped the Confederate forces and moved to Corinth in northern Mississippi near the Tennessee border. Ulysses Grant, meanwhile, moved his Union army southward along the Tennessee River during the early spring of 1862. Grant then made a costly mistake. While planning his attack on Corinth, he exposed his 42,000 troops on a rolling plateau between two creeks flowing into the Tennessee River and failed to dig defensive trenches. Johnston shrewdly recognized

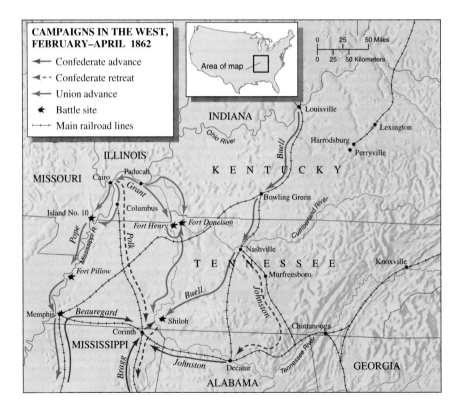

Grant's oversight, and on the morning of April 6, the Kentuckian ordered an attack on the vulnerable Federals, urging his men to be "worthy of your race and lineage; worthy of the women of the South."

The 44,000 Confederates struck suddenly at Shiloh, a log church in the center of the Union camp in southwestern Tennessee. They found most of Grant's troops still sleeping or eating breakfast; many died in their bedrolls. After a day of carnage and confusion, the Union soldiers were pinned against the river. They might well have been totally defeated had the Confederate commander, General Johnston, not been mortally wounded at the peak of the battle. His second in command called off the attack. Under the cover of gunboats and artillery at Pittsburg Landing, Grant and General William Tecumseh Sherman (who had two horses shot from under him and was himself wounded once) rallied their troops. "We've had the devil's own day," Sherman told Grant that night. "Yes," Grant noted, "but we'll lick them tomorrow." Bolstered by reinforcements, Grant took the offensive the next day, and the Confederates glumly withdrew to Corinth, leaving the Union army too battered to pursue. Casualties on both sides totaled over 20,000.

Shiloh, a Hebrew word meaning "place of peace," was the costliest battle in which Americans had ever engaged, although worse was yet to come. Grant observed that the ground was "so covered with dead one could walk across the field without touching the ground." Like so many battles thereafter, Shiloh was a story of missed opportunities and debated turning points punctuated by lucky incidents and accidents. Throughout the Civil War, winning armies would fail to pursue their retreating foes, thus allowing the wounded opponent to slip away and fight again.

After the Battle of Shiloh, the Union lost for a while the full services of its finest general. Grant had been caught napping, and many northerners were shocked by the colossal loss of life. His superior, General Henry Halleck, already jealous of Grant's success, spread the false rumor that Grant had been drinking at Shiloh. Some called on Lincoln to fire Grant, but the president refused: "I can't spare this man; he fights." Halleck, however, took Grant's place as field commander, and as a result the Union thrust southward ground to a halt. For the remainder of 1862, the chief action in the Western Theater was a series of inconclusive maneuvers punctuated by sharp engagements.

MCCLELLAN'S PENINSULAR CAMPAIGN   The Eastern Theater remained fairly quiet for nine months after Bull Run. In the wake of the Union defeat, Lincoln had replaced McDowell with General George B. McClellan, Stonewall Jackson's classmate at West Point. As head of the Army of the Potomac, McClellan set about building a powerful, well-trained army that would be ready for its next battle. When General Scott retired in November, Lincoln appointed McClellan as general-in-chief. He exuded confidence and poise, as well as a certain flair for parade-ground showmanship. His troops adored him. Yet for all of McClellan's organizational ability and dramatic flair, his innate caution would prove crippling.

Time passed, and McClellan kept building and training his army to meet the superior numbers he claimed the Confederates were deploying. His intelligence service, headed by the private detective Allan Pinkerton, tended to overestimate enemy forces. Before moving, there

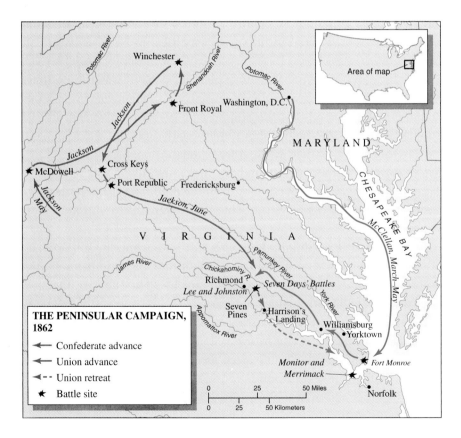

THE PENINSULAR CAMPAIGN, 1862

◄— Confederate advance

◄— Union advance

◄-- Union retreat

★ Battle site

was always the need to do this or that, to get 10,000 or 20,000 more men, always something. Lincoln wanted the army to move directly toward Richmond, keeping itself between the Confederate army and Washington. But McClellan, who dismissed Lincoln as a "well-meaning baboon," sought to enter Richmond by the side door, so to speak, up the neck of land between the York and James Rivers, site of Jamestown, Williamsburg, and Yorktown.

In mid-March 1862 McClellan's army finally embarked. The Union forces went down the Potomac River and Chesapeake Bay to the Virginia peninsula southeast of Richmond. This bold move put the Union forces within sixty miles of the Confederate capital. Before the end of May, McClellan's advance units sighted the church spires of Richmond. Thousands of Richmond residents fled the city in panic. President Davis sent his own family to a safe haven west of the city. But McClellan waited to strike, failing to capitalize on his situation.

President Jefferson Davis, at the urging of his adviser Robert E. Lee, sent Stonewall Jackson's army into the Shenandoah Valley on what proved to be a brilliant diversionary action. From March 23 to June 9, Jackson and some 18,000 men pinned down two separate Union armies with more than twice their numbers in the western Virginia mountains and at the northern end of the valley. While the Union army under General McDowell braced to defend Washington, Jackson hastened back to defend Richmond against McClellan.

On May 31 Confederate general Joseph E. Johnston struck at McClellan's forces isolated on the south bank by the flooded Chickahominy River. In the Battle of Seven Pines (Fair Oaks), only the arrival of reinforcements, who somehow crossed the swollen river, prevented a disastrous Union defeat. Both sides took heavy casualties, and General Johnston was severely wounded.

At this point, Robert E. Lee assumed command of the Army of Northern Virginia, a development that changed the course of the war. Tall, erect, and wide-shouldered, Lee projected a commanding presence. At the start of the Civil War, the West Point graduate was considered the most promising army officer in the United States. Abraham Lincoln had asked him to command the new Union army, but Lee chose to defend his native Virginia. Even though he knew the Confederacy would face a "terrible ordeal," he "did only what duty demanded." Dignified yet fiery, he was a bold commander who led by

Camp Winfield Scott, the headquarters of General McClellan during the siege of Yorktown, 1862.

example. His men loved him. Unlike Johnston, Lee enjoyed Jefferson Davis's trust. More important, he knew how to use the talents of his superb field commanders: Stonewall Jackson, the pious, fearless mathematics professor from the Virginia Military Institute; James Longstreet, Lee's deliberate but tireless "war horse"; sharp-tongued D. H. Hill, the former engineering professor at Davidson College; Ambrose P. Hill, the consummate fighter who challenged one commander to a duel and feuded with Stonewall Jackson; and J. E. B. Stuart, the colorful young cavalryman who once said: "All I ask of fate is that I may be killed leading a cavalry charge." He would get his wish.

Once in command, Lee launched a desperate attack at Malvern Hill (July 1), where the Confederates suffered heavy casualties from Union artillery and gunboats in the James River. This week of intense fighting, labeled the Seven Days' Battles (June 25 to July 1), failed to dislodge the Union forces. McClellan's army was still near Richmond. On July 9, when Lincoln visited McClellan's headquarters, the general complained that the administration had failed to support him adequately and instructed the president at length on war policies. It was ample reason to remove McClellan. Lincoln returned to Washington and on July 11 called Henry

Halleck from the West to take charge as general-in-chief, a post that McClellan had temporarily vacated. Miffed at his demotion, McClellan angrily dismissed Halleck as an officer "whom I know to be my inferior."

SECOND BULL RUN   Lincoln and Halleck ordered McClellan to leave the peninsula and join the Washington defense force, now under the bombastic John Pope, who had been called back from the West for a new overland assault on Richmond. In a letter to his wife, McClellan predicted that "Pope will be thrashed and disposed of" by Lee. As McClellan's Army of the Potomac began to pull out of the Tidewater, Lee moved northward to strike Pope before McClellan's troops arrived. Dividing his forces, Lee sent Jackson's "foot cavalry" around Pope's right flank to attack his supply lines. At Cedar Mountain, Virginia, Jackson pushed back an advance party of Federals, and then went on to seize and destroy the Federal supply base at Manassas Junction. At Second Bull Run (or Second Manassas), fought on almost the same site as the earlier battle, Pope assumed that he faced only Jackson, but Lee's main army by that time had joined in. On August 30 a crushing attack on Pope's flank drove the Federals from the field. In the next few days the Union forces pulled back into the fortifications around Washington, where McClellan once again took command and reorganized. He displayed his unflagging egotism in a letter to his wife: "Again I have been called upon to save the country." The disgraced Pope was dispatched to Minnesota to fight in the Indian wars.

ANTIETAM   Still on the offensive, Lee decided to invade the North and perhaps thereby gain foreign recognition for the Confederacy. He and his battle-tested troops pushed into western Maryland in September 1862, headed for Pennsylvania. But Lee's bold strategy was uncovered when a Union soldier picked up a bundle of cigars and discovered a secret order from Lee wrapped around them. The paper revealed that Lee had again divided his army, sending Stonewall Jackson off to take Harper's Ferry, Virginia. McClellan boasted upon seeing the captured document: "Here is a paper with which, if I cannot whip Bobby Lee, I will be willing to go home." Instead of seizing his unexpected opportunity, however, he again delayed for sixteen crucial hours, still worried—as always—about enemy strength, and Lee was thereby able to reassemble most of his tired army behind Antietam Creek. Still, McClellan was

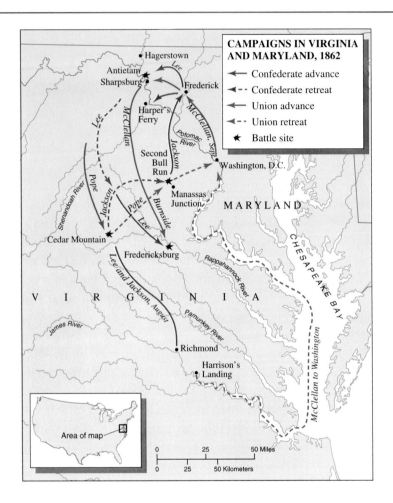

CAMPAIGNS IN VIRGINIA AND MARYLAND, 1862

← Confederate advance
◄--- Confederate retreat
← Union advance
◄--- Union retreat
★ Battle site

optimistic, and Lincoln, too, relished the chance for a truly decisive blow: "God bless you and all with you," he wired McClellan. "Destroy the rebel army if possible."

On September 17, 1862, McClellan's forces attacked, commencing the furious Battle of Antietam (Sharpsburg). With the Confederate lines ready to break, A. P. Hill's division arrived from Harper's Ferry, having marched sixteen miles to the battlefield. Bone-weary and footsore, they nevertheless plunged immediately into the fray, battering the Union army's left flank. It was a ghastly scene. "No tongue can tell, no mind conceive, no pen portray the horrible sights I witnessed this morning," a Pennsylvania soldier reported. Still outnumbered more than two to one, the Confederates forced a standoff in the bloodiest single day of the Civil War, a day participants thought would never end.

At Antietam the Union lost 2,108 dead and counted more than 10,000 wounded or missing. Lee's total losses were fewer, but they represented fully a fourth of his entire army. "God has been very kind to us this day," Stonewall Jackson declared with unintentional irony. The next day the battered Confederates slipped south across the Potomac River to the safety of Virginia.

The vainglorious McClellan insisted that he had "fought the battle splendidly," and that "our victory was complete," but Lincoln thought otherwise. Disgusted by McClellan's failure to gain a truly decisive victory, the president sent a curt message to the general: "I have just read your dispatch about sore-tongued and fatigued horses. Will you pardon me for asking what the horses of your army have done . . . that fatigues anything?" Failing to receive a satisfactory answer, Lincoln removed McClellan and assigned him to recruiting duty in New Jersey. Never again would he command troops.

Lincoln with McClellan at his headquarters at Antietam, October 3, 1862.

FREDERICKSBURG   Lee's failed invasion of the North dashed the Confederacy's hopes of foreign recognition. Yet the war was far from over. In his search for a fighting general, Lincoln now made the worst choice of all. He turned to Ambrose E. Burnside, who had twice before turned down the job on the grounds that he felt unfit for so large a command. But if the White House wanted him to fight, he would attack even in the face of oncoming winter.

On December 13, 1862, Burnside sent the Army of the Potomac across the icy Rappahannock River to assault Lee's forces, well entrenched on ridges and behind stone walls west of Fredericksburg. Confederate artillery and muskets chewed up the blue columns as they crossed a mile of open land outside the town. It was, a Federal general sighed, "a great slaughter-pen." The scene was both awful and awesome, prompting Lee to remark: "It is well that war is so terrible—we should grow too fond of it." After taking more than 12,000 casualties compared to fewer than 6,000 for the Confederates, Burnside wept as he gave the order to withdraw.

The year 1862 ended with forces in the East deadlocked and the Union advance in the West stalled since midyear. Union morale reached a low ebb; northern Democrats were calling for a negotiated peace. At the same time, Lincoln was under pressure from the so-called Radical Republicans, who were pushing for more stringent war measures and questioning the competence of the president. At the same time, General Burnside was under fire from his own officers, some of whom were ready to testify publicly to his shortcomings.

But amid the dissension the deeper currents of the war were turning in favor of the Union: in a lengthening war its superior resources began to tell. In both the Eastern and Western Theaters, the Confederate counterattack had been repulsed. And while the armies clashed, Lincoln by the stroke of a pen had changed the conflict from a war to restore the Union into a revolutionary struggle for the abolition of slavery. On January 1, 1863, he signed the Emancipation Proclamation.

EMANCIPATION

At the war's outset, Lincoln had promised to restore the Union but maintain slavery where it existed. Congress too endorsed that position. Once fighting began, the need to hold the border states in the Union dictated caution on the volatile issue of emancipation. Beyond that, several other considerations deterred action. For one, Lincoln had to cope with a deep-seated racial prejudice in the North. Where most abolitionists promoted both complete emancipation and the social integration of the races, many antislavery activists only wanted slavery prohibited from the new territories and states. They were willing to allow slavery to continue in the South and were uneasy about racial integration. Lincoln himself harbored doubts about his authority to emancipate slaves so long as he clung to the view that the states remained legally in the Union. The only way around the problem would be to justify emancipation as a military necessity.

A MEASURE OF WAR The war forced the issue. As Federal forces pushed into the Confederacy, fugitive slaves began to turn up in Union army camps, and generals did not know whether to declare them free or not. Some put the "contrabands" to work building fortifications; others set them free.

Lincoln began to edge toward emancipation. In March 1862 he proposed that federal compensation be offered any state that began gradual emancipation. The plan failed in Congress because of border-state opposition, but on April 16, 1862, Lincoln signed an act that abolished slavery in the District of Columbia; on June 19 another act excluded

Former slaves, or "contrabands," on a farm in Cumberland Landing, Virginia,
1862.

slavery from the territories, without offering owners compensation. A Second Confiscation Act, passed on July 17, liberated the slaves of all persons aiding the rebellion. Still another act forbade the army to help return runaways to their border-state owners.

To save the Union, Lincoln finally decided, complete emancipation would be required for several reasons: slave labor bolstered the Rebel war effort, sagging morale in the North needed the lift of a moral cause, and public opinion was swinging that way as the war dragged on. Proclaiming a war on slavery, moreover, would end forever any chance that France or Britain would support the Confederacy. In July 1862 Lincoln first confided to his cabinet that he was considering issuing a proclamation that under his war powers would free the slaves of the enemy. At the time, Secretary of State William Seward advised him to wait for a Union victory in order to avoid any semblance of desperation.

The time to act finally came after the Battle of Antietam. It was a dubious victory, but it did force Lee's withdrawal. On September 22 Lincoln issued a preliminary Emancipation Proclamation, in which he repeated that his object was mainly to restore the Union and that he favored proposals for paying slaveholders for their losses. But the main burden of the document was his warning that on January 1, 1863, "all persons held as slaves within any state, or designated part of a state, the people whereof shall be in rebellion against the United States, shall be then, thenceforward and forever free." On January 1, 1863, Lincoln signed the second Emancipation Proclamation, giving effect to his promise of September, again emphasizing that this was a war measure based on his war powers. He also urged blacks to abstain from violence except in self-defense, and he added that free blacks would now be received into the armed service of the United States.

REACTIONS TO EMANCIPATION   Among the Confederate states, Tennessee and the Union-controlled parts of Virginia and Louisiana were exempted from the proclamation. The Emancipation Proclamation thus freed no slaves who were within Union lines at the time. But these objections missed a point that black slaves readily grasped. "In a document proclaiming liberty," wrote the historian Benjamin Quarles, "the unfree never bother to read the fine print." Though most slaves deemed it safer just to wait for the "day of jubilee" when Union forces

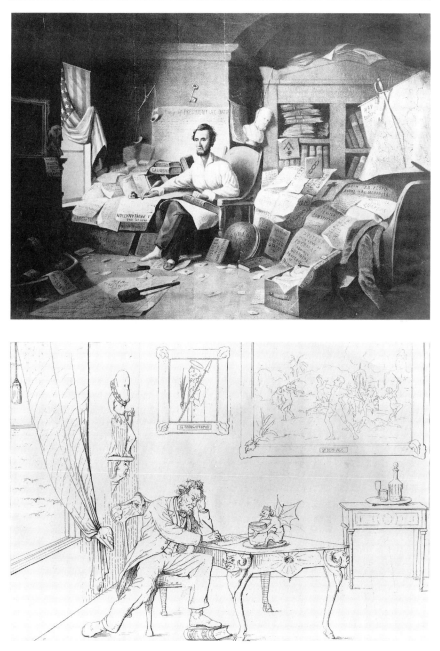

Two views of the Emancipation Proclamation. *The Union view (top) shows a thoughtful Lincoln composing the Proclamation with the Constitution and the Holy Bible in his lap. The Confederate view (bottom) shows a demented Lincoln with his foot on the Constitution using an inkwell held by the devil.*

arrived, some actively claimed their freedom. One spectacular instance was that of the black harbor pilot Robert Smalls, who one night took over a small Confederate gunboat, the *Planter,* and sailed his family through Charleston Harbor out to the blockading Union fleet. Later he served the Union navy as a pilot and still later became a congressman.

BLACKS IN THE MILITARY   From very early in the war Union commanders found "contrabands" like Smalls useful as guides to unfamiliar terrain and waterways, informants on the enemy, and at the very least common laborers. While menial labor by blacks was familiar enough to whites, military service was something else again. Though not unprecedented, it aroused in whites embedded racial fears. For more than a year, the Lincoln administration warily evaded the issue of allowing blacks in the armed forces.

Lincoln's Emancipation Proclamation reaffirmed the policy that blacks could enroll in the armed services and sparked new efforts to organize all-black units, to be led by white officers. Massachusetts organized the first northern all-black unit, the Massachusetts Fifty-fourth Regiment under Colonel Robert Gould Shaw. Rhode Island and other states soon followed suit. In May the War Department authorized general recruitment of blacks across the country. This was a

The 107th U.S. Colored Infantry.

momentous decision, for it changed a war to preserve the Union into a revolution to transform the social, economic, and racial status quo in the South. When one black soldier encountered his former master, now a prisoner of war, the former slave said, "Hello, Massa, bottom rail on top now."

By mid-1863 black units were involved in significant action in both the Eastern and Western Theaters. On July 18, 1863, Colonel Shaw, a Harvard graduate who was the son of a prominent abolitionist, led his black troops in a courageous assault against Fort Wagner, a massive earth-work barrier guarding Charleston, South Carolina. During the battle almost half of the Fifty-fourth Regiment were killed, including Colonel Shaw, who was slain while leading his men over the parapet.

The courageous performance of the Fifty-fourth Regiment, and the use of African-American units in the Vicksburg campaign, did much to win acceptance both for black soldiers and for emancipation, at least as a proper stratagem of war. Commenting on Union victories at Port Hudson and Milliken's Bend, Mississippi, Lincoln reported that "some of our commanders . . . believe that . . . the use of colored troops constitutes the heaviest blow yet dealt to the rebels, and that at least one of these important successes could not have been achieved . . . but for the aid of black soldiers."

By the end of the war, almost 180,000 African Americans served

This photograph of "Drummer" Jackson, a former slave who served in the 79th U.S. Colored Troops, was circulated to encourage African Americans to enlist.

in the regiments of the United States Colored Troops, providing around 10 percent of the Union army total. Some 80 percent of the "colored troops" were former slaves or free blacks from the South. The African-American soldiers encountered prejudice and skepticism within the Union ranks, but they persevered. Some 38,000 gave their lives. In the navy blacks accounted for about a fourth of all enlistments; of these more than 2,800 died.

As the war entered its final months, freedom emerged more fully as a legal reality. Three major steps occurred in January 1865, when both Missouri and Tennessee abolished slavery by state action and the House of Representatives passed an abolition amendment. Upon ratification by three-fourths of the reunited states, the Thirteenth Amendment became part of the Constitution on December 18, 1865, and removed any lingering doubts about the legality of emancipation. By then, in fact, slavery remained only in the border states of Kentucky and Delaware.

WOMEN AND THE WAR

While breaking the bonds of slavery, the Civil War also loosened traditional restraints on female activity. "No conflict in history," a journalist wrote at the time, "was such a woman's war as the Civil War." Women on both sides and of both races played prominent roles in the conflict, and in the process many saw their outlook and status transformed. Initially the call to arms revived heroic images of female self-sacrifice and domestic skills. Women north and south sewed uniforms, composed uplifting poetry and songs, and raised money and supplies. Thousands of northern women worked with the United States Sanitary Commission, which organized medical relief and other services for soldiers. Others, both black and white, supported the freedmen's-aid movement to help impoverished freed slaves.

In the North alone, some 20,000 women served as nurses or other health-related volunteers. Nursing was as arduous an enterprise as soldiering. A nurse working at a Maryland hospital recorded that she and her peers "endured the cold without sufficient bedding for our hard beds, and with no provision made for our fires. On bitter mornings we rose shivering, broke the ice in our pails, and washed our numb hands and faces, then went out into the raw air, up to our mess room, also without fire, thence to the wards." Perhaps the two most famous nurses were Dorothea Dix and Clara Barton, both untiring volunteers in service to the wounded and dying. Dix, the veteran reformer of the nation's insane asylums, became the Union army's first Superintendent of Women Nurses. She soon found herself flooded with applications from around the country. Dix explained that nurses should be "sober, earnest, self-sacrificing, and self-sustained" women between the ages of thirty-five and fifty who could "bear the presence of suffering and exercise entire self control" and be "calm, gentle, quiet, active, and steadfast in duty."

Clara Barton oversaw the distribution of vital medicines to Union troops and later founded the American Red Cross.

Born in 1821, Clara Barton was the fifth child of a Massachusetts family of modest means. She became an itinerant schoolteacher impatient with the gender discrimination of the day. Barton fought for equal pay and eventually became one of the first female clerks in the United States Patent Office in Washington, D.C. But she remained frustrated by her desire to find "something to do that *was* something." She discovered such fulfilling work as a nurse in the Civil War. Instead of accepting an assignment to a general hospital, she followed the troops on her own, working in makeshift field hospitals. At Antietam she came so close to the fighting that a Confederate bullet ripped through the sleeve of her dress and killed the man she was aiding.

Confederate Sally Tompkins of Richmond was equally unstinting. She and six others attended to 1,333 wounded men in her private hospital and kept all but 73 of them alive, a performance unmatched by any other hospital, North or South. Tompkins and Barton challenged both male doctors' control of battlefield medicine and male bureaucrats' efforts to restrict the nurses' sphere of operations. In this way the war experience of women helped generate greater confidence in their own abilities and produced female activists such as Annie Wittenmeyer of Iowa, who would become the first president of the Women's Christian Temperance Union, and Josephine Shaw Lowell, who would direct a variety of charitable organizations.

The departure of hundreds of thousands of men for the battlefields forced women to assume the public and private roles the men left behind. With three out of four white men of military age in the Confederate armed forces, southern women were especially forced to assume new responsibilities. In many southern towns and counties, the home front became a world of white women, children, and slaves. A resident of Lexington, Virginia, reported in 1862 that there were "no men left" in town by mid-1862.

Women suddenly found themselves in charge of households, farms, and businesses. They became farmers or plantation managers, clerks, munitions plant workers, and schoolteachers. In North Carolina in 1860, for example, only 7 percent of teachers were women. By the end of the Civil War, a majority of the state's teachers were women. Some 400 women disguised themselves as men and fought in the war; dozens worked as spies; others traveled with the armies, cooking meals, writing letters, and assisting with amputations.

Not all women, however, accepted being cast in the new roles required by the war. Many among the slaveholding elite found themselves woefully unprepared for their new duties. The Confederacy never found enough women willing to serve as nurses. Many genteel women could not cook, sew, or knit, and they balked at the idea of daily cleaning. One of them complained that she "was too delicately raised for such work." Those who still owned slaves during the war expressed reluctance at managing them alone. A few slaves took advantage of the departure of their male masters and murdered their white mistresses.

The war's unrelenting carnage and demands eventually eroded the martial enthusiasm of some home-front stalwarts. A North Carolina mother lost seven sons in the fighting; another lost four, all at Gettysburg. Women who bore such loss or who witnessed daily suffering while serving as nurses were permanently altered by the experience. Still other women experienced what a West Virginia writer described as the "long, nervous strain" of waiting for news from the front. "No matter how gentle or womanly we might be, we read, we talked, we thought perforce of nothing but slaughter." And the war's effects were enduring. The number of widows, spinsters, and orphans mushroomed. Many bereaved women on both sides came to look on the war with what the poet Emily Dickinson called a "chastened stare." Northerner Julia Ward Howe recalled that after the war ended many battle-scarred women in one way or another refused to revert to their "chimney corner life of the fifties." They struggled to find causes to serve or work to do outside the home.

GOVERNMENT DURING THE WAR

Striking the shackles from 4 million slaves and loosening the restraints on female activity constituted a momentous social and economic revolution. But an even broader revolution began as power in Congress shifted from South to North with secession. Before the war, southern congressmen had been able to frustrate the designs of both Free Soilers and Whigs. But once the secessionists abandoned Congress to the Republicans, a dramatic change occurred. Several projects that had been stalled by sectional controversy were adopted before the end of 1862. A new protective tariff was passed. A transcontinental railroad was approved to run through Omaha, Nebraska, to Sacramento, California. A homestead act granted 160 acres to settlers who agreed to work the land for five years. The National Banking Act followed in 1863. Two other key pieces of legislation were the Morrill Land Grant Act (1862), which provided federal aid to state colleges of "agriculture and mechanic arts," and the Contract Labor Act (1864), which encouraged the importation of immigrant labor. All of these had great long-term significance to the expansion of the national economy—and federal government.

UNION FINANCES Congress focused on three options to finance the war: higher taxes, printing paper money, and borrowing. The higher taxes came chiefly in the form of the Morrill Tariff on imports and excise taxes placed on manufactures and the practice of nearly every profession. A butcher, for example, had to pay 30¢ for every head of beef he slaughtered, 10¢ for every hog, 5¢ for every sheep. On top of the excises came an income tax. In 1862, Congress passed the Internal Revenue Act which created a Bureau of Internal Revenue.

But federal tax revenues trickled in so slowly—in the end they would meet only 21 percent of wartime expenditures—that Congress in 1862 resorted to printing paper money. Beginning with the Legal Tender Act of 1862, Congress ultimately authorized $450 million of the paper currency, which soon became known as "greenbacks" because of their color. The congressional decision to allow the Treasury to print paper money was a profoundly important development for the American economy, then and since. Unlike previous paper currencies issued by local banks, the federal greenbacks could not be exchanged for gold or silver. Instead, their value relied on public trust in the government. Many bankers were outraged by the advent of greenbacks. "Gold and silver are the only true measure of value," one financier declared. "These metals were prepared by the Almighty." But the crisis of the Union and the desperate need to finance the expanding civil war demanded such a solution. "I prefer gold to paper money," explained Senator John Sherman. "But there is no other resort. We must have money or a fractured Government." As the months passed, the greenbacks helped ease the Union's financial crisis without causing the ruinous inflation that the unlimited issue of paper money caused in the Confederacy.

The federal government also relied on the sale of bonds. A Philadelphia banker named Jay Cooke (sometimes tagged "the Financier of the Civil War") mobilized a nationwide machinery of agents and propaganda to sell government bonds to private investors. Eventually bonds amounting to more than $2 billion were sold. New banks formed under the National Banking Act of 1863 were required to invest one-third of their capital in the bonds and to deposit them with the Treasury Department. They were also encouraged to invest even more of their capital as security for the national bank notes they could issue.

For many businessmen, war-related ventures brought quick riches. Some suppliers and financiers bilked the government or provided shoddy goods. Not all the wartime fortunes, however, were made dishonestly. And the war-related expenditures by the Union helped promote the capital accumulation with which American businesses fueled later expansion. Wartime business thus laid the groundwork for the fortunes of tycoons such as J. P. Morgan, John D. Rockefeller, Andrew Mellon, and Andrew Carnegie and for the economic boom after the war.

CONFEDERATE FINANCES Confederate finances were a disaster from the start. In the first year of its existence, the Confederacy levied export and import duties, but exports and imports were too low to generate much revenue. It then enacted a tax of one-half of 1 percent on most forms of property, which should have yielded a hefty income, but the Confederacy farmed out its collection of the taxes to the states, promising a 10 percent rebate on the take. The result was chaos.

In 1863 the Confederate Congress passed a revenue measure that, like Union excises, taxed nearly everything. A 10 percent tax in kind on all agricultural products did more to outrage farmers and planters than to supply the army, however. Enforcement of the taxes was poor and evasion easy.

Altogether, taxes covered no more than 5 percent of Confederate costs, perhaps less; bond issues accounted for less than 33 percent; and Treasury notes for more than 66 percent. The last resort, the printing press, was in fact one of the early resorts. Altogether the Confederacy turned out more than $1 billion in paper money and sparked a steep inflation. By 1864 a turkey sold in the Richmond market for $100, flour brought $425 a barrel, home calls by doctors were $30, meal cost $72 a bushel, and bacon was $10 a pound.

CONFEDERATE DIPLOMACY   Confederate diplomacy focused on gaining foreign supplies, diplomatic recognition, and perhaps even military intervention. The Confederates indulged the pathetic hope that diplomatic recognition would prove decisive, when in fact it more likely would have followed decisive victory in the field, which never came. An equally fragile illusion was the conviction that King Cotton would lure military aid and political sympathy from countries around the world dependent upon the fiber.

The first Confederate emissaries to England and France took hope when the British foreign minister received them informally after their arrival in London in 1861; they even won a promise from France's Napoleon III to recognize the Confederacy if Britain would lead the way. But the British foreign minister refused to receive the Confederates again, partly because of Union pressures and partly out of British self-interest.

One incident early in the war threatened to upset British neutrality. In November 1861 a Union warship stopped a British ship, the *Trent*, and took into custody two Confederate agents, James M. Mason and John Slidell, en route from Havana to Europe. Celebrated as a heroic deed by a northern public still starved for victories, the *Trent* affair roused a storm of protest in Britain. London sent Lincoln an ultimatum for the captives' release. To interfere with a neutral ship on the high seas violated long-settled

American principle, and Seward finally decided to release Mason and Slidell, much to their own chagrin. As martyrs in Boston, they were more useful to their own cause than they could ever be in London and Paris.

Confederate agents in Europe were far more successful in getting supplies than in gaining official government recognition of the Confederacy as a sovereign nation. The most spectacular feat was the purchase of raiding ships designed to attack Union vessels around the world. Although British law forbade the sale of warships to belligerents, a Confederate commissioner contrived to have the ships built and then, on trial runs, to escape to the Azores or elsewhere for outfitting with guns. In all, eighteen such ships were activated and saw action in the Atlantic, Pacific, and Indian Oceans, where they sank hundreds of Yankee ships and threw terror into the rest. The most spectacular of the Confederate raiders were the first two, the *Florida* and the *Alabama*, which captured thirty-eight and sixty-four Union ships, respectively.

UNION POLITICS AND CIVIL LIBERTIES   On the home fronts, the crisis of war brought no moratorium on partisan politics, North or South. Within his own party Lincoln faced a Radical wing composed mainly of prewar abolitionists. Led by House members such as Thaddeus Stevens and George W. Julian, and senators such as Charles Sumner, Benjamin F. Wade, and Zachariah Chandler, the Radical Republicans pushed for confiscation of plantations, immediate emancipation of slaves, and a more vigorous prosecution of the war. The majority of Republicans, however, continued to back Lincoln's more cautious approach. The party was generally united on economic policy.

The Democratic party suffered the loss of its southern wing and the death of its leader, Stephen A. Douglas, in June 1861. By and large, northern Democrats supported a war for the "Union as it was" before 1860, giving reluctant support to Lincoln's policies but opposing restraints on civil liberties and the new economic legislation. "War Democrats" such as Senator Andrew Johnson and Secretary of War Edwin M. Stanton fully supported Lincoln's policies, however, while a Peace Wing of the party preferred an end to the fighting, even at risk to the Union. An extreme fringe of the Peace Wing even flirted with outright disloyalty. The "Copperheads," as they were called, were strongest in states such as Ohio, Indiana, and Illinois, all leavened with native southerners, some of whom were pro-Confederate.

Such open sympathy for the enemy provoked Lincoln to crack down hard. Early in the war he assumed emergency powers, including the power to suspend the writ of habeas corpus, which entitles people arrested to a speedy hearing. Lincoln also subjected "disloyal" persons to martial law. The Constitution said only that habeas corpus could be suspended in cases of rebellion or invasion, but congressional leaders argued that Congress alone had authority to take such action. By the Habeas Corpus Act of 1863, Congress finally authorized the president to suspend the writ. It required officers to report the names of all arrested persons to the nearest district court, and provided that if the grand jury found no indictment, those arrested could be released upon taking an oath of allegiance.

There were probably more than 14,000 arrests made without recourse to a writ of habeas corpus. Most of those arrested were Confederate citizens accused of slipping vessels through the Union blockade, or foreign nationals. But Union citizens were also detained. One celebrated case

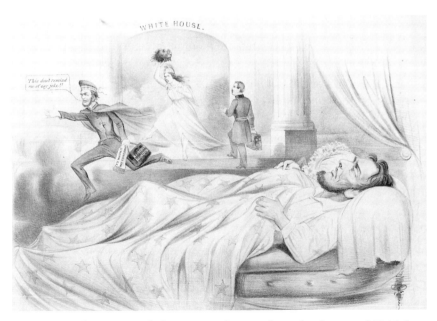

This cartoon depicts Lincoln having a nightmare about the election of 1864. In the dream, Lady Liberty brandishes the severed head of a black man at the door of the White House as General McClellan walks up the steps at the right and Lincoln runs away at the left.

arose in 1863 when Federal soldiers hustled the Democrat Clement L. Vallandigham out of his home in Dayton, Ohio. A military court condemned Ohio's most prominent Confederate sympathizer to confinement for the duration of the war because he had questioned arbitrary federal arrests. The muzzling of a political opponent proved such an embarrassment to Lincoln that he commuted the sentence, but only by another irregular device, banishment behind the Confederate lines. Vallandigham eventually found his way to Canada. In 1863 he ran as the Democratic candidate for Ohio governor *in absentia,* and in 1864 he slipped back into the country. He was left alone at Lincoln's order, took part in the Democratic national convention, and ultimately his pro-southern stance proved more of an embarrassment to the Democrats than to the president.

At their 1864 national convention in Chicago, the Democrats called for an immediate end to the war to be followed by a national convention that would restore the Union. They named General George B. McClellan as their candidate, but he distanced himself from the peace platform by declaring that agreement on Union would have to precede peace.

Radical Republicans, who still regarded Lincoln as soft on treason, tried to thwart his nomination, but he outmaneuvered them at every turn. Lincoln promoted the vice-presidential nomination of Andrew Johnson, a War Democrat from Tennessee, on the "National Union" ticket, so named to minimize partisanship. As the war dragged on through 1864, however, with Grant taking heavy losses in Virginia, Lincoln fully expected to lose the election. Then Admiral David Farragut's capture of Mobile in August and General Sherman's capture of Atlanta on September 2 turned the tide. McClellan carried only New Jersey, Delaware, and Kentucky, with 21 electoral votes to Lincoln's 212, and 1.8 million popular votes (45 percent) to Lincoln's 2.2 million (55 percent).

CONFEDERATE POLITICS Unlike Lincoln, Jefferson Davis never had to contest a presidential election. He and his vice-president, Alexander Stephens, were elected without opposition in 1861 for a six-year term. But discontent flourished as the war dragged on. Food grew scarce, and prices skyrocketed. A bread riot in Richmond on April 2, 1863, ended only when Davis himself persuaded the mob (mostly women) to disperse. After the Confederate congressional elections of 1863, the second and last in the Confederacy, about a third of the legislators were anti-administration. Although parties as such did not figure in the elections, it was noteworthy that many ex-Whigs and other opponents of secession were chosen.

Davis, like Lincoln, had to contend with dissenters. Many southern Unionists followed their states into the Confederacy reluctantly, and were receptive to talk of peace. They were less troublesome to Davis, however, than the politicians who had embraced secession and then guarded states' rights against the central government as zealously as they had against the Union. Georgia, and to a lesser degree North Carolina, were strongholds of such sentiment, which prevailed widely elsewhere as well. The states'-rights advocates challenged, among other things, the legality of the military draft, taxes on farm produce, and above all the suspension of habeas corpus. Vice-President Stephens carried on a running battle against Davis's effort to establish "military despotism," and he eventually left Richmond to sulk at his Georgia home for eighteen months.

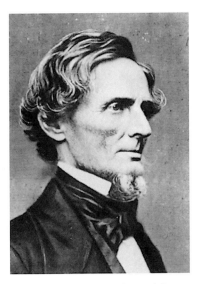

Jefferson Davis, president of the Confederacy.

Among other fatal flaws, the Confederacy suffered from an excess of dogma. Where Lincoln was the consummate pragmatist, Davis was a brittle ideologue with a waspish temper. His fundamental insecurity made him indecisive. But once he made a decision, nothing could change his mind. One southern politician said that Davis was "as stubborn as a mule." Davis could never find it in himself to admit that he had made a mistake. Such a personality was ill suited to the chief executive of an infant—and fractious—nation.

THE FALTERING CONFEDERACY

CHANCELLORSVILLE   After the Union disaster at Fredericksburg, Lincoln's search for a capable general turned to one of Burnside's disgruntled lieutenants, Joseph E. Hooker, whose pugnacity had earned him the nickname of "Fighting Joe." With a force of perhaps 130,000 men, the largest Union army yet gathered, and a brilliant plan, Hooker suffered a loss of control and failed his leadership test at Chancellorsville, Virginia, May 1–5, 1863. Lee, with perhaps half that number of troops, staged what became a textbook example of daring and maneuver. Hooker's plan was to leave his base, opposite Fredericksburg, on a sweeping movement upstream across the Rappahannock and Rapidan Rivers to flank Lee's position. A diversionary force was to cross below the town. Lee, however, sniffed out the ruse and pulled his main forces back to meet Hooker. The Union general lost sight of his opponents and panicked. At Chancellorsville, after a preliminary skirmish, Lee divided his army again, sending Stonewall Jackson's famous foot soldiers on a long march to hit the enemy's exposed right flank.

On May 2, toward evening, Jackson surprised the Federals at the edge of a densely wooded area called the Wilderness, but the fighting

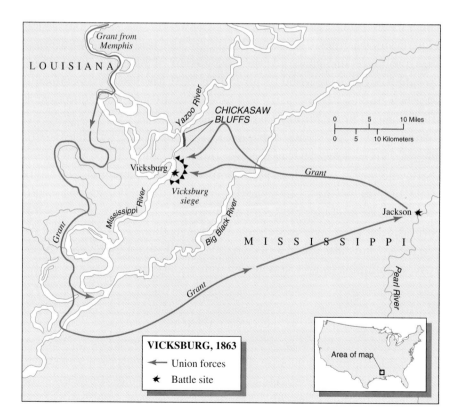

VICKSBURG, 1863

← Union forces

★ Battle site

died out in confusion as darkness fell. Jackson rode out beyond the skirmish line to locate the Union forces. Fighting erupted in the darkness, and nervous Confederates mistakenly opened fire on Jackson, who was struck by three bullets that shattered his left arm and right hand. The next day, a surgeon amputated his arm. He seemed to be recovering well, but then contracted the dreaded pneumonia. Jackson assured his surgeon that "I am not afraid to die." A few hours later he uttered his last words: "Let us cross over the river and rest under the shade of the trees." He had been an utterly fearless general famous for leading rapid marches, bold flanking movements, and furious assaults. "I have lost my right arm," Lee lamented, and "I do not know how to replace him."

The next day, Lee forced Hooker's army back across the Rappahannock. It was the peak of Lee's career, but Chancellorsville was his last significant victory—and his costliest: the South lost 1,600 soldiers. After Chancellorsville the hinges of fate began to close the door on the brief career of the Confederacy.

VICKSBURG   While Lee held the Federals at bay in the East, a reinstated Ulysses Grant had been inching his army down the Mississippi River toward the Confederate stronghold of Vicksburg in western Mississippi. Grant knew that if he could capture Vicksburg, the Union forces could gain control of the Mississippi River and thereby split the Confederacy in two. Located on a bluff 200 feet above the river, Vicksburg had withstood repeated naval attacks. Grant positioned his army about fifteen miles north of the city, but the surrounding bayous proved to be impassable, and Grant gave up the idea of a northern approach. He crossed over to Louisiana and while the navy ran gunboats and transports past the Confederate batteries at Vicksburg, he moved south to meet them at the end of April. From there Grant swept eastward on a campaign that Lincoln later called "one of the most brilliant in the world," took Jackson, Mississippi, where he seized or destroyed supplies, then turned westward and on May 18 pinned the 30,000 Confederates inside Vicksburg. He resolved to wear them down by bombarding and starving them.

GETTYSBURG   The plight of besieged Vicksburg put the Confederate high command in a quandary. Joseph E. Johnston, now in charge of the western Confederate forces, wanted to lure Grant's army into Tennessee and thereby relieve the siege of Vicksburg. Lee had another

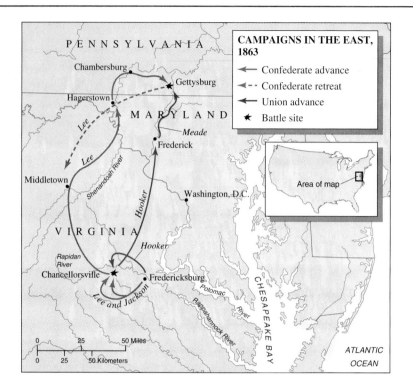

idea for a diversion. If he could win a major battle on northern soil, he might do more than save Vicksburg; he might also convince northern public opinion to end the war. In June he moved his army northward again across Maryland.

Hooker followed the Confederates, keeping his forces between Lee's army and Washington. But demoralized by defeat at Chancellorsville and quarrels with Henry Halleck, general-in-chief of Union forces, he turned in his resignation. On June 28 Major-General George G. Meade took over Hooker's command. Neither side chose Gettysburg, Pennsylvania, as the site for the war's climactic battle, but a Confederate scavenging party entered the town in search of shoes and encountered units of Union cavalry on June 30. The main forces quickly converged on that point. On July 1 the Confederates pushed the Federals out of the town, but into stronger positions on high ground to the south. Meade hastened reinforcements to his new lines along the heights. On July 2 Lee, hampered by a lack of information because of the inexcusable absence of J. E. B. Stuart's cavalry, mounted furious assaults at both the extreme left and right flanks of Meade's army, but in vain. Union general James Longstreet said that it was the "best three hours' fighting I had seen done by any troops on any battle-field."

The next day Lee staked everything on one final assault on the Union center at Cemetery Ridge. His plan suffered from a fatal problem: his generals were not unified in their support of it. As a result, Longstreet, who remained skeptical of a frontal assault, did not position his forces to assist the division led by General George Pickett that Lee had ordered to take Cemetery Ridge.

About 2 P.M. Pickett's 15,000 troops emerged from the woods into the brilliant sunlight, formed neat ranks, and began their suicidal advance uphill across open ground commanded by Union artillery. "Pickett's Charge" was as hopeless as Burnside's assault at Fredericksburg. In fact, the Union defenders shouted "Fredericksburg!"—their taunts delivered between volleys. The few Confederates who got within range of hand-to-hand combat were quickly overwhelmed. At the head of Pickett's division were the University Greys, thirty-one college students from Mississippi. Within an hour after their assault, every one of them was killed or wounded. Surveying the grisly scene, a Confederate captain confessed: "We gained nothing but glory, and lost our bravest men." As he watched the few survivors returning from the bloody field, General Lee muttered: "All this has been my fault." He then told Pickett to regroup his division to repulse a possible counterattack, only to have Pickett tartly

Harvest of Death. *T. H. O'Sullivan's grim photograph of the dead at Gettysburg.*

reply, "General Lee, I have no division now." Pickett never forgave Lee. Years later he charged: "That old man had my division slaughtered."

With nothing left to do but retreat, on July 4 Lee's dejected and mangled army, with about a third of its number gone, began to slog south through a driving rain. They had failed in all their purposes, not the least being to relieve the pressure on Vicksburg. On that same July 4, the Confederate commander at Vicksburg surrendered his entire garrison after a forty-seven-day siege. Four days later the last remaining Confederate stronghold on the Mississippi River, Port Hudson, under siege since May by Union forces, gave up. "The father of waters," Lincoln said, "flows unvexed to the sea." The Confederacy was irrevocably split. Had Meade pursued Lee, he might have delivered the *coup de grace* before the Rebels could get back across the flooded Potomac, but yet again the winning army failed to capitalize fully on its victory.

After the furious fighting at Gettysburg ended, a group of northern states funded a military cemetery for the 6,000 soldiers killed in the battle. On November 19, 1863, the new cemetery was officially dedicated. In his brief remarks, President Lincoln eloquently expressed the pain and sorrow of the brutal civil war. The prolonged conflict was testing whether a nation "dedicated to the proposition that all men are created equal . . . can long endure." Lincoln said that all living Americans must ensure that the "honored dead" had not "died in vain." In stirring words that continue to inspire, Lincoln predicted that "this nation, under God, shall have a new birth of freedom—and that government of the people, by the people, and for the people, shall not perish from the earth."

CHATTANOOGA The third great Union victory of 1863 occurred in fighting around Chattanooga, the railhead of eastern Tennessee and gateway to northern Georgia. In the late summer, a Union army led by General William Rosecrans took Chattanooga and then rashly pursued General Braxton Bragg's Rebel forces into Georgia, where they met at Chickamauga. The battle (September 19–20) had the makings of a Union disaster, since it was one of the few times when the Confederates had a numerical advantage (about 70,000 to 56,000). Only the stubborn stand of Union troops under George H. Thomas (thenceforth "the Rock of Chickamauga") prevented a general rout. The battered Union forces fell back into Chattanooga, while Bragg held the city virtually under siege from the heights to the south and east.

Rosecrans seemed stunned and apathetic, but Lincoln urged him to hang on: "If we can hold Chattanooga, and East Tennessee, I think rebellion must dwindle and die." The Union command sent reinforcements from Virginia, while Grant and Sherman arrived with more from the West. Grant, given overall command of the Western Theater of operations on October 16, pushed his way into Chattanooga a few days later, forcing open a supply route as he came. He replaced Rosecrans with Thomas. On November 24 the Federals began to move, hitting the Confederate flanks at Lookout Mountain and Signal Hill while Thomas created a diversion at the center. The Union troops took Lookout Mountain in what was mainly a feat of mountaineering, but Sherman's forces stalled at Signal Hill. On the second day of the battle, Union forces dislodged the Rebels atop Missionary Ridge.

Bragg was unable to regroup his forces until they were many miles to the south, and the Battle of Chattanooga was the end of his active career. Jefferson Davis reluctantly replaced Bragg with Joseph E. Johnston. Soon after the battle the Federals linked up with Burnside, who had taken Knoxville, and proceeded to secure their control of eastern Tennessee.

Chattanooga had another consequence. The Union victory at Missionary Ridge confirmed the impression of Grant's genius. Lincoln had at last found his general. In 1864 Grant arrived in Washington to assume the rank of lieutenant-general and a new position as general-in-chief. Halleck became chief of staff and continued in his role as channel of communication between the president and commanders in the field. Within the Union armies at least, a modern command system was emerging; the Confederacy never had a unified command.

General Ulysses S. Grant at his headquarters in City Point, now Hopewell, Virginia.

The Confederacy's Defeat

During the winter of 1863–1864, Confederates began to despair of victory. A War Department official in Richmond reported in his diary a spreading "sense of hopelessness." At the same time, Mary Chesnut of South Carolina reported that "gloom and despondency hang like a pall everywhere." Union leaders, sensing the momentum swinging their way, stepped up the pressure on Confederate forces.

The Union command's main targets now were Lee's army in Virginia and General Joseph Johnston's in Georgia. Grant personally would accompany George Meade, who retained direct command over the Army of the Potomac; operations in the West were entrusted to Grant's long-time lieutenant, William T. Sherman. As Sherman put it later, Grant "was to go for Lee, and I was to go for Joe Johnston." Grant brought with him a new strategy against Lee. Where his predecessors had all hoped for the climactic single battle, he adopted a policy of attrition. He would attack, attack, attack, keeping the pressure on the Confederates, grinding down their numbers and their will to fight. As he ordered Meade, "Wherever Lee goes, there you will go also." Grant would also

Sketch by Alfred R. Waud depicting General Philip Henry Sheridan's ride at the battle of Cedar Creek, Virginia, October 19, 1864. Artists like Waud traveled with the soldiers and rendered quick and accurate sketches of battle scenes.

wage total war, confiscating or destroying any and all civilian property of military use. It was a brutal and costly—but effective—plan.

GRANT'S PURSUIT OF LEE   In May 1864, Grant's Army of the Potomac, numbering about 115,000 to Lee's 65,000, moved south across the Rappahannock and Rapidan Rivers into the Wilderness, where Hooker had come to grief in the Battle of Chancellorsville. In the Battle of the Wilderness (May 5–6), the armies fought blindly through the woods, the horror and suffering of the scene heightened by crackling brushfires. Grant's men suffered heavier casualties than the Confederates, but the Rebels were running out of replacements. Always before when bloodied by Lee's troops, Union forces had pulled back to nurse their wounds, but Grant slid off to his left and continued his relentless advance southward, now toward Spotsylvania Court House. "Whatever happens," he assured Lincoln, "we will not retreat."

There the opposing armies settled down for five days of bloody warfare, May 8–12. But again Grant's forces slid off to the left of Lee's army and kept moving. Along the banks of the Chickahominy River, the two sides clashed again at Cold Harbor (June 1–3). Grant ordered his troops to assault the heavily entrenched Confederate lines. As the Confederates had discovered at Gettysburg, such a frontal assault was murder.

The tattered colors of the 56th and 36th Massachusetts regiments, marching through Virginia, 1864.

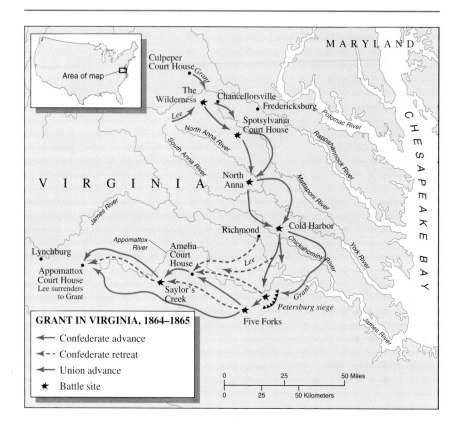

GRANT IN VIRGINIA, 1864–1865

← Confederate advance

◄-- Confederate retreat

← Union advance

★ Battle site

The Union army was massacred at Cold Harbor. In twenty minutes, almost 7,000 attacking Federals were killed or wounded. Grant later admitted that the attack was his greatest mistake. Critics called him "the Butcher" after Cold Harbor. Battered and again repulsed, Grant brilliantly maneuvered his battered forces around Lee and headed for Petersburg, south of Richmond, where the major railroads converged.

The two armies then dug in for a siege along lines that extended for twenty-five miles above and below Petersburg. Grant telegraphed Lincoln that he intended "to fight it out on this line if it takes all summer." Lincoln replied: "Hold on with a bulldog grip, and chew and choke as much as possible." For nine months the two armies faced each other down while Grant kept pushing toward his left flank to break the railroad arteries that were Lee's lifeline. During this time, Grant's troops, twice as large as the Confederate army, were generously supplied by Union vessels moving up the James River, while Lee's forces, beset by hunger, cold, and desertion, wasted away. Petersburg had become Lee's prison while disasters piled up for the Confederacy elsewhere.

SHERMAN'S MARCH   When Grant headed south, so did Sherman—toward the railroad hub of Atlanta, with 90,000 men against Joseph Johnston's 60,000. Sherman's campaign, like Grant's, developed into a war of maneuver, but without the pitched battles. Sherman kept moving to his right, but the wily Johnston was always one step ahead of him—turning up in secure positions along the north Georgia ridges, including at Kennesaw Mountain, drawing Sherman farther from his Chattanooga base, harassing the Union supply lines. But Johnston's skillful defensive tactics caused an impatient President Davis finally to replace him with the combative but reckless John B. Hood. He was a natural fighter but an inept strategist who did not know the meaning of retreat. Having had an arm crippled by a bullet at Gettysburg and most of one leg shot off at Chickamauga, he had to be strapped to his horse. Three times in eight days Hood's army lashed out at the Union lines, each time meeting a bloody rebuff. Sherman at first resorted to a siege of Atlanta, then slid off to the right again, cutting the rail lines below Atlanta. Hood evacuated the city on September 1, but kept his army intact.

Sherman now laid plans for a march through central Georgia, where no organized Confederate armies remained. His intention was to "whip the rebels, to humble their pride, to follow them into their inmost recesses, and make them fear and dread us." Hood meanwhile had hatched an equally audacious plan. He would slip out of Georgia into northern Alabama and push on into Tennessee, forcing Sherman into pursuit. Sherman refused to take the bait, although he did send a Union force led by General George Thomas back to Tennessee to keep watch. So the

William Tecumseh Sherman.

Ruins of Georgia Railroad Roundhouse at Atlanta, 1864. *In the wake of Sherman's march, abandoned locomotives and twisted rails marked the destruction in Atlanta.*

curious spectacle unfolded of the main armies moving off in opposite directions. But it was a measure of the Confederates' plight that Sherman could cut a swath of destruction across Georgia with impunity, while Hood was soon outnumbered again, this time in Tennessee.

In the Battle of Franklin (November 30), Hood sent his army across two miles of open ground. Six waves broke against the Union lines, leaving the ground strewn with Confederate dead. With what he had left, Hood dared not attack Nashville, nor did he dare withdraw for fear of final disintegration. Finally, in the Battle of Nashville (December 15–16), the Federals broke and scattered what was left of the Confederate Army of Tennessee. The Confederate front west of the Appalachians had collapsed.

During all this, Sherman's army was marching through Georgia, waging total war against the people's resources and against their will to resist. In his effort to demoralize the civilian populace, Sherman was determined to "make Georgia howl." On November 15, 1864, he destroyed Atlanta's warehouses and railroad facilities while spreading fires that consumed about a third of the city. Against the advice of Lincoln and Grant, Sherman's army of over 60,000 Midwesterners

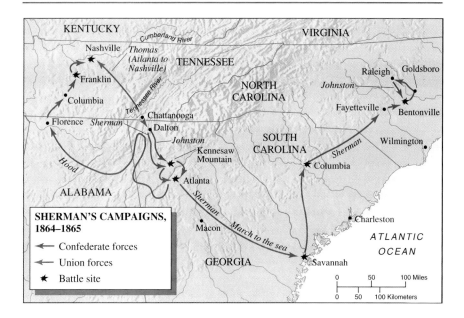

SHERMAN'S CAMPAIGNS, 1864–1865

← Confederate forces
← Union forces
★ Battle site

headed into "the bowels of the Confederacy." The Union army then moved southeast in four columns over a front twenty to sixty miles wide, living off the land and destroying any provisions that might serve Confederate forces. Bands of stragglers and deserters from both armies joined in looting along the flanks, while Union cavalry destroyed Rebel supplies to keep them out of enemy hands.

More than any other general, Sherman recognized the connection between the South's economy, its morale, and its ability to wage war. He explained that "we are not only fighting hostile armies, but a hostile people" who must be made to "feel the hard hand of war." He wanted the rebels to "fear and dread us." When, after a month of ravaging the Georgia countryside, Sherman's army arrived in Savannah on the coast, his forces had destroyed over $100 million of property, freed over 40,000 slaves, and burned many plantations. A Macon, Georgia, newspaper said Sherman was a "demon" willing to plumb the "depths of depravity" in wreaking his campaign of vengeance.

Pushing across the Savannah River into that "hell-hole of secession," South Carolina, Sherman's men wrought even greater destruction. More than a dozen towns were burned in whole or part, including the state capital of Columbia, captured on February 17, 1865. Meanwhile, Charleston's defenders abandoned the city and headed north to join a ragtag Rebel army that Joseph E. Johnston was desperately pulling together in North Carolina. Johnston mounted one final attack on Sherman's army at Bentonville (March 19–20), but that was his last major battle.

APPOMATTOX   During this final season of the Confederacy, Grant kept pushing, probing, and battering the entrenched Rebels around Petersburg, Virginia. The Confederates were slowly starving. Their trenches were filled with rats and lice. Scurvy and dysentery were rampant. News of Sherman's progress through Georgia and South Carolina added to the gloom and the impulse of weary Rebels to desert. Lee began to lay plans for his besieged, starving forces to escape and join Johnston's army in North Carolina. At Five Forks (April 1, 1865), Grant finally cut the last rail line to Petersburg, and the next day Lee's army of 35,000 emaciated men abandoned Richmond and Petersburg in a desperate flight southwest toward Lynchburg and rails south. President Davis, exhausted but still defiant, gathered what archives and treasure he could and made it out by train ahead of the advancing Federals, only to be captured in Georgia by Union cavalry on May 10.

By then the Confederacy was already dead. Lee had moved out of Petersburg with Grant in hot pursuit, and soon found his escape route cut off. On April 9 (Palm Sunday) the tall and stately Lee donned a crisp dress uniform and met the mud-spattered Grant, short and round-shouldered, in the parlor of the McLean home at Appomattox to tender his surrender. Grant, at Lee's request, let the Rebel officers keep their sidearms and permitted soldiers to keep personal horses and mules. As the gaunt, hungry Confederate troops formed ranks for the last time, Joshua Chamberlain, the Union general in charge

Robert E. Lee. *Matthew Brady took this photograph in Richmond eleven days after Lee's surrender at Appomattox.*

of the surrender ceremony, ordered his Federal soldiers to salute their foes as they paraded past. His Confederate counterpart signaled his men to do likewise. General Chamberlain remembered that there was not a sound—no trumpets or drums, no cheers or jeers, simply an "awed stillness . . . as if it were the passing of the dead." On April 18, General Joseph Johnston surrendered his Confederate army to General Sherman near Durham, North Carolina. The remaining Confederate forces surrendered during May.

A MODERN WAR

The Civil War was in many respects the first modern war. Its scope was unprecedented. One out of every twelve adult American males served in the war, and few families were unaffected by the event. Over 620,000 Americans died in the conflict, 50 percent more than in World War II. Because battlefield surgeons were constantly overworked and frequently lacked equipment, supplies, and knowledge, almost any stomach or head wound proved fatal, and gangrene was rampant. Fifty thousand of the survivors returned home with one or more limbs amputated. Disease, however, was the greatest threat to soldiers, killing twice as many as were lost in battle.

The Civil War was not neatly self-contained; it was a total war, fought not solely by professional armies but by and against whole societies. Farms became battlefields, cities were transformed into armed encampments, and homes were commandeered for field hospitals. After one battle, a woman recalled that "wounded men were brought into our house and laid side by side in our halls and first-story rooms . . . carpets were so saturated with blood as to be unfit for further use."

The Civil War was also modern in that much of the killing was distant, impersonal, and mechanical. The opposing forces used an array of new weapons and instruments of war: artillery with "rifled" or grooved barrels for greater accuracy, repeating rifles, ironclad ships, observation balloons, and wire entanglements. Men were killed without even knowing who had fired the shot that felled them.

The debate over why the North won and the South lost the Civil War will probably never end, but as in other modern wars firepower and manpower were essential factors. Lee's own explanation of the Confederate defeat retains an enduring legitimacy: "After four years of arduous service marked by unsurpassed courage and fortitude, the Army of Northern Virginia has been compelled to yield to overwhelming numbers and resources."

MAKING CONNECTIONS

- Certain fiscal measures enacted during the Civil War (when southerners were not in Congress to block them) helped fuel the postwar economic growth (see Chapter 20).

- The Confederacy's defeat had a tremendous impact on all dimensions of life in the South, as Chapter 19 (on the New South) demonstrates.

FURTHER READING

The best one-volume overview of the Civil War period is James M. McPherson's *Battle Cry of Freedom: The Civil War Era* (1988). A good introduction to the military events is Herman Hattaway's *Shades of Blue and Gray: An Introductory Military History of the Civil War* (1997). The outlook and experiences of the common soldier are explored in James M. McPherson's *For Cause and Comrades: Why Men Fought in the Civil War* (1997) and Earl J. Hess's *The Union Soldier in Battle: Enduring the Ordeal of Combat* (1997).

For emphasis on the South, turn first to Gary W. Gallagher's *The Confederate War* (1997). For a sparkling account of the birth of the Rebel nation, see William C. Davis's *"A Government of Our Own": The Making of the Confederacy* (1994). The same author provides a fine biography of the Confederate president in *Jefferson Davis: The Man and His Hour* (1992).

Analytical scholarship on the military conflict includes Joseph L. Harsh's *Confederate Tide Rising: Robert E. Lee and the Making of Southern Strategy, 1861–1862* (1998), Steven E. Wordworth's *Jefferson Davis and His Generals: The Failure of Confederate Command in the West* (1990), and Paul D. Casdorph's *Lee and Jackson: Confederate Chieftains* (1992). Lonnie R. Speer's *Portals to Hell: The Military Prisons of the Civil War* (1997) details the ghastly experience of prisoners of war.

The history of the North during the war is surveyed in Philip S. Paludan's *"A People's Contest": The Union and Civil War, 1861–1865* (1988) and J. Matthew Gallman's *The North Fights the Civil War: The Home Front* (1994).

The central northern political figure, Abraham Lincoln, is the subject of many books. Two good biographies are David H. Donald's *Lincoln* (1995) and Stephen B. Oates's *With Malice toward None* (1977). The election of 1864 is treated in John C. Waugh's *Reelecting Lincoln: The Battle for the 1864 Presidency* (1998). On Lincoln's assassination, see William Hanchett's *The Lincoln Murder Conspiracies* (1983).

Concerning specific military campaigns, see Larry J. Daniel's *Shiloh: The Battle That Changed the Civil War* (1997), Thomas Goodrich's *Black Flag: Guerrilla Warfare on the Western Border, 1861–1865* (1995), Stephen W. Sears's *Landscape Turned Red: The Battle of Antietam* (1983) and *To the Gates of Richmond: The Peninsula Campaign* (1993), James Lee McDonough and James Pickett Jones's *War So Terrible: Sherman and Atlanta* (1992), Robert Garth Scott's *Into the Wilderness with the Army of the Potomac* (1985), and Albert Castel and Laura K. Poracsky's *Decision in the West: The Atlanta Campaign of 1864* (1992).

The experience of the black soldier is surveyed in Joseph T. Glatthaar's *Forged in Battle: The Civil War Alliance of Black Soldiers and White Officers* (1989) and Ira Berlin, Joseph P. Reidy, and Leslie S. Rowland's *Freedom's Soldiers: The Black Military Experience in the Civil War* (1998). For the black woman's experience, see Jacqueline Jones's *Labor of Love, Labor of Sorrow: Black Women, Work and the Family from Slavery to the Present* (1985).

Recent gender and ethnic studies include *Divided Houses: Gender and the Civil War*, edited by Catherine Clinton and Nina Silber

(1992), Drew Gilpin Faust's *Mothers of Invention: Women of the Slaveholding South in the American Civil War* (1997), George C. Rable's *Civil Wars: Women and the Crisis of Southern Nationalism* (1989), and William L. Burton's *Melting Pot Soldiers: The Union's Ethnic Regiments* (2nd ed., 1998).

18 ❧ RECONSTRUCTION:
NORTH AND SOUTH

CHAPTER ORGANIZER

This chapter focuses on:

- the different approaches to Reconstruction.

- congressional efforts to reshape southern society.

- the role of African Americans in the early postwar years.

- national politics in the 1870s.

*I*n the spring of 1865 the cruel war was over. At a frightful cost of 620,000 lives and the destruction of the southern economy and much of its landscape, American nationalism had emerged triumphant, and nearly 4 million slaves had seized their freedom. Ratification of the Thirteenth Amendment in December 1865 abolished slavery throughout the Union. But peace had come only on the battlefields. "Cannon conquer," recognized a northern editor, "but they do not necessarily convert." Now the North faced the task of re-uniting the nation, coming to terms with the abolition of slavery, and "reconstructing" a ravaged and resentful South.

THE WAR'S AFTERMATH

In the war's aftermath, important questions faced the victors in the North: Should the Confederate leaders be tried for treason? How should new governments be formed? How and at whose expense was the South's economy to be rebuilt? Should debts incurred by Confederate state governments be honored? Who should pay to rebuild the South's railroads and public buildings, dredge the clogged southern harbors, and restore damaged levees? What was to be done with the freed slaves? Were they to be given land? social equality? education? voting rights? Such complex questions required sober reflection and careful planning, but policy makers did not have the luxury of time or the benefits of consensus.

DEVELOPMENT IN THE NORTH   To some Americans the Civil War had been more truly a social revolution than the War of Independence, for it reduced the once-dominant power of the South's planter elite in national politics and elevated the power of the northern "captains of industry." Government became more friendly to business leaders and unfriendly to those who would probe into their activities. The wartime Republican Congress had delivered on the major platform promises of 1860, which had cemented the allegiance of northeastern businessmen and western farmers to the party of free labor.

In the absence of southern members, Congress during the war had centralized national power and enacted the Republican economic agenda. It passed the Morrill Tariff, which doubled the average level of import duties. The National Banking Act created a uniform system of banking and bank-note currency, and helped to finance the war. Congress also passed legislation guaranteeing that the first transcontinental railroad would run along a north-central route from Omaha, Nebraska, to Sacramento, California, and it donated public lands and public bonds to ensure its financing. In the Homestead Act of 1862, moreover, Congress voted free homesteads of 160 acres to settlers. They only had to occupy the land for five years to gain title. The Morrill Land Grant Act of the same year conveyed to each state 30,000 acres of federal land per member of Congress from the state. The sale of some of the land provided funds to create colleges of "agriculture and mechanic arts." Such measures helped stimulate the North's economy in the years after the Civil War.

DEVASTATION IN THE SOUTH   The postwar South, where most of
the fighting had occurred, offered a sharp contrast to the victorious
North. Along the path of General William T. Sherman's army, one observer reported in 1866, the countryside "looked for many miles like a
broad black streak of ruin and desolation." Columbia, South Carolina,
said another witness, was "a wilderness of ruins," Charleston a place of
"vacant houses, of widowed women, of rotting wharves, of deserted
warehouses, of weed-wild gardens, of miles of grass-grown streets, of
acres of pitiful and voiceless barrenness." In 1866 fully one-fifth of
Mississippi's state revenues went to purchase artificial limbs for returning Confederate soldiers. The border states of Missouri and Kentucky
had experienced a guerrilla war that lapsed into postwar anarchy as marauding bands of bushwhackers turned into outlaws. The most notorious were the James boys, Frank and Jesse.

Throughout the South, property values had collapsed. Confederate
bonds and paper money were worthless; most railroads were damaged
or destroyed. Cotton that had escaped destruction was seized by federal
troops. Emancipation of the slaves wiped out perhaps $4 billion in-
vested in human flesh and left the labor system in disarray. The great
age of expansion in the cotton market was over. Not until 1879 would

The "burned district" of Richmond, Virginia, April 1865.

the cotton crop again equal the record harvest of 1860; tobacco production did not regain its prewar level until 1880; the sugar crop of Louisiana not until 1893; and the old rice industry of the Tidewater and the hemp industry of the Kentucky Blue Grass never regained their prewar status.

A TRANSFORMED SOUTH   The defeat of the Confederacy transformed much of southern society. The freeing of slaves, the destruction of property, and the free fall in land values left many planters destitute and homeless. Amanda Worthington, a planter's wife from Mississippi, saw her whole world destroyed. In the fall of 1865, she assessed the damage: "None of us can realize that we are no longer wealthy—yet thanks to the yankees, the cause of all unhappiness, such is the case."

Genteel southerners found themselves forced to rebuild lives and families without the help of slaves. Women accustomed to relying on slaves for their every need were unprepared for the tasks at hand. "I did the washing for six weeks," one tired woman wrote, "[and] came near ruining myself for life as I was too delicately raised for such hard work." Those who still had some money after the war often recruited former slaves to work as domestic servants. Now, however, they had to pay for their services.

After the Civil War many former Confederates were so embittered by defeat that they abandoned their native region rather than submit to "Yankee rule." Some migrated to Canada, Europe, Mexico, South America, and Asia. Others preferred the western territories and states. Still others moved north, settling in northern and midwestern cities on the assumption that educational and economic opportunities would be better among the victors.

Those who remained in the South found old social roles reversed. One Confederate army captain reported that on his father's plantation "Our negroes are living in great comfort. They were delighted to see me with overflowing affection. They waited on me as before, gave me breakfast, splendid dinners, etc. But they firmly and respectfully informed me: 'We own this land now. Put it out of your head that it will ever be yours again.'"

Union troops that fanned out across the defeated South were cursed and spat upon. A Virginia woman expressed a spirited defiance common among her circle of friends: "Every day, every hour, that I live increases my hatred and detestation, and loathing of that race. They [Yankees] disgrace our common humanity. As a people I consider them vastly inferior to the better classes of our slaves." Fervent southern nationalists, both men and women, planted in their children a similar hatred of Yankees and a defiance of northern rule. One mother said that she trained her children to "fear God, love the South, and live to avenge her."

LEGALLY FREE, SOCIALLY BOUND In the former Confederate states, the newly freed slaves suffered most of all. According to the black abolitionist Frederick Douglass, the former slave remained dependent: "He had neither money, property, nor friends. He was free from the old plantation, but he had nothing but the dusty road under his feet. . . . He was turned loose, naked, hungry, and destitute to the open sky."

A few northerners argued that what the ex-slaves needed most was their own land. But even dedicated abolitionists shrank from proposals to confiscate white-owned land and distribute it to the freed slaves. Citizenship and legal rights were one thing, wholesale confiscation of property and land redistribution quite another. Discussions of land distribution, however, fueled false rumors that freed slaves would get

According to a former Confederate general, recently freed blacks had "nothing but freedom."

"forty acres and a mule," a slogan that swept the South at the end of the war. Instead of land or material help, the freed slaves more often got advice and moral platitudes.

THE FREEDMEN'S BUREAU   On March 3, 1865, Congress set up within the War Department the Bureau of Refugees, Freedmen, and Abandoned Lands, to provide "such issues of provisions, clothing, and fuel" as might be needed to relieve "destitute and suffering refugees and freedmen and their wives and children." Agents of the Freedmen's Bureau were entrusted with negotiating labor contracts (something new for both blacks and planters), providing medical care, and setting up schools, often in cooperation with northern agencies such as the American Missionary Association and the Freedmen's Aid Society. The bureau had its own courts to deal with labor disputes and land titles, and its agents were further authorized to supervise trials involving blacks in other courts.

White intransigence and the failure to grasp the intensity of racial prejudice increasingly thwarted the efforts of Freedmen's Bureau agents to protect and assist the former slaves. Congress was not willing

The Freedmen's Bureau set up schools such as this throughout the former Confederate states.

to strengthen the powers of the Freedmen's Bureau to reflect such problems. Beyond temporary relief measures, no program of Reconstruction ever incorporated much more than constitutional and legal rights for freedmen. These were important in themselves, of course, but the extent to which even these should go was very uncertain, to be settled more by the course of events than by any clear-cut commitment to social and economic equality.

THE BATTLE OVER RECONSTRUCTION

The problem of reconstructing the South politically centered on deciding what governments would constitute authority in the defeated states. This problem arose first in the state of Virginia at the very beginning of the Civil War, when the thirty-five western counties of Virginia refused to go along with secession. In 1861 a loyal state government of Virginia was proclaimed at Wheeling, and this government in turn formed a new state called West Virginia, admitted to the Union in 1863. As Union forces advanced into the South, Lincoln in 1862 named military governors for Tennessee, Arkansas, and Louisiana. By the end of the following year he had formulated a plan for regular governments in those states and any others that might be liberated from Confederate rule.

LINCOLN'S PLAN AND CONGRESS'S RESPONSE Acting under his pardon power, President Lincoln issued in late 1863 a Proclamation of Amnesty and Reconstruction, under which any rebel state could form a Union government whenever a number equal to 10 percent of those who had voted in 1860 took an oath of allegiance to the Constitution and the Union and had received a presidential pardon. Participants also had to swear support for laws and proclamations dealing with emancipation. Certain groups, however, were excluded from the pardon: civil and diplomatic officers of the Confederacy; senior officers of the Confederate army and navy; judges, congressmen, and military officers of the United States who had left their federal posts to aid the rebellion; and those accused of failure to treat captured black soldiers and their officers as prisoners of war.

Under this plan, governments loyal to the Union appeared in Tennessee, Arkansas, and Louisiana, but Congress recognized them neither by representation nor in counting the electoral votes of 1864. In the absence of any specific provisions for Reconstruction in the Constitution, politicians disagreed as to where authority properly rested. Lincoln claimed the right to direct Reconstruction under the clause that set forth the presidential pardon power, and also under the constitutional obligation of the United States to guarantee each state a republican form of government. Republican congressmen, however, argued that this obligation implied that Congress, not the president, should supervise Reconstruction.

A few conservative and most moderate Republicans supported Lincoln's program of immediate restoration. The small but influential group of Radical Republicans, however, favored a sweeping transformation of southern society based on granting freedmen full-fledged citizenship. The Radicals hoped to reconstruct southern society so as to mirror the North's emphasis on small-scale capitalism. This meant thwarting the efforts of the old planter class to reestablish a caste system and keep the freed blacks in a state of peonage.

The Radicals were talented, earnest men who insisted that Congress control the Reconstruction program. To this end, they helped pass in 1864 the Wade-Davis Bill, sponsored by Senator Benjamin Wade of Ohio and Representative Henry Winter Davis of Maryland. In contrast to Lincoln's 10 percent plan, the Wade-Davis Bill required that a majority of white male citizens declare their allegiance and that only those who could take an "ironclad" oath (required of federal officials since 1862) attesting to their *past* loyalty could vote or serve in the state constitutional conventions. The conventions, moreover, would have to abolish slavery, exclude from political rights high-ranking civil and military officers of the Confederacy, and repudiate debts incurred during the conflict.

Passed during the closing day of the session, the Wade-Davis Bill never became law. Lincoln exercised a pocket veto. That is, he simply refused to sign it, but he issued an artful statement that he would accept any state back into the Union that preferred to present itself under the congressional plan. In retaliation, furious Republicans penned the Wade-Davis Manifesto, which accused the president, among other sins, of usurping power and attempting to use readmitted states to ensure his reelection.

Lincoln offered his last view of Reconstruction in his final public address, on April 11, 1865. Speaking from the White House balcony, he pronounced that the Confederate states had never left the Union. These states were simply "out of their proper practical relation with the Union," and the object was to get them "into their proper practical relation." At a cabinet meeting, Lincoln proposed to get new southern state governments in operation before Congress met in December. He described the Radical Republicans as possessing feelings of hate and vindictiveness with which he did not sympathize and could not participate. He wanted "no persecution, no bloody work," no radical restructuring of southern social and economic life.

THE ASSASSINATION OF LINCOLN   On the evening of April 14, Lincoln went to Ford's Theater and his rendezvous with death. With his trusted bodyguard called away to Richmond and with the policeman assigned to his box away from his post watching the play, Lincoln was helpless as John Wilkes Booth slipped into the presidential box. Booth, a crazed actor and Confederate zealot, blocked the door to the box and fired his derringer point-blank at the president's head. He then stabbed Lincoln's aide and jumped from the box onto the stage, crying *"Sic semper tyrannis"* (Thus always to tyrants), the motto of Virginia.

The funeral procession for President Lincoln.

The president died nine hours after he had been shot. Accomplices of Booth had also targeted Vice-President Andrew Johnson and Secretary of State William Seward. Seward and four others, including his son, were victims of severe but not fatal stab wounds. Johnson escaped injury, however, because his would-be assassin got cold feet and wound up tipsy in the barroom of Johnson's hotel.

The nation extracted a full measure of vengeance from the conspirators. Booth was pursued into Virginia and shot in a burning barn. His last words were: "Tell Mother I die for my country. I thought I did for the best." Three of Booth's collaborators were convicted by a military court and hanged, along with the woman at whose boardinghouse they had plotted. Three others got life sentences, including a Maryland doctor who set the leg Booth had broken when he jumped to the stage. President Johnson eventually pardoned them all, except one who died in prison. Apart from those cases, however, there was only one other execution in the aftermath of war: Confederate Henry Wirz, who commanded the infamous prison at Andersonville, Georgia, where Union prisoners were probably more the victims of war conditions than of deliberate cruelty.

JOHNSON'S PLAN   Lincoln's death suddenly elevated to the White House Andrew Johnson of Tennessee, a man whose state was still in legal limbo and whose party affiliation was unclear. He was a War Democrat (pro-Union) who had been put on the Union ticket in 1864 as a gesture of unity. Of humble origins like Lincoln, Johnson had moved as a youth from his birthplace in Raleigh, North Carolina, to Greeneville, Tennessee, where he became proprietor of a tailor shop. Self-educated with the help of his wife, he had made himself into an effective orator of the rough-and-tumble school, served as mayor, congressman, governor, and senator, then as military governor of Tennessee before he became vice-president. In the process he had become an advocate of the small farmers against the privileges of the large planters—"a bloated, corrupted aristocracy." He also shared the racial attitudes of most white yeomen. "Damn the negroes," he exclaimed to a friend during the war, "I am fighting those traitorous aristocrats, their masters."

Some of the Radicals at first thought Johnson, unlike Lincoln, to be one of them. Johnson had, for example, once asserted that treason "must be made infamous and traitors must be impoverished." Senator Benjamin Wade loved such language. "Johnson, we have faith in you," he promised.

"By the gods, there will be no trouble now in running this government." But Wade would soon find Johnson to be as unsympathetic as Lincoln, if for different reasons.

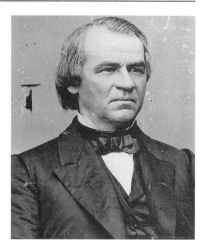

Johnson's loyalty to the Union sprang from a strict adherence to the Constitution and a fervent belief in limited government. Given to dogmatic abstractions that were alien to Lincoln's temperament, he nevertheless arrived by a different route at similar objectives. The states should be quickly brought back into their proper relation to the Union because

Andrew Johnson.

the states and the Union were indestructible. And like many other whites, he found it hard to accept the growing Radical sentiment to provide the vote to blacks. In 1865 Johnson declared that "there is no such thing as reconstruction. Those States have not gone out of the Union. Therefore reconstruction is unnecessary."

Johnson's plan to restore the Union thus closely resembled Lincoln's. A new Proclamation of Amnesty (May 1865) added to those Lincoln had excluded from pardon everybody with taxable property worth more than $20,000. These wealthy planters, bankers, and merchants were the people Johnson believed had led the South into secession. But those in the excluded groups might make special applications for pardon directly to the president, and before the year was out Johnson had issued some 13,000 such pardons.

Johnson followed up his amnesty proclamation with his own plan for readmitting the former Confederate states. In each state a native Unionist became provisional governor with authority to call a convention of men elected by loyal voters. Lincoln's 10 percent requirement was omitted. Johnson called upon the state conventions to invalidate the secession ordinances, abolish slavery, and repudiate all debts incurred to aid the Confederacy. Each state, moreover, was to ratify the Thirteenth Amendment. Lincoln had privately advised the governor of Louisiana to consider giving the vote to some blacks, "the very intelligent and those who have fought gallantly in our ranks." In his final public address he had also endorsed a limited black suffrage. Johnson re-peated Lincoln's advice. He reminded the provisional governor of Mississippi, for example, that the state conventions might "with perfect safety" extend suffrage to blacks with education or with military service so as to "disarm the adversary"—the adversary being "radicals who are wild upon Negro franchise."

The state conventions for the most part met Johnson's requirements. But Carl Schurz, a prominent Missouri politician, found during his visit to the South "an *utter absence of national feeling* . . . and a desire to pre-serve slavery . . . as much and as long as possible." Southern whites had accepted the situation because they thought so little had changed after all. Emboldened by Johnson's indulgence, they ignored his counsels of expediency. Suggestions of black suffrage were scarcely raised in the state conventions and promptly squelched when they were.

SOUTHERN INTRANSIGENCE   When Congress met in December 1865, for the first time since the end of the war, it faced the fact that new state governments were functioning in the postwar South, and they were remarkably like the old ones. Southern voters had acted with ex-treme disregard for northern feelings. Among the new legislative mem-bers presenting themselves were Georgia's Alexander H. Stephens, ex-vice-president of the Confederacy, now claiming a seat in the Sen-ate, four Confederate generals, eight colonels, and six cabinet mem-bers. The Congress forthwith denied seats to all members from the eleven former Confederate states. It was too much to expect, after four bloody years, that the Unionists in Congress would welcome ex-Confederates like prodigal sons.

Furthermore, the new southern state legislatures, in passing re-pressive "Black Codes" restricting the freedom of blacks, demon-strated that they intended to preserve slavery as nearly as possible. As one white southerner stressed, "the ex-slave was not a free man; he was a free Negro," and the Black Codes were intended to highlight the distinction.

The details of the Black Codes varied from state to state, but some provisions were common. Existing marriages, including common-law marriages, were recognized (although interracial marriages were prohibited), and testimony of blacks was accepted in legal cases involv-ing blacks—and in six states, in all cases. Blacks could own property.

They could sue and be sued in the courts. On the other hand, blacks could not own farm lands in Mississippi or city lots in South Carolina; they were required to buy special licenses to practice certain trades in Mississippi; and in some states they could not carry firearms without a license. Blacks were required to enter into annual labor contracts. Dependent children were subject to compulsory apprenticeship and corporal punishment by masters. Unemployed (vagrant) blacks were punished with severe fines, and, if unable to pay, they were forced to labor in the fields for those who paid the courts for this source of cheap labor. To many people it indeed seemed that slavery was on the way back in another guise. The new Mississippi penal code virtually said so: "All penal and criminal laws now in force describing the mode of punishment of crimes and misdemeanors committed by slaves, free negroes, or mulattoes are hereby reenacted, and decreed to be in full force."

Faced with such blatant evidence of southern intransigence, moderate Republicans in the Congress drifted toward Radical views. Having

Slavery Is Dead (?) *Thomas Nast's cartoon suggests that, in 1866, slavery was only legally dead.*

excluded the "reconstructed" southern members, the new Congress set up a Joint Committee on Reconstruction, with nine members from the House and six from the Senate, to gather evidence of southern efforts to thwart Reconstruction. Initiative on the committee fell to determined Radical Republicans who knew what they wanted: Ben Wade of Ohio, George W. Julian of Indiana—and most conspicuously of all, Thaddeus Stevens of Pennsylvania and Charles Sumner of Massachusetts.

THE RADICAL REPUBLICANS Most Radical Republicans had been connected with the antislavery cause for decades. In addition, few could escape the bitterness bred by the long and bloody war or remain unaware of the partisan advantage that would come to the Republican party from black suffrage. The Republicans needed black votes to maintain their control of Congress and the White House. Also they needed to disenfranchise former Confederates to keep them from helping elect Democrats who would restore the old southern ruling class to power. In public, however, the Radical Republicans rarely disclosed such partisan self-interest. Instead they asserted that the Republicans, the party of Union and freedom, could best guarantee the fruits of victory and that extending voting rights to blacks would be the best way to promote their welfare.

The growing conflict of opinion over Reconstruction policy brought about an inversion in constitutional reasoning. Secessionists—and Andrew Johnson—were now arguing that the Rebel states had in fact remained in the Union, and some Radical Republicans were contriving arguments that they had left the Union after all. Thaddeus Stevens argued that the Confederate states were now conquered provinces, subject to the absolute will of the victors, and that the "whole fabric of southern society must be changed." Charles Sumner maintained that the southern states, by their pretended acts of secession,

Senator Charles Sumner, a leading Radical Republican.

had reverted to the status of unorganized territories subject to the will of Congress. But few ever took such ideas seriously. Republicans converged instead on the "forfeited-rights theory," later embodied in the report of the Joint Committee on Reconstruction. This held that the states as entities continued to exist, but by the acts of secession and war, they had forfeited "all civil and political rights under the constitution." And Congress, not the president, was the proper authority to determine how such rights might be restored.

JOHNSON'S BATTLE WITH CONGRESS   A long year of political battling remained, however, before this idea triumphed. By the end of 1865, the Radical Republicans' views had gained a majority in Congress, if one not yet large enough to override presidential vetoes. But the critical year 1866 saw the gradual waning of Andrew Johnson's power and influence; much of this was self-induced. Johnson first challenged Congress in 1866, when he vetoed a bill to extend the life of the Freedmen's Bureau. The measure, he said, assumed that wartime conditions still existed, whereas the country had returned "to a state of peace and industry." Because it was no longer valid as a war measure, the bill violated the Constitution in several ways, he declared. It made the federal government responsible for the care of indigents. It was passed by a Congress in which eleven states were denied seats. And it used vague language in defining the "civil rights and immunities" of blacks. For the time being, Johnson's prestige remained sufficiently intact that the Senate upheld his veto.

Three days after the veto, however, Johnson undermined his already weakening authority with a fiery assault on Radical Republican leaders during an impromptu speech. From that point forward, moderate Republicans backed away from a president who had opened himself to counterattack. The Radical Republicans took the offensive. Johnson was "an alien enemy of a foreign state," Stevens declared. Sumner called him "an insolent drunken brute"—and Johnson was open to the charge because of an incident at his vice-presidential inauguration in 1865. Weakened by illness at the time, he had taken a belt of brandy to get him through the ceremony and, under the influence of fever and alcohol, had become incoherent.

In mid-March 1866 the Radical-led Congress passed the Civil Rights Act. A response to the Black Codes created by unrepentant southern state legislatures, this bill declared that "all persons born in the United States and not subject to any foreign power, excluding Indians not taxed," were citizens entitled to "full and equal benefit of all laws." The grant of citizenship to native-born blacks, Johnson fumed, went beyond anything formerly held to be within the scope of federal power. It would, moreover, "foment discord among the races." Johnson vetoed the bill, but this time, on April 9, 1866, Congress overrode the presidential veto. On July 16 it enacted a revised Freedmen's Bureau Bill, again overriding a veto. From that point on, Johnson steadily lost both public and political support.

THE FOURTEENTH AMENDMENT   To remove all doubt about the constitutionality of the new Civil Rights Act, the Joint Committee recommended a new constitutional amendment, which passed Congress on June 16, 1866, and was ratified by the states on July 28, 1868. The Fourteenth Amendment, however, went far beyond the Civil Rights Act.

The amendment reaffirmed state and federal citizenship for persons born or naturalized in the United States, and it forbade any *state* (the word "state" was important in later litigation) to abridge the "privileges and immunities" of citizens, to deprive any *person* (again an important term) of life, liberty, or property without "due process of law," or to deny any person "the equal protection of the laws." The last three of these clauses have been the subject of many lawsuits resulting in applications not widely, if at all, foreseen at the time. The "due-process clause" has come to mean that state as well as federal power is subject to the Bill of Rights, and it has been used to protect corporations, as legal "persons,"

A cartoon depicting Andrew Johnson as a "cruel uncle" leading two children, "civil rights" and "the freedmen's bureau," into the "veto wood."

from "unreasonable" regulation by the states. Other provisions of the amendment had less far-reaching effects. One section specified that the debt of the United States "shall not be questioned" by the former Confederate states and declared "illegal and void" all debts contracted in aid of the rebellion. Another section specified the power of Congress to pass laws enforcing the amendment.

Johnson's home state was among the first to ratify the Fourteenth Amendment. In Tennessee, which had harbored probably more Unionists than any other Confederate state, the government had fallen under Radical Republican control. The state's governor, in reporting the results to the secretary of the Senate, added: "Give my respects to the dead dog of the White House." His words afford a fair sample of the growing acrimony on both sides of the Reconstruction debates. In May and July, race riots in Memphis and New Orleans added fuel to the flames. Both incidents involved indiscriminate massacres of blacks by local police and white mobs. The carnage, Radical Republicans argued, was the natural fruit of Johnson's policy. "Witness Memphis, witness New Orleans," Senator Charles Sumner cried. "Who can doubt that the President is the author of these tragedies?"

Reconstructing the South

THE TRIUMPH OF CONGRESSIONAL RECONSTRUCTION As 1866 drew to an end, the congressional elections promised to be a referendum on the growing split between Andrew Johnson and the Radical Republicans. Johnson sought to influence voters with a speaking tour of the Midwest, a "swing around the circle," which turned into an undignified shouting contest between Andrew Johnson and his critics. In Cleveland he described the Radical Republicans as "factious, domineering, tyrannical" men, and he foolishly exchanged hot-tempered insults with a heckler. At another stop, while Johnson was speaking from an observation car, the engineer mistakenly pulled the train out of the station, making the president appear quite the fool. Such incidents tended to confirm his image as a "ludicrous boor" and "drunken imbecile," which Radical Republican papers projected. In the congressional elections, the Republicans won over a two-thirds majority in each house, a comfortable margin with which to override any presidential vetoes.

The Congress in fact enacted a new program even before new members took office. Two acts passed in 1867 extended the suffrage to African Americans in the District of Columbia and the territories. Another law provided that the new Congress would convene on March 4 instead of the following December, depriving Johnson of a breathing spell. On March 2, 1867, two days before the old Congress expired, it passed three basic laws promoting congressional Reconstruction over Johnson's vetoes: the Military Reconstruction Act, the Command of the Army Act (an amendment to an army appropriation), and the Tenure of Office Act.

The first of the three acts prescribed new conditions under which the formation of southern state governments should begin all over again. The other two sought to block any effort by the president to obstruct the process. The Command of the Army Act required that all orders from the commander-in-chief go through the headquarters of the general of the army, then Ulysses S. Grant. The Radical Republicans trusted Grant, who was already leaning their way. The Tenure of Office Act required the consent of the Senate for the president to remove any officeholder whose appointment the Senate had to confirm in the first place. The purpose of at least some congressmen was to retain Secretary of War Edwin M. Stanton, the one Radical Republican sympathizer in Johnson's cabinet. But an ambiguity crept into the wording of the act. Cabinet officers, it said, should serve during the term of the president who appointed them—and Lincoln had appointed Stanton, although, to be sure, Johnson was serving out Lincoln's term.

The Military Reconstruction Act was hailed or denounced as the triumphant victory of "Radical" Reconstruction. The act declared that "no legal state governments or adequate protection for life and property now exists in the rebel States. . . ." One state, Tennessee, which had ratified the Fourteenth Amendment, was exempted from the application of the new act. The other ten states were divided into five military districts, and the commanding officer of each was authorized to keep order and protect the "rights of persons and property." To that end he might use military tribunals in place of civil courts. The Johnson governments remained intact for the time being, but new constitutions were to be framed "in conformity with the Constitution of the United States," in conventions elected by male citizens twenty-one and older "of whatever race, color, or previous condition." Each state constitution had to provide the same universal male suffrage. Then, once the consti-tution was ratified by a majority of voters and accepted by Congress, other criteria had to be met. The state legislature had to ratify the Four-teenth Amendment, and once the amendment became part of the Con-stitution, any given state would be entitled to representation in Congress. Persons excluded from officeholding by the proposed amendment were also excluded from participation in the process.

Johnson reluctantly appointed military commanders under the act, but the situation remained uncertain for a time. Some people expected the Supreme Court to strike down the act, and no machinery existed at the time for the new elections. Congress quickly remedied that on March 23, 1867, with the Second Reconstruction Act, which directed the army commanders to register all adult males who swore they were qualified. A Third Reconstruction Act, passed on July 19, directed regis-trars to go beyond the loyalty oath and determine each person's eligibility to take it, and also authorized district commanders to remove and replace officeholders of any existing "so-called state" or division thereof. Before the end of 1867 new elections had been held in all the states but Texas.

Having clipped the president's wings, the Republican Congress moved a year later to safeguard its program from possible interference by the Supreme Court. On March 27, 1868, Congress simply removed the power of the Supreme Court to review cases arising under the Mili-tary Reconstruction Act, which Congress clearly had the right to do under its power to define the Court's appellate jurisdiction. The Court accepted this curtailment of its authority on the same day it affirmed the principle of an "indestructible union" in *Texas* v. *White* (1868). In that case it also asserted the right of Congress to reframe state govern-ments, thus endorsing the Radical Republican point of view.

THE IMPEACHMENT AND TRIAL OF JOHNSON   By 1868, Radical Republicans were convinced that not only did the power of the Supreme Court and the president need to be curtailed, but Johnson himself had to be removed from office. Horace Greeley, the prominent editor of the *New York Tribune,* called Johnson "an aching tooth in the national jaw, a screeching infant in a crowded lecture room. There can be no peace or comfort till he is out."

Johnson, though hostile to the congressional Reconstruction pro-gram, had gone through the motions required of him. He continued, however, to pardon former Confederates and transferred several of the district military commanders who had displayed Radical sympathies. Johnson was revealing himself to be a man of limited ability and narrow vision. He lacked Lincoln's resilience and pragmatism. In the process of promoting his lenient southern strategy, Johnson allowed his temper to get the better of his judgment. He castigated the Radical Republicans as "a gang of cormorants and bloodsuckers who have been fattening upon the country." During 1867, newspapers reported that the differences between Johnson and the Republicans were irreconcilable.

The Republicans unsuccessfully tried to impeach Johnson early in 1867, alleging a variety of flimsy charges, none of which represented an indictable crime. The head of the Secret Service, for example, shared rumors about an alleged presidential affair with a woman seeking pardons for former Confederates. Johnson was also accused of public drunkenness, and one congressman even tried to implicate him in the assassination of Lincoln. After listening to the hodgepodge of charges, a House member from Iowa concluded: "While the President has been guilty of many great follies and wickedness," it is better to "submit to two years of misrule . . . than subject the country, its institutions and its credits to the shock of an impeachment." But the impasse between the congressional leadership and the president continued.

At last, Johnson himself provided the occasion for impeachment when he deliberately violated the Tenure of Office Act in order to test its constitutionality. Secretary of War Edwin Stanton had become a thorn in the president's side, refusing to resign despite his disagreements with Johnson's Reconstruction policy. On August 12, 1867, during a congressional recess, Johnson suspended Stanton and named General Grant in his place. When the Senate refused to confirm Johnson's action, however, Grant returned the office to Stanton.

The Radical Republicans now saw their chance to remove the president, and they were quite explicit about their political purposes. As Charles Sumner declared, "Impeachment is a political proceeding before a political body with a political purpose." The debate in the House was clamorous and vicious. One congressman said Johnson had dragged the robes of his office through the "filth of treason." Another denounced the president as "an ungrateful, despicable, besotted traitorous man—an incubus." Still another called Johnson's advisers "the worst men that ever crawled like filthy reptiles at the footstool of

House of Representatives managers of the impeachment proceedings and trial of Andrew Johnson. Among them were Benjamin Butler (R-Mass., seated left) and Thaddeus Stevens (R-Pa., seated with cane).

power." On February 24, 1868, the Republican-dominated House passed eleven articles of impeachment by a party-line vote of 126 to 47.

Of the eleven articles of impeachment, eight focused on the charge that Johnson had unlawfully removed Stanton and had failed to give the Senate the name of a successor. Article 9 accused the president of issuing orders in violation of the Command of the Army Act. The last two articles in effect charged him with criticizing Congress by "inflammatory and scandalous harangues." Article 11 also accused Johnson of "unlawfully devising and contriving" to violate the Reconstruction Acts, contrary to his obligation to execute the laws. At the very least, it stated, Johnson had tried to obstruct Congress's will while observing the letter of the law.

The Senate trial began on March 5, 1868, and continued until May 26, with Chief Justice Salmon P. Chase presiding. It was a great spectacle before a packed gallery. Witnesses were called, speeches made, and rules of order debated. Johnson wanted to plead his case in person, but his attorneys refused, fearing that his short temper might erupt and hurt his cause. The president thereupon worked behind the scenes to win over undecided Republican senators, offering them a variety of political incentives.

As the weeks passed, the trial grew tedious. Senators slept during the proceedings, spectators passed out in the unventilated room, and poor acoustics prompted repeated cries of "We can't hear." Debate eventually focused on Stanton's removal, the most substantive impeachment charge. Johnson's lawyers argued that Lincoln, not Johnson, had appointed Stanton, so the Tenure of Office Act did not apply to him. At the same time, they claimed (correctly, as it turned out) that the law was unconstitutional.

As the five-week trial ended and the voting began in May 1868, the Senate Republicans could afford only six defections from their ranks to ensure the two-thirds majority needed to convict. In the end, seven moderate Republicans and all twelve Democrats voted to acquit. The final tally was 35–19 for conviction, one vote short of the two-thirds needed for removal from office. The renegade Republicans offered two primary reasons for their controversial votes: they feared damage to the separation of powers among the branches of government if Johnson were removed, and they were assured by Johnson's attorneys that he would stop obstructing congressional policy in the South.

In a moment of high drama, the deciding vote was cast by Edmund Ross, a first-term Kansas Republican who in the days leading up to the verdict was "hunted like a fox" by both sides. He insisted that his decision was an act of courage based on principled constitutional scruples: "If the president must step down upon insufficient proofs and from partisan considerations, the office of president would be degraded" and "ever after subordinated to the legislative will."

Historians have since discovered that Ross was not so principled: he demanded several political favors from Johnson in exchange for his vote. Whatever his motives, Ross's defection infuriated those promoting impeachment. One of his constituents fired off a bitter telegram: "Kansas repudiates you as she does all perjurers and skunks."

Although the Senate failed to remove Johnson, the trial crippled his already weak presidency. During the remaining ten months of his term, he initiated no other clashes with Congress. In 1868 Johnson sought the Democratic presidential nomination but lost to New York governor Horatio Seymour, who then lost to Republican Ulysses Grant in the general election. A bitter Johnson refused to attend Grant's inauguration. His final act as president was to issue a pardon to former Confederate president Jefferson Davis. In 1874, after failed bids for the Senate and the House, Johnson won a measure of vindication with election to the Senate, the only former president ever to do so, but he died a few months later. He was buried with a copy of the Constitution tucked under his head.

As for the impeachment trial, only two weeks after it ended, a Boston newspaper reported that people were amazed at how quickly "the whole subject of impeachment seems to have been thrown into the background and dwarfed in importance" by other events. Moreover, impeachment of Johnson was in the end a great political mistake, for the failure to remove the president damaged Radical Republican morale and support. Nevertheless, the Radical cause did gain something. To blunt the opposition, Johnson agreed not to obstruct the process of Reconstruction, and thereafter Radical Reconstruction began in earnest.

REPUBLICAN RULE IN THE SOUTH   In June 1868 Congress agreed that seven southern states had met the conditions for readmission, all but Virginia, Mississippi, and Texas. Congress rescinded Georgia's admission, however, when the state legislature expelled twenty-eight black members and seated former Confederate leaders. The federal military commander in Georgia then forced the legislature to reseat the black members and remove the Confederates, and the state was compelled to ratify the Fifteenth Amendment before being admitted in July 1870. Mississippi, Texas, and Virginia had returned earlier in 1870, under the added requirement that they too ratify the Fifteenth Amendment. This amendment, submitted to the states in 1869, ratified in 1870, forbade the states to deny any person the vote on grounds of race, color, or previous condition of servitude.

Long before the new governments were established, Republican groups began to spring up in the South, chiefly sponsored by the Union League, founded at Philadelphia in 1862 to promote support for the Union. Emissaries of the League enrolled African Americans and loyal whites, initiated them into the secrets and rituals of the order, and instructed them "in their rights and duties." Their recruiting efforts were so successful that in 1867, on the eve of South Carolina's choice of convention delegates, the League reported eighty-eight chapters, which claimed to have enrolled almost every adult black male in the state.

THE RECONSTRUCTED SOUTH

THE FREED SLAVES   To focus solely on what white Republicans did to reconstruct the defeated South creates the false impression that the freed slaves were simply pawns in the hands of others. In fact, however, southern blacks were active agents in affecting the course of Reconstruction. It was not an easy road, though. Many former Confederates continued to harbor deeply ingrained racial prejudices. They adopted a militant stance against federally imposed changes in southern society. During the era of Reconstruction, whites used terror, intimidation, and violence to suppress black efforts to gain social and economic equality. In July 1866, for instance, a black woman in Clinch County, Georgia, was arrested and given sixty-five lashes for "using abusive language" during an encounter with a white woman. A month later another black woman suffered the same punishment. The Civil War had brought freedom to the slaves, but it did not bring protection against exploitation or abuse. Many former slaves found themselves liberated but destitute after the fighting ended. The mere promise of freedom, however, raised their hopes about achieving a biracial democracy, equal justice, and economic opportunity. "Most anyone ought to know that a man is better off free than as a slave, even if he did not have anything," said the Reverend E. P. Holmes, a black Georgia preacher and former domestic servant. "I would rather be free and have my liberty."

The First African Church at Richmond, Virginia, 1874.

Participation in the Union army or navy gave many freedmen a training ground in leadership. Black military veterans would form the core of the first generation of African-American political leaders in the postwar South. Military service provided many former slaves with the first opportunities to learn to read and write. Army life also alerted them to new opportunities for advancement and respectability. "No negro who has ever been a soldier," reported a northern official after visiting a black unit, "can again be imposed upon; they have learnt what it is to be free and they will infuse their feelings into others." Fighting for the Union cause also instilled a fervent sense of nationalism. A Virginia freedman explained that the United States was "now *our* country—made emphatically so by the blood of our brethren."

Former slaves established independent black churches after the war, churches that would serve as the foundation of African-American community life. In war-ravaged Charleston, South Carolina, the first new building to appear after the war was a black church on Calhoun Street; by 1866 ten more had been built. Blacks preferred the Baptist denomination, in part because of the decentralized structure that allowed each congregation to worship in its own way. By 1890 there were over 1.3 million black Baptists in the South, nearly three times as many as any other black denomination. For many former slaves, churches were the first institutions they owned and controlled. In addition to forming viable new congregations, freed blacks organized thousands of fraternal, benevolent, and mutual-aid societies, clubs, lodges, and associations. Memphis, for example, had over two hundred such organizations; Richmond boasted twice that number.

The freed slaves, both women and men, also hastened to reestablish and reaffirm families. Marriages that had been prohibited during slavery were now legitimized through the assistance of the Freedmen's Bureau. By 1870 a preponderant majority of former slaves lived in two-parent households. One white editor in Georgia, lamenting the difficulty of finding black women to serve as house servants, reported that "every negro woman wants to set up house keeping" for herself and her family. To do so they often had little choice but to become tenant farmers, gaining access to land in exchange for a share of their crop. With little money or technical training, freed slaves faced the prospect of becoming wage laborers. Yet in order to retain as much autonomy as possible over their productive energies and those of their children on both a daily and seasonal basis, many husbands and wives chose sharecropping. This enabled mothers and wives to devote more of their time to domestic needs while still contributing to family income.

Black communities in the postwar South also sought to establish schools. The antebellum planter elite had denied education to blacks because they feared that literate slaves would organize uprisings. After the war the white elite worried that education programs would encourage both poor whites and blacks to leave the South in search of better social and economic opportunities. Economic leaders wanted to protect the competitive advantage afforded by the region's low-wage labor market. "They didn't want us to learn nothin'," one former slave recalled. "The only thing we had to learn was how to work." White opposition to education for blacks made it all the more important to African Americans. South Carolina's Mary Jane McLeod Bethune, the fifteenth child of former slaves and one of the first children in the household born after the Civil War, reveled in the opportunity to gain an education: "The whole world opened to me when I learned to read." She walked five miles to school as a child, earned a scholarship to college, and went on to become the first black woman to found a school that became a four-year college, Bethune-Cookman, in Daytona Beach, Florida.

The general resistance among the former slaveholding class to new education initiatives forced the freed slaves to rely on northern assistance or to take their own initiative. A Mississippi Freedmen's Bureau agent noted in 1865 that when he told a gathering of some 3,000 former slaves that they "were to have the advantages of schools and education, their joy knew no bounds. They fairly jumped and shouted in gladness." Black churches and individuals helped raise the money and often built the schools and paid the teachers. Soldiers who had acquired some reading and writing skills often served as the first teachers, and the students included adults as well as children. A Florida teacher reported that a sixty-year-old former slave woman in her class was so excited by literacy that she "spells her lesson all the evening, then she dreams about it, and wakes up thinking about it."

BLACKS IN SOUTHERN POLITICS   In the postwar South, the new role of African Americans in politics caused the most controversy, then and afterward. If largely illiterate and inexperienced in the rudiments of politics, they were little different from millions of propertyless whites

Black Suffrage. *The Fifteenth Amendment was passed in 1870 and guaranteed the rights of citizens, including the right to vote, regardless of race, color, or previous condition of servitude, on the federal level. But former slaves had been registering to vote and voting in large numbers in state elections since 1867, as shown here.*

enfranchised in the age of Jackson or immigrants taken to the polls by political bosses in New York and other cities after the war. Some freedmen frankly confessed their disadvantages. Beverly Nash, a black delegate in the South Carolina convention of 1868, told his colleagues: "I believe, my friends and fellow-citizens, we are not prepared for this suffrage. But we can learn. Give a man tools and let him commence to use them, and in time he will learn a trade. So it is with voting."

Several hundred black delegates participated in the statewide political conventions. Most had been selected by local political meetings or by churches, fraternal societies, Union Leagues, and black army units from the North, although a few simply appointed themselves. "Some bring credentials," explained a North Carolina black leader, "others had as much as they could to bring themselves, having to escape from their homes stealthily at night" to avoid white assaults. The African-American delegates "ranged all colors and apparently all conditions," but free mulattoes from the cities played the most prominent roles. At Louisiana's

Republican state convention, for instance, nineteen of the twenty black delegates had been born free.

By 1867, however, former slaves began to gain political influence and vote in large numbers, and this revealed emerging tensions within the black community. Some southern blacks resented the presence of northern brethren who moved south after the war, while others complained that few ex-slaves were represented in black leadership positions. Northern blacks and the southern free black elite, most of whom were urban dwellers, tended to oppose efforts to confiscate and redistribute land to the rural freedmen, and many insisted that political equality did not mean social equality. As an Alabama black leader stressed, "We do not ask that the ignorant and degraded shall be put on a social equality with the refined and intelligent." In general, however, unity rather than dissension prevailed, and blacks focused on common concerns such as full equality under the law.

Brought suddenly into politics in times that tried the most skilled of statesmen, many African Americans served with distinction. Nonetheless, the derisive label "black Reconstruction" used by later critics exaggerates black political influence, which was limited mainly to voting, and overlooks the political clout of the large numbers of white Republicans, especially in the mountain areas of the upper South, who also favored the Radical plan for Reconstruction. Only one of the new state conventions, South Carolina's, had a black majority, 76 to 41. Louisiana's was evenly divided racially, and in only two other conventions were more than 20 percent of the members black: Florida's, with 40 percent, and Virginia's, with 24 percent. The Texas convention was only 10 percent black, and North Carolina's 11 percent—but that did not stop a white newspaper from calling it a body consisting of "baboons, monkeys, mules . . . and other jackasses."

In the new state governments, any African-American participation was a novelty. Although some 600 blacks—most of them former slaves—served as state legislators, no black man was ever elected governor, and only a few served as judges. In Louisiana, however, Pinckney Pinchback, a northern black and former Union soldier, won the office of lieutenant-governor and served as acting governor when the white governor was indicted for corruption. Several blacks were elected lieutenant-governors, state treasurers, or secretaries of state. There were two black senators in Congress, Hiram Revels and Blanche K. Bruce,

A lithograph depicting five of the major black political figures of the Reconstruction period: Hiram Revels (top left) and Blanche K. Bruce (center) served in the U.S. Senate; Joseph H. Rainey (bottom left), John R. Lynch (bottom right), and James T. Rapier (top right) in the House of Representatives.

both Mississippi natives who had been educated in the North, and fourteen black members of the House during Reconstruction.

CARPETBAGGERS AND SCALAWAGS The top positions in southern state governments went for the most part to white Republicans, whom the opposition whites soon labeled "carpetbaggers" and "scalawags," depending on their place of birth. The northern opportunists who allegedly rushed South with all their belongings in carpetbags to grab the political spoils were more often than not Union veterans who had arrived as early as 1865 or 1866, drawn South by the hope of economic opportunity and by other attractions that many of them had seen in Union service. Many other so-called carpetbaggers were teachers, social workers, or preachers animated by a missionary impulse.

The "scalawags," or native white Republicans, were even more reviled and misrepresented. A Nashville editor called them the "merest trash that could be collected in a civilized community, of no personal credit or social responsibility." Most "scalawags" had opposed secession, forming a Unionist majority in many mountain counties as far south as Georgia and Alabama, and especially in the hills of eastern Tennessee. Among the "scalawags" were several distinguished figures, including former Confederate general James A. Longstreet, who decided after Appomattox that the Old South must change its ways. He became a successful cotton broker in New Orleans, joined the Republican party, and supported the Radical Reconstruction program. Other "scalawags" were former Whigs attracted by the Republican party's economic program of industrial and commercial expansion.

THE RADICAL REPUBLICAN RECORD   Former Confederates also resented the new state constitutions because of their provisions allowing for black suffrage and civil rights. Yet most remained in effect for some years after the end of Radical Republican control, and later constitutions incorporated many of their features. Conspicuous among Radical innovations were such steps toward greater democracy as requiring universal manhood suffrage, reapportioning legislatures more nearly according to population, and making more state offices elective.

Given the hostile circumstances under which the Radical governments operated, their achievements are remarkable. For the first time in most of the South, they constructed an extensive railroad network and established state school systems, however inadequate and ill-supported at first. Some 600,000 black pupils were in southern schools by 1877. State governments under the Radicals also gave more attention than ever before to poor relief and to orphanages, asylums, and institutions for the deaf and blind of both races. Public roads, bridges, and buildings were repaired or rebuilt. Blacks achieved new rights and opportunities that would never again be taken away, at least in principle: equality before the law and the rights to own property, carry on business, enter professions, attend schools, and learn to read and write.

Yet several of these Republican regimes also engaged in corrupt practices. Bids for contracts were accepted at absurd prices, and public officials took their cut. Public money and public credit were often voted to privately owned corporations, notably railroads, under conditions that invited influence peddling. Corruption was not invented by the Radical

Republican regimes, nor did it die with them. Louisiana's "carpetbag" governor recognized as much: "Why," he said, "down here everybody is demoralized. Corruption is the fashion." In three years Louisiana's government printing bill ran to $1.5 million, about half of which went to a newspaper belonging to the young governor, who left office with a tidy nest egg and settled down to a long life as a planter. At about the same time, Mississippi's Democratic state treasurer embezzled over $315,000.

WHITE TERROR   In general, however, southern whites were hostile to Republican regimes less because of their corruption than because of their inclusion of blacks. Most white southerners remained so conditioned by the social prejudices embedded in slavery that they were unable to conceive of blacks as citizens. In some places hostility to the new biracial regimes turned violent. In Grayson County, Texas, three whites murdered three freed slaves because they felt the need to "thin the niggers out and drive them to their holes."

The prototype of terrorist groups was the Ku Klux Klan (KKK), first organized in 1866 by some young men of Pulaski, Tennessee, as a social club with the costumes, secret ritual, and mumbo-jumbo common to fraternal groups. At first a group of pranksters, they soon turned to intimidation of blacks and white Republicans, and the KKK and its imitators, like Louisiana's Knights of the White Camellia, spread

This Thomas Nast cartoon chides the Ku Klux Klan and the White League for promoting conditions "worse than slavery" for southern blacks after the Civil War.

rapidly across the South in answer to the Republican party's Union League. Klansmen rode about the countryside hiding under masks and robes, spreading horrendous rumors, issuing threats, harassing African Americans, and occasionally wreaking violence and destruction.

Klansmen focused their terror on prominent Republicans, black and white. In Mississippi they killed a black Republican leader in front of his family. Three white "scalawag" Republicans were murdered in Georgia in 1870. That same year an armed mob of whites assaulted a Republican political rally in Alabama, killing four blacks and wounding fifty-four. In South Carolina the Klan was especially active. Virtually the entire white male population of York County joined the Klan, and they were responsible for eleven murders and hundreds of whippings. In 1871 some 500 masked men laid siege to the Union County jail and eventually lynched eight black prisoners. Although most Klansmen were poor farmers and tradesmen, middle-class whites—planters, merchants, bankers, lawyers, doctors, even ministers—also joined the group and participated in its brutalities.

Congress struck back with three Enforcement Acts (1870–1871) to protect black voters. The first of these measures levied penalties on persons who interfered with any citizen's right to vote. A second placed the election of congressmen under surveillance by federal election supervisors and marshals. The third (the Ku Klux Klan Act) outlawed the characteristic activities of the Klan—forming conspiracies, wearing disguises, resisting officers, and intimidating officials—and authorized the president to suspend habeas corpus where necessary to suppress "armed combinations." In 1871, the federal government singled out nine counties in upcountry South Carolina as an example, suspended habeas corpus, and pursued mass prosecutions. In general, however, the federal Enforcement Acts suffered from weak and inconsistent execution. President Grant vacillated between clamping down on the Klan and capitulating to racial intimidation. The strong tradition of states' rights and local autonomy in the South resisted federal force.

CONSERVATIVE RESURGENCE   The Klan's impact on politics varied from state to state. In the upper South it played only a modest role in facilitating a Democratic resurgence. But in the Deep South, Klan violence and intimidation had more substantial effects. In Georgia, for instance, Republicans virtually quit campaigning and voting. In overwhelmingly black Yazoo County, Mississippi, vengeful whites used violence to reverse the political balance of power. In the 1873 elections the Republicans cast 2,449 votes and the Democrats 638; two years later the Democrats polled 4,049 votes, the Republicans 7. Throughout the South the activities of the Klan weakened black and Republican morale, and in the North they encouraged a growing weariness with the whole southern question. "The plain truth is," noted the *New York Herald,* "the North has got tired of the Negro."

The erosion of northern interest in civil rights resulted from more than weariness, however. Western expansion, Indian wars, new economic opportunities, and political controversy over the tariff and the currency distracted attention from southern outrages against Republican rule and black rights. In addition, after a business panic that occurred in 1873 and the ensuing depression, desperate economic circumstances in the North and South created new racial tensions that helped undermine already inconsistent federal efforts to promote racial justice in the former Confederacy. Republican control in the South gradually loosened as "Conservative" parties—Democrats used that name to mollify former Whigs—mobilized the white vote. Old prewar political leaders reemerged to promote the antebellum Democratic goals of limited government, states' rights, and free trade. They politicized the race issue to excite the white electorate and intimidate black voters. The Republicans in the South had no effective response. They became increasingly an organization limited to blacks and federal officials. Many scalawags and carpetbaggers drifted away from the Radical Republican ranks under pressure from their white neighbors. Few of them had joined the Republicans out of concern for black rights in the first place. And where persuasion failed to work, Democrats were willing to use chicanery. As one enthusiastic Democrat boasted, "the white and black Republicans may outvote us, but we can outcount them."

Republican political control collapsed in Virginia and Tennessee as early as 1869, in Georgia and North Carolina in 1870, although North Carolina had a Republican governor until 1876. Reconstruction lasted longest in the Deep South states with the largest black population, where whites abandoned Klan masks for barefaced intimidation in paramilitary groups such as the Mississippi Rifle Club and the South Carolina Red Shirts. By 1876 Radical Republican regimes survived only

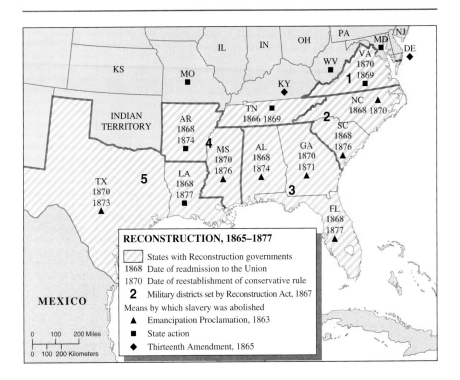

RECONSTRUCTION, 1865–1877

☐ States with Reconstruction governments
1868 Date of readmission to the Union
1870 Date of reestablishment of conservative rule
2 Military districts set by Reconstruction Act, 1867
Means by which slavery was abolished
▲ Emancipation Proclamation, 1863
■ State action
◆ Thirteenth Amendment, 1865

in Louisiana, South Carolina, and Florida, and these all collapsed after the elections of that year. Later the last carpetbag governor of South Carolina explained that "the uneducated negro was too weak, no matter what his numbers, to cope with the whites."

THE GRANT YEARS

THE ELECTION OF 1868   Ulysses S. Grant, who presided during the collapse of Republican rule in the South, brought to the White House little political experience. But in 1868 the rank-and-file northern voter could be expected to support "the Lion of Vicksburg" because of his record as a war leader. Both parties wooed him, but his falling-out with President Johnson pushed him toward the Republicans and built trust in him among the Radicals. They were, as Thaddeus Stevens said, ready to "let him into the church."

The Republican platform of 1868 endorsed the Reconstruction policy of Congress, congratulating the country on the "assured success" of the program. One plank cautiously defended black suffrage as a necessity in the South, but a matter each northern state should settle for itself. Another urged payment of the national debt "in the utmost good faith to all creditors," which meant in gold. More important than the platform were the great expectations of a soldier-president and his slogan: "Let us have peace."

The Democrats took opposite positions on both Reconstruction and the debt. The Republican Congress, the platform charged, instead of restoring the Union had "so far as in its power, dissolved it, and subjected ten states, in the time of profound peace, to military

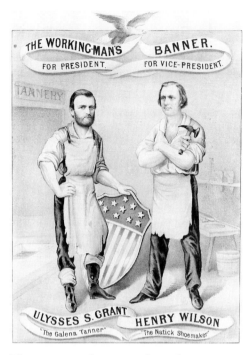

This campaign banner makes reference to the working-class origins of Ulysses S. Grant and his vice-presidential candidate Henry Wilson by depicting Grant as a tanner and Wilson as a shoemaker.

despotism and Negro supremacy." As to the public debt, the party endorsed Representative George H. Pendleton's "Ohio idea" that, since most war bonds had been bought with depreciated greenbacks, they should be paid off in greenbacks. With no conspicuously available candidate in sight, the convention turned to Horatio Seymour, war governor of New York and chairman of the convention. His friends had to hustle him out of the hall to prevent his withdrawal. The Democrats made a closer race of it than showed up in the electoral vote. Eight states, including New York and New Jersey, went for Seymour. While Grant swept the electoral college by 214 to 80, his popular majority was only 307,000 out of a total of over 5.7 million votes. More than 500,000 black voters accounted for Grant's margin of victory.

Grant had proven himself a great leader in the war, but in the White House he seemed blind to the political forces and influence peddlers around him. He was awestruck by men of wealth and unaccountably loyal to some who betrayed his trust. His conception of the presidency was "Whiggish." The chief executive carried out the laws; in the formulation of policy he passively followed the lead of Congress. This approach endeared him at first to Republican party leaders, but it left him at last ineffective and left others disillusioned with his leadership.

At the outset Grant consulted nobody on his cabinet appointments. Some of his choices indulged personal whims; others simply displayed bad judgment. In some cases appointees learned of their nomination from the newspapers. As time went by Grant betrayed a fatal gift for losing men of talent and integrity from his cabinet. Secretary of State Hamilton Fish of New York turned out to be a happy exception; he guided foreign policy throughout the Grant presidency.

THE GOVERNMENT DEBT   Financial issues dominated the political agenda during Grant's presidency. After the war, the Treasury had assumed that the $432 million worth of greenbacks issued during the conflict would be retired from circulation and that the nation would revert to a "hard-money" currency—gold coins. Many agrarian and debtor groups resisted any contraction of the money supply resulting from the elimination of greenbacks, believing that it would mean lower prices for their crops and would make it harder for them to repay long-term debts. They were joined by a large number of Radical Republicans who thought a combination of high tariffs and inflation would generate more rapid economic growth. As Senator John Sherman explained, "I prefer gold to paper money. But there is no other resort. We must have money or a fractured government." In 1868 congressional supporters of such a "soft-money" policy halted the retirement of greenbacks. There matters stood when Grant took office.

The "sound" or hard-money advocates, mostly bankers and merchants, claimed that Grant's election was a mandate to save the country from the Democrats' "Ohio idea" of using greenbacks to repay government bonds. Quite influential in Republican circles, the "sound-money" advocates also had the benefit of a deeply ingrained popular assumption that hard money was morally preferable to paper currency. Grant agreed, and in his inaugural address he endorsed payment of the national debt in gold as a point of national honor. On March 18, 1869, the Public Credit Act endorsing that principle became the first act of

Congress that he signed. Under the Refunding Act of 1870, the Treasury was able to replace 6 percent Civil War bonds with a new bond issue promising purchasers a 4 to 5 percent return in gold.

SCANDALS   The complexities of the "money question" exasperated Grant, but that was the least of his worries, for his administration soon fell into a cesspool of scandal. In the summer of 1869, two financial buccaneers, the crafty Jay Gould and the flamboyant Jim Fisk, connived with the president's brother-in-law to corner the nation's gold market. That is, they would create a public craze for gold by purchasing massive quantities of the yellow metal and convincing traders and the general public that the price would keep climbing. As more buyers joined the frenzy, the value of gold would soar. The only danger to the scheme was if the federal Treasury sold large amounts of gold. Gould concocted an argument that the government should refrain from selling gold on the market because the resulting rise in gold prices would raise temporarily depressed farm prices. Grant apparently smelled a rat from the start, but he was seen in public with the speculators. As the rumor spread on Wall Street that the president had bought the argument, gold rose from $132 to $163 an ounce. When Grant finally persuaded his brother-in-law to pull out of the deal, Gould began quietly selling out. Finally, on "Black Friday," September 24, 1869, Grant ordered the Treasury to sell a large quantity of gold, and the bubble burst. Fisk got out by repudiating his agreements and hiring thugs to intimidate his creditors. "Nothing is lost save honor," he said.

The plot to corner the gold market was only the first of several scandals that rocked the Grant administration. During the campaign of 1872 the public first learned about the financial crookery of the Crédit Mobilier, a construction company composed of the directors of the Union Pacific Railroad that had milked the Union Pacific for exorbitant fees in order to line the pockets of the insiders who controlled both firms. Union Pacific shareholders were left holding the bag. The schemers bought political support by giving congressmen stock in the enterprise. This chicanery had transpired before Grant's election in 1868, but it now touched a number of prominent Republicans. The beneficiaries had included Speaker of the House Schuyler Colfax, later vice-president, and Representative James A. Garfield, later president. Of thirteen members of Congress involved, only two were censured.

Even more odious disclosures soon followed, and some involved the president's cabinet. The secretary of war, it turned out, had accepted bribes from merchants who traded with Indians at army posts in the West. He was impeached, but he resigned in time to elude a Senate trial. Post-office contracts, it was revealed, went to carriers who offered the highest kickbacks. The secretary of the treasury had awarded a political friend a commission of 50 percent for the collection of overdue taxes. In St. Louis a "Whiskey Ring" bribed tax collectors to bilk the government of millions in revenue. Grant's private secretary was enmeshed in that scheme, taking large sums of money and other valuables in return for inside information. There is no evidence that Grant himself was ever involved in, or that he personally profited from, any of the fraud, but his poor choice of associates and his gullibility earned him widespread censure.

REFORM AND THE ELECTION OF 1872   Long before Grant's first term ended, a reaction against Radical Reconstruction and against incompetence and corruption in the administration had incited mutiny

The People's Handwriting on the Wall. *An 1872 engraving comments on the corruption engulfing Grant.*

within the Republican ranks. The Liberal Republicans favored free trade, gold to redeem greenbacks, a stable currency, ending federal Reconstruction efforts in the South, restoring the rights of former Confederates, and civil service reform. Open revolt broke out first in Missouri where Carl Schurz, a German immigrant and war hero, led a group of Liberal Republicans that elected a governor with Democratic help in 1870 and sent Schurz to the Senate. In 1872 the Liberal Republicans held their own national convention at Cincinnati that produced a compromise platform condemning the Republicans' Reconstruction policy and favoring civil service reform, but remained silent on the protective tariff. The delegates embraced an anomalous presidential candidate: Horace Greeley, editor of the *New York Tribune*, a longtime champion of just about every reform available. His image as a visionary eccentric was complemented by his record of hostility to Democrats, whose support the Liberals needed. The Democrats nevertheless swallowed the pill and gave their nomination to Greeley as the only hope of beating Grant.

The result was a foregone conclusion. Republican regulars duly endorsed Radical Reconstruction and the protective tariff. Grant still had seven carpetbag states in his pocket, generous contributions from business and banking interests, and the stalwart support of the Radical Republicans. Above all, he still evoked the imperishable glory of Appomattox. Greeley, despite an exhausting tour of the country—still unusual for a presidential candidate—carried only six southern and border states and none in the North. Grant won by 3,597,132 votes to Greeley's 2,834,125 votes, and by an electoral college vote of 286 to 66.

PANIC AND REDEMPTION   Economic distress followed close upon the public scandals besetting the Grant administration. Such developments explain why northerners lost interest in Reconstruction. Contraction of the money supply resulting from the withdrawal of greenbacks and investments in new railroads had made investors cautious and helped precipitate a financial crisis. During 1873 the market for railroad bonds turned sour as some twenty-five railroads defaulted on their interest payments. The investment-banking firm of Jay Cooke and Company, unable to sell the bonds of the Northern Pacific Railroad, financed them with short-term deposits in hope that a European market would develop. But in 1873 the opposite happened when a panic in

Vienna forced many financiers to unload American stocks and bonds. Caught short, Cooke and Company went bankrupt on September 18, 1873. The ensuing stampede of investors to exchange securities for cash forced the stock market to close for ten days. The Panic of 1873 set off a depression that lasted for six years, the longest and most severe that Americans had yet suffered, marked by widespread bankruptcies, unemployment, and a drastic slowdown in railroad building.

Hard times and political scandals hurt Republicans in the midterm elections of 1874. The Democrats won control of the House of Representatives and gained seats in the Senate. The new Democratic House immediately launched inquiries into the scandals and unearthed further evidence of corruption in high places. The financial panic, meanwhile, focused attention once more on greenback currency.

Since greenbacks were valued less than gold, they had become the chief circulating medium. Most people spent greenbacks first and held their gold or used it to settle foreign accounts, which drained much gold out of the country. The postwar reduction of greenbacks in circulation from $432 million to $356 million had made for tight money. To relieve the currency shortage and stimulate business, the Treasury reissued $26 million in greenbacks that had been previously withdrawn.

For a time the advocates of paper money were riding high. But in 1874 Grant vetoed a bill to issue more greenbacks. Then, in his annual message he called for the gradual resumption of specie payments—that is, the redemption of greenbacks in gold. This would make greenbacks "good as gold" and raise their value to a par with the gold dollar. Congress obliged by passing the Resumption Act of 1875. The payment in gold to people who turned in their paper money began on January 1, 1879, after the Treasury had built a gold reserve for that purpose and reduced the value of greenbacks in circulation. This act infuriated those promoting an inflationary monetary policy and provoked the formation of the National Greenback party, which elected fourteen congressmen in 1878. The much-debated and very complex "money question" was destined to remain one of the most divisive issues in American politics.

THE COMPROMISE OF 1877 Grant, despite the controversies swirling around him, wanted to run again in 1876, but many Republicans were not enthusiastic about Grant being the first three-term president.

James G. Blaine of Maine, former Speaker of the House, emerged as the Republican front-runner, but he too bore the taint of scandal. Letters in the possession of James Mulligan of Boston linked Blaine to some dubious railroad dealings, and these "Mulligan letters" found their way into print.

The Republican convention therefore eliminated Blaine and several other hopefuls in favor of Ohio's favorite son, Rutherford B. Hayes. Three times elected governor of Ohio, most recently as an advocate of hard money, Hayes had also made a name as a civil service reformer. But his chief virtue was that he offended neither Radicals nor reformers. As Henry Adams put it, he was "a third rate nonentity, whose only recommendation is that he is obnoxious to no one."

The Democratic convention was abnormally harmonious from the start. The nomination went on the second ballot to Samuel J. Tilden, a millionaire corporation lawyer and reform governor of New York who had directed a campaign to overthrow the notorious Tweed Ring controlling New York City politics and the Canal Ring in Albany, which had bilked the state of millions.

The 1876 campaign generated no burning issues. Both candidates favored the trend toward white conservative rule in the South. During one of the most corrupt elections ever, both candidates also favored civil service reform. In the absence of strong differences, Democrats aired the Republicans' dirty linen. In response, Republicans waved the "bloody shirt," which is to say that they engaged in verbal assaults on former Confederates and the spirit of rebellion, linking the Democratic party with secession and with the outrages committed against black and white Republicans in the South. As one Republican speaker insisted, "Every man that tried to destroy this nation was a Democrat. . . . The man that assassinated Abraham Lincoln was a Democrat. . . . Soldiers, every scar you have on your heroic bodies was given you by a Democrat!"

Early election returns pointed to a Tilden victory. He enjoyed a 300,000 edge in the popular vote and had 184 electoral votes, just one short of a majority. Hayes had 165 electoral votes, but the Republicans also claimed nineteen doubtful votes from Florida, Louisiana, and South Carolina. The Democrats laid a counterclaim to one electoral vote from Oregon. But the Republicans had clearly carried Oregon. In the South the outcome was less certain, and given the fraud and intimidation perpetrated on both sides, nobody will ever know what might have happened if, to use a slogan of the day, "a free ballot and a fair count" had prevailed.

In all three of the disputed southern states, rival canvassing boards sent in different returns. In Florida, Republicans conceded the state election, but in Louisiana and South Carolina rival state governments also appeared. The Constitution offered no guidance in this unprecedented situation. Even if Congress were empowered to sort things out, the Democratic House and the Republican Senate proved unable to reach an agreement.

Finally, on January 29, 1877, the two houses decided to set up a special Electoral Commission that would investigate and report its findings. It had fifteen members, five each from the House, the Senate, and the Supreme Court. Members were so chosen as to have seven from each major party, with Justice David Davis of Illinois as the swing man. Davis, though appointed to the Court by Lincoln, was no party regular and was in fact thought to be leaning toward the Democrats. Thus, the panel appeared to be stacked in favor of Tilden.

But as it turned out, the panel got restacked the other way. Short-sighted Democrats in the Illinois legislature teamed up with minority Greenbackers to name Davis their senator. Davis accepted, no doubt with a sense of relief. From the remaining justices, all Republicans, the panel chose Joseph P. Bradley to fill the vacancy. The decision on each state went by a vote of 8 to 7, along party lines, in favor of Hayes. After much bluster and threat of filibuster by Democrats, the House voted on March 2 to accept the report and declare Hayes elected by an electoral vote of 185 to 184.

Critical to this outcome was the defection of southern Democrats who, seeing the way the wind was blowing with the composition of the Electoral Commission, had made several informal agreements with the Republicans. On February 26, 1877, prominent Ohio Republicans (including James A. Garfield) and powerful southern Democrats struck a bargain at the Wormley House, a Washington hotel. The Republicans promised that, if elected, Hayes would withdraw the last federal troops from Louisiana and South Carolina, letting the Republican governments there collapse. In return, the Democrats promised to withdraw their opposition to Hayes, to accept in good faith the Reconstruction amendments (including civil rights for blacks), and to refrain from partisan reprisals against Republicans in the South.

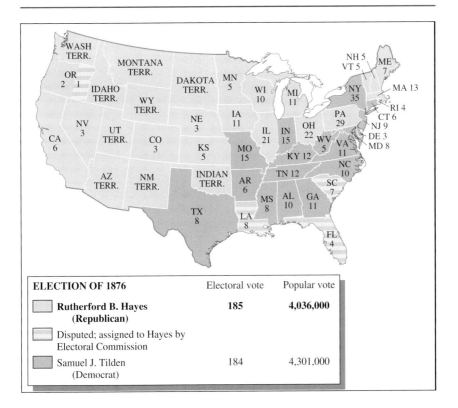

ELECTION OF 1876	Electoral vote	Popular vote
Rutherford B. Hayes (Republican)	**185**	**4,036,000**
Disputed; assigned to Hayes by Electoral Commission		
Samuel J. Tilden (Democrat)	184	4,301,000

Southern Democrats could now justify deserting Tilden because this so-called Compromise of 1877 brought a final "redemption" from the "Radicals" and a return to "home rule," which actually meant rule by white Democrats. Other, more informal promises, less noticed by the public, bolstered the Wormley House agreement. Hayes's friends pledged more support for Mississippi levees and other internal improvements, including a federal subsidy for a transcontinental railroad along a southern route. Southerners extracted a further promise that Hayes would name a white southerner as postmaster-general, the cabinet position with the most patronage jobs at hand. In return, southerners would let Republicans make Garfield Speaker of the new House. Such a deal illustrates the relative weakness of the presidency compared to Congress during the post–Civil War era.

THE END OF RECONSTRUCTION   In 1877 President Hayes withdrew federal troops from Louisiana and South Carolina, and the Republican governments there collapsed soon thereafter—along with much of Hayes's claim to legitimacy. Hayes chose a Tennessean and former Confederate as postmaster-general. But after southern Democrats failed to permit the choice of James Garfield as House Speaker, Hayes expressed doubt about any further subsidy for railroad building, and none was voted. Most of the other "Wormley House" promises were either renounced or forgotten.

As to southern promises regarding the civil rights of blacks, only a few Democratic leaders, such as the new governors of South Carolina and Louisiana, remembered them for long. Over the next three decades, protection of black civil rights crumbled under the pressure of white rule in the South and the force of Supreme Court decisions narrowing the application of the Reconstruction amendments. Radical Reconstruction never offered more than an uncertain commitment to black civil rights and social equality. Yet it left an enduring legacy, the Thirteenth, Fourteenth, and Fifteenth Amendments—not dead but dormant, waiting to be awakened. If Reconstruction did not provide social equality or substantial economic opportunities for blacks, it did create the foundation for future advances. It was a revolution, sighed North Carolina governor Jonathan Worth, and "nobody can anticipate the action of revolutions."

MAKING CONNECTIONS

- The political, economic, and racial policies of the conservatives who overthrew the Republican governments in the southern states are described in Chapter 19.

- Several of the political scandals mentioned in this chapter were related to the railroads, a topic discussed in greater detail in Chapter 20.

- This chapter ended with the election of Rutherford B. Hayes; for a discussion of Hayes's administration, see Chapter 22.

FURTHER READING

The most comprehensive treatment of Reconstruction is Eric Foner's *Reconstruction: America's Unfinished Revolution, 1863–1877* (1988). For a study of Andrew Johnson, see Hans L. Trefousse's *Andrew Johnson: A Biography* (1989).

Scholars have been fairly sympathetic to the aims and motives of the Radical Republicans. See, for instance, Herman Belz's *Reconstructing the Union* (1969) and Richard Nelson Current's *Those Terrible Carpetbaggers: A Reinterpretation* (1988). The ideology of the Radicals is explored in Michael Les Benedict's *A Compromise of Principle: Congressional Republicans and Reconstruction, 1863–1869* (1974).

The intransigence of southern white attitudes is examined in Michael Perman's *Reunion without Compromise* (1973) and Dan T. Carter's *When the War Was Over: The Failure of Self-Reconstruction in the South, 1865–1867* (1985). Allen W. Trelease's *White Terror* (1971) covers the various organizations that practiced vigilante tactics, chiefly the Ku Klux Klan. The difficulties former slaves had in adjusting to the new labor system are documented in James L. Roark's *Masters without Slaves* (1977). Books on southern politics during Reconstruction include Michael Perman's *The Road to Redemption* (1984), Terry L. Seip's *The South Returns to Congress* (1983), and Mark W. Summer's *Railroads, Reconstruction, and the Gospel of Prosperity* (1984).

Numerous works study the freed blacks' experience in the South. Start with Leon F. Litwack's *Been in the Storm So Long* (1979). Joel Williamson's *After Slavery* (1965) argues that South Carolina blacks took an active role in pursuing their political and economic rights. The Freedmen's Bureau is explored in William S. McFeely's *Yankee Stepfather: General O.O. Howard and the Freedmen* (1968). The situation of freed slave women, which was often quite different than that of freed slave men, is discussed in Jacqueline Jones's *Labor of Love, Labor of Sorrow: Black Women, Work, and the Family from Slavery to Present* (1985).

The land confiscation issue is discussed in Eric Foner's *Politics and Ideology in the Age of the Civil War* (1980), and Janet S. Hermann's *The Pursuit of a Dream* (1981), covers the Davis Bend experiment in Mississippi.

The politics of corruption outside the South is depicted in William S. McFeely's *Grant: A Biography* (1981). The political maneuvers of the election of 1876 and the resultant crisis and compromise are explained in C. Vann Woodward's *Reunion and Reaction* (1951) and William Gillette's *Retreat from Reconstruction, 1869–1879* (1979).

GLOSSARY

Agricultural Adjustment Act (1933) New Deal legislation that established the Agricultural Adjustment Administration (AAA) to improve agricultural prices by limiting market supplies; declared unconstitutional in *United States* v. *Butler* (1936).

Alamo, Battle of the Siege in the Texas War for Independence, 1836, in which the San Antonio mission fell to the Mexicans, and Davy Crockett and Jim Bowie died.

Alexander v. *Holmes County Board of Education* (1969) Case fifteen years after the *Brown* decision in which the U.S. Supreme Court ordered an immediate end to segregation in public schools.

Alien and Sedition Acts (1798) Four measures passed during the undeclared war with France that limited the freedoms of speech and press and restricted the liberty of noncitizens.

America First Committee Largely midwestern isolationist organization supported by many prominent citizens, 1940–41.

American Anti-Slavery Society National abolitionist organization founded in 1833 by New York philanthropists Arthur and Lewis Tappan, propagandist Theodore Dwight Weld, and others.

American Colonization Society Organized in 1816 to encourage colonization of free blacks to Africa; West African nation of Liberia founded in 1822 to serve as a homeland for them.

American Federation of Labor Founded in 1881 as a federation of trade unions, the AFL under president Samuel Gompers successfully pushed for the eight-hour workday.

American Protective Association Nativist, anti-Catholic secret society founded in Iowa in 1887 and active until the end of the century.

American System Program of internal improvements and protective tariffs promoted by Speaker of the House Henry Clay in his presidential campaign of 1824; his proposals formed the core of Whig ideology in the 1830s and 1840s.

Antietam, Battle of (Battle of Sharpsburg) One of the bloodiest battles of the Civil War, fought to a standoff on September 17, 1862, in western Maryland.

Antifederalists Forerunners of Thomas Jefferson's Democratic-Republican party; opposed the Constitution as a limitation on individual and states' rights, which led to the addition of a Bill of Rights to the document.

Appomattox Court House, Virginia Site of the surrender of Confederate general Robert E. Lee to Union general Ulysses S. Grant on April 9, 1865, marking the end of the Civil War.

Army-McCarthy hearings Televised U.S. Senate hearings in 1954 on Senator Joseph McCarthy's charges of disloyalty in the Army; his tactics contributed to his censure by the Senate.

Atlanta Compromise Speech to the Cotton States and International Exposition in 1895 by educator Booker T. Washington, the leading black spokesman of the day; black scholar W. E. B. Du Bois gave the speech its derisive name and criticized Washington for encouraging blacks to accommodate segregation and disenfranchisement.

Atlantic Charter Issued August 12, 1941, following meetings in Newfoundland between President Franklin D. Roosevelt and British prime minister Winston Churchill, the charter signaled the allies' cooperation and stated their war aims.

Atomic Energy Commission Created in 1946 to supervise peacetime uses of atomic energy.

Axis powers In World War II, the nations of Germany, Italy, and Japan.

Aztec Mesoamerican people who were conquered by the Spanish under Hernando Cortés, 1519–28.

Baby boom Markedly higher birth rate in the years following World War II; led to the biggest demographic "bubble" in American history.

Bacon's Rebellion Unsuccessful 1676 revolt led by planter Nathaniel Bacon against Virginia governor William Berkeley's administration because it had failed to protect settlers from Indian raids.

Bakke v. *Board of Regents of California* (1978) Case in which the U.S. Supreme Court ruled against the California university system's use of racial quotas in admissions.

Balance of trade Ratio of imports to exports.

Bank of the United States Proposed by the first secretary of the treasury, Alexander Hamilton, the bank opened in 1791 and operated until 1811 to issue a uniform currency, make business loans, and collect tax monies. The Second Bank of the United States was chartered in 1816 but was not renewed by President Andrew Jackson twenty years later.

Barbary pirates Plundering pirates off the Mediterranean coast of Africa; President Thomas Jefferson's refusal to pay them tribute to protect American ships sparked an undeclared naval war with North African nations, 1801–1805.

Barbed wire First practical fencing material for the Great Plains was invented in 1873 and rapidly spelled the end of the open range.

Battle of the Currents Conflict in the late 1880s between inventors Thomas Edison and George Westinghouse over direct versus alternating electric current; Westinghouse's alternating current (AC), the winner, allowed electricity to travel over long distances.

Bay of Pigs Invasion Hoping to inspire a revolt against Fidel Castro, the CIA sent 1,500 Cuban exiles to invade their homeland on April 17, 1961, but the mission was a spectacular failure.

Bill of Rights First ten amendments to the U.S. Constitution, adopted in 1791 to guarantee individual rights and to help secure ratification of the Constitution by the states.

Black Codes (1865–66) Laws passed in southern states to restrict the rights of former slaves; to combat the codes, Congress passed the Civil Rights Act of 1866 and the Fourteenth Amendment and set up military governments in southern states that refused to ratify the amendment.

Black Power Post-1966 rallying cry of a more militant civil rights movement.

Bland-Allison Act (1878) Passed over President Rutherford B. Hayes's veto, the inflationary measure authorized the purchase each month of 2 to 4 million dollars' worth of silver for coinage.

"Bleeding" Kansas Violence between pro- and antislavery settlers in the Kansas Territory, 1856.

Bloody shirt, Waving the Republican references to Reconstruction-era violence in the South, used effectively in northern political campaigns against Democrats.

Bonus Expeditionary Force Thousands of World War I veterans, who insisted on immediate payment of their bonus certificates, marched on Washington in 1932; violence ensued when President Herbert Hoover ordered their tent villages cleared.

Boston Massacre Clash between British soldiers and a Boston mob, March 5, 1770, in which five colonists were killed.

Boston Tea Party On December 16, 1773, the Sons of Liberty, dressed as Indians, dumped hundreds of chests of tea into Boston harbor to protest the Tea Act of 1773, under which the British exported to the colonies millions of pounds of cheap—but still taxed—tea, thereby undercutting the price of smuggled tea and forcing payment of the tea duty.

Boxer Rebellion Chinese nationalist protest against Western commercial domination and cultural influence, 1900; a coalition of American, European, and Japanese forces put down the rebellion and reclaimed captured embassies in Peking (Beijing) within the year.

Brain trust Group of advisers—many of them academics—that Franklin D. Roosevelt assembled to recommend New Deal policies during the early months of his presidency.

Branch Davidians Religious cult that lived communally near Waco, Texas, and was involved in a fiery 1993 confrontation with federal authorities in which dozens of cult members died.

Brook Farm Transcendentalist commune in West Roxbury, Massachusetts, populated from 1841 to 1847 principally by writers (Nathaniel Hawthorne, for one) and other intellectuals.

Brown v. Board of Education of Topeka (1954) U.S. Supreme Court decision that struck down racial segregation in public education and declared "separate but equal" unconstitutional.

Budget and Accounting Act of 1921 Created the Bureau of the Budget and the General Accounting Office.

Bull Run, Battles of (First and Second Manassas) First land engagement of the Civil War took place on July 21, 1861, at Manassas Junction, Virginia, at which surprised Union troops quickly retreated; one year later, on August 29–30, Confederates captured the federal supply depot and forced Union troops back to Washington.

Bunker Hill, Battle of First major battle of the Revolutionary War; it actually took place at nearby Breed's Hill, Massachusetts, on June 17, 1775.

"Burned-Over District" Area of western New York strongly influenced by the revivalist fervor of the Second Great Awakening; Disciples of Christ and Mormons are among the many sects that trace their roots to the phenomenon.

Burr conspiracy Scheme by Vice-President Aaron Burr to lead the secession of the Louisiana Territory from the United States; captured in 1807 and charged with treason, Burr was acquitted by the U.S. Supreme Court.

Bush v. Gore **(2000)** U.S. Supreme Court case that determined the winner of the disputed 2000 presidential election.

Calhoun Resolutions In making the proslavery response to the Wilmot Proviso, Senator John C. Calhoun argued that barring slavery in Mexican acquisitions would violate the Fifth Amendment to the Constitution by depriving slaveholding settlers of their property.

Calvinism Doctrine of predestination expounded by Swiss theologian John Calvin in 1536; influenced the Puritan, Presbyterian, German and Dutch Reformed, and Huguenot churches in the colonies.

Camp David Accords Peace agreement between Israeli prime minister Menachem Begin and Egyptian president Anwar Sadat, brokered by President Jimmy Carter in 1978.

Carpetbaggers Northern emigrants who participated in the Republican governments of the Reconstruction South.

Chancellorsville, Battle of Confederate general Robert E. Lee won his last major victory and General "Stonewall" Jackson died in this Civil War battle in northern Virginia on May 1–4, 1863.

Chattanooga, Battle of Union victory in eastern Tennessee on November 23–25, 1863; gave the North control of important rail lines and cleared the way for General William T. Sherman's march into Georgia.

Chinese Exclusion Act (1882) Halted Chinese immigration to the United States.

Civil Rights Act of 1866 Along with the Fourteenth Amendment, guaranteed the rights of citizenship to freedmen.

Civil Rights Act of 1957 First federal civil rights law since Reconstruction; established the Civil Rights Commission and the Civil Rights Division of the Department of Justice.

Civil Rights Act of 1964 Outlawed discrimination in public accommodations and employment.

Clipper ships Superior oceangoing sailing ships of the 1840s to 1860s that cut travel time in half; the clipper ship route around Cape Horn was the fastest way to travel between the coasts of the United States.

Closed shop Hiring requirement that all workers in a business must be union members.

Coercive Acts/Intolerable Acts (1774) Four parliamentary measures in reaction to the Boston Tea Party that forced payment for the tea, disallowed colonial trials of British soldiers, forced their quartering in private homes, and set up a military government.

Cold war Term for tensions, 1945–89, between the Soviet Union and the United States, the two major world powers after World War II.

***Commonwealth v. Hunt* (1842)** Landmark ruling of the Massachusetts supreme court establishing the legality of labor unions.

Compromise of 1850 Complex compromise mediated by Senator Henry Clay that headed off southern secession over California statehood; to appease the South it included a stronger fugitive slave law and delayed determination of the slave status of the New Mexico and Utah territories.

Compromise of 1877 Deal made by a special congressional commission on March 2, 1877, to resolve the disputed presidential election of 1876; Republican Rutherford B. Hayes, who had lost the popular vote, was declared the winner in exchange for the withdrawal of federal troops from the South, marking the end of Reconstruction.

Congress of Industrial Organizations (CIO) Umbrella organization of semi-skilled industrial unions, formed in 1935 as the Committee for Industrial Organization and renamed in 1938.

Congress of Racial Equality (CORE) Civil rights organization started in 1944 and best known for its "freedom rides," bus journeys challenging racial segregation in the South in 1961.

Conspicuous consumption Phrase referring to extravagant spending to raise social standing, coined by Thorstein Veblen in *The Theory of the Leisure Class* (1899).

Constitutional Convention Meeting in Philadelphia, May 25–September 17, 1787, of representatives from twelve colonies—excepting Rhode Island—to revise the existing Articles of Confederation; convention soon resolved to produce an entirely new constitution.

Containment General U.S. strategy in the cold war that called for containing Soviet expansion; originally devised in 1947 by U.S. diplomat George F. Kennan.

Continental Army Army authorized by the Continental Congress, 1775–84, to fight the British; commanded by General George Washington.

Continental Congress Representatives of a loose confederation of colonies met first in Philadelphia in 1774 to formulate actions against British policies; the Second Continental Congress (1775–89) conducted the war and adopted the Declaration of Independence and the Articles of Confederation.

Convict leasing System developed in the post–Civil War South that generated income for the states and satisfied planters' need for cheap labor by renting prisoners out; the convicts, however, were often treated poorly.

Copperheads Northerners opposed to the Civil War.

Coral Sea, Battle of the Fought on May 7–8, 1942, near the eastern coast of Australia, it was the first U.S. naval victory over Japan in World War II.

Cotton gin Invented by Eli Whitney in 1793, the machine separated cotton seed from cotton fiber, speeding cotton processing and making profitable the cultivation of the more hardy, but difficult to clean, short-staple cotton; led directly to the dramatic nineteenth-century expansion of slavery in the South.

Counterculture "Hippie" youth culture of the 1960s, which rejected the values of the dominant culture in favor of illicit drugs, communes, free sex, and rock music.

Court-packing plan President Franklin D. Roosevelt's failed 1937 attempt to increase the number of U.S. Supreme Court justices from nine to fifteen in order to save his Second New Deal programs from constitutional challenges.

Credit Mobilier scandal Millions of dollars in overcharges for building the Union Pacific Railroad were exposed; high officials of the Ulysses S. Grant administration were implicated but never charged.

Cuban missile crisis Caused when the United States discovered Soviet offensive missile sites in Cuba in October 1962; the U.S.-Soviet confrontation was the cold war's closest brush with nuclear war.

Crop-lien system Merchants extended credit to tenants based on their future crops, but high interest rates and the uncertainties of farming often led to inescapable debts (debt peonage).

D-Day June 6, 1944, when an Allied amphibious assault landed on the Normandy coast and established a foothold in Europe from which Hitler's defenses could not recover.

Dartmouth College v. Woodward (1819) U.S. Supreme Court upheld the original charter of the college against New Hampshire's attempt to alter the board of trustees; set precedent of support of contracts against state interference.

Declaration of Independence Document adopted on July 4, 1776, that made the break with Britain official; drafted by a committee of the Second Continental Congress including principal writer Thomas Jefferson.

Deism Enlightenment thought applied to religion; emphasized reason, morality, and natural law.

Department of Homeland Security Created to coordinate federal antiterrorist activity following the 2001 terrorist attacks on the World Trade Center and Pentagon.

Depression of 1893 Worst depression of the century, set off by a railroad failure, too much speculation on Wall Street, and low agricultural prices.

Dixiecrats Deep South delegates who walked out of the 1948 Democratic National Convention in protest of the party's support for civil rights legislation and later formed the States' Rights (Dixiecrat) party, which nominated Strom Thurmond of South Carolina for president.

Dominion of New England Consolidation into a single colony of the New England colonies—and later New York and New Jersey—by royal governor Edmund Andros in 1686; dominion reverted to individual colonial governments three years later.

Donner Party Forty-seven surviving members of a group of migrants to California were forced to resort to cannibalism to survive a brutal winter trapped in the Sierra Nevadas, 1846–47; highest death toll of any group traveling the Overland Trail.

Dred Scott v. Sandford (1857) U.S. Supreme Court decision in which Chief Justice Roger B. Taney ruled that slaves could not sue for freedom and that Congress could not prohibit slavery in the territories, on the grounds that such a prohibition would violate the Fifth Amendment rights of slaveholders.

Due-process clause Clause in the Fifth and the Fourteenth amendments to the U.S. Constitution guaranteeing that states could not "deprive any person of life, liberty, or property, without due process of law."

Dust Bowl Great Plains counties where millions of tons of topsoil were blown away from parched farmland in the 1930s; massive migration of farm families followed.

Eighteenth Amendment (1919) Prohibition amendment that made illegal the manufacture, sale, or transportation of alcoholic beverages.

Ellis Island Reception center in New York Harbor through which most European immigrants to America were processed from 1892 to 1954.

Emancipation Proclamation (1863) President Abraham Lincoln issued a preliminary proclamation on September 22, 1862, freeing the slaves in the Confederate states as of January 1, 1863, the date of the final proclamation.

Embargo Act of 1807 Attempt to exert economic pressure instead of waging war in reaction to continued British impressment of American sailors; smugglers easily circumvented the embargo, and it was repealed two years later.

Emergency Banking Relief Act (1933) First New Deal measure that provided for reopening the banks under strict conditions and took the United States off the gold standard.

Emergency Immigration Act of 1921 Limited U.S. immigration to 3 percent of each foreign-born nationality in the 1910 census; three years later Congress restricted immigration even further.

Encomienda System under which officers of the Spanish conquistadores gained ownership of Indian land.

ENIAC Electronic Numerical Integrator and Computer, built in 1944, the early, cumbersome ancestor of the modern computer.

Enlightenment Revolution in thought begun in the seventeenth century that emphasized reason and science over the authority of traditional religion.

Enola Gay American B-29 bomber that dropped the atomic bomb on Hiroshima, Japan, on August 6, 1945.

Environmental Protection Agency (EPA) Created in 1970 during the first administration of President Richard M. Nixon to oversee federal pollution control efforts.

Equal Rights Amendment Amendment to guarantee equal rights for women, introduced in 1923 but not passed by Congress until 1972; it failed to be ratified by the states.

Era of Good Feelings Contemporary characterization of the administration of popular Democratic-Republican president James Monroe, 1817–25.

Erie Canal Most important and profitable of the barge canals of the 1820s and 1830s; stretched from Buffalo to Albany, New York, connecting the Great Lakes to the East Coast and making New York City the nation's largest port.

Espionage and Sedition Acts (1917–18) Limited criticism of government leaders and policies by imposing fines and prison terms on those who acted out in opposition to the First World War; the most repressive measures passed up to that time.

Fair Deal Domestic reform proposals of the second Truman administration (1949–53); included civil rights legislation and repeal of the Taft-Hartley Act, but only extensions of some New Deal programs were enacted.

Fair Employment Practices Commission Created in 1941 by executive order, the FEPC sought to eliminate racial discrimination in jobs; it possessed little power but represented a step toward civil rights for African Americans.

Family and Medical Leave Act (1993) Allowed certain workers to take twelve weeks of unpaid leave each year for family health problems, including birth or adoption of a child.

Farmers' Alliance Two separate organizations (Northwestern and Southern) of the 1880s and 1890s that took the place of the Grange, worked for similar causes, and attracted landless, as well as landed, farmers to their membership.

Federal Trade Commission Act (1914) Established the Federal Trade Commission to enforce existing antitrust laws that prohibited business combinations in restraint of trade.

The Federalist Collection of eighty-five essays that appeared in the New York press in 1787–88 in support of the Constitution; written by Alexander Hamilton, James Madison, and John Jay but published under the pseudonym "Publius."

Federalist party One of the two first national political parties, it favored a strong central government.

Fence-Cutters' War Violent conflict in Texas, 1883–84, between large and small cattle ranchers over access to grazing land.

"Fifty-four forty or fight" Democratic campaign slogan in the presidential election of 1844, urging that the northern border of Oregon be fixed at 54°40′ north latitude.

Fletcher v. *Peck* (1810) U.S. Supreme Court decision in which Chief Justice John Marshall upheld the initial fraudulent sale contracts in the Yazoo Fraud cases; Congress paid $4.2 million to the original speculators in 1814.

Fort Laramie Treaty (1851) Restricted the Plains Indians from using the Overland Trail and permitted the building of government forts.

Fort McHenry Fort in Baltimore Harbor unsuccessfully bombarded by the British in September 1814; Francis Scott Key, a witness to the battle, was moved to write the words to "The Star-Spangled Banner."

Fort Sumter First battle of the Civil War, in which the federal fort in Charleston (South Carolina) Harbor was captured by the Confederates on April 14, 1861, after two days of shelling.

"Forty-niners" Speculators who went to northern California following the discovery of gold in 1848; the first of several years of large-scale migration was 1849.

Fourteen Points President Woodrow Wilson's 1918 plan for peace after World War I; at the Versailles peace conference, however, he failed to incorporate all of the points into the treaty.

Fourteenth Amendment (1868) Guaranteed rights of citizenship to former slaves, in words similar to those of the Civil Rights Act of 1866.

Franchise The right to vote.

"Free person of color" Negro or mulatto person not held in slavery; immediately before the Civil War, there were nearly a half million in the United States, split almost evenly between North and South.

Free Soil party Formed in 1848 to oppose slavery in the territory acquired in the Mexican War; nominated Martin Van Buren for president in 1848, but by 1854 most of the party's members had joined the Republican party.

Free Speech Movement Founded in 1964 at the University of California at Berkeley by student radicals protesting restrictions on their right to demonstrate.

Freedmen's Bureau Reconstruction agency established in 1865 to protect the legal rights of former slaves and to assist with their education, jobs, health care, and landowning.

French and Indian War Known in Europe as the Seven Years' War, the last (1755–63) of four colonial wars fought between England and France for control of North America east of the Mississippi River.

Fugitive Slave Act of 1850 Gave federal government authority in cases involving runaway slaves; so much more punitive and prejudiced in favor of slaveholders than the 1793 Fugitive Slave Act had been that Harriet Beecher Stowe was inspired to write *Uncle Tom's Cabin* in protest; the new law was part of the Compromise of 1850, included to appease the South over the admission of California as a free state.

Fundamentalism Anti-modernist Protestant movement started in the early twentieth century that proclaimed the literal truth of the Bible; the name came from *The Fundamentals*, published by conservative leaders.

Gadsden Purchase (1853) Thirty thousand square miles in present-day Arizona and New Mexico bought by Congress from Mexico primarily for the Southern Pacific Railroad's transcontinental route.

Gentlemen's Agreement (1907) United States would not exclude Japanese immigrants if Japan would voluntarily limit the number of immigrants coming to the United States.

Gettysburg, Battle of Fought in southern Pennsylvania, July 1–3, 1863; the Confederate defeat and the simultaneous loss at Vicksburg spelled the end of the South's chances in the Civil War.

Gibbons v. *Ogden* (1824) U.S. Supreme Court decision reinforcing the "commerce clause" (the federal government's right to regulate interstate commerce) of the Constitution; Chief Justice John Marshall ruled against the State of New York's granting of steamboat monopolies.

Gideon v. *Wainwright* (1963) U.S. Supreme Court decision guaranteeing legal counsel for indigent felony defendants.

The Gilded Age Mark Twain and Charles Dudley Warner's 1873 novel, the title of which became the popular name for the period from the end of the Civil War to the turn of the century.

Glass-Owen Federal Reserve Act (1913) Created a Federal Reserve System of regional banks and a Federal Reserve Board to stabilize the economy by regulating the supply of currency and controlling credit.

Glass-Steagall Act (Banking Act of 1933) Established the Federal Deposit Insurance Corporation and included banking reforms, some designed to control speculation. A banking act of the Hoover administration, passed in 1932 and also known as the Glass-Steagall Act, was designed to expand credit.

Good Neighbor Policy Proclaimed by President Franklin D. Roosevelt in his first inaugural address in 1933, it sought improved diplomatic relations between the United States and its Latin American neighbors.

Grandfather clause Loophole created by southern disfranchising legislatures of the 1890s for illiterate white males whose grandfathers had been eligible to vote in 1867.

Granger movement Political movement that grew out of the Patrons of Husbandry, an educational and social organization for farmers founded in 1867; the Grange had its greatest success in the Midwest of the 1870s, lobbying for government control of railroad and grain elevator rates and establishing farmers' cooperatives.

Great Awakening Fervent religious revival movement in the 1720s through the 1740s that was spread throughout the colonies by ministers like New England Congregationalist Jonathan Edwards and English revivalist George Whitefield.

Great Compromise (Connecticut Compromise) Mediated the differences between the New Jersey and Virginia delegations to the Constitutional Convention by providing for a bicameral legislature, the upper house of which would have equal representation and the lower house of which would be apportioned by population.

Great Depression Worst economic depression in American history; it was spurred by the stock market crash of 1929 and lasted until World War II.

Great Migration Large-scale migration of southern blacks during and after World War I to the North, where jobs had become available during the labor shortage of the war years.

Great Society Term coined by President Lyndon B. Johnson in his 1965 State of the Union address, in which he proposed legislation to address problems of voting rights, poverty, diseases, education, immigration, and the environment.

Greenback party Formed in 1876 in reaction to economic depression, the party favored issuance of unsecured paper money to help farmers repay debts; the movement for free coinage of silver took the place of the greenback movement by the 1880s.

Habeas corpus, Writ of An essential component of English common law and of the U.S. Constitution that guarantees that citizens may not be imprisoned without due process of law; literally means, "you must have the body."

Half-Breeds During the presidency of Rutherford B. Hayes, 1877–81, a moderate Republican party faction led by Senator James G. Blaine that favored some reforms of the civil service system and a restrained policy toward the defeated South.

Harlem Renaissance African-American literary and artistic movement of the 1920s and 1930s centered in New York City's Harlem district; writers Langston Hughes, Jean Toomer, Zora Neale Hurston, and Countee Cullen were among those active in the movement.

Harper's Ferry, Virginia Site of abolitionist John Brown's failed raid on the federal arsenal, October 16–17, 1859; he intended to arm the slaves, but ten of his compatriots were killed, and Brown became a martyr to his cause after his capture and execution.

Hartford Convention Meeting of New England Federalists on December 15, 1814, to protest the War of 1812; proposed seven constitutional amendments (limiting embargoes and changing requirements for officeholding, declaration of war, and admission of new states), but the war ended before Congress could respond.

Hawley-Smoot Tariff Act (1930) Raised tariffs to an unprecedented level and worsened the depression by raising prices and discouraging foreign trade.

Haymarket Affair Riot during an anarchist protest at Haymarket Square in Chicago on May 4, 1886, over violence during the McCormick Harvester Company strike; the deaths of eleven, including seven policemen, helped hasten the demise of the Knights of Labor, even though they were not responsible for the riot.

Hessians German soldiers, most from Hesse-Cassel principality (hence the name), paid to fight for the British in the Revolutionary War.

Holding company Investment company that holds controlling interest in the securities of other companies.

Homestead Act (1862) Authorized Congress to grant 160 acres of public land to a western settler, who had only to live on the land for five years to establish title.

Homestead Strike Violent strike at the Carnegie Steel Company near Pittsburgh in 1892 that culminated in the disintegration of the Amalgamated Association of Iron and Steel Workers, the first steelworkers' union.

House Un-American Activities Committee (HUAC) Formed in 1938 to investigate subversives in the government; best-known investigations were of Hollywood notables and of former State Department official Alger Hiss, who was accused in 1948 of espionage and Communist party membership.

Hundred Days Extraordinarily productive first three months of President Franklin D. Roosevelt's administration in which a special session of Congress enacted fifteen of his New Deal proposals.

Impeachment Bringing charges against a public official; for example, the House of Representatives can impeach a president for "treason, bribery, or other high crimes and misdemeanors" by majority vote, and after the trial the Senate can remove the president by a vote of two-thirds.

Implied powers Federal powers beyond those specifically enumerated in the U.S. Constitution; the Federalists argued that the "elastic clause" of Article I, Section 8, of the Constitution implicitly gave the federal government broad powers, while the Antifederalists held that the federal government's powers were explicitly limited by the Constitution.

"In God We Trust" Phrase placed on all new U.S. currency as of 1954.

Indentured servant Settler who signed on for a temporary period of servitude to a master in exchange for passage to the New World; Virginia and Pennsylvania were largely peopled in the seventeenth and eighteenth centuries by English indentured servants.

Independent Treasury Act (1840) Promoted by President Martin Van Buren, the measure sought to stabilize the economy by preventing state banks from printing unsecured paper currency and establishing an independent treasury based on specie.

Indian Peace Commission Established in 1867 to end the Indian wars in the West, the commission's solution was to contain the Indians in a system of reservations.

Indian Removal Act (1830) Signed by President Andrew Jackson, the law permitted the negotiation of treaties to obtain the Indians' lands in exchange for their relocation to what would become Oklahoma.

Industrial Workers of the World Radical union organized in Chicago in 1905 and nicknamed the Wobblies; its opposition to World War I led to its destruction by the federal government under the Espionage Act.

Internal improvements In the early national period the phrase referred to road building and the development of water transportation.

Interstate Commerce Commission Reacting to the U.S. Supreme Court's ruling in *Wabash Railroad* v. *Illinois* (1886), Congress established the ICC to curb abuses in the railroad industry by regulating rates.

Iran-Contra affair Scandal of the second Reagan administration involving sale of arms to Iran in partial exchange for release of hostages in Lebanon and use of the arms money to aid the Contras in Nicaragua, which had been expressly forbidden by Congress.

Iron Curtain Term coined by Winston Churchill to describe the cold war divide between western Europe and the Soviet Union's eastern European satellites.

Irreconcilables Group of isolationist U.S. senators who fought ratification of the Treaty of Versailles, 1919–20, because of their opposition to American membership in the League of Nations.

Jamestown, Virginia Site in 1607 of the first permanent English settlement in the New World.

Jay's Treaty Treaty with Britain negotiated in 1794 by Chief Justice John Jay; Britain agreed to vacate forts in the Northwest Territories, and festering disagreements (border with Canada, prewar debts, shipping claims) would be settled by commission.

Jim Crow Minstrel show character whose name became synonymous with post-Reconstruction laws revoking civil rights for freedmen and with racial segregation generally.

Judiciary Act of 1801 Enacted by the lame duck Congress to allow the Federalists, the losing party in the presidential election, to reorganize the judiciary and fill the open judgeships with Federalists.

Kansas-Nebraska Act (1854) Law sponsored by Illinois senator Stephen A. Douglas to allow settlers in newly organized territories north of the Missouri border to decide the slavery issue for themselves; fury over the resulting nullification of the Missouri Compromise of 1820 led to violence in Kansas and to the formation of the Republican party.

Kellogg-Briand Pact Representatives of sixty-two nations in 1928 signed the pact (also called the Pact of Paris) to outlaw war.

Kentucky and Virginia Resolutions (1798–99) Passed in response to the Alien and Sedition Acts, the resolutions advanced the state-compact theory that held states could nullify an act of Congress if they deemed it unconstitutional.

King William's War (War of the League of Augsburg) First (1689–97) of four colonial wars between England and France.

King's Mountain, Battle of Upcountry South Carolina irregulars defeated British troops under Patrick Ferguson on October 7, 1780, in what proved to be the turning point of the Revolutionary War in the South.

Knights of Labor Founded in 1869, the first national union picked up many members after the disastrous 1877 railroad strike but lasted, under the leadership of Terence V. Powderly, only into the 1890s; supplanted by the American Federation of Labor.

Know-Nothing (American) party Nativist, anti-Catholic third party organized in 1854 in reaction to large-scale German and Irish immigration; the party's only presidential candidate was Millard Fillmore in 1856.

Korean War Conflict touched off in 1950 when Communist North Korea invaded South Korea, which had been under U.S. control since the end of World War II; fighting largely by U.S. forces continued until 1953.

Ku Klux Klan Organized in Pulaski, Tennessee, in 1866 to terrorize former slaves who voted and held political offices during Reconstruction; a revived organization in the 1910s and 1920s stressed white, Anglo-Saxon, fundamentalist Protestant supremacy; the Klan revived a third time to fight the civil rights movement of the 1950s and 1960s in the South.

Land Ordinance of 1785 Directed surveying of the Northwest Territory into townships of thirty-six sections (square miles) each, the sale of the sixteenth section of which was to be used to finance public education.

League of Nations Organization of nations to mediate disputes and avoid war established after World War I as part of the Treaty of Versailles; President Woodrow Wilson's "Fourteen Points" speech to Congress in 1918 proposed the formation of the league.

Lecompton Constitution Controversial constitution drawn up in 1857 by proslavery Kansas delegates seeking statehood; rejected in 1858 by an overwhelmingly antislavery electorate.

Legal Tender Act (1862) Helped the U.S. government pay for the Civil War by authorizing the printing of paper currency.

Lend-Lease Act (1941) Permitted the United States to lend or lease arms and other supplies to the Allies, signifying increasing likelihood of American involvement in World War II.

Levittown Low-cost, mass-produced development of suburban tract housing built by William Levitt on Long Island in 1947.

Lexington and Concord, Battle of The first shots fired in the Revolutionary War, on April 19, 1775, near Boston; approximately 100 minutemen and 250 British soldiers were killed.

Leyte Gulf, Battle of Largest sea battle in history, fought on October 25, 1944, and won by the United States off the Philippine island of Leyte; Japanese losses were so great that they could not rebound.

Liberty party Abolitionist political party that nominated James G. Birney for president in 1840 and 1844; merged with the Free Soil party in 1848.

Lincoln-Douglas debates Series of senatorial campaign debates in 1858 focusing on the issue of slavery in the territories; held in Illinois between Republican Abraham Lincoln, who made a national reputation for himself, and incumbent Democratic senator Stephen A. Douglas, who managed to hold onto his seat.

Little Bighorn, Battle of Most famous battle of the Great Sioux War took place in 1876 in the Montana Territory; combined Sioux and Cheyenne warriors massacred a vastly outnumbered U.S. Cavalry commanded by Lieutenant Colonel George Armstrong Custer.

Lost Colony English expedition of 117 settlers, including Virginia Dare, the first English child born in the New World; colony disappeared from Roanoke Island in the Outer Banks sometime between 1587 and 1590.

Louisiana Purchase President Thomas Jefferson's 1803 purchase from France of the important port of New Orleans and 828,000 square miles west of the Mississippi River to the Rocky Mountains; it more than doubled the territory of the United States at a cost of only $15 million.

Lusitania British passenger liner sunk by a German U-boat, May 7, 1915, creating a diplomatic crisis and public outrage at the loss of 128 Americans (roughly 10 percent of the total aboard); Germany agreed to pay reparations, and the United States waited two more years to enter World War I.

Lyceum movement Founded in 1826, the movement promoted adult public education through lectures and performances.

Maize Indian corn, native to the New World.

Manhattan Project Secret American plan during World War II to develop an atomic bomb; J. Robert Oppenheimer led the team of physicists at Los Alamos, New Mexico.

Manifest Destiny Imperialist phrase first used in 1845 to urge annexation of Texas; used thereafter to encourage American settlement of European colonial and Indian lands in the Great Plains and Far West.

Marbury v. *Madison* (1803) First U.S. Supreme Court decision to declare a federal law—the Judiciary Act of 1801—unconstitutional; President John Adams's "midnight appointment" of Federalist judges prompted the suit.

March on Washington Civil rights demonstration on August 28, 1963, where the Reverend Martin Luther King, Jr., gave his "I Have a Dream" speech on the steps of the Lincoln Memorial.

Marshall Plan U.S. program for the reconstruction of post–World War II Europe through massive aid to former enemy nations as well as allies; proposed by General George C. Marshall in 1947.

Massive resistance In reaction to the *Brown* decision of 1954, U.S. senator Harry Byrd encouraged southern states to defy federally mandated school integration.

Maya Pre-Columbian society in Mesoamerica before about A.D. 900.

Mayflower Compact Signed in 1620 aboard the *Mayflower* before the Pilgrims landed at Plymouth, the document committed the group to majority-rule government; remained in effect until 1691.

Maysville Road Bill Federal funding for a Kentucky road, vetoed by President Andrew Jackson in 1830.

McCarran Internal Security Act (1950) Passed over President Harry S. Truman's veto, the law required registration of American Communist party members, denied them passports, and allowed them to be detained as suspected subversives.

***McCulloch* v. *Maryland* (1819)** U.S. Supreme Court decision in which Chief Justice John Marshall, holding that Maryland could not tax the Second Bank of the United States, supported the authority of the federal government versus the states.

McNary-Haugen Bill Vetoed by President Calvin Coolidge in 1927 and 1928, the bill to aid farmers would have artificially raised agricultural prices by selling surpluses overseas for low prices and selling the reduced supply in the United States for higher prices.

Meat Inspection Act (1906) Passed largely in reaction to Upton Sinclair's *The Jungle,* the law set strict standards of cleanliness in the meat-packing industry.

Mercantilism Limitation and exploitation of colonial trade by an imperial power.

Mestizo Person of mixed Native American and European ancestry.

Mexican War Controversial war with Mexico for control of California and New Mexico, 1846–48; the Treaty of Guadalupe Hidalgo fixed the border at the Rio Grande and extended the United States to the Pacific coast, annexing more than a half-million square miles of potential slave territory.

Midway, Battle of Decisive American victory near Midway Island in the South Pacific on June 4, 1942; the Japanese navy never recovered its superiority over the U.S. navy.

Military Reconstruction Act (1867) Established military governments in ten Confederate states—excepting Tennessee—and required that the states ratify the Fourteenth Amendment and permit freedmen to vote.

Minstrel show Blackface vaudeville entertainment popular in the decades surrounding the Civil War.

***Miranda* v. *Arizona* (1966)** U.S. Supreme Court decision required police to advise persons in custody of their rights to legal counsel and against self-incrimination.

Missouri Compromise Deal proposed by Kentucky senator Henry Clay to resolve the slave/free imbalance in Congress that would result from Missouri's admission as a slave state; in the compromise of March 20, 1820, Maine's admission as a free state offset Missouri, and slavery was prohibited in the remainder of the Louisiana Territory north of the southern border of Missouri.

Molly Maguires Secret organization of Irish coal miners that used violence to intimidate mine officials in the 1870s.

***Monitor* and *Merrimack* Battle of the** First engagement between ironclad ships; fought at Hampton Roads, Virginia, on March 9, 1862.

Monroe Doctrine President James Monroe's declaration to Congress on December 2, 1823, that the American continents would be thenceforth closed to colonization but that the United States would honor existing colonies of European nations.

Moral Majority Televangelist Jerry Falwell's political lobbying organization, the name of which became synonymous with the religious right—conservative evangelical Protestants who helped ensure President Ronald Reagan's 1980 victory.

Mormons Founded in 1830 by Joseph Smith, the sect (officially, the Church of Jesus Christ of Latter-Day Saints) was a product of the intense revivalism of the "Burned-Over District" of New York; Smith's successor Brigham Young led 15,000 followers to Utah in 1847 to escape persecution.

Montgomery bus boycott Sparked by Rosa Parks's arrest on December 1, 1955, a successful year-long boycott protesting segregation on city buses; led by the Reverend Martin Luther King.

Muckrakers Writers who exposed corruption and abuses in politics, business, meat-packing, child labor, and more, primarily in the first decade of the twentieth century; their popular books and magazine articles spurred public interest in progressive reform.

Mugwumps Reform wing of the Republican party which supported Democrat Grover Cleveland for president in 1884 over Republican James G. Blaine, whose influence peddling had been revealed in the Mulligan letters of 1876.

Munn v. Illinois (1877) U.S. Supreme Court ruling that upheld a Granger law allowing the state to regulate grain elevators.

NAFTA Approved in 1993, the North American Free Trade Agreement with Canada and Mexico allowed goods to travel across their borders free of tariffs; critics argued that American workers would lose their jobs to cheaper Mexican labor.

National Aeronautics and Space Administration (NASA) In response to the Soviet Union's launching of *Sputnik*, Congress created this federal agency in 1957 to coordinate research and administer the space program.

National Association for the Advancement of Colored People (NAACP) Founded in 1910, this civil rights organization brought lawsuits against discriminatory practices and published *The Crisis*, a journal edited by African-American scholar W. E. B. Du Bois.

National Defense Education Act (1958) Passed in reaction to America's perceived inferiority in the space race, the appropriation encouraged education in science and modern languages through student loans, university research grants, and aid to public schools.

National Industrial Recovery Act (1933) Passed on the last of the Hundred Days, it created public-works jobs through the Federal Emergency Relief Administration and established a system of self-regulation for industry through the National Recovery Administration, which was ruled unconstitutional in 1935.

National Organization for Women Founded in 1966 by writer Betty Friedan and other feminists, NOW pushed for abortion rights and nondiscrimination in the workplace, but within a decade it became radicalized and lost much of its constituency.

National Road First federal interstate road, built between 1811 and 1838 and stretching from Cumberland, Maryland, to Vandalia, Illinois.

National Security Act (1947) Authorized the reorganization of government to coordinate military branches and security agencies; created the National Security Council, the Central Intelligence Agency, and the National Military Establishment (later renamed the Department of Defense).

National Youth Administration Created in 1935 as part of the Works Progress Administration, it employed millions of youths who had left school.

Nativism Anti-immigrant and anti-Catholic feeling in the 1830s through the 1850s; the largest group was New York's Order of the Star-Spangled Banner, which expanded into the American, or Know-Nothing, party in 1854.

Naval stores Tar, pitch, and turpentine made from pine resin and used in shipbuilding; an important industry in the southern colonies, especially North Carolina.

Navigation Acts Passed by the English Parliament to control colonial trade and bolster the mercantile system, 1650–1775; enforcement of the acts led to growing resentment by colonists.

Neutrality Acts Series of laws passed between 1935 and 1939 to keep the United States from becoming involved in war by prohibiting American trade and travel to warring nations.

New Deal Franklin D. Roosevelt's campaign promise, in his speech to the Democratic National Convention of 1932, to combat the Great Depression with a "new deal for the American people"; the phrase became a catchword for his ambitious plan of economic programs.

New England Anti-Slavery Society Abolitionist organization founded in 1832 by William Lloyd Garrison of Massachusetts, publisher of the *Liberator*.

New Freedom Democrat Woodrow Wilson's political slogan in the presidential campaign of 1912; Wilson wanted to improve the banking system, lower tariffs, and, by breaking up monopolies, give small businesses freedom to compete.

New Frontier John F. Kennedy's program, stymied by a Republican Congress and his abbreviated term; his successor Lyndon B. Johnson had greater success with many of the same concepts.

New Harmony Founded in Indiana by British industrialist Robert Owen in 1825, the short-lived New Harmony Community of Equality was one of the few nineteenth-century communal experiments not based on religious ideology.

New Left Radical youth protest movement of the 1960s, named by leader Tom Hayden to distinguish it from the Old (Marxist-Leninist) Left of the 1930s.

New Nationalism Platform of the Progressive party and slogan of former president Theodore Roosevelt in the presidential campaign of 1912; stressed government activism, including regulation of trusts, conservation, and recall of state court decisions that had nullified progressive programs.

New Orleans, Battle of Last battle of the War of 1812, fought on January 8, 1815, weeks after the peace treaty was signed but prior to its ratification; General Andrew Jackson led the victorious American troops.

New South *Atlanta Constitution* editor Henry W. Grady's 1886 term for the prosperous post–Civil War South he envisioned: democratic, industrial, urban, and free of nostalgia for the defeated plantation South.

Nineteenth Amendment (1920) Granted women the right to vote.

Nisei Japanese Americans; literally, "second generation."

Normalcy Word coined by future president Warren G. Harding as part of a 1920 campaign speech—"not nostrums, but normalcy"—signifying his awareness that the public was tired of progressivism, war, and sacrifice.

North Atlantic Treaty Organization (NATO) Defensive alliance founded in 1949 by ten western European nations, the United States, and Canada to deter Soviet expansion in Europe.

Northwest Ordinance of 1787 Created the Northwest Territory (area north of the Ohio River and west of Pennsylvania), established conditions for self-government and statehood, included a Bill of Rights, and permanently prohibited slavery.

Nullification Concept of invalidation of a federal law within the borders of a state; first expounded in the Kentucky and Virginia Resolutions (1798), cited by South Carolina in its Ordinance of Nullification (1832) of the Tariff of Abominations, used by southern states to explain their secession from the Union (1861), and cited again by southern states to oppose the *Brown v. Board of Education* decision (1954).

Nullification Proclamation President Andrew Jackson's strong criticism of South Carolina's Ordinance of Nullification (1832) as disunionist and potentially treasonous.

Office of Price Administration Created in 1941 to control wartime inflation and price fixing resulting from shortages of many consumer goods, the OPA imposed wage and price freezes and administered a rationing system.

Okies Displaced farm families from the Oklahoma dust bowl who migrated to California during the 1930s in search of jobs.

Old Southwest In the antebellum period, the states of Alabama, Mississippi, Louisiana, Texas, Arkansas, and parts of Tennessee, Kentucky, and Florida.

Oneida Community Utopian community founded in 1848; the Perfectionist religious group practiced universal marriage until leader John Humphrey Noyes, fearing prosecution, escaped to Canada in 1879.

OPEC Organization of Petroleum Exporting Countries.

Open Door Policy In hopes of protecting the Chinese market for U.S. exports, Secretary of State John Hay unilaterally announced in 1899 that Chinese trade would be open to all nations.

Operation Desert Storm Multinational allied force that defeated Iraq in the Gulf War of January 1991.

Operation Dixie CIO's largely ineffective post–World War II campaign to unionize southern workers.

Oregon fever Enthusiasm for emigration to the Oregon Country in the late 1830s and early 1840s.

Ostend Manifesto Memorandum written in 1854 from Ostend, Belgium, by the U.S. ministers to England, France, and Spain recommending purchase or seizure of Cuba in order to increase the United States' slaveholding territory.

Overland (Oregon) Trail Route of wagon trains bearing settlers from Independence, Missouri, to the Oregon Country in the 1840s through the 1860s.

Overseer Manager of slave labor on a plantation.

Panic of 1819 Financial collapse brought on by sharply falling cotton prices, declining demand for American exports, and reckless western land speculation.

Panic of 1837 Major economic depression lasting about six years; touched off by a British financial crisis and made worse by falling cotton prices, credit and currency problems, and speculation in land, canals, and railroads.

Panic of 1857 Economic depression lasting about two years and brought on by falling grain prices and a weak financial system; the South was largely protected by international demand for its cotton.

Panic of 1873 Severe six-year depression marked by bank failures and railroad and insurance bankruptcies.

Peace of Paris Signed on September 3, 1783, the treaty ending the Revolutionary War and recognizing American independence from Britain also established the border between Canada and the United States, fixed the western border at the Mississippi River, and ceded Florida to Spain.

Pendleton Civil Service Act (1883) Established the Civil Service Commission and marked the end of the spoils system.

Pentagon Papers Informal name for the Defense Department's secret history of the Vietnam conflict; leaked to the press by former official Daniel Ellsberg and published in the *New York Times* in 1971.

Pequot War Massacre in 1637 and subsequent dissolution of the Pequot Nation by Puritan settlers, who seized the Indians' lands.

Personal Responsibility and Work Opportunity Act (1996) Welfare reform measure that mandated state administration of federal aid to the poor.

Philippine Sea, Battle of the Costly Japanese defeat of June 19–20, 1944; led to the resignation of Premier Tojo and his cabinet.

Pilgrims Puritan Separatists who broke completely with the Church of England and sailed to the New World aboard the *Mayflower,* founding Plymouth Colony on Cape Cod in 1620.

Pinckney's Treaty Treaty with Spain negotiated by Thomas Pinckney in 1795; established United States boundaries at the Mississippi River and the thirty-first parallel and allowed open transportation on the Mississippi.

Planter In the antebellum South, the owner of a large farm worked by twenty or more slaves.

Platt Amendment (1901) Reserved the United States' right to intervene in Cuban affairs and forced newly independent Cuba to host American naval bases on the island.

Plessy v. *Ferguson* (1896) U.S. Supreme Court decision supporting the legality of Jim Crow laws that permitted or required "separate but equal" facilities for blacks and whites.

Poll tax Tax that must be paid in order to be eligible to vote; used as an effective means of disenfranchising black citizens after Reconstruction, since they often could not afford even a modest fee.

Popular sovereignty Allowed settlers in a disputed territory to decide the slavery issue for themselves.

Populist party Political success of Farmers' Alliance candidates encouraged the formation in 1892 of the National People's party (later renamed the Populist party); active until 1912, it advocated a variety of reform issues, including free coinage of silver, income tax, postal savings, regulation of railroads, and direct election of U.S. senators.

Pottawatomie Massacre Murder of five proslavery settlers in eastern Kansas led by abolitionist John Brown on May 24–25, 1856.

Potsdam Conference Last meeting of the major Allied powers, the conference took place outside Berlin from July 17 to August 2, 1945; United States president Harry Truman, Soviet dictator Joseph Stalin, and British prime minister Clement Atlee finalized plans begun at Yalta.

Proclamation of Amnesty and Reconstruction President Lincoln's plan for reconstruction, issued in 1863, allowed southern states to rejoin the Union if 10 percent of the 1860 electorate signed loyalty pledges, accepted emancipation, and had received presidential pardons.

Proclamation of 1763 Royal directive issued after the French and Indian War prohibiting settlement, surveys, and land grants west of the Appalachian Mountains; although it was soon overridden by treaties, colonists continued to harbor resentment.

Progressive party Created when former president Theodore Roosevelt broke away from the Republican party to run for president again in 1912; the party supported progressive reforms similar to the Democrats but stopped short of seeking to eliminate trusts.

Progressivism Broad-based reform movement, 1900–17, that sought governmental help in solving problems in many areas of American life, including education, public health, the economy, the environment, labor, transportation, and politics.

Protestant Reformation Reform movement that resulted in the establishment of Protestant denominations; begun by German monk Martin Luther when he posted his "Ninety-five Theses" (complaints of abuses in the Catholic church) in 1517.

Pullman Strike Strike against the Pullman Palace Car Company in the company town of Pullman, Illinois, on May 11, 1894, by the American Railway Union under Eugene V. Debs; the strike was crushed by court injunctions and federal troops two months later.

Pure Food and Drug Act (1906) First law to regulate manufacturing of food and medicines; prohibited dangerous additives and inaccurate labeling.

Puritans English religious group that sought to purify the Church of England; founded the Massachusetts Bay Colony under John Winthrop in 1630.

Quartering Act (1765) Parliamentary act requiring colonies to house and provision British troops.

Radical Republicans Senators and congressmen who, strictly identifying the Civil War with the abolitionist cause, sought swift emancipation of the slaves, punishment of the rebels, and tight controls over the former Confederate states after the war.

Railroad Strike of 1877 Violent but ultimately unsuccessful interstate strike, which resulted in extensive property damage and many deaths.

Reaganomics Popular name for President Ronald Reagan's philosophy of "supply side" economics, which combined tax cuts, less government spending, and a balanced budget with an unregulated marketplace.

Reconstruction Finance Corporation Federal program established in 1932 under President Herbert Hoover to loan money to banks and other institutions to help them avert bankruptcy.

Red Scare Fear among many Americans after World War I of Communists in particular and noncitizens in general, a reaction to the Russian Revolution, mail bombs, strikes, and riots.

Redcoats Nickname for British soldiers, after their red uniform jackets.

Redeemers/Bourbons Conservative white Democrats, many of whom had been planters or businessmen before the Civil War, who reclaimed control of the South following the end of Reconstruction.

Regulators Groups of backcountry Carolina settlers who protested colonial policies; North Carolina royal governor William Tryon retaliated at the Battle of Alamance on May 17, 1771.

Report on Manufactures First secretary of the treasury Alexander Hamilton's 1791 analysis that accurately foretold the future of American industry and proposed tariffs and subsidies to promote it.

Republican party Organized in 1854 by antislavery Whigs, Democrats, and Free Soilers in response to the passage of the Kansas-Nebraska Act; nominated John C. Frémont for president in 1856 and Abraham Lincoln in 1860.

Republicans Political faction that succeeded the Antifederalists after ratification of the Constitution; led by Thomas Jefferson and James Madison, it soon developed into the Democratic-Republican party.

Reservationists Group of U.S. senators led by Majority Leader Henry Cabot Lodge who would only agree to ratification of the Treaty of Versailles subject to certain reservations, most notably the removal of Article X of the League of Nations Covenant.

Revolution of 1800 First time that an American political party surrendered power to the opposition party; Jefferson, a Democratic-Republican, had defeated incumbent Adams, a Federalist, for president.

Right-to-work State laws enacted to prevent imposition of the closed shop; any worker, whether or not a union member, could be hired.

Roe v. Wade (1973) U.S. Supreme Court decision requiring states to permit first-trimester abortions.

Roosevelt Corollary (1904) President Theodore Roosevelt announced in what was essentially a corollary to the Monroe Doctrine that the United States could intervene militarily to prevent interference from European powers in the Western Hemisphere.

Romanticism Philosophical, literary, and artistic movement of the nineteenth century that was largely a reaction to the rationalism of the previous century; romantics valued emotion, mysticism, and individualism.

Rough Riders The 1st U.S. Volunteer Cavalry, led in battle in the Spanish-American War by Theodore Roosevelt; they were victorious in their only battle near Santiago, Cuba, and Roosevelt used the notoriety to aid his political career.

Santa Fe Trail Beginning in the 1820s, a major trade route from St. Louis, Missouri, to Santa Fe, New Mexico Territory.

Saratoga, Battle of Major defeat of British general John Burgoyne and more than 5,000 British troops at Saratoga, New York, on October 17, 1777.

Scalawags Southern white Republicans—some former Unionists—who served in Reconstruction governments.

***Schenck* v. *U.S.* (1919)** U.S. Supreme Court decision upholding the wartime Espionage and Sedition Acts; in the opinion he wrote for the case, Justice Oliver Wendell Holmes set the now-familiar "clear and present danger" standard.

Scientific management Analysis of worker efficiency using measurements like "time and motion" studies to achieve greater productivity; introduced by Frederick Winslow Taylor in 1911.

Scottsboro case (1931) In overturning verdicts against nine black youths accused of raping two white women, the U.S. Supreme Court established precedents in *Powell* v. *Alabama* (1932), that adequate counsel must be appointed in capital cases, and in *Norris* v. *Alabama* (1935), that African Americans cannot be excluded from juries.

Second Great Awakening Religious revival movement of the early decades of the nineteenth century, in reaction to the growth of secularism and rationalist religion; began the predominance of the Baptist and Methodist churches.

Second Red Scare Post–World War II Red Scare focused on the fear of Communists in U.S. government positions; peaked during the Korean War and declined soon thereafter, when the U.S. Senate censured Joseph McCarthy, who had been a major instigator of the hysteria.

Seneca Falls Convention First women's rights meeting and the genesis of the women's suffrage movement; held in July 1848 in a church in Seneca Falls, New York, by Elizabeth Cady Stanton and Lucretia Coffin Mott.

"Separate but equal" Principle underlying legal racial segregation, which was upheld in *Plessy* v. *Ferguson* (1896) and struck down in *Brown* v. *Board of Education* (1954).

Servicemen's Readjustment Act (1944) The "GI Bill of Rights" provided money for education and other benefits to military personnel returning from World War II.

Settlement houses Product of the late nineteenth-century movement to offer a broad array of social services in urban immigrant neighborhoods; Chicago's Hull House was one of hundreds of settlement houses that operated by the early twentieth century.

Seventeenth Amendment (1913) Progressive reform that required U.S. senators to be elected directly by voters; previously, senators were chosen by state legislatures.

Seward's Folly Secretary of State William H. Seward's negotiation of the purchase of Alaska from Russia in 1867.

Shakers Founded by Mother Ann Lee Stanley in England, the United Society of Believers in Christ's Second Appearing settled in Watervliet, New York, in 1774 and subsequently established eighteen additional communes in the Northeast, Indiana, and Kentucky.

Sharecropping Type of farm tenancy that developed after the Civil War in which landless workers—often former slaves—farmed land in exchange for farm supplies and a share of the crop; differed from tenancy in that the terms were generally less favorable.

Shays's Rebellion Massachusetts farmer Daniel Shays and 1,200 compatriots, seeking debt relief through issuance of paper currency and lower taxes, stormed the federal arsenal at Springfield in the winter of 1787 but were quickly repulsed.

Sherman Anti-Trust Act (1890) First law to restrict monopolistic trusts and business combinations; extended by the Clayton Anti-Trust Act of 1914.

Sherman Silver Purchase Act (1890) In replacing and extending the provisions of the Bland-Allison Act of 1878, it increased the amount of silver periodically bought for coinage.

Shiloh, Battle of At the time it was fought (April 6–7, 1862), Shiloh, in western Tennessee, was the bloodiest battle in American history; afterward, General Ulysses S. Grant was temporarily removed from command.

Single tax Concept of taxing only landowners as a remedy for poverty, promulgated by Henry George in *Progress and Poverty* (1879).

Sixteenth Amendment (1913) Legalized the federal income tax.

Smith-Connally War Labor Disputes Act (1943) Outlawed labor strikes in wartime and allowed the president to take over industries threatened by labor disputes.

Smith v. Allwright (1944) U.S. Supreme Court decision that outlawed all-white Democratic party primaries in Texas.

Social Darwinism Application of Charles Darwin's theory of natural selection to society; used the concept of the "survival of the fittest" to justify class distinctions and to explain poverty.

Social gospel Preached by liberal Protestant clergymen in the late nineteenth and early twentieth centuries; advocated the application of Christian principles to social problems generated by industrialization.

Social Security Act (1935) Created the Social Security system with provisions for a retirement pension, unemployment insurance, disability insurance, and public assistance (welfare).

Sons of Liberty Secret organizations formed by Samuel Adams, John Hancock, and other radicals in response to the Stamp Act; they impeded British officials and planned such harassments as the Boston Tea Party.

South Carolina Exposition and Protest Written in 1828 by Vice-President John C. Calhoun of South Carolina to protest the so-called Tariff of Abominations, which seemed to favor northern industry; introduced the concept of state interposition and became the basis for South Carolina's Nullification Doctrine of 1833.

Southeast Asia Treaty Organization (SEATO) Pact among mostly western nations signed in 1954; designed to deter Communist expansion and cited as a justification for U.S. involvement in Vietnam.

Southern Christian Leadership Conference (SCLC) Civil rights organization founded in 1957 by the Reverend Martin Luther King, Jr., and other civil rights leaders.

Southern renaissance Literary movement of the 1920s and 1930s that included such writers as William Faulkner, Thomas Wolfe, and Robert Penn Warren.

Spanish flu Unprecedentedly lethal influenza epidemic of 1918 that killed more than 22 million people worldwide.

Spoils system The term—meaning the filling of federal government jobs with persons loyal to the party of the president—originated in Andrew Jackson's first term; the system was replaced in the Progressive Era by civil service.

Sputnik First artificial satellite to orbit the earth; launched October 4, 1957, by the Soviet Union.

Stalwarts Conservative Republican party faction during the presidency of Rutherford B. Hayes, 1877–81; led by Senator Roscoe B. Conkling of New York, Stalwarts opposed civil service reform and favored a third term for President Ulysses S. Grant.

Stamp Act (1765) Parliament required that revenue stamps be affixed to all colonial printed matter, documents, dice, and playing cards; the Stamp Act Congress met to formulate a response, and the act was repealed the following year.

Standard Oil Company Founded in 1870 by John D. Rockefeller in Cleveland, Ohio, it soon grew into the nation's first industry-dominating trust; the Sherman Anti-Trust Act (1890) was enacted in part to combat abuses by Standard Oil.

Staple crop Important cash crop, for example, cotton or tobacco.

Steamboats Paddlewheelers that could travel both up- and down-river in deep or shallow waters; they became commercially viable early in the nineteenth century and soon developed into America's first inland freight and passenger service network.

Stimson Doctrine In reaction to Japan's 1932 occupation of Manchuria, Secretary of State Henry Stimson declared that the United States would not recognize territories acquired by force.

Strategic Defense Initiative ("Star Wars") Defense Department's plan during the Reagan administration to build a system to destroy incoming missiles in space.

Student Non-violent Coordinating Committee Founded in 1960 to coordinate civil rights sit-ins and other forms of grassroots protest.

Students for a Democratic Society (SDS) Major organization of the New Left, founded at the University of Michigan in 1960 by Tom Hayden and Al Haber.

Sugar Act (Revenue Act of 1764) Parliament's tax on refined sugar and many other colonial products; the first tax designed solely to raise revenue for Britain.

Taft-Hartley Act (1947) Passed over President Harry Truman's veto, the law contained a number of provisions to control labor unions, including the banning of closed shops.

Tariff Federal tax on imported goods.

Tariff of Abominations (Tariff of 1828) Taxed imported goods at a very high rate; the South hated the tariff because it feared it would provoke Britain to reject American cotton.

Tariff of 1816 First true protective tariff, intended strictly to protect American goods against foreign competition.

Tax Reform Act (1986) Lowered federal income tax rates to 1920s levels and eliminated many loopholes.

Teapot Dome Harding administration scandal in which Secretary of the Interior Albert B. Fall profited from secret leasing to private oil companies of government oil reserves at Teapot Dome, Wyoming, and Elk Hills, California.

Tenancy Renting of farmland by workers who owned their own equipment; tenant farmers kept a larger percentage of the crop than did sharecroppers.

Tennessee Valley Authority Created in 1933 to control flooding in the Tennessee River Valley, provide work for the region's unemployed, and produce inexpensive electric power for the region.

Tenure of Office Act (1867) Required the president to obtain Senate approval to remove any official whose appointment had also required Senate approval; President Andrew Johnson's violation of the law by firing Secretary of War Edwin Stanton led to the Radical Republicans retaliating with Johnson's impeachment.

Tertium Quid Literally, the "third something": states' rights and strict constructionist Republicans under John Randolph who broke with President Thomas Jefferson but never managed to form a third political party.

Tet Offensive Surprise attack by the Viet Cong and North Vietnamese during the Vietnamese New Year of 1968; turned American public opinion strongly against the war in Vietnam.

Tippecanoe, Battle of On November 7, 1811, Indiana governor William Henry Harrison (later president) defeated the Shawnee Indians at the Tippecanoe River in northern Indiana; victory fomented war fever against the British, who were believed to be aiding the Indians.

Title IX Part of the Educational Amendments Act of 1972 that required colleges to engage in "affirmative action" for women.

Tonkin Gulf Resolution (1964) Passed by Congress in reaction to supposedly unprovoked attacks on American warships off the coast of North Vietnam; it gave the president unlimited authority to defend U.S. forces and members of SEATO.

Tories Term used by Patriots to refer to Loyalists, or colonists who supported the Crown after the Declaration of Independence.

Townshend Acts (1767) Parliamentary measures (named for the chancellor of the exchequer) that punished the New York Assembly for failing to house British soldiers, taxed tea and other commodities, and established a Board of Customs Commissioners and colonial vice-admiralty courts.

Trail of Tears Cherokees' own term for their forced march, 1838–39, from the southern Appalachians to Indian lands (later Oklahoma); of 15,000 forced to march, 4,000 died on the way.

Transcendentalism Philosophy of a small group of mid-nineteenth-century New England writers and thinkers, including Ralph Waldo Emerson, Henry David Thoreau, and Margaret Fuller; they stressed "plain living and high thinking."

Transcontinental railroad First line across the continent from Omaha, Nebraska, to Sacramento, California, established in 1869 with the linkage of the Union Pacific and Central Pacific railroads at Promontory, Utah.

Truman Doctrine President Harry S. Truman's program of post–World War II aid to European countries—particularly Greece and Turkey—in danger of being undermined by communism.

Trust Companies combined to control competition.

Twenty-first Amendment (1933) Repealed prohibition on the manufacture, sale, and transportation of alcoholic beverages, effectively nullifying the Eighteenth Amendment.

Twenty-second Amendment (1951) Limited presidents to two full terms of office or two terms plus two years of an assumed term; passed in reaction to President Franklin D. Roosevelt's unprecedented four elected terms.

Twenty-sixth Amendment (1971) Lowered the voting age from twenty-one to eighteen.

U.S.S. *Maine* Battleship that exploded in Havana Harbor on February 15, 1898, resulting in 266 deaths; the American public, assuming that the Spanish had mined the ship, clamored for war, and the Spanish-American War was declared two months later.

Uncle Tom's Cabin Harriet Beecher Stowe's 1852 antislavery novel popularized the abolitionist position.

Underground Railroad Operating in the decades before the Civil War, the "railroad" was a clandestine system of routes and safehouses through which slaves were led to freedom in the North.

Understanding clause Added to state constitutions in the late nineteenth century, it allowed illiterate whites to circumvent literacy tests for voting by demonstrating that they understood a passage in the Constitution; black citizens would be judged by white registrars to have failed.

Underwood-Simmons Tariff (1913) In addition to lowering and even eliminating some tariffs, it included provisions for the first federal income tax, made legal the same year by the ratification of the Sixteenth Amendment.

Unitarianism Late eighteenth-century liberal offshoot of the New England Congregationalist church; rejecting the Trinity, Unitarianism professed the oneness of God and the goodness of rational man.

United Farm Workers Union for the predominantly Mexican-American migrant laborers of the Southwest, organized by César Chavez in 1962.

United Nations Organization of nations to maintain world peace, established in 1945 and headquartered in New York.

Universal Negro Improvement Association Black nationalist movement active in the United States from 1916 to 1923, when its leader Marcus Garvey went to prison for mail fraud.

Universalism Similar to Unitarianism, but putting more stress on the importance of social action, Universalism also originated in Massachusetts in the late eighteenth century.

V-E Day May 8, 1945, the day World War II officially ended in Europe.

Vertical integration Company's avoidance of middlemen by producing its own supplies and providing for distribution of its product.

Veto President's constitutional power to reject legislation passed by Congress; a two-thirds vote in both houses of Congress can override a veto.

Vicksburg, Battle of The fall of Vicksburg, Mississippi, to General Ulysses S. Grant's army on July 4, 1863, after two months of siege was a turning point in the war because it gave the Union control of the Mississippi River.

Virginia and New Jersey Plans Differing opinions of delegations to the Constitutional Convention: New Jersey wanted one legislative body with equal representation for each state; Virginia's plan called for a strong central government and a two-house legislature apportioned by population.

Volstead Act (1919) Enforced the prohibition amendment, beginning January 1920.

Voting Rights Act of 1965 Passed in the wake of Martin Luther King's Selma to Montgomery March, it authorized federal protection of the right to vote and permitted federal enforcement of minority voting rights in individual counties, mostly in the South.

Wabash Railroad v. *Illinois* (1886) Reversing the U.S. Supreme Court's ruling in *Munn* v. *Illinois*, the decision disallowed state regulation of interstate commerce.

Wade-Davis Bill (1864) Radical Republicans' plan for reconstruction that required loyalty oaths, abolition of slavery, repudiation of war debts, and denial of political rights to high-ranking Confederate officials; President Lincoln refused to sign the bill.

Wagner Act (National Labor Relations Act of 1935) Established the National Labor Relations Board and facilitated unionization by regulating employment and bargaining practices.

War Industries Board Run by financier Bernard Baruch, the board planned production and allocation of war materiel, supervised purchasing, and fixed prices, 1917–19.

War of 1812 Fought with Britain, 1812–14, over lingering conflicts that included impressment of American sailors, interference with shipping, and collusion with Northwest Territory Indians; settled by the Treaty of Ghent in 1814.

War on Poverty Announced by President Lyndon B. Johnson in his 1964 State of the Union address; under the Economic Opportunity Bill signed later that year, Head Start, VISTA, and the Jobs Corps were created, and grants and loans were extended to students, farmers, and businesses in efforts to eliminate poverty.

War Production Board Created in 1942 to coordinate industrial efforts in World War II; similar to the War Industries Board in World War I.

War Relocation Camps Internment camps where Japanese Americans were held against their will from 1942 to 1945.

Warren Court The U.S. Supreme Court under Chief Justice Earl Warren, 1953–69, decided such landmark cases as *Brown* v. *Board of Education* (school desegregation), *Baker* v. *Carr* (legislative redistricting), and *Gideon* v. *Wainwright* and *Miranda* v. *Arizona* (rights of criminal defendants).

Washington Armaments Conference Leaders of nine world powers met in 1921–22 to discuss the naval race; resulting treaties limited to a specific ratio the carrier and battleship tonnage of each nation (Five-Power Naval Treaty), formally ratified the Open Door to China (Nine–Power Treaty), and agreed to respect each other's Pacific territories (Four-Power Treaty).

Watergate Washington office and apartment complex that lent its name to the 1972–74 scandal of the Nixon administration; when his knowledge of the break-in at the Watergate and subsequent coverup was revealed, Nixon resigned the presidency under threat of impeachment.

Webster-Ashburton Treaty Settlement in 1842 of U.S.-Canadian border disputes in Maine, New York, Vermont, and in the Wisconsin Territory (now northern Minnesota).

Webster-Hayne debate U.S. Senate debate of January 1830 between Daniel Webster of Massachusetts and Robert Hayne of South Carolina over nullification and states' rights.

Whig Party Founded in 1834 to unite factions opposed to President Andrew Jackson, the party favored federal responsibility for internal improvements; the party ceased to exist by the late 1850s, when party members divided over the slavery issue.

Whigs Another name for revolutionary Patriots.

Whiskey Rebellion Violent protest by western Pennsylvania farmers against the federal excise tax on corn whiskey, 1794.

Whitewater Development Corporation Failed Arkansas real estate investment that kept President Bill Clinton and his wife Hillary under investigation by Independent Counsel Kenneth Starr throughout the Clinton presidency; no charges were ever brought against either of the Clintons.

Wilderness, Battle of the Second battle fought in the thickly wooded Wilderness area near Chancellorsville, Virginia; in the battle of May 5–6, 1864, no clear victor emerged, but the battle served to deplete the Army of Northern Virginia.

Wilderness Road Originally an Indian path through the Cumberland Gap, it was used by over 300,000 settlers who migrated westward to Kentucky in the last quarter of the eighteenth century.

Wilmot Proviso Proposal to prohibit slavery in any land acquired in the Mexican War, but southern senators, led by John C. Calhoun of South Carolina, defeated the measure in 1846 and 1847.

Works Progress Administration (WPA) Part of the Second New Deal, it provided jobs for millions of the unemployed on construction and arts projects.

Wounded Knee, Battle of Last incident of the Indians Wars took place in 1890 in the Dakota Territory, where the U.S. Cavalry killed over 200 Sioux men, women, and children who were in the process of surrender.

Writs of assistance One of the colonies' main complaints against Britain, the writs allowed unlimited search warrants without cause to look for evidence of smuggling.

XYZ Affair French foreign minister Tallyrand's three anonymous agents demanded payments to stop French plundering of American ships in 1797; refusal to pay the bribe led to two years of sea war with France (1798–1800).

Yalta Conference Meeting of Franklin D. Roosevelt, Winston Churchill, and Joseph Stalin at a Crimean resort to discuss the postwar world on February 4–11, 1945; Soviet leader Joseph Stalin claimed large areas in eastern Europe for Soviet domination.

Yazoo Fraud Illegal sale of the Yazoo lands (much of present-day Alabama and Mississippi) by Georgia legislators; by 1802 it had become a tangle of conflicting claims that the U.S. Supreme Court settled in *Fletcher v. Peck* (1810).

Yellow journalism Sensationalism in newspaper publishing that reached a peak in the circulation war between Joseph Pulitzer's *New York World* and William Randolph Hearst's *New York Journal* in the 1890s; the papers' accounts of events in Havana Harbor in 1898 led directly to the Spanish-American War.

Yeoman farmers Small landowners (the majority of white families in the South) who farmed their own land and usually did not own slaves.

Yorktown, Battle of Last battle of the Revolutionary War; General Lord Charles Cornwallis along with over 7,000 British troops surrendered at Yorktown, Virginia, on October 17, 1781.

Zimmermann telegram From the German foreign secretary to the German minister in Mexico, February 1917, instructing him to offer to recover Texas, New Mexico, and Arizona for Mexico if it would fight the United States to divert attention from Germany in case of war.

APPENDIX

THE DECLARATION
OF INDEPENDENCE

WHEN IN THE COURSE OF HUMAN EVENTS, it becomes necessary for one people to dissolve the political bands which have connected them with another, and to assume the Powers of the earth, the separate and equal station to which the Laws of Nature and of Nature's God entitle them, a decent respect to the opinions of mankind requires that they should declare the causes which impel them to the separation.

We hold these truths to be self-evident, that all men are created equal, that they are endowed by their Creator with certain unalienable rights, that among these are Life, Liberty, and the pursuit of Happiness. That to secure these rights, Governments are instituted among Men, deriving their just powers from the consent of the governed. That whenever any Form of Government becomes destructive of these ends, it is the Right of the People to alter or to abolish it, and to institute new Government, laying its foundation on such principles and organizing its powers in such form, as to them shall seem most likely to effect their Safety and Happiness. Prudence, indeed, will dictate that Governments long established should not be changed for light and transient causes; and accordingly all experience hath shown, that mankind are more disposed to suffer, while evils are sufferable, than to right themselves by abolishing the forms to which they are accustomed. But when a long train of abuses and usurpations, pursuing invariably the same Object evinces a design to reduce them under absolute Despotism, it is their right, it is their duty, to throw off such Government, and to provide new Guards for their future security.—Such has been the patient sufferance of these Colonies; and such is now the necessity which constrains them to alter their former Systems of Government. The history of the present King of Great Britain is a history of repeated injuries and usurpations, all having in direct object the establishment of an absolute Tyranny over these States. To prove this, let Facts be submitted to a candid world.

He has refused his Assent to Laws, the most wholesome and necessary for the public good.

He has forbidden his Governors to pass Laws of immediate and pressing importance, unless suspended in their operation till his Assent should be obtained; and when so suspended, he has utterly neglected to attend to them.

He has refused to pass other Laws for the accommodation of large districts of people, unless those people would relinquish the right of Representation in the Legislature, a right inestimable to them and formidable to tyrants only.

He has called together legislative bodies at places unusual, uncomfortable, and distant from the depository of their public Records, for the sole purpose of fatiguing them into compliance with his measures.

He has dissolved Representative Houses repeatedly, for opposing with manly firmness his invasions on the rights of the people.

He has refused for a long time, after such dissolutions, to cause others to be elected; whereby the Legislative powers, incapable of Annihilation, have returned to the People at large for their exercise; the State remaining in the mean time exposed to all dangers of invasion from without, and convulsions within.

He has endeavoured to prevent the population of these States; for that purpose obstructing the Laws of Naturalization of Foreigners; refusing to pass others to encourage their migrations hither, and raising the conditions of new Appropriations of Lands.

He has obstructed the Administration of Justice, by refusing his Assent to Laws for establishing Judiciary powers.

He has made Judges dependent on his Will alone, for the tenure of their offices, and the amount and payment of their salaries.

He has erected a multitude of New Offices, and sent hither swarms of Officers to harass our People, and eat out their substance.

He has kept among us, in times of peace, Standing Armies without the Consent of our legislatures.

He has affected to render the Military independent of and superior to the Civil Power.

He has combined with others to subject us to a jurisdiction foreign to our constitution, and unacknowledged by our laws; giving his Assent to their Acts of pretended Legislation:

For quartering large bodies of armed troops among us:

For protecting them, by a mock Trial, from Punishment for any Murders which they should commit on the Inhabitants of these States:

For cutting off our Trade with all parts of the world:

For imposing taxes on us without our Consent:

For depriving us of many cases, of the benefits of Trial by jury:

For transporting us beyond Seas to be tried for pretended offences:

For abolishing the free System of English Laws in a neighbouring Province, establishing therein an Arbitrary government, and enlarging its Boundaries so as to render it at once an example and fit instrument for introducing the same absolute rule into these Colonies:

For taking away our Charters, abolishing our most valuable Laws, and altering fundamentally the Forms of our Governments:

For suspending our own Legislatures, and declaring themselves in vested with Power to legislate for us in all cases whatsoever.

He has abdicated Government here, by declaring us out of his Protection and waging War against us.

He has plundered our seas, ravaged our Coasts, burnt our towns, and destroyed the lives of our people.

He is at this time transporting large armies of foreign mercenaries to compleat the works of death, desolation, and tyranny, already begun with circumstances of Cruelty & perfidy scarcely paralleled in the most barbarous ages, and totally unworthy the Head of a civilized nation.

He has constrained our fellow Citizens taken Captive on the high Seas to bear Arms against their Country, to become the executioners of their friends and Brethren, or to fall themselves by their Hands.

He has excited domestic insurrections amongst us, and has endeavoured to bring on the inhabitants of our frontiers, the merciless Indian Savages, whose known rule of warfare, is an undistinguished destruction of all ages, sexes, and conditions.

In every stage of these Oppressions We have Petitioned for Redress in the most humble terms: Our repeated Petitions have been answered only by repeated injury. A Prince, whose character is thus marked by every act which may define a Tyrant, is unfit to be the ruler of a free people.

Nor have We been wanting in attention to our British brethren. We have warned them from time to time of attempts by their legislature to extend an unwarrantable jurisdiction over us. We have reminded them of the circumstances of our emigration and settlement here. We have appealed to their native justice and magnanimity, and we have conjured them by the ties of our common kindred to disavow these usurpations, which, would inevitably interrupt our connections and correspondence. They too must have been deaf to the voice of justice and of consanguinity. We must, therefore, acquiesce in the necessity, which denounces our Separation, and hold them, as we hold the rest of mankind, Enemies in War, in Peace Friends.

WE, THEREFORE, the Representatives of the UNITED STATES OF AMERICA, in General Congress, Assembled, appealing to the Supreme Judge of the world for the rectitude of our intentions, do, in the Name, and by Authority of the good People of these Colonies, solemnly publish and declare, That these United Colonies are, and of Right ought to be FREE AND INDEPENDENT STATES; that they are Absolved from all Allegiance to the British

Crown, and that all political connection between them and the State of Great Britain, is and ought to be totally dissolved; and that as Free and Independent States, they have full Power to levy War, conclude Peace, contract Alliances, establish Commerce, and to do all other Acts and Things which Independent States may of right do. And for the support of this Declaration, with a firm reliance on the Protection of Divine Providence, we mutually pledge to each other our Lives, our Fortunes, and our sacred Honor.

The foregoing Declaration was, by order of Congress, engrossed, and signed by the following members:

John Hancock

NEW HAMPSHIRE
Josiah Bartlett
William Whipple
Matthew Thornton

MASSACHUSETTS BAY
Samuel Adams
John Adams
Robert Treat Paine
Elbridge Gerry

RHODE ISLAND
Stephen Hopkins
William Ellery

CONNECTICUT
Roger Sherman
Samuel Huntington
William Williams
Oliver Wolcott

NEW YORK
William Floyd
Philip Livingston
Francis Lewis
Lewis Morris

NEW JERSEY
Richard Stockton
John Witherspoon
Francis Hopkinson
John Hart
Abraham Clark

PENNSYLVANIA
Robert Morris
Benjamin Rush
Benjamin Franklin
John Morton
George Clymer
James Smith
George Taylor
James Wilson
George Ross

DELAWARE
Caesar Rodney
George Read
Thomas M'Kean

MARYLAND
Samuel Chase
William Paca
Thomas Stone
*Charles Carroll, of
    Carrollton*

VIRGINIA
George Wythe
Richard Henry Lee
Thomas Jefferson
Benjamin Harrison
Thomas Nelson, Jr.
Francis Lightfoot Lee
Carter Braxton

NORTH CAROLINA
William Hooper
Joseph Hewes
John Penn

SOUTH CAROLINA
Edward Rutledge
Thomas Heyward, Jr.
Thomas Lynch, Jr.
Arthur Middleton

GEORGIA
Button Gwinnett
Lyman Hall
George Walton

Resolved, That copies of the Declaration be sent to the several assemblies, conventions, and committees, or councils of safety, and to the several commanding officers of the continental troops; that it be proclaimed in each of the United States, at the head of the army.

ARTICLES OF
CONFEDERATION

To ALL TO WHOM these Presents shall come, we the undersigned Delegates of the States affixed to our Names send greeting.

Whereas the Delegates of the United States of America in Congress assembled did on the fifteenth day of November in the Year of our Lord One Thousand Seven Hundred and Seventy-seven, and in the Second Year of the Independence of America agree to certain articles of Confederation and perpetual Union between the States of Newhampshire, Massachusetts-bay, Rhodeisland and Providence Plantations, Connecticut, New York, New Jersey, Pennsylvania, Delaware, Maryland, Virginia, North-Carolina, South-Carolina and Georgia in the Words following, viz.

Articles of Confederation and perpetual Union between the States of Newhampshire, Massachusetts-bay, Rhodeisland and Providence Plantations, Connecticut, New-York, New-Jersey, Pennsylvania, Delaware, Maryland, Virginia, North-Carolina, South-Carolina and Georgia.

ARTICLE I. The stile of this confederacy shall be "The United States of America."

ARTICLE II. Each State retains its sovereignty, freedom and independence, and every power, jurisdiction and right, which is not by this confederation expressly delegated to the United States, in Congress assembled.

ARTICLE III. The said States hereby severally enter into a firm league of friendship with each other, for their common defence, the security of their liberties, and their mutual and general welfare, binding themselves to assist each other, against all force offered to, or attacks made upon them, or any of them, on account of religion, sovereignty, trade or any other pretence whatever.

ARTICLE IV. The better to secure and perpetuate mutual friendship and intercourse among the people of the different States in this Union, the free inhabitants of each of these States, paupers, vagabonds and fugitives from justice excepted, shall be entitled to all privileges and immunities of free citizens in the several States; and the people of each State shall have free ingress and regress to and from any other State, and shall enjoy therein all the privileges of trade and commerce, subject to the same duties, impositions and restrictions as the inhabitants thereof respectively, provided that such restrictions shall not extend so far as to prevent the removal of property imported into any State, to any other State of which the owner is an inhabitant; provided also that no imposition, duties or restriction shall be laid by any State, on the property of the United States, or either of them.

If any person guilty of, or charged with treason, felony, or other high misdemeanor in any State, shall flee from justice, and be found in any of the United States, he shall upon demand of the Governor or Executive power, of the State from which he fled, be delivered up and removed to the State having jurisdiction of his offence.

Full faith and credit shall be given in each of these States to the records, acts and judicial proceedings of the courts and magistrates of every other State.

ARTICLE V. For the more convenient management of the general interests of the United States, delegates shall be annually appointed in such manner as the legislature of each State shall direct, to meet in Congress on the first Monday in November, in every year, with a power reserved to each State, to recall its delegates, or any of them, at any time within the year, and to send others in their stead, for the remainder of the year.

No State shall be represented in Congress by less than two, nor by more than seven members; and no person shall be capable of being a delegate for more than three years in any term of six years; nor shall any person, being a delegate, be capable of holding any office under the United States, for which he, or another for his benefit receives any salary, fees or emolument of any kind.

Each State shall maintain its own delegates in a meeting of the States, and while they act as members of the committee of the States.

In determining questions in the United States, in Congress assembled, each State shall have one vote.

Freedom of speech and debate in Congress shall not be impeached or questioned in any court, or place out of Congress, and the members of Congress shall be protected in their persons from arrests and imprisonments, during the time of their going to and from, and attendance on Congress, except for treason, felony, or breach of the peace.

ARTICLE VI. No State without the consent of the United States in Congress assembled, shall send any embassy to, or receive any embassy from, or enter into any conference, agreement, alliance or treaty with any king, prince or state; nor shall any person holding any office of profit or trust under the United States, or any of them, accept of any present, emolument, office or title of any kind whatever from any king, prince or foreign state; nor shall the United States in Congress assembled, or any of them, grant any title of nobility.

No two or more States shall enter into any treaty, confederation or alliance whatever between them, without the consent of the United States in Congress assembled, specifying accurately the purposes for which the same is to be entered into, and how long it shall continue.

No State shall lay any imposts or duties, which may interfere with any stipulations in treaties, entered into by the United States in Congress assembled, with any king, prince or state, in pursuance of any treaties already proposed by Congress, to the courts of France and Spain.

No vessels of war shall be kept up in time of peace by any State, except such number only, as shall be deemed necessary by the United States in Congress assembled, for the defence of such State, or its trade; nor shall any body of forces be kept up by any State, in time of peace, except such number only, as in the judgment of the United States, in Congress assembled, shall be deemed requisite to garrison the forts necessary for the defence of such State; but every State shall always keep up a well regulated and disciplined militia, sufficiently armed and accoutred, and shall provide and constantly have ready for use, in public stores, a due number of field pieces and tents, and a proper quantity of arms, ammunition and camp equipage.

No State shall engage in any war without the consent of the United States in Congress assembled, unless such State be actually invaded by enemies, or shall have received certain advice of a resolution being formed by some nation of Indians to invade such State, and the danger is so imminent as not to admit of a delay, till the United States in Congress assembled can be consulted: nor shall any State grant commissions to any ships or vessels of war, nor letters of marque or reprisal, except it be after a declaration of war by the United States in Congress assembled, and then only against the kingdom or state and the subjects thereof, against which war has been so declared, and under such regulations as shall be established by the United States in Congress assembled, unless such State be infested by pirates, in which case vessels of war may be fitted out for that occasion, and kept so long as the danger shall continue, or until the United States in Congress assembled shall determine otherwise.

ARTICLE VII. When land-forces are raised by any State of the common defence, all officers of or under the rank of colonel, shall be appointed by the

Legislature of each State respectively by whom such forces shall be raised, or in such manner as such State shall direct, and all vacancies shall be filled up by the State which first made the appointment.

ARTICLE VIII. All charges of war, and all other expenses that shall be incurred for the common defence or general welfare, and allowed by the United States in Congress assembled, shall be defrayed out of a common treasury, which shall be supplied by the several States, in proportion to the value of all land within each State, granted to or surveyed for any person, as such land and the buildings and improvements thereon shall be estimated according to such mode as the United States in Congress assembled, shall from time to time direct and appoint.

The taxes for paying that proportion shall be laid and levied by the authority and direction of the Legislatures of the several States within the time agreed upon by the United States in Congress assembled.

ARTICLE IX. The United States in Congress assembled, shall have the sole and exclusive right and power of determining on peace and war, except in the cases mentioned in the sixth article—of sending and receiving ambassadors—entering into treaties and alliances, provided that no treaty of commerce shall be made whereby the legislative power of the respective States shall be restrained from imposing such imposts and duties on foreigners, as their own people are subjected to, or from prohibiting the exportation or importation of and species of goods or commodities whatsoever—of establishing rules for deciding in all cases, what captures on land or water shall be legal, and in what manner prizes taken by land or naval forces in the service of the United States shall be divided or appropriated—of granting letters of marque and reprisal in times of peace—appointing courts for the trial of piracies and felonies committed on the high seas and establishing courts for receiving and determining finally appeals in all cases of captures, provided that no member of Congress shall be appointed a judge of any of the said courts.

The United States in Congress assembled shall also be the last resort on appeal in all disputes and differences now subsisting or that hereafter may arise between two or more States concerning boundary, jurisdiction or any other cause whatever; which authority shall always be exercised in the manner following. Whenever the legislative or executive authority or lawful agent of any State in controversy with another shall present a petition to Congress, stating the matter in question and praying for a hearing, notice thereof shall be given by order of Congress to the legislative or executive authority of the other State in controversy, and a day assigned for the appearance of the parties by their lawful agents, who shall then be directed to appoint by joint consent, commissioners or judges to constitute a court for hearing and determining the matter in question: but if they cannot agree, Congress shall name three persons out of each of the United States, and from the list of such persons each party shall alternately strike out one, the petitioners beginning, until the number shall be reduced to thirteen; and from that number not less than seven, nor more than nine names as Congress shall direct, shall in the presence of Congress be drawn out by lot, and the persons whose names shall be so drawn or any five of them, shall be commissioners or judges, to hear and finally determine the controversy, so always as a major part of the judges who shall hear the cause shall agree in the determination: and if either party shall neglect to attend at the day appointed, without reasons, which Congress shall judge sufficient, or being present shall refuse to strike, the Congress shall proceed to nominate three persons out of each State, and the Secretary of Congress shall strike in behalf of such party absent or refusing; and the judgment and sentence of the court to be appointed, in the manner before prescribed, shall be final and conclusive; and if any of the parties shall refuse to submit to the authority of such court, or to appear or defend their claim or cause, the court shall nevertheless proceed to pronounce sentence, or judgment, which shall in like manner be final and decisive, the judgment or sentence and other proceedings being in either case transmitted to Congress, and lodged among the acts of Congress for the security of the parties concerned: provided that every commissioner, before he sits in judgment, shall take an oath to be administered by one of the judges of the supreme or superior court of the State where the case shall be tried, "well and truly to hear and determine the matter in question, according to the best of his judgment, without favour, affection or hope of reward:" provided also that no State shall be deprived of territory for the benefit of the United States.

All controversies concerning the private right of soil claimed under different grants of two or more States, whose jurisdiction as they may respect such lands, and the states which passed such grants are adjusted, the said grants or either of them being at the same time claimed to have originated antecedent to such settlement of jurisdiction, shall on the petition of either party to the Congress of the United States, be finally determined as near as may be in the same manner as is before prescribed for deciding disputes respecting territorial jurisdiction between different States.

The United States in Congress assembled shall also have the sole and exclusive right and power of regulating the alloy and value of coin struck by their own authority, or by that of the respective States—fixing the standard of weights and measures throughout the United States—regulating the trade and managing all affairs with the Indians, not members of any of the States, provided that the legislative right of any State within its own limits be not infringed or violated—establishing and regulating post-offices from one State to another, throughout all of the United States, and exacting such postage on the papers passing thro' the same as may be requisite to defray the expenses of the said office—appointing all officers of the land forces, in the service of the United States, excepting regimental officers—appointing all the officers of the naval forces, and commissioning all officers whatever in the service of the United States—making rules for the government and regulation of the said land and naval forces, and directing their operations.

The United States in Congress assembled shall have authority to appoint a committee, to sit in the recess of Congress, to be denominated "a Committee of the States," and to consist of one delegate from each State; and to appoint such other committees and civil officers as may be necessary for managing the general affairs of the United States under their direction—to appoint one of their number to preside, provided that no person be allowed to serve in the office of president more than one year in any term of three years; to ascertain the necessary sums of money to be raised for the service of the United States, and to appropriate and apply the same for defraying the public expenses—to borrow money, or emit bills on the credit of the United States, transmitting every half year to the respective States an account of the sums of money so borrowed or emitted,—to build and equip a navy—to agree upon the number of land forces, and to make requisitions from each State for its quota, in proportion to the number of white inhabitants in such State; which requisition shall be binding, and thereupon the Legislature of each State shall appoint the regimental officers, raise the men and cloath, arm and equip them in a soldier like manner, at the expense of the United States; and the officers and men so cloathed, armed and equipped shall march to the place appointed, and within the time agreed on by the United States in Congress assembled: but if the United States in Congress assembled shall, on consideration of circumstances judge proper that any State should not raise men, or should raise a smaller number of men than the quota thereof, such extra number shall be raised, officered, cloathed, armed and equipped in the same manner as the quota of such State, unless the legislature of such State shall judge that such extra number cannot be safely spared out of the same, in which case they shall raise officer, cloath, arm and equip as many of such extra number as they judge can be safely spared. And the officers and men so cloathed, armed and equipped, shall march to the place appointed, and within the time agreed on by the United States in Congress assembled.

The United States in Congress assembled shall never engage in a war, nor grant letters of marque and reprisal in time of peace, nor enter into any treaties or alliances, nor coin money, nor regulate the value thereof, nor ascertain the sums and expenses necessary for the defence and welfare of the United States, or any of them, nor emit bills, nor borrow money on the credit of the United

States, nor appropriate money, nor agree upon the number of vessels to be built or purchased, or the number of land or sea forces to be raised, nor appoint a commander in chief of the army or navy, unless nine States assent to the same: nor shall a question on any other point, except for adjourning from day to day be determined, unless by the votes of a majority of the United States in Congress assembled.

The Congress of the United States shall have power to adjourn to any time within the year, and to any place within the United States, so that no period of adjournment be for a longer duration than the space of six months, and shall publish the journal of their proceedings monthly, except such parts thereof relating to treaties, alliances or military operations, as in their judgment require secresy; and the yeas and nays of the delegates of each State on any question shall be entered on the Journal, when it is desired by any delegate; and the delegates of a State, or any of them, at his or their request shall be furnished with a transcript of the said journal, except such parts as are above excepted, to lay before the Legislatures of the several States.

ARTICLE X. The committee of the States, or any nine of them, shall be authorized to execute, in the recess of Congress, such of the powers of Congress as the United States in Congress assembled, by the consent of nine States, shall from time to time think expedient to vest them with; provided that no power be delegated to the said committee, for the exercise of which, by the articles of confederation, the voice of nine States in the Congress of the United States assembled is requisite.

ARTICLE XI. Canada acceding to this confederation, and joining in the measures of the United States, shall be admitted into, and entitled to all the advantages of this Union: but no other colony shall be admitted into the same, unless such admission be agreed to by nine States.

ARTICLE XII. All bills of credit emitted, monies borrowed and debts contracted by, or under the authority of Congress, before the assembling of the United States, in pursuance of the present confederation, shall be deemed and considered as a charge against the United States, for payment and satisfaction whereof the said United States, and the public faith are hereby solemnly pledged.

ARTICLE XIII. Every State shall abide by the determinations of the United States in Congress assembled, on all questions which by this confederation are submitted to them. And the articles of this confederation shall be inviolably observed by every State, and the Union shall be perpetual; nor shall any alteration at any time hereafter be made in any of them; unless such alteration be agreed to in a Congress of the United States, and be afterwards confirmed by the Legislatures of every State.

And whereas it has pleased the Great Governor of the world to incline the hearts of the Legislatures we respectively represent in Congress, to approve of, and to authorize us to ratify the said articles of confederation and perpetual union. Know ye that we the undersigned delegates, by virtue of the power and authority to us given for that purpose, do by these presents, in the name and in behalf of our respective constituents, fully and entirely ratify and confirm each and every of the said articles of confederation and perpetual union, and all and singular the matters and things therein contained: and we do further solemnly plight and engage the faith of our respective constituents, that they shall abide by the determinations of the United States in Congress assembled, on all questions, which by the said confederation are submitted to them. And that the articles thereof shall be inviolably observed by the States we respectively represent, and that the Union shall be perpetual.

In witness thereof we have hereunto set our hands in Congress. Done at Philadelphia in the State of Pennsylvania the ninth day of July in the year of our Lord one thousand seven hundred and seventy-eight, and in the third year of the independence of America.

THE CONSTITUTION OF
THE UNITED STATES

WE THE PEOPLE OF THE UNITED STATES, in order to form a more perfect Union, establish Justice, insure domestic Tranquility, provide for the common defence, promote the general Welfare, and secure the Blessings of Liberty to ourselves and our Posterity, do ordain and establish this Constitution for the United States of America.

ARTICLE. I.

Section. 1. All legislative Powers herein granted shall be vested in a Congress of the United States, which shall consist of a Senate and House of Representatives.

Section. 2. The House of Representatives shall be composed of Members chosen every second Year by the People of the several States, and the Electors in each State shall have the Qualifications requisite for Electors of the most numerous Branch of the State Legislature.

No Person shall be a Representative who shall not have attained to the Age of twenty five Years, and been seven Years a Citizen of the United States, and who shall not, when elected, be an Inhabitant of that State in which he shall be chosen.

Representatives and direct Taxes shall be apportioned among the several States which may be included within this Union, according to their respective Numbers, which shall be determined by adding to the whole Number of free Persons, including those bound to Service for a Term of Years, and excluding Indians not taxed, three fifths of all other Persons. The actual Enumeration shall be made within three Years after the first Meeting of the Congress of the United States, and within every subsequent Term of ten Years, in such Manner as they shall by Law direct. The Number of Representatives shall not exceed one for every thirty Thousand, but each State shall have at Least one Representative; and until such enumeration shall be made, the State of New Hampshire shall be entitled to chuse three, Massachusetts eight, Rhode-Island and

Providence Plantations one, Connecticut five, New-York six, New Jersey four, Pennsylvania eight, Delaware one, Maryland six, Virginia ten, North Carolina five, South Carolina five, and Georgia three.

When vacancies happen in the Representation from any state, the Executive Authority thereof shall issue Writs of Election to fill such Vacancies.

The House of Representatives shall chuse their Speaker and other Officers; and shall have the sole Power of Impeachment.

Section. 3. The Senate of the United States shall be composed of two Senators from each State, chosen by the legislature thereof, for six Years; and each Senator shall have one Vote.

Immediately after they shall be assembled in Consequence of the first Election, they shall be divided as equally as may be into three Classes. The Seats of the Senators of the first Class shall be vacated at the Expiration of the second Year, of the second Class at the Expiration of the fourth Year, and of the third Class at the Expiration of the sixth Year, so that one third maybe chosen every second Year; and if Vacancies happen by Resignation, or otherwise, during the Recess of the Legislature of any State, the Executive thereof may make temporary Appointments until the next Meeting of the Legislature, which shall then fill such Vacancies.

No Person shall be a Senator who shall not have attained to the Age of thirty Years, and been nine Years a Citizen of the United States, and who shall not, when elected, be an Inhabitant of that State for which he shall be chosen.

The Vice President of the United States shall be President of the Senate, but shall have no Vote, unless they be equally divided.

The Senate shall chuse their other Officers, and also a President pro tempore, in the Absence of the Vice President, or when he shall exercise the Office of President of the United States.

The Senate shall have the sole Power to try all Impeachments. When sitting for that Purpose, they shall be on Oath or Affirmation. When the President of the United States is tried, the Chief Justice shall preside: And no Person shall be convicted without the Concurrence of two thirds of the Members present.

Judgment in Cases of Impeachment shall not extend further than to removal from Office, and disqualification to hold and enjoy any Office of honor, Trust or Profit under the United States: but the Party convicted shall nevertheless be liable and subject to Indictment, Trial, Judgment and Punishment, according to Law.

Section. 4. The Times, Places and Manner of holding Elections for Senators and Representatives, shall be prescribed in each State by the Legislature thereof; but the Congress may at any time by Law make or alter such Regulations, except as to the Places of chusing Senators.

The Congress shall assemble at least once in every Year, and such Meeting shall be on the first Monday in December, unless they shall by Law appoint a different Day.

Section. 5. Each House shall be the Judge of the Elections, Returns and Qualifications of its own Members, and a Majority of each shall constitute a Quorum to do Business; but a smaller Number may adjourn from day to day, and may be authorized to compel the Attendance of absent Members, in such Manner, and under such Penalties as each House may provide.

Each House may determine the Rules of its Proceedings, punish its Members for disorderly Behaviour, and, with the Concurrence of two thirds, expel a Member.

Each House shall keep a Journal of its Proceedings, and from time to time publish the same, excepting such Parts as may in their Judgment require Secrecy; and the Yeas and Nays of the Members of either House on any question shall, at the Desire of one fifth of those Present, be entered on the Journal.

Neither House, during the Session of Congress, shall, without the Consent of the other, adjourn for more than three days, not to any other Place than that in which the two Houses shall be sitting.

Section. 6. The Senators and Representatives shall receive a Compensation for their Services, to be ascertained by Law, and paid out of the Treasury of the United States. They shall in all Cases, except Treason, Felony and Breach of the Peace, be privileged from Arrest during their Attendance at the Session of their respective Houses, and in going to and returning from the same; and for any Speech or Debate in either House, they shall not be questioned in any other Place.

No Senator or Representative shall, during the Time for which he was elected, be appointed to any civil Office under the Authority of the United States, which shall have been created, or the Emoluments whereof shall have been increased during such time; and no Person holding any Office under the United States, shall be a Member of either House during his Continuance in Office.

Section. 7. All Bills for raising Revenue shall originate in the House of Representatives; but the Senate may propose or concur with Amendments as on other Bills.

Every Bill which shall have passed the House of Representatives and the Senate shall, before it become a Law, be presented to the President of the United States; If he approve he shall sign it, but if not he shall return it, with his Objections to that House in which it shall have originated, who shall enter the Objections at large on their Journal, and proceed to reconsider it. If after such Reconsideration two thirds of that House shall agree to pass the Bill, it shall be sent, together with the Objections, to the other House, by which it shall likewise be reconsidered, and if approved by two thirds of that House, it shall become a Law. But in all such Cases the Votes of both Houses shall be determined by yeas and Nays, and the Names of the Persons voting for and against the Bill shall be entered on the Journal of each House respectively. If any Bill shall not be returned by the President within ten Days (Sundays excepted) after it shall have been presented to him, the Same shall be a Law, in like Manner as if he had signed it, unless the Congress by their Adjournment prevent its Return, in which Case it shall not be a Law.

Every Order, Resolution, or Vote to which the Concurrence of the Senate and House of Representatives may be necessary (except on a question of Adjournment) shall be presented to the President of the United States; and before the Same shall take Effect, shall be approved by him, or being disapproved by him, shall be repassed by two thirds of the Senate and House of Representatives, according to the Rules and Limitations prescribed in the Case of a Bill.

Section. 8. The Congress shall have Power To lay and collect Taxes, Duties, Imposts and Excises, to pay the Debts and provide for the common Defence and general Welfare of the United States; but all Duties, Imposts and Excises shall be uniform throughout the United States;

To borrow Money on the credit of the United States;

To regulate Commerce with foreign Nations, and among the several States, and with the Indian Tribes;

To establish an uniform Rule of Naturalization, and uniform Laws on the subject of Bankruptcies throughout the United States;

To coin Money, regulate the Value thereof, and of foreign Coin, and fix the Standard of Weights and Measures;

To provide for the Punishment of counterfeiting the Securities and current Coin of the United States;

To establish Post Offices and Post Roads;

To promote the Progress of Science and useful Arts, by securing for limited Times to Authors and Inventors the exclusive Right to their respective Writings and Discoveries;

To constitute Tribunals inferior to the supreme Court;

To define and punish Piracies and Felonies committed on the high Seas, and Offences against the Law of Nations;

To declare War, grant Letters of Marque and Reprisal, and make Rules concerning Captures on land and Water;

To raise and support Armies, but no Appropriation of Money to that Use shall be for a longer Term than two Years;

To provide and maintain a Navy;

To make Rules for the Government and Regulation of the land and naval Forces;

To provide for calling forth the Militia to execute the Laws of the Union, suppress Insurrections and repel Invasions;

To provide for organizing, arming, and disciplining, the Militia, and for governing such Part of them as may be employed in the Service of the United States, reserving to the States respectively, the Appointment of the Officers, and the Authority of training the Militia according to the discipline prescribed by Congress.

To exercise exclusive Legislation in all Cases whatsoever, over such District (not exceeding ten Miles square) as may, by Cession of Particular States, and the Acceptance of Congress, become the Seat of the Government of the United States, and to exercise like Authority over all Places purchased by the Consent of the Legislature of the State in which the Same shall be, for the Erection of Forts, Magazines, Arsenals, dock-Yards, and other needful Buildings;—And

To make all Laws which shall be necessary and proper for carrying into Execution the foregoing Powers, and all other Powers vested by this Constitution in the Government of the United States, or in any Department or Officer thereof.

Section. 9. The Migration or Importation of such Persons as any of the States now existing shall think proper to admit, shall not be prohibited by the Congress prior to the Year one thousand eight hundred and eight, but a Tax or duty may be imposed on such Importation, not exceeding ten dollars for each Person.

The Privilege of the Writ of Habeas Corpus shall not be suspended, unless when in Cases of Rebellion or Invasion the public Safety may require it.

No Bill of Attainder or ex post facto Law shall be passed.

No Capitation, or other direct, Tax shall be laid, unless in Proportion to the Census or Enumeration herein before directed to be taken.

No Tax or Duty shall be laid on Articles exported from any State.

No Preference shall be given by any Regulation of Commerce or Revenue to the Ports of one State over those of another: nor shall Vessels bound to, or from, one State, be obliged to enter, clear, or pay Duties in another.

No Money shall be drawn from the Treasury, but in Consequence of Appropriations made by Law; and a regular Statement and Account of the Receipts and Expenditures of all public Money shall be published from time to time.

No Title of Nobility shall be granted by the United States: And no Person holding any Office of Profit or trust under them, shall, without the Consent of the Congress, accept of any present, Emolument, Office, or Title, of any kind whatever, from any King, Prince, or foreign State.

Section 10. No State shall enter into any Treaty, Alliance, or Confederation; grant Letters of Marque and Reprisal; coin Money; emit Bills of Credit; make any Thing but gold and silver Coin a Tender in Payment of Debts; pass any Bill of Attainder, ex post facto Law, or Law impairing the Obligation of Contracts, or grant any Title of Nobility.

No State shall, without the Consent of the Congress, lay any Imposts or Duties on Imports or Exports, except what may be absolutely necessary for executing its inspection Laws: and the net Produce of all Duties and Imposts, laid by any State on Imports or Exports, shall be for the Use of the Treasury of the United States; and all such Laws shall be subject to the Revision and Controul of the Congress.

No State shall, without the Consent of Congress, lay any Duty of Tonnage, keep Troops, or Ships of War in time of Peace, enter into any Agreement or Compact with another State, or with a foreign Power, or engage in War, unless actually invaded, or in such imminent Danger as will not admit of delay.

Article. II.

Section. 1. The executive Power shall be vested in a President of the United States of America. He shall hold his Office during the term of four Years, and, together with the Vice President, chosen for the same Term, be elected, as follows:

Each State shall appoint, in such Manner as the Legislature thereof may direct, a Number of Electors, equal to the whole Number of Senators and Representatives to which the State may be entitled in the Congress: but no Senator or Representative, or Person holding an Office of Trust or Profit under the United States, shall be appointed an Elector.

The Electors shall meet in their respective States, and vote by Ballot for two Persons, of whom one at least shall not be an Inhabitant of the same State with themselves. And they shall make a List of all the Persons voted for, and of the Number of Votes for each; which List they shall sign and certify, and transmit sealed to the Seat of the Government of the United States, directed to the President of the Senate. The President of the Senate shall, in the Presence of the Senate and House of Representatives, open all the Certificates, and the Votes shall then be counted. The Person having the greatest Number of Votes shall be the President, if such Number be a Majority of the whole Number of Electors appointed; and if there be more than one who have such Majority, and have an equal Number of Votes, then the House of Representatives shall immediately chuse by Ballot one of them for President; and if no Person have a Majority, then from the five highest on the List the said House shall in like Manner chuse the President. But in chusing the President, the Votes shall be taken by States, the Representation from each State having one Vote; A quorum for this Purpose shall consist of a Member or Members from two thirds of the States, and a Majority of all the States shall be necessary to a Choice. In every Case, after the Choice of the President, the Person having the greatest

Number of Votes of the Electors shall be the Vice President. But if there should remain two or more who have equal Votes, the Senate shall chuse from them by Ballot the Vice President.

The Congress may determine the Time of chusing the Electors, and the Day on which they shall give their Votes; which Day shall be the same throughout the United States.

No Person except a natural born Citizen, or a Citizen of the United States, at the time of the Adoption of this Constitution, shall be eligible to the Office of President; neither shall any Person be eligible to that Office who shall not have attained to the Age of thirty five Years, and been fourteen Years a Resident within the United States.

In Case of the Removal of the President from Office, or of his Death, Resignation, or Inability to discharge the Powers and Duties of the said Office, the Same shall devolve on the Vice President, and the Congress may by Law provide for the Case of Removal, Death, Resignation or Inability, both of the President and Vice President, declaring what Officer shall then act as President, and such Officer shall act accordingly, until the Disability be removed, or a President shall be elected.

The President shall, at stated Times, receive for his Services, a Compensation, which shall neither be encreased or diminished during the Period for which he shall have been elected, and he shall not receive within that Period any other Emolument from the United States, or any of them.

Before he enters on the Execution of his Office, he shall take the following Oath or Affirmation:—"I do solemnly swear (or affirm) that I will faithfully execute the Office of President of the United States, and will to the best of my Ability, preserve, protect and defend the Constitution of the United States."

Section. 2. The President shall be Commander in Chief of the Army and Navy of the United States, and of the Militia of the several States, when called into the actual Service of the United States; he may require the Opinion, in writing, of the principal Officer in each of the executive Departments, upon any Subject relating to the Duties of their respective Offices, and he shall have Power to grant Reprieves and Pardons for Offences against the United States, except in Cases of Impeachment.

He shall have Power, by and with the Advice and Consent of the Senate, to make Treaties, provided two thirds of the Senators present concur; and he shall nominate, and by and with the Advice and Consent of the Senate, shall appoint Ambassadors, other public Ministers and Consuls, Judges of the supreme Court, and all other Officers of the United States, whose Appointments are not herein otherwise provided for, and which shall be established by Law; but the Congress may by Law vest the Appointment of such inferior Officers, as they think proper, in the President alone, in the Courts of Law, or in the Heads of Departments.

The President shall have Power to fill up all Vacancies that may happen during the Recess of the Senate, by granting Commissions which shall expire at the End of their next Session.

Section. 3. He shall from time to time give to the Congress Information of the State of the Union, and recommend to their Consideration such Measures as he shall judge necessary and expedient; he may, on extraordinary Occasions, convene both Houses, or either of them, and in Case of Disagreement between them, with Respect to the Time of Adjournment, he may adjourn them to such Time as he shall think proper; he shall receive Ambassadors and other public Ministers; he shall take Care that the Laws be faithfully executed, and shall Commission all the Officers of the United States.

Section. 4. The President, Vice President and all civil Officers of the United States, shall be removed from Office on Impeachment for, and Conviction of, Treason, Bribery, or other high Crimes and Misdemeanors.

Article. III.

Section. 1. The judicial Power of the United States, shall be vested in one supreme Court, and in such inferior Courts as the Congress may from time to time ordain and establish. The Judges, both of the supreme and inferior Courts, shall hold their Offices during good Behavior, and shall, at stated Times, receive for their Services, a Compensation, which shall not be diminished during their Continuance in Office.

Section. 2. The judicial Power shall extend to all Cases, in Law and Equity, arising under this Constitution, the Laws of the United States, and Treaties made, or which shall be made, under their Authority;—to all Cases affecting Ambassadors, other public Ministers and Consuls;—to all Cases of admiralty and maritime Jurisdiction;—the Controversies to which the United States shall be a Party;—to Controversies between two or more States;—between a State and Citizens of another State;—between Citizens of different States;—between Citizens of the same State claiming Lands under Grants of different States, and between a State, or the Citizens thereof, and foreign States, Citizens or Subjects.

In all cases affecting Ambassadors, other public Ministers and Consuls, and those in which a State shall be Party, the supreme Court shall have original Jurisdiction. In all the other Cases before mentioned, the supreme Court shall have appellate Jurisdiction, both as to Law and Fact, with such Exceptions, and under such Regulations as the Congress shall make.

The Trial of all Crimes, except in Cases of Impeachment, shall be by Jury; and such Trial shall be held in the State where the said Crimes shall have been committed; but when not committed within any State, the Trial shall be at such Place or Places as the Congress may by Law have directed.

Section. 3. Treason against the United States, shall consist only in levying War against them, or in adhering to their Enemies, giving them Aid and Comfort. No Person shall be convicted of Treason unless on the Testimony of two Witnesses to the same overt Act, or on Confession in open Court.

The Congress shall have Power to declare the Punishment of Treason, but no Attainder of Treason shall work Corruption of Blood, or Forfeiture except during the Life of the Person attainted.

ARTICLE. IV.

Section. 1. Full Faith and Credit shall be given in each State to the public Acts, Records, and judicial Proceedings of every other State. And the Congress may by general Laws prescribe the Manner in which such Acts, Records and Proceedings shall be proved, and the Effect thereof.

Section. 2. The Citizens of each State shall be entitled to all Privileges and Immunities of Citizens in the several States.

A Person charged in any State with Treason, Felony, or other Crime, who shall flee from Justice, and be found in another State, shall on Demand of the executive Authority of the State from which he fled, be delivered up, to be removed to the State having Jurisdiction of the Crime.

No Person held to Service or Labour in one State, under the Laws thereof, escaping into another, shall, in Consequence of any Law or Regulation therein, be discharged from such Service or Labour, but shall be delivered up on Claim of the Party to whom such Service or Labour may be due.

Section. 3. New States may be admitted by the Congress into this Union; but no new State shall be formed or erected within the Jurisdiction of any other State; nor any State be formed by the Junction of two or more States, or Parts of States, without the consent of the Legislatures of the States concerned as well as of the Congress.

The Congress shall have Power to dispose of and make all needful Rules and Regulations respecting the Territory or other Property belonging to the United States; and nothing in this Constitution shall be so construed as to Prejudice any Claims of the United States, or of any particular States.

Section. 4. The United States shall guarantee to every State in this Union a Republican Form of Government, and shall protect each of them against Invasion; and on Application of the Legislature, or of the Executive (when the Legislature cannot be convened) against domestic Violence.

ARTICLE. V.

The Congress, whenever two thirds of both Houses shall deem it necessary, shall propose Amendments to this Constitution, or, on the Application of the Legislatures of two thirds of the several States, shall call a Convention for proposing Amendments, which, in either Case, shall be valid to all Intents and Purposes, as Part of this Constitution, when ratified by the Legislatures of three fourths of the several States, or by Conventions in three fourths thereof, as the one or the other Mode of Ratification may be proposed by the Congress; Provided that no Amendment which may be made prior to the Year One thousand eight hundred and eight shall in any Manner affect the first and fourth Clauses in the Ninth Section of the first Article; and that no State, without its Consent, shall be deprived of its equal Suffrage in the Senate.

ARTICLE. VI.

All Debts contracted and Engagements entered into, before the Adoption of this Constitution, shall be as valid against the United States under this Constitution, as under the Confederation.

This Constitution, and the Laws of the United States which shall be made in Pursuance thereof; and all Treaties made, or which shall be made, under the Authority of the United States, shall be the supreme Law of the Land; and the Judges in every State shall be bound thereby, any Thing in the Constitution or Laws of any State to the Contrary notwithstanding.

The Senators and Representatives before mentioned, and the Members of the several State Legislatures, and all executive and judicial Officers, both of the United States and of the several States, shall be bound by Oath or Affirmation, to support this Constitution; but no religious Test shall ever be required as a Qualification to any Office or public Trust under the United States.

ARTICLE. VII.

The Ratification of the Conventions of nine States, shall be sufficient for the Establishment of this Constitution between the States so ratifying the Same.

Done in Convention by the Unanimous Consent of the States present the Seventeenth Day of September in the Year of our Lord one thousand seven hundred and Eighty seven and of the Independence of the United States of America the Twelfth. In witness thereof We have hereunto subscribed our Names,

G⁰. WASHINGTON—Presdᵗ.
and deputy from Virginia.

New Hampshire	John Langdon Nicholas Gilman		
		Delaware	Geo: Read Gunning Bedford jun John Dickinson Richard Bassett Jaco: Broom
Massachusetts	Nathaniel Gorham Rufus King		
Connecticut	Wᵐ Samˡ Johnson Roger Sherman	Maryland	James McHenry Dan of Sᵗ Thoˢ Jenifer Danˡ Carroll
New York: . . .	Alexander Hamilton		
		Virginia	John Blair— James Madison Jr.
New Jersey	Wil: Livingston David A. Brearley. Wᵐ Paterson. Jona: Dayton	North Carolina	Wᵐ Blount Richᵈ Dobbs Spaight. Hu Williamson
Pennsylvania	B Franklin Thomas Mifflin Robᵗ Morris Geo. Clymer Thoˢ FitzSimons Jared Ingersoll James Wilson Gouv Morris	South Carolina	J. Rutledge Charles Cotesworth Pinckney Charles Pinckney Pierce Butler.
		Georgia	William Few Abr Baldwin

AMENDMENTS TO THE CONSTITUTION

ARTICLES IN ADDITION TO, and Amendment of the Constitution of the United States of America, proposed by Congress, and ratified by the Legislatures of the several States, pursuant to the fifth Article of the original Constitution.

AMENDMENT I.

Congress shall make no law respecting an establishment of religion, or prohibiting the free exercise thereof; or abridging the freedom of speech, or of the press; or the right of the people peaceably to assemble, and to petition the Government for a redress of grievances.

Amendment II.

A well regulated Militia, being necessary to the security of a free State, the right of the people to keep and bear Arms, shall not be infringed.

Amendment III.

No Soldier shall, in time of peace be quartered in any house, without the consent of the Owner, nor in time of war, but in a manner to be prescribed by law.

Amendment IV.

The right of the people to be secure in their persons, houses, papers, and effects, against unreasonable searches and seizures, shall not be violated, and no Warrants shall issue, but upon probable cause, supported by Oath or affirmation, and particularly describing the place to be searched, and the persons or things to be seized.

Amendment V.

No person shall be held to answer for a capital, or otherwise infamous crime, unless on a presentment or indictment of a Grand Jury, except in cases arising in the land or naval forces, or in the Militia, when in actual service in time of War or public danger; nor shall any person be subject for the same offence to be twice put in jeopardy of life or limb; nor shall be compelled in any criminal case to be a witness against himself, nor be deprived of life, liberty, or property, without due process of law; nor shall private property be taken for public use, without just compensation.

Amendment VI.

In all criminal prosecutions, the accused shall enjoy the right to a speedy and public trial, by an impartial jury of the State and district wherein the crime shall have been committed, which district shall have been previously ascertained by law, and to be informed of the nature and cause of the accusation; to be confronted with the witnesses against him; to have compulsory process for obtaining witnesses in his favor, and to have the Assistance of Counsel for his defence.

AMENDMENT VII.

In Suits at common law, where the value in controversy shall exceed twenty dollars, the right of trial by jury shall be preserved, and no fact tried by a jury, shall be otherwise re-examined in any Court of the United States, than according to the rules of the common law.

AMENDMENT VIII.

Excessive bail shall not be required, nor excessive fines imposed, nor cruel and unusual punishments inflicted.

AMENDMENT IX.

The enumeration in the Constitution, of certain rights, shall not be construed to deny or disparage others retained by the people.

AMENDMENT X.

The powers not delegated to the United States by the Constitution, nor prohibited by it to the States, are reserved to the States respectively, or to the people. [The first ten amendments went into effect December 15, 1791.]

AMENDMENT XI.

The Judicial power of the United States shall not be construed to extend to any suit in law or equity, commenced or prosecuted against one of the United States by Citizens of another State, or by Citizens or Subjects of any Foreign State. [January 8, 1798.]

AMENDMENT XII.

The Electors shall meet in their respective states, and vote by ballot for President and Vice-President, one of whom, at least, shall not be an inhabitant of the same state with themselves; they shall name in their ballots the person voted for as President, and in distinct ballots the person voted for as Vice-President, and they shall make distinct lists of all persons voted for as President, and of all persons voted for as Vice President, and of the number of votes for each, which lists they shall sign and certify, and transmit sealed to the seat of the government of the United States, directed to the President of the Senate;—The President of the Senate shall, in the presence of the Senate and House of Representatives, open all the certificates and the votes shall then be counted;—The person having the greatest number of votes for President, shall be the President, if such number be a majority of the whole number of Electors appointed; and if no person have such majority, then from the persons having the highest numbers not exceeding three on the list of those voted for as President, the House of Representatives shall choose immediately, by ballot, the President. But in choosing the President, the votes shall be taken by states, the representation from each state having one vote; a quorum for this purpose shall consist of a member or members from two-thirds of the states, and a majority of all the states shall be necessary to a choice. And if the House of Representatives shall not choose a President whenever the right of choice shall devolve upon them, before the fourth day of March next following, then the Vice-President shall act as President, as in the case of the death or other constitutional disability of the President.—The person having the greatest number of votes as Vice-President, shall be the Vice-President, if such number be a majority of the whole number of Electors appointed, and if no person have a majority, then from the two highest numbers on the list, the Senate shall choose the Vice-President; a quorum for the purpose shall consist of two-thirds of the whole number of Senators, and a majority of the whole number shall be necessary to a choice. But no person constitutionally ineligible to the office of President shall be eligible to that of Vice-President of the United States. [September 25, 1804.]

AMENDMENT XIII.

Section 1. Neither slavery nor involuntary servitude, except as a punishment for crime whereof the party shall have been duly convicted, shall exist within the United States, or any place subject to their jurisdiction.

Section 2. Congress shall have power to enforce this article by appropriate legislation. [December 18, 1865.]

Amendment XIV.

Section 1. All persons born or naturalized in the United States, and subject to the jurisdiction thereof, are citizens of the United States and of the State wherein they reside. No State shall make or enforce any law which shall abridge the privileges or immunities of citizens of the United States; nor shall any State deprive any person of life, liberty, or property, without due process of law; nor deny to any person within its jurisdiction the equal protection of the laws.

Section 2. Representatives shall be apportioned among the several States according to their respective numbers, counting the whole number of persons in each State, excluding Indians not taxed. But when the right to vote at any election for the choice of electors for President and Vice President of the United States, Representatives in Congress, the Executive and Judicial officers of a State, or the members of the Legislature thereof, is denied to any of the male inhabitants of such State, being twenty-one years of age, and citizens of the United States, or in any way abridged, except for participation in rebellion, or other crime, the basis of representation therein shall be reduced in the proportion which the number of such male citizens shall bear to the whole number of male citizens twenty-one years of age in such State.

Section 3. No person shall be a Senator or Representative in Congress, or elector of President and Vice President, or hold any office, civil or military, under the United States, or under any State, who, having previously taken an oath, as a member of Congress, or as an officer of the United States, or as a member of any State legislature, or as an executive or judicial officer of any State, to support the Constitution of the United States, shall have engaged in insurrection or rebellion against the same, or given aid or comfort to the enemies thereof. But Congress may by a vote of two-thirds of each House, remove such disability.

Section 4. The validity of the public debt of the United States, authorized by law, including debts incurred for payment of pensions and bounties for services in suppressing insurrection or rebellion, shall not be questioned. But neither the United States nor any State shall assume or pay any debt or obligation incurred in aid of insurrection or rebellion against the United States, or any claim for the loss or emancipation of any slave; but all such debts, obligations and claims shall be held illegal and void.

Section 5. The Congress shall have power to enforce, by appropriate legislation, the provisions of this article. [July 28, 1868.]

Amendment XV.

Section 1. The right of citizens of the United States to vote shall not be denied or abridged by the United States or by any State on account of race, color, or previous condition of servitude—

Section 2. The Congress shall have power to enforce this article by appropriate legislation.—[March 30, 1870.]

Amendment XVI.

The Congress shall have power to lay and collect taxes on incomes, from whatever source derived, without apportionment among the several States, and without regard to any census or enumeration. [February 25, 1913.]

Amendment XVII.

The Senate of the United States shall be composed of two senators from each State, elected by the people thereof, for six years; and each Senator shall have one vote. The electors in each State shall have the qualifications requisite for electors of the most numerous branch of the State legislature.

When vacancies happen in the representation of any State in the Senate, the executive authority of such State shall issue writs of election to fill such vacancies: *Provided,* That the legislature of any State may empower the executive thereof to make temporary appointments until the people fill the vacancies by election as the legislature may direct.

This amendment shall not be so construed as to affect the election or term of any senator chosen before it becomes valid as part of the Constitution. [May 31, 1913.]

Amendment XVIII.

After one year from the ratification of this article, the manufacture, sale, or transportation of intoxicating liquors within, the importation thereof into, or the exportation thereof from the United States and all territory subject to the jurisdiction thereof for beverage purposes is hereby prohibited.

The Congress and the several States shall have concurrent power to enforce this article by appropriate legislation.

This article shall be inoperative unless it shall have been ratified as an amendment to the Constitution by the legislatures of the several States, as provided in the Constitution, within seven years from the date of the submission thereof to the States by Congress. [January 29, 1919.]

AMENDMENT XIX.

The right of citizens of the United States to vote shall not be denied or abridged by the United States or by any State on account of sex.

The Congress shall have power by appropriate legislation to enforce the provisions of this article. [August 26, 1920.]

AMENDMENT XX.

Section 1. The terms of the President and Vice-President shall end at noon on the twentieth day of January, and the terms of Senators and Representatives at noon on the third day of January, of the years in which such terms would have ended if this article had not been ratified; and the terms of their successors shall then begin.

Section 2. The Congress shall assemble at least once in every year, and such meeting shall begin at noon on the third day of January, unless they shall by law appoint a different day.

Section 3. If, at the time fixed for the beginning of the term of the President, the President-elect shall have died, the Vice-President-elect shall become President. If a President shall not have been chosen before the time fixed for the beginning of his term, or if the President-elect shall have failed to qualify, then the Vice-President-elect shall act as President until a President shall have qualified; and the Congress may by law provide for the case wherein neither a President-elect nor a Vice-President-elect shall have qualified, declaring who shall then act as President, or the manner in which one who is to act shall be selected, and such person shall act accordingly until a President or Vice-President shall have qualified.

Section 4. The Congress may by law provide for the case of the death of any of the persons from whom the House of Representatives may choose a President whenever the right of choice shall have devolved upon them, and for the case of the death of any of the persons from whom the Senate may choose a Vice-President whenever the right of choice shall have devolved upon them.

Section 5. Sections 1 and 2 shall take effect on the 15th day of October following the ratification of this article.

Section 6. This article shall be inoperative unless it shall have been ratified as an amendment to the Constitution by the legislatures of three-fourths of the several States within seven years from the date of its submission. [February 6, 1933.]

AMENDMENT XXI.

Section 1. The eighteenth article of amendment to the Constitution of the United States is hereby repealed.

Section 2. The transportation or importation into any State, Territory or possession of the United States for delivery or use therein of intoxicating liquors, in violation of the laws thereof, is hereby prohibited.

Section 3. This article shall be inoperative unless it shall have been ratified as an amendment to the Constitution by convention in the several States, as provided in the Constitution, within seven years from the date of the submission thereof to the States by the Congress. [December 5, 1933.]

AMENDMENT XXII.

Section 1. No person shall be elected to the office of the President more than twice, and no person who has held the office of President, or acted as President, for more than two years of a term to which some other person was elected President shall be elected to the office of the President more than once. But this Article shall not apply to any person holding the office of President when this Article was proposed by the Congress, and shall not prevent any person who may be holding the office of President, or acting as President, during the term within which this Article becomes operative from holding the office of President or acting as President during the remainder of such term.

Section 2. This article shall be inoperative unless it shall have been ratified as an amendment to the Constitution by the legislatures of three-fourths of the several states within seven years from the date of its submission to the States by the Congress. [February 27, 1951.]

Amendment XXIII.

Section 1. The District constituting the seat of government of the United States shall appoint in such manner as the Congress may direct:

A number of electors of President and Vice-President equal to the whole number of Senators and Representatives in Congress to which the District would be entitled if it were a State, but in no event more than the least populous State; they shall be in addition to those appointed by the States, but they shall be considered, for the purposes of the election of President and Vice-President, to be electors appointed by a State; and they shall meet in the District and perform such duties as provided by the twelfth article of amendment.

Section 2. The Congress shall have the power to enforce this article by appropriate legislation. [March 29, 1961.]

Amendment XXIV.

Section 1. The right of citizens of the United States to vote in any primary or other election for President or Vice President, for electors for President or Vice President, or for Senator or Representative in Congress, shall not be denied or abridged by the United States or any State by reason of failure to pay any poll tax or other tax.

Section 2. The Congress shall have power to enforce this article by appropriate legislation. [January 23, 1964.]

Amendment XXV.

Section 1. In case of the removal of the President from office or of his death or resignation, the Vice President shall become President.

Section 2. Whenever there is a vacancy in the office of Vice President, the President shall nominate a Vice President who shall take office upon confirmation by a majority vote of both Houses of Congress.

Section 3. Whenever the President transmits to the President pro tempore of the Senate and the Speaker of the House of Representatives his written declaration that he is unable to discharge the powers and duties of his office, and until he transmits to them a written declaration to the contrary, such powers and duties shall be discharged by the Vice President as Acting President.

Section 4. Whenever the Vice President and a majority of either the principal officers of the executive departments or of such other body as Congress may by law provide, transmit to the President pro tempore of the Senate and the Speaker of the House of Representatives their written declaration that the President is unable to discharge the powers and duties of his office, the Vice President shall immediately assume the powers and duties of the office as Acting President.

Thereafter, when the President transmits to the President pro tempore of the Senate and the Speaker of the House of Representatives his written declaration that no inability exists, he shall resume the powers and duties of his office unless the Vice President and a majority of either the principal officers of the executive departments or of such other body as Congress may by law provide, transmit within four days to the President pro tempore of the Senate and the Speaker of the House of Representatives their written declaration that the President is unable to discharge the powers and duties of his office. Thereupon Congress shall decide the issue, assembling within forty-eight hours for that purpose if not in session. If the Congress, within twenty-one days after receipt of the latter written declaration, or, if Congress is not in session, within twenty-one days after Congress is required to assemble, determines by two-thirds vote of both Houses that the President is unable to discharge the powers and duties of his office, the Vice President shall continue to discharge the same as Acting President; otherwise, the President shall resume the powers and duties of his office. [February 10, 1967.]

AMENDMENT XXVI.

Section 1. The right of citizens of the United States, who are eighteen years of age or older, to vote shall not be denied or abridged by the United States or by any State on account of age.

Section 2. The Congress shall have power to enforce this article by appropriate legislation [June 30, 1971.]

AMENDMENT XXVII.

No law, varying the compensation for the services of the Senators and Representatives shall take effect, until an election of Representatives shall have intervened. [May 8, 1992.]

PRESIDENTIAL ELECTIONS

Year	Number of States	Candidates	Parties	Popular Vote	% of Popular Vote	Electoral Vote	% Voter Participation
1789	11	**GEORGE WASHINGTON**	No party designations			69	
		John Adams				34	
		Other candidates				35	
1792	15	**GEORGE WASHINGTON**	No party designations			132	
		John Adams				77	
		George Clinton				50	
		Other candidates				5	
1796	16	**JOHN ADAMS**	Federalist			71	
		Thomas Jefferson	Democratic-Republican			68	
		Thomas Pinckney	Federalist			59	
		Aaron Burr	Democratic-Republican			30	
		Other candidates				48	
1800	16	**THOMAS JEFFERSON**	Democratic-Republican			73	
		Aaron Burr	Democratic-Republican			73	
		John Adams	Federalist			65	
		Charles C. Pinckney	Federalist			64	
		John Jay	Federalist			1	
1804	17	**THOMAS JEFFERSON**	Democratic-Republican			162	
		Charles C. Pinckney	Federalist			14	

Year	Number of States	Candidates	Parties	Popular Vote	% of Popular Vote	Electoral Vote	% Voter Participation
1808	17	**JAMES MADISON**	Democratic-Republican			122	
		Charles C. Pinckney	Federalist			47	
		George Clinton	Democratic-Republican			6	
1812	18	**JAMES MADISON**	Democratic-Republican			128	
		DeWitt Clinton	Federalist			89	
1816	19	**JAMES MONROE**	Democratic-Republican			183	
		Rufus King	Federalist			34	
1820	24	**JAMES MONROE**	Democratic-Republican			231	
		John Quincy Adams	Independent			1	
1824	24	**JOHN QUINCY ADAMS**	Democratic-Republican	108,740	30.5	84	26.9
		Andrew Jackson	Democratic-Republican	153,544	43.1	99	
		Henry Clay	Democratic-Republican	47,136	13.2	37	
		William H. Crawford	Democratic-Republican	46,618	13.1	41	
1828	24	**ANDREW JACKSON**	Democratic	647,286	56.0	178	57.6
		John Quincy Adams	National-Republican	508,064	44.0	83	

Year	Number of States	Candidates	Parties	Popular Vote	% of Popular Vote	Electoral Vote	% Voter Participation
1832	24	**ANDREW JACKSON**	Democratic	688,242	54.5	219	55.4
		Henry Clay	National-Republican	473,462	37.5	49	
		William Wirt	Anti-Masonic	101,051	8.0	7	
		John Floyd	Democratic			11	
1836	26	**MARTIN VAN BUREN**	Democratic	765,483	50.9	170	57.8
		William H. Harrison	Whig	739,795	49.1	73	
		Hugh L. White	Whig			26	
		Daniel Webster	Whig			14	
		W. P. Mangum	Whig			11	
1840	26	**WILLIAM H. HARRISON**	Whig	1,274,624	53.1	234	80.2
		Martin Van Buren	Democratic	1,127,781	46.9	60	
1844	26	**JAMES K. POLK**	Democratic	1,338,464	49.6	170	78.9
		Henry Clay	Whig	1,300,097	48.1	105	
		James G. Birney	Liberty	62,300	2.3		
1848	30	**ZACHARY TAYLOR**	Whig	1,360,967	47.4	163	72.7
		Lewis Cass	Democratic	1,222,342	42.5	127	
		Martin Van Buren	Free Soil	291,263	10.1		
1852	31	**FRANKLIN PIERCE**	Democratic	1,601,117	50.9	254	69.6
		Winfield Scott	Whig	1,385,453	44.1	42	
		John P. Hale	Free Soil	155,825	5.0		
1856	31	**JAMES BUCHANAN**	Democratic	1,832,955	45.3	174	78.9
		John C. Frémont	Republican	1,339,932	33.1	114	
		Millard Fillmore	American	871,731	21.6	8	

Year	Number of States	Candidates	Parties	Popular Vote	% of Popular Vote	Electoral Vote	% Voter Participation
1860	33	**ABRAHAM LINCOLN**	Republican	1,865,593	39.8	180	81.2
		Stephen A. Douglas	Democratic	1,382,713	29.5	12	
		John C. Breckinridge	Democratic	848,356	18.1	72	
		John Bell	Constitutional Union	592,906	12.6	39	
1864	36	**ABRAHAM LINCOLN**	Republican	2,206,938	55.0	212	73.8
		George B. McClellan	Democratic	1,803,787	45.0	21	
1868	37	**ULYSSES S. GRANT**	Republican	3,013,421	52.7	214	78.1
		Horatio Seymour	Democratic	2,706,829	47.3	80	
1872	37	**ULYSSES S. GRANT**	Republican	3,596,745	55.6	286	71.3
		Horace Greeley	Democratic	2,843,446	43.9	66	
1876	38	**RUTHERFORD B. HAYES**	Republican	4,036,572	48.0	185	81.8
		Samuel J. Tilden	Democratic	4,284,020	51.0	184	
1880	38	**JAMES A. GARFIELD**	Republican	4,453,295	48.5	214	79.4
		Winfield S. Hancock	Democratic	4,414,082	48.1	155	
		James B. Weaver	Greenback-Labor	308,578	3.4		
1884	38	**GROVER CLEVELAND**	Democratic	4,879,507	48.5	219	77.5
		James G. Blaine	Republican	4,850,293	48.2	182	
		Benjamin F. Butler	Greenback-Labor	175,370	1.8		
		John P. St. John	Prohibition	150,369	1.5		
1888	38	**BENJAMIN HARRISON**	Republican	5,477,129	47.9	233	79.3
		Grover Cleveland	Democratic	5,537,857	48.6	168	
		Clinton B. Fisk	Prohibition	249,506	2.2		
		Anson J. Streeter	Union Labor	146,935	1.3		

Year	Number of States	Candidates	Parties	Popular Vote	% of Popular Vote	Electoral Vote	% Voter Participation
1892	44	**GROVER CLEVELAND**	Democratic	5,555,426	46.1	277	74.7
		Benjamin Harrison	Republican	5,182,690	43.0	145	
		James B. Weaver	People's	1,029,846	8.5	22	
		John Bidwell	Prohibition	264,133	2.2		
1896	45	**WILLIAM McKINLEY**	Republican	7,102,246	51.1	271	79.3
		William J. Bryan	Democratic	6,492,559	47.7	176	
1900	45	**WILLIAM McKINLEY**	Republican	7,218,491	51.7	292	73.2
		William J. Bryan	Democratic; Populist	6,356,734	45.5	155	
		John C. Wooley	Prohibition	208,914	1.5		
1904	45	**THEODORE ROOSEVELT**	Republican	7,628,461	57.4	336	65.2
		Alton B. Parker	Democratic	5,084,223	37.6	140	
		Eugene V. Debs	Socialist	402,283	3.0		
		Silas C. Swallow	Prohibition	258,536	1.9		
1908	46	**WILLIAM H. TAFT**	Republican	7,675,320	51.6	321	65.4
		William J. Bryan	Democratic	6,412,294	43.1	162	
		Eugene V. Debs	Socialist	420,793	2.8		
		Eugene W. Chafin	Prohibition	253,840	1.7		
1912	48	**WOODROW WILSON**	Democratic	6,296,547	41.9	435	58.8
		Theodore Roosevelt	Progressive	4,118,571	27.4	88	
		William H. Taft	Republican	3,486,720	23.2	8	
		Eugene V. Debs	Socialist	900,672	6.0		
		Eugene W. Chafin	Prohibition	206,275	1.4		

Year	Number of States	Candidates	Parties	Popular Vote	% Popular Vote	Electoral Vote	% Voter Participation
1916	48	**WOODROW WILSON**	Democratic	9,127,695	49.4	277	61.6
		Charles E. Hughes	Republican	8,533,507	46.2	254	
		A. L. Benson	Socialist	585,113	3.2		
		J. Frank Hanly	Prohibition	220,506	1.2		
1920	48	**WARREN G. HARDING**	Republican	16,143,407	60.4	404	49.2
		James M. Cox	Democratic	9,130,328	34.2	127	
		Eugene V. Debs	Socialist	919,799	3.4		
		P. P. Christensen	Farmer-Labor	265,411	1.0		
1924	48	**CALVIN COOLIDGE**	Republican	15,718,211	54.0	382	48.9
		John W. Davis	Democratic	8,385,283	28.8	136	
		Robert M. La Follette	Progressive	4,831,289	16.6	13	
1928	48	**HERBERT C. HOOVER**	Republican	21,391,993	58.2	444	56.9
		Alfred E. Smith	Democratic	15,016,169	40.9	87	
1932	48	**FRANKLIN D. ROOSEVELT**	Democratic	22,809,638	57.4	472	56.9
		Herbert C. Hoover	Republican	15,758,901	39.7	59	
		Norman Thomas	Socialist	881,951	2.2		
1936	48	**FRANKLIN D. ROOSEVELT**	Democratic	27,752,869	60.8	523	61.0
		Alfred M. Landon	Republican	16,674,665	36.5	8	
		William Lemke	Union	882,479	1.9		
1940	48	**FRANKLIN D. ROOSEVELT**	Democratic	27,307,819	54.8	449	62.5
		Wendell L. Willkie	Republican	22,321,018	44.8	82	
1944	48	**FRANKLIN D. ROOSEVELT**	Democratic	25,606,585	53.5	432	55.9
		Thomas E. Dewey	Republican	22,014,745	46.0	99	

Year	Number of States	Candidates	Parties	Popular Vote	% of Popular Vote	Electoral Vote	% Voter Participation
1948	48	**HARRY S. TRUMAN**	Democratic	24,179,345	49.6	303	53.0
		Thomas E. Dewey	Republican	21,991,291	45.1	189	
		J. Strom Thurmond	States' Rights	1,176,125	2.4	39	
		Henry A. Wallace	Progressive	1,157,326	2.4		
1952	48	**DWIGHT D. EISENHOWER**	Republican	33,936,234	55.1	442	63.3
		Adlai E. Stevenson	Democratic	27,314,992	44.4	89	
1956	48	**DWIGHT D. EISENHOWER**	Republican	35,590,472	57.6	457	60.6
		Adlai E. Stevenson	Democratic	26,022,752	42.1	73	
1960	50	**JOHN F. KENNEDY**	Democratic	34,226,731	49.7	303	62.8
		Richard M. Nixon	Republican	34,108,157	49.5	219	
1964	50	**LYNDON B. JOHNSON**	Democratic	43,129,566	61.1	486	61.9
		Barry M. Goldwater	Republican	27,178,188	38.5	52	
1968	50	**RICHARD M. NIXON**	Republican	31,785,480	43.4	301	60.9
		Hubert H. Humphrey	Democratic	31,275,166	42.7	191	
		George C. Wallace	American Independent	9,906,473	13.5	46	
1972	50	**RICHARD M. NIXON**	Republican	47,169,911	60.7	520	55.2
		George S. McGovern	Democratic	29,170,383	37.5	17	
		John G. Schmitz	American	1,099,482	1.4		

Year	States	Candidates	Party	Popular Vote	% of Popular Vote	Electoral Vote	% Voter Participation
1976	50	**JIMMY CARTER**	Democratic	40,830,763	50.1	297	53.5
		Gerald R. Ford	Republican	39,147,793	48.0	240	
1980	50	**RONALD REAGAN**	Republican	43,901,812	50.7	489	52.6
		Jimmy Carter	Democratic	35,483,820	41.0	49	
		John B. Anderson	Independent	5,719,437	6.6		
		Ed Clark	Libertarian	921,188	1.1		
1984	50	**RONALD REAGAN**	Republican	54,451,521	58.8	525	53.1
		Walter F. Mondale	Democratic	37,565,334	40.6	13	
1988	50	**GEORGE H. W. BUSH**	Republican	47,917,341	53.4	426	50.1
		Michael Dukakis	Democratic	41,013,030	45.6	111	
1992	50	**BILL CLINTON**	Democratic	44,908,254	43.0	370	55.0
		George H. W. Bush	Republican	39,102,343	37.4	168	
		H. Ross Perot	Independent	19,741,065	18.9		
1996	50	**BILL CLINTON**	Democratic	47,401,185	49.0	379	49.0
		Bob Dole	Republican	39,197,469	41.0	159	
		H. Ross Perot	Independent	8,085,295	8.0		
2000	50	**GEORGE W. BUSH**	Republican	50,455,156	47.9	271	50.4
		Al Gore	Democrat	50,997,335	48.4	266	
		Ralph Nader	Green	2,882,897	2.7		

Candidates receiving less than 1 percent of the popular vote have been omitted. Thus the percentage of popular vote given for any election year may not total 100 percent.

Before the passage of the Twelfth Amendment in 1804, the electoral college voted for two presidential candidates; the runner-up became vice-president.

ADMISSION OF STATES

Order of Admission	State	Date of Admission	Order of Admission	State	Date of Admission
1	Delaware	December 7, 1787	26	Michigan	January 26, 1837
2	Pennsylvania	December 12, 1787	27	Florida	March 3, 1845
3	New Jersey	December 18, 1787	28	Texas	December 29, 1845
4	Georgia	January 2, 1788	29	Iowa	December 28, 1846
5	Connecticut	January 9, 1788	30	Wisconsin	May 29, 1848
6	Massachusetts	February 7, 1788	31	California	September 9, 1850
7	Maryland	April 28, 1788	32	Minnesota	May 11, 1858
8	South Carolina	May 23, 1788	33	Oregon	February 14, 1859
9	New Hampshire	June 21, 1788	34	Kansas	January 29, 1861
10	Virginia	June 25, 1788	35	West Virginia	June 30, 1863
11	New York	July 26, 1788	36	Nevada	October 31, 1864
12	North Carolina	November 21, 1789	37	Nebraska	March 1, 1867
13	Rhode Island	May 29, 1790	38	Colorado	August 1, 1876
14	Vermont	March 4, 1791	39	North Dakota	November 2, 1889
15	Kentucky	June 1, 1792	40	South Dakota	November 2, 1889
16	Tennessee	June 1, 1796	41	Montana	November 8, 1889
17	Ohio	March 1, 1803	42	Washington	November 11, 1889
18	Louisiana	April 30, 1812	43	Idaho	July 3, 1890
19	Indiana	December 11, 1816	44	Wyoming	July 10, 1890
20	Mississippi	December 10, 1817	45	Utah	January 4, 1896
21	Illinois	December 3, 1818	46	Oklahoma	November 16, 1907
22	Alabama	December 14, 1819	47	New Mexico	January 6, 1912
23	Maine	March 15, 1820	48	Arizona	February 14, 1912
24	Missouri	August 10, 1821	49	Alaska	January 3, 1959
25	Arkansas	June 15, 1836	50	Hawaii	August 21, 1959

POPULATION OF THE UNITED STATES

Year	Number of States	Population	% Increase	Population per Square Mile
1790	13	3,929,214		4.5
1800	16	5,308,483	35.1	6.1
1810	17	7,239,881	36.4	4.3
1820	23	9,638,453	33.1	5.5
1830	24	12,866,020	33.5	7.4
1840	26	17,069,453	32.7	9.8
1850	31	23,191,876	35.9	7.9
1860	33	31,443,321	35.6	10.6
1870	37	39,818,449	26.6	13.4
1880	38	50,155,783	26.0	16.9
1890	44	62,947,714	25.5	21.1
1900	45	75,994,575	20.7	25.6
1910	46	91,972,266	21.0	31.0
1920	48	105,710,620	14.9	35.6
1930	48	122,775,046	16.1	41.2
1940	48	131,669,275	7.2	44.2
1950	48	150,697,361	14.5	50.7
1960	50	179,323,175	19.0	50.6
1970	50	203,235,298	13.3	57.5
1980	50	226,504,825	11.4	64.0
1985	50	237,839,000	5.0	67.2
1990	50	250,122,000	5.2	70.6
1995	50	263,411,707	5.3	74.4
2000	50	281,421,906	6.8	77.0

IMMIGRATION TO THE UNITED STATES, FISCAL YEARS 1820–1998

Year	Number	Year	Number	Year	Number	Year	Number
1820–1989	**55,457,531**	**1871–80**	**2,812,191**	**1921–30**	**4,107,209**	**1971–80**	**4,493,314**
		1871	321,350	1921	805,228	1971	370,478
1820	8,385	1872	404,806	1922	309,556	1972	384,685
1821–30	**143,439**	1873	459,803	1923	522,919	1973	400,063
1821	9,127	1874	313,339	1924	706,896	1974	394,861
1822	6,911	1875	227,498	1925	294,314	1975	386,914
1823	6,354	1876	169,986	1926	304,488	1976	398,613
1824	7,912	1877	141,857	1927	335,175	1976	103,676
1825	10,199	1878	138,469	1928	307,255	1977	462,315
1826	10,837	1879	177,826	1929	279,678	1978	601,442
1827	18,875	1880	457,257	1930	241,700	1979	460,348
1828	27,382	**1881–90**	**5,246,613**	**1931–40**	**528,431**	1980	530,639
1829	22,520	1881	669,431	1931	97,139	**1981–90**	**7,338,062**
1830	23,322	1882	788,992	1932	35,576	1981	596,600
1831–40	**599,125**	1883	603,322	1933	23,068	1982	594,131
1831	22,633	1884	518,592	1934	29,470	1983	559,763
1832	60,482	1885	395,346	1935	34,956	1984	543,903
1833	58,640	1886	334,203	1936	36,329	1985	570,009
1834	65,365	1887	490,109	1937	50,244	1986	601,708
1835	45,374	1888	546,889	1938	67,895	1987	601,516
1836	76,242	1889	444,427	1939	82,998	1988	643,025
1837	79,340	1890	455,302	1940	70,756	1989	1,090,924
1838	38,914	**1891–1900**	**3,687,564**	**1941–50**	**1,035,039**	1990	1,536,483
1839	68,069	1891	560,319	1941	51,776		
1840	84,066	1892	579,663	1942	28,781		
1841–50	**1,713,251**	1893	439,730	1943	23,725		
1841	80,289	1894	285,631	1944	28,551		
1842	104,565	1895	258,536	1945	38,119		
		1896	343,267	1946	108,721		

Year	Number	Year	Number	Year	Number	Year	Number
1843	52,496					**1991–98**	**7,605,068**
1844	78,615					1991	1,827,167
1845	114,371					1992	973,977
1846	154,416					1993	904,292
1847	234,968	1897	230,832	1947	147,292	1994	804,416
1848	226,527	1898	229,299	1948	170,570	1995	720,461
1849	297,024	1899	311,715	1949	188,317	1996	915,900
1850	369,980	1900	448,572	1950	249,187	1997	798,378
1851–60	**2,598,214**	**1901–10**	**8,795,386**	**1951–60**	**2,515,479**	1998	660,477
1851	379,466	1901	487,918	1951	205,717		
1852	371,603	1902	648,743	1952	265,520		
1853	368,645	1903	857,046	1953	170,434		
1854	427,833	1904	812,870	1954	208,177		
1855	200,877	1905	1,026,499	1955	237,790		
1856	200,436	1906	1,100,735	1956	321,625		
1857	251,306	1907	1,285,349	1957	326,867		
1858	123,126	1908	782,870	1958	253,265		
1859	121,282	1909	751,786	1959	260,686		
1860	153,640	1910	1,041,570	1960	265,398		
1861–70	**2,314,824**	**1911–20**	**5,735,811**	**1961–70**	**3,321,677**		
1861	91,918	1911	878,587	1961	271,344		
1862	91,985	1912	838,172	1962	283,763		
1863	176,282	1913	1,197,892	1963	306,260		
1864	193,418	1914	1,218,480	1964	292,248		
1865	248,120	1915	326,700	1965	296,697		
1866	318,568	1916	298,826	1966	323,040		
1867	315,722	1917	295,403	1967	361,972		
1868	138,840	1918	110,618	1968	454,448		
1869	352,768	1919	141,132	1969	358,579		
1870	387,203	1920	430,001	1970	373,326		

Source: U.S. Immigration and Naturalization Service, 1999.

IMMIGRATION BY REGION AND SELECTED COUNTRY OF LAST RESIDENCE, FISCAL YEARS 1820–1999

Region and Country of Last Residence[1]	1820	1821–30	1831–40	1841–50	1851–60	1861–70	1871–80	1881–90
All countries	8,385	143,439	599,125	1,713,251	2,598,214	2,314,824	2,812,191	5,246,613
Europe	7,690	98,797	495,681	1,597,442	2,452,577	2,065,141	2,271,925	4,735,484
Austria-Hungary	—[2]	—[2]	—[2]	—[2]	—[2]	7,800	72,969	353,719
Austria	—[2]	—[2]	—[2]	—[2]	—[2]	484[3]	63,009	226,038
Hungary	—[2]	—[2]	—[2]	—[2]	—[2]	7,124[3]	9,960	127,681
Belgium	1	27	22	5,074	4,738	6,734	7,221	20,177
Czechoslovakia	—[4]	—[4]	—[4]	—[4]	—[4]	—[4]	—[4]	—[4]
Denmark	20	169	1,063	539	3,749	17,094	31,771	88,132
France	371	8,497	45,575	77,262	76,358	35,986	72,206	50,464
Germany	968	6,761	152,454	434,626	951,667	787,468	718,182	1,452,970
Greece	—	20	49	16	31	72	210	2,308
Ireland[5]	3,614	50,724	207,381	780,719	914,119	435,778	436,871	655,482
Italy	30	409	2,253	1,870	9,231	11,725	55,759	307,309
Netherlands	49	1,078	1,412	8,251	10,789	9,102	16,541	53,701
Norway-Sweden	3	91	1,201	13,903	20,931	109,298	211,245	568,362
Norway	—[6]	—[6]	—[6]	—[6]	—[6]	—[6]	95,323	176,586
Sweden	—[6]	—[6]	—[6]	—[6]	—[6]	—[6]	115,922	391,776
Poland	5	16	369	105	1,164	2,027	12,970	51,806
Portugal	35	145	829	550	1,055	2,658	14,082	16,978
Romania	—[7]	—[7]	—[7]	—[7]	—[7]	—[7]	11	6,348
Soviet Union	14	75	277	551	457	2,512	39,284	213,282
Spain	139	2,477	2,125	2,209	9,298	6,697	5,266	4,419
Switzerland	31	3,226	4,821	4,644	25,011	23,286	28,293	81,988
United Kingdom[5,8]	2,410	25,079	75,810	267,044	423,974	606,896	548,043	807,357
Yugoslavia	—[9]	—[9]	—[9]	—[9]	—[9]	—[9]	—[9]	—[4]
Other Europe	—	3	40	79	5	8	1,001	682

Asia	6	30	55	141	41,538	64,759	124,160	69,942
China[10]	1	2	8	35	41,397	64,301	123,201	61,711
Hong Kong	—[11]	—[11]	—[11]	—[11]	—[11]	—[11]	—[11]	—[11]
India	1	8	39	36	43	69	163	269
Iran	—[12]	—[12]	—[12]	—[12]	—[12]	—[12]	—[12]	—[12]
Israel	—[13]	—[13]	—[13]	—[13]	—[13]	—[13]	—[13]	—[13]
Japan	—[14]	—[14]	—[14]	—[14]	—[14]	186	149	2,270
Korea	—[15]	—[15]	—[15]	—[15]	—[15]	—[15]	—[15]	—[15]
Philippines	—[16]	—[16]	—[16]	—[16]	—[16]	—[16]	—[16]	—[16]
Turkey	1	20	7	59	83	131	404	3,782
Vietnam	—[11]	—[11]	—[11]	—[11]	—[11]	—[11]	—[11]	—[11]
Other Asia	3	—	1	11	15	72	243	1,910
America	387	11,564	33,424	62,469	74,720	166,607	404,044	426,967
Canada & Newfoundland[17,18]	209	2,277	13,624	41,723	59,309	153,878	383,640	393,304
Mexico[18]	1	4,817	6,599	3,271	3,078	2,191	5,162	191,319
Caribbean	164	3,834	12,301	13,528	10,660	9,046	13,957	29,042
Cuba	—[12]	—[12]	—[12]	—[12]	—[12]	—[12]	—[12]	—[12]
Dominican Republic	—[20]	—[20]	—[20]	—[20]	—[20]	—[20]	—[20]	—[20]
Haiti	—[20]	—[20]	—[20]	—[20]	—[20]	—[20]	—[20]	—[20]
Jamaica	—[21]	—[21]	—[21]	—[21]	—[21]	—[21]	—[21]	—[21]
Other Caribbean	164	3,834	12,301	13,528	10,660	9,046	13,957	29,042
Central America	2	105	44	368	449	95	157	404
El Salvador	—[20]	—[20]	—[20]	—[20]	—[20]	—[20]	—[20]	—[20]
Other Central America	2	105	44	368	449	95	157	404
South America	11	531	856	3,579	1,224	1,397	1,128	2,304
Argentina	—[20]	—[20]	—[20]	—[20]	—[20]	—[20]	—[20]	—[20]
Colombia	—[20]	—[20]	—[20]	—[20]	—[20]	—[20]	—[20]	—[20]
Ecuador	—[20]	—[20]	—[20]	—[20]	—[20]	—[20]	—[20]	—[20]
Other South America	11	531	856	3,579	1,224	1,397	1,128	2,304
Other America	—[22]	—[22]	—[22]	—[22]	—[22]	—[22]	—[22]	—[22]
Africa	1	16	54	55	210	312	358	857
Oceania	1	2	9	29	158	214	10,914	12,574
Not specified[22]	300	33,030	69,902	53,115	29,011	17,791	790	789

Region and Country of Last Residence[1]	1891–1900	1901–10	1911–20	1921–30	1931–40	1941–50	1951–60	1961–70
All countries	3,687,564	8,795,386	5,735,811	4,107,209	528,431	1,035,039	2,515,479	3,321,677
Europe	3,555,352	8,056,040	4,321,887	2,463,194	347,566	621,147	1,325,727	1,123,492
Austria-Hungary	592,707[23]	2,145,266[23]	896,342[23]	63,548	11,424	28,329	103,743	26,022
Austria	234,081[3]	668,209[3]	453,649	32,868	3,563[24]	24,860[24]	67,106	20,621
Hungary	181,288[3]	808,511[3]	442,693	30,680	7,861	3,469	36,637	5,401
Belgium	18,167	41,635	33,746	15,846	4,817	12,189	18,575	9,192
Czechoslovakia	—[4]	—[4]	3,426[4]	102,194	14,393	8,347	918	3,273
Denmark	50,231	65,285	41,983	32,430	2,559	5,393	10,984	9,201
France	30,770	73,379	61,897	49,610	12,623	38,809	51,121	45,237
Germany	505,152[23]	341,498[23]	143,945[23]	412,202	114,058[24]	226,578[24]	477,765	190,796
Greece	15,979	167,519	184,201	51,084	9,119	8,973	47,608	85,969
Ireland[5]	388,416	339,065	146,181	211,234	10,973	19,789	48,362	32,966
Italy	651,893	2,045,877	1,109,524	455,315	68,028	57,661	185,491	214,111
Netherlands	26,758	48,262	43,718	26,948	7,150	14,860	52,277	30,606
Norway-Sweden	321,281	440,039	161,469	165,780	8,700	20,765	44,632	32,600
Norway	95,015	190,505	66,395	68,531	4,740	10,100	22,935	15,484
Sweden	226,266	249,534	95,074	97,249	3,960	10,665	21,697	17,116
Poland	96,720[23]	—[23]	4,813[23]	227,734	17,026	7,571	9,985	53,539
Portugal	27,508	69,149	89,732	29,994	3,329	7,423	19,588	76,065
Romania	12,750	53,008	13,311	67,646	3,871	1,076	1,039	2,531
Soviet Union	505,290[23]	1,597,306[23]	921,201[23]	61,742	1,370	571	671	2,465
Spain	8,731	27,935	68,611	28,958	3,258	2,898	7,894	44,659
Switzerland	31,179	34,922	23,091	29,676	5,512	10,547	17,675	18,453
United Kingdom[5,8]	271,538	525,950	341,408	339,570	31,572	139,306	202,824	213,822
Yugoslavia	—[9]	—[9]	1,888[9]	49,064	5,835	1,576	8,225	20,381
Other Europe	282	39,945	31,400	42,619	11,949	8,486	16,350	11,604

Asia	74,862	323,543	247,236	112,059	16,595	37,028	153,249	427,642
China[10]	14,799	20,605	21,278	29,907	4,928	16,709	9,657	34,764
Hong Kong	—[11]	—[11]	—[11]	—[11]	—[11]	—[11]	15,541[11]	75,007
India	68	4,713	2,082	1,886	496	1,761	1,973	27,189
Iran	—[12]	—[13]	—[13]	241[12]	195	1,380	3,388	10,339
Israel	—[13]	—[13]	—[13]	—[13]	—[13]	476[13]	25,476	29,602
Japan	25,942	129,797	83,837	33,462	1,948	1,555	46,250	39,988
Korea	—[15]	—[15]	—[15]	—[16]	—	107[15]	6,231	34,526
Philippines	—[16]	—[16]	—[16]	—[16]	528[16]	4,691	19,307	98,376
Turkey	30,425	157,369	134,066	33,824	1,065	798	3,519	10,142
Vietnam	—[11]	—[11]	—[11]	—[11]	—[11]	—[11]	335[11]	4,340
Other Asia	3,628	11,059	5,973	12,739	7,435	9,551	21,572	63,369
America	38,972	361,888	1,143,671	1,516,716	160,037	354,804	996,944	1,716,374
Canada & Newfoundland[17,18]	3,311	179,226	742,185	924,515	108,527	171,718	377,952	413,310
Mexico[18]	971[19]	49,642	219,004	459,287	22,319	60,589	299,811	453,937
Caribbean	33,066	107,548	123,424	74,899	15,502	49,725	123,091	470,213
Cuba	—[12]	—[12]	—[12]	15,901[12]	9,571	26,313	78,948	208,536
Dominican Republic	—[20]	—[20]	—[20]	—[20]	1,150[20]	5,627	9,897	93,292
Haiti	—[20]	—[20]	—[20]	—[20]	191[20]	911	4,442	34,499
Jamaica	—[21]	—[21]	—[21]	—[21]	—[21]	—[21]	8,869[21]	74,906
Other Caribbean	33,066	107,548	123,424	58,998	4,590	16,874	20,935[21]	58,980
Central America	549	8,192	17,159	15,769	5,861	21,665	44,751	101,330
El Salvador	—[20]	—[20]	—[20]	—[20]	673[20]	5,132	5,895	14,992
Other Central America	549	8,192	17,159	15,769	5,188	16,533	38,856	86,338
South America	1,075	17,280	41,899	42,215	7,803	21,831	91,628	257,954
Argentina	—[20]	—[20]	—[20]	—[20]	1,349[20]	3,338	19,486	49,721
Colombia	—[20]	—[20]	—[20]	—[20]	1,223[20]	3,858	18,048	72,028
Ecuador	—[20]	—[20]	—[20]	—[20]	337[20]	2,417	9,841	36,780
Other South America	1,075	17,280	41,899	42,215	4,894	12,218	44,253	99,425
Other America	—[22]	—[22]	—[22]	31[22]	25	29,276	59,711	19,630
Africa	350	7,368	8,443	6,286	1,750	7,367	14,092	28,954
Oceania	3,965	13,024	13,427	8,726	2,483	14,551	12,976	25,122
Not specified[22]	14,063	33,523[25]	1,147	228	—	142	12,491	93

Region and Country of Last Residence[1]	1971–80	1981–89	1990–99	1994	1995	1996	1997	1998[26]	1999	Total 179 Years 1820–1999
All countries	4,493,314	5,801,579	9,781,496	804,368	720,401	915,847	798,339	654,420	646,539	65,239,029
Europe	800,368	637,524	1,291,299	160,916	128,185	147,581	119,871	90,793	92,672	38,268,333
Austria-Hungary	16,028	20,152	N/A	N/A	N/A	N/A	N/A	N/A	N/A	4,338,049
Austria	9,478	14,566	5,094	499	518	554	487	291	231	1,830,266
Hungary	6,550	5,586	11,003	880	900	1,183	949	809	698	1,677,804
Belgium	5,329	6,239	5,783	516	569	651	554	421	428	215,512
Czechoslovakia[27]	6,023	6,649	7,597	642	599	561	395	342	319	152,820
Czech Republic	N/A	N/A	723	11	72	165	186	144	145	723
Slovak Republic	N/A	N/A	3,010	221	503	663	629	491	493	3,010
Denmark	4,439	4,696	5,785	606	551	608	429	457	368	375,523
France	25,069	28,088	26,879	2,715	2,505	3,079	2,568	2,352	2,209	812,201
Germany	74,414	79,809	60,082	6,992	6,237	6,748	5,723	5,472	5,201	7,131,395
Germany, East	N/A	N/A	105	N/A	N/A	N/A	N/A	N/A	N/A	105
Germany, West	N/A	N/A	7,338	N/A	N/A	N/A	N/A	N/A	N/A	7,338
Greece	92,369	34,490	15,403	1,440	1,309	1,452	1,049	863	727	715,420
Ireland	11,490	22,229	67,975	17,256	5,315	1,731	1,001	944	812	4,738,368
Italy	129,368	51,008	23,365	2,305	2,231	2,501	1,982	1,831	1,530	5,380,227
Netherlands	10,492	10,723	12,334	1,239	1,196	1,423	1,059	917	777	385,051
Norway-Sweden	10,472	13,252	15,720	1,599	1,396	1,729	1,330	1,121	1,130	2,099,489
Norway	3,941	3,612	4,618	459	420	478	372	298	308	805,290
Sweden	6,531	9,640	11,102	1,140	976	1,251	958	823	822	1,294,199
Poland	37,234	64,888	180,035	28,048	13,824	15,772	12,038	8,469	8,798	768,007
Portugal	101,710	36,365	25,428	2,169	2,615	2,984	1,665	1,536	1,071	522,623
Romania	12,393	27,361	55,303	3,444	4,871	5,801	5,545	5,112	5,686	256,648
Russia	N/A	N/A	110,921	15,249	14,560	19,668	16,632	11,529	12,347	110,921
Soviet Union[28]	38,961	42,898	126,115	6,954	6,784	3,513	2,944	6,336	5,058	3,555,042
Former Soviet Republics[29]	N/A	N/A	255,552	42,981	34,838	41,769	31,269	14,044	18,614	255,552
Spain	39,141	17,689	14,310	1,418	1,321	1,659	1,241	1,043	874	296,714
Switzerland	8,235	7,561	8,840	877	881	1,006	1,063	828	649	366,991
United Kingdom	137,374	140,119	138,380	16,326	12,427	13,624	10,708	9,018	7,690	5,238,476
Yugoslavia[28]	30,540	15,984	25,923	2,038	2,907	3,605	2,793	2,408	1,897	159,416

Former Yugoslavian States	N/A	N/A	61,389	3,338	8,242	11,777	10,688	7,954	8,494	61,389
Other Europe	9,287	7,324	822,161	94,794	89,446	105,406	84,548	59,808	62,380	1,003,225
Asia	1,588,178	2,416,278	2,965,360	292,589	267,931	307,807	265,810	219,696	199,411	8,662,661
China, People's Republic	124,326	306,108	410,736	53,985	35,463	41,728	41,147	36,884	32,204	1,284,473
Hong Kong	113,467	83,848	78,016	7,731	7,249	7,824	5,577	5,275	4,917	365,879
India	164,134	221,977	371,925	34,921	34,748	44,859	38,071	36,482	30,237	798,832
Iran	45,136	101,267	129,055	11,422	9,201	11,084	9,642	7,883	7,203	291,001
Israel	37,713	38,367	33,814	3,425	2,523	3,126	2,448	1,991	1,858	165,448
Japan	49,775	40,654	60,112	6,093	4,837	6,011	5,097	5,138	4,217	515,925
Korea	267,638	302,782	187,794	16,011	16,047	18,185	14,239	14,268	12,840	799,078
Philippines	354,987	477,485	526,835	53,535	50,984	55,876	49,117	34,466	31,026	1,482,209
Taiwan	N/A	N/A	112,464	10,032	9,377	13,401	6,745	7,097	6,714	112,464
Turkey	13,399	20,028	26,178	1,840	2,947	3,657	3,145	2,682	2,219	435,300
Vietnam	172,820	266,027	443,173	41,345	41,752	42,067	38,519	17,649	20,393	886,695
Other Asia	244,783	557,735	769,425	62,663	77,529	95,310	84,127	73,743	71,065	1,709,524
Africa	80,779	144,096	374,149	26,712	42,456	52,889	47,791	40,660	36,700	675,497
Oceania	41,242	38,401	49,040	4,592	4,695	5,309	4,344	3,935	3,676	246,858
America	1,982,735	2,564,698	4,529,512	272,178	231,466	340,487	307,449	252,965	271,336	6,546,533
Canada	169,939	132,296	138,165	16,068	12,932	15,825	11,609	10,190	8,864	142,435
Mexico	640,294	975,657	2,756,513	111,398	89,932	163,572	146,865	131,575	147,573	5,965,056
Caribbean	741,126	759,416	1,023,237	104,804	96,788	116,501	105,299	73,521	71,683	3,613,779
Cuba	264,863	135,142	170,675	14,727	17,937	26,466	33,587	17,375	14,132	909,949
Dominican Republic	148,135	209,899	365,598	51,189	38,512	39,604	27,053	20,387	17,864	833,598
Haiti	56,335	118,510	179,725	13,333	14,021	18,386	15,057	13,449	16,532	394,613
Jamaica	137,577	184,481	182,552	14,349	16,398	19,089	17,840	15,146	14,733	588,385
Other Caribbean	134,216	111,384	124,687	11,206	9,920	13,256	11,762	9,164	8,422	887,234
Central America	134,640	321,845	611,597	39,908	31,814	44,289	43,676	35,679	43,216	1,284,982
El Salvador	34,436	133,938	274,989	17,644	11,744	17,903	17,969	14,590	14,606	470,055
Other Central America	100,204	187,907	336,608	22,264	20,070	26,386	25,707	21,089	28,610	384,427
South America	295,741	375,026	569,650	47,377	45,666	61,769	52,877	45,394	41,585	1,733,132
Argentina	29,897	21,374	27,431	2,318	1,762	2,456	1,964	1,511	1,393	152,596
Colombia	77,347	99,066	140,685	10,847	10,838	14,283	13,004	11,836	9,966	412,255
Ecuador	50,077	43,841	81,204	5,906	6,397	8,321	7,750	6,852	8,904	224,497
Other South America	138,420	210,745	320,330	28,306	26,669	36,709	30,129	25,195	21,322	943,784
Other America	995	458	595	48	60	53	39	31	29	110,721
Unknown or not reported	N/A	N/A	2,486	4	2	5	197	977	1,159	269,495

Source: U.S. Immigration and Naturalization Service, 1999.

[1]Data for years prior to 1906 relate to country whence alien came; data from 1906–79 and 1984–89 are for country of last permanent residence; and data for 1980–99 refer to country of birth. Because of changes in boundaries, changes in lists of countries, and lack of data for specified countries for various periods, data for certain countries, especially for the total period 1820–1999, are not comparable throughout. Data for specified countries are included with countries to which they belonged prior to World War I.

[2]Data for Austria and Hungary not reported until 1861.

[3]Data for Austria and Hungary not reported separately for all years during the period.

[4]No data available for Czechoslovakia until 1920.

[5]Prior to 1926, data for Northern Ireland included in Ireland.

[6]Data for Norway and Sweden not reported separately until 1871.

[7]No data available for Romania until 1880.

[8]Since 1925, data for United Kingdom refer to England, Scotland, Wales, and Northern Ireland.

[9]In 1920, a separate enumeration was made for the Kingdom of Serbs, Croats, and Slovenes. Since 1922, the Serb, Croat, and Slovene Kingdom recorded as Yugoslavia.

[10]Beginning in 1957, China includes Taiwan.

[11]Data not reported separately until 1952.

[12]Data not reported separately until 1925.

[13]Data not reported separately until 1949.

[14]No data available for Japan until 1861.

[15]Data not reported separately until 1948.

[16]Prior to 1934, Philippines recorded as insular travel.

[17]Prior to 1920, Canada and Newfoundland recorded as British North America. From 1820 to 1898, figures include all British North America possessions.

[18]Land arrivals not completely enumerated until 1908.

[19]No data available for Mexico from 1886 to 1893.

[20]Data not reported separately until 1932.

[21]Data for Jamaica not collected until 1953. In prior years, consolidated under British West Indies, which is included in "Other Caribbean."

[22]Included in countries "Not specified" until 1925.

[23]From 1899 to 1919, data for Poland included in Austria-Hungary, Germany, and the Soviet Union.

[24]From 1938 to 1945, data for Austria included in Germany.

[25]Includes 32,897 persons returning in 1906 to their homes in the United States.

[26]Data for fiscal year 1998 have been revised due to changes in the count for asylees and cancellation of removal. The previously reported total was 660,477.

[27]Prior to 1993, data include independent republics; beginning in 1993, data are for unknown republic only.

[28]Prior to 1992, data include independent republic; beginning in 1992, data are for Yugoslavia only.

[29]Prior to 1992, data include previously independent republics only; beginning in 1992, data are for all former republics except Russia.

— represents zero.

NOTE: From 1820 to 1867, figures represent alien passengers arrived at seaports; from 1868 to 1891 and 1895 to 1897, immigrant aliens arrived; from 1892 to 1894 and 1898 to 1899, immigrant aliens admitted for permanent residence. From 1892 to 1903, aliens entering by cabin class were not counted as immigrants. Land arrivals were not completely enumerated until 1908. For this table, fiscal year 1843 covers 9 months ending September 1843; fiscal years 1832 and 1850 cover 15 months ending December 31 of the respective years; and fiscal year 1868 covers 6 months ending June 30, 1868.

PRESIDENTS, VICE-PRESIDENTS,
AND SECRETARIES OF STATE

President	Vice-President	Secretary of State
1. George Washington, Federalist 1789	John Adams, Federalist 1789	Thomas Jefferson 1789 Edmund Randolph 1794 Timothy Pickering 1795
2. John Adams, Federalist 1797	Thomas Jefferson, Dem.-Rep. 1797	Timothy Pickering 1797 John Marshall 1800
3. Thomas Jefferson, Dem.-Rep. 1801	Aaron Burr, Dem.-Rep. 1801 George Clinton, Dem.-Rep. 1805	James Madison 1801
4. James Madison, Dem.-Rep. 1809	George Clinton, Dem.-Rep. 1809 Elbridge Gerry, Dem.-Rep. 1813	Robert Smith 1809 James Monroe 1811
5. James Monroe, Dem.-Rep. 1817	Daniel D. Tompkins, Dem.-Rep. 1817	John Q. Adams 1817
6. John Quincy Adams, Dem.-Rep. 1825	John C. Calhoun, Dem.-Rep. 1825	Henry Clay 1825
7. Andrew Jackson, Democratic 1829	John C. Calhoun, Democratic 1829 Martin Van Buren, Democratic 1833	Martin Van Buren 1829 Edward Livingston 1831 Louis McLane 1833 John Forsyth 1834
8. Martin Van Buren, Democratic 1837	Richard M. Johnson, Democratic 1837	John Forsyth 1837
9. William H. Harrison, Whig 1841	John Tyler, Whig 1841	Daniel Webster 1841

	President	Vice-President	Secretary of State
10.	John Tyler, Whig and Democratic 1841	None	Daniel Webster 1841 Hugh S. Legaré 1843 Abel P. Upshur 1843 John C. Calhoun 1844
11.	James K. Polk, Democratic 1845	George M. Dallas, Democratic 1845	James Buchanan 1845
12.	Zachary Taylor, Whig 1849	Millard Fillmore, Whig 1848	John M. Clayton 1849
13.	Millard Fillmore, Whig 1850	None	Daniel Webster 1850 Edward Everett 1852
14.	Franklin Pierce, Democratic 1853	William R. King, Democratic 1853	William L. Marcy 1853
15.	James Buchanan, Democratic 1857	John C. Breckinridge, Democratic 1857	Lewis Cass 1857 Jeremiah S. Black 1860
16.	Abraham Lincoln, Republican 1861	Hannibal Hamlin, Republican 1861 Andrew Johnson, Unionist 1865	William H. Seward 1861
17.	Andrew Johnson, Unionist 1865	None	William H. Seward 1865
18.	Ulysses S. Grant, Republican 1869	Schuyler Colfax, Republican 1869 Henry Wilson, Republican 1873	Elihu B. Washburne 1869 Hamilton Fish 1869
19.	Rutherford B. Hayes, Republican 1877	William A. Wheeler, Republican 1877	William M. Evarts 1877

	President	Vice-President	Secretary of State
20.	James A. Garfield, Republican 1881	Chester A. Arthur, Republican 1881	James G. Blaine 1881
21.	Chester A. Arthur, Republican 1881	None	Frederick T. Frelinghuysen 1881
22.	Grover Cleveland, Democratic 1885	Thomas A. Hendricks, Democratic 1885	Thomas F. Bayard 1885
23.	Benjamin Harrison, Republican 1889	Levi P. Morton, Republican 1889	James G. Blaine 1889 John W. Foster 1892
24.	Grover Cleveland, Democratic 1893	Adlai E. Stevenson, Democratic 1893	Walter Q. Gresham 1893 Richard Olney 1895
25.	William McKinley, Republican 1897	Garret A. Hobart, Republican 1897 Theodore Roosevelt, Republican 1901	John Sherman 1897 William R. Day 1898 John Hay 1898
26.	Theodore Roosevelt, Republican 1901	Charles Fairbanks, Republican 1905	John Hay 1901 Elihu Root 1905 Robert Bacon 1909
27.	William H. Taft, Republican 1909	James S. Sherman, Republican 1909	Philander C. Knox 1909
28.	Woodrow Wilson, Democratic 1913	Thomas R. Marshall, Democratic 1913	William J. Bryan 1913 Robert Lansing 1915 Bainbridge Colby 1920
29.	Warren G. Harding, Republican 1921	Calvin Coolidge, Republican 1921	Charles E. Hughes 1921
30.	Calvin Coolidge, Republican 1923	Charles G. Dawes, Republican 1925	Charles E. Hughes 1923 Frank B. Kellogg 1925

	President	Vice-President	Secretary of State
31.	Herbert Hoover, Republican 1929	Charles Curtis, Republican 1929	Henry L. Stimson 1929
32.	Franklin D. Roosevelt, Democratic 1933	John Nance Garner, Democratic 1933 Henry A. Wallace, Democratic 1941 Harry S. Truman, Democratic 1945	Cordell Hull 1933 Edward R. Stettinius, Jr. 1944
33.	Harry S. Truman, Democratic 1945	Alben W. Barkley, Democratic 1949	Edward R. Stettinius, Jr. 1945 James F. Byrnes 1945 George C. Marshall 1947 Dean G. Acheson 1949
34.	Dwight D. Eisenhower, Republican 1953	Richard M. Nixon, Republican 1953	John F. Dulles 1953 Christian A. Herter 1959
35.	John F. Kennedy, Democratic 1961	Lyndon B. Johnson, Democratic 1961	Dean Rusk 1961
36.	Lyndon B. Johnson, Democratic 1963	Hubert H. Humphrey, Democratic 1965	Dean Rusk 1963
37.	Richard M. Nixon, Republican 1969	Spiro T. Agnew, Republican 1969 Gerald R. Ford, Republican 1973	William P. Rogers 1969 Henry Kissinger 1973
38.	Gerald R. Ford, Republican 1974	Nelson Rockefeller, Republican 1974	Henry Kissinger 1974
39.	Jimmy Carter, Democratic 1977	Walter Mondale, Democratic 1977	Cyrus Vance 1977 Edmund Muskie 1980

	President	*Vice-President*	*Secretary of State*
40.	Ronald Reagan, Republican 1981	George H. W. Bush, Republican 1981	Alexander Haig 1981 George Schultz 1982
41.	George H. W. Bush, Republican 1989	J. Danforth Quayle, Republican 1989	James A. Baker 1989 Lawrence Eagleburger 1992
42.	William J. Clinton, Democrat 1993	Albert Gore, Jr., Democrat 1993	Warren Christopher 1993 Madeleine Albright 1997
43.	George W. Bush, Republican 2001	Richard B. Cheney, Republican 2001	Colin L. Powell 2001

CREDITS

CHAPTER 1: p. 9, Peabody Museum, Harvard University; **p. 11,** from the Henry Whelpley Collection at the St. Louis Science Center; **p. 12,** Denver Convention & Visitors Bureau; **p. 17,** © Bettmann/Corbis; **p. 20,** © The British Museum; **p. 21,** Neg. No. 286821, courtesy Department of Library Services, American Museum of Natural History; **p. 25,** Courtesy of The General Libraries, The University of Texas at Austin; **p. 33,** Royal Library, Copenhagen; **p. 36,** Corbis-Bettman; **p. 39,** National Maritime Museum; **p. 41,** Corbis-Bettman.

CHAPTER 2: p. 47 *(left)* By courtesy of the National Portrait Gallery, London, and *(right)* Photo Bulloz; **p. 52,** The Huntington Library, Art Collection and Botanical Gardens, San Marino, CA; **p. 53,** Library of Congress; **p. 55,** National Portrait Gallery, Smithsonian Institution/Art Resource, NY; **p. 63,** Stadelschen Kunstinstituts Frankfurt, photo © Ursula Edelmann; **p. 65,** Courtesy, American Antiquarian Society; **p. 69,** The Warder Collection; **p. 73,** Courtesy of the John Carter Brown Library at Brown University; **p. 75,** The Library Company of Philadelphia; **p. 81,** South Caroliniana Library; **p. 85,** by permission of the British Library, shelfmark K.Top CXX1.35; **p. 87,** Courtesy of the New York State Museum, Albany, NY and the Onondaga Nation; **p. 90,** Bequest of Maxim Karolik, courtesy of the Museum of Fine Arts, Boston; **p. 92,** The Mariners Museum , Newport News, Virginia.

CHAPTER 3: p. 103 *(left, right)*, The Worcester Art Museum; **p. 106,** Connecticut Historical Society; **p. 109,** All rights reserved, The Metropolitan Museum of Art; **p. 110,** Swem Library, The College of William and Mary; **p. 112,** Swem Library, The College of William and Mary; **p. 116,** The Abby Aldridge Rockefeller Folk Art Center, Williamsburg, Virginia; **p. 117,** The Maryland Historical Society, Baltimore, Maryland; **p. 118,** Library of Congress; **p. 120,** Corbis-Bettman; **p. 122,** Corbis-Bettman; **p. 129,** Courtesy, Peabody Essex Museum, Salem, Mass.; **p. 131,** The Archbishop of Canterbury and the Trustees of Lambeth Palace Library; **p. 138,** © Collection of the New-York Historical Society; **p. 140,** The Library Company of Philadelphia; **p. 143,** courtesy of the Harvard University Portrait Collection, Bequest of Dr. John Collins

Warren, 1856. Photo by Katya Kallsen, © President and Fellows of Harvard College; **p. 144,** Courtesy, American Antiquarian Society; **p. 146,** by courtesy of the National Portrait Gallery, London.

CHAPTER 4: **p. 155,** courtesy, Henry Francis du Pont Winterthur Museum; **p. 156,** National Maritime Museum, London; **p. 161,** Courtesy of the Bostonian Society/Old State House; **p. 166,** National Library of Canada, Rare Books and Manuscripts Division, Ottawa; **p. 168,** National Archives of Canada, Negative # C3163; **p. 170,** National Archives of Canada, Negative # C43730; **p. 174,** The Historical Society of Pennsylvania, Stauffer Collection, V.6.P.499; **p. 177,** National Archives of Canada, Negative # C7079.

CHAPTER 5: **p. 185,** Private Collection; photograph Courtauld Institute of Art; **p. 190,** © The British Museum; **p. 194,** The Historical Society of Pennsylvania; **p. 196,** Courtesy of the John Carter Brown Library at Brown University; **p. 198,** Deposited by the City of Boston. Courtesy, Museum of Fine Arts Boston; **p. 200,** Library of Congress; **p. 205,** The New York Public Library, Astor, Lenox and Tilden Foundations; **p. 207,** © The British Museum; **p. 210,** Courtesy of the John Carter Brown Library at Brown University; **p. 211,** *Attack on Bunker Hill with Burning of Charlestown,* Gift of Edgar William and Bernice Chrylser Garbisch, 1953, photograph © The Board of Trustees, National Gallery of Art, Washington; **p. 215,** Courtesy, American Antiquarian Society.

CHAPTER 6: **p. 228,** Courtesy Pennsylvania Academy of the Fine Arts, Philadelphia. Gift of Maria McKean Allen and Phebe Warren Downes through the bequest of their mother, Elizabeth Wharton McKean; **p. 231,** Anne S. K. Brown Military Collection, Courtesy of the John Carter Brown Library at Brown University; **p. 234,** Frick Collection; **p. 239,** New York State Historical Association, Cooperstown, New York; **p. 246,** Yale University Art Gallery; **p. 247,** Courtesy, Henry Francis du Pont Winterthur Museum; **p. 253,** Collection of the Maryland Historical Society, Baltimore; **p. 255,** Courtesy, Massachusetts Historical Society, Boston; **p. 257,** The Library Company of Philadelphia; **p. 258,** Museum of Art, Rhode Island School of Design; **p. 260,** The Pennsylvania Academy of Fine Arts, Philadelphia. Gift of Mrs. Sarah Harrison (The Joseph Harrison Jr. Collection).

CHAPTER 7: **p. 273,** The Library Company of Philadelphia; **p. 276,** The Historical Society of Pennsylvania; **p. 280,** The Historical Society of Pennsylvania, Gratz, case 1 Box 25; **p. 282,** Library of Congress; **p. 283,** Library of Congress; **p. 287,** Independence National Historical Park Collection; **p. 293,** Library of Congress.

CHAPTER 8: **p. 297,** Library of Congress; **p. 300,** Collection of the Albany Institute of History & Art; **p. 303,** National Portrait Gallery, Smithsonian Institution,

Washington, D.C.; **p. 306,** Corbis-Bettman; **p. 308,** The Historical Society of Pennsylvania, *Certificate of the New York Mechanick Society* by Abraham Godwin (Bb 613 N489); **p. 310,** Independence National Historical Park Collection; **p. 315,** Detroit Public Library; **p. 318,** The Warder Collection; **p. 321,** Rare Book Division, The New York Public Library, Astor, Lenox and Tilden Foundation; **p. 322,** Collection of Washington University, St. Louis; **p. 324,** Courtesy of the Chapin Library of Rare Books, Williams College; **p. 326,** Collection of the Boston Athenaeum; **p. 327,** The Henry E. Huntington Library, Art Gallery and Botanical Gardens (San Marino, CA); **p. 331,** Print Collection, Miriam and Ira D. Wallach Division of Art, Prints and Photographs, The New York Public Library, Astor, Lenox and Tilden Foundations.

CHAPTER 9: **p. 341,** Library of Congress; **p. 343,** The New York Public Library, Astor, Lenox and Tilden Foundations; **p. 345,** The Cincinnati Historical Society; **p. 350,** Library of Congress; **p. 353,** From the Collections of The New Jersey Historical Society, Newark, New Jersey; **p. 357,** The New York Public Library, Astor, Lenox and Tilden Foundations; **p. 358,** © Collection of the New-York Historical Society; **p. 360,** American Museum of Natural History; **p. 362,** © Collection of the New-York Historical Society; **p. 368,** Courtesy, Massachusetts Historical Society, Boston; **p. 371,** Collection of Davenport West, Jr.

CHAPTER 10: **p. 380,** Collection of the Maryland Historical Society, Baltimore; **p. 385,** National Portrait Gallery, Smithsonian Institution, transfer from the National Gallery of Art, Gift of Andrew W. Mellon; **p. 388,** Historical Museum of Southern Florida; **p. 389,** National Archives; **p. 392,** Henry Clay Memorial Foundation; **p. 394,** Library of Congress; **p. 397,** all rights reserved, The Metropolitan Museum of Art, Rogers Fund, 1942 (42.95.7); **p. 401,** © Collection of the New-York Historical Society; **p. 403,** © Bettmann/Corbis; **p. 405,** © Collection of the New-York Historical Society; **p. 406,** © Collection of the New-York Historical Society.

CHAPTER 11: **p. 412,** Library of Congress; **p. 415,** Library of Congress; **p. 416,** National Portrait Gallery, Smithsonian Institution; **p. 418,** Boston Art Commission; **p. 420,** courtesy, American Antiquarian Society; **p. 425,** Western Historical Collections, University of Oklahoma Library; **p. 428,** © Collection of the New-York Historical Society; **p. 430,** Collection of the Boatmen's National Bank of St. Louis; **p. 432,** Library of Congress; **p. 436,** Library of Congress; **p. 437,** Library of Congress.

CHAPTER 12: **p. 446,** The Granger Collection, New York; **p. 450,** V & A Picture Library; **p. 451,** Minnesota Historical Society; **p. 454,** Collection of The New-York Historical Society, negative no. 34684; **p. 459,** Library of Congress; **p. 463,** © New York State Historical Association, Cooperstown, New York; **p. 464,** American Textile History Museum, Lowell, Massachusetts; **p. 466,** From Memoir of Samuel Slater,

Phelps Stokes, Edward S. Hawes, Alice Mary Hawes, Marion Augusta Hawes, 1937 (37.14.37); **p. 605** *(left)* National Portrait Gallery, Smithsonian Institution/Art Resource, NY, and *(right)* © Collection of the New-York Historical Society.

CHAPTER 16: p. 615, William Sidney Mount, *California News,* 1850. The Museums at Stony Brook; **p. 617,** Amon Carter Museum, Fort Worth, Texas; **p. 621,** Library of Congress; **p. 624,** Library of Congress; **p. 625,** © Collection of the New-York Historical Society; **p. 627,** Library of Congress; **p. 629,** National Portrait Gallery, Smithsonian Institution/Art Resource, NY; **p. 633,** Library of Congress; **p. 634,** Print Collection, Miriam and Ira D. Wallach Division of Art, Prints and Photographs. The New York Public Library, Astor, Lenox and Tilden Foundations; **p. 638,** National Archives; **p. 641,** GLC 5116.19 **p. 17,** Pamphlet: The Border Ruffian Code in Kansas, 1856. Courtesy of The Gilder Lehrman Collection, New York; **p. 645,** Collection of the Boston Athenaeum; **p. 647,** Library of Congress; **p. 648,** Chicago Historical Society; **p. 651,** Rare Book Division, The New York Public Library, Astor, Lenox and Tilden Foundations.

CHAPTER 17: p. 661, © Corbis; **p. 663,** © Corbis; **p. 668,** © Bettmann/Corbis; **p. 676,** © Corbis; **p. 679,** © Bettmann/Corbis; **p. 681,** Library of Congress; **p. 683** *(top, bottom),* Library of Congress; **p. 684,** © Corbis; **p. 685,** © Corbis; **p. 687,** Library of Congress; **p. 693,** Library of Congress; **p. 695,** National Archives; **p. 699,** Library of Congress; **p. 701,** © Bettmann/Corbis; **p. 702,** © Corbis; **p. 703,** Massachusetts Commandery Military Order of the Loyal Legion and the U.S. Army Military History Institute; **p. 705,** © Bettmann/Corbis; **p. 706,** Library of Congress; **p. 708,** Library of Congress.

INDEX

Page numbers in *italics* refer to illustrations.